D0810681

A GRAMMAR

OF THE

ENGLISH LANGUAGE

Volume II
SYNTAX

A GRAMMAR OF THE
ENGLISH LANGUAGE

IN TWO VOLUMES

by George O. Curme, Ph.D., Litt.D.

Volume I: Parts of Speech
Volume II: Syntax

REPUBLICATION BY

VERBATIM

Essex, Connecticut

SYNTAX

by
GEORGE O. CURME
Ph.D., Litt.D.

A
VERBATIM
BOOK

ISBN: 0-930454-01-4 (Volume II)
ISBN: 0-930454-03-0 (Set)
L. C. catalog card number: 77-87422

PRINTED IN THE UNITED STATES OF AMERICA

PREFACE

The purpose of this volume is to present a systematic and rather full outline of English syntax based upon actual usage. The book contains the fruits of many years of earnest investigation. From the beginning of these studies the great *Oxford Dictionary* has been an unfailing source of inspiration and concrete help. The author owes much also to the large works of the foreign students of our language, the grammars of Jespersen, Poutsma, Kruisinga, Gustav Krüger, and Wendt, the first three written in English, the last two in German. Moreover, there is a considerable foreign literature in the form of monographs and articles in technical language journals. The author has learned much from the keen observations of these foreign scholars, who have sharp eyes for the peculiarities of our language. He has also made extensive use of the quotations gathered by them and the many other foreign workers in this field. In the same way he has availed himself of the materials gathered by English-speaking scholars. This book could not have been made without the aid of these great stores of fact. But to get a clear, independent view of present usage and its historical development the author found it necessary to read widely for himself, in older English and in the present period, in British literature and, especially, in American literature, which has not been studied so generally as it deserves. Almost the entire important literature of the early part of the Modern English period has been read, in critical editions where such have appeared. Everywhere attention has been called to the loose structure of the English sentence at that time and to the subsequent development of our simple, terse, differentiated forms of expression — an eloquent testimony to the growing intellectual life of the English-speaking people. In the best literature of his own time the author has read so extensively that he feels that his findings have independent value. With his eyes constantly upon present usage, he has read a large number of recent novels, dramas, lectures, orations, speeches, letters, essays, histories, scientific treatises, poems, etc., from all parts of the English-speaking territory. It might seem at first glance that the novelists and dramatists are more fully represented than writers on the events of the day, politics, literature, history, science, etc., but in fact this, the calm, composed form of English speech, representing the higher unity of the language, has been very carefully studied and illustrative examples are given everywhere throughout the book, but usually without mention of the source since they represent common normal usage. In the novel and the drama, however, we find the irregular beat of changeful life, varying widely in different provinces and social strata, and, moreover, often disturbed by the exciting influences of pressing events, changing moods, and passionate feeling. An attempt has been made to give at least a faint idea of this complex life so far as it has found an expression in our language.

On the other hand, the more dignified forms of expression have been carefully treated. Good English varies according to the occasion, just as our dress varies according to the occasion. Evening dress would be out of place in playing a football game. Loose colloquial English, as often described in this book, is frequently as appropriate as a loose-fitting garment in moments of relaxation. The lesser grammarians, who so generally present only one form of English, not only show their bad taste, but do a great deal of harm in that they impart erroneous ideas of language. In this book also the language of the common people is treated. It is here called 'popular speech' since the common grammatical term 'vulgar' has a disparaging meaning which arouses false conceptions. Popular English is an interesting study. On the one hand, it has retained characteristics of our greatest masters of English, which the literary language has discarded. On the other hand, quite forgetful of its old conservatism, it boldly faces the present with its new needs and hesitates not to give an expression to them, often, like our western pioneers, opening up paths to new and better things, going forward with faith in the present and the future. Those who always think of popular speech as ungrammatical should recall that our present literary grammar was originally the grammar of the common people of England. Who today would return to our older literary English? The common people will also in the future make contributions to our language. The author, however, does not desire to emphasize too much the importance of the common people. The expressive power of our language has for the most part come from the intellectual class. Left entirely to the common people the English language would soon deteriorate. On the other hand, intellectual struggles bring to language an undesirable abstractness and intricacy of expression, while the common people bring to it a refreshing concreteness and simplicity, which appeals also to people of culture and will influence them. Our American popular speech, in general, has not proved to be very productive. It has preserved in large measure the original British forms of expression. As, however, the various British dialects have been brought together on American soil, they have not been preserved intact, but have been curiously mingled. In sections where mountains, low swampy lands, and islands have isolated tracts of country the language is often peculiarly archaic. The Negroes as a result of social isolation have preserved many old forms of expression acquired in earlier days from the whites, who themselves often spoke archaic British dialect.

Diligent use has been made of every possible means to secure an accurate, reliable insight into existing conditions in all the different grades of English speech, both as to the actual fixed usage of today and as to present tendencies. Of course, the grades of our literary language have been put in the foreground. An earnest effort has been made to treat clearly the most difficult and most perplexing questions of literary English in order that those might receive practical help who are often in doubt as to how they should express themselves.

This book is not rich in details. It treats of the general principles of English expression. The attention is directed, not to words, but to the grammatical categories — the case forms, the nominative, genitive, dative, accusative, the prepositional phrase, the indicative, the subjunctive, the active, the passive, the word-order, the clause formations, clauses with finite verb, and the newer, terser participial, gerundival, and infinitival clauses, etc. These categories are the means by which we present our thought in orderly fashion and with precision, and are intimately associated with the expression of our inner feeling. The story of the development of these categories constitutes the oldest and most reliable chapters in the history of the inner life of the English people. Serious efforts have been made everywhere throughout this book to penetrate into the original concrete meaning of these categories, in order to throw light upon the interesting early struggles of our people for a fuller expression of their inner life and to gain suggestions for their present struggles in this direction. In these excursions into older English the author in his quotations from the original sources always preserves the older form, usually in the original spelling, but in the case of writings still widely read, as the Bible and Shakespeare, the spelling has been modernized in conformity to present usage.

The author has not for a moment forgotten that English is a language without a central territory that regulates its use. It is spoken in many centers, which are becoming more and more real centers and are developing under peculiar circumstances. Hence, usage cannot be fixed in accordance with the standards of any particular center. In the erstwhile colonial centers, America, Ireland, etc., English, no longer in direct touch with the language of England, has not at all points developed in the same way. The development has proceeded unevenly in the different territories. There is no English colony or former colony that follows the British standard in every respect, so that English is characterized in every country by peculiarities of development; but as the differences are not in essential things, English is still an entity, a well-defined language with peculiar differences in the various countries. Except where something is said to the contrary, all descriptions of language in this book refer to the body of usage common to England and America. Where British and American English go different ways, each is described.

In early American English the prevailing type of expression was southern British, the language of the southern half of England and at the same time the literary language of the United Kingdom, so that at first the literary language of England and that of America had the same general character. In the eighteenth century came Scotch-Irish immigrants in large numbers, also many from the north of England. The speech of these newcomers was, of course, northern British, a conservative form of English preserving older sounds and expressions. The new settlers naturally went to the newer parts of the country west of the old colonies. Their presence there in large numbers influenced American English in certain respects. While the younger, southern British form of English remained intact for the most part on the Atlantic seaboard and in large measure also in the south generally, the modified form of it, characterized by older, northern British features, became established everywhere in the north except along the Atlantic seaboard.

On the other hand, the new things and the new needs of the New World called forth a large number of new words and new expressions. Moreover, the abounding, freer life of the New World created a new slang. Even conservative Scotch Irish had something new to offer — *will* in the first person of the future tense instead of literary *shall*. These differences in vocabulary and idiom will always distinguish the English-speaking peoples, but will not separate them. They have already stood a severe test. Between 1620 and 1800 important changes took place in the grammatical structure of English, both in Great Britain and America, but instead of drifting apart in this period of marked changes these two branches of English, at all important points, developed harmoniously together. This was the result of the universal tendency in colonial days among Americans of culture to follow in speech the usage of the mother country. The colonies had little literature of their own and were largely dependent in matters of culture upon the Old World. If it had not been for this general tendency of American culture, the language of the New World might have drifted away from that of England, for, as can be seen by American popular speech, there is a very strong tendency for English on American soil to cling to the older forms of the language. About 1800 the structure of literary English had virtually attained its present form in both territories and was in both essentially the same. That since that date no syntactical changes of consequence have taken place in either branch indicates a remarkable solidarity of structure. The English-speaking people are held together by their priceless common heritage — the English language in its higher forms in science and literature. Constant contact with these forces will keep the different peoples in touch with one another. The same English life pulsates everywhere, insuring in spite of the different conditions a similarity, if not a oneness, of evolution.

Definite unifying forces are now at work. We all feel that that is the best English which is most *expressive*, or most *simple*. These are the only principles that will be universally recognized. The drift towards simplicity is still strong and will continue strong. As many forms and concrete pictures have in the past disappeared,

yielding to simpler modes of expression, so also will they continue
to disappear in the future. We shall thus continue to lose and
gain, lose in concreteness and gain in directness. Present tendencies point to the possible ultimate loss of several valuable forms,
as *I*, *he*, *she*, *we*, *they* in certain categories, since these forms are
exposed to the leveling influences of a powerful drift, as explained
in 7 C *a*; but there is now, on the other hand, in careful language a
strong tendency to express ourselves clearly, which prompts us
to use these expressive old forms. Indeed, at the present time
this tendency is, at this point, stronger than it has been for
centuries. The desire to speak clearly and accurately is even
leading us to create new forms for this purpose, as will be shown
in this book. The territory is wide, but thinking people everywhere, even though not in actual contact with one another, will
instinctively be guided by the same general principle, will choose
that which is most expressive. Hence the author defends in this
book the recommendations of conservative grammarians wherever
they contend against the tendencies of the masses to disregard fine
distinctions in the literary language already hallowed by long
usage. On the other hand, the author often takes a stand against
these conservative grammarians wherever they cling to the old
simply because it is old and thus fail to recognize that English
grammar is the stirring story of the English people's long and
constant struggle to create a fuller and more accurate expression
of their inner life.

This book has a good deal to say of these struggles, even the
latest much censured ones, which find so little favor with conservative grammarians because they are new and violate rules that
are sacred to them. In all ages, the things of long ago have found
zealous and fanatical defenders, who are at the same time foes of
the new and unhallowed. These new things of today, however,
need no organized defense, for they are born of universal needs
and will be supported by the resistless forces of life that created
them. To the conservative grammarian all change is decay.
Although he knows well that an old house often has to be torn
down in part or as a whole in order that it may be rebuilt to suit
modern conditions, he never sees the constructive forces at work
in the destruction of old grammatical forms. He is fond of mourn-
ing over the loss of the subjunctive and the present slovenly use
of the indicative. He hasn't the slightest insight into the fine

constructive work of the last centuries in rebuilding the sub-junctive. The present nicely differentiated use of the indicative and the newly created subjunctive, as presented in this book, is recommended for careful study to those who talk about the decay of our language. The English-speaking people will chase after fads and eagerly employ the latest slang as long as it lives, for play is as necessary as work, but as long as it remains a great people it will strive unceasingly to find more convenient and more perfect forms of expression. It will do that as naturally as it breathes, and will continue to do it, so that grammarians shall occasionally have to *revise* the school grammars. The fads will pass away, but the constructive work will remain and go on. The author has spent his life in studying the growth and development of Germanic expression and has been very happy in his work. It is his ardent hope that he has presented in this book the subject of English expression in such a way that the reader may realize that English grammar is not a body of set, unchangeable rules, but a description of English expression, bequeathed to us by our forefathers, not to be piously preserved, but to be constantly used and adapted to our needs as they adapted it to their needs.

Square brackets have been uniformly used throughout this book to inclose within quotations the omitted parts of an elliptical statement. Hence they were not available for use to inclose within quotations parenthetical remarks by the author of the *Grammar*. All parenthetical remarks made by the author of the *Grammar* within quotations are inclosed in parentheses as elsewhere.

In the few instances in *Syntax* where the pronunciation of words is indicated, use has been made of the well-known Web-sterian key, so that the means of indicating pronunciation here are quite different from those employed in Volume I, where English sounds are treated scientifically. The author of *Syntax* hesitated to assume on the part of his readers the knowledge of a scientific alphabet.

The author desires to express here his feeling of obligation to his colleague, Professor James Taft Hatfield, for much aid received from him from time to time. His wide knowledge of modern English literature and his notes containing quotations from mod-ern writers illustrating characteristic forms of current English expression have been at the author's disposal, and, what is of great importance, his fine feeling for the English of our day has many times guided the author in making final decisions. The author also desires to express here his gratitude for the large number of individual quotations that have been sent to him by other friends.

The author is deeply indebted also to the following scholars, who have read the manuscript and contributed valuable remarks which have been embodied in the text or have led to important changes: the late Professor O. F. Emerson of Western Reserve University; Professor W. F. Bryan of Northwestern University; Professor J. S. Kenyon of Hiram College. The author has had the advantage of discussing several vexing questions with Sir William Craigie, the editor of the *Oxford Dictionary*. He has also received from him some valuable quotations. This acknowledgment is made without any desire to hold these and other contributors responsible for views in the book which they do not share. For assistance in reading the proofs and for useful suggestions the author desires to thank Dr. Bert Emsley of the Ohio State University; Professors W. Leopold, J. W. Spargo, F. A. Bernstorff of Northwestern University; Professor Francis E. Moran of the University of Notre Dame. Finally, the author desires to express here his deep gratitude to Dr. F. W. Scott of D. C. Heath and Company for encouraging this enterprise and for his active cooperation in putting the book into its present form.

GEORGE O. CURME

Northwestern University
Evanston, Illinois

TABLE OF CONTENTS

See analysis of contents at the head of each chapter

CHAPTER I

INTRODUCTORY

1. Syntax treats of the relations of words or groups of words to one another in sentences.

Sentences are divided into three classes — simple, compound, and complex.

THE SIMPLE SENTENCE

DEFINITION, FORMS, FUNCTIONS, ESSENTIAL ELEMENTS

2. A sentence is an expression of a thought or feeling by means of a word or words used in such form and manner as to convey the meaning intended.

The form of the sentence may be: (1) exclamatory, uttering an outcry, or giving expression to a command, wish, or desire, often closing with an exclamation point — perhaps the oldest form of the sentence; (2) declarative, stating a fact, closing with a period; (3) interrogative, asking a question, closing with an interrogation point.

The sentence has two functions: (1) It is emotive, i.e., it is an expression of will, or is an expression of emotions, attitudes, intentions, and moods present in the speaker or to be evoked in the listener. (2) It makes a statement, or, in the case of a question, calls for a statement. The question belongs not only here but also to (1) since it contains an expression of will. Compare **43 I A** (last par.).

It is usually considered that there are two essential elements in every sentence — the subject and the predicate: *Lead sinks.* The subject is that which is spoken of. The predicate is that which is said of the subject. In a normal sentence both subject and predicate are present, but sometimes the one or the other or both may be absent and yet the sentence may be a complete expression of thought. See *a* below.

a. Sentences Lacking the One or the Other or Both of the Essential Elements. In accurate thinking we often need a large vocabulary and intricate grammatical form; but language also adapts itself readily to the simpler needs of practical life, where action, tone, and the situation are often more expressive than words and grammatical form.

Still, as in primitive speech, a single word in connection with the proper tone or the situation conveys our meaning and thus constitutes a complete sentence: *O! Ouch! Yes. No. 'Glass.* Handle with care.' *Beautiful! Hurry!* If we call out *'Fred!'* to indicate that he should come, we pronounce in loud prolonged tones *Fred* as a dissyllable. If we scold him we pronounce *Fred* as a monosyllable and raise the tone of the voice. Short terse expression was not only characteristic of primitive speech when language was undeveloped, but it is still widely used. In all such cases the expression of the thought is perfect. The sentences, though brief, are complete. In the setting in which they appear, not a word, not a syllable is lacking. A learned grammarian with mistaken enthusiasm might desire to expand these brief utterances into full sentences, but in spite of his grammatical skill the language would be bad, for it would violate good usage. We do not here usually employ full sentences, and for a good reason. Fuller expression would be incomplete expression, for it would mar the thought, take something vital away from it. Thus such brief sentences are as complete as those of exact scientific language, where, however, the speaker, removed from everyday life, must express himself fully if he would describe accurately the hidden forces he is studying.

In older languages there was often no verb and survivals of this older type of sentence are still common: *Nobody here? Everybody gone?* Compare **6 B** *a.* In older speech there was sometimes no subject, expressed or understood. See **4** II B.

The oldest form of the sentence contained only one word, which, however, was a complete sentence, not a word in its modern sense, for a word is a later development in language growth than a sentence. This oldest type of sentence still survives in case of exclamations, as *Ouch!* and the simple imperative forms, as *Go!* In course of time successive sentences often stood in such close relation to each other that the different *sentences* developed into *words: See! Fire! Yonder!* becoming *See the fire yonder!*

CHAPTER II

THE SUBJECT

3. Case and Position of the Subject. In Old English, the subject and its article and modifying adjectives were in the nominative case. Today only certain pronouns, *he, she,* etc., have a distinctive nominative: '*He* inspires.' Noun, article, and adjectives now have here the common form: '*A fine big mind* inspires.' In Old English, the noun had a fuller inflection than now and its article and modifying adjectives had still more distinctive case forms, since in this early period they were needed to make clear the grammatical relations, for then the grammatical relations were not indicated as now by the word-order. In the course of the Old English period the tendency to indicate the grammatical relations by the word-order grew stronger and stronger. The subject was put into the first place, the verb was placed next or near the subject, then came the object and adverbial elements.

Later, after this new word-order had become established in the subject and object relations, noun, article, and modifying adjectives gradually lost their distinctive case forms, for in the new order of things *form* was slighted as not being a vital factor in expressing the thought. In the literary language the personal, relative, and interrogative pronouns have retained their old distinctive case forms better than nouns and adjectives, but also in these pronouns the tendency to level away the distinctive nominative and accusative forms to a common form for both these relations has become strong in our colloquial and popular speech, as described in **7 C** *a* and **11 2** *e*.

a. SURVIVALS OF OLDER WORD-ORDER. The new word-order with the subject in the first place did not come into use at any particular date, but has been gradually gaining ground throughout the centuries. Even in our own day, however, it has not entirely supplanted the old Germanic principle of placing the emphatic or important word in the first place without

3

regard to its grammatical function. Hence, we still often find an emphatic or important word in the first place in a sentence or proposition: '*Hánd* me that book!' '*Nówhere in the wórld* is there such a place for an idle man as London.' 'He quickened his pace and *só* did I.' 'These *mén!* how I detest them!' For fuller treatment see **35** 1 and 2.

Also in a question, where a noun subject does not in normal usage introduce the sentence, the noun subject is in lively language often nevertheless put into the uncommon first place. Under the pressure of thought or feeling the subject here springs forth first as the most important thing before the usual grammatical structure occurs to the mind, and is later repeated in the usual position of the subject in the form of a personal pronoun: '*Your friénds*, what will *théy* say?' (F. C. Philips, *One Never Knows*, I, 52). Similarly, in declarative sentences the subject thus often springs forth suddenly before it is felt as a subject and is then repeated in the form of a personal pronoun, especially earlier in the period, when the literary language was not so subject to logical and formal requirements as today, and still very commonly in popular and colloquial speech: 'The *Lórd your Gód*, which goes before you, *hé* shall fight for you' (*Deut.*, I, 30). 'Now, they ain't many women that would just let a man stand up like that and give her daughter away under her nose, but *mý wife*, shé's been well trained' (William Allen White, *A Certain Rich Man*, Ch. VIII). If such a subject is a clause of any kind, it must be repeated in the form of the neuter pronoun *it:* '*Getting to truth — it's* like warming cold hands at a fire; isn't it?' (Robert Hichens, *Mrs. Marden*, Ch. VI). Often the whole predicate thus suddenly springs forth with only a light pronominal subject, later followed by the logical subject: '*It* leaves a nasty taste in the mouth, *this scheme*' (F. C. Philips, *One Never Knows*, II, 221).

On the other hand, in case of intransitives and passives the subject is often withheld for a time, sometimes even until the end of the sentence, in order to create the feeling of suspense and thus direct attention more forcibly to it: 'Many years ago when I was a mere lad there lived in this house a *lonely old man, of whom I desire to tell you an interesting story.*' 'In the center of the room, under the chandelier, as became a host, stood the *head of the family*, old Jolyon' (Galsworthy, *The Man of Property*, Ch. I). 'Behind him had come in *a tall woman, of full figure and fine presence, with hair still brown* — Lady Valleys herself' (*id.*, *The Patrician*, Ch. I). 'From mere cuttings have been grown *some of the finest rosebushes I have.*' Similarly, sometimes in the subordinate clause: 'No sooner was the last lodge of the Western drive left behind than there came into sudden view *the most pagan bit of landscape in all England*' (Galsworthy, *The Patrician*, Ch. VII). 'But more exactly and more boldly was the real reaction of the press was indicated by *Punch's* cartoon of a phœnix, bearing the grim and forceful face of Lincoln, rising from the ashes *where lay the embers of all that of old time had gone to make up the liberties of America*' (Ephraim Douglass Adams, *Great Britain and the American Civil War*, II, p. 239).

As in these examples, the emphatic subject that stands at the end of a proposition or clause should be lengthy and heavy enough to form a proper balance to what precedes. In accordance with this principle a short subject, even though stressed, does not usually follow a compound tense, mood, or voice form of a verb. In an independent proposition a short emphatic subject often follows a simple form of a verb: 'First comes the músic.' Compare **35** 1 (6th par.). Not so commonly now as formerly after a compound tense, mood, or voice form of a verb: 'Then was seen a stránge síght.' This is still less commonly found in a subordinate clause: 'As he spoke, he moved across to the sapling, *where was fastened his hórse*' (Mary Johnston, *The Long Roll*, Ch. II) (or more commonly *where his hórse was fastened*). After *there* (**4** II c), however, a short, emphatic subject usually stands at the end of the subordinate clause: 'Where there is a *will* there is a way.' 'I do not believe that there has ever been a more *lóvely dáy.*'

Usually it is not possible to place an emphatic subject after a transitive verb since the subject could not be distinguished from the object, but sometimes where the thought would not be endangered this old word-order still survives: 'At last there reached his ear far down the woodland path the *sounds of voices and laughter*' (James Lane Allen, *The Choir Invisible*, Ch. XXI).

4. Forms of the Subject. The complete subject often consists of a group of words: '*The stately ship* dropped her anchor.' The noun around which the other words are grouped is called the *subject word*, in this sentence *ship*. The subject word is always in the nominative case.

I. *Particulars as to the Form of the Subject.* The form of the subject may be that of:

a. A noun: 'The *sun* is shining.'

b. A pronoun: '*He* is writing.' For peculiar uses of pronouns as subject see II, p. 7.

c. An adjective or participle used as a noun: 'No *good* will come of it.' '*Rich* and *poor* rejoiced.' 'Ruler and *ruled* were alike discontented with the turn of affairs.' 'The *dying* and the *wounded* were cared for.' Compare **58**.

d. The prepositional infinitive, in older English also the simple infinitive: '*To err* is human, *to forgive* divine.' 'To know my deed, 't were best not *know* myself' (*Macbeth*, II, ɪɪ, 73).

The use of the simple infinitive is still common in old saws: 'Better (= it is better) *bend* than *break*.' 'Better *ask* than *go* astray.' After [*it is*] *better* it still lingers on even in common everyday language: 'I mustn't be too hasty; it would be better *wait* a few days, till the end of the term, or even till we come home from the seaside, then *pack* her off' (Hubert Henry Davies, *The Mollusc*, Act II).

In popular Irish English, the simple infinitive is here still well preserved, so that it is still quite common: 'It would be best for us *follow* after the rest of the army of the Whiteboys' (W. B. Yeats,

The Unicorn from the Stars, Act III). As here Irish English often preserves older English usage.

The preservation of the simple infinitive here in many cases probably results from our feeling the form to be an imperative, as can be seen by the tone or in the written language sometimes by the punctuation: '*Kill* or *be killed, eat* or *be eaten*, was the law' (Jack London, *The Call of the Wild*, Ch. VI). 'Better not *say* too much to the parents at present!' (De Morgan, *When Ghost Meets Ghost*, Ch. III). In colloquial speech, however, the old simple infinitive is still often used where it cannot be interpreted as an imperative: 'All she has to do is *come* here' (George Ade, *Hand-Made Fables*, p. 29). 'She's awful. The only thing she hasn't done is *bob* her hair' (Tarkington, *Napoleon Was a Little Man*). 'I'm not a general. All I can do is *trust* the men who are' (S. V. Benét, *John Brown's Body*, p. 220).

   e. The gerund, usually as a parallel construction to the prepositional infinitive without an essential difference of meaning: '*Seeing* is believing,' or '*To see* is to believe.' '*To see* with one's own eyes men and country is better than *reading* all the books of travel in the world' (Thackeray) or '*to read* all the books of travel in the world.' Compare **50** 4 *a.*

   f. Any other part of speech: 'the *ups* and *downs* of life must be taken as they come.' '*Under* is a preposition.' 'The *pros* and *cons* must be considered.' '*I* is a pronoun.'

A pronoun may also be used as a noun in quite a different sense, namely, as a noun representing a person: 'Even it was hinted that poor *I* had sent a hundred pounds to America' (Thackeray, *Samuel Titmarsh*, Ch. XII). 'There is none so sick as, brought to bed, that robust *he* that ever has scorned sickness' (A. S. M. Hutchinson, *This Freedom*, p. 207).

Instead of the usual nominative of the pronoun to serve as the common form of the noun the accusative is often employed where the pronominal form used follows the verb, but also often elsewhere in accordance with the general tendency described in **7** C *a:* 'There was little *me*, astride on his bare back' (Hall Caine, *The Christian*, I, 334). 'In his place, I (a young lady) might have been just as bad, if I had been a *him*, you know' (De Morgan, *The Old Madhouse*, Ch. XXVIII). 'He viewed it (i.e., the play) as an awful lark, especially when the *Him* and the *Her* of it eat their little *dîner-de-noce* together' (*ib.*, Ch. XXX). The accusative is usually employed if an accusative to which it refers has preceded it: 'Flat, stupid uninteresting people, every one of whom has, behind a personality which does not appeal to us — important *us* — a story of some sort' (*ib.*, Ch. V).

g. A group of words: '*Two times two* is four.' '*Early to bed, early to rise* makes man healthy, wealthy, and wise.' 'In my time, *good in the saddle* was good for everything.'

h. A whole clause: '*Whoever knows him well* respects him.' For the different forms that a subject clause with a finite verb may have, see **21.** Gerundial clauses are a common characteristic of English: '*My friend's* (or simply *his*) *deceiving me* was a sad disappointment to me.' For the proper form of the subject of the gerund see **50 3.** The subject may be also an infinitive clause with an expressed subject: '*For me to back out* now would be to acknowledge that I am afraid.' Compare **21 e.**

II. *Peculiar Use and Meaning of Certain Pronominal Forms When Employed as Subject.* Attention is directed here to the following points of English usage.

A. SITUATION 'IT' AS SUBJECT. *It* is much used as subject to point to a person or thing that is at first presented in only dim outlines by the situation, but is often later identified by a predicate noun: '*It's John,* or *Anna,* or *the boys,*' or '*It's the boys,* isn't *it?*' (uttered by someone upon hearing approaching steps). 'Somebody sat behind him. A little later I saw that *it* was his brother.' 'Somebody sat behind him, but I couldn't see who *it* was,' but 'There were several sitting behind him, but I couldn't see who *they* were.' 'Who is *it* (or *he*)?' (referring to some gentleman who has just entered the room), but 'Who are *they?*' (referring to two or more). *It* is often a substitute for a noun obvious from the situation or the context: '*It* is twenty miles to Chicago.'

B. IMPERSONAL 'IT.' We now say '*It* rained yesterday,' but in Gothic, the oldest Germanic language, there was no *it* here. The verb had no subject at all. The original idea here was to call attention to an activity or a state without any reference whatever to a definite subject. In Gothic there were few such verbs, but in oldest English and German this group had become large, since the original idea of calling attention to an activity or state without any reference whatever to a definite subject had appealed more and more to English and German feeling as a convenient and valuable means of expression. Difficulties, however, arose in using this growing construction. These impersonal verbs in most cases introduced the sentence, a position which was beginning to be characteristic of questions requiring *yes* or *no* for an answer. To avoid the impression of a question and to comply with the established convention of associating a subject with the verb, *it* was early introduced as subject.

This *it* is related to situation *it* (A) in that it refers to a given situation, but it does not point to a definite or an indefinite person or thing.   As it does not indicate a definite or an indefinite person or thing, it is practically meaningless.   This *it*, though containing no real meaning, serves the useful purpose of giving the statement the outward form of an ordinary declarative sentence with an expressed subject, thus making it possible to preserve under changed conditions a useful old construction perfectly intact, for the insertion of the meaningless *it* in no way impaired the spirit of the old construction.   In older English, the original form of impersonal verbs without *it* lingered on for a long while wherever the verb would not stand in the first place and thus make the impression of a question: 'Now es day' (Hampole, early fourteenth century) = 'Now *it* is day.'   It even lingers still, but is no longer understood: 'Today is the first of January.'   The fact that we do not employ *it* after *today* here shows clearly that we do not feel *it* as subject of *is*, for we now regularly employ *it* as the formal subject of an impersonal verb. This usage became fixed in the course of the Middle English period. We here now construe *today* — once felt as an adverb — as a noun, the subject of *is*, so that the construction has ceased to be impersonal.

The *it*-form often competes here with the *there*-form (see C, p. 9), an entirely different construction in which *there* is an anticipatory subject pointing to the following real subject: '*It* snowed heavily last night' or '*There* was a heavy snow last night.'   The words 'snowed heavily' have the same meaning as 'was a heavy snow,' although the construction of the expressions is quite different, *snowed* being a verbal predicate and *snow* a subject.   The mind thus often employs two quite different means to express the same thought.   There is often no difference of meaning between the two means of expressing a thought: 'The ship *sails* tomorrow' or 'The ship *will sail* tomorrow.'   Even though the meaning is the same, there is sometimes a difference of coloring in the two means, as here in the *it*-form and the *there*-form. 'Was *snow*' with the concrete noun *snow* with its picture of the earth covered with a white mantle is a more lively expression than the abstract verb *snowed*.   We still say '*It frosted heavily* last night' alongside of '*There was a heavy frost* last night,' but '*It dewed* heavily' has been replaced by '*There was* a heavy *dew*.'   Instead of '*It* is dewing' we now say '*Dew* is falling.'   This fondness for the concrete as shown by employing a concrete noun in preference to an abstract verb is one of the striking features of modern English, often found also in other categories, as in 6 A *b*.

Also in other meanings the old impersonal construction is not so common as it once was.   We now often prefer a construction with a definite subject: '*It* wanted but a very few days (object of *wanted*) before that blissful one when Foker should call Blanche his own' (Thackeray, *Pendennis*, I, Ch. XXXVIII), but in Ch. XXXII 'There still wanted *half an hour* (subject of *wanted*) till dinner.' Where there is a reference to persons, there has long been a tendency to abandon the impersonal construction with certain verbs, since it is often desired to represent a definite person or thing as subject and thus indicate that the person is passing through an experience or that a definite person or thing is conceived as affecting the person. Thus older '*me* hungreth' has become '*I* hunger,' or more commonly '*I* am hungry,' since the subject is conceived as suffering. '*Me* (dative) thinks' (= it seems *to me*) and '*I* think' seem to us today to be two constructions with the same verb. Originally the two verbs had different forms. After the two verbs had in Middle English become identical and were felt as one, the personal construction here as so often elsewhere gradually supplanted the impersonal. In archaic language, however, the impersonal construction survives in the form of *methinks*. In Shakespeare's 'Woe is me' *woe* was felt as a noun, subject of the verb, just as we now feel it, but in the older form of the construction — 'Me is [it] wo' — it was an adverb governing the dative *me*, and the verb *is* was impersonal with the subject *it* always suppressed as the dative introduced the sentence. Likewise in *if* [*it*] *you please* we now construe *you* as subject and say *if you please*. Of course, older usage often lives on in dialect and hence is often reflected in our realistic literature: 'Don't you say almost every day "This and that will happen, *please* (subjunctive = *may it please*) God"' (*Adam Bede*, Ch. II, 29). Sheridan's 'How is *it* with you?' (*The Critic*, I, 2, A.D. 1779) has been replaced by 'How are *you?*' Similarly, older 'How fares *it* with you?' though still used in poetic language, as in 'How fares *it* with the happy dead?' (Tennyson, *In Memoriam*, XLIV), is now usually replaced by the personal construction where the word still survives in this meaning: 'A man might go farther and *fare* worse.' 'We shall see hereafter how *he* fared on his errand' (Freeman, *Norman Conquest*, IV, XVII, 77). Although the personal construction is displacing the older *it*-form, the latter is still common in many set expressions: '*it* is late,' '*it* is twelve o'clock,' '*it* is stormy, smoky,' etc.

C. ANTICIPATORY '*IT*' AND '*THERE*.' When we desire to call especial attention to the subject, we often withhold it for a time, causing the feeling of suspense.

Where the subject is an emphatic noun or important group of words, *there* is much used at or near the beginning of the sentence as anticipatory subject, pointing forward to the following real subject, the emphatic noun or important group of words: 'There once lived in this house *a very interesting old man.*' 'At that moment there came *a knock at the door.*' 'There is always *the possibility — the possibility, I say — of being All, or remaining a particle, in the universe*' (Thoreau, *Journal*, I, p. 486). Compare **3** *a* (4th par.). For especial emphasis the subject word (**4**) is sometimes placed before *there is* (*are*), followed by the modifiers of the subject: '*Some bodies* there are that, being dead and buried, do not decay' (Thoreau, *Journal*, V, p. 10). '*Men* there are yet living who have seen him, on many a day in the early seventies, riding his horse up Main Street, clad in the colorful garb of the past' (Percival J. Cooney, *The Dons of the Old Pueblo*, Epilogue). Always so in a question: '*What* is there to do?'

When there is no predicate noun in the sentence, anticipatory *there* is used to point to a following gerund used as the real subject: 'There is *no getting along* with him.' 'There is *no telling* what will happen.' In older English, *it* was used here instead of *there:* 'Cosin, *it* (now *there*) is *no dealing* with him' (Marlowe, *Edward the Second*, l. 904, about A.D. 1591, ed. 1594). But when there is a predicate noun or adjective in the sentence, *it* is the usual anticipatory subject pointing to a following gerundial subject clause: 'It is useless, of no use, no use, no good *your saying anything*' (or with general indefinite reference *saying anything*). Compare **21** *e* (5th par. from end).

Anticipatory *it* is also used to point to a following subject *that*-clause or a subject infinitive clause (**21** *e*): '*It* is necessary *that you exert yourself*' (or *to exert yourself*). '*It* is useless, of no use, no good *for you to say anything*' (or *your saying anything*, or with general indefinite reference *to say anything*, or *saying anything*). Here *use* and *good* are predicate nouns. If anticipatory *there* is used here, *use* and *good* are subjects followed by a prepositional phrase of specification: '*There* is no use, no good *in saying anything, in your saying anything*,' or sometimes, 'There is no use *of your saying anything.*' The *there* and *it* constructions are often blended: '*There* is no use *your telling me that you are going to be good*' (Oscar Wilde, *Dorian Gray*, Ch. XIX), instead of the correct '*There* is no use *in your telling me* that you are going to be good.' Compare **21** *e* (5th par. from end).

Differing from impersonal *it*, anticipatory *it* has a little concrete force, since it points to a definite subject, namely, the following infinitive, gerund, or substantive clause. The concrete force was very slight in oldest English, for the *it* was often omitted, likewise situation *it* (A), which is still often omitted, as illustrated in **5** *d*. The situation in both constructions made the thought clear. Anticipatory *it* was early introduced where, as in the preceding examples, the verb would otherwise stand in the first place, for the verb in the first place was beginning to be felt as characteristic of a question. The older type of sentence without anticipatory *it* lingered for centuries where some word or words preceded the verb: 'Of swich (such) thing [it] were goodly for to telle' (Chaucer, *Prologue of the Nonne Preestes Tale*, 13). In course of time anticipatory *it* has become well established, as it has been found helpful in indicating the grammatical relations, but older usage without *it* still occurs occasionally, even when the omission of *it* brings the verb into the first place. Older usage without *it* is best preserved in quaint dialect : '[*it*] Used to be he couldn't abide to eat a bite after the sun had set' (Maristan Chapman, *The Happy Mountain*, Ch. I). This older usage sometimes occurs in the literary language: 'One of his pistols, loaded, was already in his suitcase. [*it*] Remained only to be positively assured, on some occasion, that the Captain carried no gun' (*Red Book*, April, 1922, p. 112). Similarly, anticipatory *there* is sometimes suppressed, as in older English: 'From Texas came Pitzer, James, and Jeff Chisum, his brothers, to help him in his business. [*there*] Came, too, to reign over his household for years as chatelaine, Miss Sallie Chisum, his niece, daughter of James Chisum, as pretty a girl as ever set fluttering the hearts of the rough-riding cavaliers of the Pecos country' (Walter Noble Burns, *The Saga of Billy the Kid*, Ch. I).

Anticipatory *it* is also used when it is desired to emphasize a predicate adjective or noun, provided, however, that the logical subject is a singular noun denoting a lifeless thing, or is a clause. The sentence is introduced by *it*, followed shortly by the predicate adjective or noun in accordance with the old Germanic principle of putting the emphatic word in or near the first place: '*It* is astónishing the amount of unadulterated sun a man can stand when he is making hay.' '*It* is hárd wórk keeping the grass green this time of year.' '*It* is immatérial what names are assigned to them.' '*It* is vílely unjúst, men closing two-thirds of the respectable careers to women!' (Sir Harry Johnston, *Mrs. Warren's Daughter*, Ch. III). '*It* was my twó bróthers who did it.' Where the emphatic predicate in a sentence containing a subject clause is a noun denoting a person, we always employ anticipatory *it* when the desire is to identify, as in the last example; but when the desire is to describe, we may say with Shakespeare '*It* is a góod divíne that follows his own instructions' (*Merchant of Venice*, I, II, 15), or now more commonly we replace *it* by a personal pronoun that can indicate gender and number: '*He* is a góod divíne who follows his own instructions.' Compare **21** *c*.

On the other hand, if the logical subject is a noun denoting a person or is a plural noun or pronoun, we use an appropriate personal pronoun as anticipatory subject: '*He* is a bríght bóy, *that little brother* of yours.' '*They* are very engáging péople, *the French Canadians!*' '*They* are no órdinary hóuses, *those*' (Dickens, *Pickwick*, Ch. XXI).

After the analogy of the emphatic predicate adjectives and nouns found in sentences which are introduced by anticipatory *it* and followed later by a formal subject in the form of a subject clause, as described on page 11, it has become common to make any noun, adverb, or adverbial phrase or clause emphatic by converting it into an emphatic predicate introduced by *it is* (or *was*) and followed by the subject of the sentence in the form of a subject clause. Thus an emphatic subject may become formally the predicate of the sentence: 'It is not *Í* that am to blame,' instead of '*Í* am not to blame.' Compare **21** *c* and *e*. Similarly, emphatic adverbs, adverbial phrases, etc., may become formally the predicate of the sentence, as shown by the following examples and more fully in **21** *c* and **22** *a:* '*It is séldom* that I ever see him any more,' instead of 'I *séldom* see him any more.' '*It was on this condítion* that I went,' instead of 'I went *on this condítion*.' '*It was hére* that it happened,' instead of 'It happened *hére*.' The common use of adverbs and adverbial phrases as a predicate, as described in **7 F**, has facilitated the development of this curious but useful construction.

Though this construction with an emphatic word at the beginning of the sentence after the formal introduction *it is, it was*, etc., is not infrequent in the literary language, it is especially characteristic of popular Irish English, where it attracts attention not only by its exceedingly great frequency but also by the extremes to which the principle is carried. For instance, any element in a subordinate clause can be brought to the beginning of the sentence, although the subordinate clause itself less this element follows the principal proposition: 'It is *yoursélf* I am come here purposely to meet with' (Lady Gregory, *The Bogie Men*, p. 15). 'Is it *to shóot me* you are going?' (*id., The Full Moon*). The formal introduction *it is* sometimes drops out: 'A little shóp they are saying she will take for to open a flour store' (*ib.*). In Irish English, *it is* is often placed before an emphatic predicate adjective which expresses an attribute of a person, where in the literary language the adjective itself must stand in the first place, in accordance with the old Germanic principle described in **35 1**: 'It is *próud* she must be to get you' (Yeats, *Cathleen ni Houlihan*) = literary '*Próud* she must be to get you.'

In accordance with the old Germanic principle described in 35 1, 2, a predicate verb is placed in the first place in the case of an imperative: '*Hánd* me that book!' In older English also in the case of a question requiring *yes* or *no* for an answer: '*Knóws* he the wickedness?' (Shakespeare, *King Lear*, IV, II, 92). Today we prefer to secure emphasis in questions by the employment of another old Germanic principle. We introduce the sentence by an unstressed auxiliary, which contains the outward form of predication, and withhold for a time the real predicate, a predicate infinitive or participle, thus creating a feeling of suspense, which imparts emphasis: '*Does* he *knów* the wickedness?' '*Did* he *cóme?*' corresponding to older '*Cáme* he?' Compare 6 A *d* (2).

In oldest English it was still quite common in narrative to put the verb in or near the first place, since in narrative the idea of action often becomes prominent, or a form of the verb *be* was brought forward to call attention to a past state of things. Much later, Chaucer still uses this word-order with fine effect: '*Ran* Colle our dogge, and Talbot, and Gerland, *Ran* cow and calf, and eek (also) the verray hogges' (*The Nonne Preestes Tale*, 563). This old usage survives in choice lively narrative style: '*Came* Christmas by which, at the outset, everybody knew it (i.e., the war) would be over, and it was not over. *Came* June, 1915,' etc. (Hutchinson, *If Winter Comes*, p. 256). '*Came* days of storm, days and nights of storm, when the ocean menaced us with its roaring whiteness, and the wind smote our struggling boat with a Titan's buffets' (Jack London, *The Sea-Wolf*, Ch. XXVII). Since, however, this word-order with the verb in the first place had even in Old English become intimately associated with the idea of a question, it gradually became normal usage to place an adverb before the verb to differentiate narrative from interrogation. Thus by a simple device we can still in narrative keep the verb near the beginning of the sentence. We now employ here *there* at the beginning of the narrative and later on *then:* '*There sailed* a bold mariner over the sea. . . . *Then came* unfavorable winds.' '*There was* once a king.' In older English, before the verb *be* we sometimes find *it* instead of *there:* '*It was* an English lady bright. . . . And she would marry a Scottish knight' (Scott, *Last Minstrel*, VI, XI). *There* is used not only in narrative style to enable the verb to be brought near the beginning of the sentence, but it is employed also at the beginning of the sentence to announce the later appearance of an emphatic noun subject: '*There* never was in all the history of the world a gréater blúnder.' See 3 *a*.

D. PRONOUNS USED AS GENERAL OR INDEFINITE SUBJECT. The pronouns *one, we, you* are much used here with the same general or indefinite force: 'As long as *one* is young, *one* easily acquires new friends.' '*We* don't like to be flatly contradicted.' '*You* don't like to be snubbed.'

We often use *they* here, but with a somewhat narrower meaning, since it usually refers to a smaller circle or one remote, always excluding the speaker and the person addressed, hence often used by the speaker to assert something modestly, representing it as coming from others: 'In fashionable society *they* talk of the impending nuptials of the Duke of Clarence.' 'In that crowd *they* mostly play cards.' 'In Japan *they* generally marry without love.' '*They* say best men are moulded out of faults' (Shakespeare).

When a writer or speaker desires to refer to himself modestly, there is a tendency at present to employ the indefinite *one* instead of the sharply precise *I* or *me:* '*One* (or *a person, a fellow*) *doesn't* (instead of *I don't*) like to be treated that way.' 'Under such circumstances you might offer to help *one*' (or *a fellow* instead of *me*).

E. EDITORIAL '*WE.*' The first person plural is often used by authors and speakers instead of the first person singular, and the possessive *our* instead of *my,* the author or speaker thus modestly turning the attention away from himself by representing his readers or hearers as accompanying him in thought: 'Thus far *we* have been considering only the outward condition of things at Luther's birth, now *we* are to turn (or let *us* turn) our attention to his early home influences.' A speaker or writer often modestly employs *we* since he speaks also for those associated with him: '*We* (the editor speaking for the editorial staff) owe an apology to the public for not noticing this work on its first appearance.' In these examples *we* still has the original associative force, but it now often refers to only one: '*We* (the reviewer of the book) do not say that everything in these essays is as good as what *we* have quoted.' 'It will be easier to explain this later on, when *we* have said something about what is called the history of language' (Wyld, *The Growth of English,* Ch. I, 8). The Plural of Modesty in its earliest forms is very old, for we find a quite similar usage in classical Latin.

Instead of *we* some authors employ here a noun with the third person of the verb: 'The *author* would remark,' etc.

F. PLURAL OF MAJESTY. Of later origin than editorial *we* is the associative *we* first used in the third century in imperial decrees; in that period of Roman history when two or three rulers reigned together and hence were associated in the official proclamations. Later, whenever the political power was centered in one emperor the old *we* was retained, so that although the associative force was present, since the ruler included his advisers, the associative *we* developed into royal *we*, the Plural of Majesty, since the ruler

spoke of himself in his official announcements in the plural instead
of the singular, as 'We decree' instead of 'I decree.' This usage
spread to the different European courts and was common in the
Old English period.

G. WE = YOU. *We* is often used with the force of *you:* 'Are
we downhearted today?' Often sarcastically: 'How touchy *we*
are!' 'Oh, ain't *we* select since *we* went to that hen college!' (Sinclair Lewis, *Babbitt*, Ch. II, II) (retort of a boy to his sister, who has
graduated from Bryn Mawr, and on the occasion in question has
spoken to him sarcastically).

H. THOU, THEE, YE, YOU. In Middle English, it was still
possible to express the idea of number in the personal pronouns of
the second person. In the singular, *thou* was used as subject and
thee as dative and accusative object, while in the plural *ye* served
as subject and *you* as dative and accusative object. These grammatical functions for *ye* and *you* were widely observed until the
middle of the sixteenth century, and survive in the Biblical and
higher poetical language of our time. In the fourteenth century,
however, the form *you* — with reference to one or more — sometimes replaced *ye* in the subject relation in the usual intercourse
of life, and later in the course of the sixteenth century became more
common here than *ye*. Occasionally we find the opposite development in older English — *ye* was used instead of *you* in the object
relation: 'I do beseech *ye*' (*Julius Cæsar*, III, I, 157). In older
English, *ye* is thus not infrequently used in both the subject and
the object relation, often in the form of *ee: 'D'ee (do ee)* know this
crucifix?' (Middleton and Rowley, *The Spanish Gipsie*, III, III,
40, A.D. 1661). 'I commend me *t'ee*, sir' (Chapman, *The Gentleman
Usher*, III, II, 208, A.D. 1606). This usage survives in British
dialect. The outcome of this development for the literary language
is *you* for nominative, dative, and accusative. In Biblical language
ye is now uniformly employed as nominative and *you* as dative and
accusative, as can be seen in the present text of the King James
Version of the Bible. In the original text of this version this usage
was not so uniform, as there were in it a number of *you's* where we
now find *ye*. Both *ye* and *you* are here still always plural forms as
originally.

The use of the plural forms *ye* and *you* for reference to one person
is closely related to the use of the plural of majesty *we* described in
F above. As a ruler often spoke of himself in the plural, others in
addressing him felt that they should employ the plural form. After
this model it became general in continental Europe to address by a
plural form every individual of high rank in church and state. At
last, plural form became a mark of politeness in general and was

used in speaking to an equal as well as to a superior. This new usage arose in England in the thirteenth century under the influence of French, which here followed the continental Latin usage. The new polite form of addressing one person by the plurals *ye* and *you* did not at once displace the older usage of employing *thou* and *thee* here. For a long while the old and the new forms often alternated with each other, but gradually the new form was distinctly felt as more polite. Thus, in older English, the forms were often differentiated. *Thou* was used in familiar intercourse, and *you* employed as a polite form in formal relations. In Pecock's *Donet* (about A.D. 1449) the father, throughout the book, addresses his son by *thou* and *thee*, while the son out of deference uses *ye* and *you* to his father. The British dialects of the South and South Midland still distinguish between *thou* or *thee* used in intimate relation and *you* or *ye* (often written *ee*) employed in polite language in more formal intercourse. In the eighteenth century, Richardson in his *Pamela* lets Lady Davers use *thou* to her brother in moments of strong emotions and employ *thou* to Pamela in moments of anger and tenderness. This usage survives in British dialects.

In the standard prose English of the eighteenth century, *thou* and *thee* were entirely replaced by *you*, so that the form of polite address became general in the common intercourse of life, the one form *you* serving without distinction of rank or feeling for one or more persons and for the nominative, dative, and accusative relations. The lack of clearness here has called forth in the popular speech of America, Australia, and Ireland a plural ending for this form to indicate more than one, *yous* (or *youse* and in Ireland also *ye, yees, yez, yiz*): 'He'll settle *yous* (= you kids), *yous guys*.' It is not unknown in British English. Horace Walpole in a letter to Miss Mary Berry, March 27, 1791, in speaking of her and her sister Agnes writes playfully: 'I have been at White Pussy's (i.e., Lady Amherst's) this evening. She asked much after *yous*.' This advantage, however, is sometimes lost through the popular tendency to simplify, i.e., to employ *yous* also as a singular: 'So! At last I found *youse*' (cartoon in *Chicago Tribune*, Sept. 16, 1923).

In the southern states, *yóu all* is used as the plural of *you:* 'He'll settle *yóu all*.' The genitive *yóu all's* is also in use: '*yóu all's* business.' *Yóu all* may be addressed to a single person provided the form is felt as a plural comprising a definite group of individuals: 'Do *yóu all* (addressed to a clerk representing the different members of the firm) keep fresh eggs here?' (Alphonso Smith, *The Kit-Kat*, Vol. IX, p. 27). The *all* in *you all* is often reduced to *'ll*, as it is only weakly stressed: 'Boys, I want *you'll* to stop that noise' (*ib.*). In the literary language *you áll* is used, but the stressed *all* indicates that the thought is different from the normal southern use of *yóu all*, which is simply a plural of *you:* '*You áll* are wrong,' or 'You are *áll* wrong.' In popular speech *you uns* is often used as the plural of *you.* The genitive is *you uns'*. In certain British dialects *you together* is used as plural of *you.* In the literary language and in ordinary colloquial speech we bring out the plural idea here by placing some plural noun after *you:* 'you gentlemen,' 'you boys,' 'you kids,' etc.

The older universal use of *thou* and *thee* in the singular and *ye* and *you* in the plural to all persons has survived in the higher forms of poetry and elevated diction, where the thoughts soar, but in the realistic forms of poetry the actual language of everyday city and country life holds almost complete sway, even where the thoughts rise somewhat from earth, the poet forgetting that the language of earth keeps us on earth: 'Oh, when I was in love with *you*, Then I was clean and brave, And miles around the wonder grew, How well did I behave' (Housman, *A Shropshire Lad*, XVIII). Thus the old poetic forms, long used to elevate thought and feeling, are in our own time breaking down; it may be because the poetic elevation of thought and feeling that once gave them meaning is no longer present.

In older English, *thee* is sometimes seemingly used as a nominative subject, where in fact it may be an ethical dative (**12 1 B** *c*): 'Hear *thee* (possibly an ethical dative, but now felt as a nominative), Gratiano!' (*Merchant of Venice*, II, II, 189). This same form is also sometimes found in older English as a real nominative, perhaps after the analogy of *you*, which has one form for all the cases: 'How agrees the devil and *thee* about thy soul?' (Shakespeare, *I Henry IV*, I, II, 127). 'What hast *thee* done?' (Marlowe, *Jew*, 1085, about A.D. 1590, ed. 1636). 'If *thee* wilt walk with me, I'll show thee a better' (words of a young Quaker to Benjamin Franklin, as quoted in Franklin's *Autobiography, Writings*, I, p. 255). This usage lingered much later in popular speech: 'I know *thee* dost things as nobody 'ud do' (George Eliot, *Adam Bede*, Ch. IV).

Thou and *thee* are still used by Quakers, often with the nominative form *thee* in connection with the third person of the verb, as explained in **8 I 1** *h*: '*Thou art not* (or now more commonly *thee's not*) consistent.' The Quaker address originally had a deep meaning in that it was used toward all men irrespective of rank, and hence emphasized their equality, but it has become a mere symbol of sect since society in general recognized this democratic principle by the employment of *you* without respect to social station.

5. Omission of the Subject. In general every sentence must have a subject expressed, but usage admits of certain irregularities. The subject is omitted:

a. As a rule in imperative sentences: 'Hand me that book.' Compare **45** 1 a, b, c.

b. In the first person in a few set expressions: 'Thank you.' 'Hope to see you again.' In colloquial American the subject I is usually omitted in the expression 'I say' employed to call attention to what is about to be said: 'Say, do you know who that is?' It is omitted also when 'I say' is employed as an exclamation: 'Say! won't it be glorious?' In British English, I is usually expressed in both uses of 'I say.'

c. Grammarians usually say that a subject governing a preceding possessive genitive is suppressed if the same word is used shortly before or after: 'Of the three autos *William's* [auto] is the best.' 'John's hair is darker than *his sister's* [hair is].' 'So did his maiden sister, Miss Monica Thorne, than *whose* [heart] no kinder heart glowed through all Barsetshire' (Trollope, *Dr. Thorne*, II, Ch. XXIV). The common impression that words are omitted here, as indicated above in brackets, is in a scientific sense erroneous. The genitive in all such cases, as here *William's, his sister's, whose*, has in English developed into a possessive pronoun. This can be clearly seen in such cases as '*Yours* is the greater treason, for *yours* is the treason of friendship.' Here *yours* is a possessive pronoun, pointing forward to the governing noun *treason*. No noun can be supplied after *yours*, hence there is no omission here. In the other cases there is likewise in the exact sense no omission since the genitives have become possessive pronouns. For fuller information see **57** 5 a.

d. As in oldest English, there is still often no subject expressed since it is suggested by the context. From a modern point of view we may supply as subject situation *it* (**4** II A) or some other pronoun. This old construction is most common after *as* and *than:* 'Come as soon *as* [*it*, i.e., the coming, *is*] possible.' 'He described the affair *as* [*it*, i.e., the description] *follows*.' 'The conditions are *as* [*what*] *follows*' (or sometimes *as* [*they here*] *follow*). 'As many *as* [*they*] *came* were caught.' In older English, the subject was often omitted after an *as* which introduced a degree clause of modal result (**29** 2): 'I was seized by a fever which grew so upon me *as* (now *that it*) forced me to a resolution of seeking my physician at London' (John Donne, *Letter to Mrs. Cokain*, Aug. 24, 1628). The pronoun *what* is often omitted: 'He never reads as much *as* [*what*] *is* required of the class.' 'He accomplished more *than* [*what*] *was* expected of him.' Even though the subject is omitted, anticipatory *there* (**4** II C) is often employed after *than* and *as* to point forward, as it were, to the following omitted subject: 'One would say that there were fewer flowers just now *than there* have been' (Thoreau, *Journal*, II, p. 282).

Similarly, the pronominal object is often omitted here: 'Bring as many of them as you can find.' 'He bought more of them than he needed.' There is no object in the subordinate clause here since the meaning is made clear by the words *many* and *more* of the principal proposition.

The predicate is likewise often suppressed since it is implied in some word in the principal proposition, especially in a predicate adjective: 'Out of this war (between the North and the South) we emerged more *homogeneous* as a people than we had ever been before' (Henry Watterson, *Editorial*, May 11, 1909). 'I am as *well* as I have ever been.'

Similarly, an adverb is often suppressed: 'He works harder than he did as a young man.'

Earlier in the period, a *what* was sometimes inserted in all these grammatical relations to fill the vacancy that was felt: 'On the twentieth of the last February there came on a snow, which, being added unto what had covered the ground a few days before, made a thicker mantle for our mother than *what* (subject) was usual' (Thoreau, *Journal*, VIII, p. 163). 'I think I laughed heartier then than *what* (adv. acc.) I do now' (Scott, *Heart of Midlothian*, Ch. XXX). This *what* is a marked feature of current popular speech; 'I'm more in earnest than *what* you are.' 'I hope you can walk quicker than *what* you eat.' *What* is now never inserted here in the literary language.

In older English, omissions of pronouns were very common in the subordinate clause where a preceding word suggested the meaning of the sentence. This older usage survives only in set expressions, as here after *as* and *then* and in relative clauses: 'The book *I* hold [*it*] *in my hand* is an English grammar.' Compare **19** 3 (3rd par.), **23** II.

There is sometimes a difference of meaning between the form of expression with the subject suppressed and that with the subject expressed: 'The neighbors were kind *as could be*' (Julia Peterkin, *Scarlet Sister Mary*, Ch. XXIX), but 'On this occasion the gruff old fellow was as kind *as he could be.*'

e. Subject Omitted when Verb is Used Absolutely. In 'For whosoever hath, to him *shall be given*' (*Matthew*, XIII, 12) the subject of the principal proposition is omitted as the verb is used absolutely (**46**, 2nd par.), i.e., without regard to a subject.

THE PREDICATE

FORMS OF THE PREDICATE

6. The predicate can be:

A. **A Finite Verb of Complete Predication:** 'Birds *sing.*' 'Dogs *bark.*' 'Riches *pass* away.' 'Mary *writes* neatly.' 'Mary *writes* beautiful letters.' Verbs of complete predication are often not complete of themselves and need some other word or words, as in the last two examples, to make the meaning complete, but the term 'verb of complete predication' is not entirely without inner justification. Such verbs stand in contrast to copulas (B, p. 26), which in a mere formal way perform the *function* of predication and do not in an actual sense predicate. Verbs of complete predication, on the other hand, predicate, say something of the subject; they present

20

a general line of thought which is basic even if it has to be often supplemented by details. The verb with all its modifiers constitutes the complete predicate.

The verb is not always a simple word, as in the preceding examples, but is often made up of an auxiliary and another verb-form, both together usually called the verb-phrase: 'I *have* just *finished* my work.' 'I *shall* soon *finish* my work.' 'I *cannot finish* my work today.' Though the auxiliary has finite form as far as possible and the verb proper is in a formal sense dependent, the verb proper contains the basic thought.

In oldest English, the verb usually stood at or near the end of the sentence. This withholding of the verb for a time created the feeling of suspense and thus made the verb prominent. Later, it often became desirable to make important modifiers of the verb prominent by suspending them for a time, so that the verb was gradually crowded out of the end position. See **35** 1 *a*. We have, however, never lost all feeling for the old principle of rendering the verb emphatic by withholding it for a time: 'Many things we gladly remémber, others we gladly forgét.'

a. VERB OFTEN UNIMPORTANT. The verb often becomes quite an unimportant element in a sentence and on account of the overtowering importance of some other part of the predicate is so little felt that it may be omitted: '[take your] Hats off!' '[sit] Down in front!' A part of the verbal predicate is often suppressed since it is suggested by the context: 'Have you done it?'—'Of course, I have [done it].' 'Then, I take it, there had been — er — ?'—'An estrangement. Yes, there had [been]' (Pinero, *The Thunderbolt*, Act I). 'They [have] been comin[g] here a long time' (Meredith Nicholson, *Blacksheep*, p. 21). '[have] You seen Elmer again?' (Edith Wharton, *The Custom of the Country*, Ch. IV). '[did you] Get my wire?' (Edwin Balmer, *Breath of Scandal*, Ch. XIII). '[it would] Serve you right if Red (name) wouldn't answer your old letter' (J. P. McEvoy, *The Potters*). '[would you] Like to know him?' (Pinero, *Sweet Lavender*, Act I). 'But I guess I [had] better go in' (Tarkington, *Gentle Julia*, Ch. XX).

In lively narrative the suppression of the verb often imparts to the description the idea of a brisk movement of events: 'Down the gorge and over the bridge at the bottom of it' (Wallace, *Ben Hur*, VIII, Ch. VIII). Similarly, in imperative sentences: 'The horses — and quickly!' (*ib.*, VIII, Ch. IX).

In older English, the infinitive of a verb of motion was often thought unnecessary after an auxiliary, where according to present usage it must stand: 'Thou shalt [go] to prison' (Shakespeare). In Scotland, North Ireland, and in parts of America this old usage is still quite common after *to want* (= *to wish*): 'I want [to get] off.' 'I want out.' 'I want in.' 'Belgium *wants in* this protective arrangement' (from an editorial in *Chicago*

Tribune, Nov. 10, 1919, p. 8). 'Who said I *wanted back?*' (*ib.*, cartoon, Sept. 19, 1923). It is also still commonly and widely preserved after the full verb *let* (= *allow*) in certain set expressions: (to a conductor on a street car) 'Let me off at 12th Street!' Dickens in his *Barnaby Rudge,* Ch. XVII, uses it after the modal auxiliary *let* (**43** I A), where it now seems odd to us: 'Let us to supper, Grip!' Here and there the old construction occurs elsewhere in recent literature, indicating that there is still some feeling for it: 'I'll into the kitchen!' (Alfred Noyes, *The Torch-Bearers,* p. 109). It survives generally in the proverb 'Murder will out.' In certain dialects, as in Scotch English, it is still widely used: 'We'll jist awa' up the stair an' luik' (George Macdonald, *Robert Falconer,* Ch. X).

b. FINITE VERB REPLACED BY NOUN. There is a marked tendency in English to clothe the chief idea of the predicate in the form of a noun instead of a finite verb: 'The matter is *under consideration,*' instead of 'The matter is *being considered.*' 'After dinner we *had a quiet smoke,*' instead of 'We *smoked quietly.*' 'I got a *good shaking up,*' instead of 'I was *shaken up thoroughly.*' 'We got *a good snub.*' Similarly, there is a strong tendency to clothe the chief idea of the predicate in the form of a noun instead of an infinitive which depends upon an auxiliary and hence contains the real verbal meaning: 'Let me *have a try,*' instead of 'Let me *try it.*' 'I'll *make a try* (instead of *try*) at least not to be a disgrace to my Alma Mater' (Mary R. S. Andrews, *The Eternal Masculine,* p. 381). '*Let's have a good swim!*' All these cases indicate a reluctance in colloquial speech to predicate by means of a full verb, since this method is felt as too formal, too scientific, precise. In colloquial language there is here as elsewhere a tendency to more concrete forms of expression. A noun seems nearer to popular feeling than the more abstract verb. The verbs that are used here in colloquial speech are all of the nature of the copulas described in B. They merely serve to connect the predicate noun, the real predicate, with the subject.

c. USE OF 'DO' TO AVOID THE REPETITION OF A VERB. In all the different periods of English a form of *do* has been employed as a pro-verb to avoid the repetition of a verb that has just been used: 'If competition advances as it *has done* for several years.' 'He has never acted as he *should have done.*' 'He behaves better than you *do.*'

In many cases this usage is more modern, coming from the omission of the infinitive in the periphrastic *do*-form (*d*) of the verb: 'Shall I ask him?' — '*Dó* [ask him]!' or 'O please *dó* [ask him]!' 'Did you tell him?' — 'Of course I *did* [tell him]' or 'I surely *did* [tell him].'

d. USE OF THE PERIPHRASTIC FORM WITH 'DO.' In the present and the past tense of verbs of complete predication the simple verb is often replaced by a periphrastic form made up of *do* and a dependent infinitive: 'Thus conscience *does make* (= *makes*) cowards of us all' (Shakespeare); originally according to **46** (next to last par.) '*causes a making* of cowards out of us all.' At first, *do* was a full verb with an infinitive as object. Later, it lost its concrete force and became a mere periphrastic auxiliary. In older English, as in the example from Shakespeare, there was usually no clear difference of meaning between the simple and the

periphrastic form. Sometimes the periphrastic form was chosen because
it was a clearer past tense form, as in 'For my vesture they _did cast_
(instead of simple _cast_) lots' (_John_, XIX, 24); sometimes for the sake of
dignity, euphony, rhythm, emphasis, often from mere caprice. This older
use of the periphrastic form without a clear differentiation from the
simple form survives in poetry and in Biblical, liturgical, and legal language. The _do_-form of the verb is now used only in the present and the
past tense, but in early Modern English it was sometimes employed also
in the present perfect and the past perfect, especially in Scotland: 'as I
afore _haue done discus_' (Lauder, _Tractate_, 340, A.D. 1556) = _have discussed._
The infinitive following the past participle _done_ was sometimes attracted
into the form of the past participle: 'Remember . . . How that my
50wth I [_have_] _done forloir_' (past participle instead of the infinitive _forleir_
'lose') (Dunbar, XXII, 2) = 'Remember that I have lost my youth.'
'Thay ar Wolfis and Toddis, quha . . . _haue_ violentlie _done brokin_
(instead of _break_) the dyk of the Scheipfald' (Burne, _Disput._, 78, V,
A.D. 1581) = 'They are wolves and foxes who _have_ violently _broken_ the
wall of the sheepfold.'   Both forms of this construction are still found in
popular southern American English: 'I [_have_] _done tell_ you 'bout Brer
Rabbit makin' 'im a steeple' (Joel Chandler Harris, _Nights with Uncle
Remus_, p. 97). 'I 'speck I [_have_] _done tole_ (instead of _tell_) you 'bout dat'
(_ib._, p. 97). 'I've _done found_ (instead of _find_) it' (Margaret Prescott Montague, _Up Eel River_, p. 182). The past participle resulting from attraction
is now much more common than the older infinitive form. This attraction
takes place also after the past tense _done:_ ' 'Tain't so mighty long sence I
done tole (instead of _tell_) you 'bout ole Mr. Benjermin Ram' (Joel Chandler
Harris, _Nights with Uncle Remus_, p. 297). Compare **49** 4 C (1) _a_ (last par.).
   The periphrastic form with _do_ was rare in Old English, but began to
become common in the fourteenth century and was at its height between
1500 and 1700. After the periphrastic and the simple form had long been
used interchangeably, a desire for more accurate expression led to a differentiation of their meaning. This had become possible since the periph-
rasis had come to be felt as an analytic form and, like other analytic
forms, could assume different shades of meaning according to the stress,
as explained on page 24. Present usage became fixed about 1750, but with
certain verbs the old simple forms lingered on even in plain prose long
after they had elsewhere passed away; indeed here and there linger still,
especially in set expressions, as _if I mistake not, I care not, I doubt not, I
know not, what say you? what think you?_ etc. Of course, the poet makes
still more liberal use of the old forms when it suits his purpose. In popular
speech there is a tendency to employ the _do_-form with the copula _be_ in
declarative sentences, which is contrary to literary usage: 'Some days
she _do be_ awful about her food' (Dorothy Gerard, _The Eternal Woman_,
Ch. XV).
   In plain prose we now employ _do:_
   (1) In the present and the past tense of a verb of complete predication
when it stands in a question, a declarative statement, or an entreaty
where there is a desire to emphasize the idea of actuality, the truthfulness

of a claim, realization or a desire of realization: '*Dídn't* he work?' '*Díd* he work?' '*Dóes* he cheat?' 'I still maintain that you *didn't dó* it.' — 'But I *díd* do it.' 'Why don't you *wórk?*' — 'I *dó* work.' 'I am so happy to learn that you *dó* intend to come.' '*Dó* finish your work!' (desire of realization). Compare (3), p. 25, 1st paragraph (end).

The employment of a stressed *do* to emphasize the idea of actuality is in accordance with the general tendency in English to emphasize the idea of actuality, realization, or modality by the use of a stressed auxiliary: 'Why are you not studying?' — 'I *ám* studying.' 'You have done that before.' — 'I *háven't.*' 'Now I shall tell your mother. Mark my words, this time I *sháll* tell your mother' (Bennett, *Old Wives' Tale*, II, Ch. IV). 'He hasn't come yet, but he *wíll* come.' 'Why don't you dó it?' — 'I *cán't.*' 'I haven't done it yet, but I feel that I *shóuld* do it.' We have discovered the possibility of using our analytic verbal forms in such a way as to shade our thought. In these compound forms the auxiliary merely performs the formal function of predication, gives the time relations, or colors the thought. The verbal meaning lies in the participle or infinitive. If we desire to emphasize the verbal meaning, we stress the part of the verb that contains the verbal meaning, i.e., the participle or infinitive; but if we desire to emphasize the idea of actuality, truthfulness, realization, or modality, we stress the auxiliary: 'Why aren't you *wórking?*' — 'I *ám* working.' 'Why don't you *wórk?*' — 'I *dó* work.' This great advantage of our analytic forms has been the active factor in extending their use. Compare **37** 3.

The copula and the auxiliaries, which in single propositions, like the preceding examples, are much used to emphasize the idea of actuality, truthfulness, are now also employed with the same force in double propositions, where the copula or auxiliary stands in the second shorter statement, reaffirming the truth of the preceding longer statement. The shorter proposition consists of only two words, a subject, repeating the preceding subject in the form of a pronoun or a more explicit noun, and a predicate, repeating the preceding verbal predicate in the form of a copula or an auxiliary, which is sometimes only moderately stressed, sometimes, in language charged with feeling, strongly stressed in connection with a strong stress upon the repeated subject, so that there results a double stress, as so often elsewhere in lively speech: 'He was odd, *was the Captain.*' 'But it's a cunning devil, *is that machine* (type machine)! — and knows more than any man that ever lived' (Mark Twain, *Letter to Orion Clemens*, Jan. 5, 1889). 'Dick had his Bible out and was praying volubly. He had been well brought up, *had Dick*' (Stevenson, *Treasure Island*, Ch. XXXII). 'He had a particular taste, *Mr. Glenarm had*' (Meredith Nicholson, *The House of a Thousand Candles*, Ch. III, p. 43). 'I did not know him. I really *didn't*' (Joseph Conrad, *Chance*, Ch. II). 'The Shipping Master swung round on his stool and addressed me as "Charles." *He did*' (*ib.*, Ch. I). 'Alexandra! Can't you see he's just a tramp and he's after your money? He wants to be taken care of, *hé dóes*' (W. S. Cather, *O Pioneers!* p. 167). 'I love him, *Í do*.' Similarly, we repeat a modal auxiliary to emphasize the idea of modality: 'John must *dó* it, he just *múst.*' 'John can *dó* it, I just know he *cán.*' 'John can *dó* it, *cán't* he?' 'John can't *dó* it, *cán* he?'

(2) The *do*-form is used also in the present and the past tense of a verb of complete predication when it stands *in an entreaty*, or *in a question*, or *in a declarative sentence with inverted word-order* where there is a desire to stress the activity or to inquire after or to state simple facts without any intention of emphasizing the idea of actuality: 'Do *finish* your work!' 'Does he *beliéve* it?' 'How's (= how does) it *stríke* you?' (Jack London, *The Sea-Wolf*, Ch. VII). 'Did you *sée* him do it?' 'What's he *sáy?*' 'What did he *ánswer?*' 'Where did he *cóme* from?' 'When did he finally *gó?*' 'Bítterly did we *repént* our decision.' 'Never did I *sée* such a sight!' In such entreaties and questions and in such declarative statements with inverted word-order the verbal meaning is usually quite prominent and hence the verb is usually stressed. In contrast to older English, we now use the *do*-form here, so that by stressing the infinitive we can emphasize the verbal meaning pure and simple.

The *do*-form was so often used in questions for the sake of securing a pure verbal form to stress and emphasize that it has become associated with interrogative form and is now used in all questions, even where the verb is not emphatic: '*Whére did* you buy it?' '*Whóm did* you meet?' The old simple forms are now only used in questions when the subject is an interrogative pronoun: '*Who met* you?' In older English, the simple forms could be used also when some other word was subject: '*Discern'st thou* aught in that?' (Shakespeare, *Othello*, III, III, 101). The old simple forms are still used for archaic effect in historical novels: '*Saw* you ever the like?' (Wallace, *Ben Hur*, Ch. X). Also in certain dialects, as in Scotch English, the old simple forms are still used: 'What *paid* ye for't?' (George Macdonald, *Robert Falconer*, Ch. XXI). The older simple form survives widely in the literary language in the case of *have*, especially in England: '*Have* you swordfish?' alongside of the more common *do*-form, '*Do* you *have* swordfish?' In indirect questions the old simple form is preserved with all verbs: 'When *did* you *come* back?' but 'I asked him when he *came* back.'

(3) *Do* is employed also in the negative form of questions, declarative statements, and commands when simple *not* is the negative, only, however, in the present and past tense of verbs of complete predication, of course, therefore not in the case of the copula *be*, the tense auxiliaries, the modal auxiliaries *can*, *must*, etc., the auxiliary-like verb *ought*, often also the auxiliary-like verbs *need* and *dare*, both of which, however, may take *do;* usually also not in the case of *have* in unemphatic statements: 'He *doesn't live* here,' but 'He *isn't* here.' 'I *do not* often *forgét* it,' but 'I *must not forget* it.' 'I *do not go* home till eight,' but either 'I *need not go* home till eight' or 'I *do not need to go* home till eight.' 'She *dared not tell* (or *to tell*) him,' or 'She *did not dare tell* (or *to tell*) him.' 'I *haven't* it with me,' but in emphatic statement 'I *do nót have* it with me,' where, however, in colloquial speech we may employ also the form without *do:* 'You have it with you.' — 'I *háven't.*' In commands and entreaties: '*Don't tóuch* me!' '*Don't have* a thíng to *dó* with him!' '*Dón't go* yet!'

In negative commands and in positive and negative entreaties *do* is used also with the copula *be*, as *do* has become associated with negative commands and both positive and negative entreaties: '*Don't* be late!' '*Dón't yóu* be late!' '*Dó* be reasonable!' '*Dón't* be unreasonable!' In popular speech *do* is used also elsewhere with *be:* 'Now, boy, why *don't* you *be* perlite and get up and give one of these young ladies a seat?' (*Punch*).

Thus in negative statements there is usually an auxiliary, *do* or some auxiliary of tense or mood or auxiliary-like verb. In all such cases, as explained more fully in **16** 2 *d*, the sentence adverb *not*, like other sentence adverbs, stands after the auxiliary immediately before the real verbal element, the infinitive or participle. The *do*-form is chosen in the case of verbs of complete predication in order that the sentence adverb *not* may stand in its natural place before the real verbal element. In case of the auxiliaries *has, may, can*, etc., the *not* follows the auxiliary regularly and thus comes into its natural position before the real verbal element.

Although in negative statements the old simple forms have disappeared from simple prose, the charm of the beautiful older simplicity often asserts itself in the language of our better moments: 'We cannot do wrong to others with impunity. Our conscience *résts not* until the wrong be righted.'

B. Predicate a Verb of Incomplete Predication + Complement.
The predicate may be also a verb of incomplete predication in connection with a predicate complement, the verb assuming in a mere formal way the *function* of predication, the complement, noun or adjective, serving as the real predicate: 'The whale *is a mammal*.' 'Man *is mortal*.' A verb of incomplete predication is called a copula, or linking verb. The verb *be*, the oldest and most common of the copulas, has in most cases nothing whatever of its original concrete meaning, so that it for the most part is employed today not to convey sense but merely to perform a function, to indicate predication, connecting the subject with the real predicate. Concrete meaning, however, often enters into *be*, but it is usually inconspicuous, so that the form is felt as a copula, connecting a subject with the real predicate: 'The book *is* (= *is lying*) on the table.' 'He *is* (= *is sitting*) on the veranda.' 'He *is* (= *is standing working*) in his workshop.' Sometimes, however, the force is more concrete. For examples see **7** D 3.

There are at present a large number of copulas, or linking verbs, in English, verbs in various stages of development toward the copula state, all containing more or less of their original concrete meaning, so that, though all are copulas, they are all more or less differentiated in meaning from one another and from the copula *be*. A number of them are serving not only as copulas, but also as full verbs, preserving in certain meanings their original concrete force: 'The cow has *run*, or *gone* (full verbs), into the barn,' but 'The cow has *run*, or *gone* (copulas = *become*), dry.' As copulas they indicate a state, continuance in a state, or entrance into a state. Simple state: 'He *is* sick.' 'He *is* a great master.' Continuance in a state: 'He *continues* obstinate.' 'He *keeps* still.' Entrance into a state may call attention to the first point or the final point in a development. First point: 'He *became* (or *got*) sick.' 'He (i.e., Keats) now also *commenced* poet' (J. R. Lowell, *Literary Essays*, I, p. 224). Final point: 'He *became* (or *went*) blind.' 'He *became* a great master.' As the predicate is often a verbal adjective, a past or present participle, the copulas are often employed as auxiliary verbs. As auxiliary of the passive voice: 'Our house *is* painted every year.' Here *is* has the force of *gets*, an old meaning that it has had for many centuries, hence the literal meaning is, 'Our house enters every year into the painted state.' In colloquial speech *get* is often used here: 'Our house *gets* painted every year.' Compare **47** *b*. As auxiliary of aspect (**38** 1) indicating duration: 'He *is* working.' 'He *keeps on* working.'

The most common copulas are: *appear, bang* (Door *banged* shut), *become, blow* (Door *blew* open), *blush* (She *blushed* red; see also **7** A *d*), *break* (He *broke* loose or free), *break out, bulk, burn* (Clay *burns* white), *burst out, catch* (**7** F), *chance, come, commence, continue, cut up* (British Eng. = *turn out to be:* He *cut up* rough, i.e., showed resentment), *eat* (The cakes *eat* crisp, i.e., prove to be crisp when eaten), *fall, feel, flame* (His face *flamed* redder), *flash* (He *flashed* crimson with anger), *flush* (Her cheeks *flushed* red; see also **7** A *d*), *fly* (Door *flew* open), *get, go, go on, grow, happen, hold, keep, keep on, lie, live, look, loom, make* (see (3) and (4), p. 28), *prove, rank, remain, rest, ring, rise, run, seem, shine, show, sit, smell, sound, spring* (**7** B *a*), *stand, stay, strike, take* (colloquial American in '*take* ill, sick'), *taste, turn, turn out, wax, wear* (Coat *wears* thin), *work* (Button *works* loose). *Appear, seem*, and often *look*, though copulas, differ from the others in that they have subjunctive force, casting more or less doubt upon the statement. See **44** I (last par.).

All these copulas are intransitive verbs and differ only in this respect from the copula-like verbs in A *b*, which are for the most part transitives.

There are four classes in these intransitives: (1) Those originally intransitive: 'He *fell* ill.' 'What I ate *lies* heavy on my stomach.' 'He *stands* high in the community.' (2) Verbs originally transitive which have become intransitive since their object is so often omitted that it is no longer felt: 'The room *struck* [one as] cold and cheerless' (Phillpotts, *The Secret Woman*, Ch. II). 'When George Herbert *left off* [being] courtier and took orders, he burnt his earlier love-poetry' (G. H. Mair, *English Literature*, p. 84). (3) Somewhat different from the verbs in (2) are reflexive verbs which have dropped their reflexive object since they have developed intransitive meaning, as described in **46**: 'He felt much depressed,' originally 'He felt himself much depressed.' 'I felt such a fool' (A. Marshall, *The Squire's Daughter*, Ch. VI). 'He is *making* (for *making himself*) merry over us.' 'Seen by the strong light of the window, her face *showed* [itself] sallow in tone' (Ellen Glasgow, *Life and Gabriella*, Ch. I). (4) On the other hand, the transitive *make* often retains its object but loses so much of its concrete force that it is felt as a copula with the meaning *become*, *turn out to be:* 'She will *make* him a good wife.' We here still dimly feel *wife* as an object, but we cannot put the sentence into the passive with *wife* as subject, which shows that *wife* is virtually a predicate noun after the copula *make*. Here the former object *wife* does not drop out, as the objects in (3), because it has received a new function, while in (3) the objects drop out since they no longer have a function and have become useless. In form, however, *wife* is still an object, as we can see by the simple dative object *him* before it. (5) As described in **46**, intransitives often acquire passive force: 'This cloth *feels* (i.e., is felt as being) soft.' On the other hand, as passive force is often found in intransitive form we sometimes use intransitive form instead of passive: 'He *took* ill' instead of 'He *was taken* ill,' just as we often say 'The first consignment *sold* out in a week' instead of 'The first consignment *was sold* out in a week.' In the case of both *feel* and *take*, however, their concrete meaning and passive force are not as prominent as their function of copula to introduce a predicate adjective.

The old linking verb *worth* (= *be, become*) has passed out of common use, now usually replaced by other copulas: 'Woe *worth* the chase (dative), woe *worth* the day (dative), That costs thy life, my gray' (Scott, *Lady of the Lake*, I, ix, 166) = 'Woe be to the chase, woe be to the day,' etc.

    a. Appositional Type of Sentence or Clause. The use of a copula represents an advanced stage of language development. Originally it was sufficient merely to place the predicate complement alongside the subject without any formal sign of predication. Colloquial speech teems with examples of the older type of sentences: 'Our sister *dead?*' 'Everybody *gone?*' 'Everything *in good condition*.' This primitive type of sentence, which simply consists in placing the predicate complement alongside the subject, is called the appositional type of sentence. The predicate adjective may not only follow the subject, but it very often precedes it: 'A *sad* experience!' '*Good* work!' '*Poor* fellow!' In many cases, as in the last example, for instance, this old appositional type of sentence is firmly fixed in English usage, and can scarcely be changed into the later conventional form with an expressed copula. The old type is most common where there is a strong expression of feeling, as in the last example.

In the prehistoric period of Indo-European, before it split up into different languages, the finite verb of complete predication had become established to indicate that the subject is acting, acted upon, or resting in a certain condition. Where the predicate was a noun, adjective, adverb, or prepositional phrase, the old appositional type of sentence still in general remained in common use. But even in this prehistoric period the copula *be* was often used to connect the subject with a predicate noun, adjective, adverb, or prepositional phrase. This verb was chosen because in its historical development it had at this time lost a good deal of its original concrete meaning and yet retained its verbal *form*. The loss of concrete meaning and the retention of its verbal endings made it possible to employ it as a formal means to introduce the predicate noun, adjective, adverb, or prepositional phrase, for by virtue of its verbal form it possessed the power of predication as in its earlier days when it was a verb of complete predication, and moreover could indicate the relations of time and *mood*, two important features not found in the older appositional type of sentence.

From the very start the new type of sentence with the copula has been closely associated with formal accurate language, hence is employed in the calm flow of thought in declarative sentences and hasn't such exclusive sway in loose colloquial speech or where strong feeling is involved. Of course, the old type is common in old saws which often preserve faithfully older forms of expression. In many of these old saws we can see that this primitive type can in spite of its simple structure often indicate clearly the complicated grammatical relations of complex sentences: '[if something is] Out of sight, [it soon comes] out of mind.'

This old type of predication without a copula is still common in the headlines of our newspapers: SNOWDEN'S STAND CRITICIZED (*The New York Times*, Aug. 17, 1929). Still common also in advertisements: 'Money back guarantee in every package.'

On the other hand, it is still common in choice poetic prose, where it often possesses a peculiar charm: 'Blossom week in Maryland! The air steeped in perfume and soft as a caress: the sky a luminous gray interwoven with threads of silver, flakings of pearls and tiny scales of opal! All the hillsides smothered in bloom — of peach, cherry and pear!' (F. Hopkinson Smith, *The Romance of an Old-Fashioned Gentleman*).

It is best preserved in the subordinate clause. In the predicate accusative (15 III 2) construction: 'She boiled *the egg hard*' = 'She boiled the egg *that it became hard*.' 'The President made *him a general*' = 'The President disposed so *that he became a general*.'

But it is not at all confined to the cases where the predicate of the subordinate clause is an adjective or a noun. It is widely used also where the predicate of the clause has the force of a verb of complete predication: 'I wrote to *him to come*' = 'I wrote to him *that he should come*.' This terse old type of predication without a finite verb is described in detail in 20 3.

In popular Irish English it is employed more widely than in the literary language, the infinitive or participle here usually serving as predicate. It can be used in any kind of subordinate clause: (subject clause) 'It is not fitting *McDonough's wife to travel without company*' (Lady Gregory, *McDonough's Wife*). (conditional clause) '*I to have money or means in my hand*, I would ask no help' (*ib.*). It is especially common here in the second of two propositions connected by *and*, where, according to **19** 3, the second proposition is felt as logically subordinate: 'What way wouldn't it be warm *and it* (i.e., the sun) *getting high up in the South*' (causal clause) (J. M. Synge, *The Well of the Saints*, p. 1).

C. **Predicate Appositive.** The predicate may be also a verb of complete predication in connection with a predicate complement, usually called predicate appositive: 'He came home *sick*.' '*Tired and sleepy*, I went to bed.' 'She asked him *in tears* to come again.' 'He came home *very much depressed*.' 'The two persons who had entered the house *friends* left it *with feelings of alienation*.' 'Leslie reached Edinburgh *a general without an army*.' 'He died *the* (or *as the*) *richest man* in the state.' 'This successful enterprise will go down in local history *as representing the best that our town can do*.' For the use of *as* here, see **7** A *b* (3) and **7** B *c*.

The predicate appositive often not only adds a remark about the subject but also has the force of an adverbial clause, thus sustaining relations to both the subject and the principal verb: 'She sat at the window *sewing*' (with the force of an adverbial clause of attendant circumstance). '*Being sick* (= *as I was sick*), I stayed at home.' '*Having finished my work* (= *after I had finished my work*), I went to bed.' The wide use of the predicate appositive in this category is one of the most characteristic features of our language. Compare **48** 2 (5th par.).

The predicate appositive is also found with passives: 'Even *as a young boy*, he was regarded as very promising.'

The predicate appositive is, of course, also found after *be* when the verb is in fact not a copula but a verb of complete predication: 'He is (is lying) at home *sick*.'

The predicate complement is used not only with verbs of complete predication but also with a predicate noun or adjective: 'He is a good neighbor, always *ready* to lend a helping hand and do a good turn.' 'She was like a bird, *full* of joy and music.' '*Far* from being kind, he was most cruel.'

Also limiting adjectives are used as predicate appositive: 'But there is a little redness, a kind of tendency to inflammation around them (i.e., the eyes), and she is likewise slightly marked with the small pox; *both* which blemishes were then imperceptible' (Mrs. Eliza Fay, *Letter*, April 24, 1779), now 'which blemishes were then *both* imperceptible,' or '*both* of which blemishes were then imperceptible.' 'There had ridden along with this old princess's cavalcade two gentlemen, who *both* were greeted with a great deal of cordiality' (Thackeray, *Henry Esmond*, I, Ch. XII), or 'who were *both* greeted with a great deal of cordiality,' or '*both* of whom were greeted with a great deal of cordiality.' 'They were *all, both, each,* or *themselves*, wrong.' 'The others were *all* killed' or '*All* the others were killed.' The word-order *all the others* in the last example shows clearly that *all* is developing toward the estate of an attributive adjective, but at the same time indicates its origin as a predicate appositive. We say *his whole* (attributive adj.) *time*, but *all his time, half his time, all these books, half these books*, since a predicate appositive cannot stand between a limiting adjective and the governing noun. Similarly, we say *these two books*, but *both these books*. After the analogy of *two of these books* we now say also *both of these books, all of these books, half of these books*, and 'He sent me some beautiful ties, *all of which*, however, were too small for me,' or with the old appositional construction, 'He sent me some beautiful ties, *which*, however, were *all* too small for me.' These limiting adjectives may be used also as predicate appositive to an object: 'I have the letters *all* together.' 'I have already paid Messrs. McCrea and Maire *half* their account' (George Mason, *Letter to George Washington*, Feb. 17, 1775). 'I've not said *half* what I've got to say.'

On the other hand, *half* is often used as a noun, preceded by a limiting adjective and followed by a partitive genitive: *my half of the money*. 'I've not said *the half of what I've got to say*.'

The nouns *half, third, quarter*, etc., are often used as predicate appositive to a subject or an object, standing before the subject or the object: '*My half the melon* is good.' '*My half the money*' (George Mason, *Letter to George Washington*, Feb. 17, 1775). 'Were I but capable of interpreting to the world *one half the great thoughts and noble feelings* which are buried in her grave!' (John Stuart Mill, *On Liberty*, 1). 'The fleet did not have *a quarter the number* of boats it should have had' (Theodore Roosevelt, *The Rough Riders*, Ch. II).

Where the predicate is an adjective or a participle, we avoid the adjective *half* in the predicate appositive relation, since it would be felt here as an adverb: '*Half of them* were dead,' not '*They* were *half* dead,' for *half* is here felt as an adverb.

The peculiar word-order connected with *many* and *some* in older English shows that they were predicate appositives: 'as there be *gods many* and *lords many*' (*I Cor.*, VIII, 5); 'the letters . . . Of *many our contriving friends*' (Shakespeare, *Antony and Cleopatra*, I, II, 188); 'the fate of *some your servants*' (Ben Jonson, *Sejanus*,

V, i, 59, A.D. 1616). We now say *many of our contriving friends,*
some of your servants. For the further discussion of the predicate
appositive see **10** II 2 H *b*.

7. Predicate Complement or Appositive. The predicate complement or appositive may be:

A. A NOUN:

a. In the nominative after verbs of incomplete predication and
after passives:

(1) After the copulas enumerated in **6** B or after their infinitives
and gerunds: 'Socrates was *the son* of a sculptor.' 'They fell *a prey*
to the angry waves.' 'He (Silas Marner) felt *a reformed man,* de-
livered from temptation' (George Eliot). 'What big *girls* you're
both getting' (A. Marshall, *The Eldest Son,* Ch. II). 'She looks *a
lady,*' but *look* is a transitive verb with an accusative object in
'She looks *compassion, daggers,*' 'She would have said more; she
looked *the remainder,*' 'Some women use their tongues — she look'd
a lecture' (Byron, *Don Juan,* I, xv). 'Sir Leslie Stephen had the
double advantage of both being and looking *a man of letters.*'
'"The Scarlet Letter" remains *the greatest work* of the kind in the
English language.' 'I shrank from grateful words which would
have sounded *payment*' (Meredith). 'They turned *Catholics* from
sincere conviction.' 'The boy will turn out *a marvelous man.*'

In accordance with the old Germanic principle described in **3** *a*
the predicate noun may for emphasis sometimes still stand in the
first place: 'Cantánkerous cháp Roger always was!' (Galsworthy,
The Man of Property, p. 24). Compare **35** 1 (7th par.).

The infinitive *be* is often added to the finite form of a number of
these verbs which have considerable concrete force in order to
mark them more clearly as copulas: 'He *seemed* (or *seemed to be*) a
happy man.' 'Young Pen *looked to be* a lad of much more consequence than he was really' (*Pendennis,* I, Ch. XVIII). 'He *lived
to be* a very old man.' 'He *rose to be* president of the company.'

After the verbs *let, bid,* the simple infinitive of these copulas is
used to connect the predicate noun or adjective with the accusative
subject: 'Let me *be* your friend.' 'I bade him *be* a good boy.' 'I
bade him *be* quiet.' After other verbs the copula in infinitive
clauses usually has the prepositional form: 'He never expected *to
become* a criminal.' 'I want you *to remain* my friend.' As *he,* the
subject of the principal proposition in the first example, is a
nominative, so the predicate of the infinitive clause, *criminal,* is also
in the nominative. In the second example, as the subject of the
infinitive clause is the accusative *you,* so the predicate of the clause,
friend, is also in the accusative. Distinctive forms, of course, are
found only in the case of pronouns, which are regularly in the

accusative in the predicate if the subject of the clause is an accusative: 'He thought Richard to be *me*.' 'A boy whom I believed to be *him* just passed me.' 'I believed it to be *her*.' 'They supposed us to be *them*.' '*Whom* do you suppose them to be?' The predicate accusative becomes nominative after a passive: 'It was at first thought to be *he*' (or in loose colloquial speech usually *him*, as explained in 7 C *a*). In the active form of statement the infinitive clause is not so common here as a full clause with a finite verb: 'He thought Richard was *I*' (or in loose colloquial speech usually *me*, as explained in 7 C *a*).

On the other hand, if the complement is predicated of the genitive subject of a gerund, it is in the nominative: 'I was sure of its being *he*' (or in loose colloquial speech *him*, as explained in 7 C *a*).

A noun is often predicated of a direct accusative object without the aid of a copula — an objective predicate accusative: 'The President made him *a general*.' This is the appositional type of predication described in 15 III 2.

(2) After the passive forms of the transitives (see 15 III 2) which take a predicate accusative in the active, as in 'The President made him a *general*': 'He was made *a general*.' 'He was appointed *agent*.' 'He was called *John*.' 'He was called *bad names*.' 'He was acclaimed *king*.' 'The Amsterdam Congress (of Socialists) must be written *a failure*' (*Times* Correspondent).

b. The predicate nominative is introduced by *as:*

(1) After the intransitive *appear:* 'This appears to me *the* (or *as the*) *only way* out of the difficulties.'

(2) After the passive forms of *look upon, look at, consider, regard, greet, treat,* and all others (for list see 15 III 2 A) which in the active take a predicate accusative introduced by *as* (see (3) below), as in 'I look upon him *as a worthy man*': 'He is looked upon *as a worthy man*.' 'He is regarded *as our* (or considered *our*, or less commonly *as our*) *most trustworthy man*.'

(3) After a copula + complement and after intransitives of complete predication and after passives, *as* is often placed before a predicate appositive, although in accordance with older usage *as* is still often, especially in poetry, lacking here, as sometimes also in the two preceding categories: '*As a teacher*, he is a stern disciplinarian.' 'Methinks you breathe Another soul; your looks are more divine; You speak *a heroe* (now in plain prose *as a hero*), and you move *a god*' (now in plain prose *as a god*) (Dryden, *All for Love*, I, I, 435, A.D. 1678). 'She acted *hostess* (more commonly *as hostess*) at the ducal parties' (Elinor Glyn, *The Reason Why*, Ch. VII). 'One of those robust natures and incisive constitutions to which doubt figures *as a sickness*' (Morley, *Voltaire*, 11). 'Lincoln was

born *a* (or *as a*) poor farmer's *boy* and died *President* (or *as President*) of the United States.' 'People are not born *carpenters*, but sometimes they are born *painters*.' 'He was detested *as a Tory*.' 'He was shunned *as a man of doubtful character*.'

Here *as* (from *all so*, i.e., *quite so*) as a determinative (**27 2**, last par.) points as with an index finger to the following noun which expresses the idea in mind, thus always indicating *oneness with, identity*. For more information about its origin see **15** III 2 A. This *as* stands in contrast to the predicate appositive adjective *like* that takes after it a dative object (**11 2 g**): '*As a true friend* he stood by me to the end,' but '*Like a friend* he came to me and exchanged a few words with me, but I knew that he was inwardly not friendly disposed toward me.' The *as* here expresses complete identity, oneness with, while *like* indicates mere similarity. Latin *qua* (ablative fem. sing. of the relative pronoun *qui*, hence = [*in the way*] *in which*, i.e., with the meaning of *in the capacity of*) is sometimes used with the force of an emphatic *as:* 'He does it, not *qua* father, but *qua* judge.'

c. Instead of introducing the predicate complement by *as*, as in *b*, we still after a few verbs in certain set expressions employ a prepositional phrase introduced by the preposition *for*, a usage once more common than now: 'He passes *for an accurate scholar*.' 'Analogy goes *for very little* in the pronunciation of English.' 'He was taken *for his brother*.' 'If thou losest the prize, thou shalt be scourged out of the lists *for* (or *as*) *a wordy and insolent braggart*' (Scott, *Ivanhoe*, Ch. XIII). The verbs which in **15** III 2 A sometimes take *for* in the active, of course, take it sometimes in the passive.

In older English, *for* was used here in connection with the predicate *what* and the verb *be*, where *what* and *for* have the force of *what kind of*, as *was für* in German: '*What* is he *for a fool* that betroths himself to unquietness?' (Shakespeare, *Much Ado About Nothing*, I, III, 49). '*What* is she *for a woman?*' (Dryden, *Marriage à la Mode*, I, I). This older usage survives here and there in popular speech.

d. After an intransitive copula containing the idea of growth, development, or a change of position or condition, the predicate complement indicates the final stage of the development or the new position or state: 'I speculated how it would look when the youth grew *a man*' (Mrs. Craik, *Domestic Stories*, I, Ch. V, 251). 'He became *a rich man*.'

The simple predicate complement is common only after *become*. In a few expressions the nominative is used after *turn, blush, flush:* 'She turned *a livid white*.' 'She blushed, flushed, *a deep rose color*.'

Usually a preposition or, after certain verbs, the infinitive form *to be* stands before the predicate complement to indicate more clearly the idea of a final stage or a new position or state: 'From a robust and vigorous infant I grew *into a pale and slender boy.*' 'When the boy grows *to man,* and is master of the house, he pulls down that wall and builds a new and bigger' (R. W. Emerson, *The Conduct of Life,* p. 34). 'You've suddenly turned *into a woman* and *into a very clever one.*' 'Something *got into my throat,*' in contrast to 'Something *was in my throat.*' 'The machine *got to running* (gerund) smoothly,' in contrast to 'The machine *was running* (predicate participle) smoothly,' but sometimes, as explained in **50** 4 *c dd,* we find simple *get* here instead of *get to:* 'If I *get lying* (predicate participle) awake tonight, I shan't,' etc. (De Morgan, *Joseph Vance,* Ch. X, p. 74). 'She grew up *to be a lovely woman* like her mother.' 'He rose *to be inspector* of police.' 'He lived *to be a very old man.*' 'A rumor does not always *prove* (or *prove to be*) *a fact.*'

e. *Predicate Genitive.* After the verbs *be, become, seem, feel,* a predicate genitive is used to express several ideas also found in the attributive genitive, namely, *characteristic, origin, possession, material,* and sometimes the *partitive* idea, now usually with the prepositional form of the genitive except in the case of the possessive genitive, although the old simple genitive was once common in most of these relations: 'I am quite *of your opinion.*' 'This matter is *of considerable importance.*' 'We are *of the same age.*' 'Be *of good cheer.*' 'He seems (to be) *of a sound mind.*' 'I feel *of no use* to anybody.' 'He was not *of the poor class.*' 'Render therefore unto Cæsar the things which are *Cæsar's,* and unto God the things which are *God's*' (*Matthew,* XXII, 21). '*God's* is the quarrel' (Shakespeare, *Richard the Second,* I, ii, 37). 'Nature has denied him (i.e., Lord Curzon) the wit that is *Lord Rosebery's*' (*Athenæum,* 17/7, 1915). ''Tis *mine* To speak' (Wordsworth, *The Prelude,* XIII, 12). 'It is not *ours* (or in simpler language *for us,* or in colloquial speech often *our business*) to criticize them.' 'The house is *of stone.*' 'But ye believe not, because ye are not *of my sheep*' (*John,* X, 26).

The old simple genitive of possession is still very common when it points backward or forward to a preceding or following noun or pronoun, but here, as in **57** 5 *a,* it is often to be construed as a possessive pronoun, like *mine, hers,* etc.: 'The book is *my brother's,* not mine.' Compare **57** 5 *a.* The prepositional genitive of characteristic often develops here into an adjective, as is indicated by the frequent dropping of *of,* which converts the group of words into a compound adjective, as in **10** I 2: 'The plank is not [*of*] *the right width.*' 'The chimneys are [*of*] *the same height.*' 'The two boys

are [*of*] *the same size, age.*' 'My face became [*of*] *a very bad color.*'
'The door was [*of*] *a dark brown.*' 'This ring is [*of*] *a pretty
shade.*' 'It's [*of*] *no use.*' 'I only wish I could do it again; then
I should feel [*of*] *some use*' (Galsworthy, *Saint's Progress*, 205).
'Don't be [*of*] *any trouble* to him.' '[*of*] *What benefit* are all these
experiments?' '*What age* is she?' '*What part of speech* are these
words?' '*What price* is this article?' '*What* are potatoes today?'
Similarly, in the appositional relation after a governing noun
where the appositive has the force of a predicate: 'She is a gawky,
slipshod, untidy child, with hair [which is *of*] *the color* of tow.'

An objective predicate genitive of characteristic is used after
show, make, represent, regard, etc.: 'He showed himself *of noble
spirit,*' or 'He showed himself *to be of noble spirit.*' The *of* of the
genitive here is often suppressed as in the predicate genitive and
for the same reason: 'He made the two planks [*of*] *the same width.*'
'He painted the door [*of*] *a green color.*' '[*of*] *What color* shall I
paint the door?' After some verbs the objective predicate genitive
is introduced by *as:* 'I regard this *as of great importance.*' See also
15 III 2 A. The objective predicate genitive here, as the objective
predicate accusative in **15** III 2, is joined to its subject, the object
of the principal verb, without the aid of a copula, since the statement is felt to be of the old appositional type of sentence described
in **6** B *a,* where the predicate is placed alongside of the subject like
an appositive without the aid of a finite verb.

The genitive — usually introduced by *as* — is often used as a
predicate appositive after intransitives of complete predication:
'This consideration ought to weigh *as of value* to you.'

B. PREDICATE ADJECTIVE AND PARTICIPLES. The predicate
complement or appositive may be an adjective or a participle:

a. Adjective or Participle as Complement. The adjective or
participle may be predicated of a noun or pronoun in the nominative, here usually standing after a copula (**6** B) or after the passive
forms of the transitives (**15** III 2), which in the active take a noun
or a pronoun as a direct object and an adjective or a participle as
objective predicate, as in 'He knocked *him crazy*': 'The verdict
appears [to be] *just.*' 'He is *rich.*' 'He became *happy.*' 'He was
not a man who bulked (or figured) *large* in the thoughts of his
contemporaries.' 'It came *easy* to me.' 'She fell *ill.*' 'He feels
uneasy.' 'He got quite *angry.*' 'Much of our best literature goes
virtually *unread.*' 'The offer holds *good* for a month' (Mildred E.
Lambert, *American Speech*, Oct., 1928). 'He kept *silent.*' 'The
meat keeps *good.*' 'She keeps *well.*' 'He lived to be eighty years
old.' 'He looks *healthy.*' 'The shadow of these things it was that
had suddenly fallen upon her spirit, and loomed *thick* and *dark*

between her and the friend of her early years' (Allen Raine).
'The rumor proved [to be] *true*.' 'He ranks *high* as a general.'
'All services rank *the same* with God' (Browning). 'He remained
silent.' 'He will not rest *content* with these victories.' 'It is only
where he drops the grand style that his verse really rings *true*.'
'Our ammunition is running *short*.' 'Oldish gentlefolks run *fat* in
general' (George Eliot, *Silas Marner*, Ch. XI). 'He seems to be
contented.' 'The joy shone *clear* and *warm* on her face.' 'It shows
white from here.' 'He sits *tight*' (slang). 'It smells *bad*' (adj.)
but 'It smells (i.e., stinks) *badly*' (or *disgustingly*) (adverbs).
'I feel *bad*' (not *badly*). 'Your sentence sounds *well* (adj.), *bad*.'
'It sounds *good* to hear your voice again.' 'It sounded *harsh* to
me.' 'But, then, evening came, and the stars sprang *alight*' (Sarah
Gertrude Millin, *God's Stepchildren*, Ch. II, I). 'On this question
we two stand *alone*.' 'Stay *quiet* for a little while.' 'It tastes
sour.' It turned *cold*.' 'The rumor turned out *false*' (or *to be
false*). 'My father waxed *hotter* and *hotter*.' 'He was knocked
crazy.' 'The egg was boiled *hard*.' 'He was found *dead*.' For
the insertion of *to be* in a number of these sentences see A *a* (1).

We still often find here the old verbless appositional type of
sentence described in **6 B *a*:** *The little rascal! The poor fellow!
A beautiful sight! A sad fate!* In narrating indirectly such direct
outbursts of feeling we often give them in part narrative form by
the use of the copula as formal predicate, but instead of converting
the adjective into a predicate adjective we often under the influence of the original strong impression retain its original attributive
form, so that we say 'Indeed it was a beautiful sight!' instead of
'Indeed the sight was beautiful!' and 'Mary's (or hers) was a sad
fate!' instead of 'Mary's (or her) fate was sad!'

The governing substantive does not always stand in the predicate, as in these examples, but often serves as the subject, standing
in the first place, the adjective standing in the predicate, not as a
simple predicate adjective, but in substantive form (57 1) with the
suffix *one* referring back to its governing noun, so that the adjective is in reality not a predicate adjective, for we always feel its
relation to its governing noun: 'The sight is indeed *a beautiful one!*'

Though we thus often replace the simple predicate adjective by
more expressive attributive and substantive forms, we are, on the
other hand, fond of it in connection with a complementary prepositional phrase as a more forcible form of statement than a transitive verb with an accusative object: 'You *are forgetful of* (= *forget*)
the fact that,' etc. 'I *was ignorant of* (= *didn't know*) these facts.'
'Inaccuracy *is fruitful of* (= *produces*) error.' 'His style *is provoca-
tive of* (= *provokes*) controversy.' This usage is very common in

learned speech and often tends away from simplicity in the direction of bombast.

The adjective or participle may be predicated also of a direct accusative object: 'It made him *angry*.' 'She boiled the egg *hard*.' 'I saw him *making* a kite.' This is the so-called objective predicate adjective or participle. Compare 15 III 2 and 15 III 2 A. As can be seen by the last example, the participle here often has the force of a finite verb. Compare 48 2 (3rd par.).

The predicate adjective is often found in the infinitive and the gerundial construction without reference to a definite subject since the reference is general: 'To be *cheerful* is the habit of a truly pious mind.' 'The desire of being *happy* reigns in all hearts.'

aa. Predicate Noun with the Force of an Adjective. In the predicate a noun often loses its concrete force, representing no longer an individual person, but now a general abstract idea, often without an article: 'He was *fool* (= *foolish*) enough to marry her.' 'He was not *blunderer* enough to betray his thought.' 'He was more *hero* than *scoundrel*.' 'He was *master* of the situation.' 'The child is *father* of the man.' 'If I were *sovereign*, I would rule that,' etc. 'He looked at me and, *heavy* and *strong man* as he was, he thought it wiser to speak me fair.' 'Under such strokes a courageous heart may turn *coward*.' 'He turned *traitor*.' 'Even irreligious people don't feel *week-day* on Sundays' (Hichens). 'The highest genius is splendidly *spendthrift*; it is only the second order that needs to be niggardly' (A. Symonds, *Browning*, quoted from Wendt's *Syntax*, I, p. 115). 'that I may rest assur'd Whether yond troops are *friend* or *enemy*' (*Julius Cæsar*, V, III, 18).

Where, as in the last example, there is a reference to more than one, the idea of a number of individuals is usually present to our feeling, so that we more commonly put the noun in the plural in spite of its abstract nature: 'Whether yonder troops are *friends* or *enemies*.' 'They were *masters* of the situation.' 'Are we not *men* enough to face things as they are?' (John Burroughs, *Accepting the Universe*, p. 11). In 'I am *friends* with him' the plural idea is so strong that the predicate noun is plural although the formal subject is singular. In a few set expressions, however, as a survival of older usage, the abstract idea is still stronger than the conception of different individuals, so that the noun, like an adjective, keeps its singular form: 'They stood *sentry*.' 'Two girls sat *sentinel* beside her' (M. H. Hewlett, *The Forest Lovers*, 237). 'They turned *Christian*' (Kipling, *Plain Tales*, 11). Jespersen in his *English Grammar*, II, p. 166, cites two more examples after *turn*: 'Enthusiasts have tried the experiment of turning *husbandman*' (Gissing, *Henry Ryecroft*, 188). 'Young gallants with no intention to turn *husband*' (Walter A. Raleigh, *Shakespeare*, 161). The definite article imparts here abstract force, so that it is used with the singular even where the reference is to more than one: 'They were too much *the lady* to make up to a gentleman who so obviously did not want them' (J. M. Barrie, *Tommy and Grizel*, 23). Of course, often used also where the reference is to one: 'He (J. Ramsay MacDonald) looked *the prime minister*' (Edward Price Bell, *Why MacDonald Came to America*, p. 25).

The predicate noun here does not usually agree with its subject in gender, but the masculine form, as the more abstract of the two genders, is employed with reference to both sexes: 'The King's wife was in reality *king*.' 'She was *master* of the situation.' 'She is *Jew*, through and through.' 'Nightfall saw her *victor* (objective predicate; see **15** III 2 A) in this domestic contest.' In such sentences, however, as 'As for Mary, she was *mistress* of herself enough to whisper to Elizabeth' (Jane Austen, *Pride and Prejudice*), the feminine form *mistress* becomes natural since we are influenced in our feeling by the accompanying *herself*. Of course, the feminine form is regularly employed when the predicate noun refers to something specifically feminine: 'She is more *mother* than *wife*.' 'Sheila was very *woman*, and one Paris gown and the prospect of more had lifted her from the depths to the heights' (Rupert Hughes, *Clipped Wings*, Ch. XXXI).

In a few expressions the definite article is used with the noun to indicate a particular noticeable state of things: 'I am not quite *the thing* (= *well*) today.' 'Blue socks are now *the thing*' (= *proper, in vogue*). 'What's *the matter* (= *amiss*) with him?' 'She has something *the matter* (objective predicate = *amiss*) with her spine.'

On the other hand, modified nouns used as attributive adjectives, as described in **10** I 2, are often used in the predicate, and, as pure adjectives, are invariable: 'He is *high church*.' 'I'm *west country* myself.' 'The Windfields felt hopelessly *small town*' (Rupert Hughes, *Clipped Wings*, Ch. XXXI). 'His evidence was too *first hand*' (Galsworthy, *Man of Property*, II, Ch. X). 'He is *first rate* as a cricketer' (George Bernard Shaw). Compare **7** A *e* and **10** I 2.

b. Predicate Complement Introduced by 'As' or 'For.' Instead of the simple adjective or participle the predicate is in certain instances, as in the case of nouns, introduced by *as* or *for:* 'He is generally regarded *as honest, as defeated*,' etc. 'He passes *for rich*.' 'He was left *for dead*.' 'He was taken up *for dead*,' quite different in meaning from 'He was taken up *dead*.' 'This should be taken *for granted*.'

c. Adjective or Participle as Predicate Appositive. The adjective or participle is associated as predicate appositive (**6** C) with an intransitive or transitive verb of complete predication: 'He died *young*.' '*Unfortified* by philosophy and *unconsoled* by religion, he perceived the arrival of the end with tears and lamentations.' Compare **6** C.

The predicate appositive is in certain cases introduced by *as:* 'Those who vote for this measure go on record *as being* willing to further public interests at the expense of their own.'

C. Predicate Pronoun, or Adverb 'So' instead of Pro-

NOUN. The predicate complement may be a pronoun: 'It was *he*.' 'It was *they*.' 'It was *we*.' In colloquial speech the accusative is often used here. See *a*, p. 41.

The predicate complement may be a pronoun, referring to some preceding sentence or description, or to the idea contained in a preceding noun, adjective, verb, or prepositional phrase: '*Thát* (or *súch*) was the close of a remarkable life.' 'The thing is to be free all around in this world, and only the poor can be *thát*' (Phillpotts, *Forest*, Ch. III). 'He is the author of the article, but he does not desire to be knówn as *such*.' ' "They must be curious creatures." — "They áre *that*," said Humpty Dumpty' (Lewis Carroll, *Through the Looking-Glass*). 'She is a queen, and looks *it*.' 'She is very tired, and looks *it*' (or *so;* see 3rd par. below). 'But I call no Man bad till *súch* he's found' (Robert Rogers, *Ponteach*, I, IV, A.D. 1776), but now more commonly, 'till he's found to bé *that*' (or *so;* see 3rd par. below). 'He is patient, *which* you never are.' 'She did it without murmuring, like the brave girl *which* (or *that*) she was.' 'I tried to stop him, madman *as* he was.'

That and sometimes *such* (now not so commonly as formerly) can be used thus also as objective predicate (**15** III 2): 'His sister is tactful, but I couldn't call hím *that*.' 'He is honest, and you will always find him *thát*' (or sometimes *súch*, or *so;* see 2nd par. below).

If the indefinite pronoun *one* is used as predicate, it does not refer back to an idea as do *such*, *that*, and *it*, but points indefinitely to a person or thing: 'He was a notorious miser, and looked *one* generally' (Reade, *The Cloister and the Hearth*, Ch. I). In older English, *such* was used here, and is sometimes still so used. Compare **57** 5 *b*.

Instead of a predicate pronoun we often employ the adverb *so* as predicate, especially in connection with *if* and *why* and in referring with emphasis to the idea contained in a preceding adjective, noun, or prepositional phrase: 'John, I hope you have not forgotten the butter. *If* [that is] *só*, you must go back and get it.' 'I don't like my teacher.' — 'Why [is that] *só?*' 'He is poor, and *só* am I.' 'He is a Catholic, and *só* am I.' 'Is he a faithful friend?' — 'He certainly has proved *so*.' Although *so* is often emphatic, *that* conveys still greater emphasis: 'To feel with them, we must be like them; and none of us can be *thát* without pains' (Ruskin, *Sesame*, I).

Sometimes both *it* and *so* can be put to good use in the same sentence: 'She is shy, but it is a peculiarity of hers that she never looks *it* and yet is intensely *so*.'

The form *so* is, in general, the more common of the two; but, in contrast to older usage, now generally drops out when the copula *be*, or in a compound tense its tense auxiliary, in accordance with 6 A *d* (1), is strongly stressed, or *not* is stressed: 'Are you ready?' — 'I ám.' 'He used to be rich, but ísn't any more.' 'You are my true friend, and always háve been.' 'He is willing, but I am nót.' Similarly, in questions which merely express surprise: 'It is already done!' — 'Ís it?' but in older English, as in the preceding cases, with *so:* "Twas agreed betwixt us, before,' etc. — 'Wás it *so?*' (Wycherley, *The Gentleman Dancing-Master*, V, I, 11, A.D. 1673). 'Just now you wished to talk.' — 'Ah, díd I *so?*' (George H. Boker, *Francesca da Rimini*, V, I, A.D. 1856). 'I pray that it may be *só*, but I cannot think that it ís *so*' (now usually omitted) (Miss Braddon, *Lady Audley*, Ch. XXIII, A.D. 1862).

The adverb *so* is used not only as an ordinary predicate but often also as an objective predicate: 'She made life interesting just because she found it *so.*' 'Things are in good shape, and I like to have (or keep) them *so.*' 'Is Beauty beautiful, or is it only our eyes that make it *so?*' 'No man is poor that does not think himself *so.*' 'The present scribe is no snob. He is a respectfully brought-up old Briton of the higher middle class — at least, he flatters himself *so*' (Du Maurier, *Trilby*, I, 196).

On the other hand, *it* is often in colloquial speech used in the predicate without reference to anything that has preceded — predicative situation *it* (4 II A). When in a difficult situation someone after much fruitless discussion makes a bright suggestion the others remark: 'That is *it*' (= *the thing to do*). If a wrong motive has been ascribed to one's act, one replies: 'No, that is not *it*' (= *the right explanation*). Predicate *it* here often has the meaning of *superior, acme, point of perfection:* 'Did he know his Greek?' — 'I should say so. He was *it*' (*Dialect Notes*, II, p. 42). Often in an unfavorable sense: 'He thinks he is *it*.' 'For barefaced lying you are really *it*' (*Pocket Oxford Dictionary*). Predicative *it* often precedes the copula so that the emphatic subject may stand at the end: 'In the dance *it* (= *the important thing*) is grace. In a cigarette *it* is taste' (advertisement). Compare 21 *b* (2nd par.), 21 *e* (10th par.).

a. Case of the Predicate Pronoun. Where there are distinctive case forms, the predicate pronoun should be in the nominative and in choice language usually is, but in popular and loose colloquial speech there has persisted since the sixteenth century a tendency to employ here the accusative of personal pronouns as the predicate complement after the copula: 'It wasn't *them*' (Tarkington, *Penrod and Sam*, Ch. IV). 'No, it's *us*' (E. Poole, *The Harbor*, p. 61). 'I say it is *him* or nobody for you' (Hardy, *The Mayor of Casterbridge*, Ch. XXX). 'Some one said, "That's *him!*"'

(Hutchinson, *If Winter Comes*, p. 369). Under the influence of attraction we often find the accusative here in good authors in serious style: 'It is not *me* [whom] he misjudges' (Winston Churchill, *The Inside of the Cup*, p. 501), but 'It is *I* who keep Mr. Hodder in the Church' (*ib.*, p. 512). Here *me* has been attracted into accusative form under the influence of the suppressed accusative relative which should follow it. The use of the accusative in the literary language is not confined to cases of attraction, as in this example, but there is a tendency to use it elsewhere, as in colloquial speech.

The tendency here towards the accusative is in part explained by the position of the pronoun after the verb, a position which in general is closely associated with the accusative. We not infrequently find even the subject in the accusative when it follows the verb: 'Here be *them* [that] haue beene amongst souldiers' (Ben Jonson, *Euery Man in His Humour*, V, ii, 4, A.D. 1601, ed. 1616). 'And damn'd be *him* that first cries, "Hold, enough!"' (Shakespeare, *Macbeth*, V, viii, 34). 'Come and dine with us. There'll only be *us* three' (Sir Harry Johnston, *Mrs. Warren's Daughter*, Ch. I). In colloquial speech, where the verb precedes the subject, the pronominal subject is often in the accusative and the verb, as in **8 I 1 *h***, is in the third person singular, whatever may be the person of the pronoun: 'Here are you and Mr. Farr, both of you whole-time schoolmasters; here's Sir Eliphaz toiling night and day to make cheap suitable homes for the masses; *here's me* (instead of *here am I*) an overworked engineer' (H. G. Wells, *The Undying Fire*, p. 87). 'Now *there's you* (instead of *there are you*), burning yourself out 'cos your high principles won't let you,' etc. (Sir Harry Johnston, *Mrs. Warren's Daughter*, Ch. XIV).

Where an appositive noun stands between a pronominal subject and the verb and thus hides, as it were, the subject and weakens our feeling for its force, we sometimes employ the accusative for the subject instead of the correct nominative: 'All *us* girls think it ever so romantic' (Meredith Nicholson, *The House of a Thousand Candles*, Ch. IX, p. 127), instead of the correct 'All (predicate appositive; see **6 C**, 6th par.) *we* girls think,' etc., or '*We* girls all think,' etc., or 'All *of us* girls think,' etc.

Where there is no finite verb expressed, there is a widespread drift in colloquial speech, and sometimes even in the literary language, to employ the accusative without regard to the grammatical relations: 'Those men have other feelings than *us* who have nothing suffered' (Thomas Paine, *Common Sense*, p. 43, A.D. 1776). 'I don't know, Frank, what the world is coming to or *me either*' (Thackeray, *The Newcomes*, I, Ch. XXIX), instead of *what I*

am coming to either. 'Who talked it over?' — 'Why, *him* and
her and *me*, of course' (De Morgan, *Somehow Good*, Ch. IX, p. 85).
'"I guess you ain't a New Yorker, huh?" Mike said. — "*Me*, no."'
(Edna Ferber, *Half Portions*, p. 64). 'There was that in the room
as we entered which was stronger *than us all*' (Mrs. Gaskell, *Cranford*, 22) = *than we all were*. 'There's not a soul in my house
but me (= *but I*) tonight' (Hardy, *Far from the Madding Crowd*,
Ch. XXXIV). Other examples are given in **27** 2 *a*, **29** 1 A *a, aa*,
and **31** (5th par.).

The plain drift of our language is to use the accusative of personal pronouns as the common case form for the nominative and
accusative relations; just as in nouns there is here no formal distinction. In the best grade of colloquial speech it is still firm usage,
however, to employ the nominative as subject when it stands immediately *before* the verb, as in '*I* am tired.' In popular speech
the accusative is used even here when there are two or more subjects connected by a conjunction: 'This is the last Sabbath-day
that *him* and *me* will be under the same roof' (Mrs. Oliphant, *The
Laird of Norlaw*, I, 30). '*You* and *him* is nice fallas, 'deed *ye* are'
(Manx dialect). '*Him* and *me* is friends, yes, *we* are' (*ib.*). In
popular speech in general the pronoun for the first person sometimes retains the nominative form: '*Him* and *I* (or *I* and *him*) were
there.' The accusative is sometimes used here even when there is
but a single subject: '*Her'll* be sixteen come Martinmas' (M. E.
Francis, *Honesty*, I, Ch. II). In Manx dialect it is common to say,
'*Them* is good,' but usually '*They, we, ye*, are good.' Similarly,
in the nominative absolute construction (**17** 3 A) the subject in
popular speech usually has the form of the accusative: 'It will be
a very good match for me, m'm, *me* being an orphan girl' (H. G.
Wells, *The Country of the Blind*, p. 16). Irish English preserves
the older nominative here. Compare **17** 3 A.

The wide use of the accusative for the nominative, described in
detail above, is unfortunate, for, as illustrated in **29** 1 B *a*, it is
sometimes ambiguous. The expressive power of our language
should not become impaired. It is to be hoped that all who are
interested in accurate expression will oppose this general drift by
taking more pains to use a nominative where a nominative is in
order. Compare **31** (5th par.). It is gratifying to observe that
this careless usage, though still common in colloquial speech, is in
general less common in our best literature than it once was.

Opposed to the general tendency to employ the accusative instead of the nominative is the use of the nominative instead of the
accusative, especially where other words connected by a conjunction stand between the pronoun and the governing preposition or

verb, obscuring the grammatical relations: 'He went with John and *I*.' In older literary English, this error sometimes crept into the language of prominent writers: 'All debts are cleared between you and *I*' (Shakespeare, *The Merchant of Venice*, III, ii, 321). 'Why, Macro, It hath beene otherwise between you and *I*' (Ben Jonson, *Sejanus*, V, viii, 203, A.D. 1605, ed. 1616). 'Let you and *I* cry quits' (Hughes, *Tom Brown*, I, iii, A.D. 1857). This error is still common in popular speech: 'As soon as he saw Dorothy and *I*' (Anita Loos, *Gentlemen Prefer Blondes*, Ch. II).

D. PREDICATE INFINITIVE. There are three classes of infinitives here:

1. *Normal Prepositional Form.* There are two groups:

a. The prepositional infinitive is used after the copulas: 'To be good is *to be* happy.' 'To represent him as a man of stainless virtue is *to make* him ridiculous.' 'He seems *to have* ability.' 'He seems *to want* to do it.' 'He appeared *to desire* it.' 'I happened (or chanced) *to look* in that direction and caught him in the act of doing it.' What is now a nominative subject of the verb *happen* or *chance* was in older English a dative of interest (**12** 1 B *b*): 'It hapned *me* fall in with an vgly Captain' (Thomas Nashe, *The Vnfortvnate Traveller*, Works, II, p. 217, A.D. 1594), now 'I happened to fall in with an ugly captain.' This change from dative to nominative is in accordance with the modern tendency to represent the person standing in relation to an action as doing, passing through an experience, rather than as involved in the action or as affected by it. Compare **4** II B (4th par.). The word after *happen* is now a predicate infinitive linked to the subject by the copula *happen*, while in older English it is a subject infinitive, sometimes with its old simple form, as in the example from Nashe. Compare **4** *d*. The *to*-infinitive was more common.

Descriptive force is sometimes imparted here by employing as predicate a present participle or the progressive form of the infinitive: 'Her whole being seemed *hanging* (or *to be hanging*) on his words' (Galsworthy, *The Country House*, I, Ch. VII). 'Instead of offering any explanation, he seemed *waiting* (or *to be waiting*) for her to say something' (Christopher Morley, 'Thunder on the Left,' in *Harper's Magazine* for Sept., 1925, p. 400).

b. The prepositional infinitive is employed after the passive forms of two groups of verbs: (1) verbs of finding, making (= compelling), knowing, perceiving, and others with similar or related meanings; (2) verbs of believing, thinking, saying, reporting, teaching, recommending, allowing, advising, commanding, ordering, and the like. Examples: 'He was finally found *to be sleeping*' (a fact), or 'He was found *sleeping*' (with descriptive force).

'He was never found *to neglect* his work.' 'He was made *to shut* the door.' 'He was known *to do* it.' 'He was believed *to be* rich.' 'It was ordered *sent* (or *to be sent*) to my house.' 'He was ordered (asked, requested, or told) *to do* it.' These two passive groups correspond to the two active ones described in **15** III 2 B and **24** III *d*, except that the passive is not used with the verbs of wishing and desiring in **24** III *d*. Instead of the present tense of the progressive active infinitive a present participle with descriptive force is often used, and instead of the present passive infinitive a perfect participle without a difference of meaning, as illustrated above.

The use of the infinitive after passive form is characteristic of modern English. We can now usually convert active into passive form by merely putting the object of the person into the nominative, changing the active to the passive voice, and retaining the rest of the predicate without change, as if the words formed a compound or group-word (**63**): (active) 'He told me to do it'; (passive) 'I was told to do it.' Compare **15** I 2 *a*. If, however, we use a simple infinitive in the active, we employ the prepositional form in the passive, for this construction is modern, and in modern infinitival constructions we regularly use the prepositional form: 'I saw him *do* it,' but in the passive 'He was seen *to do* it.' Occasionally, however, the simple infinitive of the active is retained in the passive, as illustrated in **15** III 2 B *a*.

2. *Modal Form.* After the copulas *be, remain, fall*, and in a few expressions *seem*, the infinitive often assumes a peculiar modal force in the predicate, expressing the necessity, possibility, or fitness of an action: 'The letter is *to be* (i.e., *must be*) *handed* to him in person.' 'An account of the event is *to be* (i.e., *can be*) *found* in the evening papers.' 'Women are not easily *to be read*' (Hichens, *Ambition*, Ch. XXXIV) (*cannot be easily read*). 'Such women are *to* (i.e., *ought to*) *be admired*.' 'That remains *to be seen*.' 'Having placed so much to its (i.e., the motor omnibus's) credit, however, there falls *to be considered* a totally different aspect of the case' (II. *London News*, No. 3896, 1068 *a*). This same modal force is also found in attributive clauses where the infinitive has the force of a predicate: 'There are still serious difficulties *to be overcome*' (= *which are to be overcome, must be overcome*). 'He has given me much *to think about*' (= *that I should think about*). Compare **23** II 11 (2nd par.).

The idea of necessity, so often found here in the infinitive, has many shades of meaning. It indicates that something must take place in accordance with the will of a person or of Destiny, or as the outcome of events or a natural development, or in accordance with some plan or agreement: 'John, you are *to* (or must) *be* up by six.' 'What am I (or do you want me) *to do* next?' 'We are *to* (or must, or are destined to) *toil* and *moil* here below.' 'I am *to* (or must) *become* a burden to you all.' 'He is at last *to receive* his merited reward.' 'He is yet *to meet* his equal.' 'We are all *to meet* next week to settle the question.' 'There is a circus *to be* here next week.' There is often future force here, but it is mingled with the modal. The modal force is often found also in abridged attributive relative clauses (**23** II 11), where the infinitive has the force of a predicate, although there is here, of course, no copula before it: 'She dreamed impossibly of a spirituality *never to be hers*' (= *which was never to be hers*). 'She did not realize that she, *now or about to be a social power* (= *who was now or about to be a social power*), was to do,' etc. (Hope, *Intrusions of Peggy*, 57). 'She desires to flee from the wrath *to come*' (= *which is to come*). There is often future force here in connection with the modal, as in the last example.

The modal force of the infinitive is often found also in abridged accusative (**24** III *d*) and prepositional (**24** IV *a*, 2nd par.) clauses where the *to*-infinitive is felt as predicated of some word in the principal proposition: '*I* don't know what *to do*' (= *I am to do*, or *should do*). 'I'll tell *you* how *to do it*' (= *you should do it*). 'I told *him* where *to find it*' (= *he could find it*). 'I showed *him* how *to do it*' (= *he should do it*). 'I shall tell *him* when *to go*' (= *he should go*). '*I* am thinking of what *to do* (= *I should do*) next.'

In older English, the modal infinitive was sometimes employed after the present participle and gerund *being* in an abridged participial or gerundial clause, where present usage requires a full clause with a finite verb: 'John *being to go* your way, I am willing to write, because he is so willing to carry anything for me' (Richardson, *Pamela*, I, *Letter V*), now '*Since John is to go* your way, I am willing,' etc. 'This particular circumstance of her *being to come* so soon' (Jane Austen, *Emma*, II, Ch. I), now 'This particular circumstance that she *is to come* so soon.'

In Old English, the infinitive here usually had passive meaning, so that a number of the sentences given above in which the infinitive has active force represent modern usage and indicate that this construction has extended its boundaries. Originally the infinitive was a noun and could not express the idea of voice. In Old English, the infinitive here usually had clear passive meaning, but the form was active, although elsewhere passive form had come into use to express the passive idea. The infinitive here was still felt as a noun, object of the preposition *to*. In the fourteenth century the infinitive here began to be felt as a verb, and sometimes assumed passive form: 'The menaces of Fortune ne ben nat for *to dreden* (active form with passive force), ne the flaterynges of hir *to ben desired'* (passive form and force) (Chaucer, *Boethius*, II, I), now 'The menaces of Fortune are not *to be dreaded*, nor are her flatteries *to be desired*.' The development of passive form for passive meaning was naturally facilitated by the fact that the infinitive here sometimes had active force, so that passive form was needed to distinguish passive from active meaning. The gradual development of passive form for passive meaning made it possible to employ active form freely for active meaning: 'How *am I to (can I) pay* such a debt?' 'He is *to come* back tonight.' Other examples of infinitives with active form and meaning are given on page 46. There are, however, a few survivals of older usage with active form and passive meaning: 'This house is *to let*.' 'He is *to blame* for it.' 'He seems *to blame* for it' with modal force, while in passive form 'He seems *to be blamed* for everything that goes wrong' there is no modal force at all. In abridged attributive relative clauses, active form with passive meaning is still common: 'He is not a man *to trifle with*' (= *that can be trifled with*). Compare **23** II 11. Sometimes, however, active and passive form here have a little different meaning: 'This is the man *to send*' (= *that should be sent*), but 'This is the man *to be sent*' (= *that in accordance with our plan will be sent*).

As in **4** II B (last par.), there has been a change of subject here since the Old English period wherever there was in Old English a dative of reference (**12** 1 B *a*): 'Ac *us* is to smeagenne þaet Drihten on þaere costunge nolde his þa myclan miht gecyþan' (*Blickling Homilies*, p. 33, tenth century), now 'But *we* are to consider that the Lord in his temptation did not desire to reveal his great power.' The newer construction is a marked characteristic of Modern English, but it began to appear in Middle English: 'He wist (knew) what *he* was to do' (Wyclif, *Selected Works*, I, 120).

3. *Form to Express Purpose*. After a copula an infinitive *to*-clause is sometimes used as a predicate to indicate purpose: 'John *is* now with us *to help us with our work*.' 'I *have been* down town *to buy a new hat*.' In all such cases the copula has considerable concrete meaning. In older English, *be* was used here as a pure copula without any concrete force, where we now replace the *to*-infinitive by a present participle, copula and *to*-infinitive in older English being used much as the progressive form: 'AMIENS. He *hath been* all this day *to look you* (now *has been looking for you*). JAQUES. And I *have been* all this day *to avoid him*' (Shakespeare, *As You Like It*, II, v, 33) (now *have been avoiding him*).

E. PREDICATE GERUND. The gerund is often used as a predicate, usually as a parallel construction to the prepositional infinitive without an essential difference of meaning: 'To build

upon any other foundation (than religion) is *building* upon sand'
(Southey) (or '*to build* upon sand'). Compare **50** 4 *b*.
   F. PREDICATE ADVERB AND PREPOSITIONAL PHRASE. In general, adverbs and prepositional phrases modify adjectives, adverbs,
and verbs of complete predication as adverbs proper, but a large
number of adverbs and prepositional phrases are used as adjectives
— as attributive adjectives, or as predicate complements standing
after a linking verb, or as predicate appositives (**7** C) following a
verb of complete predication. The use of adverbs and prepositional phrases in the attributive relation is described in **10** I 2 and
10 VI. The following examples illustrate their use as predicate
complement and predicate appositive.
   Predicate complement: 'The matter is quite *otherwise.*' 'Is Mr.
Smith *in?*' 'My day's work is *over.*' 'Don't strike a man when he is
down.' 'He is *down and out.*' 'He is *out* for a walk.' 'The sun is *up.*'
'He was *up* early this morning.' 'He is *up* in mathematics.' 'I am
up with him now. I was *behind him* for a while, but I have caught
(linking verb) *up* with him.' 'Smallpox is *about.*' 'He is *about*
(adverb, not preposition, for the prepositional infinitive cannot
now stand after a preposition) to take the step.' 'He seems *about*
(adverb) to take the step.' 'The car is *in good condition*' (predicate prepositional phrase). 'The nation is *at peace.*' 'I must be
about (preposition) *my Father's business*' (*Luke*, II, 49). 'The
trend is *in this direction.*' 'The trend of both statements was *to
the effect* that in this critical hour friends of law and order should
stand by the President' (*Chicago Tribune*, Dec. 29, 1929). 'The
book is *up to* (compound preposition) *date.*' 'He is not *up to his
task.*' 'I am *up to his tricks.*' 'He is *up to some mischief.*' 'It is
up to you to do something.' The predicate is often a prepositional
gerundial clause: 'He is *about taking the step.*' 'He seems *about
taking the step.*' 'He is *on the point of* (compound preposition) *taking the step.*' 'He is *above doing such things.*'
   Predicate appositive: 'The fruit arrived *in good condition.*' 'He
came home *out of humor.*'
   In many compounds the preposition *on* is reduced to *a*, as in
abreast, afoot, aglow, ashore, away, etc., all originally prepositional
phrases, hence freely used as predicate complement or as predicate
appositive. Predicate complement: 'He is *asleep, ashore, away,*'
etc. Predicate appositive: 'He is lying on the sofa *asleep.*' 'He
came home all *aglow* with enthusiasm.'
   An adverb or a prepositional phrase can be predicated also of an
accusative object, i.e., can be an objective predicate (**15** III 2 A):
'I should not wish it *otherwise.*' 'I found everything *in good condition.*' There is no copula here. For an explanation see **15** III 2.

CHAPTER IV

AGREEMENT BETWEEN SUBJECT AND PREDICATE

8. The predicate agrees — wherever the form will permit — with the subject in number, person, gender, and case. On account of the lack of distinctive forms the verb often cannot be brought into agreement with the subject; but, so far as the form will permit, present usage requires strict concord. Older usage was not so strict.

I. NUMBER

1. If the subject is singular, the verb is also singular: 'The tiniest *hair casts* a shadow.'

a. The verb which follows situation *it* (4 II A) or an anticipatory subject *it* that points to a following clause is always singular, even though the reference is to more than two: 'Where does all that noise come from?' — '*It's* the children playing upstairs.' 'It *was* my brothers who were struck.' ''*Twas* men I lack'd' (Shakespeare, *II Henry VI*, III, ɪ, 345). Compare 4 II C.

b. If a subject in the singular is associated by means of *with, together with, as well as, no less than, like, but, except,* with other words which logically though not formally constitute a part of the subject, the subject is now with our present strong feeling for form usually in the singular, although the plural is often found here in older English and is sometimes still used: 'But *godliness* with contentment *is* great gain' (*I Timothy*, VI, 6), but sometimes with a plural verb if the idea of number is prominent: '*Old Sir John with half-a-dozen more are* at the door' (Onions, *Syntax*, p. 31), where, however, to most speakers and writers *and* is more natural than *with*, or *is* is more natural if *with* is employed. '*The island of Australia*, with Tasmania, *constitutes* the Commonwealth of Australia.' '*The bat* together with the balls *was* stolen.' '*Justice*, as well as mercy, *allows* it.' '*The girl*, as well as the boys, *has* learned to ride' and of course '*The girls*, as well as the boy, *have* learned to

49

ride.' '*Man*, no less than the lower forms of life, *is* a product of the evolutionary process.' '*The conquest* of the air, like all the conquests that man has made over the elements, *is* taking a costly toll of human life.' '*Nothing* but dreary dikes *occurs* to break the monotony of the landscape.' '*Nobody* but John and William *was* there.' '*Nobody*, except his most intimate friends, *knows* of it.'

c. It is often very difficult, indeed, to determine whether the noun which precedes the copula is the subject or the predicate complement. Professor Jespersen has given us a good practical rule for use in perplexing cases: 'The subject is comparatively definite and special, while the predicate is less definite, and thus applicable to a greater number of things' (*The Philosophy of Grammar*, p. 150). In common practice, however, many find it difficult to distinguish subject and predicate here. The present tendency is to avoid a decision on this perplexing point by regulating the number of the copula by a mere formal principle — namely, as the nominative before the copula is often the subject, it has become the rule to place the copula in accord with it, whether it be a subject or a predicate. 'Her *children* (subject) *are* her sole care.' 'Her principal *anxiety* (predicate, but felt as subject) *was* her children.' 'The chief *curse* (predicate, but felt as subject) *is* taxes.' On the other hand, as the noun which follows the copula is often the subject, we frequently, especially in older English, find the copula in accord with it: 'All that we found of the deer *were* the ragged hide, some patches of hair, cracked bones, and two long ears' (Zane Grey, in *Harper's Monthly*, Aug., 1925). 'What it (i.e., the air) unquestionably did contain *were* carbon monoxide gas and prussic acid gas' (E. E. Free, 'The Origin of Life,' in *Forum*, Oct., 1925). 'His pavilion round about him *were* dark waters and thick clouds of the skies' (*Psalms*, XVIII, 11). 'The wages of sin *is* death' (*Romans*, VI, 23). As far as the form is concerned, we might interpret *wages* here as a singular, subject of *is*, for it is often used as a singular in older English, as illustrated in 2 *f*, p. 58. But, according to the rule given above, it is the predicate and *death* the subject.

d. Collective nouns take a singular verb or a plural verb, according as the idea of *oneness* or *plurality* is uppermost in the mind: '*The multitude*, unacquainted with the best models, *are* captivated by whatever stuns or dazzles them' (Macaulay). '*The assembly was* dissolved.' '*Congress were* (now *was*) pleased to order me an advance of two quarters' salary' (Thomas Jefferson, *Letter to Samuel Osgood*, Oct. 5, 1785). '*The Senior Class requests* (i.e., as a unit) the pleasure of your company,' but '*The Senior Class are* unable to agree upon a president.' '*The choir* knelt and covered *their* faces' (Bennett, *Old Wives' Tale*). The point of view sometimes shifts within one and the same sentence, so that the verb is now singular, now plural, although the reference in the different cases is to the same noun: ' There *was* a grand *band* hired from Rosseter, *who*, with *their* wonderful wind-instruments and puffed-out cheeks, *were themselves* a delightful show to the small boys' (George Eliot, *Adam Bede*, 233). Aside from cases where the idea of oneness is quite pronounced, there is in general still a tendency in English — now, however, not so strong as formerly — to employ a plural verb with a collective noun. Of course, sometimes here formal forces counteract this general tendency. The singular is sometimes chosen for the sake of a contrast or a parallelism: ' Although *he* himself presumably *knows* what are the thoughts and ideas which *he is* trying to express, his *audience does* not.' 'The *Mary Rogers was* strained, the *crew was* strained, and big *Dan Cullen*, master, *was* likewise strained' (Jack London, *When God Laughs*). Compare **59 1**.

Similarly, if a group of words, especially a partitive group, conveys the idea of plurality, a number of individuals, the verb is in the plural, even though the governing noun is singular, while the verb is singular if the group conveys the idea of oneness: 'The greatest *part* of these years *was* spent in philosophic retirement,' but 'The greatest *part* of the Moguls and Tartars *were* as illiterate as their sovereigns.' In '*A large number* of the garrison *were* prostrate with sickness' and 'There *are a large number* of things that I desire to say' *number* is now felt not as a collective noun but as a component of a compound numeral, the indefinite pronoun *a large number* with plural force, so that the verb is in the plural. In older English, *number* was sometimes treated as a singular noun in accordance with its singular form: 'In the Chirche above in heven *is a noumbre* of greete seintis' (Wyclif, *Selected Works*, II, 309, A.D. 1380). This treatment of *number* as a singular noun is still found occasionally where a writer follows the outward form rather than the inner meaning: 'Chicago has as many more (models) and besides these there *is* probably *an equal number* of occasional sitters, transients' (Beecher Edwards, 'Faces That Haunt You,' in *Liberty*, May 22, 1926).

e. The singular is the regular form after the indefinite or general pronouns *each one, everybody, everyone, anyone, either, nobody, neither*, etc., since they are now usually felt as presenting the subject separately: '*Each* of us *must live* his or her (**60 1 d**) life.' '*Everyone has* his hobby.' '*Either* of the expressions *is* correct, but the former is more common than the latter.' '*Neither has* a wife.' In older English, the plural was common here, as the tendency was then strong to give expression to the plural idea logically contained in these words: '*Everyone* in the house *were* in their beds' (Fielding, *Tom Jones*, Book VII, Ch. XIV). This usage survives in loose colloquial and popular speech. Compare **61** 1 *a*. After *neither*, however, the plural verb is still found also in the literary language alongside of the singular. On account of the strong plural idea logically contained in it, the plural verb was common in older English and is still found in good authors: 'Thersites' body is as good as Ajax', when *neither are* alive' (Shakespeare, *Cymbeline*, IV, II, 252). '*Neither* of the sisters *were* very much deceived' (Thackeray). '*Neither* of us *are* dukes' (H. G. Wells, *The New Machiavelli*, p. 316). Compare 2 *c*, p. 56.

None, originally singular, may also be classed here when the reference is to one person: '*None has* more keenly felt them' (Stevenson). It is common in older English, and is still used in choice language, but is now largely replaced by *no one* or *nobody*. It is now quite common, however, as a plural with a plural verb: '*None are* so deaf as those that will not hear.'

Just as the singular is usually found after the pronouns *each one*, *everyone*, *either*, *neither*, it is also usually employed after the adjective forms *each*, *every*, *either*, *neither*, although the reference is to more than one: '*Every* boy *is taught* to read and write.' '*Either* expression *is* correct.' '*Neither* speech *is* to exceed fifteen minutes.'

f. For the number of the verb after *kind of*, *sort of*, see **59** 7.

g. A plural personal pronoun, subject of a plural verb, often has for its antecedent a singular noun modified by *many a*: 'But yesterday I saw *many a brave warrior*, in all the pomp and circumstance of war, marching to the battlefield. Where *are they* now?'

h. The principle that the verb should agree with the subject is very often not recognized in popular speech. Here in the present indicative the third person singular is used for all persons and both numbers, in accordance with the tendency to level away the inequalities within a category, provided distinctive form is not absolutely necessary to the thought: I *says*, you *says*, he *says*, we *says*. In dialect *thou* (**4** II H) likewise has a verb in the third person after it: 'Thou's not acting right' (Stanley Houghton, *Hindle Wakes*, Act II). This usage is common also in the language of Quakers: '*Thee* (**4** II H) *is* wrong about that.' In older English, more commonly with *thou* as subject: 'How *comes thou* Into truth if thou hast not beene led by ye spirit of truth?' (George Fox, *Journal*, p. 313, A.D. 1657).

NOTE. — This use of the verbal ending *s* for all persons and numbers was originally a dialectic feature of Northern English. In the Old English period the oldest ending for the second person singular of the verb was *s*. In this early period the *s* often spread to the second person plural, and then further spread to the other persons of the plural and to the third person singular, so that in the Old English period *s* was often used in the North for all persons and numbers except the first person singular. In Middle English, the *s* spread in the North also to the first person singular, so that the *s* was sometimes used for all persons and numbers: 'as I before you *has* talde' (*Cursor Mundi*, 14135, A.D. 1300), now 'as I *have* told you before.' 'O gode pertre *comes* god peres' (*ib.*, 37), now 'From a good pear tree *come* good pears.'

This *s* was destined to play an important part in the literary language. In Middle English it spread to the northern part of the Midland, where it was used in the East in the third person singular and in the West in the third person singular and often also in the plural. In both sections, however, the old *th* continued to be used alongside of it in the third person singular. The *s* at this time had not yet reached London, and thus it did not affect Chaucer's customary language. But he was well acquainted with it, and in his *Reues Tale* let the two Northern clerks employ their Northern *s* in characteristic manner, using it for all persons and numbers: 'And forthy (therefore) *is* I come' (111). 'How *fares* thy faire doghter and thy wyf?' (103). In one instance Chaucer used an *s*-form on his own account for the sake of the rime. Later, the *s*-ending became established in London and the South generally. Many people from the North and the northern Midland came to the growing national capital to live and, of course, brought with them their handy *s*-ending, which by reason of its marked superiority in ease of utterance appealed to the people there as it had appealed previously to the people of the North. It affected at first only colloquial speech, while in literary prose the older and more stately *th* maintained itself for a time. Shakespeare employed *s* in the prose of his dramas, where the tone is colloquial, while the translators of the Bible used *th* throughout as more appropriate for a serious style. The poets often employed *s* on account of its warmer tone or for the sake of rime or meter. After the time of Shakespeare *s* gradually became established in all styles of the literary language, but only in the third person singular, not in the other persons of the singular and throughout the plural as in northern English.

In older literary English, however, *s* was not entirely confined to the third person singular. Just as the *s* in the North spread from the second person singular to the plural and to the other persons of the singular, the literary *s* of the third person singular, from the late fifteenth to well into the eighteenth century, occasionally spread to other forms, especially to the second person singular and the third person plural: 'Syker, *thou's* (i.e., *thou is*) but a laesie loord' (Spenser, *The Shepheards Calender*, July, 33, A.D. 1579) = 'Surely, you are a lazy lubber.' 'Why *bends thou* thus thy minde to martir me?' (Kyd, *The Spanish Tragedie*, III, IX, 6, A.D. 1585–1587). 'What are *they that comes* here?' (Richard Edwards, *Damon and Pithias*, 376, A.D. 1571). 'Your *commissionars telz* me' (Queen Elizabeth, *Letters to James VI*, 44). This usage survives in the literary language in jocular imitations of popular speech in the case of *says I, says you* instead of *said I, said you*, parenthetical insertions in a quotation to indicate the author of the language: '"It was folly and ingratitude, Mr. Brough," *says I*, "I see it all now"' (Thackeray, *Samuel Titmarsh*, Ch. VI). It survives also in the second person singular after *thee* in the language of the Quakers, as described in *h*, p. 52.

In popular speech we find for all persons and numbers not only *does* but also *do* after the analogy of a number of other auxiliaries (*may, can,* etc.) which have no *s* in the third person singular: 'They always *does* it' (Dickens, *Martin Chuzzlewit*). 'It *do* seem hard' (Masefield, *The Everlasting Mercy*). In older English, this *do* occurs sometimes in the literary language: 'He *do* confess himself to speak of this third kind' (Philpot, *Exam. and Writ.*, 335, A.D. 1553). 'He *do*' not hear me I hope' (Ben Jonson, *Euery Man out of His Humour*, Inductio, 351, A.D. 1600). In loose colloquial speech, the negative form *don't* is still widely used as an auxiliary for all persons and numbers: 'I, you, he, we, they, *don't* believe it.' In the Isle of Man *hev* is used for all persons and numbers: 'I, thou, he, we, *hev*' (= *have*). For the peculiar use of the uninflected form of the verb in the east Midland of England for all numbers and persons of the present tense see Accidence, **56** 4 *b*. This usage is common also in American Negro dialect: 'Dish yer chicken-nabber *look* lak (like) he dead' (Joel Chandler Harris, *Nights with Uncle Remus*, p. 20). 'Gawd always *lub* (for *loves*) de righteous' (Du Bose Heyward, *Porgy*, p. 32).

In the past tense there is also in the literary language, aside from the poetic second person singular, no ending for person or number, except that the plural of *was* is *were:* I *said*, you *said*, he *said*, we *said*, etc., but: I *was*, you *were*, he *was*, we *were*, you *were*, etc. In older English, leveling took place even in the case of *was*, which was sometimes used for both singular and plural, and for all persons. Thus *was* was sometimes used with the subject *thou* instead of *wast:* 'Where *was thou* born?' (Marlowe, *The Jew of Malta*, 892,.about A.D. 1590, ed. 1636). *Was* was most frequently employed for *were* with the subject *you* where the reference was to only one individual: 'Pray, Sir, how *was* you cured of your love?' (Fielding, *Love in Several Masques*, Act. IV, Scene II). Of this once very common construction Noah Webster says on page 92 of his *Philosophical and Practical Grammar* (A.D. 1807): 'The compilers of grammars condemn the use of *was* with *you* — but in vain. The practice is universal, except among men who learn their language by books. The best authors have given it their sanction, and the usage is too well established to be altered.' The use of *was* for reference to more than one was much less widespread, but it has become common in current popular speech: 'we, you, they, *was*.' But also the older literary usage of employing in the second person *was* for reference to one and *were* for more than one occurs here: you *was* (sing.), you *were* (pl.).

2. If the subject is plural, or if there are several subjects, the verb is plural: 'The *boys* in our class *are* more numerous than the girls.' 'A strong *wind* and a full *sail bring* joy to the sailor.'

a. When the verb *precedes* a number of subjects, it is often in the singular, especially in older English: 'And now *abideth* faith, hope, charity, these three' (*I Cor.*, XIII, 13). This usage lingers on in poetry: 'It is man's age-long struggle to draw near His Maker, learn His thoughts, discern His law — A boundless task in whose infinitude, As in the unfolding light and law of love, *Abides* our hope and our eternal joy' (Alfred Noyes, *The Torch-Bearers*, p. 230). Plain prose usage here today favors strict agreement of the verb with its subject, hence the plural is now the natural form of the verb. There is often a hesitation to use a plural verb because it does not harmonize with the nearest subject: 'There *is* little illustration and no side-lights of suggestion' (G. W. Lewes, *Aristotle*, Ch. I, p. 20), instead of 'There *is* little illustration and there *are* no side-lights of suggestion.'

In older English, as illustrated on page 53, a singular verb was not infrequently used with a following plural subject, a usage which survives in popular speech. Survivals still occasionally occur also in the literary language after *there is, there exists*, etc.; i.e., in certain set expressions where the mind is not on the alert: '*There exists*, sometimes only in germ and potentially, sometimes more or less developed, the same tendencies and passions which have made our fellow-citizens of other classes what they are' (M. Arnold, *Culture and Anarchy*, Ch. III). 'Here there *does* seem to be, if not certainties, at least a few probabilities, that,' etc. (H. G. Wells, *Mankind in the Making*, Ch. III).

When the subjects precede, the verb sometimes stands in the singular, agreeing with the last of a number of subjects, usually, however, only when this part of the subject serves as a climax to the whole of the subject or summarizes the different subjects: 'Your interest, your honor, God himself *bids* you do it' (Onions, *An Advanced English Syntax*, p. 31). 'Her knights and dames — her court *is* there' (Byron, *Parisina*).

In older English, a singular verb is often found after two or more singular subjects where we now employ a plural verb. The singular form of the verb here was defended on the ground that the verb agrees with one subject and is understood with the other or the others. Noah Webster in his *Philosophical and Practical Grammar* (A.D. 1807) defends thus the following sentence: 'Nor were the young fellows so wholly lost to a sense of right as pride and conceit *has* (now *have*) since made them affect to be' (*Rambler*, No. 97).

b. In case several coördinate singular subjects represent the same person, the verb is in the singular, often also when they are felt as forming a distinct collective idea, a close union or oneness of idea: 'My *colleague* and dear *friend* (one person) *is* near death's door.' '*Slow* and *steady* (one person or animal that is slow and steady) *wins* the race.' '*To mumble over the past, to live on the classics*, however splendidly, *is* senility' (H. G. Wells). '*To make*

life worth living and *to raise the standard of comfort sounds* well'
(G. Peel). 'A *cart* and *horse* (felt as a unit) *was* seen at a distance.'
'The *sum* and *substance* of the matter *is* this,' etc. 'The *long* and
short of it *is*,' etc. Aside from a few expressions, the singular is
not now so common as formerly where the different subjects form
a collective idea.

On the other hand, when each of a number of singular noun
subjects is considered separately, the verb is in the singular: 'A
fever, a mutilation, a cruel disappointment, a loss of wealth, a loss
of friends, *seems* at the moment untold loss' (Emerson). 'The
author, the wit, the partisan, the fine gentleman, *does* not take the
place of the man' (*id.*). 'Not enjoyment, and not sorrow, *Is* our
destined end or way' (Longfellow, *Psalm of Life*). 'Either sex and
every age *was* engaged in the pursuits of industry' (Gibbon, *Roman
Empire*, Ch. X). 'Every boy and girl *is* taught to read and write.'
'Many an orator and essayist *has* pointed out the supreme value to
manhood of the hard grinding conditions under which such boys
grow up' (Theodore Clarke Smith, *James A. Garfield*, I, p. 35).

c. In connection with the conjunctions *not only — but* (*also*),
either — or, neither — nor, partly — partly, etc., the different subjects are considered singly, and hence the verb agrees with one of
them — the one next to it — and is understood with the others:
'Not only the *children are* ill, but also the mother.' 'Not only
arms and arts, but *man* himself *has* yielded to it' (i.e., the pen).
'Either John or *William is* to blame.' 'Either the mayor or the
aldermen are to blame.' 'Neither the girls nor *John is* to blame.'
'Neither she nor *John is* to blame.'

After *neither — nor* we still often find the plural verb after singular subjects since there has long been a tendency to give formal
expression to the plural idea which always lies in the negative form
of statement: 'And neuer sithen nouther the kyng of Ermonye ne
the countree *weren* neuer in pees' (Mandeville, *Travels*, Ch. XVII,
about A.D. 1410–1420) = 'Since that time neither the King of
Armenia nor the country *have been* at peace.' 'Neither search
nor labor *are* necessary' (Johnson, *Idler*, No. 44, A.D. 1759).
'Neither he nor his lady *were* at home' (George Washington,
Diary, Dec. 2, 1789). 'Neither Leopardi nor Wordsworth *are*
of the same order with the great poets who made such verses
as . . .' (Matthew Arnold). 'Neither painting nor fighting *feed*
men' (Ruskin). 'It (i.e., Matthew Arnold's *Thyrsis*) does not
carry the same conviction of distress that *Lycidas* does; neither
the friendship nor the sorrow *seem* so profound' (Robert Bridges,
'Poetic Diction in English,' in *Forum*, May, 1923, p. 1539).
Compare these examples with those in 1 *e*, p. 51. Similarly, after

not . . . *either — or*, which has the force of *neither — nor:* 'I do not think either Montaigne or Johnson *were* good judges' (Lord Avebury). We sometimes find the plural after *or* since the speaker or writer feels that the statement, though at any one time applicable to only one of two or more things, holds good for them all: 'My life or death *are* equal both to me' (Dryden). 'A drama or an epic *fill* the mind and one does not look beyond them' (Matthew Arnold, *Essays in Criticism*, II, p. 135). 'Acting, singing, or reciting *are* forbidden them' (H. G. Wells). 'What *are* honor or dishonor to her?' (Henry James). 'Language is the medium of literature as marble or bronze or clay *are* the materials of the sculptor' (Sapir, *Language*, p. 237). The expression *one or two* always requires the plural: 'There *are one or two* subjects on which you are bound to have but one opinion' (Ruskin). After *a word or two* the singular is often used since we feel the collective force: 'Only a word or two *is* (or *are*) needed here.' Where the subjects are personal pronouns of different persons there is considerable fluctuation in present usage. See II, p. 60.

d. If the subject of the sentence is the name of a book, drama, newspaper, country, or in general any title, proper name, the verb is usually in the singular: '"The Virginians" *is* a good story.' '"The Liars" *was* produced yesterday at the Criterion.' '"The Times" *reports*,' etc. 'The United States *is* the paradise of the workman,' but often also the plural: 'The United States of America, which *reckon* 20,000,000 of people' (Emerson, *English Traits*, 26). See also **59 2.**

e. If a single plural subject or several singular or plural subjects are felt as forming the idea of a firm mass or fixed amount, the verb is in the singular: '*Nearly thirty shillings was* paid for a pound of tea in 1710.' 'Oh, there'*s bushels* of fun in that!' (Eugene Field, *Poems of Childhood*, 'The Drum'). '*The fifty miles was* (or *were*) covered by the winner in four hours, fourteen minutes, and forty-five seconds.' '*Thirty minutes is* sufficient for a good sermon.' '*Four years has* seemed a long time to you but a very short time to us' (Woodrow Wilson, June 12, 1910). 'Three times (adverbial element) 3 *is* (or *are*) 9.' 'Three times 3 quarts of water *is* 9 quarts.' 'Three times 3 oranges *are* 9 oranges.' '2 and 2 *is* (or *are*) 4.' '2 quarts of water and two more quarts *is* 4 quarts.' '2 oranges and 2 oranges *are* 4 oranges.' '4 from 6 (phrase used as subject) *leaves* (not *leave*) 2,' but '6 less (or minus) 4 *is* (or *are*) 2,' in which 'less 4' and 'minus 4' are prepositional phrases with adverbial force. '20 divided by 5 (phrase used as subject) *equals* (not *equal*) 4.' '5 *is* contained in 15 three times,' or 'There *are* three 5's in 15.' 'There *was* two hundred dollars in the purse,' but 'There *were* two hundred-dollar bills in the purse.' 'Three-fourths of the surface of the earth *is* sea,' but 'Three fourths of our old college class *are* married.'

f. Nouns that are plural in form but singular in sense, such as *gallows, news, measles, mumps, smallpox* (for *small pocks*), usually take a verb in the singular: '*This sad news was* brought to him at once.' 'Few diseases provide a more favorable chance for consumption to develop than *does measles*' (Thos. S. Blair, *Public Hygiene*, p. 307). Some nouns, such as *amends, means, odds* (now usually a plural, except in the meaning of *difference*), *pains, tidings* (more commonly a plural), are sometimes used as plurals, sometimes as singulars: 'What'*s the odds?*' but '*The odds are* against us.' '*Great pains have* (or *has*) been taken,' or '*Much pains has* been taken.' '*All possible means have* been adopted,' or '*Every means has* been tried.' 'Then *come* (less commonly *comes*) tidings that,' etc. Sciences in *-ics*, as *mathematics, economics, physics*, etc., are usually felt as singulars, but the names of practical matters, as *athletics, gymnastics, tactics, politics*, are usually felt as plurals: '*Mathematics is* (sometimes *are*) not his strong point.' '*Physics is* mainly the science of the transformation of energy.' '*Politics are* my only pleasure' (Oscar Wilde, *An Ideal Husband*, Act I), but also the singular is used here where the idea of oneness is pronounced: '*Politics makes* strange bed-fellows.' In older English, *wages* was a plural form with singular force: 'Their daily *wages is* so small' (Sir Thomas More, *Utopia*). *Wages* is now a plural: 'But I shall be able to manage till my first quarter's *wages come* in' (George Moore, *Esther Waters*, Ch. III). The singular *wage* is often used: *a living wage* or *living wages*. Compare **59** 2.

Alms, eaves, and *riches* (from Old French *richesse*), though in older English singular forms, are now felt and treated as plurals: 'Where *riches are*, some *alms are* due.' 'The *eaves are* not yet finished.'

Lots of or *lots, heaps of* or *heaps*, though originally plural nouns, are now felt as indefinite pronouns expressing an indefinite number or amount, so that, when used as subject expressing an indefinite amount, they take a singular verb: 'There *is lots of* fun and there'*s lots* to follow.' 'There *was heaps of* fun' (Alec Waugh, *Loom of Youth*, III, Ch. VIII). Compare Parts of Speech, **7** 5.

3. Where there are an affirmative and a negative subject, the verb agrees with the affirmative: '*Virtue*, not rolling suns, the mind *matures*' (Young, *Night Thoughts*).

4. The verb is in the plural where a singular abstract subject is modified by two or more adjectives connected by *and* which

clearly indicate that two or more things are meant: *'Sacred and profane wisdom agree* in declaring that "pride goeth before a fall."' The abstract subject here retains its singular form since it cannot as an abstract noun take a plural. Similarly, we employ a singular subject and a plural verb when the subject is a mass word modified by two adjectives connected by *and:* *'Good and bad butter are* things quite different to our taste.'

Of course, the verb is in the plural where there is an article or other limiting adjective before each of the descriptive adjectives to indicate that two persons or things are described: *'The red and the white rose are* both beautiful.' Similarly, the verb is in the plural after a singular noun modified by two possessive adjectives referring to different persons: *'Your and my wife* (or more commonly *your wife and mine) are* good friends.' Compare **10 I 4** and **57 5 *a.***

5. After the group *more than* there is a difference of usage according to the meaning. The usual form of expression is the singular verb since *more than* is felt as an adverb, as equivalent to *not merely;* but others feel *more* as a plural indefinite pronoun and employ the plural verb: 'More than one *has* (or *have) found it so.'* Of course, the plural is used when the words are separated: 'More *have* found it so than just he.'

Similarly, *less than* is often felt as an adverb: 'There were *less than* (adverb) sixty (= sixty people) there,' or 'There were fewer (plural pronoun) than sixty there.'

6. The predicate noun agrees with the subject in number: *'The Puritans* (subject) were the King's most exásperated *énemies,'* or in order to emphasize the subject 'The King's most exasperated *enemies* were the *Púritans.'* For the position of the subject see **3,** p. 3.

a. The predicate noun does not agree with the subject if it is the name of a material or is a collective or an abstract noun: *'Ye are the salt of the earth'* (*Matthew,* V, 13). *'The Swedes* are *a Germanic people.'* *'Good children* are *the joy* of their parents.' Concrete nouns in the predicate assume a general abstract force and then often do not agree with the subject, as illustrated in **7 B *a aa.***

7. The verb is in the singular if its subject is a clause: *'That they were in error in these matters is* now clear to us and probably also to their warmest friends.' Similarly, a group of words containing a single thought or picture takes the singular form of the verb: *'Early to bed and early to rise makes* a man healthy, wealthy, and wise.' *'Three such rascals hanged in one day is* good work for society.' Compare **17 3 B.**

II. PERSON

A few difficulties arise with regard to the form of the verb when pronouns of different persons are used as subjects:

1. When two or more subjects of different persons are in apposition, the verb agrees with the first of them since it is felt as containing the leading idea: '*I*, your master, *command* you.'

2. Where there are an affirmative and a negative subject, the verb agrees with the affirmative: '*I*, not you, *am* to blame,' or '*I am* to blame, not you.'

3. Where there are subjects of different persons connected by *or* or *nor*, most grammarians prescribe that the verb should agree with the nearest subject: 'Either he or *I am* in the wrong.' 'Either we or *John is* in the wrong.' 'Neither he nor *I am* in the wrong.' 'Neither we nor *John is* in the wrong.' In our ordinary English, however, this construction is not now common, for most people desire to avoid the annoying necessity of making a choice between the two persons. Hence the most common usage now is to separate the sentence into two distinct propositions, each with a verb or one with a verb and one elliptical in form: 'Either *he is* in the wrong or *I am*.' 'We are not in the wrong, nor [*is*] *John* either.' The wide currency of this usage indicates that most people dodge the necessity of making a choice between the two persons as though it were an educational test which they dreaded to meet. This diffidence stands in marked contrast to the fearless directness which in similar cases elsewhere often urges us to express ourselves tersely at whatever cost, since we feel that it is better to speak by guess than to become systematically awkward in expression. In colloquial and popular speech many people, feeling this awkwardness, place the subjects together and employ a plural verb, which, though often incorrect, always avoids the clash of the different persons: 'Either he or *I are* in the wrong.' After *nor*, however, the plural occurs also in the literary language, for here it is logical, as often elsewhere after *neither* or *neither — nor:* 'Neither *Isabel* nor *I are* timid people' (H. G. Wells, *The New Machiavelli*, p. 436). 'Neither *you* nor *I are* ever going to say a word about it' (Marion Crawford, *Katherine Lauderdale*, I, Ch. XV).

In a number of cases the force of *or* is not really disjunctive, so that the rule does not apply at all and we must be guided by the sense: 'There *are one or two irregularities* to be noted.' Here *one or two* has the force of an indefinite number, hence the verb is in the plural. In 'The scriptures, or Bible, are the only authentic source' (Bishop Tomline) the words 'or Bible' are a mere explanation of 'Scriptures,' which is the real subject.

In the above examples *either* and *neither* are construed as conjunctions, so that they do not influence the form of the verb. But
sometimes they are treated as pronouns employed as subject of
the verb and followed by two appositives: '*Either* he or I *is* in
the wrong.' '*Neither* my dog nor I *is* for sale' (Thomas Nelson
Page, *John Marvel, Assistant*, Ch. XXVI). '*Neither* you nor I *is*
necessary to the progress of that great Methodist Church' (Sinclair
Lewis, *Elmer Gantry*, Ch. XVIII, IV). Of course, the verb is
here always in the third person, agreeing with its subject *either* or
neither.

III. GENDER

The predicate noun can assume a form in accordance with the
natural sex of the person or animal represented by the subject,
provided such forms are elsewhere in common use for persons or
animals: '*He* is a *count*.' '*The animal* is a *bull*.' '*She* is a *countess*.'
In general, we have few such special forms for males and females,
and hence usually employ the same form for both males and
females: '*He* is a *teacher*.' '*She* is a *teacher*.' '*She* is a good *friend*
of mine.' Sometimes we can put a word such as *woman, lady, man,
girl, boy*, etc., before the predicate noun to indicate sex: 'She is
the only *woman* competitor.' 'She is the best *lady* (better *woman*)
physician in the city.' 'It's a *woman* friend of mine.' 'It's a
man friend of mine.' 'It's a *boy* actor.' 'It's a *she* goat, a *he*
goat.' For a fuller treatment see **60 1** *b*.

IV. CASE

The predicate noun or pronoun agrees with a nominative subject in case and thus both stand in the nominative: 'It is *I*,'
but in colloquial speech we often hear the accusative here: 'It
is *me*.' See **7 C** *a*. '*Who* (predicate) are the men working on
the roof?' — 'They are *the tilers*.' Where there is a reference to
a name already mentioned, a predicate pronoun is used: 'Jesus
therefore went forth, and said unto them, Whom seek ye? They
answered, Jesus of Nazareth. Jesus said unto them, I am *he*'
(*John*, XVIII, 4–5). Today we may still in such a case say
'I am *he*,' or perhaps more commonly 'This is *he*,' but in colloquial speech we sometimes replace the pronoun by a noun: 'I
am *the man* [you're looking for],' or 'I am *your man*.'

A noun or pronoun predicated of an accusative is in the accusative. For examples see **7 A** *a* (1), 4th par.

A noun or pronoun predicated of the genitive subject of a gerund
is in the nominative. For an example see **7 A** *a* (1), next to last par.

Also the genitive is used in the predicate. See **7 A** *e*.

CHAPTER V

SUBORDINATE ELEMENTS OF A SENTENCE

9. The subordinate elements of a sentence are called modifiers. They are divided into the following general classes:

1. *Attributive Adjective Modifiers,* which modify a noun or a pronoun.

2. *Objective Modifiers,* which modify a verb, an adjective, or an adverb.

3. *Adverbial Modifiers,* which modify a verb, an adjective, or another adverb. It is often difficult to distinguish an adverbial from an objective modifier as both kinds of modifiers modify verbs, adjectives, and adverbs. In this book the term *object* is used where the relation to the modified word is close. The expression *adverbial modifier* is employed to indicate a less close relation. Compare **14** *a,* **24** IV, **24** IV *a,* **25** 1.

Thus modifiers are classified according to their function. Recent grammarians under Jespersen's influence speak also of the 'rank' of the modifier. In 'exceedingly prompt action' *action* is called the principal, *prompt* the secondary word or adjunct, *exceedingly* the tertiary word or subjunct.

ATTRIBUTIVE ADJECTIVE MODIFIERS

10. Attributive adjective modifiers are treated as follows:

I. ADHERENT AND APPOSITIVE ADJECTIVE AND PARTICIPLE

The attributive adjective stands either before or after its governing noun; in the former position called *adherent*, in the latter position *appositive*, adjective. As will be shown on page 64, the appositive adjective is much nearer the nature of a predicate adjective than is the adherent adjective.

Adherent and appositive adjectives which modify verbal nouns are in a formal sense adjectives, but they have the force of adverbs: 'his *late* arrival,' 'his last visit *here*.'

The inflectional forms of the adjective and their use are treated in **52–56**. Other matters are presented below.

1. **Position and Stress.** The adjective in the attributive relation usually precedes the governing noun, is a little less strongly stressed, and normally has descriptive force: 'this *little bóy*.' This is descriptive stress. The adjective, when important to the thought, is often strongly stressed, but yet a little less strongly

than the governing noun: 'This is *bláck ingrátitude!'* Here we have emphatic stress, usually indicated in this book by two marks of chief stress, although the second accent is a little stronger. If the adjective is more strongly stressed than the governing noun and precedes it, it usually has distinguishing or classifying force: 'the *líttle bòok*, not the *bíg one'* (distinguishing stress). ' *Líttle mìnds* (classifying stress) always think so.' *'Bíg wòrds* seldom go with *góod dèeds'* (classifying stress).

A participle usually follows the governing noun as an appositive when its verbal force is marked, but of course stands before the noun when felt as an adherent adjective: 'He dropt his chin like a *màn shót'* (H. G. Wells) (= *like a man who has just been shot*, or *like a man after he has been shot*). Adjectives in *–ble* are often treated as participles since they contain a good deal of verbal force: *gòrges nearly impássable, sùfferings unspéakable, the only pèrson vísible*, and after the analogy of such expressions also *with all the solèmnity póssible, the bèst stỳle póssible*, etc. This word-order and stress has descriptive force, hence often is used when the participle is stressed, for the stressed participle before the noun would have classifying force, as in *an unhéard of crìme*, while in fact attention is here usually directed toward an act: *the resùlt arríved at* (with descriptive force = *the result which has been arrived at*). 'The crowd round a couple of *dògs fíghting* is a crowd masculine mainly with an occasional active, compassionate woman.' 'In the world's view a *wòman sóiled* is a *wòman spóiled'* (Hall Caine). ' *Bòys neglécted* were *bòys lóst'* (Kipling). This word-order is sometimes used by good authors in the case of adjectives in the hope of securing a striking effect through the unusual position of the adjective, but the marked classifying force does not harmonize with the descriptive stress: 'After Snòbs Mílitary Snòbs Clérical suggest themselves' (Thackeray), instead of the more natural and forceful 'After Mílitary Snòbs (classifying stress and force) Clérical Snòbs suggest themselves.'

On the other hand, it is both natural and common to place stressed adjectives after the noun when they have descriptive force: 'a *làugh músical but malícious'* (Mrs. H. Ward). *'Calculàtions quíck and ánxious* passed through the young wife's brain' *(id.).* Such adjectives, like participles, are felt as descriptive appositives rather than as adherent adjectives, i.e., as explanatory additions with the force of a descriptive, subordinate, attributive clause, which always follows the governing noun. A single adjective frequently stands after an indefinite pronoun with this force: 'Sòmething [which is] *néw*, nòthing [which is] *extraórdinary*, èverything [which is] *Énglish.'* 'I can't believe ànything [which is] *múch* can happen.' 'Let Jenny marry sòmebody [who is] *rích*.' Similarly, nouns used as adjectives: 'sòmething *silk*.' 'Èverything *métal* was intolerable to the touch.' But a single adjective stands much less commonly with this force after a noun. A single adjective clings tenaciously to its place before the noun, and can in only comparatively few instances stand after the noun in native English expression; but when two adjectives are united by a conjunction, as in the first two examples in this paragraph, they often follow the governing noun. This position is also common when a single adjective is modified, or when there are a number of adjectives not connected by conjunctions, for in these cases, as in the case of two adjectives connected by a conjunction, the adjective or adjectives after the noun are felt as appositives: 'It was a plàn *so stúpid* that no one approved of it.' 'It was a beautiful deed *worth remembering*.' 'It was an army *a hundred thousand strong*.' 'He was a man *very just in all his dealings with his fellows*.' 'She is a woman *inferior to none in unselfish service*.' 'When observing this Chinese peasantry, you seem to be watching a community of ants, *persistent, untiring, organized;* only the ants are men, *physically strong, assiduous, resourceful, adaptable, cheerful*.'

The modified adjective or participle is often *before* the noun where we should upon first thought expect to find it *after* the noun: 'a many times explòded érror,' 'too còstly a sácrifice,' or 'a too còstly sácrifice,' 'so hàrsh an ánswer.' 'I am as gòod a schólar as he.' In these and many similar examples we prefer adherent form and thus put the noun after the adjective or participle in order to make the noun more prominent in accordance with the usual character of adherent descriptive groups. But to call attention to the adjective and yet give it descriptive force, we employ the appositional form: 'in wèather as inclément as that on the day previous.'

On the other hand, we may say 'a too còstly sácrifice' when we desire descriptive force and 'a too cóstly sàcrifice' when we desire to convey classifying force. Notice the classifying force in the following example: 'True, Wolf Larsen possessed intellect to an unusual degree, but it was directed solely to the exercise of his savage instincts and made him but *the more fórmidable a sàvage*' (Jack London, *The Sea-Wolf*, Ch. XXIII). As *so* + a stressed adjective often has descriptive force; it is often found in the appositional construction when it is more strongly stressed than the governing noun: 'a pòwer so stróng,' 'pèople so unéducated,' etc. If, however, the adjective is not a descriptive (**51** 2) but a limiting (**51** 2) adjective the adherent form may be freely used without destroying the descriptive force: 'so múch mòney,' 'so féw pèople,' 'so mány bòoks.'

Sometimes an adjective must be placed after the noun to avoid a clash of different numbers: 'one of the greatest export articles of Norway, perhaps *the greatest*' (Fowler, *Modern English Usage*, p. 402), not 'one of the greatest, perhaps *the greatest*, export articles of Norway.' 'One of the finest poems of an equal length produced of recent years, if not *the finest*' (*ib.*), not 'one of the finest, if not *the finest*, poem of an equal length produced of recent years.'

a. A SINGLE UNMODIFIED ADJECTIVE AFTER THE NOUN. In a number of set expressions under French influence a single unmodified adjective has become established in the position after its governing noun: the Prèsident eléct; fèe símple; the sùm tótal; còurt mártial; the bòdy pólitic; Pòet Láureate; Pòstmaster Géneral; from tìme immemórial; dèvil incárnate, etc. A few such groups have arisen under Latin influence: Gòd Almíghty; thìrd person plúral, etc. Not only the word-order in such groups but also the stress is in most cases foreign, for the accent upon the second member, i.e., the descriptive stress, is in marked contrast to its distinguishing or classifying force, as can be seen in comparing the Latin group *Àsia Mínor* with the native English *Gréater New Yòrk*. These foreign groups with a stressed adjective after the noun should not be confounded with native English groups with the same word-order and stress but with descriptive force: the amòunt dúe (= the amount which is due); the amòunt overchárged; the wreck of Fèbruary lást; Frèderick the Gréat; Chàpter Í (usually read and spoken *One* instead of *The First* under the influence of the written Roman character). 'A màn déad is a màn déad, and there is an end of the matter' (Macaulay) = 'A man if he is once dead is a man who is dead for good.'

A few of these cases of post position of the adjective are very old: mother dear; Grace dear, etc. Originally the adjective was a substantive here and this original usage is still very common; of course in modern form with a limiting adjective before the descriptive: 'Oliver, my dear' (Dickens).

2. Nouns, Adverbs, Phrases, and Sentences Used as Adherent Adjectives.

One of the marked features in English is the great freedom with which nouns, adverbs, phrases, and sentences can stand before a noun in adjective function: a *stòne* brídge; a *bòy* lóver; a *bàby* bóy; the *Smith* résidence; the *pòet* philósopher; *foreign lànguage* instrúction; a *twèlve-pound* páckage; a *clòck-work* tóy; a *làrge-scale* máp; the *United States* góvernment; a *cat and dòg* lífe (compare similar example in 3rd par.); the *dòwn* stróke; the *abòve* árgument; the *thèn* sécretary; his *àlmost* ímpudence; in *àfter* yéars; an *òut-and-out* fáilure; an *up-to-dàte* díctionary; that *nèver-to-be-forgòtten* lóok; these *not-to-be-avòided* cùrrent expénses; my *nèxt-door* néighbor; a *quarter-past-sèven* tráin; a *wòrld-wide* reputátion; the *ùnderground* ráilroad; a *pèn and ink* dráwing; a *matter-of-fàct* mán; a *mòney-back* guarantée; in a *free-and-èasy*, *gò-as-you plèase* sort of wáy; the most *stày-at-home* pérson that I ever heard of; a very *gò-ahèad-looking* lìttle pórt; a *drỳ-as-dùst* stúdy; a *pày-as-you-gò* pólicy. Similarly, if we drop the *of* in a predicate genitive it is because we feel the words following the *of* as a predicate adjective: 'The children are exactly [of] *the same age*.' 'Do I look [to be of] *my age?*' '[of] *What color* shall I paint your door?' after the analogy of 'Shall I paint your door *white?*' (objective predicate). Compare **7 A** *e*.

In all the groups in the preceding paragraph the second member, always a noun, is more heavily stressed than the first member, which is now felt as an adjective, i.e., descriptive stress prevails. These groups which normally have descriptive stress should not be confounded with groups that normally have distinguishing or classifying stress upon the first member, which is always a noun or has a noun as its basic element: *héadàche; wéll wàter; cánnon bàll; artíllery fìre; insúrance còmpany; bóy-lòver* (i.e., *a lover of boys*, in contrast to *a bòy lóver*, a youthful lover); a *bárgain còunter;* an *ármy òfficer;* a *bóok revìew;* a lively *good róads agitàtion;* a new *drý-goods stòre,* etc.   The first member in these groups was originally always stressed, hence these rigid formations were compounds or group-words (**63**).   But the marked feature in a large number of these formations as we now use them is that, in contrast to older usage, the stress is no longer rigid.   While in many cases we usually stress the first member when the group has classifying force, we do not hesitate to shift the accent to the second member when we desire to impart descriptive force: '*Good ròads agitátion* will lead to *good ròads legislátion*.'   We today feel the first member of a large number of the formations as an adjective which modifies the second member, hence we treat the first member as an adjective, stressing it to impart classifying force, but stressing the following noun to impart descriptive force.   Of course, the adjectives in the preceding paragraph may, like other adjectives, be stressed more heavily than their governing noun when the desire is to impart classifying force: *bóy sìngers;* a *pen-and-ínk dràwing;* the productions of his *áfter yèars;* an *up-to-dáte dìctionary.*   The oldest groups in the preceding paragraph, such as *stòne brídge* (in Old English *stán-brỳcg*), were originally compounds or group-words and hence were rigid formations with stress upon the first member, but later the feeling that the first member describes rather than classifies broke up the old formation and led to the shifting of the stress upon the second member, so that we now feel the first member as an adjective.   The groups described at the beginning of this paragraph had the same origin, but the peculiar oneness of meaning in some of them has preserved their old rigidity of form. In general, however, most of them are developing in the same direction as the groups in the preceding paragraph.

Adjectives are often formed from the plural of nouns: the *Niagara Falls* post office; a lively *good roads* agitation; *harbors* legislation (*Chicago Tribune*, Jan. 10, 1930); the fierce Kiowa, Comanche and other *plains* tribes (Milo Milton Quaife in 'Historical Introduction' to Kendall's *Narrative of the Texan Santa Fé Expedition*); a big *arms* budget (*Chicago Tribune*, Dec. 29, 1929); a *two-thirds* majority; the *customs* officers; the *five-powers* parley (*Chicago Herald-Examiner*, Jan. 5, 1930); an *auto-sales* cabinet; the *expenditures* committee (*Chicago Daily News*, Feb. 3, 1930); the *house rules* committee (*ib.*); the *Highways* Committee (*Review of Reviews*), etc. In most cases the singular is more common here: the *parcel* (sometimes *parcels*) post; a *ten-dollar* bill; a *fifty-dollar* suit; a *two-trouser* suit; a *two-cent* stamp; a *two-horse* carriage; *22-carat* gold; a *two-volume* novel; a *five-act* play; the *five-power* naval conference; the national *rose* show, etc. We often feel the genitive as an adjective: a *this year's* loon (Thoreau, *Journal*, XI, p. 309); a new *beginner's* Latin book; obvious *printer's* (also *printers'*) errors; a *cat and dog's* life; a new *old men's* home; a pleasant *five minutes'* talk; a *lovers'* quarrel; a *boys'* school; a very good *girls'* school. 'No mere *bankers'* plan will meet the requirements, no matter how honestly conceived. It should be a *merchants'* and a *farmers'* plan as well' (Woodrow Wilson, August 7, 1912). Compare 10 II 2 F *a, b*.

In English there is one common restriction to placing attributive elements before the governing noun. If the attributive modifier is an infinitive phrase, it must follow the governing noun, aside from a few passive infinitive phrases, such as those given in 2, p. 66: 'all time *to come*,' 'the new measures *to save coal*,' etc.

Adverbs and prepositional phrases often modify nouns as appositive adjective elements (10 I 1): 'the tree *yonder*,' 'the book *upon the table*.' Compare 10 VI, 10 IV.

3. **Repetition of Limiting Adjective.** If the limiting adjective modifies two nouns, both representing the same person or thing, or parts of a whole, it should be used only once; while, on the other hand, if the nouns represent different persons or things that it is desired to contrast or to mark as distinct and separate, the limiting adjective should be repeated before each noun: 'He is *the* guardian and natural protector (one person) of the lad,' but '*The* teacher and *the* guardian (two persons) of the lad were discussing his case together.' '*A* German and English dictionary,' or '*a* German-English dictionary' (one book), but '*a* German and *an* English

dictionary' (two books); '*the* red and white rose' (one rose with two colors), but '*the* red and *the* white rose' (two roses, each with only one color); '*the* red and white roses' (a number of roses, each of which is red and white), but '*the* red and *the* white roses' (a number of roses, some of which are all red and others of which are all white); (felt as belonging together) '*the* King and Queen,' '*my* knife and fork,' '*this* watch and chain,' '*the first* and second verses of the song'; '*a* horse and cart,' but '*I* bought *a* horse and *a* cart' (the horse and the cart not belonging together) and '*A* fair and *a* brunette woman were sitting inside the stagecoach.'

However, even where the reference is to different individuals, the second limiting adjective is often, for convenience' sake, dropped, provided no ambiguity would arise: '*the* old and new worlds,' '*the* English and German languages' instead of '*the* old and *the* new world,' '*the* English and *the* German language.' '*A* doctor and nurse were provided for them.' The omission of the limiting adjective becomes even necessary here to prevent awkwardness if there stands before both of the coördinated adjectives one or more adjectives which belong to them both: '*a peculiar neuter* nominative and accusative singular in –*d: id*,' etc. (Lane, *Latin Grammar*, p. 86).

One advantage accrues to us from the non-inflection of the adjective; namely, that the same adjective may modify a singular and a plural, so that we need not repeat it: '*some particular* chapter or chapters.'

On the other hand, the article is often repeated, not to make the thought clear, but to emphasize the individual words: 'Becky took an interest in everything appertaining to the estate, to the farm, the park, the gardens, and the stables' (Thackeray, *Vanity Fair*).

4. Noun Modified by Two Possessive Adjectives Connected by 'And.' On the one hand, the noun here often denotes a person or thing associated jointly with two or more different persons: 'I shall not cease to be *their* and *your* affectionate friend.' 'Let it be *your* and *my* gift.'

On the other hand, the noun here often denotes different persons or things: '*Your* (or sometimes *yours;* see **57** 5 *a*) *and my wife* (or more commonly and more clearly *your wife and mine*) are good friends.' '*Your* (or sometimes *yours*) *and my house* (or more commonly and more clearly *your house and mine*) are the only ones where good music is cultivated.' The context usually makes the thought clear. Plural form is sometimes employed here to express the plural idea: '*Mine* (or more commonly *my*) and *her* souls (or *my* and *her soul*, or more commonly *my soul and hers*) rushed together' (Browning, *Cristina*, VI). We regularly say 'Your and

my favorite *books'* when we mean 'Your favorite *books* and mine.'
Here again the latter expression is more common and also clearer.
Compare **57** 5 *a*.

5. **Logical Relations of the Adjective to Its Governing Substantive.** The attributive adjective has the force of a predicate,
i.e., it is something predicated of the governing noun.   The attributive adjective, however, as in 'the *cruel* man,' differs from
the predicate adjective, as in 'The man is *cruel*,' in that it indicates that the thought is incomplete, while the predicate adjective
indicates that the clause or sentence is complete.   As explained in
6 C, the predicate appositive adjective sustains relations to both
the subject and the principal verb, and thus often has the force of
an adverbial clause: '*Cruel* beyond belief (= *as he was cruel beyond
belief* — adverbial clause of cause), he didn't listen to their pleadings.'   The adherent and the appositive attributive adjective often
have the same force as the predicate appositive adjective when they
modify a subject: 'The *cruel* man, or the man, *cruel* beyond belief,
didn't listen to their pleadings' = 'The man didn't listen to their
pleadings, *as he was cruel* or *cruel beyond belief*' (adverbial clause
of cause).   'This *old* woman still dolls herself up like a young lady'
= 'This woman still dolls herself up like a young lady, *although she
is old*' (adverbial clause of concession).

6. **Orthographical Form.**   English orthography often does not
distinguish between a simple attributive adjective in an ordinary
syntactical group and an attributive adjective as a component of
a group-word (**63**) or compound.   Thus in *pràctical jóker* the adjective *practical* does not modify *joker* but is a component of the
derivative *pràctical jóker* = *pràctical jóke* + *–er*.   *Nèw and sècond-
hand bóoksèller* is a group-word = *nèw and sècond-hand bóok
+ séller*.   *Dìrty clóthes bàsket* is usually a compound = *dìrty
clóthes + básket*, but it may also be an ordinary syntactical group
= *a dìrty clóthes-bàsket*.

II. Attributive Genitive

A noun or pronoun in the genitive may modify a noun.

1. **Form, Position, and Stress.**   Oldest English had more genitive forms than the language of today.   We now have only two
distinctive forms, the prepositional genitive with *of* and the older
form in –*s*.   The genitive –*s* is now always written '*s*, but it is pronounced in two different ways: (1) After sibilants pronounced *ez*,
i.e., with a pronounced *e* followed by a *z*-sound, as in *Jones's*.
(2) Elsewhere pronounced as a simple *s* or *z*, as in *Smith's, John's*.
Originally, the *s*-genitive ending was always *es* (with pronounced

e), and even as late as Shakespeare's time the old ending *es* occurs, not only after sibilants, but also occasionally after non-sibilant sounds: 'as white as *whalĕs* bone' (*Love's Labor's Lost*, V, II, 332). Where in present-day English the old long genitive in *–es* is used after other sounds than sibilants, it is a mere literary form employed in poetry for the sake of the meter: 'My eyes for beauty pine, My soul for *Goddĕs* grace' (Bridges, *Shorter Poems*, Book IV, 9). In actual speech the old long genitive ending *es* with pronounced *e* survives only after sibilants; elsewhere it is reduced to a simple *s*.

About 1380 the *e* of the old genitive ending *es* began to disappear in written English, at first in words of more than one syllable: 'the *Pardoners* Tale' (Chaucer, *Ellesmere* MS.); '*Joseps son*' (*The Pepysian Gospel Harmony*, 46, about A.D. 1400); '*resons* dom' (Pecock, *Folewer*, p. 10, about A.D. 1454); 'the *Emperours* counsail' (Thomas Cromwell, *Letter to Pate*, May 11, 1540). At the close of the sixteenth century simple *s* is the usual genitive ending also in monosyllabic nouns: 'in *Gods* care' (Chettle, *Kind-Hartes Dreame*, p. 22, A.D. 1592).

As can be seen by the preceding examples, the apostrophe was not usually associated with the genitive ending in older English. This old genitive *s* without an apostrophe is preserved in *its* (**57** 5 *a*), *his, hers, ours, yours, theirs*. In the case of nouns singular '*s* began to appear about 1680, gaining ground at first only slowly. About a century later plural *s*' began to be used. The apostrophe in '*s* does not always indicate that a sound is suppressed, for we often pronounce '*s* as *es*, thus suppressing nothing, as in *Jones's*. The apostrophe came into use here at a time when the *his*-genitive, as in '*John his* book,' was widely used, competing with the *s*-genitive. The *s*-genitive was doubtless felt by many as a contraction of the *his*-genitive, which strengthened the tendency to place an apostrophe before the genitive ending *s*. This theory does not explain the use of '*s* after a feminine or a plural noun. The '*s* spread by analogy from masculine nouns to feminines and plurals.

The *his*-genitive occurs occasionally in Old English: '*Enac his* bearn' (*Numbers*, XIII, 29) = '*Anak's* sons.' In older English alongside of the *his*-genitive were a *her*-genitive and a *their*-genitive: '*Mary her* books,' '*the boys their* books.' Also these genitive forms occur in Old English. The genitive with *his, her*, and *their* became common between 1500 and 1700: '*my lord his* gracious letteres' (Thomas Cromwell, *Letter to Thomas Arondell*, June 30, 1528); '*Mars his* true moving' (Shakespeare, *I Henry VI*, I, II, 1.); 'in those 12 years of Sr. *Tho. Smith his* government'

(*The Tragical Relation of the Virginian Assembly*, A.D. 1624);
'*William Bradford his* wife' (Bradford, *History of Plymouth Plantation*, p. 410, A.D. 1630–1648); '*Mr. Dudley his* house' (Winthrop,
Journal, Oct. 31, 1632); '*at William Morse his* house' (Increase
Mather, *Remarkable Providences*, A.D. 1684). 'Then I took my
children and one *of my sisters hers*' (*The Captivity of Mary Row-
landson*, p. 2, A.D. 1682). 'For my Sowle, *my Father* and *Mother
their* Sowles' (Thomas Cromwell, *Testament*, July 12, 1529).
After the seventeenth century the genitive with *his, her*, and
their gradually disappeared from the literary language, but it
survives in popular speech: 'in *George the First his* time' (Thackeray, *Pendennis*, I, Ch. XXII).

The genitive in '*s* is still, as in older English, often, especially in
poetic language and in poetry, used with nouns designating lifeless things, but it is much more commonly employed with nouns
designating living beings: 'the *sun's* rays,' '*John's* hat,' 'the *boy's*
hat,' etc. The '*s* is added also in the plural if the plural does not
end in –*s:* '*men's* shoes,' '*children's* shoes.' The plural in –*s* takes
only the apostrophe: 'the *boys*' hats,' etc. Names of persons
and common nouns denoting persons which end in a sibilant
usually in the written language take here in the genitive singular '*s*, which is spoken *əz:* 'Mrs. *Adams's* wrapper' (Tarkington, *Alice Adams*, Ch. IX). 'The Duke sat at his *hostess's*
right' (Edith Wharton, *The Age of Innocence*, Ch. VIII). But
the plural genitive takes only the apostrophe, which is added to
the full plural form in –*es:* 'the *Adamses*' small veranda' (*Alice
Adams*, Ch. VII). The genitive plural of words not ending in a
sibilant adds the apostrophe to the plural in simple –*s:* 'the
Gaunts' cottage' (Galsworthy, *The Freelands*, Ch. XXXVIII).
Sometimes, however, we find a separate genitive ending, as in
the singular, an '*s* added to the regular plural: 'I ran over to
the *Flemings's*' (Meredith Nicholson, *A Reversible Santa Claus*,
Ch. V). In dialect the genitive of the plural *folks* ends thus quite
commonly in –*es:* 'bizzy wid udder *fo'ks's* doin's' (Joel Chandler
Harris, *Uncle Remus*, p. 68). Often also in the case of other
plurals in –*s:* 'the *farmers's* cows' (Wright, *The English Dialect
Grammar*, p. 265).

The genitive singular of words ending in a sibilant not infrequently still, as often in Middle English and early Modern English,
has no ending, but now in the written language takes an apostrophe: '*Cards*' pride' (Hugh Walpole, *Fortitude*, p. 80). This
usage is general in the case of *Jesus*' and ancient names in –*es*, as
Xerxes', *Socrates*', etc. Quite commonly so also in the case of
designations of lifeless things in certain set expressions, especially

before a word beginning with *s*, as *sake*, to avoid bringing near together three *s*-sounds, as in 'for old *acquaintance*' sake,' 'for *goodness*' sake,' 'for *conscience*' sake.' In older English, in these set expressions with *sake* the *s* was suppressed even in words not ending in a sibilant, which was an unconscious shortening of the long *s* resulting from such expressions as 'for sport[*s*] sake' (Shakespeare, *Henry IV*, I, ii, 77). It looks as though the long genitive ending –*es* had disappeared in Middle English and early Modern English after sibilants, but alongside of this shortened genitive was a *his*-genitive. As the *his* of the *his*-genitive was weakly stressed, it had about the same pronunciation as the old genitive ending –*es* and might often have been confounded with it, so that in many cases the form might have been a genitive in –*es*. However that may be, the genitive in –*es* is now the usual form here though it is written –'*s: Jones's*.

The forms with suppressed –*s* in all the cases described above are survivals of older usage. The dropping of the genitive ending was facilitated by analogies that existed in older inflection. In many Middle English nouns the genitive did not have a distinctive ending. Such a genitive survives in *Lady*, as in *a Lady chapel, a Lady altar*, etc., i.e., *My Lady's chapel, altar*, etc., but it is today felt as an adjective. After the analogy of such old genitives without a distinctive genitive ending many nouns dropped their genitive ending, so that such endingless genitives are characteristic of older English. Later, under the influence of the general feeling that the grammatical relations here should be expressed clearly, the genitive *s* was not only restored to those nouns that once had it, but it was given also to the nouns that did not have a distinctive ending. Though this new development is at present strong, there are a number of fluctuations where older usage lingers on alongside of the new, as described above. In British dialect of the North Country the endingless genitive is still common: 'my *father*' brother.' This genitive occurs often also in American Negro dialect: '*King Deer*' daughter' (Joel Chandler Harris, *Nights with Uncle Remus*, p. 69), 'fer *Gawd*' sake' (Du Bose Heyward, *Porgy*, p. 168).

Also the prepositional genitive with *of* is often used with nouns denoting living beings and is moreover the usual form for nouns denoting lifeless things: *John's hat; Job's patience* and *the patience of Job; a man's leg*, but only *a leg of a table*.

Originally, i.e., in primitive Indo-European, the genitive did not have a distinctive form, but was distinguished from its governing noun by placing it before the governing noun and by stressing it more heavily. This older type is still well preserved in numerous compounds and group-words (**63**): *sún-rìse = the rìsing of the sún; wáter-pòwer = pòwer of wáter*, etc. Even in the prehistoric period the inflected simple genitive had come into wide use and was of course very common in oldest English, but it was still as in the prehistoric period placed before the governing noun and in many cases was still stressed more heavily. Little by little the heavily stressed simple inflected genitive was removed in the Old English period from the position *before* the less heavily stressed governing noun to the place *after* it, and was later for the most part gradually replaced by the prepositional genitive, as explained below.

The less heavily stressed simple inflected genitive remained before the governing noun and is still there. Thus the inflected genitive that stands before the governing noun usually has a weaker stress than its governing noun, while the genitive after the governing noun has a heavier stress: *Mr. Smìth's new hóuse*, but *the new hòuse of Mr. Smíth*. This is the normal stress in genitive groups wherever the stress is descriptive. The old stressed simple inflected or uninflected genitive before the governing noun is still preserved wherever there is a strong desire to distinguish or classify; now pronounced with a little extra force to convey this meaning: (with distinguishing force) *Jóhn's hàt, not Wílliam's; the táble-lèg, not the cháir-lèg;* (with classifying force) *a chíld's lànguage; a chíld's vòice; a gírl's hàt; wáter-pòwer; hórse-pòwer; stéam-pòwer; a cháir-lèg; a táble-lèg.* Of course, we can often put an extra strong stress upon the second member in order to distinguish it: *Jòhn's hàt, not his bàll.* In the case of both persons and things we can distinguish and classify also by means of the prepositional genitive by placing, according to the meaning, a little stronger stress upon the first or the second member of the genitive group: (with distinguishing force) *the lèg of the táble, not the lèg of the cháir; the lèg of the tàble, not the tòp; the hèlmets of the ófficers, not thòse of the common sòldiers;* (with classifying force) *the lànguage of a chíld,* or *a chíld's lànguage; the pàtience of Jòb.* But if in any of these cases the stress upon the second member is stronger than that upon the first member, yet not extra strong, the force is descriptive: 'The hèlmet of this ófficer is broken.' 'The lànguage of this chíld is quite undeveloped.'

In Old English, there were several simple genitive forms: *-es* for many masculines and neuters; *-e* for certain feminines; *-an* for certain masculines, feminines, and neuters, etc. Although in oldest English, the simple genitive was the usual form, the new prepositional genitive was in certain categories coming into use by reason of the strong concrete force of *of*, originally meaning *from*, which indicated more graphically the ideas of separation, source, and origin than the simple genitive. Thus, people began to say 'He walks in the strength *of God*' instead of 'He walks in *God's* strength,' since the words *of God*, i.e., *from God*, vividly brought out the idea of man walking and struggling on earth, at the same time drawing strength from a higher source. Later, when Old English inflection began to lose its distinctive case forms, the unclear simple genitives were, without regard to gender, replaced, on the one hand, by the clear simple genitive in '*s* and, on the other hand, by the clear prepositional genitive with *of*. The tendency toward the prepositional genitive, which originally was the result of a strong desire for *concrete* expression, later became a formal trend toward *clearer* expression. Thus we feel the prepositional genitive with *of* today only as one of the two genitive forms without a vivid feeling for the origin of the preposition *of*.

a. S-Genitive Associated with the Conception of Life. As the prepositional genitives after the governing noun were usually designations of things, the prepositional genitive has become associated with designations of things and the form in −*s* with designations of living beings. This distinction between living and lifeless things is, however, not closely observed. We quite often in choice English still employ the genitive in −*s* in cases of *unstressed* designations of things to impart descriptive force and at the same time stress the governing noun: 'When I think of all the sorrow and the barrenness that has been wrought in my life by want of a few more pounds per annum than I was able to earn, I stand aghast at *mòney's* signíficance' (Gissing, *Henry Ryecroft*, V, p. 15). 'It was apparently felt that, for the sake of the *mìnd's* péace, one ought not to inquire into such things too closely' (Arnold Bennett, *The Old Wives' Tale*, IV, Ch. IV, p. 82). 'A *bòok's* chánces depend more on its selling qualities than its worth.' The old genitive in −*s* cannot be freely used here. The thing must usually have some sort of individual life like a living being, but this idea of life may be very faint. It is faintest when the name of a thing is used as the subject of a gerund, where it is often not felt at all: 'There is now no further danger of the *hòuse's* séttling.' Of course, the idea of life is often strong: 'the òcean's róar'; 'Trùth's greatest víctories,' etc. On the other hand, under similar conditions, we often use the stressed genitive in −*s* to impart distinguishing force: 'for Héaven's sàke'; 'at déath's dòor'; 'Dúty's càll,' etc.

b. Double Genitive. The simple form in −*s* is still widely used when the genitive stands before the governing noun, but in the position after the governing noun it has been entirely replaced by the form with *of*, for it would here not be felt as a genitive but as a plural. We may, however, quite often use the terminational genitive of personal pronouns after the governing noun provided we place the prepositional genitive sign *of* before the terminational genitive, so that it becomes clear that the form in question is a genitive: 'þi neghbur wijf yerne noght at haue,

Ne aght *of his*, ne mai, ne knaue' (*Cursor Mundi*, l. 6479, about A.D. 1300) = 'Yearn not to have your neighbor's wife, nor property *of his* (= *that is his*), nor his maiden, nor his servant.' In this old example and similar ones in this same book the clear genitive sign *of* is put before *his*, since in this and all similar genitives, as *yours*, *mine*, etc., the genitive force is not felt, since these forms are also used as possessive pronouns in the nominative, dative, and accusative relations. The combination of *of* and the old genitive, *his*, *hers*, *yours*, *theirs*, etc., makes a clear genitive. This double genitive is usually preferred to the form with *of* + accusative, as *of him*, *of her*, etc., since there is usually a strong desire to express here after the governing noun the idea of personal possession that is so prominent in the old inflectional genitive found before the governing noun. Hence the double genitive is strictly limited to reference to a definite person or definite persons: 'a friend *of mine*,' 'this friend *of ours*,' 'the friend *of mine* of whom I spoke yesterday,' 'these friends *of mine*,' 'a remark *of hers*,' etc., not 'a friend *of me*, *of us*,' etc. But we say 'a beautiful picture (i.e., likeness) *of her*' in contrast to 'a beautiful picture *of hers*' (i.e., that belongs to her). The usual idea in the double genitive is that of possession, as in 'that great weakness *of his*,' or the closely related idea of origin, authorship, as in 'this remark *of his*.' But the partitive idea often mingles with that of possession: 'a friend *of mine*,' 'an admirer *of hers*.' In course of time there has become associated with the double genitive a marked liveliness of feeling, so that it now often implies praise or censure, pleasure or displeasure: 'that dear little girl *of yours*,' 'that kind wife *of yours*,' 'this broad land *of ours*,' 'that ugly temper *of hers*,' 'that ugly nose *of his*.' 'Thus Professor Blackie, in that vituperative book *of his*, "The Natural History of Atheism" . . . says . . .' (John Burroughs, *The Light of Day*, Ch. VI).

From the very start the double genitive has been in use also with nouns, for it is often desirable to employ here the old terminational genitive with its strongly pronounced personal force: 'Sertes . . . Haue we noght þan (for *tan*) o þe kinges' (*Cursor Mundi*, l. 4907) = 'We surely have taken nothing *of the King's*.' It is also here absolutely necessary to insert the clear genitive sign *of*, or otherwise the genitive group would be felt as an appositional element, not as an attributive genitive. The double genitive here has come into wide use, but it is still strictly confined to definite reference and, differing from usage with pronouns, can be used of only a single definite person, for the plural form here is to the ear usually identical with the singular: 'this remark *of Carlyle's*,' 'a threat *of my father's*,' 'the battered schoolbook *of Tom's*.' The plural form is quite rare: 'in some old retreat of his or his *friends*' ' (John Burroughs, *Far and Near*, p. 162). The apostrophe here makes clear the thought of the author, but in the spoken language the thought is usually ambiguous when the double genitive is a common class noun — unless the context makes the reference clear. The ear, unaided by the situation, cannot detect whether the form is singular or plural. Hence, the use of the double genitive with nouns is largely confined to proper names and such titles of relationship as have the force of proper names, as in the first three examples. In many cases, however, the double genitive of titles of relationship, as 'the beauty *of my sister's,*' is not clear to the ear, unless the situation makes the reference clear. Although the double genitive with nouns is in general subject to ambiguity, many, desirous of its lively effect, take their chances with it, trusting to the situation to help them out: 'It was no fault *of the doctor's*' (Washington Irving). The *of*-genitive is here, as often elsewhere, a clearer form, and is often preferred.

The double genitive and the *of*-genitive of nouns are often used side by side without any differentiation of meaning: 'a play *of Shakespeare's*' (or *of Shakespeare*). But the forms are gradually becoming differentiated. The double genitive is associated with liveliness of feeling, expressing the idea of approbation, praise, censure, pleasure, displeasure: 'this appropriate remark *of Mrs. Smith's,*' 'that really beautiful speech *of your wife's,*' 'that ugly remark *of her father's,*' etc.

c. POSITION OF GENITIVE AMONG OTHER ATTRIBUTIVE MODIFIERS. The genitive usually stands first among the attributive modifiers which follow the governing word: 'The desire *of my hèart* for péace.' The genitive precedes the other modifiers because it is least stressed, but it of course stands last when it is the most important element: 'this sudden appearance amid my corrupt, and heartless, and artificial life of *so much innocence,* and *so much lóve,* and *so much simplícity* — they fell upon my callous heart like the first rains upon a Syrian soil' (Disraeli, *Contarini Fleming*, 150). Another attributive element sometimes precedes the genitive because it contains a word which points back to something that precedes and hence comes as early as possible: 'the presence in such a spot *of a crew* of foreign adventurers' (R. L. Stevenson, *The Merry Men*, 47).

2. **The Categories of the Attributive Genitive.** The attributive genitive expresses different classes of ideas briefly described in the following articles. These categories are not all peculiar to the attributive use, but several of them are found also in the genitive which is used in connection with verbs, adjectives, and participles, and rests upon the same original genitive idea — the general idea of sphere described on page 78 and in **13 3**. Thus D and H (pp. 81, 85) are often closely related to the genitive after verbs described in **13 3**. See D and H *a*. Also the common genitive of origin and possession described in A and B and the genitive of characteristic described in F *a* are not only used as attributive forms but are employed also as the predicate complement of the verb *be*, as illustrated in **7 A** *e*. In Old English, the genitive after verbs and adjectives was the simple genitive. The genitive here survives only in the form of the *of*-genitive. As we do not now feel the *of*-genitive here as a genitive, but construe it as a prepositional object, we no longer have a live feeling for the old, once common, genitive after verbs and adjectives. We now usually think of the genitive as an attributive adjective element modifying nouns or pronouns. Compare **13**

1, 2, 3. The attributive genitive categories are treated below at considerable length.

A. GENITIVE OF ORIGIN, representing a person or thing as associated with another person or thing in the relation of source, cause, authorship: the sòn *of the kíng, the kìng's* són; *this wòman's* chíldren, the chìldren *of this wóman;* the devastàtions *of the wár; this wàrrior's* déeds, the dèeds *of this wárrior; Tàcitus'* Ánnals, the Ánnals *of Tácitus; Dìckens's* wórks, the wòrks *of Díckens; Shàkespeare's* wórks, the wòrks *of Shákespeare; the Oxford Professor of Pòetry's* ináugural lécture. The same idea is found in the genitive used in the predicate with verbs. See **7 A e.**

a. This one use of this case form has given to it the name of *genitive* (from Latin genitivus, *pertaining to generation or birth*), which has become a fixed name not only for this use but also for all the following relations expressed by the same case form.

b. If two names are connected by *and* and represent persons that are joined together in authorship, business, or a common activity the second name alone assumes the genitive ending: '*Steevens and Malone's* Shakespeare,' 'in *William and Mary's* reign,' but of course *Steele's and Addison's works* when we are speaking of the separate sets of two different authors.

B. POSSESSIVE GENITIVE. This is a broad category that may have developed out of the general idea of 'sphere,' which in the prehistoric period and still in oldest English was a common meaning of the genitive employed with verbs, as described in **13 3,** as well as the source of a number of the attributive possessive genitive meanings which have come down to us from this older period, namely, possession, inherence, a belonging to, association with, or relation to, indicating various relations between nouns much as prepositions indicate relations between nouns and verbs: *my bròther's* hóuse, the hòuse *of my bróther* (literally, the house in the sphere of my brother, i.e., the house owned by my brother); *the hèro's* cóurage, the còurage *of the héro* (literally, the courage in the sphere, the nature of the hero); *life's* déepest próblems, the dèepest próblems *of lífe* (literally, the deepest problems in the sphere of life); *Sòcrates'* wísdom, the wìsdom *of Sócrates; Mr. Jònes's* áuto, the àuto *of Mr. Jónes; the King of Éngland's* private próperty; *Whàt do you call him's* són; *the writer's mòther's* máiden nàme; *last Màg's* stórms; the lèaves *of the trées;* the strèets *of the cíty;* the còolness *of évening;* the snòws *of wínter; the sùn's* ráys, the ràys *of the sún; the èarth's* míghty ones, the mìghty ones *of éarth; the shìp's* síde; *the cìty's* wéalth; *the nàtion's* prospérity; *the dày's* wórk; in *The Tìmes's* opínion, in the opìnion of 'The Tímes,' in the opìnion of *The Tímes; Éngland's* aristócracy, the

aristòcracy *of Éngland; the dòg's* máster, the màster *of the dóg* (literally, master in the sphere of the dog, not *a master owned by the dog*);
the bòy's fáther, the fàther *of the bóy* (literally, father in the sphere
of, with reference to the boy, not *a father owned by the boy*); the
chìef *of police* (literally, chief in the sphere of the police); the kìng
of the lánd.

This is a very common category, to which A, C, F, G are closely
related. The same idea is found in the genitive used with verbs.
See **7 A** *e.*

The possessive genitive is often closely related to the partitive
genitive: 'the leg *of the table*' (possessive or partitive genitive).
The two genitives here have the same form and practically the
same meaning, but in case of personal pronouns there has long
been a tendency to differentiate here form and meaning, namely,
to employ *his, her,* etc., in the possessive relation and *of him, of
her,* etc., in the partitive relation, stressing the idea of an integral
part, as described more fully in H, p. 85: '*His hair, his eyes,*'
etc., but 'She was the daughter of a lumberjack and woodcraft
was bred into the very fiber *of her*' (*Saturday Evening Post*, July 29,
1916). 'The man had something in the *look of him*' (Browning,
An Epistle). 'I do it for the honor *of it.*' As this differentiation
has not become thoroughly established, we still more commonly
employ here the old undifferentiated forms *his, her,* etc., for either
the possessive or the partitive relation: '*his* eyes' and 'The
man had something in *his* look.' But we now always use the
form with *of* when the pronoun is modified by a relative clause:
'Then first I heard the voice *of her* to whom the Gods Rise up
for reverence' (Tennyson, *Œnone*, l. 105). In older English, the
simple possessive genitive, *her, his,* etc., could be used here. See
23 II 8 *a.*

In this category descriptive stress with the accent upon the
second member prevails, but we not infrequently find distinguishing stress: nőbody's bòok; somebody élse's bòok; for péace'
sàke; for héaven's sàke; for héalth's sàke; for ríghteousness' sàke;
for Jésus' sàke; at déath's dòor; Fórtune's trìcks, the trìcks of
Fórtune; Wílliam's àuto, not Jóhn's. Also classifying stress is
common, sometimes in connection with the genitive in −*s*, sometimes with the old uninflected form: bírd's-nèst; rát's tàil or
ràt-tàil; swăn's nèck; pígskìn; góose-fèather; hórse-hìde, etc.
Compare **63.**

The possessive genitive may be also a genitive clause, as illustrated in **24 I.**

   a. Adverbs Inflected Like Nouns. Adverbs, or adverbial expressions,
are now often inflected like nouns: '*yèsterday's* máil,' '*this wèek's* máil,'

'the heavy màil *of last wéek*'; '*tomòrrow's* dínner'; '*yesterday èvening's* néwspaper.' Or, of course, to distinguish, '*yesterday ĕvening's* nèwspaper,' etc.

b. Inflection of Nouns Connected by 'And.' If two or more names connected by *and* represent persons that are joined together in possession, the second or last name alone assumes the genitive ending: '*John and William's* uncle'; '*John, William, and Mary's* uncle.' 'We paid a visit to *Messrs. Pike and White's* works.' '*My father and mother's* Bible.'

But we must give each genitive its genitive –*s* if there is no joint possession: '*My father's and my mother's* birthdays both fall in June, two days apart.' In older English, however, even where there was no joint possession the last genitive often alone took the ending, as a firm differentiation of usage had not yet taken place: 'Thou Must . . . bear the palm for having bravely shed Thy *wife and children's blood*' (Shakespeare, *Coriolanus*, V, iii, 113), now *thy wife's and thy children's blood*.

c. Omission of Governing Noun. The word for house or place of business is often omitted: 'I was at *Smith's* [house or place of business].' 'Go to *the baker's.*' 'Mary has written to say that she is going to spend all her Christmas holidays at her dear *aunt* (compare *b*) *and uncle's.*'

The governing noun is regularly omitted when the possessive genitive points forward or backward to a preceding or following governing noun, for the genitive here is now felt as a possessive pronoun, like *mine, hers,* etc., as explained in **57** 5 *a:* 'John's auto is larger than *William's and mine.*'

d. Group Genitive. It is usually taught that in such expressions as '*the King of England's* private property' the inflectional genitive –*s* is placed at the end of the group *King of England* because these words are felt as a unit with the force of a single word. This conception, however, cannot here be the compelling force that has brought about this construction, for we never say '*The king of Englands* now have less political power than formerly,' treating the group *king of England* as one word, adding the plural –*s* at the end. The real reason for placing the genitive –*s* at the end of the group *the King of England* is simply to avoid ambiguity, for if –*s* were added to *King* the form would be felt as a plural, since –*s* now always conveys a plural idea where it is not immediately followed by the governing noun. The oneness of idea in *King of England* made it possible to add the –*s* to the end of the group and the ambiguity that would otherwise arise suggested this course, but in this same group of words *king*, not *England*, has the plural sign in the nominative plural in the subject relation: 'The *kings of England* now have less political power than formerly.'

Until about 1500 it was common to say 'the King's property of England.' Here and there this old usage lingered on after that date for a time: 'the Archbishop's grace of York' (Shakespeare, *I Henry IV*, III, ii, 119). In such expressions as 'the King's property of England' the later tendency to bring together the words that naturally belonged together, i.e., to say *the King of England*, separated *King* from the governing noun *property*, which made it necessary to add the genitive ending to *England*, so that the *-s* might here as elsewhere stand immediately before the governing noun. In the plural in the subject relation it was not thus necessary to add the *-s* to *England* so that the old historic form of expression was here not disturbed. Where there is no ambiguity, the old historic genitive singular with the *-s* at the end of the proper word is still found in the language of children: 'It ain't *either's* of us revolaver' (Tarkington, *Penrod and Sam*, Ch. IV). This compact genitive construction is much more forceful than the literary form of expression 'The revolver doesn't belong to either of us.'

e. Unclear Old Genitive Forms. There is a force in the compact simple genitive that appeals to us. The loss of distinctive genitive form here in a number of pronouns and limiting adjectives has weakened English expression. In older English, a natural fondness for the simple genitive often led to its use even where the genitives were uninflected pronouns and limiting adjectives that could not indicate the grammatical relations: '*Both their* (in Middle English *bother their* or *their bother*, hence with a clear genitive form) *several talents* were excessive' (Fielding, *Tom Jones*, III, 45), now *the several talents of both of them*. This older usage is best preserved in the subjective genitive category in connection with the gerund: 'Your mother will feel *your both* going away' (Mrs. Gaskell, *Wives and Daughters*, Ch. XVI). 'Isn't it dreadful to think of *their all* being wrong!' (Sir Harry Johnston, *The Man Who Did the Right Thing*, Ch. II).

It is also well preserved in the possessive category in such expressions as *both our lives*, *both our minds*, but we now feel the old genitives as plural limiting adjectives. This new interpretation early led to putting a following singular governing noun into the plural: 'were you *both our mothers*' (Shakespeare, *All's Well*, I, III, 169), now 'were you *the mother of both of us*.' This old usage survives in popular speech: 'She is *both their mothers*,' i.e., 'the mother of both of them.' 'It is *both their faults*.' In the literary language it lingers on in *for both their sakes*, *for both our sakes*. Similarly, when *of* is inserted after *all*, *both*, *none*, etc., to give expression to the partitive idea: 'I'm taking the trouble of writing this true history *for all of your benefits*' (Hughes, *Tom Brown's School-Days*, I, VI), instead of the correct *for the benefit of all of you*. 'A painful circumstance which is attributable to *none of our faults*' (Thackeray, *Pendennis*, II, Ch. XXXV), instead of the correct *the fault of none of us*.

C. SUBJECTIVE GENITIVE, which represents a living being as associated with an act in the relation of author: '*Mòther's* lóve for us children.' 'We have all heard *dúty's* càll' (or the càll *of dúty*). 'From our house we can hear the *òcean's* róar' (choice prose or poetry; or more commonly the ròar *of the ócean*). Compare **20 3** (6th, 7th, and 8th parr.).

The old uninflected genitive is common here: *sún-rìse*, *éarth-quàke*, *héart-thròb*, *snáke-bìte*, etc. Compare **63**.

D. OBJECTIVE GENITIVE, which denotes the object toward

which the activity is directed: 'devoting much time *to the chíl-dren's educátion'* (or *the educátion of the chíldren*); 'the cìty's cáp-ture by the Japanese,' 'the càpture of the cíty by the Japanese'; '*Cæ̀sar's múrderers,*' 'the mùrderers of Cǽsar.' 'Old Lord Ancoat's death, which followed within a month or two, was has-tened on by the shock of *his sòn's lóss*' (Mrs. H. Ward) = 'the loss *of his son.*' 'The feeling of *Ȅmily's lóss* does not diminish as time wears on' (Mrs. Gaskell). 'WOMAN IS HUNTED AS *MAN'S* SLAYER' (headline in *The Sun*, New York, Aug. 7, 1929). 'Costa Rica, Salvador, and Honduras stoutly objected to *the treaty's* ratification' (*The Sun*, New York, Sept. 5, 1929).

The objective genitive may be a full genitive clause or an abridged infinitival or gerundial clause, as illustrated in **24 I** and *a* thereunder.

The prepositional genitive is the rule in this category, but, as can be seen by examples given above, the old simple genitive still lingers on. The prepositional form sometimes differentiates the objective from the subjective genitive: 'I hate the sight *of him*' (objective genitive), but '*His* (subjective genitive) sight is failing.'

This genitive is often closely related to the adverbial genitive of specification described in **13 3**: 'They counted on a complete destruction *of the enemy*' = *with reference, with regard to the enemy,* literally, *in the sphere of the enemy.*

The old uninflected genitive is still common here in group-words (**63**): *gate*-keeper, *money*-maker, *woman*-hater, *child*-study. In the case of words not ending in *s* in the plural, there is a tendency here to give a formal expression to the plural idea: *lice*-exterminator, etc.

As the possessive adjectives are derived from the genitive of the personal pronouns they still often have various meanings of the genitive, hence also sometimes the force of an objective geni-tive: *my* (= genitive of origin) son, *my* (= a possessive genitive) book, *my* (= a subjective genitive) love of God, *my* (= an objec-tive genitive) punishment.

E. GENITIVE OF MATERIAL OR COMPOSITION, denoting that of which something consists: a cròwn *of thórns;* an ìdol *of góld;* rài-ment *of* cámel's *hair;* a hèrd *of cáttle;* a gròup *of chíldren;* a flòck *of bírds;* a swàrm *of bées,* etc. The old uninflected simple genitive is still in part preserved: *stóne*-hèap, or a hèap *of stónes; sánd*-pìle, or a pìle *of sánd; thórn*-hèdge; *dúng*-hìll, etc. The old uninflected genitive was once much more common here. In most cases it has been construed as an adjective, as is indicated by its loss of stress: a stòne brídge (in Old English stánbryceg); an ìron píllar; a còpper kéttle, etc. Compare **10 I 2** (2nd par.) and **63**.

The old inflected s-genitive is now not used in this category.
This genitive category is closely related to H.
F. DESCRIPTIVE GENITIVE. This genitive is closely related to
the possessive genitive and some of the examples given below
might be classed there. There are two groups:

a. *Genitive of Characteristic.* With classifying force and stress:
a wŏman's vòice, or the vòice *of a wŏman; a chĭld's* lànguage, or
the lànguage *of a chĭld; a măn's* ròughness, or the ròughness *of a
măn; a lădy's* glòve; *a wŏman's* còllege; *a măn's* shòe; *a gĕntle-
man's* shòe; *mĕn's* shòes; *chĭldren's* clòthing; *a wŏrld's* fàir. We
often feel the classifying genitive that precedes its governing noun
as an adjective, as can be seen by the fact that the preceding
adjective modifies the governing noun, not the genitive: 'obvious
printer's (or *printers'*) errors.' Compare **10 I 2** (3rd par.).
With descriptive force and stress: a màn *of stérling cháracter;*
a nèwspaper *of hígh ránk;* thìngs *of thís sórt;* a màtter *of consíder-
able impórtance;* the Gòd *of lóve;* a màn *of áction;* a spìrit *of háte.*
Sometimes, however, in these descriptive groups the first member
has such a strong logical force that it is stressed, regularly so
after numerals: 'A mán *of àction* and a wóman *of àction* proceed
in quite different ways.' 'She is worth tén *of hèr dàughter,* tén *of
yòu.'*
If we employ a prepositional genitive here with classifying
force, we must stress the second member a little more than usual,
or the group will be construed as having descriptive force: thc
pàtience *of Jŏb;* the lànguage *of a chĭld.* Instead of a genitive here,
we often use an adjective with classifying stress: a màn *of hĭgh
temper,* or a *hĭgh-tempered* màn; a wòman *of kĭnd heart,* or a *kĭnd-
hearted* wòman. The compound adjective has come into wide
use here both to describe and to classify: 'He lives in a beautiful
fòur-hundrcd-dollar-a-month hóuse' (descriptive), but 'Every cavalry officer must be a good *cross-cŏuntry* rìder' (classifying). Compare I 2, p. 66.
b. Quite similar is the *Genitive of Measure:* a *five mìnutes'* tálk;
an *hòur or two's* deláy, or a delày *of an hóur or two;* a *three hòurs'*
deláy, or a delày *of three hóurs;* a *mònth's* rént. Instead of the
inflected genitive we often employ the old uninflected genitive,
especially when the measure is other than that of time: a *thrèe-hour*
deláy; a *tèn-pound* báby; a *tèn-foot* póle; a *five-mile* wálk; the
tèn-mile rów across the harbor (John Burroughs, *Far and Near,*
p. 252), etc. We sometimes feel the inflected genitive here so
strongly as an adjective that we treat it as an adjective, adding
one in substantive function: 'The higher course is *a two years'*

one' (London Times, Educational Supplement, 8/8, 1918). The old uninflected genitive is now usually felt as a compound adjective: 'A *five-minute* tàlk would be more appropriate than *a thírty-minute one.*'

A classifying genitive is used in units of measurement — a possessive or an objective genitive with classifying stress: (possessive genitive) 'a *bŏat's* lèngth'; 'at a distance of two *shĭp's* lèngths' (Sir C. P. Butt in *Law Times Rep.*, LIII, 61/1); 'a *hăir's* brèadth'; (objective genitive) 'a *stŏne's* thròw'; 'within *two stŏnes'* thròw of the club' (Galsworthy, *The Country House*, 263), or better 'within *two stŏne's* throws.' Apart from the genitive relation we usually employ compound or group-word (**63**) form with non-inflection of the first element in such units of measurement: 'within three *bŏwshòts'* (Kipling); i.e., 'three shots *with the bow'* (attributive prepositional phrase).

G. APPOSITIVE GENITIVE, explaining the preceding governing word: the vìce *of intémperance;* the gìft *of sóng;* the àrt *of prínting;* the tèmple *of the bódy;* the pèriod *of the Reformátion;* the tìtle *of Dúke;* the Dùchy *of Láncaster;* the Repùblic *of Fránce;* the Stàte *of Illinóis;* the cìty *of Chicágo;* the nàme *of misánthropist;* the cry *of 'Wólf, wólf';* a confused cry *of 'The King is bleeding!';* a verdict *of 'death from natural causes.'*

Except in proper names, as *St. Pául's* Cathèdral, *St. Jámes's* Pàrk, *St. Jámes's* Squàre, often in elliptical form, *St. Paul's* [Cathedral], *All Saints'* [Church], *St. James's* [Theater], *St. Bartholomew's* [Hospital], etc., the old simple genitive is now used here only in poetic language: *tréason's* chàrge (Scott, *Marmion*, II, VIII); *lífe's* jòurney; *lífe's* fitful fèver; *Tíme's* fleeting rìver, etc. The simple genitive of certain proper names is used only in poetic language: *Álbion's* Isle; *Érin's* Isle; *Zíon's* Cìty; *Twéed's* fair rìver, or more commonly, according to the second paragraph below, the fair rìver *Twéed*, etc. Notice that the appositive genitive, whether it follows or precedes the governing noun, usually has the stress.

The possessive genitive is the starting point of this genitive category, as can be seen in 'the blessing *of a good education*,' where the genitive can be construed either as a possessive or as an appositive genitive.

Alongside of this appositive construction is another. The appositive is placed after the governing noun, agreeing with it in case: the ànimal *mán;* the bìrd *héron;* the màmmal *whále;* the preposìtion *with;* the dèmon *rúm;* Kìng *Hénry;* Càrdinal *Mánning;* Làke *Míchigan*, etc. In oldest English, the stressed appositive, of course, preceded the governing noun: *'Témese* strèame'

(Bede), now often 'the rìver *Thámes*,' since the stressed word in a normal descriptive group stands last. Compare III 1 B, p. 91. The old word-order, however, is still often used here, but the stress is the new descriptive: *the Thàmes Rìver.* Many groups still have thus the old English word-order with the new stress, as *Hùdson Rìver; Bèring Séa; St. Gòthard Túnnel; Pànama Canál,* etc. The old word-order has been preserved through a change of conception and a consequent change of stress. The proper name is now felt as a descriptive adjective and has accordingly lost its strong stress, so that it must stand before the more strongly stressed governing noun as other descriptive adjectives. But *Státe Strèet, Wábash Àvenue, Dráke Hòtel,* etc., with distinguishing stress.

Chaucer sometimes has alongside of the appositive genitive form the older appositional construction of two nouns agreeing in case: *the citee of Rome* (*The Nonne Preestes Tale,* 549); *Thebes the citee* (*The Knightes Tale,* 76). We now say *the river Jordan* or *the Jordan River,* but in older English, we find also *the river of Jordan* (*Mark,* I, 5). We now say *Lake Erie,* etc., but the appositive genitive form occurs in a few names: *the Lake of Tiberias, the Sea of Galilee,* etc.

The appositive genitive may be also a genitive clause, as illustrated in **23 I**.

a. The appositive genitive is often added to a noun, not to define its meaning more accurately, but to indicate a class to which a thing or person belongs that has just been characterized as an individual by the governing noun: the ráscal *of a làndlord;* a jéwel *of a cùp;* a béast *of a nìght;* a fráil slíp *of a wòman;* a brúte *of a hùsband;* his térmagant *of a wìfe;* a lóve *of a chìld;* a dévil *of a hùrry,* etc. This construction is not known in Old English. It has come into the language from the French. Originally, it came from the Latin appositive genitive, which is an outgrowth of the possessive genitive, as in 'scelus viri' *rascal of a man,* i.e., a rascal who belongs to the class represented by man; 'monstrum mulieris' *monster of a woman,* i.e., monster who belongs to womankind. All feeling for this origin has been lost, for the common class noun after *of* can now be replaced by a proper name: 'Where is that béast *of a Fìngal?*' = 'Where is that béast Fìngal?'

H. PARTITIVE GENITIVE, denoting the whole of which only a part is taken: a pìece *of bréad;* the hàlf *of my próperty;* a glàss *of wáter;* òne *of my friends;* twò *of the bóys.* 'Have you a còpy *of this bóok?*' In these descriptive groups the idea of quantity or part often becomes logically so important that we must stress the first member: 'Edward the Confessor was mòre *of a mónk* than a kíng,' but 'He is now móre *of a hỳpocrite* than ever before.' 'He

isn't *múch of a lìnguist.'* 'He is *sómething of an advènturer.'* 'She
is *a bít of a coquètte.'* 'He is *the héad* (or *the very lífe,* or *the sóul*)
of the ènterprise.'

In rather poetic language, it has long been common to employ
a stressed noun here to denote the part and the unstressed genitive
of a personal pronoun to denote the whole, where the whole is a
person or thing and the part the material body or some part of
it, or, on the other hand, an immaterial part or some characteristic feature: *þe sáule of hìm* (*Old English Homilies,* I, 163, latter half
of twelfth century). 'Fetch thou *the córpse of hèr* and bury her
by her husband the noble King Arthur' (Malory, *Le Morte d'Arthur,* XXI, 2). 'He is tender to impression at the surface, but
there is too much *máss of hìm* to be moved' (Ruskin, *Modern
Painters*). 'They were his environment, these men, and they
were moulding *the cláy of hìm* into a more ferocious thing than
had been intended by nature' (Jack London, *White Fang*). 'She
was the daughter of a lumberjack and woodcraft was bred into
the very fíber of hèr' (*Saturday Evening Post,* July 29, 1916). 'The
chief quality of Burns is *the sincérity of hìm'* (Carlyle). *'The píty
of it àll* (= *the pitiable feature of his life*) is that he had to die without seeing the fruits of his work.' 'I do not remember that I then
had any pity for him (the chipmunk). I think I rather enjoyed
the sport of hunting him. That is *the bóy of it'* (John Burroughs,
Field and Study, Ch. IX).

In a number of expressions the partitive genitive of personal
pronouns is also common in plain prose, usually, however, without
the poetic meaning of the preceding examples, merely stressing
the idea of an integral part: 'That will be the énd *of it,* the lást of
it.' In a vague way we feel life and death as parts of us, vital
parts of our human experience: 'I couldn't do it for *the lífe of mè.'*
'That will be *the déath of yòu.'* In all the above examples, where
we think of a whole and some part of it, the partitive genitive is
closely related to the possessive genitive. Compare B, p. 79.

The partitive genitive may be also a clause, as illustrated in
23 I.

a. Nature of the Attributive Partitive Genitive. The Old English attributive partitive genitive was closely related to the adverbial genitive
of specification (**13** 3): 'Heora *heriges* þær wæs mycel of slægen' = *With
regard to their army there was a large part slain.* This old genitive was
early construed also as an attributive genitive, and this conception still
survives: *'Of their army* a large part was slain,' or 'A large part *of
their army* was slain.' In older English, however, the old genitive of
specification was here often also construed as a partitive genitive subject
or object, and later was replaced by a nominative for the subject relation

and by an accusative for the object relation: 'There is *gold* and *siluer* (subject) gret *plentee*' (pred. appos.) (Mandeville). '*Sound* (subject) there was *none* (pred. appos.) only that faint stir that never quite dies of a country evening' (Galsworthy, *The Country House*, p. 26). '*Silver* and *gold* (object) have I *none*' (pred. appos.) (*Acts*, III. 6). '*Affection* (object) she had *none*' (pred. appos.) (James Payne, *Not Wooed but Won*, I, 68). '*Paternal relatives* (object) Goodwin has as good as *none*' (pred. appos.) (Gissing, *Born in Exile*, 41).

On the other hand, with certain verbs the old use of the genitive as partitive object or predicate tarried a long while and in poetic and solemn style still lingers on: 'When the woman saw that the tree was good for food . . . she took *of the fruit* thereof' (*Genesis*, III, 6). 'Ye believe not, because ye are not *of my sheep*' (*John*, X, 26).

b. Partitive Genitive Replaced by the Appositional Construction. Instead of the genitive we often find apposition after certain words: a little *bréad;* twò dòzen *éggs,* dózens *of èggs;* a great màny *chíldren;* a fèw *bóys;* twò thousand *dóllars,* thóusands *of dòllars;* fòur mìllion *péople,* míllions *of pèople;* thrèe score *yéars* and ten, scóres *of tìmes.* In older English, the appositional construction here was more widely used than now: 'no mòrsel *bréd*' (Chaucer); 'a bàrel *ále*' (*id.*), etc. This construction arose in the period of the decay of older inflection. A simple genitive often did not have a distinctive form, so that it appeared to stand in apposition with the governing noun. Later, the true genitive was restored by replacing the appositive by the clear modern prepositional genitive. The old construction, in general, has been retained only where the governing noun has been construed as an adjective.

Another, quite different, appositional construction, the predicate appositional construction described in **6 C**, has, in a number of cases, been replaced for the most part by the partitive genitive: 'your broder, *the worthyest knighte of the world one*' (Malory, *Le Morte d'Arthur*, Book XVI, Ch. XV, fifteenth century), now '*one of the worthiest knights of the world*'; 'the receipt of *Two your letters*' (Thomas Cromwell, *Letter to Sir Thomas Wyatt*, Feb. 13, 1539), now 'the receipt of two *of your letters*.' 'He offered unto him the choise in marriage of *eyther the sisters*' (Sir Philip Sidney, *Arcadia*, Book IV, p. 133, A.D. 1593), now *either of the sisters.* 'His stature did exceed the height of *three the tallest* of mortal seed' (Spenser, *The Faerie Queene*, I, VII, VIII), now 'three *of the tallest*.' 'My father, king of Spain, was reckon'd *one The wisest prince* (now 'one *of the wisest princes*') that there had reign'd by many A year before' (Shakespeare, *Henry the Eighth*, II, IV, 48). 'The letters . . . Of *many our contriving friends*' (*id., Antony and Cleopatra*, I, II, 188), now 'the letters of many *of our contriving friends*'; 'the fate of *some your servants*' (Ben Jonson, *Sejanus*, V, I, 59, A.D. 1616), now 'the fate of some *of your servants*.' 'He does not believe *any the most Comick Genius* (now 'any *of the most comic geniuses*') can censure him for talking on such a Subject at such a Time' (Addison, *Spectator*, No. 23, p. 2, A.D. 1711). 'To me and *many more my countrymen*' (William Dunlap, *André*, Act III, A.D. 1798), now 'many more *of my countrymen*.' Where the noun after the appositive is in the plural, this appositional construction survives in colloquial speech: 'Aunt Fannie saw a newspaper from *one the places* where Aunt Julia's visiting her school room-mate' (Tarkington, *Gentle Julia*, Ch. XVI). '*None the girls* are going.' In the case of *each* we may say: 'She kissed *them each*' (or *each of them*).

In a few cases this old appositive has become an attributive adjective: 'to *other my poore kynnesfolkes*' (Thomas Cromwell, *Testament*, A.D. 1529), now 'to my *other* poor kinsfolk'; 'with *other the great men* of Scotland' (Burton, *Scot. Abr.*, I, I, 18, A.D. 1864), now 'with the *other* great men of Scotland.' With the original word-order: 'strict adherence to *every the minutest part* of their customs and religion' (Mrs. A. M. Bennett, *Juvenile Indiscretions*, V, 117, A.D. 1785), now 'strict adherence to every *minutest part*,' etc.; '*any plainest* (from older *any the plainest*) man who reads this' (Trollope, *Framley Parsonage*, Ch. XIV). After possessive adjectives *every* has become a real attributive adjective: 'He watched her *every* movement.'

c. Blending. In the partitive category there is a tendency, once much more common than now, to blend the genitive with some other construction, resulting in illogical expression: 'His versification is by far the most perfect *of any English poet*' (Saintsbury, *Nineteenth Century Literature*, 268), a blending of 'His versification is the most perfect *of all English poets*' and 'His versification is more perfect than that *of any English poet.*' The omission of the word *other* after *any* in the last example is a form of blending still common. In comparisons where there is present the idea of a group or class, the superlative represents the group as complete, while the comparative represents the separation of one or more from all the others in the group. Hence we should say 'is the most perfect *of all English poets*,' or 'is more perfect than that *of any other English poet.*'

d. Genitive of Gradation. This is now felt as a variety of the partitive genitive: 'the Kíng *of kìngs* and Lórd *of lòrds*' (*I Timothy*, VI, 15), 'the bóok *of bòoks.*' 'But it was not enough for Frances, who found her mind looking for the wórd *of wòrds* that would express her own meaning to her own satisfaction' (May Sinclair, *The Tree of Heaven*, Ch. XVIII). This genitive has come from the Hebrew through the medieval Latin of the church.

III. APPOSITION

1. Apposition Proper. A noun which explains or characterizes another noun is placed alongside of it, and from its position is accordingly called an *appositive* (i.e., placed alongside of): 'Smith, *the banker.*'

The idea of apposition is expressed also by the appositive genitive, so that here apposition and the appositive genitive compete with each other, as illustrated in II 2 G. Another common appositional category is that of a sentence or clause explaining a preceding word, now divided into two distinct groups, called attributive substantive clause and attributive adjective clause. The former is still felt as an appositive. Its use is described at length in **23** I. The latter, though now felt as an adjective relative clause, was once an appositive, and traces of its older function are still to be seen in both literary and popular speech, as described in **23** II. There is still another common appositional category, the prepositional infinitive, which competes with the appositional genitive and the appositional clause: 'your plan *to go yourself* (or *of going yourself*, or *that you should go yourself*) doesn't please me.'

Attributive appositives were originally only loosely connected with the headword; words added by way of explanation or in oldest English often preceding the headword on account of their importance. In course of time a close relation has in many cases developed between headword and appositive, so that they now form a close group with the accent upon the second member. Hence there are now two groups of appositives, namely, those loosely connected and those closely attached.

A. LOOSE APPOSITION. Where the appositive noun follows the headword in a rather loose connection with the force of a descriptive (**23** II 6) relative clause, it agrees, if possible, with the headword in number and gender, but not always in case: 'Mary, *the belle* of the village'; 'the Smiths, *the friends* of my youth.' The appositives *belle* and *friends* may here be regarded as agreeing with their headword in number, gender, and case.

Often, however, the appositive does not agree with its headword in case since it is felt as a nominative, the predicate of an abridged relative clause: 'There was only one close carriage in the place, and that was old Mr. Landor's, [who was] *the banker*' (George Eliot). 'And these footsteps dying on the stairs were Charley's — [who was] *his old friend* of so many years!' (De Morgan, *The Old Madhouse*, Ch. XXIV). In Old English, the appositive was usually in the genitive when the headword was in the genitive: 'on *Isais* bec *þæs witegan*' (*Luke*, III, 4) = 'in the book of the wordis *of Isaye the prophete*' (Purvey's ed., A.D. 1388) = 'in the book of the words *of Isaiah the prophet*' (Revised Version, A.D. 1881). As can be seen in these translations, the genitive form of the appositive has for the most part been replaced by the nominative, always so after an *of*-genitive, as in these examples. The *of*-genitive is never used as an appositive. The simple genitive is sometimes impossible, in which case the nominative must be used: 'These words were Cicero's, *the most eloquent* of men.' The appositive in all these examples indicates the identity of a person, but where it indicates the identity of a place, a shop, or a residence expressed by a genitive, it too is in the genitive to make clear that the reference is to a place, not to a person: 'I bought the book at *Smith's, the bookseller's*' (= at Smith's store, the bookseller's store). But if we feel the reference is to a person, we may use the nominative, though it is not so common as in older English: 'I bought the book at Smith's *the bookseller*.' The nominative, however, is the usual form here where the appositive consists of parts connected by a conjunction, or is a noun modified by a prepositional phrase: 'at Smith's, *the bookseller and stationer*'; 'at Smith's, *the bookseller on Main Street*.' On the other hand, the headword and the appositive sometimes form a compound noun, as described below, and as a compound take the genitive sign at the end: 'I bought the book at *Smith the bookseller's*.'

The appositive sometimes stands in rather close relations to the headword, especially when the latter is a pronoun, but the headword and the appositive do not entirely fuse, as in B, p. 91, so that a slight pause separates them: 'we *poor fellows*.' 'He died in 1859, leaving his property to one *Ann Duncan*.' The relation between *one* and the following name, however, is sometimes so close that the two words form a compound, the second component, the name, assuming the genitive ending: 'We breakfasted at *one Goldens*' (George Washington, *Diary*, Oct. 14, 1794).

The appositive is often introduced by *as:* 'I have thought of you as your sister might think and spoken to you *as my brother*' (Hall Caine). The headword is here often a possessive adjective, which was originally the genitive of a personal pronoun and still implies a personal pronoun in the genitive case: 'Guildford now found himself restricted to *his* business *as a judge* in equity' (Macaulay). The appositive is here regularly in the nominative as in the first two examples given in the second paragraph of A, p. 89, where the headword is a noun in the genitive.

The appositional idea often disappears entirely, headword and appositive merging into a compound, as in B, p. 91, so that the new unit, like a simple noun, takes inflection at the end, usually so when the governing noun follows it: *Nixon the hátter* (Thomas Hughes, *Tom Brown's School-Days*). 'We stopped at *Mr. Bàrton the clérgyman's* house for a drink of water.' The name and the following appositive often become so closely associated that both together blend into one name: *Tòm the Píper, Pèter the Gréat, Pèter the Hérmit*, etc. The stress in all these cases is descriptive, i.e., rests upon the last member. If we desire to classify here, we must stress the second member a little more than usual to distinguish it from the usual descriptive stress: 'I have spoken of *Tènnyson the pŏet*, I now desire to speak of *Tènnyson the măn*.'

Similarly, if we desire to distinguish: 'Nìxon the hătter, not Nìxon the drúggist.'

a. *Pronouns as Appositives.* An appositive pronoun usually agrees with its headword, noun or pronoun, in case: 'Mother, who should go, John or *I?*' 'Mother, whom do you want, John or *me?*' There is a tendency here in colloquial language to employ the accusative, especially strong in personal pronouns of the first person: 'Which would you rather took you over the crossing? *Me* (instead of *I*) or Papa?' (May Sinclair, *Mary Olivier*, p. 88). 'We're not like ordinary people, *us* (instead of *we*) Cardinals' (name) (Hugh Walpole, *The Captives*, p. 15). 'Will we — *us* (instead of *we*) two — go to lunch on Sunday to meet Mr. Snaith?' (De Morgan, *The Old Madhouse*, Ch. VII). Compare **7 C a.**

b. *Appositive to a Sentence.* An appositive in the form of an explanatory remark often belongs to the whole sentence: 'I, like many another, am apt to judge my fellow men in comparison with myself, *a wrong and a foolish thing* to do.' The appositive may be in the plural if it is felt as referring to two or more *ideas* in the preceding sentence: 'You are *humane* and *considerate, things* few people can be charged with' (Pope, *Letter*).

The appositive sometimes precedes the sentence: 'He (the Indian Chief Logan) had changed, and not for the better, as he grew older, becoming a sombre, moody man; *worse than all*, he had succumbed to the fire-water, the curse of his race' (Theodore Roosevelt, *The Winning of the West*, Vol. I, Ch. VIII). Often introduced by *as:* '*As a first step*, I secured my vast property, so that the income would be certain' (Wallace, *Ben Hur*, I, Ch. V).

On the other hand, a substantive clause may serve as an appositive to a single substantive: 'Here and there a cleft in the level land occurs, *what they call a "chine" in the Isle of Wight*' (Mrs. Gaskell, *Sylvia's Lovers*, Ch. IV).

B. CLOSE APPOSITION. The appositive may be a proper name and enter into such close relations with the preceding headword that it forms with it a group with the stress upon the last member, i.e., the appositive: Kìng *Édward*, Jòhn *Smíth*, my frìend *Jónes*, Ùncle *Tóm*, Profèssor *Brówn*, the apòstle *Pául*, the Vìrgin *Máry*, the stèamer *Ocean Bríde*, Mòunt *Étna*, Làke *Michigan*, the rìver *Thámes*, Càpe *Hátteras*, Fòrt *Wáyne*, Pòrt *Árthur*, etc.

The appositive here assumes the inflection if it precedes a governing noun: at my friend *Smith's* house; at Uncle *Tom's* house; at Banker *Smith's* house.

The stress here is usually descriptive, i.e., rests upon the second member. Of course, we must stress the first member if we desire to classify: 'I desire here to speak, not of the *pöet Tènnyson*, but of the măn.'

In many cases the appositive is not a proper name, but a noun with a similar force, namely, a word or expression representing a thing as an individual, not as a member of a class: the lètter *á;* the fìgure *5;* the vèrb *gó;* the preposìtion *in;* dèmon *Rúm;* the old saying *'First come, first served.'* 'On her tombstone stood the words *"Thy will be done."'* The close relation here between the appositive and the headword cannot always be indicated by the stress, since the appositive is often, as in the last two examples, not a single word but a thought as a whole, which may expand into an entire clause or sentence.

In oldest English, the appositive here stood before the head-word: *'Ælfred* cyning' = 'King Alfred.' Traces of this older usage are still to be found. See II 2 G.

2. **Improper Apposition.** The appositional construction was often in older English improperly used instead of the partitive genitive. This older usage with the traces it has left behind is described in **10** II 2 H *b.*

IV. A PREPOSITIONAL PHRASE AS MODIFIER OF A NOUN

A noun or pronoun may be modified by a prepositional phrase, which usually follows it: (with the force of a descriptive adjective) 'a girl *with black hair'* (= *a black-haired girl*); (with the force of a limiting adjective) 'the book *on the table.'* After verbal nouns the attributive phrase is in a formal sense an adjective element, but logically it is an object, or an adverb: 'a mother's love *for her children'* (with the force of an object); 'a walk *in the evening'* (with the force of an adverb of time).

In the early stage of language development there were no prepo-sitions. The modifier was simply placed *before* the governing noun, the word-order alone indicating that the one noun was de-pendent upon the other. This primitive type of expression is still found in group-words (**63**) and on account of its convenient form is still widely used: a *rát*tràp = a tràp for ráts; *hórse*whìp = whìp for the hórse; *tóoth*brùsh = brùsh for the téeth. As this con-struction originated in the period before the introduction of in-flection, the plural idea is usually not formally expressed. In *clóthes*hòrse, *clóthes*brùsh, however, the plural idea has found a formal expression.

a. ATTRIBUTIVE PREPOSITIONAL CLAUSE. In attributive elements the preposition may stand not only before a noun, but also before a clause. There are many prepositions that can stand before a clause intro-duced by an indefinite relative pronoun, adjective, or adverb: 'He always has a clear insight *into what is needed.'* 'I haven't the slightest information

as to what plans he has made, as to where he is going.' Compare **23** I
(4th par.).

After, before, and *since* often seem to stand as prepositions before a
clause not introduced by a pronoun of any kind. Originally the determinative (**56** A) pronoun *that* stood after the preposition, pointing as with
an index finger to the following explanatory clause: 'The day *after* or
before [*that:*] *he came* was very beautiful.' 'The long lonesome period
since (a contraction of *sith than* + *s;* see **27** 3, 6th par.) *we last met* has
depressed me very much' (literally, *since that: we last met*). Gradually
after that, before that, since came to be felt as conjunctions introducing an
attributive clause. Later, *that* disappeared after *after* and *before,* leaving
to *after* and *before* the function of conjunction. Compare **27** 3 (7th par.).

V. An Infinitive as Modifier of a Noun

A noun may be modified by a prepositional infinitive. There
are different categories:

1. The infinitive has its original force, i.e., is still a prepositional
phrase with the literal meaning of the preposition *to:* 'Power *to
forgive sin*' (literally, *power in the direction of forgiving sin*); 'a
strong impulse *to do it*' (literally, *toward doing it*). See also **50** 4 *d.*

2. The attributive infinitive has often developed the force of a
relative clause: 'He was the first man *to come*' (= *who came*).
'The King has no children *to succeed him on the throne*' (= *who
can succeed him*). 'That's the way *to do it*' (= *in which you
should do it*). 'This is the fourth case of lockjaw *to occur* (= *which
has occurred*) within a week.' 'This road car is the latest *to be
offered* to the public.' 'They had no windows *to speak of*' (George
Eliot). As the relative force here is quite strong the relative pronoun is often inserted: 'It is the glory of Trinity that she has an
abundance of famous men *from whom to select*' (or in older simpler form *to select from*). See also **23** II 11.

3. The attributive infinitive often has the force of an appositive.
With loose connection: 'I am conscious that a duty devolves upon
me, *to omit no detail.*' With close connection: 'He didn't even do
me the honor *to come in*' (or *of coming in,* the infinitive competing
here with the appositive genitive).

It often takes the place of an appositive clause: 'Your plan *that
I should go* (or *for me to go*) doesn't please me.' See also **23** I *a.*

VI. An Adverb as Modifier of a Noun

An adverb may modify a noun: (1) as an appositive (**10** I 1)
adjective: 'the room *above,*' 'the tree *yonder,*' etc.; (2) as an
adherent (**10** I 1) adjective: 'the *down* stroke.' Compare **10** I 2.

VII. A Clause as Modifier of a Noun

A clause may modify a noun: 'The thought *that we shall help him* gives him courage.' 'The boy *who is standing by the door* is my son.' For much fuller description of usage here see **23** I and II.

a. Logical Relation of Attributive Clause to Governing Noun. An attributive clause, though formally connected only with its governing noun, often has logical relations to the principal verb: 'A boy *who would do a thing like that* (with the force of an adverbial conditional clause) would be laughed at.' 'We took the dear little fellow, *who was daily getting worse* (with the force of an adverbial clause of cause), to the hospital.' Compare I 5, p. 70.

OBJECTIVE MODIFIERS

ACCUSATIVE OBJECT

11 1. Form, Position, and Stress. As explained in **3**, page 3, the old distinctive accusative forms of nouns have disappeared. The personal pronouns have fuller inflection than nouns, but they, in part, too, have lost their old accusative and dative forms, as described in detail in Accidence, **35** *b*. The word-order now in part indicates the accusative and dative functions, as is illustrated in detail below, but the function itself, i.e., the peculiar rôle that the word plays in the sentence, is always important. Sometimes the function alone distinguishes accusative and dative: 'They chose *him* (acc.) king,' but 'They chose *him* (dat.) a wife.' English is here at its simplest. Form disappears entirely. The position of the noun or pronoun does not reveal its function. Here function alone distinguishes accusative and dative. The position, however, of noun or pronoun in connection with function often helps to distinguish case.

If there is only one object, it is in most cases an accusative and stands in the position after the verb: 'He broke *a glass*.' If it becomes necessary to employ a dative object after the verb, we must usually employ the distinctive dative form with *to*, for otherwise it would be construed as an accusative: 'Robin Hood robbed the rich to give *to the poor*.' Where the function is clear, however, the older simple dative is sometimes still heard in England and is even common in America, which is here, as so often elsewhere, tenacious of older forms of expression: 'The reason we wired *you* yesterday' (Pinero, *The Thunderbolt*, Act I). 'Wire, write *me* at once.' 'He has already told *me*.' 'Ten minutes suffice *me* (or *to me*) to dress.' The unaccented simple dative still often survives in the passive: 'No consideration was shówn *me*' (or *to me*), but 'No consideration was shown *to mé*.'

If there are two objects, the dative, or indirect object, stands immediately after the verb, then comes the accusative, or direct object: 'He loves *her*' (acc.), 'He loves his *mother*' (acc.), but 'He gave *her* (dat.) a *book*' (acc.), 'He gave the *house* (dat.) a new *coat* (acc.) of paint.' If the dative ever for any reason follows the accusative, as for instance when it is to be emphasized, when it is to be modified by a clause, or when it serves as a sentence modifier (**12** 1 B *a b*), it now usually, as illustrated more fully in **12** 1 A B *a b*, takes the prepositions *to*, *for*, *on*, or *from* before it to indicate the dative relation: 'I will lend it *to yóu*, but not to *hím*.' 'He gave his *friend* (dat.) a *book*' (acc.), but 'He gave a *book* (acc.) *to his friend* (dat.) who is visiting him.' 'He held my horse (acc.) *for me*' (sentence dat.). 'He shut the door *on me'* (sentence dat.; in older English also *to me* or the simple dative). 'He stole a watch (acc.) *from me'* (sentence dat.). The old simple sentence dative sometimes still follows the verb: 'Kindly cash *me* this check,' or 'Kindly cash this check *for me.*' Compare **15** I 2 (3rd par.). The old simple dative also not infrequently follows the verb when the accusative precedes the verb: 'What would you recommend *me?'* 'Everyone is a moon, and has a dark side which he never shows *anybody'* (or *to anybody*). Compare **15** I 2 (last par.).

The dative form with *to* must in general be used to mark the dative relation clearly in cases where doubt might arise: 'I told *him* (dat.) that I should come' (a *that*-clause in the acc. relation), but 'I indicated *to him* that I should come,' because *to indicate* usually takes an accusative object, and hence a dative that follows it must be clearly marked as such. The dative form with *to*, however, is sometimes used even where it is not necessary to make the thought clear, especially in a choice literary style: 'He (Columbus) *gave to the world* (or simply *the world*) the knowledge of a new land' (Elbridge S. Brooks, *A Trip to Washington*). Compare **15** I 2 (next to last par.).

Dative before accusative has always been the common word-order in English in normal expression, and, as can be seen from the preceding examples, this order is still well established. But this order has never been common if there are two personal pronouns as objects, or if there are an accusative of the pronoun and a dative of the noun. As the ideas of reference and personal interest which lie in the dative here are prominent and the stress is usually a little stronger and hence also a factor, the dative still as in oldest English stands in the more important final position in the group: 'He gave it *to mé.*' 'She asked him for it and he gáve *it tò her.*' 'I gave it *to his móther.*' In such examples as the last, where the accusative is a weakly stressed pronoun and the dative a noun, the dative by reason of its heavier weight invariably follows the lighter accusative. The placing of the accusative pronoun in the final place in the group in harmony with the normal word-order dative before the accusative is still, as in oldest English, rather uncommon: 'Officers and men Levied a kindly tax upon themselves. Pitying the lonely man, and gave *him* it' (Tennyson, *Enoch Arden*). Sometimes even in colloquial speech: 'If you really have it, show *me it'* or more commonly 'Shów it *tò me,'* since the word-order, dative of a personal pronoun after the accusative of a personal pronoun, has become fixed here, now usually with the modern dative form, but in England very often still as in older English with the simple dative: 'Show it *me'*

(Pinero, *Sweet Lavender*, Act II). Sometimes also in American English: 'I give it *you* beforehand' (Oemler, *Slippy McGee*, Ch. V). On the other hand, if the accusative is a stressed demonstrative it stands in the important final position in the group: 'I tòld him *thát.*' 'He gàve me *thís.*'

2. **Meaning and Use of the Accusative with Verbs.** In an early stage of our language the accusative could be used with adverbial force after intransitive verbs of motion to indicate a concrete goal. This old usage survives only in the case of *home:* 'He went *home.*' This old accusative after intransitive verbs of motion is somewhat better preserved where the idea of goal appears in an abstract figurative sense, namely, in the case of the simple infinitive, an old verbal noun here in the accusative of goal, employed in Old English, and even still in the colloquial speech of our time after the imperative and the infinitive of *go* and *come* to indicate the goal, i.e., end, purpose, of the verb of motion: 'Go *get* it!' (Dr. Bert Emsley in a communication to the author, July 5, 1930). 'You'd better go *lie* down' (Tarkington, *The Magnificent Ambersons*, Ch. IV). 'I'll make May and Lola and their partners come *sit* in this little circle of chairs' (*id.*, *Seventeen*, Ch. XXVII). 'Women could go *hang* (see **46**, 7th par.), because she did not want them' (W. J. Locke, *The Glory of Clementina*, Ch. II). Elsewhere we now usually employ here the prepositional infinitive: 'She went upstairs *to lie* down.'

Although the accusative of goal is no longer common after intransitives of motion, it has from the earliest times been common after transitives to indicate the goal, the object actually hit or affected by the activity, or the thing representing the goal, the real object of the activity, i.e., the result, effect: 'to hit, reach, or toe *a mark*,' 'to paint *a house*,' 'to burn *a house*,' 'to build *a house*' (the goal, the result of the activity), 'to sketch *a house*' (the goal, result of the activity). After the analogy of such transitives that take an accusative of result, the accusative is used after many verbs usually intransitive to indicate a result of the activity or something exhibited by it: 'to weep *tears*,' 'to look *compassion, daggers, death*,' 'to breathe *simplicity*.'

Out of the idea of the accusative as an object in these more or less concrete relations has come the more abstract conception that the accusative is the proper case form of a noun or pronoun employed to complete the meaning of the verb, i.e., to make its meaning special: 'I see *a bird.*' 'I hear *the voices* of children.' 'I felt *the truth* of the remark.' 'I guessed *the riddle.*' A common complement of verbs is the cognate accusative, i.e., an accusative of a meaning cognate or similar to that of the verb, repeating and also explaining more fully the idea expressed by the verb: 'to sleep the *sleep* of the righteous,' 'to fight a good *fight*,' 'to live a sad and lonely *life*,' 'to sing *a song*.' Similarly, verbs are much used with an object that denotes a thing which is closely associated with the activity expressed by the verb: 'to play *cards*,' 'to talk *shop, politics, dogs*,' etc., 'to jump *a fence*,' 'to skip *the country, two pages*,' 'to ride *a horse*,' 'to flee *the country*,' 'to depart *this life*.' 'Edgar sits *a horse* as well as any young man in England' (Mrs. Sherwood, *H. Milner*, III, V). 'She did not take any instruction herself or go through the evolutions or maneuvers, but merely sat *her horse* like a martial little statue and looked on' (Mark Twain, *Joan of Arc*, II, Ch. IV). 'The hen will sit *seventeen of her own eggs*' (*Journal R. Agric. Soc.*, III, II, 525).

In modern times the list of transitive verbs has been greatly increased by the addition of a large number of verbs originally intransitive which took a prepositional object, as '*to depend upon* a man,' '*to laugh at* a person,' '*to talk over* a matter.' In course of time the preposition here has become attached to the verb as an integral part of it, so that the object is no longer a prepositional object but a direct object of the compound verb. This becomes apparent in the passive, where the object becomes subject and the preposition remains with the verb: 'They were *laughed at* by everybody.'

A transitive verb, its object, and the preposition attached to the object are often felt as a unit forming a compound transitive: 'We *lost sight of* the boat in the fog,' or in passive form, 'The boat *was lost sight of* in the fog.'

a. METONYMIC OBJECT. The object is often metonymic, i.e., indicates not the real object but something which stands in close relation to it: 'He wiped off the dust' (real object) and 'He wiped off the table' (metonymic object).

b. 'IT' AND 'SO' AS OBJECT. In a large number of expressions the accusative object is *it*, which originally was in many instances a concrete reference to a definite thing or a definite situation, but is now also often a convenient complement of transitive and intransitive verbs without definite reference, leaving it to the situation to make the thought clear: 'You will catch *it*' (i.e., reproach, punishment). 'We *footed* (in slang *hoofed*) *it*.' 'I am going to rough *it*.' 'That's going *it* rather strong.' 'I will have *it* out with him.' 'He tries to lord *it* over us.'

Where the construction is more or less complicated, *it* is often used as an anticipatory object, pointing forward to a following full object clause or an abridged, infinitival or gerundial, object clause: 'I soon brought *it* about that he thought better of it.' 'I found *it* difficult to refuse him his request.' 'Rumor has *it* he is going to leave town.' 'I suppose you think *it* odd my having gone to church.'

On the other hand, *it* often points backward to a preceding dependent clause or an independent proposition: 'If I get home by eight o'clock, I call *it* good luck. 'He spoke very sharply to me. I shall not forget *it* soon.' Frequently, however, the adverb *so* is used instead of *it*, pointing backward, referring to the contents of the preceding proposition, especially after verbs of saying, thinking, hearing, fearing, hoping, doing, etc.: 'Did your brother receive the letter?' — 'I think *so*.' 'Will he keep his promise?' — 'I hope *so*.' 'I'll send it tomorrow if I can arrange to do *so*.'

c. REFLEXIVE OBJECT. A reflexive pronoun is often added to transitive verbs to indicate that the subject acts upon himself: 'He dressed *himself* quickly,' 'We all love *ourselves* more and hate *ourselves* less than we ought.' In older English, the personal pronouns were used as reflexive pronouns. This older usage lingers on in Shakespeare, although the new forms are more common: 'A (= he) bears *him* like a portly gentleman' (*Romeo and Juliet*, I, v, 68). Even in plain prose, however, the older simple accusative is still the rule after prepositions which express local relations in a literal sense: 'I have no money with *me*.' 'The two brothers had only a dollar between *them*.' 'We see the stars above *us*.' 'He shut the door behind *him*.' 'The horse sprang over the precipice bearing its rider with *it*.' 'Look about *you!*' but in a figurative sense 'Look into *yourself!*' and 'He asked me about *myself*.' Usage sometimes fluctuates here according as we feel the force of the preposition as literal or figurative: 'The teacher took it upon *him* or *himself* to punish the lad.' Compare **56 D** (next to last par.).

The reflexive form can refer only to the subject of the proposition or clause in which it stands. Hence, if the pronoun in a subordinate clause refers to the subject of the principal proposition, a personal pronoun is used: 'I believed him to be deceiving *me*' but 'I believed him to be deceiving *himself*.'

After the plural of majesty *we* and editorial *we*, it is now customary to employ *ourself* as the usual reflexive with reference to a single person in contradistinction to *ourselves* with reference to more than one: 'We feel that in this place we lay *ourself* open to the inquiry whether Mr. Winkle was whispering, during this brief conversation, to Arabella Allen' (Dickens, *Pickwick*, Ch. XXX).

In the headings of newspapers simple *self* is much used for *himself* or *herself:* 'G. W. Howard, Author, Kills *Self*' (*Chicago Tribune*, Nov. 21, 1922).

One of the marked characteristics of English is the tendency to drop the reflexive pronoun: 'He dressed quickly.' 'Oil will not unite with water.' For fuller discussion see **46.**

d. RECIPROCAL OBJECT. The pronouns *each other* and *one another* are placed after the verb to indicate that the relations between or among the persons designated by the subject are mutual. Although good writers often use these two forms promiscuously, there is a tendency to use the former for reference to two persons and the latter for reference to two or more: 'These two doctors hate *each other.*' 'We all at last understood *one another.*' In older English, the components of each of these compound forms were felt as distinct words and hence were often separated. This older usage persists: '*Each* looked at the *other*' instead of 'They looked at *each other.*' 'The roosters of the neighborhood are calling *one* to the *other*' (or *to one another*). This older usage is most common, as in these examples, when the pronoun is the object of a preposition. For fuller treatment see Accidence, **37** *a, b, c.*

In older English, the long reflexive pronouns were sometimes used for reciprocal pronouns: 'Get thee gone; tomorrow We'll hear *ourselves* (instead of *each other*) again' (Shakespeare, *Macbeth*, III, IV, 31). Although this old usage has in general passed away, it is still often found after the prepositions *among* and *between*, perhaps prevails here: 'They quarreled *among themselves*' (but *with one another*). 'We are still quarreling *among ourselves.*' 'They resolved *between themselves* to start immediately.'

As in *c* the pronominal object here is often omitted: 'Our elbows touched' (or touched *each other*). 'We met (or, sometimes, met *each other*) at the post office.' 'We soon came to a place where two roads crossed' (or crossed *each other*). See **46.**

e. INTERROGATIVE AND RELATIVE '*WHOM*' AS OBJECT. The interrogative objective *whom* is used in careful language: 'For what or *whom* was she waiting?' (Galsworthy, *The Man of Property*, p. 302). '*Whom* did you meet?' 'I asked him *whom* he met' (an indirect question). '*Whom* do you mean?' 'I asked him *whom* he meant.'

In current colloquial speech, as in older literary English, it is still quite common to use *who* as an invariable form for both the subject and the object relation: '*Who* (subject) was there?' '*Who* (object) did you meet?' Likewise in early modern literary English: 'Hor. My lord, I think I saw him yesternight. — Haml. Saw? *Who?*' (Shakespeare, *Hamlet*, I, II, 190). 'To *who*, my lord?' (*id., King Lear*, V, III, 248).

This usage is explained in part by a natural tendency to avoid inflection here, as the other interrogative words, *where, when, whence*, etc., which stand in the same position as *who*, are all invariable. The use of the nominative *who* here as the invariable form for subject and object in contrast to the employment of the accusative *me, him, her, us, them*, etc., elsewhere as the invariable form, as described in **7 C** *a*, has probably come from the fact that the accusative *whom* here in the subjective relation standing immediately before the verb, as in '*Whom* came?' would be unnatural and contrary to all precedent, while the nominative *who* before the verb in the object relation, as in '*Who* did they meet?' is not unnatural, since the nominative usually stands before the verb. Moreover, the use of the nominative *who* as object is never ambiguous, since the inverted word-order, as in '*Who* did they meet?' indicates clearly that *who*, like *when, where*, etc., as in '*Where* did they meet?' modifies the verb and hence cannot be the subject. The common use of *who* as object in direct questions made it natural to use the same form in indirect questions: 'Do you know *who* the property belongs to?' (Gissing, *The House of Cobwebs*).

We sometimes find *who* for *whom* in substantive clauses, where indefinite relative *who*, which introduces the substantive clause exactly like interrogative *who* in indirect questions, has come under the influence of interrogative *who:* 'I don't know *who* you mean' (A. Trollope, *Harry Heathcote*, p. 15). In 'It feels like a fight, but I don't know *who's* fighting *who*' (Hugh Walpole, *The Captives*, p. 455), the second *who* is used after the analogy of the second *who* in 'I couldn't see *who* was *who*.'

Earlier in the period *who* for *whom* is found also when used as a relative pronoun with an antecedent: 'in company with General Lee, *who* I requested to attend me' (George Washington, *Diary*, Oct. 19, 1794). This older usage still occurs in careless language, as in 'The burthen of her talk is "my Collin," *who* she makes out to be the most angelic babe' (Mrs. Craik).

In general, however, the use of *who* for *whom* is receding in all functions in the literary language.

f. PASSIVE FORM OF STATEMENT. In changing a sentence from the active to the passive the accusative becomes nominative and the nominative is put into the accusative after *by*, in older English *of:* '*The boy* is beating *the dog*' (active), but in the passive '*The dog* is being beaten *by the boy*.' 'Ye shall be hated *of* all men' (*Matthew*, X, 22). 'He was devoured *of* a long dragon' (Bacon, *Essays*).

In normal narrative, the modifier of the verb is usually important and stressed, so that in sentences with an important modifier of the verb the active is the natural form of statement, since the modifier of the verb can often be put in the form of an object and placed in the important end position: 'Last night the frost took *áll my prétty flówers*.' On the other hand, the passive is often more appropriate when the verbal activity is prominent, since in this form the verb stands last or near the end: 'Last night my pretty flowers were all *destróyed*.' The idea of active agent or cause is best stressed by employing passive form and putting the word denoting the agent or the cause at the end: 'The dog was killed *by his ówn máster*.' 'I was hurt *by his abrúpt mánner*.' When we desire to give especial emphasis to the thing effected, we employ passive form and put the subject representing the thing effected at or near the end: 'From the instant that the lips of the little old lady touched Jill's there was sealed *a bónd*' (Temple Thurston, *The City of Beautiful Nonsense*, III, Ch. VIII). But not only the end position is important, the first place is also used for emphasis, especially in excited language, where the thing that is on our mind springs forth first. In the case of persons or things affected the passive form is here appropriate since we can put them into the first place: '*My prétty flówers* were all destroyed last night.' We can use also active form here by putting the person or thing affected into the first place in the form of an exclamation and referring to them later by a pronoun with the grammatical form required by the construction: '*My prétty flówers!* the frost destroyed *them* áll last night.' Compare 3 *a*.

The speaker or writer often employs the passive expressly to avoid mention of the participants: 'Some things *have been said* here tonight that ought not to have been spoken.'

Passive form is often chosen merely to avoid a change of subject: 'The young couple returned and *were pardoned* by the baron on the spot.'

g. OBJECT OF AN ADJECTIVE OR ADVERB. The object treated above is in all instances the object of a verb. *Worth* is the only adjective that governs the accusative: 'This book is worth *reading*.'

In 'He sat opposite [to] *me*,' *me* is a dative after the adjective *opposite*, as indicated by the suppressed *to*. Similarly, in 'He is like (adjective) *his father*,' the object is a dative, as can be seen in poetry and in older English, where the dative form occurs: 'Sweet sleep, were death like *to thee*' (Shelley). 'For ye are like *unto whited sepulchres*' (*Matthew*, XXIII, 27). Likewise, the seeming accusative after the adverb *near*, as in *near me*, is in fact a dative, for we say *nearer to me* and *next to me*. These adjectival and adverbial forms that govern the dative are now, however, often felt as prepositions. Compare **50** 4 *c bb.*

The genitive is the usual construction after *worthy*, but the accusative occasionally occurs: 'The Englishman into whose soul these tales have not sunk is not *worthy the name*' (Hughes, *Tom Brown*, II, Ch. II, 226), usually *worthy of the name*. In older English, the accusative was more common: 'It was a thought happy and *worthy Cæsar*' (Ben Jonson, *Sejanus*, V, VIII, 59 A.D. 1603). Adjectives now usually take a dative, genitive, or prepositional object. See **12** 1 A, **13** 3, **14.**

h. ACCUSATIVE OBJECT A FULL OR ABRIDGED CLAUSE. The accusative object often has the form of a clause with a finite verb: 'I demand *that he go at once*.' For the different forms that an accusative clause with a finite verb may have see **24** III. The accusative clause may also have the form of an infinitival or a gerundial clause, as described in **24** III *d.*

DATIVE OBJECT

12 1. Form and Use.

A. AFTER VERBS, ADJECTIVES, AND NOUNS. The old dative which is used after transitive verbs as an indirect object in connection with a direct object in the accusative is well preserved. Its present form and position in the sentence are treated in **11** 1.

Old English had alongside of the simple accusative also a simple dative object, employed not only as an indirect object in connection with a direct accusative object, as at present, but also much used after many verbs as the only object. As a single object it competed with the accusative, but, as described below, it had a little different meaning, which naturally associated it with certain verbs where the peculiar dative force came into play. This old dative used as a single object has been largely displaced by the accusative. In Old English, the accusative represents the object — a person or a thing — as affected by an activity, especially in a literal, material sense. The single dative in Old English represents a person as involved or concerned in an activity directed *toward* him and intended to affect him either in a mere material way or more commonly in an inner sense. If the dative object was a thing, it was felt as having interests like a person. The difference of meaning between dative and accusative was often not great, since both objects completed the meaning of the verb. Later, the difference in form between the two cases entirely disappeared, so that it became difficult to distinguish a dative object from an accusative. Where an object after verbs governing the dative, such as *thank, help, injure, please, displease, believe, threaten, oppose, serve, advise*, etc., was felt as completing the meaning of the verb, the old dative has been displaced by the accusative. Thus we say today 'He thanks *his friend*,' not 'He thanks *to his friend*.' 'The teacher helps *the beginners*,' not 'The teacher helps *to the beginners*.' 'The frost injures *the plants*,' not 'The frost injures *to the plants*.' The old dative began to be treated as an accusative about 1200. But the feeling for the old dative lingered for a long while after the old native English verbs and the new foreign verbs with the same meaning, as is shown by the employment of the new clear dative form with *to*, which was in use elsewhere: 'Yf Y do not the workis of my fadir, nyle ʒe bileue *to me;* but if Y do, thouʒ ʒe wolen not bileue *to me*, bileue ʒe *to the workis*' (*John,* X 37, John Purvey's ed., A.D. 1388) = 'If I do not the works of my Father, believe *me* not. But if I do, though ye believe not *me*, believe *the works*' (King James Version). 'Thou schalt worschipe thi Lord God, and *to hym* (now simple *him*) aloone thou schalt serue' (*Luke,* IV, 8, Purvey's ed.). The dative disappeared here later because its function was not at this point as clearly differentiated from the accusative as it was elsewhere.

In spite, however, of the decided victory of the accusative in this category of single object the dative maintained itself in a very large number of words where the idea of a person involved or concerned in an activity was strongly pronounced: 'A new thought came *to me*.' 'Recently much has happened *to us*.' 'He has yielded *to me* in this matter.' 'He apologized *to me,* cringed *to me*, deferred *to me*, bowed *to me*, submitted *to me*, surrendered *to me*.' 'He got down on his knees *to me*.' 'Religion itself is forced to truckle *to worldly policy*.' 'He read *to me,* sang *to me*, wrote *to me*, complained *to me*.' 'He proposed *to her*.' 'It never occurred *to me* before.' 'Much genuine pleasure accrued *to them* from their kindness.' 'It belonged *to me.*' 'This is all that remains *to me* of my inheritance.' 'The property has fallen *to his son.*' The dative has been preserved here because it is felt not as completing the meaning of the verb but rather as modifying the statement as a whole. The dative as a sentence modifier, or sentence object, does not of course compete with the accusative and has not been influenced by it. This common dative is treated in detail in B, p. 106.

To express the dative idea here it became necessary to give it a new form, for dative and accusative had become identical in form, and a single object after a verb would be construed as an accusative. Hence, as in these examples, the preposition *to* was placed before the noun to indicate the dative relation. Even in oldest English, *to* was thus often placed before a noun denoting a person, but at this early period it has a more concrete meaning than the old simple dative, indicating that the person was involved or concerned in the activity in an outward, literal sense, as in 'I spoke *to him,*' 'I called *to him,*' while the simple dative suggested an inner relation, as in 'I preached *to them*' (in Old English, a simple dative). As in the first two of these three examples, *to* in older English often combined the idea of outward and inner relations, so that later when the dative and accusative had become identical in form and it became necessary to create a new, clear dative, it was easy and natural to employ *to* also like the old simple dative to indicate inner relations, as in the many examples given above.

The dative is well preserved also in other categories where there is no competition between accusative and dative, as after nouns and adjectives. After nouns made from verbs which in oldest English governed the dative or which by virtue of their meaning would have governed the dative if they had been in use, the dative construction is well preserved, and indeed has experienced an extensive development beyond its original boundaries: 'The teacher helps (in Old English, with dative, now with accusative) *the beginners,*' but 'a help *to beginners.*' 'The frost injures *the plants,*' but 'injury *to plants.*' The dative is also well preserved after adjectives: 'He was helpful *to me.*' 'The frost is injurious *to plants.*' 'It lyketh to *your fader* and *to me* that I yow wedde' (Chaucer, *The Clerkes Tale,* 289), now 'It pleases *your father* (acc.) and *me* (acc.) that I marry you,' but after the participial adjective the old dative is still in full use: 'It is pleasing *to your father* and *to me,*' etc. 'Never wolde he do nothynge that scholde *to hym* displese' (Merlin, 123, about A.D. 1440), now 'that should displease *him*' (acc.), but after the participial adjective the dative is the common construction: 'It is displeasing *to him.*' In a few cases we find the simple dative after adjectives, as illustrated in **11 2 *g*.**

B. SENTENCE DATIVE. As explained in A (3rd par.), the dative is well preserved where it modifies not the verb alone but the sentence as a whole. This dative, sometimes still with its old simple form but usually in prepositional form with *to, unto, for, from,* or *on,* falls into three groups:

a. Dative of Reference. This dative denotes the person to whom the statement seems true, or with reference to whom it holds good: '*To me* the old house doesn't seem like home any more.' 'That doesn't seem true *to me* now as it once did.' '*To me* she is pretty.' 'What is that *to me?*' 'He never made *me* such excuses.' 'Am I not any more the same man *to whom* once all doors stood open?' 'The dress is too long *for her.*' 'I bet *you* five dollars (adv. acc.) that you can't do it' (acc. clause).

b. Dative of Interest. This dative denotes the person to whose advantage or disadvantage the action results: 'The umbrella stood *me* in good stead.' 'It will last *the owner* a lifetime.' 'He made *me* a whistle.' 'She made *her boy* a new coat.' 'She looked *him* tenderly in the eyes.' 'Ruin seemed to be staring *him* in the face.' 'You must not look *a gift horse* in the mouth.' 'He has already done *me* a good deal of harm.' 'He has done a good deal of harm not only *to me* but *to many others,*' where, as often elsewhere, the idea of interest mingles with that of reference. 'Please hand *me* that book.' 'He lent *me* his book.' 'He lent a book *to me* and also one *to John.*' 'Inasmuch as you have done it *unto* (in plain prose usually *to* or *for*) one of the least of these my brethren, ye have done it *unto me*' (*Matthew,* XXV, 40). 'I shall do all I can *for you.*' 'I want you to run an errand *for me.*' 'His heart beat *for all humanity.*' The use of *for* here instead of the simple dative or the dative with *to* indicates the desire for a clearer expression of the idea of advantage, for *to* is used also to denote disadvantage. Often, however, *for* itself denotes disadvantage: 'I'll break his head *for him.*' 'She'll turn your head *for you.*' 'He's setting a trap *for you.*' 'Who digs a pit *for others* may fall into it himself.'

To express more clearly the idea of disadvantage, we sometimes use *from* instead of the simple dative or the dative with *to:* 'He stole a watch *from me,*' i.e., *from me to my loss,* the concrete idea of *from* mingling with the abstract idea of loss. 'The horse ran away *from me,*' i.e., ran away *to my loss,* discomfiture. In colloquial speech we often find such expressions as 'The fire has gone out *on me.*' 'He has gone back *on me.*' 'I found out something about him and I wrote and told him so, and he got my letter and just called me up and tried to make up with me again, and I hung up *on him*' (J. P. McEvoy, *The Potters*). 'Every three years he's raised the rent *on us*' (Basil King, *The Side of the Angels*, Ch. I). 'He shut the door *on me*' (in older English, also *to me* or the simple dative). The development here from the dative to the preposition *on* (= *against*) indicates the desire for a clearer expression of the idea of disadvantage, injury. On account of its distinctive form the *on*-dative is spreading in this meaning in colloquial speech. It is especially common in popular Irish English, which at this point is doubtless influencing American colloquial usage.

The old simple dative is most common in connection with a direct object: 'She made *her boy* a new coat.' In the case of reflexive datives here, the old short form (see **11** 2 *c*), i.e., the personal pronoun instead of the reflexive, is still, especially in colloquial speech, often used in the first and second persons instead of the long literary form: 'I bought *me* (or *myself*) a new hat.' 'Did you buy *you* (or *yourself*) a new hat?' Formerly the short form was much used also in the third person: 'Let every soldier hew *him* down a bough' (*Macbeth*, V, IV, 4). Today we usually employ here the long form on account of the ambiguity of the short form: 'He bought *himself* a new hat.' But in popular speech the old short form is still common: 'Rutheney here, she never even stops to ax Link may she ride in to town — she jest ketches *her* a nag and lights out' (Lucy Furman, *The Quare Women*, Ch. II). In all these cases the reflexive dative is more common in popular speech than in the literary language, so that in the former it is still often employed where in the latter it has disappeared: 'I want *me* a woman [who] can milk' (*ib.*, Ch. V).

Earlier in the period, a weak, almost pleonastic, dative of interest was often used after *sit, lie,* and verbs of motion and fearing: 'I sit *me* down a pensive hour to spend' (Goldsmith, *Traveller*, 32). 'He walked *him* forth along the sand' (Byron, *Siege of Corinth*, XIII, 17). 'I dread *me*, if I draw it (i.e., the lance-head), you will die' (Tennyson, *Lancelot and Elaine*, 511). 'I fear *me*, tis about faire Abigall' (Marlowe, *The Jew of Malta*, I, 904, A.D. 1633). ''Faith, for the worst is filthy; and would not hold taking, I doubt (= fear) *me*' (Shakespeare, *Timon of Athens*, I, II, 159). After these verbs, especially after *to lie down* and *sit down*, this old dative still lingers: 'He had lost his way and *lain him down* to die' (Jerome, *Three Men in a Boat*, Ch. X, 127). 'Nor did his eye lighten with any pleasurable excitement as he *sat himself* (sometimes, as here, the new long dative instead of the old short form) *down* in a shadowy corner' (Tarkington, *Penrod and Sam*, Ch. IV).

Earlier in the period, and sometimes still, there is an old redundant accusative, distinguishable from this old dative by neither form nor significance, for both dative and accusative have scarcely an appreciable meaning: 'I *remember me of* (now simple *remember*) that day.' 'I *repent me of* (now simple *repent*) my suspicions.' The accusative is here sometimes construed as a dative of interest, so that the *of* drops out: 'I do not repent *me* those dallyings in enchanted fields' (J. M. Barrie, *The Little White Bird*, Ch. IX).

c. *Ethical Dative.* In older English, and sometimes still, a simple dative is employed to denote the person who has or is expected to have an emotional or sympathetic interest in the statement: 'Whip *me* such honest knaves' (*Othello*, I, i, 49). 'Why, he would slip *you* out of this chocolate-house, just when you had been talking to him — as soon as your back was turned — whip he was gone!' (Congreve, *The Way of the World*, I, I, 241, A.D. 1700). 'The main things are to be able to stand well, walk well, and look with an eye at home in its socket: — I put *you* my hand on any man or woman born of high blood' (Meredith). 'Has anything happened to you?' — 'No, Ralph, but something may happen to you if you don't heed *me* what I say' (Hall Caine). Today there is little feeling for this once common construction. Instead of saying 'That was *you* a joy!' we now usually say 'That was a joy, I tell you!' and instead of 'Now heed *me* that' we say 'Now I want you to heed that!' We can sometimes, however, employ the prepositional dative with *for:* 'There's a fine fellow *for you!*'

2. **Original Meaning of the Dative.** The dative seems originally to have denoted in a literal sense *direction toward*, which can often still be felt after transitive verbs and adjectives: 'He sent *me* a book,' or 'He sent the book *to me*.' 'He was kind *to me*,' i.e., manifestations of kindness were directed *toward me*. Thus originally both accusative and dative indicated a goal or an object toward which an activity was directed. Even in oldest English, however, we find the two forms in general differentiated in meaning as we know them today, so that the accusative often indicates that a person or thing is affected in a literal, exterior sense, while the dative indicates that a person or thing is affected in an inner sense, or that a person is involved in an act or statement as his material or higher interests are connected with the act or statement: 'That caused *me* (dat. indicating that the person is affected inwardly) *pain*' (acc. of result). 'That gave *the cause* (dat. in-

dicating vital inner interests) a mortal blow' (acc.). 'He was unfriendly *to me*' (indicating direction of feeling toward inner things, i.e., a personality). 'He sent help *to me* (dat. indicating *direction toward* in a literal, but also an inner, sense) in my distress.' In all these cases the present prepositional dative corresponds to the simple dative in Old English. Wherever the noun after *to* is now an object in a literal exterior sense we find also in Old English *to* followed by a dative: 'He went *to town*.' 'He sent a messenger *to town*.' In Old English, *to* with the dative was employed to express the old original concrete idea of *direction toward;* the simple dative was used to denote the newer derived idea of *direction toward* in an inner sense. Later, as the simple dative lost its distinctive form, the prepositional dative took its place wherever ambiguity might arise. The older distinction in meaning had to be sacrificed to the obvious necessity of indicating the dative relation clearly. Compare 1 A (4th par., p.105) and **14** (3rd par.).

GENITIVE OBJECT

13 1. Functions of the Genitive. Today we usually think of the genitive as an attributive adjective element modifying nouns or pronouns, but in Old English it was widely employed also to modify verbs and adjectives. As seen in 3, p. 110, the genitive is still used after verbs and adjectives; but it survives here only in the form of the *of*-genitive, which we here no longer feel as a genitive but now construe as a prepositional object, so that the old, once common, conception of the genitive as a modifier of verbs and adjectives has been lost. The fact that the genitive after verbs and adjectives now never takes the simple *s*-form has dulled our feeling for it as a genitive and also for its original close relation to the attributive genitive. The older conception of the genitive as a modifier of nouns, pronouns, verbs, and adjectives indicates that the genitive in all these different functions had the same general meaning — some shade of the general idea of sphere, as described in 3, p. 110, and in **10** II 2. The fact that we no longer have a live feeling for this old meaning has helped to blunt our feeling for the original close relation between the attributive genitive and the genitive after verbs and adjectives.

2. Form of the Genitive. In Old English, the simple genitive was used as the object of a large number of verbs and a smaller number of adjectives. Today, the simple genitive used as object has been entirely replaced by the prepositional genitive with *of*: 'When I felt *of his heart*, there was no beat.' 'He is worthy *of* respect.' 'The glass is full *of water*.'

3. **Meaning of the Genitive.** The original meaning of the genitive is unknown, but a study of the older periods where the genitive was much more used than now seems to indicate that the central idea of this case is *in a sphere:* 'I am thinking *of my father, of my duty,*' i.e., my thoughts are in the sphere of my father, my duty. 'They robbed him *of his money,*' in the sphere of his money, with respect to his money, or now more commonly felt as containing the idea of separation. 'They complained *of their hard lot,*' in the sphere, matter of, with respect to their hard lot. This shade of the genitive, the genitive of specification, is still very common: 'I reminded him *of his promise.*' 'He accused me *of untruths.*' 'The glass is full *of water,*' in the sphere of water, with respect to water.

In older English, *to hope, yearn, thirst, wait* took the genitive of goal, which represents some object or thing as the goal of the activity, the sphere in which it acts, now replaced by a prepositional object after *for:* 'Death waites *of* (now *for*) no man's will' (George Whetstone, *Life of Gascoigne,* I, IV, A.D. 1719). The new accusative is used alongside of the old genitive of goal after *admit, allow, approve, conceive,* and sometimes *accept,* and a little earlier in the period also *remember* and *recollect:* 'The scope of this book does not admit *of the discussion of details*' (or with the accusative *the discussion of details*). 'I remember *of* (now omitted) *detesting* the name of Cumberland' (Sir Walter Scott).

The partitive genitive object, now replaced by the accusative, was not uncommon earlier in the period: 'She went to it, smelled *of it* (now usually simple *it* or *at it*), and ate it' (Defoe, *Crusoe,* I, IV). In American colloquial speech, however, the old partitive genitive object is well preserved with a few verbs: 'She tasted *of it,* felt *of it,* smelled *of it.*' Also in the literary language the old genitive is sometimes used when it is desired to raise the tone a little above that of every day: 'Since people give *of their time,* will they not give also *of their money?*'

The prepositional genitives in all these cases correspond to the Old English simple genitive, but they are not felt today vividly as genitives. They are mere fragments of a shattered construction which gives no clear outline of older usage. Many older genitives which represented the activity as *missing of, desiring of, coveting of, forgetting of an object* are now replaced by accusatives, which represent the activity as *missing, desiring, coveting, forgetting an object,* since we today put the single object that completes the meaning of a verb in the accusative. Just as in **12 1 A,** a single dative object was not able to compete successfully with a single accusative object, so here a single genitive object is not able to compete with a single accusative object, since the old habit of distinguishing between the meaning of the two cases did not prove as strong as the simpler principle of placing, without regard to meaning, a single object uniformly in the accusative, the case most commonly used as object when there is only one. Elsewhere, where the accusative did not compete with the genitive as object, namely, after adjectives and participles, the genitive object is better preserved. Thus, though we no longer *miss of, desire of, forget of,* etc., we still are *desirous of, forgetful of,* etc.

Some of the old simple genitives after verbs have been replaced by prepositional objects. Thus we today say 'we yearn *for* (or *after*) *sympathy,*' 'we long *for rest,*' 'we laugh *at a person*' instead of employing a genitive or an accusative object, since the idea of an outward direction of an activity toward a person or thing is strong in our feeling and demands a formal expression by some preposition with a concrete force. Compare **14.** The use of different prepositions in the last three examples indicates a desire to interpret the genitive object, both the old simple genitive and the newer form with *of.* The genitive in course of time had taken on so many shades of meaning that the thought was not always clear.

Where the genitive has been retained, namely, the genitive of specification, in all periods of the language the most common category and still deeply rooted in English feeling, as in *to complain of, to accuse of, to remind of,* etc., also after adjectives, *mindful of, thoughtful of, sure of, guilty of,* etc., the *of* is now felt by most people as a preposition, not as a sign of the genitive, although the absolute rigidity of the construction, the impossibility of replacing *of* by another preposition with the same meaning, such as *about, with reference to, with regard to,* clearly indicates that the prepositional genitive is in fact intact. The construction with *of* has been retained here because *of* has the same meaning as *of* used elsewhere as a preposition, thus making the thought clear and preserving the old construction at least in external form.

Not a single instance of the old simple genitive object has been preserved. Thus the genitive as object in both its older and its newer form has passed out of the vivid consciousness of English-speaking people. The genitive object has become an accusative object or a prepositional object, the latter at least to the feeling of most people. The dative has been better preserved, in part because its meaning is simpler, in part because the simple dative rests upon a simple, clear principle of word-order, deeply rooted in English feeling, namely, *the dative precedes the accusative,* as in 'He gave *the house* a new coat of paint.'

PREPOSITIONAL OBJECT

14. Growth, Development, and Present Use of the Prepositional Object. Preposition and noun together form a prepositional object that serves as the object of a verb or an adjective, i.e., serves to complete the meaning of a verb or an adjective. For many centuries there has been a steady trend toward the prepositional object. Verbs and adjectives which once required a simple genitive or dative object now take a prepositional object. This is a trend toward more concrete expression. The Old English words for *thirsty, eager, greedy* took a simple genitive, which, as described in **13** 3, often meant *in the sphere of, with regard to*, often also designated a goal and had still other meanings, so that the thought was not always clear. But in the three words under consideration there is always the clear idea of the outward direction of an activity of the mind toward something. This idea has found a concrete expression in the language, for we now say *thirsty, eager, greedy for* or *after*. After the decay of the inflections, the old genitive was in part preserved for a while in the form of the prepositional genitive with *of*, so that forms like *eager of*, etc., tarried for a time, only, however, to be entirely replaced later by the more concrete forms *eager for, eager after*, etc. Similarly, the Old English words for *to yearn, hope, long, strive, thirst, ask, beg*, etc., required a simple genitive, but in modern English these verbs take a preposition which gives a more concrete expression to the idea of an outward direction of an activity toward an object: *to yearn for; to hope for; to long for; to strive for*, etc. The first evidences of this new trend appear in Old English.

The dative as object after adjectives and as indirect object after transitive verbs is much better preserved than the genitive object, but the prepositional object has made some inroads also upon it, since an appropriate preposition sometimes expresses more concretely the idea of *direction toward* than *to*, which not only denotes *direction toward* but also indicates inner relations, as described in **12** 2: 'He is cold, hostile, unfriendly, friendly *to me*' (or also *toward me*). Some adjectives do not take *to* at all but the more concrete *at*: 'He is mad, angry *at me*.' Likewise, after verbs *at* has a more concrete force than the dative with *to* or the simple dative: 'He threw the matter up *to me*' (in an inner sense), but 'He threw a stone *at me*' (in a literal exterior sense). 'He threw (or tossed) *me* a dollar,' but 'He threw a stone *at me*.' These last sentences show clearly that our ancestors, while they have destroyed a good deal of the older frame of their language and rebuilt it, working constructively along new lines, have often wisely retained features of the old framework, fitting them into the new structure.

In our English of today, we make a liberal use of prepositions, but ours is not by any means entirely a prepositional language, as has been claimed. The seemingly prepositional element *of*, so often used in the attributive genitive categories, is in fact at present not a preposition, but a case sign, and this new genitive with *of* is just as much a case form as the older simple case forms. Likewise, the *to* of the modern dative form is not a preposition but the dative case sign. Just as modern English has used concrete prepositional elements to reconstruct its new case forms, so did prehistoric Indo-European, from which English has sprung, once use concrete elements to construct its cases. The stages of the English development all lie open to view. On account of the loss of its inflections English was forced to employ the concrete prepositions *of* and *to* as the best available forms to make a clear genitive and a clear dative. This employment to indicate abstract relations has gradually robbed both *of* and *to* of a good deal of their original concrete force and they are becoming mere case signs. We are right in the midst of the development, however, not at the end of it, for both *of* and *to* are still often used as concrete prepositions. Similarly, *for, on, upon, from,* all still felt as prepositions with concrete force, are not infrequently used to form the dative case, as illustrated in **12** 1 A, B *a, b;* **15** I 2. Prepositions that have lost their original concrete force and are now used to indicate case relations are called inflectional prepositions.

a. PREPOSITIONAL PHRASE AS OBJECT, OR AS ADVERBIAL ELEMENT. It is difficult to distinguish the prepositional phrase in the object relation from the prepositional phrase in the adverbial relation, since there is never a difference in form and no fundamental difference in function. In general, we call the phrase an object when its relation to the verb, adjective, or participle is very close, so close that it is necessary to complete its meaning. The relation of the adverbial phrase to the verb, adjective, or participle is less close. For illustrative examples see **24** IV, **24** IV *a,* **25** 1.

b. OBJECT OF THE PREPOSITION A GERUND. The object of the preposition may be not only a noun or a pronoun but also a gerundial clause, one of the tersest and most convenient constructions in the language: 'I am counting on *his finishing the work tomorrow.*' This is a short cut to avoid a clumsy *that*-clause: 'I am counting on it *that he finish the work* tomorrow.' But the gerundial clause is often replaced by an infinitive or *that*-clause if the idea of a wish is present: 'I am longing *for a good cheerful letter from him,*' or 'I am longing *for him to write me a good cheerful letter,*' or 'I am longing, hoping *that he may write me a good cheerful letter.*' Compare **50** 4 *d.*

c. OBJECT OF THE PREPOSITION A CLAUSE. In modern English the object of the preposition may be also a full clause introduced by an indefinite relative pronoun or adverb: 'He thanked me for *what I had done for him.*' 'She is sorry for *what she said.*' Compare **24** IV. Sometimes the full clause has no formal introduction: 'My head has been people-tired, I think, but my heart is just satisfied with being full of *"I'm so glad you're better"'* (Clyde Fitch, *Letter*, 1904). Compare **24** IV (7th par.).

d. PASSIVE FORM. The verb before a prepositional object was originally intransitive, but in modern English the preposition has in many cases become so closely attached to the verb that we feel it as a part of the verb and thus transfer to the new compound verb its function of governing the object and so convert the old intransitive into a transitive. Hence such verbs with closely attached prepositions can assume passive form: *The steamer ran into a sailboat;* in passive form *A sailboat was run into by a steamer.*

DOUBLE OBJECT

15. An accusative, dative, genitive, or prepositional object may not only each be used singly after a verb, but two objects may be employed, one an accusative, to denote the direct object of the verb, and one a dative, genitive, accusative, or a prepositional object, which stands in various relations to the verb, or some other word, or the sentence as a whole, as described below. Sometimes one object is a dative, the other a prepositional object.

I. DATIVE AND ACCUSATIVE

1. Description of the Construction. This construction is found after a great many verbs, especially those with the general meaning of giving, buying, guaranteeing, devoting, dedicating, consecrating, adapting, pardoning, forgiving, bringing, sending, handing, throwing, telling, teaching, saying, answering, revealing, mentioning, remembering, writing, telephoning, telegraphing, owing, selling, paying, remitting, refunding, refusing, denying, promising, allying, betrothing, introducing, doing, making or causing, explaining, wishing, showing, singing, playing (to play one a trick), saving (to save one a good deal of trouble), yielding, etc. The accusative denotes the direct object, the person or thing affected or produced, and the dative the indirect object, the person or thing to whose advantage or disadvantage the action accrues, or the person to whom the statement seems true or with reference to whom it holds good, or the person who has or is expected to have an emotional or sympathetic interest in the statement, where, however, often in the case of an indirect object, beneath these, the predominant meanings of the dative, somewhat of the old original concrete idea of *direction toward* (12 2), is still felt.

a. In older English, the verb *learn* belonged to this list, as it was often used with the force of *teach:* 'Bob this morning begg'd me to *learn him lattin*' (Philip Vickers Fithian, *Journal*, March 14, 1774). This usage survives in popular speech.

2. **Form, Position, and Stress.** The principal rules for the form and position of the dative in this construction are given in **11 1**, but there are still other points that need attention. We can say 'He threw *mé* not *Jóhn* the ball,' or 'He threw *mé* the ball, not *Jóhn*' (dat.). The latter form is here made clear only by the parallelism of the accent, for if we say *'Hé* threw me the ball not *Jóhn'* (nom.) the meaning is quite different. We can either say: 'He threw *mé* and *Jóhn* down some apples,' or we may prefer 'He threw down some apples *to mé* and *Jóhn*,' for by withholding the dative until the end of the sentence we create the feeling of suspense and thus make it more prominent. Of course, for the same reason the accusative often stands in the last place: 'He threw me and John down some fine *ápples.'* The other important position is the first place: *'To a wóman* the consciousness of being well dressed gives a sense of tranquillity which religion fails to bestow' (Helen Choate). *'To mé* he didn't say a single word.'

We can say 'He threw the ball up *to me*,' or 'He threw *me* up the ball,' but we can only say 'He threw the matter up *to me*,' for we do not feel *to me* as an indirect object. The expression *to throw up a matter* is felt as a unit, a set verbal phrase, which as a whole takes a single dative object. Many such set verbal phrases take a single dative object, usually a prepositional dative, since a simple dative according to **12 1 A** has prepositional form.

The dative of reference (**12 1 B** *a*) usually has the prepositional form, but sometimes the old simple dative occurs: 'He never made such excuses *to me*,' or *'To mé* he never made such excuses,' but we say also 'He never made *mé* such excuses.' Many of the set verbal phrases referred to above might be classed here: 'They showed their heels *to the enemy.'* 'They declared war *upon them.'* Verbs of disguising, hiding, withholding take a prepositional dative of reference with *from:* 'He hid the matter *from me.'* 'He withheld *from me* the truth.' The dative of interest (**12 1 B** *b*) usually has the modern prepositional form, but we sometimes find the old simple dative: 'He cut off a piece of bread *for me*,' or 'He cut *me* off a piece of bread.' Many of the datives found in the set verbal phrases mentioned above might be classed as datives of interest: 'When I was down, he turned his back *upon me.*' 'He played a mean trick *on me,*' or 'He played *me* a mean trick.' Examples of the ethical dative are given in **12** 1 B *c.* The datives of reference and interest and the ethical dative do not differ in inner meaning from the dative of the indirect object. They all contain the idea of personal interest or reference and all contain traces of the original meaning of *direction toward.* They all may be used in connection with an accusative object as in these examples, but the dative of indirect object stands in closer relation to the verb than the other datives, which modify the verbal phrase, i.e., the verb with all its other modifiers, rather than the verb alone, or are often felt as sentence modifiers: 'He sent *me* (indirect object) a book.' 'She made *me* (dative of interest) a cake.' 'He never made *mé* (dative of reference) such excuses.' Often, however, the line of demarcation is not clear: 'He sent *mé* (dative of reference or indirect object) notice, too.' The ethical dative is often an out-and-out sentence modifier, but like an indirect object it is often associated with a direct object, as in the examples in **12** 1 B *c.*

English feeling demands a clear dative form: 'Give back *to Ireland* her nationality, her individual existence, and soothe thereby the wounded pride,' etc. (Asquith). Here the prepositional dative *to Ireland* is required because *to give back* usually takes as object a single accusative. We could easily say here: 'Give *Ireland* (simple dat.) back her nationality,' etc., because *to give* is usually found with a dative object followed by an accusative. This sensitiveness of English feeling for a clear dative is a marked feature of the language, which has often been overlooked by foreign and native English grammarians. In such expressions as 'Mr. Wells, *whom* competent critics have given a niche among future classics,' the simple dative is common as the proximity of *have given* makes it clear that the form is a dative, while in 'Tiberius, *to whom* Christ commanded that tribute should be given,' the prepositional form is necessary to give clear expression to the dative idea. Even in the former example a clear expression of the dative relation by the clear dative form *to whom* does not sound unnatural. In choice language, of course, more care is taken to give the dative a distinctive form than in loose colloquial speech. With nouns and also pronouns, aside from the relative pronoun, an initial dative regularly takes the prepositional form in order that at the very outset the grammatical relations may become clear: '*To me* he owes nothing.' '*To whom* did you give the apple?' In older English, the simple dative could stand in the first place and this older usage lingers on, especially in poetry: 'And *me* that morning Walter show'd the house' (Tennyson, *Princess*, Prologue).

If a stressed accusative is put into the first place for emphasis, or if a relative or interrogative pronoun, which must always introduce the clause or sentence, is in the accusative, the indirect object is left at or near the end of the sentence or clause separated from the accusative, which under other circumstances would follow it. The simple dative is still often used here, since the word-order is quite fixed and shows plainly that the form is a dative: 'This much I must tell *you*.' 'He never got back the money which he had lent *them*' (or *to them*). 'I thanked him for the position which he had procured *me*' (or *for me*). 'What would it be right to pay *the waiter?*' (or *to the waiter*). The simple dative is often used at the end of a relative clause even though the preceding relative pronoun in the accusative has been suppressed: 'a little jacket [which] she was knitting *me*' (Anne Douglas Sedgwick, *The Little French Girl*, Ch. V) (or *for me*).

a. Passive Forms of Statement. There are here two forms, the first a favorite in the literary language, the second, in colloquial speech, but often also preferred in choice expression. The accusative becomes nominative and the dative is retained, either in its old simple or its new prepositional form; the latter regularly when the dative is stressed: '*Ample warning* was given *them*,' but '*Ample warning* was given *to thém*, but not *to mé*.' Or the dative becomes nominative and the accusative is retained: '*They* were given *ample warning*.' Only the simple dative can become nominative, so that we do not say: '*I* was suggested this,' for in the active we say 'He suggested this *to me*,' with the prepositional form.

The use of a nominative in the passive corresponding to a dative in the active began in early Middle English. In the thirteenth century we find not only the nominative in the passive corresponding to the simple dative in the active, but we find also the accusative of the active retained in the passive: *He was ileten blood* (*The Ancren Riwle*, 112), literally, *He was let blood*, i.e., *was bled*, corresponding to the active *The phisicien let him* (dat.) *blood*, i.e., *The physician bled him*. There was at this time alongside of this construction an older construction out of which it had developed: '*Him* was ileten blood.' Here *him* is dative and *blood* is nominative, the subject of the sentence. The new construction arose out of the older one in such sentences as '*The Duke* was ileten blood,' where, as the form was not distinctive, *Duke*, a dative, was construed as a nominative, the subject of the verb. This construction began in such set expressions, where the accusative of the active had entered into such close relations with the verb that it had formed a compound with it and hence was retained in the passive form of statement. From such set expressions with a retained accusative object in the passive it gradually became common in colloquial speech to retain in the passive the accusative of the active. This old construction is more widely used in American and Irish English than in English proper, although it is also there quite common. Similar to the retained object in this construction is the retained object found elsewhere in passive constructions: 'He *took no notice of me*,' in passive form 'I *was taken no notice of*,' where *take no notice of* is felt as a compound, so that the accusative object *no notice* of the active is retained in the passive.

In colloquial speech there is another passive form. The subject is always a person, the verb is an active form of *have* or *get*, which has as object a thing and as objective predicate a perfect participle, which contains the passive force: 'I *have* (or *get*) *something given* me (or to me) every birthday.' 'I *have* just *had given* me (or to me) *a fine new knife*.'

b. *Accusative Object a Full or Abridged Clause*. The accusative object is often a full clause with a finite verb: 'I wrote him *that he should come*.' For the different forms that an accusative clause with a finite verb may have see **24 III**. The accusative object may have also the form of an infinitival or a gerundial clause, as described in **24 III** *d*.

II. Accusative of the Person and Genitive of the Thing

In this construction the accusative denotes the person or thing directly affected, and the genitive expresses the idea of specification, which is now often felt as denoting separation, deprivation: 'to accuse *someone of a crime*,' i.e., with respect to a crime; 'to acquit *someone of a charge*'; 'to persuade *someone of the wisdom of a course of action*'; 'to suspect *someone of treason*'; 'to possess *one's self of a thing*'; 'to assure *someone of one's sincerity*'; 'to remind *someone of something*'; 'to strip *a bush of leaves*,' literally, *with respect to leaves*, but now felt as indicating deprivation; 'to free *someone of a burden*'; 'to ease *someone of a care*'; 'to purge or cleanse *one's self of sin*'; 'to divest *someone of his honor*'; 'to deprive *someone of his liberty*.'

In Old English, the simple genitive was used here in exactly the same way as the prepositional form of today, but the list of verbs was larger. The old genitive of specification had so many meanings that the thought was often unclear, and this unclearness finally led to clearer expression. Thus older *ask* with the simple genitive of specification has disappeared and is now represented by *ask someone for something*, or *for somebody*, *ask someone about something* or *somebody*, or *after somebody*. The *of* in the modern genitive of specification as found in the above examples is now probably felt as a preposition by most people, so that the construction now passes for a prepositional object. The construction, however, corresponds so closely to the Old English accusative and simple genitive and is even today so set and rigid, not admitting readily of the substitution of another preposition with the same meaning, as *about, with respect to*, in the place of *of*, that it seems in fact a fragment of the old accusative and genitive category in modern form.

a. The genitive object may have the form of a clause with a finite verb: 'This convinces me *of his innocence*' (or *that he is innocent*). For the different forms that the genitive clause with a finite verb may have see **24 I.** The genitive object may have also the form of an infinitival or a gerundial clause, as described in **24 I** *a.*

b. Passive Form. In the passive form of statement the accusative becomes nominative, and the genitive object is retained: '*He* was robbed *of his money.*'

III. DOUBLE ACCUSATIVE

1. Accusative of the Person and Accusative of the Thing. This construction is now in common usage reduced to the verbs *ask, lead, take, envy:* 'I asked *him his name*' (or *the price*, or *the reason*, or *the way*). 'Ask *the cabman the fare.*' 'He led *them a lively dance*' (or *chase*). 'She leads *him a dog's life.*' 'I took *her a drive.*' 'I envy *him his luck.*'

Sometimes *banish, debar, dismiss, excuse, expel* take a double accusative object, one of the person, one of the thing, which has arisen through the dropping of the preposition *from* (or, in older English, *of*) which usually stands before the object of the thing: 'We banish *you our territories*' (Shakespeare, *Richard the Second*, I, III, 139), now usually *from our territories.* 'He debarred *himself every kind* of amusement' (W. Godwin, *The Adventures of Caleb Williams*, II, Ch. VII, A.D. 1794). 'They dismissed *them the society*' (Defoe, *Crusoe*, II, IV, 72, A.D. 1719), now usually *from the society.* 'He expelled *him the house*' (Lytton, *The Caxtons*, III, Ch. VII), now usually *from the house.* This type arose under the temporary influence of the two objects with *forbid*, the first of which was originally a dative, but was sometimes felt as an accusative: 'I forbade *him the house.*' 'His mother forbade *him wine.*' This construction has disappeared for the most part with all these verbs except *forbid*, which still has the original dative and accusative after it, as can be seen in the passive form of statement: '*To all the children* wine has been absolutely forbidden.' 'Wine is forbidden *him.*' '*He* is forbidden wine.'

After *hear, kiss,* and *strike* (or *hit*) there are two objects, probably a double accusative, but the first object may be construed as a dative of interest (**12 1 B** *b*): 'I heard *the boys their lessons*' (common in England, but little used in America). 'I kissed *her good night*.' 'I struck (or hit) *him a hard blow*.'

a. *Passive Form.* In the passive, the accusative of the person becomes nominative and the accusative of the thing is retained: '*He* was asked *his opinion*.' '*He* is led *a dog's life*.' '*She* was taken *a drive*.' '*He* was envied *his luck*.' '*Who*, had they dared to imitate him, would have been banished *society*' (Disraeli, *Vivian Grey*, VII, IX, A.D. 1826), now usually *from society*. '*You* are debarred *correspondence* for the present' (Scott, *Waverley*, Ch. LXII). 'She saw her husband, *who* was afterwards dismissed *the service* (now usually *from the service*), a strong and powerful man, pine and waste,' etc. (Lytton, *Eugene Aram*, Ch. VII). '*He* was excused *the entrance-fee*' (*Oxford Dictionary* under *Excuse*, 7). '*The boys* were heard *their lessons*.' '*He* was struck *a hard blow*.'

2. Accusative of the Direct Object and an Objective Predicate. This construction differs from the double object in 1, p. 119, in that the two accusatives together form logically a clause in which the first accusative performs the office of subject and the second accusative the office of predicate: '*The President made him the head of the navy*' (= *that he became the head of the navy*). '*The people made him president*.' '*They called him a traitor*.' '*The parents have named the baby Thomas*, but they of course call *him Tommy*.' '*The pastor baptized him Thomas*.' '*I have always found him a true friend*.' '*I saw him come*.' The simple infinitive here, as in the last example, is the accusative of an old type of verbal noun which still is, as in the prehistoric period, without an article before it.

The two accusatives in all these and similar examples were originally the direct objects of the verb. As the construction is very old there has gradually come about a close association between the two accusatives, so that the second one is now felt as a predicate to the first one, its subject. The predicate is here joined to its subject without the aid of a copula, since the statement is now felt to be of the old appositional type of sentence described in 6 B *a*, where the predicate is placed alongside of the subject like an appositive without the use of a finite verb.

We sometimes insert the copula here between subject and predicate, as in other sentences where a noun, pronoun, or adjective is predicated of the subject: 'I deem him *an honest man*' (or *to be an honest man*). 'But *what a parcel* of fools he would think us for getting in such a stew about him!' (De Morgan, *The Old Madhouse*, Ch. X), but with *to be* when the objective predicate is a pronoun: 'He thought *Richard to be me*,' or in the form of a full clause with finite verb: 'He thought Richard was *I*,' or in loose colloquial speech usually *me*, as explained in **7 C *a***. The insertion of *to be* before the accusative predicate was facilitated by the close relation of the objective predicate construction in force and meaning to that of the accusative with the infinitive, described in **24 III *d***, when the infinitive is the verb *be*. On the other hand, the construction of the infinitive with the accusative is often influenced by the objective predicate construction in that it is often without *to be:* 'I ordered my bill [to be] made out.'

The objective predicate is not only a noun in the accusative, but it is often also a noun in the genitive of characteristic, an adjective, participle, adverb, or prepositional phrase. For convenience the objective predicate is here treated in two groups.

A. The Objective Predicate a Noun or Pronoun in the Accusative, a Noun in the Genitive of Characteristic, an Adjective, Participle, Adverb, or Prepositional Phrase. 'The king dubbed *his son a knight*.' 'Willersley and I professed *ourselves Socialists*' (H. G. Wells, *The New Machiavelli*, p. 134). 'Mr. Crabfield did his duty by Lucius Mason, and sent *him* home at seventeen *a handsome, well-mannered lad*' (Trollope, *Orley Farm*, I, Ch. II). 'I thought *it a fraud, just, possible*.' 'I consider *what he did a gratuitous interference*.' 'He showed *himself of noble spirit*.' 'She boiled *the eggs hard*.' 'He wore *his coat threadbare*.' 'He laughed *himself sick*.' 'I consider *what he said irrelevant*.' 'I found *him sleeping*.' 'I kept *him waiting*.' 'I'll stop *him circulating* (or *from circulating*) *these reports*.' 'I pictured *myself careering into fame*.' 'I started *the clock going*.' 'His (Garfield's) journal shows *him* constantly *going* there (i.e., the library) for information' (Theodore Clarke Smith, *James A. Garfield*, II, p. 752). 'I have *some money coming* to me yet.' 'I consider *the matter settled*.' 'I got *my work done* before six o'clock.' 'I at last got *the machine running*' (or *to running*, or *to run*). 'I shall have *the machine running* by the time you get back.' 'I found *him there*.' 'Have *the children in* by nine o'clock.' 'I found *everything in good condition*.' The copula is now often expressed here: 'I have always found *him to be a true friend*' (or *to be of a friendly disposition*). 'I have always found *him to be reliable*.' We employ the same forms after verbal nouns except that we use as direct object an objective genitive (**10 II 2 D**) instead of an accusative: 'They were men who consecrated their lives to the preservation *intact of what had been wrought out in blood and sweat by the countless generations of sturdy freemen who had gone before them*' (Woodrow Wilson, Dec., 1902). For the use of the predicative present participle here see **50** 3 (3rd par. from end).

In oldest English, the predicate noun was not so often a plain accusative as today. It was usually introduced by *to* or *for*. The *to* represents the new state as the result of a development or as the purpose of the action, while *for* represents the new state as entirely or seemingly identical with the conception of it held by the person in question. These older conceptions are often found later and in part still survive: in Old English 'to crown *him to king*' (transformation into a new state), now 'to crown *him king*.' 'The seven had her *to wife*' (*Mark*, XII, 23), indicating purpose, now 'The seven had her *as wife*.' *For* is still used in a large number of expressions: 'They took him *for* his brother.' 'Though Helen laughs at me now *for* a coward, before I've been in a fight, she won't laugh at me afterwards' (J. T. Trowbridge, *The Drummer Boy*, Ch. I). 'The Reverend Hussell Barter was arrested by the sight of a couple half-hidden by a bushy plant; he knew them *for* Mrs. Bellew and George Pendyce' (Galsworthy, *The Country House*, p. 46). 'Yet he knew himself *for* a greater idiot because he had not been able to tell Walter the truth' (Tarkington, *Alice Adams*, Ch. XVI). 'He gave me this book *for* a Christmas present.' 'You will have Miss Sharp one day *for* your relation' (Thackeray, *Vanity Fair*, I, Ch. XIV). 'All the rest hooted and jeered at her *for* a witch' (A. R. Hope, *Stories of English Schoolboy Life*, p. 8).

The modern favorite here, *as*, first appeared in Old English, but did not become common until much later. In Old English, the single determinative *swa*, i.e., *so*, later *as*, or the double determinative *swa swa* (**27** 2), i.e., *so so*, is sometimes used here. The single or double *so* points as with a single or double index finger to the following explanatory noun, thus indicating that this noun expresses the idea in mind. In Chaucer we find the single *so*-form combined with the old *for*, i.e., *as for:* 'Thy doghter wol (will) I take . . . *as for* my wyf' (*The Clerkes Tale*, 251). In the corresponding nominative relation, described in **7 A b** (3), Chaucer uses simple *as*, but long before Chaucer's time we find an occasional use of simple *as* also in the accusative relation. Now for centuries in both the nominative and the accusative relation *as* has been gradually replacing older *to* and *for*, while on the other hand the simple accusative is still quite common, especially with certain verbs. Present usage is fluctuating and uneven. We say 'They selected him *president*' (or more commonly *for president*, or *to be president*), 'I believe the man *insane*' (or *to be insane*), while we prefer 'He turned water *into wine*' to 'He made the water *wine*' (*John*, IV, 46), and yet inconsistently in the case of an adjective say 'It turned his hair *gray*' rather than 'It turned his hair *to gray*.'

As can be seen by the last example, in the case of nouns we still often have a lively feeling for the old idea of transformation. We now use *to* or *into*: 'His presence will soon melt her resolution *into thin air again*.' 'They never put their aims *into practice*.' Also *at* and *on* may be used: 'We set him *at liberty*.' 'He'll never set the Hudson *on fire*.' 'It was what put Cit's back up so two years ago that set me *on thinking* (in popular speech *a-thinking*) *it*' (De Morgan, *The Old Madhouse*, Ch. XXV), or often *to thinking it*, or often simply *thinking* (present participle used as objective predicate) *it*. However, we now often express the idea of change and transformation also by a simple accusative: 'They made, proclaimed, elected, him *king*.' This is not natural Germanic expression, but represents Latin and Old French influence, which in a number of words has become natural modern English, but in many other cases Germanic usage has prevailed.

Where the idea of transformation is not involved, the latest form, the one with *as*, is spreading at the expense of the simple accusative as well as the form with *for*: 'It's no sinne to deceiue a Christian; For they themselues hold it *a principle*, Faith is not to be held with Heretickes' (Marlowe, *The Jew of Malta*, II, 1074–1075, about A.D. 1590, ed. 1633); but 'It would be almost impossible to exaggerate the effect which these schools have had in the gradual process of realizing that ideal of a national speech which the country holds *as its standard*' (Krapp, *The English Language in America*, I, 29, A.D. 1925). *As* is most widely used where the objective predicate is a noun: 'I acknowledge myself *defeated*' (or *as defeated*), but usually 'I acknowledge myself *as an offender*.' *As* has already become established in a large number of expressions, and is often used in others: 'We all regard him *as very skilful*' (*as a very skilful man*). 'I regard this *as of great importance*.' 'They represent him *as a reliable man*' (*as reliable*). 'I consider him still *a child*' (or less commonly *as a child*). 'I think her *the most confounded flirt in London*' or 'I regard her *as the most confounded flirt in London*.' Verbs having a preposition closely attached to them uniformly take *as*: 'I always think of him *as the most potent force* in my entire life.' 'I look upon him *as my best friend*.' It is used also after verbal nouns: 'The selection of Smith (objective genitive) *as chairman* pleases everybody.'

Notice the difference of meaning between *as*, denoting complete identity, oneness with, and the preposition *like*, denoting mere similarity: 'Large minds treat little things *as* little things and big things *as* big things,' but 'He treats his wife *like* a child.'

a. Passive Form. In the passive, the first accusative becomes nominative, and the predicate word or phrase is retained as in the active, with the exception that the predicate accusative becomes nominative: 'He was elected *president.*' 'He is reputed *the best physician in town*' (or *to be the best physician in town*). 'He was called *hard names.*' 'It is thought *to be a fraud.*' 'It was at first thought *to be he*' (or in loose colloquial speech *him,* as explained in **7** C *a*). 'He was found *guilty*' (or *to be guilty*). 'The egg was boiled *hard.*' 'We were all set *laughing*' (or *to laughing*). 'He is looked upon *as a reliable man.*' 'Everything was found *in good condition.*' 'I have often been taken *for my brother.*'

b. Instead of the first accusative we often employ a full clause or an abridged, infinitival or gerundial, clause, which, however, is usually preceded by a formal anticipatory accusative, namely, *it:* 'You think *it* odd *that I went to church*' (or *for me to have gone to church,* or *my having gone to church*).

B. AN INFINITIVE AS OBJECTIVE PREDICATE. After the verbs *let, leave* (in popular speech = *let*), *bid, make, have, see, behold, notice, look at, observe, perceive, watch, find, feel, hear, overhear, listen to,* the objective predicate is usually a simple infinitive, but after *bid, make, have, feel, see, observe, find,* we sometimes employ also the infinitive with *to,* indeed regularly — except after *bid, make, have* — if the infinitive is the copula *be,* and after *help* and *know* we employ either the simple infinitive or the prepositional form, the latter especially in careful language: 'I let him *go.*' 'He let (or in popular speech *left*) *go* [his hold] of it.' 'Let (in popular speech *leave;* see **43** I A) him *come* in.' 'Bid him *come* in.' 'He bade her *to take* (usually simple *take*) courage' (A. Trollope, *Dr. Wortle's School,* p. 88). 'Thou hast made the earth *to* (common in early Modern English) *tremble*' (*Psalms,* LX, 2). 'After an exciting subject which has made the general tongue *to* (now little used) *wag* . . . then start your story' (Meredith, *Harrington,* Ch. XXXI). 'I made him *do* it.' 'I made him *be* quiet.' 'I love your sister as you'd have one *love*' (Robert Browning). 'It really grieves me to have you *be* so naughty' (Mrs. H. B. Stowe, *Uncle Tom's Cabin,* Ch. XXV). 'An idiot is a human being, sir, and has an immortal soul, I'd have you *to* (perhaps more commonly omitted) *know*' (Marion Crawford, *Katherine Lauderdale,* I, Ch. VI). 'I shall have (i.e., cause) him *do* (sometimes *to do*) it,' differing in thought from the two following sentences, which have the same construction but another meaning, expressing not a causing but a suffering or experiencing: 'I had the gypsies *steal* my hens' and 'I have had many scholars *visit* me from time to time.' 'I saw him *come.*' 'He saw three figures advancing arm in arm. He waited till they came within the radius of a lamp; then, seeing them *to be* those of Miltoun (name) and a footman, he at once has-tened forward' (Galsworthy, *The Patrician*, p. 43). 'Look at Glor-vina *enter* a room, and compare her with that poor Mrs. Osborne' (Thackeray, *Vanity Fair*, Ch. XLIII). 'Oh, look at him *run!*' (Frank Norris, *The Octopus.*) 'I observed, watched, him *work.*' 'He had perceived one human being after another *reveal* quite nakedly their tumultuous feelings' (Hugh Walpole, *The Duchess of Wrexe*, Ch. IX). 'I have always found him *to be reliable.*' 'You'll never find him *neglect* (or *to neglect*) *his work,*' but always with *to* in the following entirely different constructions 'I couldn't find it (anticipatory object) in my heart *to refuse*' (accusative object) and 'I find plenty *to do*' (see **7 D 2**). 'Did you ever feel anything *sting* like that?' 'I heard him *come.*' 'I overheard him *tell* his mother about it.' 'It was my privilege a few years ago to listen to Sir Ernest Shackleton *speak* of his expedition across the Antarctic continent' (Irving Babbitt, *Rousseau and Romanticism*, p. 277). 'I never knew him *to be* careless with his work.' 'I never knew anyone *do* (usually *to do*) so much in so short a time' (Mrs. H. Ward, *Miss Bretherton*, Ch. VII). 'I helped him *do* (or especially in careful language *to do*) it.'

The present participle is often used here instead of the infinitive, usually, however, with a little different meaning. The infinitive states a fact, while the participle has descriptive force: 'I saw *him do it*' (a fact), but 'I saw *him working in the field*' (descrip-tive). The participle is regularly used after *to catch*, as the force here is always descriptive: 'I caught him *doing it.*' Compare **48 2** (4th par.).

The subject of infinitive or participle usually precedes, but if important or long, it often follows: 'I heard come booming up the river *what I suppose was the sound of cannon fired in Lowell to celebrate the Whig victory*' (Thoreau, *Journal*, V, p. 507).

Passive force is now often imparted to the objective predicate here, although originally this was impossible, since the infinitive was a noun. The verbal force of the infinitive is now so strong that we give it passive form after *let* and *bid* when we feel it as hav-ing passive force: 'He wouldn't let her wound *be dressed.*' 'In his busiest days Alfred found time to learn the old songs of his race by heart, and bade them *be taught* in the palace school' (Green, *Short History*, p. 51). After the other verbs we often employ a perfect passive participle to state a fact and a present passive participle to impart descriptive force: 'I have never known it *done* (or *to be done*) right.' 'I had (in colloquial speech often *got*) a new coat *made.*' 'I saw, watched, the net *hauled* in' (fact), or '*being hauled* in' (descriptive). In fact the perfect passive participle in this construction is an elliptical present passive infinitive with the infinitive *be* suppressed. The *be*, however, is actually expressed only after *let, bid*, and often after *know*. It is sometimes found in older English after other verbs in this group: 'Whuch of ʒou seih me *be maad?*' (*Lyff of Adam and Eve*, p. 2, fourteenth century) = 'Who of you saw me *made?*' 'Mercy, humanity call loudly that we make our now despised power *to be felt*' (William Dunlap, *André*, Act III, A.D. 1798). We usually suppress *be* here because the copula has not as yet become established before an objective predicate.

The construction with *have* or *get* and the perfect passive participle which represents the subject as planning the action, as in 'I *hád* (or *gót*) a new suit *made*,' is quite different from the construction with *have* and *get* and the perfect passive participle which represents the subject as suffering from the action of another or of fate: 'I *had* (or *got*) my right leg *húrt* in the accident.' Notice that *had* or *got* are stressed in the first example, while they are only lightly stressed in the second. There is a clear difference of meaning between stressed and unstressed *had* and *got*. Similarly, there is a difference of meaning between 'They *háve* (or *gét*) their work done' ('They employ others to do their work') with stressed *have* or *get* and 'They have their work *dóne*' ('Their work is done') and 'They get things *dóne*' ('They accomplish a good deal') with unstressed *have* and *get*.

In older English, and sometimes still, we find here instead of the new passive form the old active, a present active infinitive or participle with passive force: 'I heard *say* (now *it said*) your lordship was sick' (Shakespeare, *II Henry IV*, I, II, 108). 'I never heard *tell* (now usually *it said*) that we were put here to get pleasure out of life' (Conan Doyle, *Refugees*, 231). 'Annie seem'd to hear her own death-scaffold *raising*' (Tennyson, *Enoch Arden*, 175). 'I caught him (i.e., the lawyer Barclay) palavering with a juror the other day while we had a case *trying*' (William Allen White, *A Certain Rich Man*, Ch. VI). Compare **46** (close of next to last paragraph).

The use of *to* before the active and passive forms of the infinitive here with certain verbs indicates that the accusative and the infinitive are felt as abridged infinitive clauses, as in **24** III *d*, but in the case of the other verbs of this group the development in this direction is not yet so complete. The abridged clauses in **24** III *d* have the full force of a clause with a nominative subject and a finite verb, but these infinitive clauses without *to* before the infinitive sometimes have a somewhat different force, so that 'I heard the bells ring' is different in meaning from 'I heard that the bells rang.' The infinitive *ring* here is still, as originally, the object of the verb *heard*. In most cases, however, the difference between these clauses is not so great, often indeed is very slight, as in 'I've never known him *to neglect* (or *neglect*) his work' and 'I've never known *that he has neglected his work.*' This accounts for the tendency to place *to* before the infinitive here. Earlier in the period and in Middle English, we often find here *for to* instead of *to:* 'It maketh al my drede (dread) *for to dyen'* (die) (Chaucer, *The Nonne Preestes Tale*, 342).

a. Passive Form. In the passive statement, the direct object becomes nominative and the infinitive or the present participle is retained, the infinitive usually with its prepositional form, sometimes, however, with its simple form, especially in set expressions where the simple infinitive, so closely associated with the active form, is also employed after the passive: (active) 'I saw him *do* it,' but in the passive: 'He was seen *to do* it.' But sometimes with simple infinitive after a passive: 'The younger children were let *sleep* on' (Hardy, *Tess of the D'Urbervilles*, Ch. LII). 'I know it could be made *do*' (De Morgan, *The Old Madhouse*, Ch. II). Compare **7 D 1** *b*. Of course, to impart descriptive force here we employ a present participle: 'A funeral procession was seen *approaching.*'

b. Instead of employing *have* with a dependent infinitive to indicate that a person or thing suffers from an act, we simply use in the case of *spring* the intransitive transitively: 'The boat *sprang a leak*,' i.e., *had a leak start.*

IV. ACCUSATIVE OF THE PERSON OR THING AND A PREPOSITIONAL PHRASE

This is a very common type: 'He laid *the book upon the table.*' 'He wrote *a book about his experiences in the war.*'

a. PASSIVE FORM. In the passive, the accusative becomes nominative, and the prepositional phrase is retained: '*A long book* was written by him *about his experiences in the war.*'

V. DATIVE OF THE PERSON AND A PREPOSITIONAL PHRASE

This is not so common a type as the preceding one: 'He wrote *me about his experiences* in the war.' 'He wrote, telegraphed *me* (or *to me*) *for help.*' 'He told *me about his visit* to you.'

a. PASSIVE FORM. In the passive the dative becomes nominative and the prepositional phrase is retained: '*I* was told *about his visit to you.*' Such verbs as *write, telegraph*, etc., require a *to* in the passive to indicate clearly the idea of direction toward: 'I was *written to, telegraphed to* for help.' The *to* in such expressions is now felt as a part of the verb, forming with it a compound.

ADVERBIAL MODIFIERS

16 1. Form and Function of Adverbial Modifiers. An adverbial modifier may assume the form of an adverb, a prepositional phrase or clause, or a conjunctional clause: 'He entered *quietly.*' 'Polish it *well.*' 'He entered *in haste*' (prepositional phrase). 'I could see the bird's loaded beak *from where I stood*' (prepositional clause). In the last example a preposition and its dependent clause together form an adverbial element. It is very much more common for a clause to form an adverbial element with the help of a subordinating conjunction: 'He entered *as soon as he had taken off his overcoat.*' The adverbial conjunctional clause is treated in **25–34.**

An adverb, as indicated by its literal meaning, *joined to a verb,* is an appositive to a verb, i.e., is placed before or after a verb to explain its meaning in the case at hand more clearly, much as an adjective as an appositive is placed before or after a noun to explain it: 'The girl is improving *remarkably.*' The same form is used as an appositive to an adjective or another adverb and here is also called an adverb, although of course it is here not true to its name: 'The girl is *remarkably* beautiful.' 'The girl is improving *remarkably* fast.' An adverb, however, modifies not only thus a single word, but often also a prepositional phrase, a subordinate clause, or an independent statement as a whole: 'He has traveled *entirely* around the world.' 'He is *almost* across the river.' 'He lives *a mile* (adverbial accusative) beyond our house.' 'I arrived *soon* after it happened.' 'I did it *only* because I felt it to be my duty.' For sentence adverb see 2 *a*, p. 130.

Adverbs often occur as the first component of compounds: *up*root, *over*turn, *under*done, *out*lying, *tight*-fitting, *mis*judge, *re*turn, *co*öperate, etc. The adverb *not* is usually replaced here by *un*-: *un*able, etc. In many foreign words the negative here is *in*- (or *im*-) or *dis*-: *in*convenient, *im*possible, *dis*obey. Some of these adverbs, *mis*-, *un*-, *re*-, *co*-, etc., which are not now used outside of compounds, are called prefixes.

An adverbial element modifies a verb, adjective, or other adverb by adding to it some circumstance of place, time, manner, degree, condition, concession, purpose, or means. Though usually different in meaning from a genitive, dative, accusative, or prepositional object, it always performs the same function, i.e., modifies a verb, adjective, or adverb. The adverbial modifier differs from an object in that its relation to the modified word is less close. For illustrative examples see **24 IV, 24 IV** *a*, **25 1**. There is a close relation between adverbs and prepositions. For explanation see **62**.

Adverbs are often used as nouns: 'The *ups and downs* of life.' 'The *ins* (the party in power), the *outs*' (the party out of power). 'He knows *the ins and outs* (details) of every political move.' Nouns made from adverbs are very common in prepositional phrases: until *tomorrow*, after *tomorrow*, since *yesterday*, etc. Compare **62** (3rd par.).

Adverbs are often used as pronouns: 'I saw him a year ago, but since *then* (used as demonstrative pronoun) we haven't met.' 'I saw him a year ago, since *when* (used as relative pronoun) I haven't seen anything of him.' Compare **23 II 6** (next to last par.), **62** (3rd par.). In older English, adverbs were often used as pronouns in prepositional phrases in which the preposition followed the adverb, adverb and preposition usually being written together as parts of a compound: *therein*, now *in it*; *therewith*, now *with it*; *wherein*, now *in what* (interrogative) or *in which* (relative); *wherewith*, now *with what* (interrogative) or *with which* (relative); etc. A few of the old adverbial compounds, however, have survived in common use where they have acquired a special meaning, such as *therefore* (**19** 1 *e*), *whereupon* (**23** II 6, next to last par.). In poetical and legal language the old adverbial compounds are still widely used in their original meaning and function. Compare Parts of Speech, **7** 1 *b* and **7** 4 *a*.

Adverbs are often used as adjectives. See **7** F and **10** I 2.

2. Position and Stress of Adverbs. An adverb can freely stand in almost any position except between a verb and its direct object, where it is much less common than elsewhere: '*Yesterday* I met your father,' 'I *yesterday* met your father,' 'I met your father *yesterday*,' but not 'I met *yesterday* your father.' This usage rests upon the principle that an adverbial element is usually more important than a direct object and, like important elements in general, gravitates toward the end. Sometimes, however, where the direct object by reason of its bulk or its logical force is heavier or more important than the adverbial element, it, of course, follows: 'I read the letter agáin,' but 'After an absence of fifty years I have just seen again the déar óld hóme of my chíldhood.'

a. SENTENCE ADVERBS. An adverbial element is often more heavily stressed than a verb and then usually follows it: 'He àcted prómptly.' 'All that I have lèarnt fárther is, that the populace were going to burn the house' (Horace Walpole, *Letter to Miss Mary Berry*, July 10, 1789). In many cases, however, the adverbial element does not modify the verb directly but the sentence as a whole. In this case the adverbial element usually precedes the verb, verbal phrase, or predicate noun or adjective and has a weaker stress, for in English, when we call attention in any way to the thought as a whole, the verb, verbal phrase, or predicate noun or adjective is strongly stressed, since it is felt as the basic element of the statement: 'He *èvidently* thóught so.' 'He *at lèast* thínks so.' 'He not only beliéves in such books, but he *even* réads them to his children.' 'He *àbsolutely* líves from hánd to móuth.' 'She *àlways* lets him háve his wáy.' 'The blossoms *quite* (= *entirely*) cóver the tree.' 'A man should be *quite* (= *entirely*) cértain what he knows and what he doesn't know.' 'It was *quite* (= *truly*) a disappóintment to me.' 'I *quite* (= *positively*) líke him' (*Concise Oxford Dictionary*). 'I *rather* (= *somewhat*) féar that he won't come.' 'The performance was *rather góod, rather a fáilure.*' In certain dialects the adverb *pure* (= *absolutely;* compare **54** 2 *a*, last par.) is common here: 'Gal, you *pure outdánced* yourself' (Julia Peterkin, *Scarlet Sister Mary*). 'What you done *pure cúts* my heartstrings' (*ib.*).

Under the influence of strong emotion, the sentence adverb is often strongly stressed; but this stress, resting on an adverb standing before a strongly stressed verb, indicates that it is a

sentence stress, not a stress upon an adverb belonging to the verb
alone and thus emphasizing some detail of the predicate: 'I
útterly scórn your proposition.'

The position of the lightly stressed sentence adverb before a
heavily stressed verb, or, under the influence of strong emotion,
a heavily stressed sentence adverb before a heavily stressed verb,
are marked characteristics of current English, and the distinct
feeling for the meaning of the adverb in this position has helped
bring about the split infinitive (**49** 2 *c*): 'I hope to *èven* deféat
him,' after the analogy of 'He *èven* deféated him.' 'She wishes
to *útterly* forgét her past,' after the analogy of 'She would *útterly*
fórget her past.'

In a compound form made up of an infinitive or participle and
an auxiliary, the sentence adverb stands either after or before the
auxiliary, but usually in accordance with the fixed principle that
it stands before the accented form of the compound verb: 'I
have *always* trústed your judgment' (George Bernard Shaw, *You
Never Can Tell*, Act III). 'We shall *soon* knów,' 'We may *soon*
knów.' The stress upon the part having the verbal meaning, as
in these examples, is the normal stress; but if we desire to emphasize, not the verbal meaning, but the idea of actuality, as described
in **6** A *d* (1), we accent strongly the auxiliary: 'I *always* háve
trusted your judgment.' 'Refined policy *ever* hás been the parent
of confusion and *ever* wíll be so, as long as the world endures'
(Burke). 'I *really* múst go and stop this' (George Bernard
Shaw, *You Never Can Tell*, Act III). Similarly, we usually place
the sentence adverb after or before the copula according to the
stress: 'I am *always* cáreful,' or 'I *always* ám careful.'

This principle, however, has not become thoroughly established
yet, for after the analogy of usage with the simple tenses we sometimes without reference to the stress of the compound verbal
forms place the sentence adverb between the subject and the
verbal form having the personal ending: 'He ordered breakfast
as calmly as if *he never had* (instead of *he had never*) léft his home.'
'*He undoubtedly has* (instead of *he has undoubtedly*) wórked
hárd.' In the passive, however, two participles, the one indicating the passive idea, the other the verbal meaning, usually form a
unit, so that the sentence adverb cannot stand between them
before the stressed participle, but for the most part stands before
the participial unit: 'I have *undoubtedly been decéived*,' or, of
course, 'I *undoubtedly* have been decéived,' for we can always put
the sentence adverb between subject and verb. But even in the
case of these participial units we must put the adverb between
the participles before the accented verbal form wherever the ad-

verb indicates the manner or degree of the verbal activity: 'I have undoubtedly *been gróssly decéived.*' 'She has always *been gréatly admíred.*' As in these examples, there are often two adverbs, one standing in the usual position before the passive auxiliary, the other, an adverb of manner or degree, standing between the two participles before the accented verbal form.

Although these positions of the sentence adverb are very common, they are in principal propositions not the only ones. We sometimes find the sentence adverb at the very beginning of the sentence, or after the verb at or near the end of the sentence; in the former case followed by a slight pause and in the latter case preceded by a pause, which in both cases marks the adverb or adverbial element as a sentence modifier: '*Unfortunately* (pause), the message never arríved,' 'The message, *unfortunately*, never arrived,' or 'The message never arrived (pause), *unfortunately.*' '*At least* (pause) he thinks so,' 'He *at least* thinks so,' or 'He thinks so (pause) *at least.*' '*In my opinion* (pause) they are wise.' 'It is therefore wholly undesirable that the children of the poor should be laboriously schooled to imitate all its peculiarities — its vices as well as its virtues (i.e., the vices and virtues of the literary language); *rather* (**19** 1 c) they should be encouraged to honor their local dialect' (George Willis, *The Philosophy of Speech*, p. 191). '*Please* (pause) go and order a cab!' or 'Go and order a cab (pause), *please!*' Here *please* is a subjunctive (*may it please you*) used as a sentence adverb. Instead of *please* we may use *if you please.* Thus also in other cases we may use a short sentence or clause as a sentence adverb: 'He is quite trustworthy, *I think*,' or '*I think* he is quite trustworthy.' '*I dare say* things will, somehow or other, turn out for the best.' '*Maybe* (for *it may be*) he will come tomorrow.' In popular and colloquial speech we often find *like* with the force of the choicer *as it were:* '[They (i.e., the rich men's sons) don't know how to spend it (i.e., money) properly. They're like chaps who can't carry their drink because they aren't used to it.] The brass gets into their heads, *like*' (Stanley Houghton, *Hindle Wakes*, Act III). The use of an *if*-clause as sentence adverb is especially frequent: 'Their (i.e., loose colloquialisms) employment, *if high example counts for anything*, is a standard habit of the language' (H. L. Mencken, *The American Language*, VI). The subordinate clause has its sentence adverb like a principal proposition: 'I do not approve of what *I assume* will be the trend of your education.'

The English negative is a sentence adverb and, like other sentence adverbs, is normally weakly stressed and stands between subject and predicate: 'I *never* dó such things.' In case there is an auxiliary of any kind in the sentence the negative *not* or *n't*, like other sentence adverbs, stands before the stressed verbal form: 'He has*n't* cóme yet.' 'He does*n't* dó such things.' 'He ca*n't* dó such things.' The perfect infinitive without *to* is usually considered as a unit, so that the negative stands before the unaccented tense auxiliary of the infinitive: 'He can *scarcely have arrived* by this time.' 'He can *scarcely have béen there.*' 'He had spoken late, but he need *not have spóken* at all.' 'You need *not have tóld* me that.' Other sentence adverbs than negatives may stand before the unaccented tense auxiliary, or, as so often elsewhere, before the accented verbal form, or, as in a simple tense, between subject and verb: 'He must *surely* have séen him,' or 'He must have *surely* séen him,' or 'He *surely* must have séen him.' In the passive, however, two participles, the one indicating the passive idea, the other the verbal meaning, usually form a unit, so that the sentence adverb cannot stand between them before the accented verbal form, but for the most part stands before the participial unit: 'He must *surely have been séen,*' or 'He *surely* must have been séen.' But even in the case of these participial units we must put the adverb between the participles before the stressed verbal form wherever the adverb indicates the manner or degree of the verbal activity: 'He must undoubtedly have *been gróssly decéived.*' 'She must undoubtedly have *been sevérely tríed.*' As in these examples, there are often two adverbs, one standing before the passive auxiliary, the other, an adverb of manner or degree, standing before the stressed verbal form.

In abridged infinitival or participial clauses the subject is usually understood, so that the negative stands before the verbal form: 'He promises *not to do it again,*' or now sometimes with split infinitive (**49** 2), since there is a tendency here to place the sentence adverb immediately before the stressed verb, as in the full clause: 'There can be nothing to — to *nót tálk* about between you and me, dear mother' (De Morgan, *Alice-for-Short*, Ch. XXXV), as in 'There can be nothing between you and me, dear mother, that we can *nót tálk* about.' '[I] Always figured somebody'd come along with the brains to *not léave* education to a lot of bookworms' (Sinclair Lewis, *Babbitt*, Ch. II), as in 'I always figured that somebody would come along with enough brains that he would *not léave* education to a lot of bookworms.' The drift of present usage is evidently in this new direction, though it is not yet so strong as in the case of other sentence adverbs, where it has become very strong. Compare **49** 2. In the compound form of the infinitive the negative usually stands before *to*, or now sometimes in accordance with the new drift, after the auxiliary, as in the full clause: 'He claims *not* (or *never*) *to have seen her before*,' or sometimes *to have not* (or *never*) *seen her before*, as in 'He claims *that he has not* (or *never*) *seen her before*.' Other sentence adverbs than negatives stand either before *to* or more commonly after the auxiliary before the accented verbal form, as so often elsewhere. For examples see **49** 2 *c.*

In abridged participial clauses, *not* stands before the present participle: '*Not knowing the road*, I lost my way.' When the participle is in a compound form, the *not* regularly stands before the compound as it does before the simple form, but other sentence adverbs stand either after or before the auxiliary, as in the full clause: '*Not having seen him for a long time*, I didn't recognize him,' but either '*Having never seen him before*, or less commonly *Never having seen him before*, I, of course, didn't recognize him,' just as we can say either '*As I had never seen him before*, or less commonly *As I never had seen him before*, I, of course, didn't recognize him.'

Of course, the negative, like other sentence adverbs, is strongly stressed when the statement as a whole is stressed: 'I *néver* did it.' 'I have *nót* done it.' The auxiliary takes the stress where *not* has merged into it: 'I *dídn't* do it.' 'I *cán't* do it.'

The adverb *enough* was originally the adverbial accusative (**16** 4 *a*) of the indefinite pronoun *enough* and stood, as a sentence adverb, at the end of the sentence, the most common position of the sentence adverb in oldest English. Although in Old English it sometimes preceded an adjective or adverb, like an ordinary adverb, it now, as originally, follows it: 'It is hot *enough*.'

In questions introduced by a strongly stressed interrogative word, the interrogative is often followed by a sentence adverb, an expression denoting surprise, impatience, or displeasure, usually *in the world*, *on earth*, and in British colloquial speech often also *ever*, which is often improperly written as a part of the preceding interrogative: 'What *in the world* did he want?' or in British English also '*Whatever* (or better *What ever*) did he want?' 'Where *in the world* did he go?' or in British English also '*Wherever* (or better *Where ever*) did he go?' 'Why *on earth* didn't you say so?' or in British English also '*Whyever* (or better *Why ever*) didn't you say so?' *Ever* is sometimes used in American English: '*Whatever* has got into you?' (Hal G. Evarts, *Saturday Evening Post*, May 28, 1927, p. 9). 'Why, there's Ab Knuckles! What next? *However* did anybody get him to a party?' (C. B. Kelland, *Saturday Evening Post*, Feb. 26, 1927, p. 72), or more commonly 'How did anybody *ever* get him to a party?' 'Surely you'll admit

that you like having your own bath.' — '*Whoever* said I didn't?'
(Willa Cather, *The Professor's House*, p. 34).

b. DISTINGUISHING ADVERBS. Although the negative is a sentence adverb and as such normally stands before the verbal form, it is sometimes felt as a distinguishing adverb, i.e., as belonging to some particular word, phrase, or clause which is prominent in the situation as a whole, and is then placed immediately before this word, phrase, or clause: '*Hé* did it, not *Í*.' 'He hit *mé*, not *hím*.' 'He did it for the love of the cause, not *for personal gáin*.' 'I did it because I felt it to be my duty, not *because I was compélled to do it*.'

A number of sentence adverbs and conjunctive (**19** 1) adverbs, namely, *only, solely, simply, merely, just, particularly, especially, even, also, at least, exactly* (or *precisely*), etc., are often, like *not*, used as distinguishing adverbs, and are then placed immediately before the word, phrase, or clause which they distinguish; sometimes, however, differing from *not*, are placed after a single word which they distinguish: 'All were there, *only Jóhn* (or *Jóhn only*) was missing.' 'If you want it, you have *only to say so*.' 'I have been influenced *sólely by this consideration*.' 'I came *just to see you*.' 'I did it *simply* (or *merely*) *because I felt it to be my duty*.' 'Almost all of them arrived on time, *even Jóhn*' (or *Jóhn even*). 'William thinks so, *also Jóhn*' (or *Jóhn also*). 'None of them will go; *at least Jóhn* (or *Jóhn at least*) will not.' '*Whát exactly* (or *Exactly whát*) paganism was we shall never know.' 'We never knew *precisely whý* he left.'

Two distinguishing adverbs, *alone* (= *only*) and *too* (= *also*), regularly follow the emphatic word: '*Jóhn alone* knows about it.' '*Í, too*, have troubles.'

The sentence adverb *quite* (= *truly*), like a distinguishing adverb, is often used before another word than a predicate. Here it indicates that the circumstances are such as to justify the use of the word before which it stands: 'It took place at *quite* an *éarly* hour.' 'A ship sailing northwards passes *quite súddenly* from cold into hot water' (Herschel, *Essays*, 342). '*Quite a crówd* had already gathered about him.' 'There were *quite a féw* there' (ironic popular American = 'There were *quite a large númber* there'). 'He knows *quite a líttle* about it' (ironic popular American = 'He knows *quite a good déal* about it').

c. USE OF '*ONLY*.' Of the adverbs discussed here *only* has the greatest freedom of position, since as a distinguishing adverb it may stand before or after any word that is to be distinguished, and as a sentence adverb it may stand in the usual position of the sentence adverb, i.e., before a stressed verb or a stressed predicate noun, adjective, participle, or infinitive: '*Only* Jóhn passed in Latin.' 'John passed *only* in Látin.' 'He *ónly* (sentence adverb = *barely*) pássed in Latin.' 'He stayed *only* a wéek' (or a wéek *only*), but to emphasize the predicate, 'He *only* (sentence adverb) stáyed a week.' 'He is *only* wóunded, not kílled.' 'We *only* belíeve as deep as we líve' (Emerson, *Art*). 'The mind that lies fallow but a single day sprouts up in follies that are *ónly* to be kílled by constant and assiduous culture' (Addison). As in the last four examples *only* regularly stands before a stressed verb or a stressed predicate participle or infinitive. The stressing of the verb or the predicate participle or infinitive indicates that the attention is called to the basic element in the sentence, not to some detail, and suggests the placing of *only* as a sentence modifier before the basic element of the statement, the verb, or the predicate participle or infinitive. Where the predicate is a stressed adjective, we may put *ónly too* or *áll too* before it when we desire to express our regret at having to acknowledge the truth of the statement: 'The report proved *ónly too* (or *áll too*) trúe.' But if we stress the predicate very heavily, much more heavily than *only too*, the form *only too* is not a sentence adverb but an intensifying adverb with the force of *exceedingly:* 'I shall be *only too* thánkful if you accept my invitation.'

d. HISTORICAL EXPLANATION OF THE POSITION OF 'NOT.' In oldest English, the negative was *ne*, which was often strengthened by *not* (originally the same as *nought*, from Old English *nowiht*, i.e., *not a whit*). As *ne* was weakly stressed, it later, in the fifteenth century, dropped out of common everyday speech, leaving to *not* the office of negative. In poetry *ne* lingered on in occasional use into the nineteenth century: 'Whilome in Albion's isle there dwelt a youth, Who *ne* in Virtue's ways did take delight' (Byron, *Childe Harold*, I, II, A.D. 1812). Originally, *ne* stood before, and *not* after, the verb, which explains the occasional position of *not* in poetry and choice prose after the verb, as in older English: 'pomp that fades *not*' (Wordsworth). In older English, of course, *ne* stood before the verb: 'pomp that *ne* fadeth *not*.' After *ne* had dropped out and *not* had thus become a sentence adverb, there naturally arose a tendency to place *not* before the verb, the usual place for sentence adverbs: 'They sweat, they blunder, they bounce and plunge in the Pulpit, but all is voyce and no substance: they deafe men's eares, but *not* edifie' (Thomas Nashe, *Christs Teares ouer Iervsalem*, Works, II, p. 123, A.D. 1593). 'It *not* appears to me that,' etc. (Shakespeare, *II Henry IV*, IV, I, 107). 'I *not* doubt t'effect All that you wish' (Ben Jonson, *Catiline*, I, I, 418, A.D. 1611). This form of negative statement did not spread, since there was something unnatural about it. As *not* usually had followed the finite form of the verb, and in the case of auxiliaries still maintained this position, as in 'He can*not* come,' 'He has *not* come,' it gradually became usual to employ instead of a simple verb the periphrastic form with the auxiliary *do*, placing *not* after the auxiliary as in the case of other auxiliaries: 'He does*n't* work.' Thus in all these examples *not*, as in older English, still in a formal sense stands *after* the finite verb; but as such auxiliaries are today not felt as true verbs, *not* in reality stands *before* the real verbal element, the part containing the verbal meaning, i.e., infinitive or participle, just as other sentence adverbs stand before infinitive or participle and just as older *ne* as a sentence adverb stood before the real verb. As explained in **6** A *d*, our ancestors had a free choice between 'He works' and 'He does work.' In negative statements, they finally chose for normal expression the auxiliary form, in order that *not*, like other sentence adverbs, might stand before the verb.

e. CONTRACTIONS OF 'NOT.' Since *not* is usually lightly stressed, like older *ne* and sentence adverbs in general, it naturally loses something of its form and often, thus reduced, becomes attached to the preceding auxiliary or copula as an enclitic: 'He *doesn't* like it,' 'they, I, you *don't* like it'; in popular and loose colloquial speech 'he *don't* like it.' 'He *isn't* rich,' 'we, you, they *aren't* rich.' As can be seen by the examples, there is in the literary language no contraction with *n't* after *am*. In the declarative form, however, we can contract *am* to *'m: 'I'm* not rich.' In interrogative form contraction does not take place here in the literary language at all. In colloquial speech *am I not?* or *am not I?* often becomes *ain't I?* or *aren't I?* — the latter regarded as choicer by many in England and by some in America: 'I'm such a catch, *ain't* I?' (A. Marshall, *Exton Manor*, Ch. V). 'Well, man alive, I'm bound to know, *aren't* I?' (Hutchinson, *If Winter Comes*, p. 101). '*Aren't* I silly to weep?' (Francis R. Bellamy, *The Balance*, Ch. XX). The first person singular form *aren't* is a leveled form, after the analogy of *we aren't, you aren't, they aren't*. Similarly, the first person singular *ain't* is after the analogy of *we ain't, you ain't, they ain't*, where *ain't* is corrupted from *aren't*. As the *r* in *aren't* is not pronounced in England before a consonant, we often find this form written *an't*, especially a little earlier in the period, as in Smollett and Dickens. Of course, the *r* is still silent in England, but it is now usually written. In Ireland the contraction *amn't* is sometimes used instead of *ain't* in the first person singular: '*Amn't* I after telling you she's a great help to her mother?' (Lennox Robinson, *The Whiteheaded Boy*, Act I,

p. 9). The tendency to level, as seen in the case of *ain't* in colloquial speech in the first person singular, is still stronger in popular speech where the general drift, as described in **8 I 1** *h*, is to disregard the grammatical relations and use one form for all persons and numbers: 'I don't, you don't, he don't, we don't,' etc.; 'I ain't (or an't), you ain't (or an't), he ain't (or an't), we ain't (or an't),' etc. In popular speech *ain't* is employed also for contractions of *not* with forms of *have*, but it is here a variant of *hain't* with the *h* dropped: 'I *ain't* (or *hain't*) got it, he *ain't* (or *hain't*) got it, we *ain't* (or *hain't*) got it' = 'I *haven't* got it,' etc. In Negro dialect *ain't* is often used instead of *don't:* 'Mus' be dey *ain't* know dis is pay-day' (Du Bose Heyward, *Porgy*, p. 184). Also used instead of *won't:* 'Stick tuh dem, an' you *ain't* git into no trouble' (*ib.*, p. 57). Sometimes *ain't* is used as a pure negative adverb = *not:* 'I might be *ain'* changed on de outside, but I sho is changed on de inside' (Julia Peterkin, *Scarlet Sister Mary*, Ch. XXVI).

As contractions are, in general, so common in colloquial speech, there is a tendency in a choice style to write the full form *not* instead of the common contractions. This is appropriate where the tone is dignified and stately. As *not* is a sentence adverb and is naturally weakly stressed, it ought not in ordinary prose to be inappropriate to write the form as we speak it, provided we employ the correct contractions, but convention often controls us more than our natural feeling, so that we often write out *not* in full where we contract it in the spoken language. Of course, we also in colloquial speech stress *not* strongly in emphatic statements, for we always have a keen sense for its meaning: 'I did nót do it.' The contracted forms first began to appear about 1660 and soon came into wide use.

3. **Negatives.** The usual negative now is *not*. 'He is *not* working.' 'He is *not* strong.' In Scotch and North English this negative has the form of *no* or *nae* (*ne*), both forms weakened to *na* when used enclitically after auxiliaries: 'There's *no* (= *not*) a window in it' (J. M. Barrie, *Tommy and Grizel*, Ch. V). 'But I'm *nae* (=*not*) sure that *ee* (*he*) *didna* (*did not*) for a' that' (G. Macdonald, *Alec Forbes*, Ch. LXVIII).

Notice the use of *not* in elliptical expressions: 'I hope [that it is] not [so].'

There is an older negative, *no* (Old English *nā*, from the older negative *ne* 'not' and *ā* 'ever'), originally an emphatic form (= *not at all*, *by no means*), which we still use; now, however, not as an adverb as originally, but as the equivalent of a sentence: 'Are you going tomorrow?' — '*No.*' It sometimes still has its original emphasis, but is normally without stress, as we now have no feeling for its original meaning.

This old emphatic form, now much reduced in force, is used also as a common adverb with the meaning of *not* in one common category, namely, as a modifier of a comparative: 'Mr. Buck, the tutor, was *no* better a scholar than many a fifth form boy.' 'He is *no* more to be trusted than you are.' 'He is *no* more an officer than I am.' 'I have *no* more to say.' 'The transaction is *no* less than a swindle.' 'There were *no* (or *not*) less than five hundred people present.'

The negative adverb *no* also occurs occasionally elsewhere in a few set expressions, where, however, *not* is now more common: 'Have I done it or *no?*' (Hardy, *Life's Little Ironies*, p. 139). 'It was a question of whether or *no* she were worth it' (Haggard, *She*, p. 159). 'She would go to London whether he liked it or *no*' (Mrs. H. Ward, *Fenwick's Career*, p. 172). In older English, also the form *non(e)* occurs here, so that it seems probable that *no* and *none* in such set expressions were originally the adjective *no* used substantively (**57** 1): ' "Wheþer ar þei Cristen," he seide, "or non?" ' (R. Brunne, *Chron. Wace*, 14909, A.D. 1330). ' "I will," she sayde, "do as ye councell me: Comforte or *no*" ' (*Generydes*, 2588, A.D. 1440).

In poetry and elevated language instead of *no* we sometimes use *nay*, of Danish (i.e., old Norse) origin. It is here employed to introduce a contradiction to a preceding statement: 'You do not care for me.' — '*Nay*, I do care for you.' In this use it often assumes positive force, since in taking back a preceding word or statement we often substitute in its stead a stronger expression: 'Hundreds, *nay* thousands, perished.'

The adverb *no* should be distinguished from the limiting adjective *no*, which is of somewhat different origin, as described in **57** 5 *b*: '*no* money, *no* patience.' *No* is used also as a noun, and as such has a plural: 'The *noes* have it.'

Also the accusative singular of the neuter pronoun *none* is used as an emphatic negative adverb before a comparative: 'He was *none* the worse for his fall.' See also 4 *a*, p. 144, and **57** 5 *b* (last par.).

a. DOUBLE NEGATION AND PLEONASTIC EXPRESSION WITH NEGATIVES. In older literary English, as in current popular speech, two or three negatives were felt as stronger than a single negative, on the same principle that we drive in two or three nails instead of one, feeling that they hold better than one: 'I *can't* see *no* wit in her' (Lamb in a letter to Coleridge in 1797). 'I *don't* know *nothing* about it' (current popular speech). Under Latin influence, we have come to feel that two negatives make an affirmative statement, although we still in an answer say *no, no,* to strengthen our negative reply. Even in the literary language, however, there is a survival of older usage after verbs like *doubt, wonder,* which are affirmative in form but negative in meaning. We sometimes still use the negative *but* after these words when preceded by a negative, not feeling that the two negatives make the statement affirmative without the help of *but,* so that *but* is really pleonastic: 'I do not doubt *but that* (now usually simple *that*) you are surprised.' 'I wouldn't wonder *but* (now usually suppressed) Hannah's up-stairs all the while, splitting her sides' (St. John Ervine, *John Ferguson,* Act II). A little earlier in the period the list of these verbs was larger. See **24** III for examples. Not feeling that *but* (= *only*) is a negative, we sometimes put *not* before it, so that here *not* is pleonastic: 'It will *not* take but a few moments to dispose of it' (Mr. Blanton, of Texas, in the House, Aug. 12, 1919). On the other hand, not feeling that *help* is negative with the force of *avoid,* we often say, 'I won't do any more *than I can* (instead of the correct *can't*) help,' after the analogy of *than I have to* or *than I must.*

    b. RHETORICAL QUESTION INSTEAD OF A NEGATIVE STATEMENT. A rhetorical question often replaces a negative statement: 'Would you do better if you were in my place?' = 'You would not do better, if you were in my place.' Compare **23** II 1 (last par.).

    4. Form of Simple Adverbs. Adverbs have in part no distinctive form, as in the case of *here, there, then, when, where, why, late, straight, far, near, close, quick, slow, fast, high, low, much, little, very, right, wrong, cheap, just, well,* etc.; in part they have the distinctive suffix *–ly,* as in *rapidly, diligently, hurriedly, powerfully,* etc.; also often in the case of some of the words in the first group, which have a form in *–ly* alongside of their simple form, as in *slowly, quickly, highly, rightly, cheaply,* etc. Sometimes the two forms are differentiated in meaning: 'I'll go as *high* as a hundred dollars,' but 'The wood is *highly* polished.' 'He aimed *higher,*' but 'We ought to value our privileges more *highly.*' 'He sat up *late,*' but 'He died *lately.*' 'He works *hard,*' but 'I could *hardly* hear him.' 'He lives *near* us, *nearer* to us,' but 'It is *nearly* done.' 'He is *real* (colloquial for *very*) good,' but 'He is *really* (sentence adverb) good.' 'The bird is now flying quite *low,*' but 'He bowed *lowly* before the duchess,' i.e., bowed humbly and respectfully. 'You know *jolly* (slang for *very*) well,' but 'He smiled *jollily.*' 'Speak *loud* and distinctly,' but 'He boasted *loudly* of his power.' With certain adverbs we use the simple form after the modified word and the form with *–ly* before it: 'He guessed *right,*' but

'He *rightly* guessed that it was safe.' 'He spelled the words *wrong*,' but 'the *wrongly* spelled words.' Earlier in the period the old simple form was often used where we now employ the form in *-ly*: 'to haue him stand in the raine till he was *through* (or *thorough*) wet' (Thomas Nashe, *The Vnfortvnate Traveller*, Works, II, p. 246, A.D. 1594), now '*thoroughly* wet'; but the old simple form is preserved in *thorough*bred, *thorough*going, etc. 'She is not *near* (now *nearly*) so small as I had expected' (Horace Walpole, *Letter to Miss Mary Berry*, Sept. 25, 1793). *Scarce* was widely used in early Modern English, but is now employed only in rather choice language, yielding to *scarcely* in normal speech.

In older English, many adverbs had the suffix *-e*, which distinguished them from the corresponding adjectives. In the fifteenth century, after this ending had disappeared, many adjectives and adverbs had the same form. For a long while there has been a tendency to distinguish the adverb from the adjective by giving it the suffix *-ly*, as indicated above. The old simple form, though often replaced by the new form in *-ly*, often remains firm before an adjective or participle: *líght yèllow*, *dárk blùe*, *déad drùnk*, *précious lìttle*, *míghty delìghtful*, *búrning hòt*, *réd hòt*, *stárk nàked*, *prétty brìght*; *néw làid* eggs, *módern bùilt* house, *fóreign bòrn* citizens, etc. These are in large measure modern formations, but they belong to the old group-word (**63**) type of expression, for which we still have a lively feeling. In the old group-word, the modifying word always precedes the governing word, so that the word-order of itself makes the grammatical relations clear and hence the lack of a distinctive adverbial ending is not keenly felt. But here, as also elsewhere, as described in **63**, distinctive grammatical forms are sometimes introduced: an *uncommon* or *uncommonly* fine fellow; *terrible* or *terribly* strong; an *exceeding* or *exceedingly* great joy; a *newly* married pair; the *newly* appointed chaplain, etc. We should distinguish between 'a *góod-nàtured* boy,' where the group-word *gòod náture* has been converted into a derivative adjective by means of the suffix *-ed*, and 'a *wéll behàved* boy,' where *behaved* is an adjective participle and *well* the modifying adverb. Similarly, we say 'a *hígh-tèmpered* man,' but '*híghly sèasoned* food.' In many cases we can construe a group of words according to either of these two types, hence we often find a difference of usage: *ill-mànnered*, 'the *mosl swéetly mànnered* gentleman alive' (Disraeli, *Endymion*, III, III, 25), but also *géntle-mànnered*, *símple-mànnered*. In both constructions the stress shifts to the second component in the predicate: 'He is *gòod-nátured*.' 'He is *wèll behàved*.'

On the other hand, after verbs, where the word-order is always different from that required in group-words, the tendency is to give the adverb its distinctive suffix: '*wíde*-òpen,' but 'He àdvertises *widely*'; '*tíght*-fìtting,' but 'He clàsped his hands *tíghtly* together.'

While in literary and good colloquial language the form with –*ly* is becoming ever more firmly fixed, loose colloquial and popular speech still clings tenaciously to the older type of expression without –*ly*, especially in American and Irish English: 'I wánted to do it *bad* (instead of the usual good colloquial form *badly*) enough, and if it was to do over again I wóuld' (Mark Twain, *Joan of Arc*, Book I, Ch. IV). 'He (a certain dog) isn't anyway *near* (instead of literary *nearly*) as full-blooded as Duke' (Tarkington, *Penrod Jashber*, Ch. I). 'I beat them *easy*' (instead of the literary form *easily*), but also in good English with the short form in 'to take it *easy*' and 'to let one off *easy*.' This conservative tendency in colloquial and popular speech to employ the old type is especially noticeable in the case of sentence adverbs (see 2 *a*, p. 130), where in the literary language the form with –*ly* is most firmly established: 'It *sure* (in the literary language *surely*) will help.'

In older English, –*ly* was often added to adverbs formed from adjectives in –*ly*, and this older usage survives in a few adverbs: *holily*, *jollily* (see 4, p. 140), *sillily*, *wilily*. In general, –*ly* is now avoided here as awkward, although elsewhere there is a strong tendency toward it on account of its distinctiveness. The present tendency in this particular group is to employ the adjective also as an adverb, as in *early*, *daily*, *hourly*, *friendly*, *kindly*, *only*, etc. In many other words, however, we avoid such adverbs, as we feel their lack of distinctive form.

It is common to form an adverb out of a compound adjective provided the final element in the compound is an adjective form: *world-wide*, adv. *world-widely*; *high-minded*, adv. *high-mindedly*. If the final element is a noun we must employ the compound adjective also as an adverb: 'a *first-rate* (adj.) machine.' 'I am getting along *first-rate*' (adv.).

a. GENITIVE, DATIVE, AND ACCUSATIVE USED ADVERBIALLY. In oldest English, nouns in the genitive, dative, and accusative were often used adverbially. The old adverbial genitive survives in a few nouns and adverbs in the literary language and in a much larger number in popular speech: must *needs*, *nowadays*, *once* (i.e., *ones*, from *one*), *twice* (formerly *twyes*), *thrice*, *unawares*, *afterward* (especially in America) or *afterwards*, *backward* or *backwards*, *forward* or *forwards*, *onward* or less commonly *onwards*, *seaward* or *seawards*, *sideways*, *always*, etc.; in popular speech *anywheres*, *somewheres*, *nowheres*, etc., instead of the literary forms *anywhere, somewhere, nowhere,* etc.   In colloquial speech it is still common in a few nouns to indicate repeated occurrence, but it is now felt as an accusative plural: 'returning *nights* to his home' (F. J. Mather, *Chaucer's Prologue,* p. vii). 'Farmer Spurrier could see the plow at work before he got out of bed *mornings*' (H. C. O'Neill, *Told in the Dimpses,* p. 28). After the analogy of such common expressions we now often use this plural accusative: 'The museum is open *Sundays*' (or *on Sundays*). The modern prepositional genitive is used in 'of a morning,' 'of an evening,' 'of a Sunday afternoon,' 'of late years,' 'of rainy afternoons,' etc. In popular speech an excrescent *t* is often added to the genitive form *once: wunst.* While the literary language rejects the genitive form with excrescent *t* here, it has adopted it in the case of *amongst* and *whilst,* adverbial genitive forms now used alongside of *among* and *while* as preposition and subordinate conjunction.

The old dative plural survives in *whilom* (= *formerly*), now only used in poetry or archaic language. It is the old dative plural form of the noun *while,* used adverbially: '*Whilom* she was a daughter of Locrine' (Milton, *Comus,* 827). It is sometimes, like certain other adverbs, used also as an adjective: 'his *whilom* associates.'

The old adverbial accusative of extent is well preserved in the case of nouns: 'They remained *a long while, three years.*' 'It is *a long way* off.' 'He went *the full length.*' 'That went *a long way* toward remedying the evil.' 'He walked *two miles.*' 'He will not swerve a hair's *breadth* from the truth.' 'The lake is *three miles* wide.' 'He is *fourteen years* old.' 'The garden is *one hundred and seventy feet* long.' 'He towers *head* and *shoulders* above his contemporaries.' 'The sober sense of the community are *heart* and *soul* with the Chief of Police in his crusade.' 'Vivisection must be abolished *root* and *branch.*' In early Modern English, the genitive was not infrequently used here instead of the accusative, and this older usage still lingers in popular speech, which here, as in the first paragraph, is quite fond of the genitive as a more distinctive form: 'He'd given up sea-faring And moved quite *a way's* inland' (Amy Lowell, *East Wind,* p. 188, A.D. 1926). 'It seems *a long ways* off.'

The adverbial accusative of extent is common also in the case of indefinite pronouns, especially *a bit, every bit, a lot, lots, a sight* (colloquial and popular), and *whatever* in the meaning *at all,* also with other indefinites when used in connection with *too* or a comparative: 'Wait *a bit.*' 'I am *every bit* as good as you.' 'I am not *a bit* tired.' 'I have *a lot* (or *lots*) more to tell you.' 'I have

lots more things to show her' (Clyde Fitch, *Letter*, Feb. 10, 1903).
'It is *a long sight* better' (*Concise Oxford Dictionary*), or more
commonly '*a darn sight* better.' 'There is no doubt *whatever*.'
'Is there any chance *whatever?*' 'I cannot see anyone *whatever*.'
'No one *whatever* would have anything to do with him.' '*What*
(= *to what extent* or *in what way*) is he the better for it?' 'The
help came *none* too soon.' 'It is *much* too large.' 'The tri-
umphant people haven't *any* too much food' (*Westminster Gazette*, No. 7069, 6*a*). 'He is *none* the worse for his fall.' 'The
baby is dying slowly but *none* the less surely.' 'He is resting *all*
the better for it.' 'Is he resting *any* the better for it?' 'Is he resting *any* better today?' 'I began to think that it was of no use
crying *any* more.' 'She is not *any* less beautiful today than she
has ever been.' 'Isn't it *any* later than that?' or in American
colloquial speech also: 'Is that *all* the later it is?' '*Nothing*
daunted, he began again.' 'He is *a little* better.' 'He is *much*
better, *much* taller.' *Much* and *little* are often used outside of the
comparative: 'I don't care *much* about it.' 'I care *little* about it.'
Much is often used sarcastically: '*Much* (= *not at all*) you care
about my feelings!'

In general, *any*, *some*, *none*, except with *too* and the comparative, are now not so common in England as earlier in the period,
but in American colloquial speech there is still a great fondness
for these forms: 'I slept *none* that night,' or 'I didn't sleep *any*
that night.' 'If our readers are *any* like ourselves, we think they
cannot help laughing' (*Analectic Magazine* [Phila.], IX, 437,
A.D. 1817). 'A tall fellow . . . stammers *some* in his speech'
(runaway advertisement in *Mass. Spy*, April 28, 1785). 'I walk
some every day.' This usage survives also in Scotland: 'You
will quarrel *nane* with Captain Cleveland' (Scott, *Pirate*,
Ch. XVIII). 'Having slept scarcely *any* all the night' (Hugh
Miller, *Scenes and Legends*, XXX, 450). Scotch influence has
strengthened the conservative American tendency here. It occasionally occurs in English writers after verbs: 'He may walk *some*,
perhaps — not much' (Dickens in Forster's *Life*, III, IV). In
American slang *some* often assumes strong intensive force: 'The
papers will make it *some* hot for you' (Robert Herrick, *Memoirs
of an American Citizen*, p. 310).

Similarly, the accusative of the comparatives *more*, *less*, and
the superlatives *most*, *the most*, *least*, *the least* are much used
adverbially: 'If indiscretion be a sign of love, you are *the most*
a lover of anybody that I know' (Congreve, *Love for Love*, I, II,
354, A.D. 1695); now more commonly '*the most* a lover of all
that I know,' or '*more* a lover than any other person that I know.'

The old adverbial accusative of goal (**11** 2) after verbs of motion is preserved in *home:* 'He went *home*.' 'They brought the charge *home* to him.' 'I was *home* by six.' In the last example the verb of motion is not expressed, but the idea of motion is implied. In popular speech *home* is improperly used where there is no idea of motion implied: 'Jane was *home* (for literary *at home*) all last week.' In compounds, however, *home* is used also in the literary language where there is no idea of motion implied: *home-made, home-grown, home-brewed*, etc. *Home* is here an old uninflected locative (**62,** next to last par.) meaning *at home*. This type of expression has come down to us from the prehistoric period.

The accusative of definite and indefinite time is common: 'I go to Europe *every two years*.' 'The money was paid *the following day*.' '*First thing* in the morning he smokes a cigarette' (Krapp, *A Comprehensive Guide to Good English*). 'He often goes round *the last thing* to make sure that all is right' (*Routledge's Every Boy's Annual*). 'I met him *one day* on the street.' Also the accusative of way: 'Step *this way*, please!' 'I will take you *another way*.' Also the accusative of price: 'This hat cost *five dollars*.'

The adverbial accusative construction has replaced others less common and even some once common, since we now feel that the accusative is the natural case form of a noun that completes the meaning of the verb. It is now much used to denote manner: 'He came *full speed*.' 'The blindfolded man ran *full tilt* into the fence.' 'Have it *your own way*.' 'The windows of the tower face *both ways*.' 'Having sampled America [*in*] *that way*, Europe believes and trusts America' (Woodrow Wilson, July 4, 1919). 'She ran her fingers comb *fashion* through her hair.' 'Let us go *shares, halves!*' 'I came in and went to bed *the same* as usual.' 'Then why do you come *your frowning high and mighty airs* with me?' (William Heyliger, *American Boy*, Sept., 1927, p. 34). 'You can't come *it* with me.' In colloquial speech *sure thing* is often used as an intensive form of colloquial *sure* (= literary *surely*): 'Now that you boys know what the expedition is going to face are you still anxious to go along?'—'*Sure thing*' (Victor Appleton, *Don Sturdy in Lion Land*, Ch. IV). Also to indicate time, where in more careful language we find a preposition: '*What* (or *at what*) time do you go?' Also to indicate place in certain set expressions, but rarely with a single unmodified noun: 'He struck me on the head,' but 'He smote them *hip* and *thigh*.' 'Bind them *hand* and *foot!*' In the concrete language of popular speech the adverbial accusative of a modified noun is often used instead of an adverb: 'I looked *every place* (instead of literary *everywhere*) for it.' '*What place* (instead of literary *where*) would we run?' (Synge, *The Well of the Saints*, Act III).

In many distributive expressions, the noun following *a* is now construed as an adverbial accusative of extent, but the *a*, though now felt as an indefinite article, is in fact the reduced form of the preposition *on:* 'I visit him twice *a year.*' 'A robin frequently raises two broods *a season.*' This construction was originally confined to expressions of time, as in these examples, but it now has much wider boundaries: 'His terms are a penny *a line.*' 'She asks five dollars *a lesson.*' 'I paid six dollars *a pair* for my shoes.' The definite article is sometimes used here instead of the indefinite: 'She sold her corn at ten shillings *the bushel*' (Winthrop, *Journal*, April 27, 1631). 'Wheat was at twenty shillings *the quarter*' (Macaulay, *History*, I, Ch. III). 'Five cents *the copy*' (*The Saturday Evening Post*, Aug. 8, 1925). 'How much is salmon *the can* now?' (Zona Gale, *Miss Lulu Bett*, Ch. I). We now feel *can* in the last example as an accusative of extent; but, perhaps originally, it was a nominative, an appositive to *salmon*. Most of these expressions, except those indicating time, may have originated in this way.

b. 'THIS' AND 'THAT' USED ADVERBIALLY. In the fifteenth century the principle of employing the accusative of indefinite pronouns adverbially to indicate extent or degree was extended to the definite pronouns *this* and *that:* '*This* (or *that* or *thus* or *so*) much I hold to be true.' This usage is best established in the case of '*this* much' and '*that* much,' but in colloquial language it has spread much farther: 'I've never been *this* sick before.' 'He didn't get home until after one o'clock, and his mother told him if he ever came home *that* late again she would punish him severely.' On account of the accuracy of expression here adverbial *this* and *that* are sometimes employed in the literary language, in spite of the protests of grammarians: 'Oh, Mimo! how could you let him sit on the grass! Zara exclaimed reproachfully, when he got *this* far' (Elinor Glyn, *The Reason Why*, Ch. XV). 'I didn't think he was *that* young' (Jack London, *Martin Eden*, I, Ch. II). Also used like *so*, pointing to a following clause of result: 'I'm *that* hungry, I could eat a dog' (Hall Caine, *The Woman Thou Gavest Me*, Ch. IV). Quite commonly in popular speech: 'I was just *that* pleased I set down an' bust out cryin'' (Alice Hegan Rice, *Mrs. Wiggs of the Cabbage Patch*, Ch. VII).

The demonstrative *that* is thus often used adverbially, but the demonstrative *such*, which has a somewhat similar meaning, always remains an adjective, although often classed as an adverb.

That it is an attributive adjective when it stands before a descriptive adjective is shown by the fact that it can never be used when there is no noun after the descriptive adjective, i.e., when the descriptive adjective is used predicatively: '*such* severe weather,' but not 'The weather is *such* severe.'

c. ADVERBIAL USE OF 'THE.' The old neuter instrumental case of the determinative and demonstrative *that* still survives in the form of *the* in two common constructions: (1) In clauses of degree expressing proportionate agreement: 'This stone gets *the* harder *the* longer it is exposed to the weather.' See **29** 1 A b for a more detailed description of this construction. (2) As a determinative adverb of cause standing before a comparative, indicating cause, however, in only a formal way, pointing forward to a following clause or phrase of cause which contains the real cause: 'His unkindness hurt me all *the* more *because I had been previously so kind to him*' (or *because of my previous kindness to him*). 'The indications of inward disturbance moved Archer *the* more *that he too felt that the Mingotts* (name) *had gone a little too far*' (Edith Wharton, *The Age of Innocence*, Ch. V). 'I think a little *the* worse of him *on this account*.' 'She clung *the* more fiercely to her father *for having lost her lover*.' The cause is often not thus formally expressed in a clause or phrase of cause but implied in something that has preceded: '*Sir Arthur looked sternly at her*. Her head only dropped *the* lower.' '*If she were silent* there was one listener *the* more.' Compare **30** a.

5. **Comparison of Adverbs:**

a. RELATIVE COMPARISON. Adverbs are compared much as adjectives, as described in **54–55**. A few monosyllabic adverbs add *–er* in the comparative and *–est* in the superlative: *fast, faster, fastest*. 'He climbed *higher*.' 'He lives *nearer* us.' 'Come up *closer* to the fire.' 'John worked *hardest*.' 'He couldn't speak *finer* if he wanted to borrow' (George Eliot). 'I can't stay *longer*.' 'I would *sooner* die than do it.' Also the dissyllabics, *often, easy, early*, are compared by means of endings: 'He is absent *oftener* than is necessary.' '*Easier* said than done.' 'You ought to have told me *earlier*.'

Earlier in the period, terminational comparison was often used where we now employ *more* and *most*: 'There is almost no man but he sees *clearlier and sharper* (now *more clearly and sharply*) the vices in a speaker then (now *than*) the vertues' (Ben Jonson, *Discoveries*, p. 19, A.D. 1641).

Most adverbs are now compared by means of *more, most* and *less, least: rapidly, móre rapidly, móst rapidly; rapidly, léss rapidly, léast rapidly.*

aa. Irregularities. A few irregularities in the form occur, corresponding closely to those found in adjectives:

well	better	best
ill, illy (obs.), badly	worse	worst
much	more	most
little	less	least
near, nigh (**54** *a aa*)	nearer, nigher	nearest, nighest, next
far	farther, further	farthest, furthest
late	later	latest, last
	rather (comparative	
	of obs. *rathe,* 'soon')	

One of the outstanding features of popular speech is the use of *good* for *well:* 'I don't hear *good*' (instead of *well*).

bb. Newer Forms of Expression. Besides the normal usage described on page 147 there is another which is quite common in colloquial speech and occurs sometimes in the literary language. The superlative is formed by employing the adverbial neuter accusative of the noun made from the adjective superlative preceded by the definite article: 'All good and wise Men certainly take care To help themselves and families *the first*' (Robert Rogers, *Ponteach,* I, IV, A.D. 1776). 'I am going . . . to Havre, whence I shall get *the quickest* to Southampton' (Charlotte Smith, *Emmeline,* IV, 55, A.D. 1788). 'Of all my books I like this *the best*' (Dickens, *David Copperfield,* Preface). 'He was the greatest patriot in their eyes who brawled *the loudest* and who cared *the least* for decency' (*id., Martin Chuzzlewit,* Ch. XVI). 'It is impossible to say whose eyes would be *the widest* opened' (Henry Arthur Jones, *The Divine Gift,* Dedication, p. 49). 'My father liked this *the best*' (*Alfred, Lord Tennyson, A Memoir by His Son,* 3, 245). 'We are sure that those who have known Sommerset *the longest* will thoroughly enjoy Mr. Hutton's pages' (*Athenæum,* Dec. 28, 1912). 'Great souls are they who love *the most,* who breathe *the deepest* of heaven's air, and give of themselves most freely' (William Allen White, *A Certain Rich Man,* Ch. XXII). 'Of all the orders of men they fascinate me *the most*' (H. L. Mencken, *Prejudices,* Series III, p. 217).

This form is now spreading also to the comparative: 'He runs *the faster* (instead of the simple *faster*). 'This led him to consider which of them could be *the better* spared' (Dickens, *Martin Chuzzlewit,* Ch. XXXIII). 'I hardly know who was *the more* to blame for it' (L. M. Montgomery, *Anne of Avonlea,* Ch. XXIII). 'Ruth could not tell which she liked *the better*' (Lucy Fitch Perkins, *The Children's Yearbook,* p. 17).

In the case of the analytic form with *most, least, more, less,* this adverbial neuter accusative cannot be used at all. We often, however, add the adverbial ending *–ly* to the analytic adjective, superlative or comparative, preceded by the definite article, thus marking the form clearly as an adverb: 'If it be true that such meat as is *the most dangerously* earned is the sweetest' (Goldsmith, *Natural History*, VI, 82, A.D. 1774). 'It was difficult to say which of the young men seemed to regard her *the most tenderly*' (Thackeray, *Pendennis*, II, Ch. XX). 'Standing here between you the Englishman, so clever in your foolishness, and this Irishman, so foolish in his cleverness, I cannot in my ignorance be sure which of you is *the more deeply damned*' (George Bernard Shaw, *John Bull's Other Island*, Act IV).

In the relation of sentence adverbs the adverbial neuter accusative form of the superlative is replaced by an adverbial phrase, consisting of the preposition *at* and the noun made from the adjective superlative preceded by the definite article: 'I cannot hear from Dick *at the earliest* before Tuesday' (Mrs. Alexander, *A Life Interest*, II, Ch. XVIII), or '*At the earliest* I can't hear from Dick before Tuesday.'

When it is not the actions of different persons that are compared but the actions of one and the same person at different times and under different circumstances, we employ the adverbial neuter accusative of the noun made from the adjective superlative preceded by a possessive adjective: 'Two women shrieked *their loudest*' (Thackeray, *Pendennis*, II, Ch. XXXVIII). 'Carver smiled *his pleasantest*' (R. D. Blackmore, *Lorna Doone*, Ch. XXVIII). An adverbial phrase with the preposition *at* is sometimes used instead of the adverbial accusative: 'He led me in a courtly manner, stepping *at his tallest*, to an open place beside the water' (*ib.*, Ch. XXI). In the relation of sentence adverb this prepositional phrase form is quite common and freely used both with the simple and the analytic superlative, especially the latter: 'Even at *his ungainliest and his most wilful*, Mr. Thompson sins still in the grand manner' (*Academy*, April 14, 1894, 303). 'Nature *at her most unadorned* never takes that air of nakedness which a great open unabashed window throws upon the landscape' (*Atlantic Monthly*, March, 1887, 324).

b. ABSOLUTE SUPERLATIVE. This superlative of the adverb is formed from the absolute superlative of the adjective (**54** 2 *a*): 'Mary's mother is *a most béautiful woman*' and 'Mary's mother sings *most béautifully*.'

The absolute superlative is sometimes formed by employing the adverbial neuter accusative of the noun made from the adjective superlative preceded by the definite article: 'I do not *the léast* mind it' (*Alfred, Lord Tennyson, A Memoir by His Son*, 4, 72). 'It does not matter *the léast*' (Florence Montgomery, *Misunderstood*, Ch. IV).

Instead of this form we often use a prepositional phrase containing a simple superlative of an adjective in attributive use, standing before a noun or the simple superlative used as a noun and preceded by the definite article: 'The letter was written *in the kindest spírit.*' 'That does not concern me *in the léast.*' Compare **54** 2 *a* (3rd par.).

Instead of a superlative here we more commonly use a positive modified by *very, exceedingly, absolutely,* etc.: 'She sings *véry beautifully.*' In colloquial and popular language, the intensive adverbs, *awfully, dreadfully, terribly,* etc., are common, sometimes without the suffix *–ly* before an adverb: 'The work is moving *awfully slow.*' 'I lived *mighty comfortably.*'

To express an absolutely high degree of activity in connection with a verb, we place *very* before an adverb of degree, such as *much, greatly,* etc.: 'He is suffering *very much.*' To express an absolutely high degree of a quality, we place *very* before the positive of the adjective: '*very sick, very pleasing, a very distressed* look.' But instead of saying 'I was *very much pleased, very greatly distressed,*' many incorrectly say 'I was *very pleased, very distressed,*' feeling *pleased* and *distressed* as adjective rather than as verbal forms, which they are. Similarly, we should use *too much, too greatly* before verbal forms, not simple *too:* 'I was *too much* (or *too greatly*) discouraged by this failure to try again.'

INDEPENDENT ELEMENTS

17. Independent elements are words, phrases, or clauses which are not related grammatically to other parts of the sentence, or which stand all alone without sustaining any grammatical relation to some word understood. A historical study of these words shows that some of them were originally dependent. See 3 A, p. 152.

1. Interjections. The simplest interjections, such as *oh!* (usually *O* when not followed by a punctuation mark), *ouch!* belong to the oldest forms of spoken language and represent the most primitive type of sentence. Compare 2 *a*, p. 1. The large number of interjections now in use shows that they are as useful in modern life as in primitive times; indeed more useful, more needed, for the range of feeling is wider and the desire for varied expression greater: *ah!* (surprise or satisfaction), *bah!* or *pooh!* (disdain), *botheration!* (vexation), *bravo!* (approving, encouraging), *goody!* (joy), *alas!* (literary form expressing disappointment, grief) or *dear me!* or *oh, dear me!* (colloquial), *gee whillikers!* (surprise), *jumping geraniums!* (vexation, surprise), *why!* (expressing discovery, objection, hesitancy, protest at the simplicity of a question), *well!* (expressing astonishment, relief, concession, resumption of talk), etc.

They are often embodied in modern sentences, without any grammatical relations to the other words, but imparting a distinct shade of meaning to the sentence as a whole: '*Oh,* when will he come?'

The accusative is found in a few exclamations: '*Dear me!*' '*Unhappy me!*' Compare *f,* p. 6.

2. **Direct Address.** The name of a person who is called is often spoken alone without other words. Like interjections, such names are independent sentences of a primitive type, which, though a single word, can in connection with the situation and an appropriate accent convey a thought, as in *John!* spoken in loud tone and prolonged vowel to call him into the house, or *John!* spoken quickly with a short vowel and angry tone when we scold him. They are also often inserted in a modern sentence, without grammatical relation to the other words, but serving the useful purpose of arousing the attention of someone: '*John,* I've brought something home for you.' Originally and still in the classical languages of antiquity, nouns thus used in direct address stood in a special case called the vocative. Later, the nominative was used for this purpose; always so in English.

3. **Absolute Nominative.** An absolute nominative, i.e., a nominative without grammatical relations to the principal proposition, is often used in English. There are four groups:

A. IN ADVERBIAL CLAUSES: '*My task completed* (= *after my task was completed*), I went to bed.' '*Off we started, he remaining behind*' (= *while he remained behind*). The nominative here forms with the words with which it is connected a clause in which it is the subject, and a following participle, adjective, or noun is the predicate. The predicate here now usually follows the subject, but in older English and in poetry it often precedes: '*All loose her negligent attire, all loose her golden hair,* Hung Margaret o'er her slaughtered sire' (Scott, *Last Minstrel,* I, 10). This order is occasionally found in prose. See examples in *a, c,* and *d,* pp. 154, 155, 156. In one category, *f,* it is still employed regularly.

In Old English, the words in the adverbial clause stood in the dative, employed here in imitation of the Latin ablative. The Old English dative and the Latin ablative were in fact not used here absolutely since they stood in an adverbial relation to the principal verb, in that the words in the dative and ablative formed an adverbial clause in which the noun was subject, the accompanying participle, adjective, or noun was predicate, and the dative or ablative was the sign of subordination to the principal verb. This is the old appositional type of clause described in **6 B** *a,* where the predicate is placed as an appositive alongside of the subject without the use of a copula. Later, when the inflections lost their distinctive case forms, the dative, no longer distinguishable as such, was construed as a nominative, an absolute nominative, since its form does not indicate any relation to the principal proposition. In the literary language, irregularly here and there under foreign influence, the objective case of the personal pronouns continued for a long while to be used here as a nearer approach to the original constructions than the nominative, lingering on into the seventeenth century: '*Him* destroyed for whom all this was made, all this will soon follow' (Milton, *Paradise Lost*, IX, l. 130). On the other hand, the nominative of pronouns was used here in Middle English by Chaucer, and later this case gradually became established.

Originally, the adverbial clause was always without a copula, as was the rule for the old appositional type, but it is now often conformed to the modern type by the insertion of the copula between subject and predicate: 'He *being* absent, nothing could be done.' 'My task *being* completed, I shall go to bed.' 'Mr. Smith *being* the toastmaster, I think we may expect an enjoyable time.' The copula is now the rule where the predicate of the clause is an adjective, noun, adverb, or prepositional clause, but in older English the copula was lacking here: '*Thou away*, the very birds are mute' (Shakespeare).

The scope of the nominative absolute construction has been greatly enlarged by the development of strong verbal force in the participle. Originally, the perfect participle could be used here only when it denoted a state, i.e., when it had adjective force, as in the first example in A, p. 152. The perfect participle in this example has passive force, but with intransitives it had active force if it denoted a finished state resulting from the action: 'These obstacles *removed* and the right time *come* for action, we proceeded with energy.' Here we still have the original condition of things. The two participles, *removed*, now felt as a passive, and *come*, felt as an active, are without any formal signs of tense and voice. They still have their old adjective form. But the verbal force is now so strongly felt in participles that we often give them forms for tense and voice, and hence we may also say here: 'These obstacles *having been removed* and the right time for action *having come*, we proceeded with energy.' Although the old adjective form without a sign for tense or voice is still common when the participle has passive force, we now usually give it a tense sign when its force is active: 'Our luggage *arrived* (or now more commonly *having arrived*), I was dressed in a few minutes.' 'The clock *having struck*, we had to go.' We might construe *arrived* as an adjective, since it denotes a state, but *struck* has only verbal force. Thus we can clearly see that the participle has often developed into a verb with full verbal meaning, but as yet it has no forms for person, number, or mood, and though it can indicate tense and voice it hasn't as many tense forms as the finite verb. On the other hand, it is a terse and convenient construction for all practical purposes. For the most part, however, it has become established in the literary language better than in colloquial and popular speech.

Originally, the predicate here was a noun or an adjective, or a participle with adjective force. As we have just seen, the participle has often developed into a verb. The predicate may now be also an adverb or a prepositional phrase: 'The meal *over*, prayers were read by Miss Miller' (Charlotte Brontë, *Jane Eyre*, Ch. V). 'John being *away*, Henry had to do his work.' 'He went off, gun *in hand*.' In older English, and sometimes still, we find the prepositional infinitive used here as predicate: 'I send you today three fourths of the sum agreed upon between us, the rest *to follow* within a month.' In popular Irish, the infinitive has come into wide use here, so that it can be employed in every kind of subordinate clause, in conditional clauses, temporal clauses, etc.: (conditional clause) 'It would not be for honor *she to go without that much*' (Lady Gregory, *McDonough's Wife*). As explained in **19** 3, such clauses are often introduced by *and:* 'Little it will signify, *and we to be making clay* (temporal clause = *when we shall be moldering in the grave*), *who* was it dug a hole through the nettles or lifted down the sods over our heads' (*ib.*).

Instead of the nominative of a personal pronoun we often find here in popular and colloquial speech the accusative, as so often elsewhere in constructions where there is no finite verb, as described in **7** C *a:* 'It will be a very good match for me, m'm, *me* being an orphan girl' (H. G. Wells, *The Country of the Blind*, p. 16). 'You wouldn't expect anything else, would you, *me* (instead of the choicer *I*) being here like this, so suddenly, and talking face to face with you' (Arnold Bennett, *Sacred and Profane Love*, Act I, p. 25). 'It is strange he hasn't married with all his money, and *him* (instead of the choicer *he*) so fond of children' (Kate Douglas Wiggin, *Rebecca of Sunnybrook Farm*). The accusative subject here is, of course, of entirely different origin from the accusative subject in A (2nd par., p. 153).

The following relations are expressed by this absolute construction:

a. Time: '*My task having been finished*, I went to bed.' '*Tea over and the tray removed*, she again summoned us to the fire.'

In older English, a preposition was often placed before this construction to make the time relations clearer: 'I . . . commytted them vnto ward (prison) where they now do remayne *till your gracious pleasure knowen*' (Thomas Cromwell, *Letter to Henry VIII*, July 23, 1533). '*After my instructions dispatched,* I came away in haste' (Sir William Temple, *Letter,* Sept. 6, 1665). '*Upon the peace concluded between the Dutch and the same Indians,* she was restored to the Dutch governor' (Winthrop, *Journal,* July 5, 1646). Compare **20** 3 (next to last par.).

Sometimes, as often in older English, the predicate precedes the subject: 'She's to be married, *turned Michaelmas*' (George Eliot, *Silas Marner,* II, Ch. XVII). Compare *c.*

b. Cause: '*The rain having ruined my hat,* I had to get a new one.' Compare **30** *b* (4th par.).

The nominative absolute construction is often replaced here by a prepositional phrase: 'She is lonesome *with her husband so much away.*' Compare *a* (2nd par., p. 154) and **20** 3 (next to last par.).

c. Condition and Exception: 'And in a little while you will come back to me, will you not?' — 'Yes, dear, *God willing.*' '*Family for family,* a group of small-holders will absorb a much greater amount of industrial produce than the same number of persons, farmer and laborer, in normal proportions, in the large-farm system' (Noel Skelton, *The Quarterly Review,* July, 1925, p. 198). 'As yet few have done their full duty, *present company excepted.*'

There were formerly two word-orders in the absolute construction, not only here in the clause of condition and exception, but also in clauses of cause, time, concession, etc. The predicate could not only, as in the preceding examples, follow the subject (either a noun or a clause), but could also precede it. Clause of cause: 'Therefore *seene* (now *seeing;* see 4, p. 158) *you thinke it not gude to inuade,* my councell is that we campe still on the bordures' (Holinshed, *History of Scotland,* 309, A.D. 1577–1586). Clause of condition: 'It is enough, *considered how easy it is to copy out words from other Dictionaries*' (*Gentl. Mag.,* LVIII, 1153, A.D. 1778). It is still preserved in conditional clauses after a few participles, *except* (contracted from *excepted;* see also **31** 1 *d aa*), *granted, given, settled,* etc.: 'The whole kingdom, *except a small corner* (or *a small corner excepted*), was subjected to the Turkish yoke.' '*Granted then these correspondences* between Spenser on the one hand and Aristotle and his immediate successors on the other, we may pass to an inquiry into our poet's indebtedness to the tradition of Christian ethics that derives from the Greek philosopher' (H. S. V. Jones, *The Journal of English and Germanic Philology,* p. 288, July, 1926). '*Given the choice* of a fine home without a car and a modest one with a car, the latter will win' (William Ashdown in *Atlantic Monthly,* June, 1925). '*Given such a principle and such a method,* it follows that the function of any textbook is to remain in the background until needed' (D. D. Farrington, *The Essay.* Introduction). The subject may be a clause: '*Once settled that teachers must hold the views on all controversial matters that suit the particular community,* what persons of independent thought and action will become and remain teachers?' (American Federation of Teachers, July 11, 1925). This old word-order occurs occasionally also in *a,* p. 154, and *d,* p.156, and is even employed regularly in *f,* p. 157.

This old word-order survives also with the participles *during, pending, notwithstanding* and the adjective *save* (originally with the meaning 'safe,' 'intact,' 'excepted'), but the feeling for the original construction has disappeared, since the old word-order, no longer understood, has obscured the original grammatical relations. Since these words now stand before a noun or a pronoun, except sometimes *notwithstanding*, as in *this notwithstanding*, they are now often construed as prepositions; *during*, *pending*, *notwithstanding* regularly so, *save*, felt by some as a preposition, by others as a conjunction introducing an elliptical clause of exception, as described in **31**. Similarly, since the original construction is no longer understood, *except* is construed by some as a preposition, by others as a conjunction of exception; by still others as the imperative of the transitive verb *except*. See **31**.

When the subject is a clause, this old word-order is still employed also with the past participles *provided, given, granted* as predicate: 'I will come *provided that I have time.*' '*Given that he and they have a common object*, the one test that he must apply to them is as to their ability to help in achieving that object' (Theodore Roosevelt, *The Strenuous Life*, p. 74). '*Granted* (or *granting*) *that he had the best intentions*, his conduct was productive of great mischief.' As past participles do not now usually stand before a clause and hence are not recognized here as predicate in an absolute nominative construction, *provided that, given that, granted that* are for the most part felt as conjunctions introducing a subordinate clause, *provided that* and *given that* introducing a clause of condition, *granted that* introducing a clause of concession, as in the last example, or a clause of condition. Compare **31** and **32**.

The nominative absolute construction is often replaced in the clause of condition by a prepositional phrase: '*With conditions in every way favorable*, he might succeed.' Compare **20** 3 (next to last par.).

d. Attendant Circumstance: 'He entered upon the new enterprise cautiously, *his eyes wide-open*,' or here more commonly with a prepositional phrase *with wide-open eyes*, or *with eyes wide-open*.

Instead of an adjective element in the predicate relation we often find an adverb or a prepositional phrase or both, for adverbs and prepositional phrases are now quite commonly used as predicates: 'He sat at the table, *collar off, head down*, and *pen in position*, ready to begin the long letter' (or *with collar off, head down*, etc.). The absolute nominative here before a prepositional phrase is more common and natural than anywhere else: 'He lay on his back, *his knees in the air, his hands crossed behind his head*' (or *with his knees in the air*, etc.). The form with *with* was common in Old English and the older stages of all the Germanic languages and is still everywhere in common use. It is native English. Compare **20** 3 (next to last par.).

Especial attention is here called to the frequent use of the prepositional infinitive as predicate, which is only a particular application of the common employment of a prepositional phrase as predicate: 'He made a will bequeathing all he possessed to his niece, Mrs. Joyce, the interest for her sole use, the principal *to revert* to her eldest son after her death.' Sometimes the absolute nominative follows the prepositional phrase, i.e., contrary to ordinary usage the predicate of the clause precedes the subject of the clause: 'She stands before him with the dressing gown on her arm, *in her eyes an ódd lóok*' (Francis R. Bellamy, *The Balance*, Ch. IX). This word-order emphasizes the subject of the clause.

e. Manner Proper: 'He put on his socks *wrong side out.*' The absolute construction is often replaced here by a prepositional phrase: 'He put on his socks *with the wrong side out.*' Compare **20** 3 (next to last par.).

f. Concession, usually with the predicate of the clause before the subject: '*Granted the very best intentions,* his conduct was productive of great mischief.' '*Whatever the immediate outcome of the political and financial crisis in France,* it is certain that sooner or later the French people must deal with the results of their government's post-war policies in some drastic way' (*Chicago Tribune,* April 8, 1925). Compare **32** 2 (7th par., last example).

The absolute construction is often not possible in this category. It is then usually replaced by a prepositional phrase: '*Even with conditions quite unfavorable,* he would succeed.' The prepositional construction is often used even where the absolute construction is possible: 'Art is always art, poetry is always poetry, *in whatever form*' (Harold Williams, *Modern English Writers,* p. 296), or *whatever the form.*

B. NOMINATIVE ABSOLUTE IN SUBJECT CLAUSES. We often find, especially in colloquial speech, an absolute nominative in subject clauses, where the absolute nominative serves as the logical subject of the clause, and a participle, adjective, or prepositional phrase as the logical predicate: 'I pray you let me have the dayt of the marriage of my cosyn Hair and your daughter . . . and *ye thus doing* bynds me to doe you as great a pleasure' (*Plumpton Correspondence,* p. 215, A.D. 1515). 'I avoided him . . . my reasons are that *people seeing me speak to him* causes a great deal of teasing' (Swift, J., 493, quoted from Jespersen's *On Some Disputed Points,* S. P. E., Tract No. XXV). '*My two big sisters having now charge of things in the house* makes it much easier for Mother.' '*Three such rascals hanged in one day* is good work for society.' '*These difficulties overcome* makes the rest easy.' 'But *things being as they are* makes other things, which would have been different otherwise, different from what they would have been' (Sir Walter Raleigh, *Letter to John Sampson,* May 4, 1905). '*She and her sister both being sick* makes hard work for the rest of the family.' '*Women having the vote* reduces men's political power.' '*He saying* (present participle) *he is sorry* alters the case,' or more commonly '*His saying he is sorry* alters the case.' 'It is vilely unjust, *men closing two-thirds of the respectable careers to women!*' (Sir Harry Johnston, *Mrs. Warren's Daughter,* Ch. III). '*John and Henry rough-housing every night* is enough to destroy the strongest nerves.' '*Her hand in his* gave him strength to speak' (De Morgan, *Somehow Good*, Ch. XLVI). The principal verb here is, of course, always in the singular, since its subject is a clause. Other examples in **21** *e* (last 4 parr.). Compare **50** 3 (next to last par.).

In older English, the prepositional infinitive often serves here as predicate: 'If itt happen *the rent to be behynde*' (*Lincoln Diocese Documents*, p. 172, May 19, 1534). 'It happened immediately *Ferardo to retourne home*' (John Lyly, *Euphues*, Works, I, 242, A.D. 1578). '*I to bear this* is some burden' (Shakespeare, *Timon*, IV, III, 266). In popular Irish English the *to*-infinitive has come into wide use here as predicate: (speaking to his wife who lies dead before him) 'It is a bad case *you to have gone and to have left me*' (Lady Gregory, *McDonough's Wife*). 'A great wonder *he not to have come*, and this the fair day of Galway' (*ib.*). Compare **21** *e* (7th par.).

The subject clause in all these cases is of the old appositional type found in A and described in **6** B *a*. The predicate participle, prepositional phrase, or infinitive lies alongside of the subject, predicating without the aid of a copula.

C. ABSOLUTE NOMINATIVE IN PREDICATE CLAUSES: 'Cities are *man justifying himself to God*' (De Voto, *The Crooked Mile*, p. 405).

D. ABSOLUTE NOMINATIVE IN APPOSITIVE CLAUSES: 'Well, that is just our way, exactly — *one half of the administration always busy* getting the family into trouble, *the other half busy* getting it out again' (Mark Twain, *Letter to Mrs. Grover Cleveland*, Nov. 6, 1887).

4. **Absolute Participles.** In English, the predicate appositive construction with a present participle is a very common type of abridged adverbial clause: '*Taking* all things into consideration, I must regard my life as a happy one' = 'If I take all things into consideration, I must regard my life as a happy one.' The abridged participial clause usually has a subject which is identical with that of the principal proposition and as a predicate appositive expresses the adverbial relations of condition, cause, etc. A number of these clauses have in course of time become set adverbial elements of condition, cause, concession, etc., and are no longer thought of in connection with a definite subject any more than is any other adverb: '*Taking all things into consideration* (no longer an appositive to the subject but an adverbial element of condition), his life is a happy one.' If we try to analyze such a clause we can, of course, find no definite subject since it no longer has relations to the subject of the principal proposition. As it has no definite subject, we feel that it has an indefinite or general

subject = *if one takes all things into consideration.* 'There are certain proposals for future educational policy, which, *omitting details* (= *if one omits details*), may be summarized as follows' (*Manchester Guardian,* VII, 8, 150). '*Generally speaking* (= *if one may speak in a general sense*), boys are a nuisance.' 'They suffered little, *considering the exposure*' (or *that they were badly exposed*). '*Judging from the lengthy notes used by them,* the occasion was deemed of great importance.' The absolute present participle in such clauses of condition has become quite common where the subject is indefinite, as in these examples. Where the reference is indefinite, infinitive, gerund, and participle are often without an expressed subject. Compare **31** 2.

Because the subject is indefinite, the absolute participle is common in two other categories — in clauses of concession and in clauses of cause: '*Even granting the best intentions on his part* (or *that he had the best intentions;* concession), his conduct was productive of mischief.' 'The roads in Guernsey are good, which is not to be wondered at, *seeing the abundance of granite*' (or *that there is an abundance of granite;* cause). Compare **32** 2 and **30** *b* (3rd par.).

Like the present and the past participle in 3 A *c*, p. 155, the present participle here stands before a noun or a clause, but it has not, as in the case of these participles, developed into a preposition or a conjunction. There has been no change here in the word-order. It stands before its object like other present participles, and we still feel it as a present participle, only it is used absolutely without a subject expressed or understood. We feel that there is no need of a subject, as the reference is indefinite. Compare **32** 2 and **30** *b* (3rd par.).

In a number of cases an adjective present participle with its accusative or prepositional object often becomes detached from nouns and for convenience of expression is attached to a verb, thus becoming a preposition: 'He made me a communication *concerning* (adjective participle) my friend,' but 'He communicated with me *concerning* (preposition) my friend.' 'A peculiar effect *owing* (adjective participle) to the presence of light,' but '*Owing to* (preposition) unfavorable weather I was unable to proceed.' Thus have arisen also the prepositions *regarding, touching, including,* etc. Compare **62** (5th par.).

Thus the detached, 'dangling' or 'hanging,' participle has become established here and there in certain categories. It is found also in a few set expressions: 'The vote of condolence was passed *standing.*' '*Beginning* with the July number, it is intended materially to widen the scope of this Quarterly' (*Oxford and*

Cambridge Review). '*Talking of subscriptions,* here is one to which your lordship may affix your name.' In general, however, although occasionally found in good authors, it is felt as slovenly English in spite of its frequency in colloquial speech: '*Being not yet fully grown,* his trousers were too long.' In older English, the dangling participle was more widely used than today. It was employed even by careful writers where it cannot now be used: 'In their meals there is great silence and grauitie, *vsing* wine rather to ease the stomacke then (now *than*) to load it' (John Lyly, *Euphues and His England,* Works, II, p. 194, A.D. 1580).

CHAPTER IX

CLASSES OF SENTENCES

18. Sentences are divided according to their structure into three classes — simple, compound, and complex. A simple sentence contains but one independent proposition. A compound sentence contains two or more independent propositions. A complex sentence contains one independent proposition and one or more subordinate clauses. As the simple sentence has already been discussed there remain only the compound and the complex sentences to be treated.

THE COMPOUND SENTENCE
CONNECTIVES

19. The compound sentence consists of different independent propositions or members. These members may be two or more simple sentences, or one member may be a simple sentence and the others complex sentences, or there may be any combination of simple and complex sentences. These members are usually connected in the following ways:

1. **Coördinating Conjunctions.** The members are connected by coördinating conjunctions. The commonest are *and, or, but, for:* 'John is in the garden working *and* Mary is sitting at the window reading.' The members of a compound sentence, however, are not always thus complete, each with subject and finite verb, for a natural feeling for the economy of time and effort prompts us, wherever it is possible, to contract by employing a common verb for all members, so that the conjunctions connect only parts of like rank: not 'John is writing *and* Mary is writing,' but 'John *and* Mary are writing,' or 'John *and* Mary are both writing,'

or 'Both John *and* Mary are writing.' 'I bought paper, pen, *and* ink.' 'John writes fast *but* neatly.' Care must be taken in contracting when one subject is used with two different verbs each of which stands in a different compound tense: 'All the debts *have been* or *will be* paid,' or 'All the debts *have been* paid or *will be*,' but not 'All the debts *have* or *will be* paid.' Sentences containing these conjunctions, however, are often not an abridgment of two or more sentences, but a simple sentence with elements of equal rank, connected by a conjunction: 'The King *and* Queen are an amiable pair.' 'She mixed wine *and* oil together.'

Coördinating conjunctions also link together subordinate clauses of like rank: 'The judge said that the case was a difficult one *and* that he would reconsider his decision.'

Besides the pure connectives mentioned in 1, p. 161, there are many adverbs which perform not only the function of an adverb but also that of a conjunction. Coördinating conjunctions and conjunctive adverbs may be divided into the following classes:

a. Copulative, connecting two members and their meanings, the second member indicating an addition of equal importance, or, on the other hand, an advance in time and space, or an intensification, often coming in pairs, then called correlatives: *and; both — and; equally — and; alike — and; at once — and; not — nor* (or *neither*, or *and neither*); *not* (or *never*) *— not* (or *nor*) . . . *either* (or in older English, and still in popular speech, *neither*); a positive or negative proposition *— and nobody* (or *not*, or *nor*, or in older English, *ne* instead of *nor*) . . . *either* (or in older English, and still in popular speech, *neither*, or both words may be suppressed); in elliptical sentences where the subject or finite verb is expressed in only one member and understood elsewhere *no* (or *not*, or *never*) *— or* (or often *nor* when it is desired to call separate attention to what follows and thus emphasize); *not — no more*, employed when it is desired to repeat a preceding sentence with a new subject, usually with inverted word-order and a stressed subject after *no more*, but with normal word-order and a stressed verb when it is merely desired to corroborate a preceding negative statement; *neither — nor* (now replaced after a negative by *either — or*, but a little earlier in the period also found after a negative), but in elliptical sentences where the subject or finite verb is expressed in only one member and understood elsewhere we sometimes still, as in older English, employ here *neither — or*, especially where there is no emphasis or contrast involved; instead of *neither — nor* sometimes in poetry a positive first member followed by a second introduced by *nor*, which imparts its negative force to the first member; *neither — nor — nor*

(with three or more members instead of two); in older English
no(u)ther — nor instead of *neither — nor; nor — nor* in poetic or
older English, now usually *neither — nor; neither — neither,* in
poetic or older English, now usually *neither — nor; ne — ne,* in
older English, now *neither — nor; not only — but* (or more commonly *but also* or *but . . . too); too; as well as* or *and — as well;*
also, and also, in older English also *eke; moreover, and moreover;*
and withal (= *and moreover*); *as also* or simple *as* (= *moreover,*
and likewise), especially in older English; *again; later; further,*
furthermore; besides; likewise, and likewise; even; indeed; let
alone, to say nothing of, not to say anything of, not to mention;
still more; still less (in older English also simple *less*) or *much less;*
in the first place; first, firstly, secondly, etc.; *finally; then* (**27 3,**
last par.); *first — then; now — now; sometimes — sometimes; at*
times — at times; partly — partly; what with — and what with
= *somewhat* (i.e., *in part*) *on account of — and somewhat* (i.e., *in*
part) *on account of,* often with elliptical form, *what with — and,*
or instead of this elliptical form others, often *what between —*
and (a loose colloquial and popular blending of *what with — and*
and *between — and*) and sometimes *what of — and; on the one*
hand — on the other (hand); *at least,* etc.

Examples:

He can *both* sing *and* dance.
He can sing *and* dance *both.*
This he published in 1779, a performance in one so young *equally* sur-
prising *and* admirable.
He went to sleep *alike* thankless *and* remorseless.
The book is *alike* agreeable *and* instructive.
The Prime Minister was *at once* detested *and* despised.
I am not obliged to tell everybody, *nor* (or *neither*) am I obliged to
keep it a secret.
John was *not* there; *nor* was James (or *neither* was James, or *and*
neither was James, or *and* James was *not either*).
'I am *not* fond of parties.' — 'I am *not* fond of them *either*' (or *Nor* I
either).
CLAUD. — I did *never* think that lady would have loved any man.
LEON. — No, *nor* I *neither* (Shakespeare, *Much Ado About Nothing,* II, III,
98) (now *nor* I *either*).
You see the little beggar's *never* been to church before. I do*n't* go in
town *neither* (now usually *either*), but I think it's right in the country to
give a good example (Thackeray, *Pendennis,* I, Ch. XXII).
I am going *and* nobody can prevent it *either* (or *nor* can anybody prevent
it).
At least, and at last, I was off the sea, *nor* had I returned thence
empty handed (Stevenson, *Treasure Island,* VIII).

It has*n't* done me much good, *nor* anyone else *either*.

I do*n't* deny it was a good lay and I'll *not* deny *neither* (popular language for *either*) but what, etc. (Stevenson, *Treasure Island*, XX).

Then shall Cadwallin die; and then the raine (reign) Of Britons eke with him attonce shall dye; *Ne* shall the good Cadwallader, with paine or powre, be hable it to remedy (Spenser, *The Faerie Queene*, III, III, XL).

I can get *no* rest by night *or* (or *nor*) by day.

He is *not* brilliant *or* (or *nor*) attractive.

There was *not* a cat *or* (or *nor*) a dog in town that night that was not given a warm shelter.

I want *no* promises, *nor notes* (more emphatic than *or notes*); I want money.

I will *not* do it, *nor consider it* (more emphatic than *or consider it*).

I have *never* spoken *or* (or more emphatically *nor*) written to him.

'I can't make out how it came about.' — '*No more can I*' (Mrs. Gaskell, *Wives*) (or more commonly *Nor can I*).

'Harriet, my dear, you've gone too far — we had no right to pry into Mr. Preston's private affairs.' — '*No more I hád*' (*ib.*) (or more commonly *I knów I hádn't*).

Neither she *nor* I saw him.

Some evils which *neither* he *or* (now *nor*) she foresaw (Sterne, *Tristram Shandy*, III, VII).

I am suffering *neither* from one *or* (now more commonly *nor*) from the other (Trollope, *The Duke's Children*, 2, 140).

Great brother, thou (usually *neither* thou) *nor* I have made the world (Tennyson, *Idylls of the King, The Last Tournament*, l. 203).

Neither duty, *nor* honor, *nor* gratitude has any possible claim on him.

Thou hast *neither* heat, affection, limb, *nor* beauty (Shakespeare, *Measure for Measure*, III, I, 27).

There was *no* respite *neither* (now *either*) by day *nor* (now *or*) night for this devoted city (Southey, *Peninsular War*, II, 131, A.D. 1827).

Nobody knows *either* him *or* his family.

Nor sun *nor* wind will ever strive to kiss you (Shakespeare).

It shall *not* be forgiven him, *neither* in this world, *neither* in the world to come (*Matthew*, XII, 32).

Ne is thy fate, *ne* is thy fortune ill (Spenser, *The Faerie Queene*, III, III, XXIV).

At fifteen he was *not only* fit for the university, *but* carried thither a classical taste and a stock of learning which would have done honor to a Master of Arts (Lord Macaulay).

Not only the mother *but also* the children are sick.

'There is *not* only concision in these lines *but also* elegance' (or '*but* elegance *too*') or 'There is *not only* concision in these lines, there is *also* elegance' (or 'there is elegance, *too*').

I have promised to go. I am going to do it, *too*.

It will be my endeavor to relate the history of the people, *as well as* the history of the government.

'He must irrevocably lose her *as well as* the inheritance,' or 'He must irrevocably lose her *and* the inheritance *as well*.'

Some books are still written in Latin, and some scholars speak it. It is *also* used in our time as the language of the Roman Catholic Church (West, *A Latin Grammar*, p. 4).

Take this, *and* my very best thanks *also*.

The wolf is hardy and strong, *and withal* one of the cleverest of animals (or *and* one of the cleverest of animals *withal*).

Wherefore, that I might show them what kindness I could, *as also* that I might have a full opportunity to observe the extraordinary Circumstances of the Children, and that I might be furnished with Evidence and Argument as a Critical Eye-Witness, I took the eldest of them home to my House (Cotton Mather, *Memorable Providences*, The First Exemple, Sect. XVII).

We must abide our opportunity, And practise what is fit, *as* what is needful (Ben Jonson, *Sejanus*, I, II, 172, A.D. 1603).

Again (often, as here, at the beginning of a paragraph, continuing the discussion), man is greater by leaning on the greatest (Emerson, *Trust*).

'The attorney general *further* holds that,' etc. (*Chicago Tribune*, March 26, 1925), or with greater emphasis, '*Further* (or *furthermore*), the attorney general holds that,' etc.

John dislikes me; he *even* told me so.

The birds here are very numerous. *Indeed*, they often rise in a dense cloud that hides the sun.

Not even dogs were unkind to him, *let alone* human beings.

The house is uninhabitable in summer, *let alone* in winter.

And the scare (of cholera) has produced a rigid quarantine that has upset all commercial relations, *to say nothing of* (or *not to say anything of*, or *not to mention*) the serious interruptions of passenger traffic (Bret Harte, *Letter to His Wife*, Sept. 17, 1892).

It is scarcely imaginable how great a force is required to stretch, *still more* break, this ligament.

I do not even suggest that he is negligent, *still less* (or *much less*) that he is dishonest (*Oxford Dictionary*).

You never fought with any, *lesse* (now *still less*, or *much less*) slcw any (Ben Jonson, *Magnetic Lady*, III, III, A.D. 1632).

We played a little while longer; *then* we went home.

First think, *then* act.

What with his drinking *and what with* his jealousy (or *what with* his drinking *and* his jealousy), he wore himself out.

'*What between* the trenches *and* alarms we never have a moment to ourselves.' The *what* should be suppressed here.

What of Excise Laws *and* Custom Laws *and* Combination Laws *and* Libcl Laws, a human being scarcely knows what he dares do or say (Corbett, *Cott. Econ.*, § 108, A.D. 1823).

My interests at present are twofold: *on the one hand* my flowers claim me early in the morning, *on the other* (*hand*) I am absorbed in language studies the rest of the day.

He is very poor, *at least* he has not the wherewithal to buy proper clothes for his wife and family.

b. DISJUNCTIVE, connecting two members but disconnecting their meaning, the meaning in the second member excluding that in the first: *or*, in older English also *either* or *outher* (= *or*) and in questions *whether — or* with the force of simple *or; or . . . either; either — or; either — or — or* (with three or more members instead of two); *or — or*, in older English and still in poetry, in older English also *other — or; other — other, outher — or, outher — outher else, either — either;* the disjunctive adverbs *else, otherwise,* or *or*, or *or else*, in older English *outher else.*

The employment of *whether* here as a conjunction in older English is explained by its original use as an interrogative pronoun with the force of *which of the two:* '*Whether* is greater, the gold or the temple that sanctifieth the gold?' (*Matthew*, XXIII, 17). Examples of its later use as a conjunction are given among the examples below.

Examples:

Is he guilty *or* innocent?

Can the fig tree, my brethren, bear olive berries? *either* (now *or*) a vine, figs? (*James*, III, 12).

Pray, Sir, *whether* (now suppressed) do you reckon Derrick *or* Smart the better poet? (Boswell, *Life of Johnson*, IV, 159).

Whether then (both words now suppressed or replaced by *Say*), Master Tommy, do you reckon it more honest to use your own faculties *or* those of others? (*Punch*, 1872, Vol. I, III).

If John said so *or* William *either*, I could believe it.

Either he *or* I must go.

A narrative has to do with a narration of events, *either* past, present, *or* to come.

At different times the American government has been carried on without the coöperation of the Vice-President. *Either* he has resigned through ill-health, *or* has died while in office, *or* has succeeded to the presidency.

Alike *or* when *or* where they shone *or* shine, *or* on the Rubicon *or* on the Rhine (Pope, *Essay on Man*, IV, 245–246).

This idle sort . . . which hitherto *other* (now *either*) poverty hath caused to be thieves, *or else* now be *other* (now *either*) vagabonds *or* idle serving men and shortly will be thieves (Sir Thomas More, *Utopia*, 58).

No, no, Eubulus, but I will yield to more than *either* I am bound to grant, *either* (now *or*) thou able to prove (John Lyly, *Euphues*, 193).

He cannot be in his right senses, *else* (or *otherwise*, or *or*, or *or else*) he would not make such wild statements. Compare **31** 1 *d dd.*

Seize the chance, *else* (or *otherwise*, or *or*, or *or else*) you will regret it. Compare **31** 1 *d bb.*

Either — or often has the force of *both — and:* 'John is as steady as *either* Henry *or* William.'

c. ADVERSATIVE, connecting two members, but contrasting their meaning: *but, but then, only* (= *but, but then, it must however be added that*), *still, yet, and yet, however* (in older English *howsoever*, surviving in dialect as *howsumever, howsomdever*), *on the other hand, again, on the contrary, conversely, rather, notwithstanding, nevertheless* (replacing older *nath(e)less*), *none the less* (replacing older *not the less*), *all the same, though, after all, for all that, at the same time; and withal, yet withal,* or *but withal* (= *at this same time, for all that, notwithstanding); in the meantime, meanwhile,* etc.; in older English *howbeit* (= *yet;* see *Mark,* V, 19).

Examples:

He is small *but* strong.

The commander-in-chief has not been quite successful, *but then* he has essayed a difficult task.

He wanted to take precedence of all the Lowland gentlemen then present, *only* my father would not suffer it (Scott, *Waverley,* Ch. XV).

He makes good resolutions, *only* he never keeps them.

She is devilish like Miss Cutler that I used to meet at Dundum, *only* fairer (*Vanity Fair,* I, Ch. IV).

She has wronged me, *and yet* I wish to do her justice.

'I want to go very much; *still* (conjunction) I do not care to go through the rain'; but *still* is an adverb in 'It is raining *still.*'

'I miss him, *yet* I am glad he went'; but *yet* is an adverb in 'It hasn't quit raining *yet.*'

'The studio contained some armor and pottery of no special value. There was, *however,* a fine old cabinet at the end of the room' (or 'There was a fine old cabinet at the end of the room, *however,*' or '*However,* there was a fine old cabinet at the end of the room').

Miss Raeburn's dress was a cheerful red, verging on crimson. Lady Winterbourne, *on the other hand,* was dressed in severe black.

Charles is usually cheerful; sometimes, *again,* he is very despondent.

I have not nearly done. *On the contrary,* I have only just begun.

Very free word-order is possible only in inflected languages. *Conversely,* absolute fixed order occurs only in languages devoid of inflection.

The old man is no coward; *rather,* he is a man of high spirit.

I denied myself everything. *Notwithstanding,* the old skinflint complained without ceasing.

He is always chin-deep in debt. *Nevertheless* (or *none the less*), he is always jolly.

The expression is ungrammatical; *all the same* it is a part of the common tongue.

'The sheep which we saw behind the house were small and lean; in the next field *though* (coördinating conjunction) there were some fine cows'; but *though* is a subordinating conjunction in '*Though* it never put a cent of money into my pocket, I believe it did me good.'

In coming home we got caught in the rain and became wet through and through. *After all* I don't mind it, as we had a fine time.

He often loses his temper and can become unreasonable. *For all that* we like him, as he has some fine traits.

These persons are a moving mass of scarfs and furs and overcoats, *and* shivering *withal*.

It (book) is very stimulating and sound to the core — *yet* difficult reading *withal* (James Gibbons Huneker, *Letter*, Aug. 23, 1900).

'He confessed that his master was rather severe, *but withal* a good man' (or '*but* a good man *withal*').

He was now undergoing many hardships. His brother *in the meantime* was having an easy time.

d. CAUSAL, adding an independent proposition explaining the preceding statement, represented only by the single conjunction *for:* 'The brook was very high, *for* a great deal of rain had fallen over night.' Compare **30** *a* (next to last par.).

Although the independent causal proposition usually has declarative form, it sometimes has the form of a direct question: 'I had no twinge of compunction, *for was this not fulfilment?*' (Ray Stannard Baker, *Adventures in Contentment*, Ch. V).

e. ILLATIVE, introducing an inference, conclusion, consequence, result, namely, *thérefore* (originally the same word as *therefór*, but since A.D. 1800 differentiated from it in spelling and stress in accordance with meaning), *on that account, consequently, accordingly, for that reason, so, then, hence, thence* (= *hence*, but not so common), etc.

Examples:

No man will take counsel, but everybody will take money; *therefore* money is better than counsel (Swift).

The factory was burned down last night; *on that account* (or *consequently*) many workmen are thrown out of employment.

The thing had to be done. *Accordingly* we did it.

There was no one there, *so* I went away.

'I am here, you see, young and sound and hearty; *then*, don't let us despair!' (or '*don't* let us despair, *then!*').

When the blood becomes viscous, it is difficult for the heart to pump it through the capillaries. *Hence* the blood pressure increases.

A vast and lofty hall was the great audience-chamber of the Moslem monarch, *thence* called the Hall of the Embassadors (Washington Irving).

f. EXPLANATORY, connecting words, phrases, or sentences and introducing an explanation or a particularization: *namely, to wit, viz.* (short for Latin *videlicet*, the *z* indicating a contraction, as in *oz.* for *ounce*), *that is* (when it precedes, often written *i.e.*, for Latin *id est*), *that is to say, or, such as, as, like, for example* (often written *e.g.*, which is for Latin *exempli gratia*), *for instance, say, let us say.*

Examples:

There were only two girls there, *namely*, Mary and Ann.

Among the building stones in New England three kinds are of especial value, *namely*, granite, marble, and slate.

There is but one way of solving the difficulty — *namely*, to publish both articles.

'He has an enemy — *to wit*, his own brother' (or much more commonly '*namely*, his own brother').

There is now ample accommodation for them here, no less than five hospital ships being available, *viz.* (or *namely*), Maine, Spartan, Nubia, Lismore, and Avoca.

The play was flung on 'cold' — *that is*, without an out-of-town try-out.

A great deal of the forest of the West is on government land, and to prevent it from being wasted, our government has set apart what are called 'forest preserves.' *That is*, the forest is kept, or reserved, by the government, so that no one can cut down the trees without permission.

My wife suggested my going alone, *i.e.*, with you and without her.

The Navy is the first line of defence; *that is to say*, it is not till the Navy has been beaten that the shores of England can be invaded.

I passed some time in Poet's Corner, which occupies an end of one of the transepts, *or* cross aisles, of the Abbey.

She possessed certain definite beauties, *such as* (or simple *as*, or *like*) her hair.

The mistletoe grows on various trees, *such as* oaks, poplars, birches.

Michael, who all the time was dreading many unfortunate events, *as* for the cabman to get down from his box and quarrel about the fare, or for the train to be full, or for Stella to be sick during the journey (Mackenzie, *Youth's Encounter*, Ch. V).

The drama of literary moralizing is growing increasingly, *as* witness the plays by Mr. Shaw, Mr. Barker, Mr. Galsworthy (*Bookman*).

She gave me a good deal of miscellaneous information, *as* that William's real name was Mr. Hicking (J. M. Barrie, *The Little White Bird*, Ch. VIII).

We designate odors by the objects from which they come, *e.g.*, violet, orange, etc.

Such changes in the level of the land are even now in progress in many places, though the process is so slow that usually years, and even centuries, must pass before the changes become evident. *For instance* (or *for example*), the land along the coast of New Jersey is sinking at the rate of about two feet a century, while that around Hudson Bay is rising.

I have often heard this pronunciation, *for instance* in New York.

Take a few of them, *say* a dozen or so.

Any country, *let us say* Sweden, might do the same.

2. **Pronouns and Adverbs as Conjunctions.** The connection between the members may be made by placing at the beginning of the sentence a stressed personal pronoun, possessive adjective, or demonstrative proncun or adverb referring back to the preceding proposition: 'In this crisis I have often thought of the old home, of Father, of Mother. *That* was a good place to start out in life from. *Their* life has always been an inspiration to me, *their* example a sure guide. *There* at least in memory I shall still often tarry. *Them* I shall often consult.' Demonstrative adverbs are very frequent here. Examples of *then* so used are given in 1 *a*, p. 165.

3. **Parataxis.** Sometimes there is no formal link binding the members together since the logical connection forms a sufficient tie. Upon close investigation, however, it will become clear that such apparently independent propositions are not absolutely independent. One of the propositions often stands in some grammatical relation to the other, such as that of subject or object, or in an adverbial relation, such as that of cause, purpose, result, concession, condition: 'The best way is *you ask the man himself*' (subject clause). '*"I am not sure of it"* (object clause), he replied.' 'Hurry up; *it is getting late*' (cause). 'They gave him a large sum of money; *he was to keep still, you know*' (purpose). 'The crops were very poor this year; *the prices of food are high*' (pure result). '*I could have poisoned him* (modal result) I was so mad to think I had hired such a turnip' (Mark Twain, *Letter to His Daughter Clara*, Sept. 29, 1891). '*Let him talk* (concession), it'll do no harm.' '*Do it* (condition), you'll never regret it.'

Such sentences represent an older order of things which was once more general than now. In the earliest stage of the parent tongue from which the various Indo-European languages have come, there were no subordinating conjunctions as now, i.e., no formal expression had as yet been found for the idea of subordination of one proposition to another. This placing of a subordinate proposition alongside of a principal proposition without a formal sign of subordination is called parataxis. The development of a distinctive formal sign of subordination in the form of conjunctions and relative pronouns — hypotaxis, as it is called — is characteristic of a later stage of language and belongs to the individual life of the different languages after the migration of the different peoples from their original home. It has required many centuries to develop the present hypotactic forms, but actual subordination, although without a formal expression, was present at a very early stage of language growth, as can still be seen in the old verbless type of sentence preserved in old saws:

Out of sight out of mind = 'If something is out of sight, it soon passes out of mind.'

An early stage of formal hypotaxis, asyndetic hypotaxis, i.e., hypotaxis clearly marked in thought and form but not yet indicated by a separate word such as a conjunction or a relative, is still quite common in English in relative clauses that do not have a relative pronoun: 'The book *I hold* [*it*] *here in my hand* is an English grammar.' In this old construction, of the two originally independent sentences one of them, lying alongside of the other in close relation to it, often even as in this example literally embedded in it, is so markedly dependent logically and also formally dependent by reason of its peculiarly abridged and close-linked form that it is no longer felt as an independent sentence but as a relative clause. Compare **23** II. An imperative sentence that precedes another sentence is often logically subordinate to it. It often has the force of a conditional clause: '*Do it*, you will never regret it.' The imperative sentence often has the force of a concessive clause: '*Let him be the greatest villain in the world*, I shall never cease to have an interest in him.' Likewise a question is often degraded to a subordinate conditional clause: '*Is any among you afflicted?* let him pray. *Is any merry?* let him sing psalms' (*James*, V, 13). Now usually without the question mark: '*Had I the time*, I would go.'

In general, the formal hypotactic stage was preceded by coordination, the connection of sentences by pronouns, adverbs, and coördinating conjunctions, as described in 1 *a, b, c, d, e,* 2, pp. 162–170. Coördination often indicates a close relation between two words or two propositions, the context frequently showing clearly that one of these is subordinate to the other: *nice and warm* = *nicely warm.* '*A little farther, and* (= *when they had gone a little farther,* a clause of time) they turned off to the left in the direction of an olive orchard' (Wallace, *Ben Hur*, VIII, Ch. VIII). '*Give him an inch, and* (= *if you give him an inch,* a clause of condition) he'll take a mile.' 'You should try *and be reasonable*' (= *to be reasonable,* an abridged infinitive clause in the object relation). 'You will come *and see us*, won't you?' (= *to see us,* an abridged adverbial infinitive clause of purpose). 'Go *and fetch them for me*' = 'Go *fetch me them*' (*Genesis*, XXVII, 13), an adverbial infinitive clause of purpose containing an old simple infinitive, once more common here. 'You have been *and moved my papers!*' (*Concise Oxford Dictionary*) = 'You have been *to move my papers*,' the old infinitive of purpose construction described in **7** D 3 = 'You have been moving my papers!' 'Can you touch pitch *and not be defiled?*' (= *without being defiled,* a gerundial clause of result).

Instead of an infinitive clause of result (**38** 2 *b ee*, 4th par.), as in 'If you are not more careful, you are going *to lose your knife*,' we often employ a coördinated proposition: 'Why did I have to go *and lose my rifle?*' (Victor Appleton, *Don Sturdy among the Gorillas*, Ch. XIX). 'I cannot keep these plants alive *and I have watered them well, too*' (= *although I have watered them well*, an adverbial concessive clause). In older literary English, an independent proposition which is coördinated by *and* to a preceding independent proposition is often used instead of a dependent relative clause: 'A good man was ther of religioun, *And was a poure persoun of a town*' (Chaucer, *Canterbury Tales*, Prologue, 477) (= *who was a poor parson of a town*). Coördination instead of a dependent relative clause is still widely used in Irish English dialect, as illustrated below.

As can be seen by the above examples, coördination with *and*, though a very old construction, is still in colloquial and popular speech often more common than the hypotactic form of statement, which in general is now more common in accurate literary language. In popular Irish English every possible kind of subordination is expressed by connecting two propositions by *and*. That the proposition following *and* is now felt as subordinate is frequently shown by putting it in the old appositional type (**6** B *a*) without a finite verb, the regular form in Irish English for every subordinate clause: 'What way wouldn't it be warm, *and it* (i.e., the sun) *getting high up in the South?*' (J. M. Synge, *The Well of the Saints*, p. 1) (causal clause). 'I'm told it's a great sight to see a man hanging by his neck; but what joy would that be to ourselves, *and we* (an old blind couple) *not seeing it at all*' (*ib.*, p. 10) (conditional clause). 'Is it a niggard you are grown to be, McDonough, *and you with riches in your hand?*' (Lady Gregory, *McDonough's Wife*) (concessive clause). 'Ah, what sort at all are the people of the fair, to be doing their bargaining *and she being stark* (i.e., lying dead) *and quiet!*' (*ib.*) (temporal clause). 'Did you not hear his reverence, *and he speaking to you now?*' (J. M. Synge, *The Well of the Saints*, p. 79) (relative clause). This appositional type of clause after *and* was a common construction in Gaelic. Hence it became thoroughly established in early Irish English, for Irish expression was influenced here not only by Gaelic but also by literary English, which at this time had the same construction: 'What mortall fools durst raise thee to this daring, *and I alive!*' (Beaumont and Fletcher, *The Maids Tragedie*, IV, I, 70, A.D. 1622) (= *while I am alive*). 'Because we could not free Captain Hawkins and other voluntaries of what they had done, we were to send a small present to Monsieur

D'Aulnay in satisfaction of that, *and so all injuries and demands to be remitted and so a final peace to be concluded*' (Winthrop, *Journal*, Sept. 20, 1646) (= *that thus all injuries and demands might be remitted and a final peace be concluded*, purpose clause). It occurs sometimes still in literary English: 'If it is miserable to bear when she is here, what would it be, *and she away?*' (Dickens, *David Copperfield*, Ch. XVI) (= *if she were away*). 'Think, while we sit In gorgeous pomp and state, gaunt poverty Creeps through their sunless lanes, and with sharp knives Cuts the warm throats of children stealthily *And no word said*' (Oscar Wilde, *The Duchess of Padua*, Act II) (= *without a word being said*, a gerundial clause of result).

The older construction of coördination cannot as accurately as hypotaxis give expression to many fine shades of meaning required in exact thinking, but it is by reason of its simple directness often more forceful than the younger, more exact construction of hypotaxis, and consequently is still, even in the literary language, widely used in lively style. An illustration of this is given in 2, p. 170. Likewise the oldest construction here, parataxis, still has its distinct advantage in lively style with quick movement, as in old saws, imperative sentences, and questions as illustrated by the examples given on opposite page. In lively description, although the sentences are as elsewhere more or less connected logically, hypotaxis plays an inconspicuous rôle. On the one hand, parataxis is the favorite where the movement is rapid, as in *I came, I saw, I conquered*. On the other hand, coördination is in place where different objects are presented for the sake of making the picture more impressive, or different activities are described separately in their natural sequence in order to depict the march of events in a stately or impressive way: 'We have ships, *and* men, *and* money, *and* stores' (Webster). '*And* the rain descended, *and* the floods came, *and* the winds blew, *and* beat upon that house; *and* it fell; *and* great was the fall of it' (*Matthew*, VII, 27). Again, coördination is much more expressive when there is feeling to be conveyed: 'Three thousand years *and* the world so little changed!' (Thoreau, *Journal*, I, p. 31); more expressive than hypotactic: 'Although three thousand years have passed since Homer's times, the world has changed very little.'

On the other hand, parataxis is often loose and clumsy and for a long time has been yielding to hypotaxis, which expresses our thought more compactly and conveniently. In **26** in the description of the development of the clause of place introduced by the conjunction *where* we have an apt illustration of the compactness of hypotaxis as against the looseness of parataxis.

CHAPTER X

THE COMPLEX SENTENCE

SUBORDINATE CLAUSE

20 1. Complex Sentence, Function, and Form of Subordinate Clauses. The complex sentence consists of a principal clause and one or more subordinate clauses. This is true, however, in only a general sense. In an exact sense there is often no principal clause at all: '*Whoever comes* will be welcome.' Here one of the essential elements of the sentence, the subject, has the full form of a subordinate clause, but there is no principal clause in the sentence distinct from the subordinate clause. The so-called principal clause is merely the predicate. Not only an essential element but also a subordinate element can have the form of a clause: 'I have heard *that he has come*.' Here the object has the form of a clause, an object clause. The subordinate clause may also be merely a modification of some word within one of the component elements of the sentence: 'The book *which I hold in my hand* is an English grammar.' Here the clause is not the subject but only a modifier of it, hence is an adjective clause.

According to their grammatical function, subordinate clauses are divided into subject, predicate, adjective, object, adverbial clauses. These clauses may be reduced to three if we divide them according to the part of speech which they represent: (1) *substantive* clauses, i. e., clauses with the functions of a substantive, including *subject, predicate, object* clauses, and such *adjective* clauses as represent a noun in the attributive relation of appositive, genitive, or prepositional phrase, as described in **23** I; (2) *adjective* clauses; (3) *adverbial* clauses.

A subordinate clause is usually employed to indicate dependency of thought. It completes the meaning of the principal proposition, or it modifies it or some word in it. Formally it is distinguished by a distinctive conjunction or connective, such as *that, when, while, where, who, which,* etc., or, where there is no conjunction or connective, by the slightness of the pause before it and by the quicker enunciation, as in 'He told me *he saw you do it*' and 'Give me the book *you hold in your hand.*' Often, however, the thought in the subordinate clause is as independent as in the principal proposition. Subordinate clause form here is sometimes employed to indicate a close association with the act of the principal proposition: 'I had scarcely stepped out of the house *when* (indicating a closer association of the two acts than *then*) *I heard a shot within.*' Sometimes it expresses a contrast: 'She is diligent, *while* (or *whereas*) *he is lazy.*' Frequently it is employed merely as a convenient means of joining one independent statement to another: 'I handed it to John, *who* (= *and he*) *passed it on to James.*' 'One lost a leg, another an arm, *while* (= *and*) *a third was killed outright.*' *While* with the force of *and* has become a marked feature in recent journalistic language, but has not yet become established in choice expression.

2. **Position of Subordinate Clauses.** As each subordinate clause which is not merely a modifier of some word within one of the component elements of the sentence has a definite function as if it were a simple word, its position in the sentence is regulated by the same principle that determines the position of a simple word with the same function and logical force. For instance, just as an emphatic noun subject stands at the end of the sentence, as explained on page 1, an emphatic clause subject assumes the end position: 'The best way is *you ask the man himself.*' A subordinate clause may follow or precede the principal proposition: 'He stole my watch *while I was asleep*' or '*While I was asleep* he stole my watch.'

A subordinate clause often modifies, not the principal proposition, but a preceding subordinate clause or some element in it, the two subordinate clauses forming a complex subordinate clause. 'Late one afternoon *when I was in the garden near the end of the vineyard, where there was a bird box,* I suddenly heard the loud, emphatic note of a bluebird.' In complex subordinate clauses there is not always a succession of subordinate clauses as here.

but often one of the subordinate clauses is embedded in the other,
as illustrated in **21** (last par.), **23** II 6 *a*, **24** III (last par.).

3. Abridged Clauses. The various kinds of subordinate clauses
are the result of a long development, and represent the active
efforts of the English mind in its countless practical struggles
for fuller expression to adapt from emergency to emergency the
available historical materials of the language to the more accurate
processes of thought that became necessary in its growing intellectual life. Alongside of these involved structures are simpler
forms of expressions which in their first beginnings belong to the
earliest stage of language growth. There is still preserved in
old saws a very primitive type of complex sentence which is verbless and conjunctionless and yet as complete in its expression
as a modern complex sentence with its highly developed hypo-
tactical form: 'Right or wrong — my country' = 'Whether the
cause be right or wrong, I shall stand by my country.' 'Better
dead!' (Galsworthy, *The First and the Last*, Scene III) = 'It
would be better if he were dead!' 'Out of sight, out of mind' =
'If something is out of sight, it soon passes out of mind.' These
sentences are forms of the old appositional type of expression
described in **6** B *a*. Today there is usually a finite verb in every
principal proposition and in every subordinate clause, and the
latter is introduced by a conjunction, but in these old sentences
there is no finite verb and no conjunction. The grammatical
relations are made clear by simply placing one part of the sentence
alongside of the other.

The particular forms of the old appositional type given above
are not now common, but other forms of the old type of predication without a finite verb have become general favorites in the
subordinate clause in the style of everyday practical life, where
their vigor and simplicity have a strong appeal. Their great
practical value was discovered centuries ago, so that now for a
long time they have been developing into convenient terser types
of easy expression alongside of the more intricate clause formations which we employ in more formal and exact language. While
these simpler constructions are, in general, characteristic of colloquial speech, they are not at all confined to it. Their good qualities
are appreciated in every style. A few of these constructions, as indicated on page 177, are more common in literary than in colloquial
style, for their compact form often becomes desirable there in
concise language. These simpler types of expression are treated
in the following articles alongside of the fuller and more precise
clause formations. They are given under the caption of abridgment in the various kinds of clauses treated below and are often

elsewhere spoken of as 'abridged' or 'contracted' forms. Although these abridged clauses are in their original form older than the fuller clause structures and hence in a historical sense cannot be said to be abridged from them, the terms 'abridged' or 'contracted' are not inappropriate, for the more compact structures have long been intimately associated with the fuller, more involved structures, and in contrast to their fuller form are now felt as abridgments or contractions.

English has gone much farther than the other Germanic languages in preserving these old forms and developing them into types of expression capable of wide use. Particularly terse is the predicate appositive participial construction, where the participle and its modifiers form an abridged clause in which the participle is the logical predicate, and the subject of the principal proposition is the logical subject, the clause as a whole indicating some adverbial relation, as time, cause, manner, etc., which can be determined only from the connection, since this relation is not formally expressed in the clause itself: '*Going down town* (= *when I was going down town*), I met an old friend.' '*Having finished my work* (= *after I had finished my work*), I went to bed.' '*Being sick* (= *as I was sick*), I stayed at home.' This is the old appositional type of clause described in **6 B** *a.* The thought is not expressed accurately by means of intricate grammatical form, but is merely suggested by associating the participle with the subject of the principal proposition. Compare **48** 2 (5th par.).

Two or more participial clauses can be coördinated, linked by coördinating conjunctions or unlinked, but one of them cannot now, as sometimes in older English, be replaced by a clause with a finite verb: 'I haue reade of Themistocles, *which* (now *who*) hauing offended Philip, the king of Macedonia, and *could no way* (now *being in no way able to*) *appease his anger*, meeting his young sonne Alexander, tooke him in his armes' (John Lyly, *Euphues and Atheos*, Works, I, p. 303, A.D. 1580).

Sometimes the conjunction employed in the full subordinate clause is used also in the abridged participial clause to indicate more clearly the different adverbial relations, such as time, place, cause, concession, condition, restriction — an improvement introduced in the sixteenth century: (concession) 'For lovers' hours are long, *though seeming short*' (Shakespeare, *Venus and Adonis*, 842). (concession) 'One hears now and then of a serious-minded Eastern girl who, *though having grown up in the Eastern tradition*, distrusts the preponderantly feminine atmosphere of the woman's college that has been chosen for her' (Olivia Howard Dunbar in

Forum for Nov., 1923, p. 2049). (restriction) 'The inquiry, *so far as showing that I have favored my own interests*, has failed.' Such clauses are the result of a blending of the full and the abridged clause. In the following sentence from Thomas Nashe's *The Vnfortvnate Traveller*, Works, II, p. 220, A.D. 1594, it can be seen how much clearer the thought often becomes by the insertion of the conjunction used in the full clause: 'The whelpes of a Beare neuer growe *but* [*when*] *sleeping*.' Further illustrations are given in **26** *a*, **27** 5, **28** 2 *b*, **28** 3 *a*, **28** 5 *d*, **29** 1 A *c*, **30** *b*, **31** 2, **32** 2. This construction, though useful, has not manifested a tendency to spread beyond the boundaries indicated by the references just given.

A more accurate form of the old appositional type of clause is the gerundial construction. Often a preceding preposition indicates clearly the relation to the principal proposition: 'I am opposed to *John's going to their house*.' 'I was mortified by *her* (or *Mary's*) *treating him so unkindly*.' The predicate of the clause is the verbal noun, the gerund. The gerund without verbal endings of any kind becomes a full verbal predicate, though in fact a noun, by merely being placed as a noun alongside of its dependent possessive adjective, or its dependent noun in the genitive, or now often, as explained in **50** 3, a dependent noun in the accusative, which serves as its logical subject. The preposition which precedes the abridged clause is the sign of subordination to the principal proposition. If the subject of the gerund is the same as that of the principal verb it is not expressed: 'I am fond *of doing this*.' Likewise if the subject is general or indefinite: 'There is a strong feeling in the ward against *making him alderman again*.' In older English, the subject of the gerund was often expressed even though it was the same as that of the principal verb: 'Since *her* (now suppressed) being at Lambton, she had heard that Miss Darcy was exceedingly proud' (Jane Austen, *Pride and Prejudice*, III, Ch. II). Also elsewhere the gerundial construction is a clear, accurate type of expression. As subject the gerundial clause precedes the principal verb; as object it follows the verb, so that the grammatical relations are always easily discernible. The gerund, as we use it today, is one of the tersest and most convenient constructions in the language and little by little has come into wide use. An outline of its present extensive functions is given in **50** 3.

Verbal nouns often form with the genitive a clause of the appositional type: '*After the king's death* (= *after the king died*) many changes were made in the government.' 'You can easily observe *the decline of his mental power*' (= *that his mental power* *is declining*). Here the genitive is the subject of the clause, and the verbal noun is the predicate. The subject of the clause is often implied in a noun or pronoun in the principal proposition: *'After the loss of his fortune* (= *after he lost his fortune*) he had to change his manner of living.'* This type is chiefly literary.

Abstract nouns often form with a genitive a clause of the appositional type: 'I recognize *the man's ability'* (= *that the man is able*). 'I question *the truth of the statement'* (= *whether the statement is true*). Here the genitive is the subject of the clause, and the abstract noun is the predicate with the force of a predicate adjective. Chiefly literary.

A widely used appositional type of clause is the infinitive construction. The infinitive without verbal endings of any kind becomes a full verbal predicate, though originally a noun, by merely being associated with some noun or pronoun near it: *'I* hope *to finish* the work this evening' = 'I hope *that I may finish* the work this evening.' The subject of the infinitive *to finish* is implied in *I*, the subject of the principal proposition. A brief history of the development of the infinitive construction into a convenient new type of subordinate clause is given in **49 2 a**. Also the form of the subject of the infinitive is discussed there. An outline of the present extensive use of the infinitive is given in **49 4**.

Another form of the appositional type of clause is the absolute nominative construction described in **17 3 A, B, C, D**.

Not unlike the preceding forms of the appositional type of clause is the use of a prepositional phrase as a clause: 'He put on his socks *with the wrong side out'* (= *so that the wrong side was out*). *'Even with conditions unfavorable* (= *even though the conditions were unfavorable*) he would succeed.' 'He said it *with tears in his eyes'* (= *at the same time that tears were in his eyes*). The first noun in each prepositional phrase is the subject of the abridged clause; the adverb, adjective, or prepositional phrase after the subject is the predicate; and the introductory preposition is the sign of subordination to the principal verb.

The old objective predicate construction described in **15 III 2** and **15 III 2 A** is still a widely used form of the appositional type of clause: 'He got *the machine to running.'* = 'He got the machine so *that it ran.'* 'She boiled *the egg hard.'* = 'She boiled the egg *that it became hard.'* 'The President made *him a general.'* = 'The President disposed so *that he became a general.'* Here the object of the principal verb serves also as the subject of the subordinate clause. The predicate of the clause is a prepositional phrase, an adjective, a participle, or a noun. Compare **28 5 d** (next to last par.), **48** 2 (2nd and 3rd parr.). The construction is common in all styles.

a. ELLIPTICAL CLAUSES. In contrast to abridged clauses are elliptical clauses, which have the same structure as full clauses, only that the finite verb is suppressed: 'She is regarded more highly than he [is regarded].' In an abridged clause there is nothing suppressed that belongs to its structure.

SUBJECT CLAUSE

21. Conjunctions. The subject clause is usually introduced by: *that*, in popular speech often replaced by *as* (**27** 2, 2nd par.); sometimes *because* or in older English *for that* instead of *that* when the subject clause contains a reason for an act or a state of things; *lest*, after nouns expressing fear, sometimes still as in older English used instead of *that;* after verbs of saying, telling, relating sometimes *how* instead of *that;* *but, but that,* or in colloquial speech *but what,* instead of the more common *that* after *not improbable, not impossible, cannot be doubted;* in older English *but, but that* after *it is odds* (= *the chances are*), now usually *that; since, before, till,* see p. 190; the indefinite relative (**23** II 1, 2, 3) pronouns *who* (in older English also *who that), that, as* (= *who), who(so)ever, whoso* (in older English), *what* (in older English also *what that), what(so)ever, whatso* (in older English), *which, whichever;* the indefinite relative adjectives *which, what, whichever, whatever;* the indefinite relative adverbs *where, when, whither* (in a choice literary style, usually replaced by *where,* or often, especially in England, the more accurate *where . . . to),* *whence* (in a choice literary style, usually replaced by *where . . . from, from where,* or sometimes *from whence), why* (in older English also *why that), how* (in older English also *how that), whether* (originally a pronoun meaning *which of the two)* or *if; whether — or whether; whether — or,* used when the second member has its subject, or its verb, or both, suppressed; in indirect questions introduced by interrogative pronouns, adjectives, and adverbs, *who, which, what, where, when, whither, whence, why, how;* in indirect exclamations introduced by *what a, how.*

In substantive clauses — subject, object, and attributive substantive clauses (**23** I) — indirect questions are a common feature.

Attention is called here to the examples of indirect questions given below and in **23** I and **24** III, since their true nature has often been misunderstood and false impressions have been spread by the common definition that 'an indirect question is a substantive clause introduced by an interrogative word.' By 'interrogative word' most grammarians mean the *who, which, what, where, when, why, how,* or *whether* which stands in a substantive clause. These words are a very old class of indefinites which have come down to our time with their original force unimpaired in principal propositions and substantive clauses. As pure indefinites they are still widely used to introduce a substantive clause: 'It is not known *who* did it, *when* he did it, *how* he did it.' They are here called indefinite relative (i.e., conjunctive) pronouns or adverbs. They are interrogatives only when they call for an answer directly or indirectly. Direct question: '*Who* did it?' An indirect question is an indirect way of asking a question, as in 'Tell me *who* did it,' or an indirect report of a question, as in 'I asked *who* did it.' These forms never cease being indefinites. Their use as interrogatives in direct and indirect questions is only a special function which they often perform. In countless expressions, however, these words, *who, what, when,* etc., are not interrogatives and have not developed out of interrogatives, as is so often claimed. For instance, in a sentence like 'I saw plainly *who* struck him' *who* indicates that the identity of the person doing the striking was known to the speaker but unknown to the hearer, so that it contains an element of indefiniteness and is properly called an indefinite. It is surely not an interrogative, as so often claimed, for there isn't here the slightest suggestion of an interrogation. Similarly, the conjunctions *whether* and *if,* often used to introduce an indirect question, are also frequently employed merely to indicate indefiniteness, doubt, uncertainty as to the occurrence of an act: Indirect question: 'I asked him *whether* (or *if*) *he had seen it.*' Mere indefiniteness, uncertainty: 'I do not know *whether* (or *if*) *he has seen it.*' 'He has not yet said *whether* (or *if*) *he will do it.*' 'I'll go see *whether* (or *if*) *he has* returned.' Compare **23** I.

The idea of indefiniteness is also closely associated with interrogative form of any kind and is often the chief element in it, so that we often in deliberative and speculative (**23** II 1, last par.) questions employ interrogative form merely to express indefiniteness, doubt, without any thought of eliciting an answer: 'Have I a right to do this?' (deliberative question). 'Is he lying or telling the truth?' (speculative question). Hence, instead of the usual form of a substantive clause introduced by an indefinite we often employ interrogative form: 'The thing I want to know is *what* (relative) *I can do to improve my health,'* or more graphically in the form of a deliberative question, *What can I do to improve my condition?* or more simply in the form of a noun, *a means of improving my health.* 'The thing I want to know is *what* (relative) *the cause of the disturbance really is,'* or more graphically in the form of a speculative question, *What is really the cause of the disturbance?* Similarly, instead of a clause introduced by the indefinite *whether* or *if* we sometimes employ interrogative form: 'She cast about among her little ornaments to see *could she sell any to procure the desired novelties,'* instead of *whether* (or *if*) *she could sell any,* etc. Often in popular Irish English: 'I stood outside, wondering *would I have a right to walk in and see you, Pegeen Mike'* (J. M. Synge, *The Playboy of the Western World,* Act I), instead of *whether* (or *if*) *I had a right,* etc. 'Leave your hand off me and open the room door, and you will see *am I telling you any lie'* (Lady Gregory, *McDonough's Wife*), instead of *whether* (or *if*) *I am telling you any lie.* Compare **24** III *c.* We often speak the clause introduced by the indefinite *if* or *whether* with rising intonation, thus combining the indefinite with question form to emphasize the idea of indefiniteness: 'He says I secretly do believe, but that I am perverse and fight against my convictions. I wonder *if* I do?' (Robert Hichens, *Mrs. Marden,* Ch. V).

In substantive clauses indefinites and interrogatives both have relative (i.e., conjunctive) force, serving as indefinite relatives and interrogative relatives, but for convenience the two groups are here distinguished as relatives and interrogatives. Relatives: 'It is not known *who* did it, *when* he did it, *how* he did it, *whether* (or *if*) he did it.' Interrogatives: 'I asked him *who* did it, *when* he did it, *how* he did it, *whether* (or *if*) he did it.' The interrogatives introduce indirect questions.

The subject clause usually has declarative form, but sometimes it appears in the form of a command or a question: 'Our thought has been "*Let every man look out for himself*"' (Woodrow Wilson, March 4, 1913). Examples of question form are given above and on page 185.

Examples of Subject Clauses:

'It is best *that he go'* (or more commonly *that he should go*), but originally 'The best (predicate) is *that: he should go,'* where *that* is subject, a determinative (**56** A) pointing to the following explanatory appositional clause.

It would seem — to look at the man as he sat there — *that he had grown old before his time* (Mrs. Wood, *East Lynne,* I, Ch. I).

That he was in error will scarcely be disputed by his warmest friends.

It's only natural *as* (popular form for *that*) *I shudn't git things clear at fust*, seeing as you've kept me in the dark this two month (Sheila Kaye-Smith, *Green Apple Harvest*, p. 49).

The occasion (of his discontent) was, *because he had bound himself for divers years and saw that, if he had been at liberty, he might have had greater wages* (Winthrop, *Journal*, Aug. 6, 1633).

The deputy would not suffer them to come, neither did [he] acquaint the governor with the cause, which was, *for that Salem and Sagus had not brought in money for their parts* (*ib.*, Nov., 1633).

The reason why I was alone in the mountains on this occasion was *because, for the only time in all my experience, I had a difficulty with my guide* (Theodore Roosevelt, *An Autobiography*, Ch. II).

My only terror was *lest my father should follow me* (George Eliot, *Daniel Deronda*, I, III, Ch. XX).

'Tis told *how* (= *that*) *the good squire gives never less than gold.*

Is it probable *that he will come today?*

It is not impossible *that* (or now less commonly *but, but that*, or *but what*) *I may alter the complexion of my play.*

It could not be doubted *that* (or now less commonly *but, but that*, or *but what*) *his life would be aimed at.*

It is odds when he spits *but that* (now usually simple *that*) *all his teeth flie in thy face* (John Lyly, *Midas*, III, II, 70, A.D. 1592).

It is odds *but* (now usually *that*) *you touch somebody or other's sore place* (Chesterfield, *Letters*, II, CLVII, 116, A.D. 1748).

'It is odds *that he will do it*' (*Oxford Pocket Dictionary*), now usually 'The odds are *that he will do it.*'

As in the last seven examples, *it* often points forward to the following subject clause in both declarative and interrogative sentences, but in questions *which of the two*, or in older English *whether* (as in *Matthew*, IX, 5), points forward if the reference is to two clauses: 'Which of the two is more probable, *that he will come himself*, or *that he will send a substitute?*'

Although *that*, or its substitutes *how*, or *but*, or *but that* are the most common conjunctions, the other connectives are not infrequent: '*Who* (relative pronoun) *goes light* travels fast' (proverb).

Who (or now more commonly *he who*, or in colloquial speech still more commonly *a man, fellow, woman who*) *does a thing like that* cannot be trusted.

Is there *who* (more commonly *any one who*) '*mid these awful wilds has . . . heard . . . Soft music?* etc. (Wordsworth, *Descriptive Sketches*, 340).

'*Whom* (now more commonly *those*) *the gods love* die young,' and in older English after this model 'When *him* (instead of *he whom*) *we serve's* away' (Shakespeare).

It is he *that* (or *who*) *did it.*

It is he *that I am so anxious about* (or *about whom I am so anxious*).

'Handsome is *that* (= *he who;* see **23** II 10 *a*, last par.) *handsome does*' (proverb), or sometimes here the relative pronoun *as* instead of *that:* 'Handsome is *as handsome does*' (De Morgan, *Somehow Good*, Ch. VI).

There are *that* (now *those that*, or *those who*) *dare* (Shakespeare, *Henry the Eighth*, V, I, 40).

'The question I want to ask is, *Who* (interrogative) *is he?'* (direct question), or in the form of an indirect question *who he is.*

'The great mystery now is, *who* (relative) *he is,'* or more graphically in the form of a speculative question, *Who is he?*

It is not known *who* (relative) *he is.*

Whoever (relative) *calls* must be admitted.

It is not yet known *what* (relative) *they did.*

It has often been asked *what* (interrogative) *I meant* (indirect question).

What (plural relative) *have often been censured as Shakespeare's conceits* are completely justifiable (Coleridge).

What he says goes.

Whatever (relative) *he talks on* will prove interesting.

'*Which course we are to take* will be announced soon,' but where the thought is more indefinite we say '*What* (or *whatever*) *changes we make in our plans* will be announced later,' or a little more definitely, '*Whichever of these three plans he approves* will be the one we adopt' (relatives).

'It is not yet known *which*, or *what* (relatives), *road he took,*' or '*which* (relative) *of the roads he took.*' 'It has often been asked *which*, or *what* (interrogatives), *road he took,*' or '*which* (interrogative) *of the roads he took.*'

Where (relative adverb) *he is weakest* is in his facts (*Concise Oxford Dictionary*).

'It is immaterial *where or when* (relatives) *he goes,*' but when the relative adverb becomes quite emphatic, the subject clause comes to the front, so that the relative adverb may stand at the beginning of the sentence, and the anticipatory *it*, of course, drops out: '*Well, where that rolling-pin's got to* is a mystery' (Compton Mackenzie, *The Altar Steps*, Ch. III).

It has often been asked *where and when* (interrogatives) *he went.*

'The most important question (or thing that concerns us) now is *when* (relative) *he will return,*' or more graphically in the form of a speculative question (**23** II 1, last par.), *When will he return?*

It was a bond of union *when I learned that he was friendless as I* (Doyle, *The Memoirs of Sherlock Holmes*, p. 156).

It is not known *where* (relative) *he came from.*

It has often been asked *where* (interrogative) *he came from.*

It is immaterial *why* (relative) *he did it.*

It has often been asked *why* (interrogative) *he did it.*

It could easily be seen *how* (relative) *he did it.*

Is that *how* (relative) *you look at it?*

It has often been asked *how* (interrogative) *he did it.*

It is doubtful *whether*, or *if* (relatives), *he is coming.*

The first question I put to him was *whether*, or *if* (interrogatives), *he would do it* (indirect question).

It is immaterial *whether* (relative) *he comes himself, or whether he sends a substitute* (or *whether he comes himself or sends a substitute*).

It has often been asked *whether* (interrogative) *he will come himself, or whether he will send a substitute.*
It is not known *whether* (relative) *he did it or not.*
It occurred to me *what a nice stroke of business it would be to offer my services to them* (*Cassel's Magazine*, May, 1894, p. 425).
How strong is the hold which universities and public schools together have upon the English mind, to what an extent their influences dominate the men who in turn are entrusted with the administration of the country, may be judged by the following estimate (Escott, *England*).

The subject clause is sometimes complex, i.e., consists of a principal and a subordinate clause, the one being embedded in the other: 'What the South wants above all things is just *what General Grant says let us have,* and that is peace' (Henry Watterson, *Editorial*, Nov. 9, 1868). Here the principal clause of the subject clause, *General Grant says,* is embedded in the subordinate clause.

a. OMISSION OF 'THAT.' As in the original paratactic (**19** 3) construction, *that* is still often omitted: 'It was natural *they should like each other.' 'There are,* it seems, *few people present who are interested in this subject.'* 'It is to be hoped *nothing serious has happened.'* The omission of *that* always takes place when the principal clause is embedded in the subject clause, as in the second example. Elsewhere, however, the *that* should not be omitted if it is needed to keep the thought clear, i.e., to indicate the oneness of the words in the subject clause and to maintain the integrity of the group as a distinct grammatical element in contradistinction to other elements in the sentence. It is especially needed when the clause stands in the first place, but it is also often useful elsewhere.

b. POSITION AND STRESS. If a predicate noun or adjective is emphatic it is often placed near the beginning of the sentence after anticipatory *it,* is stressed, and pronounced with falling intonation — here indicated by a period — while the subject clause stands at the end: 'It is at least a *probability.,* or *probable.,* that he will come tomorrow.' If the subject clause is emphatic it stands at the end, while the predicate — word or clause — is in the first place, is unstressed, and is followed by the verb, which is spoken with rising intonation — here indicated by a raised period: 'The probability is· *that he will come tomorrow.'* 'The fact is· *he has already come.'* 'As she sat down she took up her yarn and needles. It was a sweater, I think. What matters is· *that her hands moved swiftly and deftly'* (Meredith Nicholson, *Lady Larkspur*, Ch. II, p. 56. The emphasis upon the subject clause — the full or the abridged clause — is in writing often indicated by setting the clause

off by a comma or a colon: 'It seems to me the idea of our civilization, underlying all American life, is, *that men do not need any
guardian*' (Wendell Phillips, *Harper's Ferry*). 'Something must be
done to relieve congestion. That something is: *widening the gates*'
(Editorial in *Chicago Tribune*, Feb. 27, 1925).

The unemphatic predicate here is often situation *it* (7 C, last
par.): 'The queer part of it was that Miss Waters didn't seem
to be really mean. *It* (= the cause of her trouble-making) was
just that she couldn't mind her own business' (Fannie Kilbourne
in *American Magazine*, Sept., 1925). 'He used to grumble at his
ill-luck and his small bag. *It* (= the cause of his ill-luck) was not
that he lacked skill with his gun. He was a good shot, but he
absolutely disregarded caution in stalking' (Ernest Brooks in
McClure's Magazine, Sept., 1925).

There is often an anticipatory *this*, which is spoken with rising
intonation, thus pointing forward to the following subject clause,
which is then usually without a conjunction: 'But the purpose
of this epistle is this˙: mother's having a few people in for dinner
before we go over to Lovell's dance; will you come?' (Edwin
Balmer, *The Breath of Scandal*, Ch. I, p. 6). 'Of course you can
see something has happened. It's this˙ — Captain Orwyn has
been killed in the war' (Robert Hichens, *Mrs. Marden*, Ch. IX).

c. EMPHASIS AND ATTRACTION. In accordance with the principle described in 4 II C, we can make any noun or pronoun in a
sentence emphatic by making it formally the predicate of a sentence introduced by anticipatory *it*. Of course, also a subject
can in this way be made emphatic: Instead of 'Í am not marvelous. Yóu are marvelous' we may say: 'It's not Í that *am* (instead of the correct *is*) marvelous. It's yóu that *are* (instead of
the correct *is*) marvelous' (Arnold Bennett, *Sacred and Profane
Love*, Act I). The correct third person occurs sometimes: 'It is
not I that *does* it' (Cameron Mackenzie, *Mr. and Mrs. Pierce*,
Ch. III). 'Is it you that's going to be married, or is it Edith?'
(Shaw, *The Doctor's Dilemma*, 229). ''Tisn't I that *wants* to spoil
your home' (Galsworthy, quoted from Jespersen's *Modern English Grammar*, III, 90, where there are other examples). The
correct third person was employed by Chaucer, and has long been
in limited use: 'It am I that *loveth* so hote (hotly) Emelye the
brighte' (*The Knightes Tale*, 878). As in the example from Bennett, a peculiar attraction now usually takes place when the subject
or object of the subordinate clause represents the same person or
thing as the predicate noun or pronoun of the principal proposition. The emphatic subject of the principal proposition here
becomes formally an emphatic predicate, and the subordinate

clause, which is really a subject clause, is construed as an attributive relative clause, so that only such relative pronouns can be used here as are used in the attributive relative clause; and the verb, if the relative is subject, must agree in person and number with the false antecedent, the predicate of the principal proposition. Similarly, 'It is his searching questions *that* (or *which*) *confuse me*,' instead of the correct *what confuse me*. If there are a positive and a negative antecedent, the verb usually agrees with the positive form: 'It is *yóu*, not *Í*, who *are* afraid to pursue this subject further' (Willa Cather, *A Gold Slipper*).

In questions, of course, the emphatic predicate here stands in the first place wherever it is an interrogative pronoun or adverb: '*Whó* is it that needs me?' '*Whén* is it that you need me?'

In Old English, a determinative (**56** A) often stood in such sentences before the subject clause, pointing to it: 'Hwæt is *se* þe þe sloh?' (*Matthew*, XXVI, 68, A.D. 1000); literally, 'Who is that one there: [he] struck you?' In the King James Version the English form of this passage is: 'Who is *he* that smote you?' Here *he* corresponds closely to Old English *se*. It is not a personal pronoun, but a determinative serving as an anticipatory subject, pointing to the following subject clause. This anticipatory subject indicates the sex. This type of expression is now little used where it is simply desired to identify. In Old English, there was another type of expression. The anticipatory subject was a neuter form, and the subject of the subject clause was suppressed: 'Hwa is *þæt* þe slog?' (Rushworth MS.) = 'Who was *that* struck you?' As can be seen by the translation, this old type of expression is still common in our colloquial language. We now use the old neuter *that* or the modern *it* in interrogative form, but regularly *it* in declarative form: 'Who was that *just came in?*' 'What's that *you say?*' (Cameron Mackenzie, *Mr. and Mrs. Pierce*, Ch. VIII). 'Who was it *told you that?*' (A. Marshall, *Watermeads*, Ch. II). 'What is it *moves this body?*' (Alfred Noyes, *The Torch-Bearers*, p. 240). 'It was this infernal fellow *completely upset me*' (Meredith, *Rhoda Fleming*, Ch. XXI). 'Prothero (name) had first set him doubting, but it was Benham's own temperament *took him on to denial*' (H. G. Wells, *The Research Magnificent*, Ch. III). 'But that is not it (now *it is not that*) *I intend to speak of here*' (Hobbes, *Leviathan*, II, XXVI, 137, A.D. 1651). When the predicate of the principal proposition is a pronoun in the first or second person, the verb of the subject clause is usually attracted into the person and the number of the predicate pronoun, as in the examples in the first paragraph, where the relative pronoun is expressed: 'No, 'tis you *dream*' (Dryden, *All for Love*, I, i, 335,

A.D. 1678). "'Tis thou *hast dragged* My soul, just rising, down again to Earth' (Thomas Godfrey, *The Prince of Parthia*, II, VI, A.D. 1765). The correct third person has long been in limited use: "'Tis I, sir, *needs* a good one' (Middleton-Rowley, *The Spanish Gipsie*, III, II, 124, A.D. 1661). It has even become common in popular Irish English: 'Is it yourself *has brought* the water?' (Synge, *The Well of the Saints*, Act I). 'Is it you *is* Mary Doul?' (*ib.*). 'Isn't it yourself *is* after playing lies on me?' (*ib.*).

In the literary language the subject of the subject clause is now usually expressed in this type: 'Who was it *just went out?*' or in literary form 'Who was it *that* (or *who*) *just went out?*' 'What was it *that caused* the disturbance?' 'What was it *which Wulf had recognized in Hypatia* which had bowed the old warrior before her?' (Kingsley, *Hypatia*, p. 193). 'Assuredly it was a daring thing *which she meant to do*' (Marion Crawford, *Katherine Lauderdale*, I, Ch. VI). 'It was my two brothers *that* (or *who*) were hurt.' We thus often use *it* even where we point to persons, provided the desire is to identify, as in the last example; but when the desire is to describe, we may say with Shakespeare '*It* is a good divine that follows his own instructions' (*Merchant of Venice*, I, II, 15); or more commonly we replace *it* here by a personal pronoun that indicates gender and number: '*He* is a good divine who follows his own instructions.'

The emphatic subject that has become a formal predicate for sake of emphasis is often modified by a relative clause, so that there are two relative clauses, the first a real relative clause, the second in reality a subject clause: 'It is only women who live alone that can know what it is to yearn to have a man's strong arm.'

The predicate noun may be made emphatic in the same way as the emphatic subject: 'What you see yonder is my *néw hóuse*,' or 'It is my *néw hóuse* that you see yonder.' Here, as in case of an emphatic subject, the subject clause assumes the form of a relative clause. Compare **4** II C and **22** *a*.

Also dative and prepositional objects and adverbial elements may be made emphatic in this way, but here the subject clause has the regular form of a subject clause introduced by the conjunction *that*, or without a conjunction: 'It was *to yóu* that I gave it,' not 'It was *to yóu* to whom I gave it,' as we sometimes hear and read; but where the predicate is a nominative 'It was *yóu that* (relative pronoun) I gave it to' (or *to whom* I gave it). 'It is *to yóu* [that] he objects' (Henry James, *The Wings of the Dove*, Book II, Ch. I). 'It is *upon yóu* that I depend.' 'It was *thén* that the unexpected turn in our affairs cáme,' or to emphasize the subject of the clause: 'It was *thén* [that] came the unexpécted túrn in our affairs.' ''Twas *thén* [that] Came hórror, as to the House of Mirth, again' (William E. Leonard, *Two Lives*, p. 32). 'It wasn't *this mórning*, it was *yésterday* that I saw him.' 'It was *with gréat difficulty* that I got him to come along.' 'It was *when I was a mére lád* that I first met her.' '*Whére* is it [that] mothers learn their love?' (John Keble). Instead of using *that* in the subject clause, as in these examples, we use *since* and *before* in sentences containing an adverbial element indicating duration of time: 'It is (or has been) a *lóng tíme since* I have seen him' = 'I haven't seen him for a *lóng tíme.*' 'It is (or has been) *mány mónths since* I have seen him.' 'It will be *wéeks before* his disappearance will attract attention' = 'His disappearance will not attract attention *for wéeks.*' *That* is often employed here instead of *since*, usually differentiated in meaning from it; the clause introduced by *since* indicating that the action is past, the clause introduced by *that* indicating that the action is still continuing: 'It is now *fóur yéars since* I have studied this question,' but 'It is now *fóur yéars that* I have studied (or have been studying) this question.' 'It is now *fóur yéars that* I have meditated this work' (Byron, *Marino Faliero*, Preface). In connection with *ago*, however, *that* indicates a point of time in the past: 'It was *fóur yéars ago that* he died.' 'It is *fóur yéars since* (simple *since*, not *ago since*, as is often spoken and written) he died' calls attention to a period of time. In older English, the subject clause was sometimes introduced by *till* or *until* instead of *before:* 'It was not *lóng till* (in England now usually *before*) he set about turning this new knowledge to account' (Carlyle, *Schiller*). In the *Oxford Dictionary* this usage is represented as now confined, in England, to dialect, but to many Americans *till* is still a common form, often used alongside of *before.* Not only adverbs and adverbial phrases may thus be stressed but also adverbial clauses, as illustrated in **22** *a.*

d. REPEATED SUBJECT. Sometimes still, as in older usage, there stands in the principal proposition when it is preceded by the subject clause a personal pronoun, which points to the preceding subject clause and in a word sums up its contents, thus binding the two propositions more firmly together: 'Whoever calls, *he* must be admitted.' Today the subject clause by reason of its distinctive form is so clearly felt as such that it is usually not considered necessary to indicate this relation by the use of a personal pronoun in the nominative pointing back to it. Where, however, an emphatic compound subject, consisting of two or more full or abridged clauses, introduces the sentence, it is customary to place a *that* at the beginning of the principal proposition to point back to the preceding compound subject: 'To know how others stand, that we may know how we ourselves stand; to know how we ourselves stand, *that* we may correct our mistakes and achieve our deliverance — *that* is our problem' (Matthew Arnold, *The Modern Element*).

e. ABRIDGMENT OF SUBJECT CLAUSE. This clause can be abridged to an infinitive clause with *to* when there is some word in the principal proposition which can serve as the subject of the infinitive or can indicate it: 'It is stupid of you *to say it*.' The subject is often implied in a preceding possessive adjective: 'It is *my* earnest desire *to do it*.' '*My* way is *to act* and *let others do the talking*.' Provided the context makes the reference clear, the infinitive can be employed even though there is no word in the principal proposition that can serve as its subject: 'The great difficulty [for us] now is *how*, or *when*, or *where, to cross the river*.'

The infinitive with *to* can be used also when the subject of the clause is general or indefinite, in which case the subject is usually understood: 'It is wise *to be cautious*.'

When the infinitive has a subject of its own, we introduce the clause by *for . . . to*, putting the subject into the accusative and placing it between *for* and *to:* '*For me to back out now* would be to acknowledge that I am afraid.' 'All that I want is *for somebody to be thinking about me*' (Arnold Bennett, *The Glimpse*). To emphasize the subject of the infinitive we often withhold it for a time, placing it after the infinitive and inserting a formal anticipatory subject, *there* (**4 II C**), after *for:* 'It is impossible *for there ever to be a conflict between our two countries*.'

The *to*-infinitive is old, but it was long limited in its development since it could only be used when there was some word in the principal proposition which could serve as its subject, or when its subject was general or indefinite, as described above. Its compact convenient form, however, won it favor, so that in the fourteenth century there arose a desire to extend its boundaries, i.e., to use it with a subject of its own if there was no word in the principal proposition to serve as its subject: 'It is no maystrye *for a lord To dampne a man* withoute answere or word' (Chaucer, *The Legend of Good Women*, 400) = 'It is no great feat *for a lord to condemn a man* without answer or word.' The *for* + noun here represents an older simple dative of reference, which, as illustrated in **12 1 B** *a*, is still sometimes used. This group of words with the force of the old simple dative of reference is still widely employed: 'It was hard *for me* to understand him.'

Closely related to this dative is the dative of interest, which was likewise a simple form in Old English, and is even sometimes

still used in its simple form, as illustrated in **12** 1 B *b*. In its
modern form with *for* + accusative the dative of interest was
common with Chaucer and is still much used: 'It is bet *for me*
To sleen myself than been defouled thus' (*The Frankelyns Tale*,
693) = 'It is better *for me* to slay myself than to be violated thus.'
Both the dative of reference and the dative of interest are sentence
datives and modify the whole sentence, but there is always here a
logical relation between the dative and the following infinitive,
so that the dative is often felt as the subject of the infinitive.
This led in Chaucer's time to the use of the modern dative, i.e.,
for + accusative, as the subject of the infinitive. The *for* + noun
in the quotations from Chaucer is still near a real dative, but
gradually the use of this form became freer, so that in time it
became common to use *for* + noun or pronoun as the subject of
an infinitive when there was no word in the principal proposition
which could serve as its subject.

Alongside of the infinitive with *for . . . to* there thrived in
this early period and for centuries afterwards a competing con-
struction, the *to*-infinitive with an absolute accusative as subject:
'Thanne (then) schal y (I) haue al that [it] is necessarie *me to
knowe*' (Pecock, *The Donet*, p. 93, A.D. 1449). This construction
arose under Latin influence, and followed the Latin quite closely:
'Forsothe it is li3ter *heuene and erthe to passe*' (*Luke*, XVI, 17,
Purvey's ed., A.D. 1388), corresponding to the Latin version,
'Facilius est autem *coelum et terram praeterire*,' later replaced by
'It is easier *for heaven and earth to pass*' (King James Version).
This construction was used not only by scholars, but not infrequently also by literary men: 'It is a greet folye *a womman to
haue a fair array outward and in herself* [been] *foul inward*' (Chaucer, *The Persouns Tale*, 935). The simple accusative here has
disappeared from the literary language. An accusative is found
here in popular speech, but it is of quite different origin, resulting
from the popular tendency to employ the accusative instead of
the nominative, which, as described in the next paragraph, was
once common here: 'I felt as if it was a great compliment *him*
(for *he*) *to come in* friendly like and take a chair and talk to you
and me' (M. O. W. Oliphant, *The Second Son*).

As the absolute accusative that arose under Latin influence was
foreign to native English expression, it was replaced in early
Modern English by the more familiar absolute nominative (**17** 3 B):
'*I to bear this* is some burden' (Shakespeare, *Timon of Athens*,
IV, III, 266), now '*For me to bear this* is some burden.' This
construction has been supplanted in the literary language by
the competing construction of the infinitive with *for . . . to*

described on page 191, but it survives in popular speech. It is especially common in popular Irish English: '[it is] A great wonder *he not to have come* and this the fair day of Galway' (Lady Gregory, *McDonough's Wife*). This construction was carried to Ireland by British colonists in the seventeenth century, where it easily became established in Irish English, as it corresponded closely to Gaelic expression.

There is another infinitive construction with *for to* of entirely different origin, which first appeared in Old English, as described in **33 2**. The *to* of the infinitive originally indicated purpose or end. As in the course of time *to* had lost much of its original concrete force, *for*, with the same meaning, was placed before the *to* to bring out more clearly in purpose clauses the idea of purpose or end. But early in the thirteenth century the new double form *for to* met the fate of simple *to*, i.e., lost its concrete force, so that from this time on it was long used alongside of *to* without the slightest differentiation as a mere parallel form in all the categories in which simple *to* could be used, i.e., in subject clauses, object clauses, etc.: 'And of swich thing were goodly *for to telle*' (Chaucer, Prologue of *The Nonne Preestes Tale*, 13), now 'It would be pleasant *to tell* such a thing.' As this old use of *for to* instead of simple *to* had nothing whatever to recommend it and was even of positive harm since there was another *for to* with different function, as described on page 191, it gradually in course of centuries disappeared from the literary language. It lives on, however, in popular speech: 'It's not manners *for t'*help oursel's' (Mrs. Gaskell, *Sylvia's Lovers*, Ch. XXVI).

The simple infinitive was often used here in older English. See **4** *d*, p. 5. This older literary usage is still common in Irish English: 'It is best for you *give* in to their say' (Lady Gregory, *McDonough's Wife*). Often also in all parts of the English-speaking territory in colloquial speech: 'All she has to do is *come* here' (George Ade, *Hand-Made Fables*, p. 19). In many cases, however, the simple infinitive is retained, since it is felt and interpreted as an imperative. See **4** *d*, p. 5, for examples.

As in *b* (2nd par.) the sentence is sometimes introduced by an unemphatic predicate, situation *it* (**7** C, last par.). The *to* of the infinitive is in colloquial speech usually suppressed: 'I was no match for him, It (= *the thing to do*) was just *dodge* an' *run* for me' (Amy Lowell, *Selected Poems*, p. 180). This form is often felt as an imperative, as can be seen by the punctuation: 'It's *tramp! tramp! tramp!* I've covered more mileage than th' mailman looking for the lady in black' (Harold Teen Cartoon in *Chicago Tribune*, Feb. 19, 1929).

The infinitive construction is often replaced by the gerund: '*To have done one's duty* (or *Having done one's duty*) is a great consolation in misfortune.' '*To live near a large town* (or *Living near a large town*) is an advantage for a farmer.' The sentence here is often introduced by an anticipatory *it*, pointing forward to the real subject standing at or near the end, which by being withheld for a time, creating suspense, becomes emphatic: 'It is dangerous *to play with explosives*' (or *playing with explosives*). 'It is no use, or of no use, or useless, *to say anything*, or *for me*, or *for you*, or *for Father*, to say anything, or *my*, or *your*, or *Father's saying anything.*' 'What use (or of what use) is *it to say anything?*' 'It was very strange *for me getting* a letter from him dated Haddington' (Jane Welsh Carlyle, *Letter to Jeanie Welsh*, Sept. 12, 1843) (or more commonly *for me to get*). '*My daughter's staying so late* worries me,' or '*The staying of my daughter so late* worries me.' The noun predicate in such sentences can become subject without a change of meaning: 'There is no *use* (or no *good*) (subject of sentence) in saying (or to say) anything' instead of 'It is no *use* (or no *good*) (predicate of sentence) saying (or to say) (subject) anything.' The *it* and *there* constructions are often blended: 'There is no use *saying* (or *to say*) anything.' Compare **4** II C.

The regular subject clause with a conjunction followed by a nominative subject and a finite verb is often replaced by the old appositional type of clause described in **17** 3 B, which here consists of a subject in the absolute nominative followed by a predicate in the form of an appositional adjective or participle: '*Things going right* is to me real poetry' (or is to me poetical). 'It's not a bit of use *you tálking*, I shan't wear it again' (Arnold Bennett, *Old Wives' Tale*, II, Ch. II). 'It was no use *men being ángry with them for damaging the links*' (*London Times*, 1913). In the last two examples the subject clause stands at the end for emphasis. Other examples in **17** 3 B.

To make room for an emphatic predicate adjective, noun, or pronoun near the head of the sentence, this subject clause is often put at the end with an anticipatory subject *it* at the beginning: 'It is vílely unjúst, *men closing two-thirds of the respectable careers to women*' (Sir Harry Johnston, *Mrs. Warren's Daughter*, Ch. III). Often the subject of the participle is not expressed but merely implied in the emphatic predicate of the principal proposition: 'I do not say these things for a dollar, or to fill up the time while I wait for a boat: it is yóu *talking* (= *who are talking*) just as much as myself — I act as the tongue of you' (Walt Whitman, *Leaves of Grass*, p. 89). 'It was always yóu *teasing me'* (= *who teased me*) (Eleanor Carroll Chilton, *Shadows Waiting*, p. 57).

As in *c*, a subject clause here, such as in the first example in the second paragraph on page 194, may be converted into an emphatic predicate after *it is:* 'It is *things góing ríght* that is poetical' (Chesterton, *The Man Who Was Thursday*, Ch. I).

In the case of impersonal expression the subject clause here as elsewhere has no real subject, only a mere formal subject *it:* '*It being Sunday* complicates matters,' or in gerundial form '*Its being Sunday* complicates matters.'

PREDICATE CLAUSE

22. Conjunctions. The predicate clause performs the function of a predicate noun or adjective: 'Serious trials are to the soul *what storms are to the atmosphere*' (= purifying agents).

The predicate clause is introduced by *who* (= *the man* or *boy, woman,* etc.), *what, why, as, where* (*a*), *when* (*a*), *before* (*a*), *after* (*a*), *because* (*a*), *that.*

Examples:

'He was not *who* (now more commonly *the man*) *he seemed to be,*' but regularly in the accusative relation *He was not the man I took him to be.*

Reputation is *what we seem;* character is *what we are.*

We are not *what we ought to be.*

They looked *what they were* — the sisters, the wives, the mothers of strong men (Vachell, *Quinneys'*, 42).

And this is *why I sojourn here* (Keats, *La Belle Dame Sans Merci*, XII).

Things are not always *as they seem to be.*

That was *where he failed* (*Oxford Dictionary*).

That is *where he lives.*

Now is *when I need him most.*

'This (or that) is *what he meant.*' 'Is that *what he meant?*'

That is *what we agreed on.*

That sometimes introduces a predicate clause which explains a determinative *so* that stands in the principal proposition: 'Yet *so* it is, *that people can bear any quality in the world better than beauty*' (Steele, *Spectator*).

There is sometimes a *that* in the principal proposition, pointing back as a demonstrative to a *what* in the preceding predicate clause, a survival of older usage when the propositions had more independent force than today and needed to be more closely linked by demonstratives in order that the relation between the members might be pointed out. The poet is fond of these older more concrete forms of expression: '*What* the leaves are to the forest, *That* to the world are children' (Longfellow). Compare **26** (2nd par. under Examples).

In all the preceding examples the predicate clause is a nominative clause, predicated of a subject; but as it can be predicated of an accusative object, it can be also an accusative clause: 'I found it to be *what I wanted*.'

In **8 I 1 c** it has been shown how difficult it often is to determine whether the noun before the copula is the subject or the predicate complement. It is also often difficult to determine whether the clause before the copula is a subject or a predicate clause. The general rule for determining the grammatical relations given in **8 I 1 c** will prove useful also here: '*What he said* (subject clause) was a blessing to us all.' 'It matters little how a man dies. *What matters* (predicate clause) is how he lives.'

a. POSITION AND STRESS. Just as any noun, adverb, or adverbial phrase may become an emphatic predicate by being stressed and put into the first part of the sentence after *it is*, so may any clause become an emphatic predicate clause by being placed at the beginning after *it is*, followed immediately by the subject in the form of a *that*-clause: 'It was *where we now stand* that we parted.' 'It was *when I was a mere lad* that I first met her.' 'It was *before her mother died* that I first met her.' 'It was *after her mother died* that I first met her.' 'It is only *because I regard it as absolutely necessary* that I take such harsh measures.' After a causal clause employed as an emphatic predicate, we sometimes instead of a subject clause employ an independent statement introduced by adversative *but*, since we desire to palliate the deed: 'I know it's because one is bad — *but* the minute one has to be grateful one isn't' (De Morgan, *Joseph Vance*, Ch. X). Compare **4 II C** (6th par.) and **21 c**.

The principal verb is stressed by putting it in an unusual position, especially by forming a predicate clause in which *what* is subject and the emphatic verb is predicate, in accordance with a principle observable elsewhere that a verb inclines more to stress in a subordinate than a principal proposition: 'Manners are what (plural) *véx* or *sóothe, corrúpt* or *púrify, exált* or *debáse, bárbarize* or *refíne* us' (Burke). 'Truth is what *húrts*.' 'The factories are what (plural) *blácken up* the city so.' This form is also used to emphasize the subject, since it is a convenient device to put the subject in an unusual position: 'That is what *Í* think' instead of '*I* think that.' If, however, the emphatic subject is a thought it can be put into a *that*-clause and placed at the end of the sentence while an unemphatic predicate *what*-clause introduces the proposition, followed by the verb spoken with rising intonation, here indicated by a raised period: 'What I am glad to hear is · that he is fond of music.'

b. COMPLEX PREDICATE CLAUSE. The predicate clause is often complex, i.e., consists of a principal proposition and a subordinate clause, the one being often embedded in the other: 'But that is not *what I sent for you to tell you*' (Robert Hichens, *Mrs. Marden*, Ch. XII). Here the principal proposition of the complex predicate clause, *I sent for you*, is embedded in the subordinate clause.

c. ABRIDGMENT OF PREDICATE CLAUSE. We often use the gerundial construction instead of a predicate clause with a finite verb: 'That is *hitting the nail on the head*.' Prepositional predicate clauses are common: 'He seems *about taking the step*.' See **7** F, **50** 4 *c dd*.

CHAPTER XIII

ATTRIBUTIVE ADJECTIVE CLAUSES

23. There are two classes — the attributive substantive clause and the attributive relative clause.

ATTRIBUTIVE SUBSTANTIVE CLAUSE

23 I. An understanding of the nature of a direct and an indirect question is necessary to appreciate the form and meaning of some of the examples of this clause given below. A general description of the nature of an indirect question is presented in **21** and **23 II 1** (last par.). This subject is discussed also in **24 III.** The attributive substantive clause is often a direct or an indirect question: 'We hope you will answer in your next letter our oft repeated question, *How did you accomplish it?*' (direct question), or *how you accomplished it* (indirect question). The forms employed to introduce direct and indirect questions in attributive substantive clauses are also used to introduce other attributive substantive clauses, namely, indefinite relative clauses, where there is not the slightest reference to a question or an answer, as in 'His explanation of *how* (indefinite relative adverb) *he accomplished it* (indefinite relative clause) is very interesting.' There is, however, a close relation between these interrogative and indefinite relative (**21**, 4th par.) forms. Both groups were originally indefinites and still retain their original meaning. An interrogative is an indefinite that assumes the additional function of asking information concerning indefinite relations. The interrogative, however, never ceases to be an indefinite. Indeed, we often, instead of employing an indefinite relative, use the form of a question, although we do not expect an answer. Deliberative question (**23** II 1, last par.): 'What shall I say to him when he comes?' Speculative question (**23** II 1, last par.): 'What could he have meant?' On the other hand, the question often loses every trace of a desire for an answer, also every trace of indefiniteness, doubt, and becomes declarative, expressing the idea of an emphatic contrary assertion — a rhetorical question: 'What's the use of trying?' = 'There is no use in trying.' Some questions, such as 'What is the meaning of life?' are either speculative or rhetorical. All the above shades of meaning appear in the attributive substantive clause: 'Next comes the question *what you want it for*' (indirect question) or in direct form, *What do you want it for?* 'The question often comes up in my mind *what he wanted it for*' (indirect speculative question), or in direct form, *What did he want it for?* 'The question often comes up in my mind *what I shall say to him when he comes*' (indirect deliberative question), or in direct form, *What shall I say to him when he comes?* 'The question often comes up in my mind *what the use is of trying*' (indirect rhetorical question), or in direct form, *What's the use of trying?*

For the most part, attributive substantive clauses are appositional or genitive clauses, but a large number are prepositional.

A noun that modifies another noun or a pronoun is usually in the genitive, but if the modifier is a full clause the most common construction is the appositional, the clause lying alongside of the governing noun or pronoun as an appositive: 'The hope *of his recovery* is faint,' but 'The hope *that he may recover* is faint.' The genitive clause, however, is often used when the clause is introduced by exclamatory *what a* or an indefinite relative pronoun, adjective, or adverb. Objective genitive: 'He soon gave proof *of what a wonderful leader he was.*' 'One evening of each week was set aside for the reception *of who(so)ever chose to visit him.*' 'I shall make note *of whom copies are to be sent to,*' or *of to whom copies are to be sent.* 'I am in favor of the purchase *of whatever books you may need.*' 'We can count on Father's sanction *of whichever course* (or *whichever of these courses*) *we may choose.*' '.His description *of how he did it* is interesting.' Partitive genitive: 'This gave us a taste *of what was to follow.*' Possessive genitive: 'The force and clearness *of what was said* depended so much on how it was said.' Appositive genitive: 'We are not investigating the question (= subject) *of whether he is trustworthy,*' or in the form of simple apposition *whether he is trustworthy.*

The prepositional clause is sometimes introduced by the

conjunction *that* preceded by a preposition and anticipatory *it* as its object: 'There was no doubt *about it that he took the money.*' Usually, however, prepositional clauses are introduced by an indefinite relative pronoun, adjective, or adverb: 'I haven't the least interest *in what he is doing, in what views he holds.*' 'I have little insight *into what he is doing, into what motives are swaying him.*' 'We have no definite information yet *as to which route* (or *which of .these routes) he will take.*' 'Can you give me any information *as to whether he will come, as to when he will come?*' Compare **10** IV *a.* The preposition is often omitted: 'She had no idea [*as to*] *why she thought of him thus suddenly,*' or '[*as to*] *Why she thought of him thus suddenly* she had no idea' (Galsworthy, *Freelands,* Ch. VIII). 'I am in doubt [*as to*] *whether I should buy or sell.*'

The appositional clause is introduced by different conjunctions, or is sometimes without such introduction, and can, moreover, be introduced by both interrogatives and indefinite relatives: 'The thought *that we shall live on after death in another better world* consoles many.' 'I'd a feeling *as* (popular for literary *that) maybe you cud give me,*' etc. (Sheila Kaye-Smith, *Green Apple Harvest,* p. 35). 'There can be no question (or doubt) *that* (or sometimes *but,* or *but that) she was lovely,*' or in the form of a prepositional clause, 'There can be no doubt *about it that she was lovely.*' 'We ought to discuss carefully the vital question (or problem) *whether* (relative) *we can do it or not,*' or more graphically in the form of a deliberative question, *Can we do it?* or more simply in the form of the appositive genitive of a noun, *of our ability to do it.* 'I have often asked myself the question *whether* (interrogative) *I have the right to do it*' (indirect deliberative question), or in direct form, *Have I the right to do it?* 'We now come to the two main questions (or problems), *what* (relative) *the cause of the disturbance is, and who* (relative) *the proper person would be to remove it,*' or more graphically in the form of a deliberative question, *What is the cause of the disturbance, and who would be the proper person to remove it?* 'But tell me one thing now: *What was that awful shadow I saw?*' (Mark Twain, *Joan of Arc,* I, Ch. VII) (direct question). 'I now put the question to you plainly, *Will you come or not?*' (direct question). 'I insisted on an answer to my question *whether he was coming or not*' (indirect question). 'I should like to say to you one important thing, *You should go slow in this matter*' (polite command), or in stronger language, *Go very slow in this matter!* 'I should like to say to him one important thing, *he should go very slow in this matter*' (indirect polite command), or in stronger language, *let him go very slow in this matter.*

Appositional clauses, as can be seen by the examples on page 201, are for the most part introduced by conjunctions, especially the following: *that;* after the noun *fear* sometimes still, as in older English, *lest* instead of *that;* after *no doubt* usually *that,* or now less commonly *but, but that,* or *but what; as,* in popular speech often replacing *that; whether,* now a conjunction, but in older English a pronoun = *which of the two,* as in *Matthew,* IX, 5. The use of *lest* after the noun *fear,* and the use of *that, but that,* or *but what* after the noun *doubt,* and *as if* after the noun *look,* shows that the noun is influenced by the corresponding verb, as also in the case of most of the other conjunctions employed here, so far as the nouns are derived from verbs: 'I was in mortal *fear lest* (or more commonly *that*) *he should see me.*' 'The good people of the place had no doubt *that* (or *but,* or *but that,* or *but what*) *the end had really come.*' 'I never had a doubt *but what you would* [*do it*]' (Winston Churchill, *Coniston,* Ch. VII). 'There was in his eye a look *as if he would annihilate me.*' The appositional clause, however, often follows the noun directly, as appositive clause without a connective: 'His fear *he might never accomplish anything* is torturing him a good deal.' Also appositional clauses in the form of direct or indirect questions or in the form of relative clauses introduced by relative pronouns, adjectives, or adverbs frequently occur; also appositional commands, as illustrated in the preceding paragraphs.

There often stands before the *that*-clause an explanatory co-ordinating conjunction, *as, such as, namely, to wit,* etc., thus indicating that an additional remark is about to be made, a remark not bearing upon the preceding statement as a whole but upon only a single noun in it, hence appearing in the form of an attributive appositional clause: 'She gave me a good deal of miscellaneous information, *as that William's real name was Mr. Hicking*' (J. M. Barrie, *The Little White Bird,* Ch. VIII).

a. ABRIDGMENT OF ATTRIBUTIVE SUBSTANTIVE CLAUSE. The attributive substantive clause can often be abridged to an infinitive clause with *to* when its subject is general or indefinite, or is implied in some word in the principal proposition: 'The time *to do something* has at last come.' 'Now arises the question *of how to do it.*' 'Then he went out to the sunshine of that morning with the whole world before him and his choice *of what to do with it.*' 'Your plan *to go yourself* doesn't please me.' 'But one course was open to me — *to cut his acquaintance*' (Thackeray, *Snobs,* Ch. I). Compare **50** 4 *d* and **10** V 3. In colloquial speech the *to* of the infinitive is often omitted in the appositional relation: 'There was only one thing for me to do — *regain hold of the reins of the government*'

(*Chicago Tribune*, Feb. 24, 1929). The absence of *to* here indicates in many cases, as in this example, that the form is felt as an imperative.

When there is no word in the principal proposition that can serve as the subject of the infinitive, it has a subject of its own introduced by *for:* 'Your plan *for me to go* doesn't please me.' 'The time had come *for the parting words to be spoken over the dead*' (Oliver Wendell Holmes, *Elsie Venner*). Even when there is some word in the principal proposition that might serve as the subject of the infinitive, the infinitive often has a subject of its own to remove all ambiguity and make the thought perfectly clear: 'I sent him the money in time *for it to reach him on Monday.*' The origin of the *for*-construction is explained in **21** *e.* In the appositive relation the *for . . . to* clause, just as the full *that*-clause, is often introduced by an explanatory conjunction, *as, such as, namely,* etc.: 'Michael, who all the time was dreading many unfortunate events, *as for the cabman to get down from his box and quarrel about the fare, or for the train to be full, or for Stella to be sick during the journey*' (Mackenzie, *Youth's Encounter*). Compare **50** 4 *d* and **10** V 3.

The infinitive here, except in the cases stated in **50** 4 *d*, can be replaced by the gerund. The gerund does not have an expressed subject if the subject of the principal proposition or some word in it can serve as its subject: 'Your plan *of going* yourself doesn't please me.' If there is no word in the principal proposition that can serve as the subject of the gerund, it has a subject of its own, usually a genitive of a noun or a possessive adjective (originally a genitive of a personal pronoun), or now often also the accusative of a noun or pronoun, as described in **50** 3: 'The hope of *John's* — or *his*, or *John's brother* (acc.) — *coming* cheers us.'

The gerund is not only common as an attributive genitive, as in these examples, but also in an attributive prepositional phrase after most prepositions: 'He is experiencing much joy on account of *his sister's* — or *her*, or *his sister's son* (acc.) — *coming.*' For limitations to this usage see **50** 4 *d* (last par.).

The gerundial clause is often used as an appositive: 'That is just our way, *always arriving too late*,' or *always to arrive too late.*

The appositive is sometimes an absolute nominative clause (**17** 3 D): 'Well, that is just our way, exactly — *one half of the administration always busy* getting the family into trouble, *the other half busy* getting it out again' (Mark Twain, *Letter to Mrs. Grover Cleveland*, Nov. 6, 1887).

CHAPTER XIV

ATTRIBUTIVE RELATIVE CLAUSE

23 II. This clause was originally an appositional construction, as can still be seen by the form which it often has: '*The book I hold [it] in my hand* is an English grammar.' 'I want to show you my books, especially *those I've recently acquired [them].*' Here *the* and *those* each point as a demonstrative, or more accurately a determinative (**56 A**), to a following explanatory appositional clause. Such a clause has the full force of a subordinate relative clause, but there is in it no relative pronoun. The preceding

204

determinative points to it and serves the same purpose as a relative; only it stands in the principal proposition and points to the following dependent clause, while a relative pronoun stands in the dependent clause and points back to the antecedent in the principal proposition. Such a clause without a relative pronoun is called an asyndetical (without a connective) relative clause. As can be seen by the forms in brackets, the pronoun that belongs to such a clause is a personal pronoun, not a relative. The suppression of the personal pronoun here leads us to look to what precedes for the connection. This suppression of the pronoun is the old primitive way of indicating that the clause is subordinated to what precedes. The asyndetic relative construction is found only rarely in Old English and Old German. The writers of this early period, accustomed to the Latin type of clause with an expressed relative pronoun, carefully avoided a relative clause without a relative pronoun. The construction has disappeared in Modern German, but it is widely used in present-day English. As it has long been used in Danish, it seems quite probable that in the older period the large Scandinavian population of Great Britain helped establish the construction in English. Its present wide use is described in 10, page 233.

In Old English, we often find a double determinative in accordance with older English fondness for double expression, as seen also in the use of two negatives instead of one and the use of double determinatives in the adverbial clause constructions described in **25, 26, 27 2.** Double expression indicates a desire to make thought and feeling clearer. As, in oldest English, determinatives were only spoken gestures, they were often, like gestures in general, freely applied, as we shall see in the course of this discussion. The old double determinative form is still often employed, but we no longer feel it as such: 'I'll lend you *the* pen I write with [it],' or with double expression of the determinative 'I'll lend you *the* pen *that* I write with [it].' We do not now feel *the* and *that* as a double determinative, pointing as with two index fingers to the following explanatory clause, but construe *that* as a relative pronoun standing in the relative clause, pointing back to the antecedent *pen* in the principal proposition. As the old determinative *that* stood immediately before the explanatory remark it became closely associated with it, gradually forming with it a subordinate clause and serving as its connective, linking it to the principal proposition and thus developing into a relative pronoun. The form of the clause, however, is the old determinative, for the preposition *with* stands at the end of the clause with its pronominal object *it* suppressed. For the peculiar form that such prepositions

used to have see 62 4 (next to last par.). If the clause here were
a real relative construction the preposition would stand before the
relative pronoun, as in 'I'll lend you the pen *with which* I write.'

We now feel also *as* (from *all so*, i.e., *quite so*) as a relative
pronoun, but it was originally a determinative, like *that*, with
which it competed and still competes. Though now felt as a
relative, it still always has the old determinative construction
with the preposition at the end of the clause: 'Let us discuss only
such things *as* we can talk *of* freely.' This is the old double determinative construction, the determinatives *such* and *so* originally
pointing as with two index fingers to the following explanatory
clause: 'Let us discuss only *such* things, *so* (= *of this character*):
we can talk of [them] freely.' Also our two common relative
pronouns *who* and *which* have developed out of a determinative
construction, as will be described in detail in 1 and 3, pp. 208–212,
215–217. In choice language they now usually take the newer relative construction after prepositions, especially *who*, which already
in early Middle English was here felt as a relative pronoun, but
in colloquial speech they may still have here the old determinative form, especially *which*, which still as in older English is intimately associated with this form: 'I should like to introduce to
you the gentleman *of whom I spoke*' (or sometimes *whom I spoke
of*). 'I'll lend you the pen *with which I write*' (or often *which I
write with*). Farther on we shall see also other traces of the former
determinative character of *who* and *which*.

In Old English, the personal pronoun in the subordinate clause
was not always suppressed, as in the examples given above, for
it was sometimes necessary to express it, especially when in the
dative or genitive, to bring out the grammatical relations clearly:
'þæt is se Abraham *se him* engla god naman niwan asceop' (*Exodus*,
380), literally, 'It was that Abraham, *that one*, the God of the
angels gave *him* a new name.' Here the determinative is an
inflected form. After the uninflected determinative *þe* the personal
pronoun was employed still more freely, as it was often felt as
helpful to make the grammatical relations clear: 'þam witgum
þe God self þurh *hi* spec to hys folce' = 'to the prophets, *those:*
God himself spoke through *them* to his people.' Also *þæt* was often
used as an uninflected determinative, and could be followed by
a personal pronoun: 'And þær is mid Estum an mægþ *þæt hi*
magon cyle gewyrcan' (King Alfred, *Orosius*, 21, 13) = 'There
is among the Esthonians a tribe, *that one* (= *such a one*): they
can create cold.' In Middle English, invariable *that* superseded
se and *þe*, but the old determinative construction remained intact
throughout the period, and was still in literary use in Shake-

speare's time, especially in the genitive relation: 'Therynne woneþ a wyȝt *that* wrong is *his* name' (*Piers Plowman*, C, II, 59, about A.D. 1362–1395) = 'Therein lives a fellow, *that one:* Wrong is *his* name.' 'Name me a profest poet *that his* poetry did ever afford him so much as a competencie' (Ben Jonson, *Poetaster*, I, II, 59, about 1601, ed. 1616). Also *which* was used here as a determinative: 'þe kynges dere sone, *which* alwey for to do wel is *his* wont' (Chaucer, *Troilus*, II, 318) = 'the King's dear son, *that one* (= *such a one*): always to act right is *his* wont,' now '*whose* wont is always to act right.' This old genitive construction is preserved in popular speech, both with *that* and with *which:* 'There's two fellows *that their* dads are millionaires' (Sinclair Lewis, *Babbitt*, Ch, II, I). 'Mrs. Boffin, *which her* father's name is Henery' (Dickens, *Our Mutual Friend*, I, Ch. V). Also with *who:* 'The fellow *who* you don't know *his* name' (Sinclair Lewis, *Babbitt*, p. 122).

In Middle and early Modern English, however, the old determinative construction, with the personal pronoun in the subordinate clause expressed, was not confined to use in the genitive relation, but was sometimes employed also in the nominative and accusative relations, flourishing especially in long descriptive clauses. The determinatives were at first *that* and *which*, later also *who:* 'A knight ther was and that a worthy man, *That* (= *such a one*), fro (= from) the tyme that he first bigan to ryden (= ride) out, *he* loved chivalrye' (Chaucer, *Prologue*, l. 43). 'þis is he *which þat* (= *that one*) myn vncle swereth *he* mot be ded' (*id.*, *Troilus*, II, 654). 'Pyrithian of Thessayle was there among all other, *the whiche* (= *that one*) whan he apperceeyuid that euerich (= everyone) hadde well eten and dronken raysonably, *he* stood up,' etc. (Caxton, *History of Jason*, p. 8, A.D. 1477). 'Anger is like A full hot horse, *who* (= *such a one*) being allow'd his way, Selfmettle tires *him*' (Shakespeare, *Henry the Eighth*, I, I, 133). 'It is a massy wheel . . . *which* (= *such a one*), when *it* falls, Each small annexment, petty consequence, Attends the boisterous ruin' (*id.*, *Hamlet*, III, III, 17). 'For charity is that fire from heaven, *which* (= *namely such a one*), unless it does enkindle the sacrifice, God will never accept *it* for atonement' (J. Taylor, *Worthy Communicant*, London, 1678, IV, I, 197).

In the literary language, this loose old determinative type of expression disappeared about the close of the eighteenth century, having been replaced by the compact relative construction with a relative pronoun pointing back to the antecedent in the principal proposition. In the transitional period from the old to the new, the new relative clauses were often construed in accordance with

Latin models and were often quite un-English. Since the old determinative was now, under the influence of Latin idiom, construed as a relative pronoun, the following personal pronoun or pronouns were felt as superfluous and were simply dropped without any attempt to recast the clause, resulting frequently, as in Latin, in bringing together in the same subordinate clause a relative pronoun and an adverbial conjunction or another relative pronoun, a construction still unknown in natural English, as it has always been, but in this earlier time in learned language under Latin influence quite common and in archaic style still lingering on: 'And this man began to do tristily (boldly) in the synagoge, *whom whanne* Priscille and Aquila herden, they token hym' (*Acts*, XVIII, 26, John Purvey's edition, A.D. 1388). 'And he began to speak boldly in the synagogue, *whom when* Aquila and Priscilla had heard, they took him unto them' (King James Version), corresponding to the older type '*who when* Aquila and Priscilla had heard *him*, they took him unto them.' 'Captain Neal sent a packet of letters to the governor, *which when* the governor had opened [it] he found it came from Sir Ferdinando Georges' (Winthrop, *Journal*, June 25, 1631). 'And you are to know that in Hampshire they use to catch Trouts in the night by the light of a Torch or straw, *which when* they have discovered [them] they strike [them] with a Trout spear' (Izaak Walton, *Compleat Angler*, p. 128, A.D. 1653). 'To send for a Comission, *which if* [it] could or could not be Obteyned by a certain day, they would proceed Comission or no Comission' (Thomas Mathew, *Bacon's Rebellion*, p. 7, July 13, 1705). 'These were works *which, though* I often inspected [them], I did not accurately study [them]' (H. F. Clinton, *Literary Reminiscences*, 24, A.D. 1818). 'Now the third joy of making, the sweet flower Of blessed work, bloometh in godlike spirit; *Which whoso* plucketh [it] holdeth for an hour The shriveling vanity of mortal merit' (Bridges, *The Growth of Love*, 26, A.D. 1913).

On the other hand, the old determinative construction survives in popular speech: 'He'd been a-making a tremendous row the night afore a-drinking, and a-singing, and *wanting to fight* Tom and the post-boy; *Which* I'm thinking he'd have had the worst of *it*' (Thackeray, *Pendennis*, Ch. V). 'Brer Rabbit 'spond' (responded) dat he smell sump'n' *which it* don't smell like ripe peaches' (Joel Chandler Harris, *Nights with Uncle Remus*, p. 125). 'The road from Nice to Monte Carlo is called the Grand Corniche, *which* I don't know what *it* means' (Ring Lardner, *The Riviera*).

1. **Development of the Relative Pronoun 'Who.'** Out of the double determinative construction with indefinite *who*, in its

original form *swa hwa swa*, i.e., *so who so*, literally, *that somebody
that one*, has developed our common relative pronoun *who*, which
in accord with its original meaning refers only to persons: '*Swa
hwæne swa* ic cysse se hyt is' (*Matthew*, XXVI, 48, tenth century)
= Modern English 'It is he *whom* I kiss,' but literally, in the
spirit of the old determinative construction = '*That somebody
that one* I kiss [him], he it is.' The two determinatives point to
the following explanatory clause 'I kiss.' The speaker here chooses
for a relative the indefinite *so who so* since the person in question
is as yet unknown to the men addressed, but the speaker has a
definite person in mind, namely, Jesus, so that the sense is quite
different from the vague general meaning usually found in *so who
so*. The indefinite determinative *who*, which here replaces older
definite *that*, suggests in a general indefinite way the idea of a
person, but at the same time points to the following explanatory
clause, so that in fact the reference becomes definite. This passing
from the unknown to the known was a new means of expression
here that soon found favor. Compare **26** (6th par.) and **27** 1. The
old indefinite form *so who so* was later reduced to *who so*. Alongside of *who so* with the determinative *so* there was another indefinite
form in use, *who that* with the determinative *that*: 'Aʒaines kinde
Gaþ *hwa þat* swuche kinsemon ne luueð' (*Old English Homilies*,
p. 275) = '*Who ever* does not love such a kinsman goes against
nature.' Gradually the two forms became differentiated, so that
who so was used for indefinite reference and *who that* for definite
reference. In archaic language *whoso* is still used for indefinite
reference. In normal speech it is now replaced here by *whoever*.
Although *who that* was in early Modern English sometimes still
used for indefinite reference, it was already in Middle English more
commonly employed for definite reference, referring to a definite
antecedent: 'the sighte of hir *whom that* I serve' (Chaucer, *The
Knightes Tale*, 373). Here *who that* points to a definite person
just as our modern *who*. *Who that* differs from *who* in the retention
of the old determinative *that*. The retention of the determinative
shows that there was still some feeling left for the old determinative
construction. While, on the one hand, the relative *who* pointed
backward to the antecedent, the determinative *that*, on the other
hand, indicated that the relative was also associated with the
following clause, linking it to the antecedent. But as *who* here
soon developed more fully in the direction of a true relative pronoun, closely associated with both the antecedent and the following clause, linking the latter to the former, the *that*, no longer
having a real function, disappeared. But even in Shakespeare's
day, *who* had not entirely lost its old determinative nature, as

clearly seen in the quotation from *Henry the Eighth*, I, ɪ, 133, given on page 207.

In Old English, alongside of the indefinite *so who so* was a simple indefinite *who* with the same meaning, which will be discussed below at more length. This simple indefinite *who*, in exactly the same manner as *so who so*, developed definite meaning, so that we find it in Middle English after a definite antecedent as a parallel form to the *who that* described in the preceding paragraph: 'He nadde (= ne hadde) bote *an doȝter wo* miȝte is eir be' (Robert of Gloucester, *Chronicle*, Rolls, 1977, A.D. 1297), literally, 'He had but a daughter who could be his heir.' 'My lady *whom* I love and serve' (Chaucer, *The Knightes Tale*, 285). 'And thei camen, not oonli for Jhesu, but to se *Lazarus, whom* he hadde reisid fro deth' (*John*, XII, 9, John Purvey's ed., A.D. 1388). Our present relative pronoun *who* has come in part from this *who* and in part from *who that* by the suppression of *that*.

The definite relative *who* first appeared in the thirteenth century, but was comparatively little used before the sixteenth. Its use was at first largely confined to the objective form *whom*, as in all the examples given above, except in the one from Robert of Gloucester. It was not much used in the nominative relation, for in this earlier period indefinite *who* was here still quite common. The usual relatives were *that* and *which;* but after *who* had acquired definite force it rapidly came into favor, for it had a great advantage over its competitors — it referred only to persons — hence for reference to persons was a clearer form.

On the other hand, the old determinative construction *so who so*, out of which the relative *who* developed, did not disappear, but in modified form, now *whoso*, or more commonly *who(so)ever* instead of *so who so*, is still widely used, not like relative *who* pointing backward to an antecedent, but still a determinative pointing to the following explanatory remark, forming with it a substantive or a concessive clause (**21, 32,** 8th par.) and serving as its connective, binding it to the principal proposition, hence a real relative pronoun, though having no antecedent — an indefinite relative pronoun: 'He welcomed *whoever* (with stronger indefinite force *whosoever*) came.' 'He stopped *whom(so)ever* he met.' '*Whoseever* it is, I mean to have it.' In older English, the determinative *that* is sometimes used here instead of *so:* 'Play *who that* can that part' (Sir Thomas Wyatt, *Poems*, 18 (3), sixteenth century). Compare first paragraph.

Alongside of this compound determinative there is the simple determinative *who*, which now, as in Old English, has the same indefinite force, only not so general and vague, often approaching definiteness, but on the other hand with the same determinative force, pointing to the following explanatory remark, forming with it a substantive clause and serving as its connective, binding it to the principal proposition, hence a real relative pronoun, though having no antecedent — an indefinite relative pronoun: '*Who* (or more indefinitely *whoever*) *goes light* travels fast'; literally, '*That somebody:* [*he*] *goes light* travels fast.' 'I always felt that, talk *with whom I would,* I left something unsaid which was precisely what I most wished to say.' '"Really" replied Mr. Povey with loftiness *as who should say* "What an extraordinary thing that a reasonable creature can have such fancies!"'' (Arnold Bennett, *Old Wives' Tale,* Ch. I). 'It is not known *who* did it,' i.e., the identity of the author of the act is not known. In 'I saw *whom* he struck' and 'I saw *who* struck him' the identity of the person struck and the person who did the striking is known to the speaker but not to his hearers. In the preceding examples the indefinite *who* stands within the relative clause, serving as its relative, i.e., conjunctive, pronoun, binding the subordinate clause to the principal proposition, but in the following example it stands in the principal proposition as an indefinite determinative with the force of *that one* only that the reference is indefinite: 'Vengeance is his or *whose* he sole appoints' (Milton, *Paradise Lost,* V, 808), now usually *that one's.* Compare **56** A (3rd par.).

This indefinite *who* often has an indefinite antecedent: 'He makes no friend *who* never made a foe' (Tennyson). This usage occasionally occurs in older English: 'A hwam mai *he* luue treweliche hwa ne luues his brother?' (*Old English Homilies of the Twelfth and Thirteenth Centuries,* I, 274) = 'Ah, whom can *he* truly love *who* does not love his brother?' In older English, *who that* was often used instead of simple *who:* 'Repreve *he* dredeth never a del *Who that* beset his wordis wel' (Chaucer, *The Romaunt of the Rose,* 5261) = 'He dreads not reproof at all *who* sets his words well.' As can be seen by the translation of this example we now drop the determinative *that* here. In plain prose we today avoid the indefinite antecedents *he, she, they.* Thus instead of *he who, she who, they who,* we usually say in plain prose *a man who, a boy who, a woman who, a girl who, those who.* We especially avoid here *she who.* *He who, she who, they who* are still used in choice literary English. Compare 5, p. 220, Examples, 2nd par.

Closely related with this indefinite *who* and developed out of it is interrogative *who.* It was quite natural that in asking questions in primitive Germanic a word was employed which indicated that the relations of the person in question were indefinite, unknown to the speaker. Interrogatives, however, have never ceased to be indefinites. These indefinites often assume the special function of calling for an answer in an indefinite situation: '*Who* did it?' The interrogative is used also in indirect questions, i.e., to ask a question in an indirect way, as in 'Tell me *who did it*,' or to report a question indirectly, as in 'He asked me *who did it*.' Our grammarians, however, often regard as an indirect question the subordinate clause of such sentences as 'I saw *who did it*' and 'We shall soon know *who did it*.' In the former example *who* indicates that the identity of the person doing the act is known to the speaker but not to the hearer. In the latter example *who* indicates that the identity of the person doing the act is unknown to both the speaker and the hearer. In both examples there is in *who* an element of indefiniteness, but not the slightest suggestion of an interrogation. An interrogative is an intensive indefinite indicating that the indefiniteness has impressed the mind so strongly that an intellectual reaction has set in which has demanded an explanation. Interrogative form, however, is often employed not to elicit an answer but merely to express doubt — a deliberative or speculative question. Deliberative: 'What shall I (or am I to) do?' 'To our son there are only two courses open, both connected with great difficulties. Which shall he take?' (a question not calling for a categorical answer but introducing a deliberation). Speculative: 'What can it mean?' 'Will he come?' The question often loses every trace of a desire for an answer, also every trace of doubt, and becomes declarative, expressing the idea of an emphatic contrary assertion — a rhetorical question: '*Who* could have foreseen it?' = '*No one* could have foreseen it.' 'When doctors disagree *who shall decide?*' = '*No one can decide*.' Rhetorical questions are often charged with different kinds of feeling. Disapproval: 'Who told you to do that?' Indignation aroused by inconsiderate treatment: 'Who do you think I am?' Compare **21** (2nd and 3rd parr.) and **23** I.

2. **Development of the Relative Pronoun 'What.'** In exactly the same way as the relative *who* developed out of the indefinite double determinative *so who so*, as described in 1 above, relative *what* has developed out of the double determinative construction with indefinite *what*, in its original form *swa hwæt swa*, i.e., *so what so*, literally, *that something that*. As in the case of *so who so*, described above, the determinatives *so — so* have disappeared: 'Now this was not all *what* G. B. wanted' (W. Black, *Sunrise*, I, 302). Also as in the case of the *who*-construction there are two types: the older one with a relative *what* pointing not backward to an antecedent but forward to a following explanatory clause; the younger

one with a relative *what* pointing backward to an antecedent, as
in the example from Black just given. The older form is still a
very common construction, now with *–so* or more commonly
–(so)ever instead of older *so — so*, pointing to the following explanatory remark, forming with it a substantive clause (**21, 24** III,
IV) and serving as its connective, binding it to the principal
proposition, hence a real relative pronoun, though having no
antecedent — an indefinite relative pronoun: 'His mother gives
him *whatever* (or archaically *whatso*, or with stronger indefinite
force *whatsoever*) *he asks for*.' The accusative of this indefinite,
like the accusative of other indefinites, as described in **16** 4 *a*,
is often used adverbially, with the force of *at all:* 'There is no
doubt *whatever* about it.' 'No one *whatever* would have anything
to do with him.' 'I cannot see anyone *whatever*.'

What(so)ever is used also adjectively, standing before its governing noun and pointing as a determinative to the following
explanatory remark, forming with it and its governing noun a
substantive clause and serving as its connective, binding it to
the principal proposition, hence a real relative, though having
no antecedent — an indefinite relative adjective: 'Even the fisher-
men armed themselves with *whatever weapons* they could procure.'

Whatever, whether pronoun or adjective, is very common in
substantive clauses, but it is often used also in adverbial concessive clauses (**32**): 'I am going to pursue this course, *whatever it
may cost, whatever sacrifice it may demand*.' It is sometimes employed also in adjective clauses. See 6 below, 5th and last parr.

Alongside of this compound determinative there is the simple
determinative *what*, which now, as in Old English, has the same
indefinite force, only not so general and vague, often approaching
definiteness, but with the same determinative force, pointing to
the following remark, forming with it a substantive clause and
serving as its connective, binding it to the principal proposition,
hence a real relative pronoun, though having no antecedent —
an indefinite relative pronoun: 'His mother gives him *what*
(or more indefinitely *whatever*) *he asks for*.' 'I saw *what* (something
seen by the speaker but as yet unknown to the persons addressed)
he held in his hand.' This *what* is often used elliptically: 'Something is the matter, but I don't know *what* [*it is*].' 'I'll tell you
what [*the thing to do is*]. We should take that fellow down a peg.'

What is widely used in substantive clauses, also as an indefinite
adjective with the same determinative and relative force: 'I
gave him *what* money I had with me.' 'Come yourself and bring
along with you *what* men you can induce to come.' *What*, or
what a, often expresses a high degree of some quality or a large

amount: 'I want to tell you *what a* time we had.' 'We all know *what a* liar he is, *what* liars they are.' 'You can't realize *what* trouble we have had.' *Whatever* is more indefinite than *what:* 'I'll see to it that you get *whatever* money you may need.' Adjective *what* was originally a pronoun. The noun following it was a genitive, so that the form was: 'I gave him *what of money* I had with me.' Since the genitive in older English was often an indistinctive simple form, the grammatical relations became obscured, so that the genitive was construed as the common case, and *what* was taken for an adjective.

The substantive (**57** 1) forms of the adjectives *what, what a*, and *whatever* are often used in substantive clauses as indefinite relative pronouns, always with a definite antecedent but with only an indefinite reference to it: 'I have only a little money with me, but *what* I have is at your disposal.' 'I am short of them and *what* I have are bad.' 'He is always making costly blunders, but we cannot foresee just *what ones* he will make next.' 'Each time he makes a new excuse. It will be interesting to hear *what one* he will offer next.' 'We surely needed friends, and we now realize *what a one* we have found in Mr. Benton.' 'His mother has overlooked all the mistakes he has made in the past, and will probably overlook *whatever ones* he will make in the future.' *Whatever* is used also in concessive clauses: '*Whatever* the defects of American universities may be, they disseminate no prejudices' (*American Notes*, III, A.D. 1842).

What is used also in principal propositions as an interrogative or exclamatory pronoun or adjective: '*What* did he say?' '*What* impression did he make?' '*What* weather!' '*What a* day!' 'Oh, *what* trouble we have had!' Also *what one(s)* is used as an interrogative or exclamatory pronoun. 'You have read many interesting German books. *What ones* would you recommend as the best twenty-five?' 'To be sure we have found a house for rent, but *what a one!*' Also indirect questions are common: 'I asked him *what* he was doing.'

Who and *what* were originally singulars, but *who* is now used in all its functions also as a plural: '*Who were* there?' 'I do not know *who were* there.' Sometimes also *what:* '*What have* been censured as Shakespeare's conceits *are* completely justifiable' (Coleridge, *Lectures on Shakespeare*). '*What appear*, from the point of view expressed in these pages, to be its shortcomings *are* emphatically the shortcomings of its type' (Olivia Howard Dunbar in *Forum* for Nov., 1923, p. 2049). 'I outlined *what seem* to be the seven dominant fears that have inspired and have been inspired by this literature of despair' (Glenn Frank in *Cen-*

tury, for Sept., 1925, p. 626). Less frequently *whoever:* '*Whoever allow themselves* much of that indulgence, *incur* the risk of something worse' (J. S. Mill, *On Liberty*). Often, however, in the predicate: 'I am not afraid of them, *whoever* they are.'

What in the old *so what so* construction had such pronounced determinative force, usually pointing forward to something following, that it did not develop relative force, pointing backward to an antecedent, as in the case of *who*. The same conditions, however, were present, as in the case of *who*, so that we have a few traces of a development in the direction of a pure relative pointing backward, both in the case of simple *what* and *what* accompanied by a determinative: 'Til she had herd *al what* the frere sayde' (Chaucer, *The Somnours Tale*, 493). 'Every lover thoughte, That *al* was wel *what so* he seyde and wroughte' (*id.*, *Troilus and Criseyde*, III, 1799). Later, the determinative *so* here was always dropped: 'anything *what* (now *that*) thou wilt' (Ben Jonson, *Euery Man out of His Humour*, V, III, A.D. 1600). 'That *what* (now usually *which*) we falsely call a religious cry is easily raised by men who have no religion' (Dickens, *Barnaby Rudge*, Preface). 'To peruse everything *what* went into the "Post"' (H. Sydnor Harrison, *Queed*, Ch. VII). That which leads to the use of *what* here instead of *which* is a tendency to differentiate *which* and *what* by employing *what* when the reference is general or indefinite. This employment of indefinite *what* as a relative, pointing backward to an antecedent, though not widespread or common, is old, for it is found in late Old English; but its strong determinative force, its normal use to point forward to something following, prevented its common use and its final establishment in the language as a relative pointing backward to an antecedent. Thus while *who* is usually a relative pointing back to an antecedent, *what* is rarely so. It is usually a different kind of relative, a form pointing forward to something following and at the same time as a relative binding it to the principal proposition. In popular speech, however, *what* may point back to a definite antecedent, even to one representing a person or persons: 'I can't see that the *man what's* willing to remain poor all his life has any pride at all' (George Moore, *Esther Waters*, Ch. VI). 'This is them two *sisters what* tied themselves together with a handkercher' (Dickens, *Our Mutual Friend*, I, Ch. III).

3. **Development of the Relative Pronoun 'Which.'** In the same manner in which *who* developed out of the indefinite double construction with *swa hwa swa*, i.e., *so who so*, the relative *which* developed out of the indefinite double determinative construction with *swa hwilk swa*, i.e., *so which so*, the determinatives *so — so*

pointing, as the double determinatives described above, to the following explanatory clause. Instead of the determinatives *so — so* we often find others in older English, especially *the* and *that*, as in *the which, which that, the which that,* the usual forms in Middle English, referring to either persons or things. *The which* began to appear in Old English: 'an of þæm gebundenum, þone suœ huœlcne hia gigiuudon' (*Mark*, XV, 6, Lindisfarne MS.), literally, 'one of the prisoners, that one, the one they desired.' This is the oldest example of *the which*. In this oldest form the *so* after *which* has disappeared. This passage in the Corpus MS. reads: 'ænne gebundenne *swa hwylcne swa* hi bædon.' In Middle English this form appears as *which that*, where the first determinative *so* has dropped out and the second has been replaced by the determinative *that*. In both of these old examples there is an antecedent, an indefinite one, but yet an antecedent, so that *which, the which, which that*, standing as they do between antecedent and subordinate clause, can now easily develop into a relative pronoun binding the subordinate clause to the antecedent. As the meaning here often became more definite these forms were later frequently used with the force of our modern *which* or *who:* 'this wyde world *which that* men seye is round' (Chaucer, *The Frankelyns Tale*, 500); 'felawes *the whiche that* he had knowe in olde dawes' (*id.*, 452) = 'fellows *whom* he had known in former days.' As *which* from now on usually followed a noun or pronoun, it gradually developed into a relative pronoun, pointing back to the preceding noun or pronoun; hence the determinatives *the* and *that* used in connection with *which* disappeared, since they lost their original function and had thus become useless. Where the reference was to definite persons *which* was gradually replaced by *who* or *that*. In early Modern English *which* was still lingering on here.

The old indefinite force of *which*, however, survives in adjective function in substantive clauses (**21, 24** III, IV), where there is not a reference to a definite antecedent but only a general or indefinite reference: 'I do not know *which* way he went.' *Whichever* is still more indefinite: 'You may take *whichever* book you like.' As in the case of the adjectives *what* and *whatever* described in 2, p. 212, the adjectives *which* and *whichever*, though referring to no definite antecedent, have become true relative adjectives, binding the clause in which they stand to the principal proposition. *Which* and *whichever* differ from *what* and *whatever* only in indicating a little less degree of indefiniteness. The indefiniteness of *which* is also preserved in questions, direct and indirect: '*Which* book did you take?' 'I asked him *which* book he took.'

The substantive (**57** 1) forms of the adjectives *which* and *which-*

ever are often used in substantive clauses (**21, 24** III, IV) as indefinite relative pronouns, frequently with a definite antecedent but with only an indefinite reference to it: 'As I have not read all the new books, I cannot tell *which one* (or *which ones*) I like best.' 'Here are some new books. You may have *whichever one* (or *whichever ones*) you choose.' 'Several Smiths live here. I don't know *which one* you refer to.' These forms often point forward to a following noun or pronoun: 'I don't know *which* of these books he would rather have.' 'You may have *whichever* of these books you choose.' 'I don't know *whích óne* of them did it, but sóme óne of them did it.' *Which* and *which one(s)* are used also as interrogatives: '*Which* of you did it?' '*Which* (or *which one*) of these bóoks is yours?' '*Which* of these books are yours?' Other examples in **57** 3 (last par.). Indirect question: 'I asked him *which* of the books he wanted.' 'I asked him *which one* of the men he meant.' In all of these cases *which* may refer to persons or things. Originally, *which* could always refer to persons or things.

Indefinite relative *whichever*, whether pronoun or adjective, is used also in adverbial concessive clauses (**32**): 'He will find difficulties, *whichever* way (or *whichever* of these ways) he may take.' It is sometimes employed also in adjective clauses, as illustrated in 6 below, 5th and last parr.

While adjective *which* is, in general, indefinite and without an antecedent, it is sometimes definite, referring back to a definite antecedent, where it is a definite relative adjective: 'We traveled together as far as Paris, at *which* place we parted company.'

4. **Other Determinative Constructions.** Out of the determinatives just described have developed not only our relative pronouns but also other connectives, among them the most common conjunctions, *that*, *as*, and *what*: 'I know *that* he is faithful'; originally 'I know *that*: he is faithful,' the *that* pointing forward to the following explanatory appositional clause. In colloquial and popular speech, *what* with the same determinative force as *that* is often used instead of *that* after *but*: 'Not a day passes *but what* (or in the literary language *but that*, or simple *but*) it rains.' 'I cannot say *but what* (or *but that*, or simple *but*) you may be right.' In popular speech we often find *as* here instead of *that*, just as we often in popular speech find *as* instead of relative *that*: 'He told us *as* (for *that*) "Gospel" meant "good news"' (George Eliot, *Adam Bede*, Ch. II). Although this little word *as* is frequently used in popular speech where it is not employed in the literary language, its field in colloquial and literary English is an exceedingly wide one, altogether too wide, embracing so many meanings

that the thought is not always apparent at a glance. A bird's-eye
view of its uses is given in **27 2**. This wide range of meanings
indicated by *as* is explained by its original determinative nature,
which was simply to point, leaving it to the connection to make
the thought clear. This is also true of the conjunction *that*, ex-
determinative, like *as*. Just as the indefinite *who*, as described
in 1, p. 208, developed into a determinative and then into a relative
pronoun with the force of *that*, so the indefinite *how* — from the
same stem as *who* — developed into a determinative and then
into a conjunction with the force of *that*, attaining to its final stage
of development very early, even in Old English, much earlier than
who: 'I saw *how* (= *that*) he was falling behind in the race.'

In Middle English, the determinative *that* was so often associated
with a preceding word, as in the *who that*, *which that* described
above, linking this word to the following subordinate clause, that
it was construed as a sign of subordination and was attached to
other words which originally were not followed by a determinative, such as interrogatives: 'If men wolde axe (ask) me *why
that* god suffred men to do yow (you) this vileinye' (Chaucer,
Melibeus, 38).

5. **List of Relative Pronouns Used in Attributive Relative
Clauses**: *that* for persons and things, except after *that* where we
now usually say *that which*, thus avoiding the repetition of *that*,
although *that that* was quite common a little earlier in the period;
at, the worn-down form of *that*, once widely used in the literary
language of Scotland and North England, still surviving in northern English dialect, where it is now often written *ut; who* for
persons; in older English sometimes *the who* (as in Shakespeare's
Winter's Tale, IV, IV, 538) instead of simple *who; which* for things,
referring to some definite thing or things, or to something indefinite; in older literary English and current popular speech also
referring to persons; *the which*, once a common form competing
with *which* without a difference of meaning, now only rarely used
and then restricted largely to descriptive clauses, both when used as
a relative pronoun and as a relative adjective; *whichever* (see 6 below, 5th and last parr.); *what*, earlier in the period sometimes referring to an indefinite pronoun, *nothing, all, everything, that*, etc., and
sometimes still so used, but far less commonly than *that* and *which*,
the latter the usual form after the indefinite pronoun *that; what*,
widely used when the reference is to a following statement or the
thought contained in a following adjective, as illustrated in 6 below; *whatever* (see 6 below, 5th and last parr.); *but* (or sometimes *but
he, but she*, etc., instead of simple *but*) or in colloquial speech *but
what*, both forms with the meaning of *that not, which not, who not,*

but usually only employed after a negative or a question in the
subject relation, much less commonly in the object relation; *as*,
in older English more widely used as a relative than now, still
the regular form after *such*, although also *that*, *which*, and *who*
are still, as in older English, used here occasionally; *as*, now the
regular form after *the same* in elliptical clauses without a finite
verb, in older English, however, also *that*, while in the full clause
with finite verb we employ *that*, *which*, *who*, or much less commonly *as; as*, sometimes elsewhere in elliptical clauses; *as*, still
much used in descriptive clauses where the reference is to the
thought contained in some preceding or following proposition or
word; *as*, still common in the predicate relation where the reference is to a preceding noun; moreover, a number of adverbs or
conjunctions, *where* (in older English also *there*, *there as*, *there that*,
where as, *where that*), *whence*, or sometimes *from whence* (both
restricted to poetry and choice prose, elsewhere replaced by *from
which*), *thence that* (in older English = *whence*), *whither* (in poetry
and choice prose, elsewhere replaced by *to which*), *when*, *while*,
why, also a large number of others, once common but now little
used except in poetry or in exact, especially legal, language, such
as *whereby*, *wherein*, *whereof*, etc.   In popular speech *as* (**27** 2) or
what often replace *that* or *who:* 'They've got a friend *as* (or *what*)
will help 'em.'   In older English, we find *as* here also in the literary
language, after determinatives, not only after *such* and *the same*,
as described above for present usage, but also after *that*, *those*,
the: 'I have not from your eyes *that* gentleness And show of love
as I was wont to have' (Shakespeare, *Julius Cæsar*, I, II, 33).
'*Those as* sleep and think not on their sins' (*id., The Merry Wives*,
V, v, 57).   'I did not imagine these little coquetries could have
the ill consequences *as* I find they have' (*The Spectator*, 87).   Of
all the above relatives only *who* is declined: nominative *who*,
genitive *whose*, dative and accusative *whom*, the same form in each
case serving as singular and plural.

But and *but what* originated in adverbial clauses of pure result
(**28** 5, **28** 5 *b*) in sentences where the meaning permitted the clause
to be construed either as a clause of result or as a relative clause:
'Nobody knew him *but* (or *but that*, or *but what*) he loved him'
(adverbial clause of pure result), or '*but* (or *but what*, relative pronouns used as subject) loved him' (relative clause).   'Nobody
read the book through *but* (or *but that*, or *but what*) it impressed him
favorably' (adverbial clause of pure result), or '*but* (or *but what*,
relative pronouns used as object) it impressed favorably' (relative
clause).   The relative clause is now differentiated in form from
the adverbial clause of result by the suppression of the personal

pronoun, *he, she, it,* the relative pronoun *but* or *but what* serving as subject or object. The differentiation of the two clauses was not so complete in older English as it is now.

Examples:

'The boy *who is standing by the door*'; 'a boy *that will do such a thing*'; 'the boy *whose father died yesterday*'; 'the two little boys *whose parents are dead*'; 'the boy *with whom you play,*' or 'the boy *you play with*'; 'a boy *that you should play with,*' or 'a boy *you should play with*'; 'the boy *whom you struck,*' or 'the boy *you struck*'; 'the man *to whom you referred*' (or *whom you referred to,* or *that you referred to,* or *you referred to*); 'the book *that* (or *which*) *is lying on the table*'; 'Dumas the Elder, *than whom* there never was a kinder heart,' where in harmony with fixed usage *whom* stands after *than* instead of the correct *who,* in accordance with a general tendency, not so firmly fixed in the literary language elsewhere, to employ the accusative of a pronoun instead of the nominative in clauses and phrases which do not contain a finite verb, as illustrated in **7 C** *a.*

'You could scarcely have told from the peace that dwelt upon them which was *she that* (choice language) had sinned' (Bret Harte, *The Outcasts of Poker Flat*); likewise '*he that* had sinned,' or in plainer language nearer colloquial speech '*he,* or *she, who* had sinned,' but in colloquial speech for both *he who* and *she who* usually *the one who,* since there is a strong tendency here to avoid the use of *he* or *she* as a *definite* determinative: 'this gentleman and *the one who* is standing by the window'; 'this lady and *the one who* is standing by the window.' But we cannot use *the one* where there isn't a preceding noun to which it can refer. Here, in colloquial speech, we usually employ a noun preceded by the definite article, which together serve as a definite determinative instead of *he* or *she:* '*the gentleman,* or *lady,* who is standing by the window.' Of course, we can freely use *he* or *she* before *who* when they are not determinatives: 'We were speaking last night of a man who has been asking for us here. His visits have alarmed the servants, but there is nothing to fear from him. You know it is rather *he* (not a determinative but a predicate pronoun) *who seems to fear us*' (subject clause). Where *he* (*she,* or *they*) is an *indefinite* determinative pointing forward to something following, we say in the singular, '*He who* (*she who,* or in choice poetic language *he that, she that,* but in colloquial speech usually *one who, a man who, a woman who, a fellow who, a girl who*) would do such a thing would not deserve respect,' but in the plural we usually prefer '*Those who* (now largely replacing in plain prose older, once common, *those that, they that, such as*) would do such a thing would not deserve respect,' although *they who* (now largely replacing older *they that*) still occasionally occurs, especially in choice, poetic language: '*They who* had most admiringly begged Percy Bresnahan for his opinions were least interested in her facts' (Sinclair Lewis, *Main Street,* p. 448), but especially in beautiful language, as in 'Great souls are *they who* love the most, who breathe the deepest of heaven's air, and give of themselves most freely' (William Allen White, *A Certain Rich Man,* Ch. XXII). '*Those* have most power to hurt us *that* (now usually *whom*) we love' (Beaumont and Fletcher, *The Maids Tragedie*, V, III, 129, A.D. 1622). '*They that* (now *those who* or *they who*) seek immortality are not onely worthy of leave but of praise' (Ben Jonson, *Discoveries*, p. 11, A.D. 1641). 'Poetry in this latter age hath prov'd but a meane mistresse to *such as* (or *those who*) have wholly addicted themselves to her. *They who* (now more commonly *those who*) have but saluted her on the by, and now and then tendred their visits, she hath done much for' (*ib.*, p. 27). To express the idea of kind or quality we often employ the qualitative determinative *such:* 'Let *such* teach others *who* (now usually *as*) themselves excel' (Pope, *Essay on Criticism*, 15). When a restrictive clause follows *such*, as in this example, *those* is often used in colloquial speech as a qualitative determinative instead of *such*, since the restrictive clause is felt as indicating with sufficient clearness the idea of quality, and *such* is avoided as a literary word: 'Mention especially the intelligent and *those who* (or in more exact formal language *such as*) want to study literature as an end, not a means' (Sir Walter Raleigh, *Letter to Percy Simpson*, Dec. 13, 1913). The singular qualitative determinative *such a one* is common when there is a preceding noun to which it can refer: 'I have had some good *teachers* but never *such a one* as [is] Professor Jones.' When there is no such preceding noun to which it can refer, the qualitative determinative *such a one* is a literary form, replaced in simple prose by *someone* or *a man* (*woman, boy, girl*): 'Associate with *such a one* as you can look up to,' or 'Associate with *someone*, or *a man* (*woman, boy, girl*), you can look up to.'

In every society, however seemingly corrupt, there are those (= some) *who* have not bowed the knee to Baal (Hughes, *Tom Brown's School-Days*, 193).

The book *which* I hold in my hand is an English grammar.

Our Father *which* art in heaven (*Matthew*, VI, 9).

(She) had been told it herself by Mrs. Mudberry, *which* kept a mangle (Dickens, *Pickwick*, Ch. XXXIV).

Uh man *w'ich* steal is uh man *w'ich* enter anodduh man' house een de dead ub night (Gonzales, *The Black Border*, p. 72).

All *that* I have is at your disposal.

It was *that* (something definite, just referred to) *which* killed him.

He always does *that* (determinative) *which* the hour demands, not that *which* he would fain do.

There was that (= that indefinite something) about him *that* (now more commonly *which*) did not please her (Julia Kavanagh, *Queen Mab*, I, 105).

There was that in Lady Jane's innocence *which* rendered light talking impertinence before her (Thackeray, *Vanity Fair*).

I fear nothing *what* (now usually *that* or *which*) can be said against me (Shakespeare, *Henry the Eighth*, V, I, 125).

Now this was not all *what* (usually *that*) G. B. wanted (W. Black, *Sunrise*, I, 302).

That *what* (usually *which*) we falsely call a religious cry is easily raised by men who have no religion (Dickens, *Barnaby Rudge*, Preface).

. . . to peruse everything *what* (usually *that* or *which*) went into the 'Post' (H. Sydnor Harrison, *Queed*, Ch. VII).

No leader worthy of the name ever existed *but* (or *but what*) was an optimist.

There is almost no man *but hee* (old nominative of *but*, now more commonly simple *but* or *but what*) sees clearlier (**16 5 a**) and sharper the vices in a speaker then (now *than*) the vertues (Ben Jonson, *Discoveries*, p. 19, A.D. 1641).

Not one great man of them, *but he* (old nominative form of *but*, but now more commonly simple *but*) will puzzle you, if you look close, to know what he means (Ruskin, *Selections*, I, 172).

There is not a touch of Vandyck's pencil *but* (used as relative pronoun in the object relation) he seems to have reveled on (*ib.*, I, 261).

No ill luck stirring *but what* lights on my shoulders (Shakespeare, *Merchant of Venice*, III, I, 98).

Not that I think Mr. M. would ever marry anybody *but what* had some education (Jane Austen, *Emma*, 29).

Not a soul in the auditorium or on the stage *but what* lived consummately during those minutes (Arnold Bennett, *Leonora*, Ch. VI).

No words *but what* seemed to him violent and extreme would have fulfilled his conception of the danger he had escaped (Galsworthy, *The Country House*, 71).

I have not from your eyes *that* (now *such*) gentleness *as* I was wont to have (Shakespeare, *Julius Cæsar*, I, I, 33).

I can't serve with *that* (now *such*) *cheerfulness as formerly* (Addison and Steele, *Spectator*, 366) (or *the same cheerfulness as formerly*).

Such books as (predicate) *this* [is], or *such men as he*, are rare.

I made *such* alterations *as* occurred to me.

Such only *who* (usually *as*) have been in parishes that have been for generations squireless and also in those where a resident family has been planted for centuries can appreciate the difference in general tone among the people (S. Baring-Gould, *Old Country Life*, Ch. I).

Only *such* intellectual pursuits *which* (or *that*, but usually *as*) are pleasant (Sarah Grand, *Ideala*, 229).

Tony turned his eager attention to *such* pleasures *that* (or more commonly *as*) could be obtained in that sociable place (A. Marshall, *Anthony Dare*, Ch. I).

The children get the same food *as* I [get].

I really couldn't put up with living in the same place *as* that fellow after what had happened.

Such was thy zeal to Israel then, the same *that* (now *as*) now to me (Milton, *Paradise Regained*, III, 413).

He sits in the same row *that* (or *as*) we do.

When we saw the engine enter the tunnel on the same track *that* (or *as*) we were on, we believed our last hour had come.

He is entangled in the same meshes *that* (or *which*) held me.

He is the same man *that* (or *whom*) we met yesterday.

His air *as* [*was that*] of not having to account for his own place in the social scale was probably irritating to Urbain (Henry James, *The American*, Ch. XIII).

Between her eyes was a driven look *as* [*was*] *of one* who walks always a little ahead of herself in her haste (Edna Ferber, *So Big*, Ch. I).

He granted her wish, good fellow *as* (or *that*) he was.

The place *where* I saw him last; this delightful country *whither* (still a favorite in choice, poetic language, but in plain prose usually replaced by *to which*) we should like to make a tour; a corner *whence* (or *from whence;* in choice, poetic language, but in plain prose usually replaced by *from which*) *there was no escape;* the day *when I was there;* the pauses *while we are thinking of the right word.*

It is a gentil pasture *ther* (now *where*) thou goost (Chaucer, *The Prologe of the Monkes Tale*, 45).

. . . this Tartre king, this Cambinskan, Roos fro his bord, *ther that* (now simple *where*) he sat ful hye. Toforn him gooth the loude minstralcye, Til he cam to his chambre of parements, *There as* (now simple *where*) they sownen diverse instruments (Chaucer, *The Squires Tale*, 258–262).

To Engelond been they come the righte wey, *wher as* (now simple *where*) they live in joye and in quiete (Chaucer, *The Tale of the Man of Lawe*, 1032).

I shall show you the chambre *where as* (now simple *where*) he slepeth (Lord Berners, *Huon*, I, p. 102, A.D. 1534).

'Tis his Highness' pleasure You do prepare to ride unto Saint Alban's, *Where as* (now simple *where* or *at which place*) the King and Queen do mean to hawk (Shakespeare, *II Henry VI*, I, II, 56).

Y must [go back] to the erthe *thennes that* y come fro (*Knight de La Tour*, 36, A.D. 1450).

That is the reason *why* (or *that*) he cannot succeed.

Is there a certain test *whereby words of native English origin can be known from others?*

6. **Descriptive and Restrictive Relative Clauses.** There is a tendency in English at present to distinguish between descriptive relatives, introducing a descriptive, independent fact, and restrictive relatives, introducing a clause confining or limiting the application of the antecedent. Descriptive clauses stand in a loose relation to the antecedent and hence are separated by a pause, indicated in print by a comma, while restrictive clauses are quite closely linked to the antecedent in thought, so that they follow immediately without pause, and hence are not usually cut off by a comma: 'I like to chat with John, *who* is a clever fellow,' but 'What is the name of the boy *that* brought us the letter?' 'Next winter, *which* you will spend in town, you know, will give you a good opportunity to work in the library,' but 'The next winter *that* you spend in town will give you a good opportunity to work in the library.' There is often a double restriction, the second

relative clause restricting the antecedent as restricted by the first
relative clause: 'How seldom do we find a man *that has stirred up
some vast commotion who does not himself perish, swept away in it*'
(Carlyle, *Heroes and Hero-worship*, 127). The descriptive relative
clause is in a formal sense a dependent clause; but it does not in
any way limit the application of the antecedent, so that it is
logically an independent proposition. Compare **20** 1 (3rd par.).
In a descriptive relative clause the relative pronoun must be expressed, for its suppression might change the thought or obscure
the expression: 'This fact, *which* you admit, condemns you,' not
'This fact, you admit, condemns you,' which is another thought.

Who, that, and *which* are all used in restrictive clauses; *who*
with reference to persons, *that* with reference to persons and things,
which now usually with reference to things. A number of grammarians, however, recommend here the exclusive use of *that*, both
for persons and for things: 'Here is the boy *that* did it.' 'Here is
the book *that* he lost.' But there is another tendency here, which
has been growing for centuries and is now often stronger than the
tendency to distinguish the restrictive relative clause by the use
of *that*. It is the tendency to express the idea of personality by
the use of *who* and the idea of lack of life or personality by the use
of *which*. The tendency to express personality is now strong even
in restrictive clauses: 'He was not a man *who* allowed his taste
to be warped when he knew for solid reasons that it was sound'
(Galsworthy, *The Man of Property*, p. 304). It was not possible
in Old English, with all its wealth of form, to express this fine
shade of meaning. The tendency in restrictive clauses to use
which to express lack of life or personality is not so strong as the
tendency to employ *who* to express personality, but it is growing:
'There is much *which* will be unpleasing to the English reader;
much *which* the Indian will dislike; but there is nothing *which*
can be seriously questioned' (*Cambridge Review*). On the other
hand, the choice of pronoun here is often determined by formal
considerations. After the interrogative *who* we always employ
that on merely formal ground, to prevent the repetition of *who:*
'*Who that* has the spirit of a man would suffer himself to be thus
degraded?' *That* being impossible, we must employ *whom* or
which in prepositional constructions wherever the preposition is
placed at the beginning of the clause: 'There is no man for *whom*
I have sincerer respect.' 'He bitterly regretted that the little
estate on *which* he had set his heart had slipped out of his hand.'
That can also not be used in the genitive and must be replaced
here by *whose*, the genitive of *who*. In popular speech, however,
as a survival of older usage, explained on page 207, *that* and *which*

are used in the genitive relation by placing a possessive adjective after *that* or *which*, *that* or *which* together with the possessive adjective having the force of *whose:* 'There's two fellows *that their* (= *whose*) dads are millionaires' (Sinclair Lewis, *Babbitt*, Ch. II, I). 'Mrs. Boffin, *which her* (= *whose*) father's name was Henery' (Dickens, *Our Mutual Friend*, I, 75). In the literary language where the reference is to things, *which* is replaced in the genitive relation by *whose*, or we may employ the prepositional genitive, *of which*, as described in 7 (last par.) below.

Who, that, and *which* have until recently been used also in descriptive clauses, but at present there is a tendency, not yet fixed usage but a growing tendency, to replace *that* here by *who* for persons and by *which* for things: 'He is with his youngest son, *who* is accompanying him on his walk.' 'This book, *which* only appeared about a year ago, has already gone through several editions.' This new usage is much more common with reference to persons than to animals and things, where we still often find *that:* 'For the first few weeks she spoke only to the goat, *that* was her chiefest friend on earth and lived in the back garden' (Rudyard Kipling, *The Light That Failed*, Ch. I, 5). 'Once he piped up a kind of country love-song, that he must have learned in his youth' (Stevenson, *Treasure Island*, Ch. III, 28). *Which* is usually employed when an attributive relative adjective in connection with a governing noun is used instead of a relative pronoun: 'We traveled together as far as Paris, at *which place* we parted company.' We now only rarely use here *the which*, once, however, a common form, competing with *which* in all its uses: 'He brought him unaccountable presents of knives, pencil-cases, gold-seals, *the which* tokens of homage George received graciously, as became his superior merit' (Thackeray, *Vanity Fair*, I, Ch. V).

In early Modern English *the who* was sometimes used in descriptive clauses instead of simple *who:* 'Where you may Enjoy your mistress, from *the whom*, I see, There's no disjunction to be made' (Shakespeare, *The Winter's Tale*, IV, iv, 537).

In descriptive clauses where the reference is indefinite some indefinite relative pronoun in *–ever* must be used; *whatever* with vague indefinite force and *whichever* with much less indefinite meaning: 'Someone in the crowd, *whoever* it was, demanded fair play.' 'I'll send you one of my boys, *whichever of them* (or *whichever one*) you prefer.' 'He stumbled over something, *whatever* it was, and fell.' 'You may use either of the expressions, *whichever* sounds best to you.'

In descriptive clauses that refer to a thought, an idea, whether contained in a proposition, a group of words, or a single noun or adjective, *which* is used with reference to a preceding statement or a single noun or adjective, while with reference to a following statement or a single noun or adjective we now usually employ *what*, though in older English, and sometimes still, *which* occurs: 'I am getting gray and wrinkled, *which is not particularly cheering.*' Only rarely now with *the which* instead of simple *which:* 'She said with thin lips, "Why, even all this time you have been deceiving me!" *the which* egged on, in that vile way in which exchanges of a quarrel are as knives sharpening one against the other, Keggo's inflamed retort, "The more fool you! Little fool!"' (A. S. M. Hutchinson, *This Freedom*, p. 167). 'We talked a long while about our boyhood days, *after which we had a good dinner.*' 'My brother is a good business man, *which I am not.*' 'My brother is a millionaire, *which I am not.*' 'When overwrought, *which he often was*, he became acutely irritable' (Charlotte Brontë, *Villette*, Ch. XXX). 'I've seen their Capital, their Troops and Stores, Their Ships, their Magazines of Death and Vengeance, And, *what is more*, I've seen their potent King' (Robert Rogers, *Ponteach*, III, III, A.D. 1766). 'He praised the wine of the country and *what was more to the purpose*, gave us the opportunity of tasting it.' 'And, *which* (now usually *what*) *is worse*, all you have done Hath been but for a wayward son' (Shakespeare). 'I found also, *which* (now usually *what*) *appeared to me to be an unlucky measure*, that the former had issued his warrants against one Herman Husbands' (George Washington, *Diary*, Oct. 20, 1794). '(I was) also abused, and taken amiss, and, *which* (now usually *what*) *vexed me most of all*, unknown' (Blackmore, *Lorna Doone*, Ch. LXIV). Adjective *which* in connection with an appropriate governing noun can refer to the thought contained in a preceding proposition: 'She had forgotten to wind it up, *which omission* indicated that the grocer had perturbed her more than she thought' (Arnold Bennett, *Old Wives' Tale*, II, 133).

On the other hand, *that* is the usual form in restrictive clauses where the reference is to the thought contained in a preceding adjective: 'On that day she looked the happiest *that I had ever seen her.*' The *that* may be suppressed: 'Louise was sitting in a deep chair, looking the happiest [*that*] *I had ever seen her*' (Mary Roberts Rinehart, *The Circular Staircase*, Ch. XXXIV).

The adverbs *when*, *as* (**17** 2), *whereupon*, and *whereat* are used as relative pronouns in descriptive clauses where the reference is to a preceding statement or the idea contained in a preceding word, the first two forms often, the other two not now so commonly as formerly, *as* also where the reference is to a following statement: 'The whole nation was jubilant, *when, like a bolt from the blue, news arrived of a serious reverse.*' 'I met him a month ago, *since when I haven't seen anything of him.*' 'He was an Englishman, *as* (or *which*) *they perceived by his accent.*' 'You behave like a madman, *as* (or *which*) *you are.*' 'Nor was the testimony of Lord Justice Rigby less important, showing, *as* (in such a parenthetical remark more common than *which*) *it did,* that the officers of the army are not visionary philanthropists.' 'Robin Hood replied that he had some two or three hundred head of cattle, *whereupon* (or *after which*) *the sheriff said that he should like to ride over and look at them.*' 'The inventor . . . said that . . . he would demonstrate by his own model that some day navigation would be by steam: *whereat* (or *at which*) *they all kindly laughed at him for a dreamer*' (J. L. Allen, *Choir Invisible*, II).

When the reference in descriptive clauses is indefinite, *whatever* and *whichever* (less indefinite than *whatever*) must be used to refer to a thought contained in some preceding word or words: 'He is one of the moderns, *whatever that may mean.*' 'The leper looked or listened, *whichever he was really doing,* for some seconds.'

a. COMPLEX RELATIVE CLAUSES. Both restrictive and descriptive clauses may be complex, i.e., may consist of a principal proposition and a subordinate clause, the one sometimes being embedded in the other: 'It is a fine opportunity, *which I would seize if I were not otherwise engaged.*' 'Shakespeare's mind may be likened to that modern machine *into which if a thousand voices speak it will treasure up and redeliver the words.*' 'Samuel Dale was a typical farmer of that part of the country with his fifty or sixty acres of land, *the capital to work which had come from fish*' (Compton Mackenzie, *The Altar Steps*, Ch. VII). In this example the relative *which* stands as an object in the attributive infinitive clause that modifies *capital,* which is the subject of the principal proposition of the complex clause. The relative often stands in a substantive clause which is the subject, predicate, or object of the verb or predicate adjective in the principal proposition of the complex clause: 'I now desire to speak of Pericles, *whose aim was, it has been said, "to realize in Athens the idea which he had conceived of human greatness."*' 'That is a statement *which I believe I can prove*' (or *which I am sure I can prove*). In this sentence and many similar ones the clause is only in a formal sense complex, for we feel such expressions as *I believe, I am sure* as sentence adverbs, as explained in **16** 2 *a* (p. 132).

b. DESCRIPTIVE RELATIVE CLAUSE INTRODUCED BY 'As.' In older English, *as* with the force of *as being* often stood before the relative pronoun introducing a descriptive clause: 'That which is of itselfe is the thing which we cal God, beyond whome nothing can bee imagined and by whome all things both are and have bene, *as which* (= *as being things which*) could have no beeing of themselves' (Sir Philip Sidney, *Trewnesse of the Christian Religion*, Ch. II, A.D. 1587). *As who* was similarly used.

c. 'AND WHICH,' 'AND WHO,' 'BUT WHICH,' 'BUT WHO.' These forms now usually follow only a noun modified by a relative clause, but sometimes, especially earlier in the present period, they follow a noun modified in other ways: 'the sign of the Bell, an excellent house indeed, *and which* (now usually simple *which*) I do most seriously recommend' (Swift). 'A man well looking for his years, *and who* Was neither much beloved, nor yet abhorr'd' (Byron, *Don Juan*, I, 65), now usually 'a man who was well looking for his years, and was neither much beloved nor yet abhorred.' 'In the case of calls within the London area, *but which* require more than three pennies, the same procedure is followed' (recent writer), now usually 'In the case of calls which are within the London area but require more than three pennies, the same procedure is followed.'

7. **Personality and Form.** Current English stresses the idea of personality much more than older English. Even a little earlier in the period *who* was used of animals, while we today usually employ *that* or *which* here since we feel the absence of personality: 'Though the weather is raw and wintry and the ground covered with snow, I noticed a solitary robin, *who* (now *that*) looked as if *he* needed to have *his* services to the Babes in the Woods speedily requited' (Thoreau, *Journal*, I, p. 21). The relative is always near the antecedent, hence the incongruity of placing a personifying form alongside of a noun designating a being without personality is more keenly felt than in the case of personal pronouns, which stand farther away: 'We have one cow *that* (or *which*) we highly prize. *She* is a Jersey.' With children the idea of individuality increases with their age. We say 'the last child *which* was born,' but 'our only child *who* is now at college.'

The idea of personality varies considerably in collective nouns denoting persons. We employ *which* here wherever the idea of oneness or a mass or masses is more prominent than that of a number of independent individuals: 'The Garth *family, which* was a large one,' etc. (George Eliot, *Middlemarch*, 217). 'His mother had ten children, of *which* he was the oldest' (*Scribner's Magazine*, XXXV, 114), but 'Every faction is attended by a crowd of camp-followers, an useless and heartless *rabble who prowl* round its line of march' (Macaulay). 'He instructed the *crowds which* surrounded him,' but '*People who* have enjoyed good educational opportunities ought to show it in their conduct and language.'

In older English, after the names of cities, countries, and other organizations implying persons, *who* was often used as relative, but it has been entirely replaced here by *which*, since the idea of organization is now uppermost in the mind: 'France, *which* is in alliance with England; that party in England *which*,' etc.

Similarly, we often employ *which* after a noun denoting a person where we desire to express the idea of estate, rank, dignity rather than to speak of a person: 'He is exactly the man *which* such an education was likely to form' (Trollope, *The Warden*, Ch. II). 'He was surprised to find that he had come out upon quite a different Clark from the one to *which* he had been accustomed' (Barry Pain, *The Culminating Point*). 'He did not understand, and could not without giving up his own idea of her, the May Gaston *which*, as she said, he had made for himself' (A. Hope). 'Most of the critics have been kind. I only saw one *which* was not' (Sir Henry Jones, *Letter*, May 29, 1919). *Which* is especially common here in the predicate relation: 'Like the clever girl *which* she undoubtedly was' (Benson, *Relentless City*, 84). 'He is not the man *which* his father wants him to be.' *That* might be used instead of *which* in all of these examples. Although *which* and *that* are both used here, *which* is the more distinctive form and is, in general, winning out, but in the predicate relation *that* and also *as* are still quite common: 'But Hilda, like the angel of mercy *that* she was, whispered,' etc. (Grant Allen, *Hilda Wade*, Ch. I, 19). 'I will do my best to stop you, madman *as* you are' (Thackeray, *Newcomes*, I, Ch. XXIX). We often omit the relative here where it would not impair the thought: 'It is a part of Torrence's business to counsel widows, which he does like the honorable man [that] he is' (Meredith Nicholson, *Lady Larkspur*, Ch. II, p. 69).

When the relative refers to both persons and things we cannot, of course, in one word indicate both personality and lack of it, hence we here choose the colorless *that*, which can refer both to living beings and lifeless things: 'He spoke largely of the men and the things *that* he had seen.' Of course we cannot use *that* after prepositions, where we must use *which*. See 8, p. 230.

In sharp contrast to the principle of indicating personality or the lack of it, which now prevails in the use of the nominative and objective cases of the relative, as described above, is the employment of the genitive *whose* for reference to persons, animals, and living and lifeless things: 'the man *whose* watch was stolen,' 'a dog *whose* name is Carlo,' 'the tree *whose* top was trimmed,' 'the house *in whose shade* (or *in the shade of which*) we sit.' Where the reference is to lifeless things, colloquial language prefers the new prepositional genitive *of which*, although the convenient old form *whose* is still not infrequent. In poetry and choice prose the old form is still the favorite: 'a little white building *whose* small windows were overgrown with creepers' (Galsworthy, *The Patrician*, p. 40). The use of *whose* for persons and things is the survival of older usage, which knew nothing of the differentiation described above. In the genitive the convenient agreeable form has thus far proved stronger in our feeling than the logical distinctions which sway us in the nominative and objective relations. Even in choice language, however, the genitive is only in limited use, for it cannot be used at all in the relation of an objective genitive: 'In its sensuous purity this woman's face reminded him of Titian's "Heavenly Love," *a reproduction of which* (not *whose reproduction*) hung over the sideboard' (Galsworthy, *The Man of Property*, p. 301).

8. **Case of Relative and Its Agreement with Its Antecedent.** The relative pronoun performs a double function: It is a pronoun in the clause in which it stands and is also a connective joining the clause in which it stands to the governing noun. As a pronoun it has the case required by its function in the relative clause, i.e., is subject, direct or indirect object, or a genitive limiting some noun in the clause: 'The man *who* (subject) was sick is now well.' 'The boy *whom* (object of the verb of the clause) I trusted has proved worthy of my confidence.' 'The boy of *whom* (object of the preposition *of*) I spoke yesterday will soon be here.' 'The boy to *whom* (indirect object) I gave a knife has lost it.' 'The boy *whose* (genitive limiting *knife*) knife was lost has bought another.' In loose colloquial speech we sometimes hear *who* as accusative instead of the correct *whom*. See **11 2 e.**

As a connective or conjunctive pronoun the relative has relations to its antecedent, with which it agrees in gender, number, and person. Gender: 'The boy *who* is standing by the gate is my brother,' but 'The book *which* lies upon the table is a history.' For the use of *whose* with reference to both persons and things see **7** (last par.) above. *That* is the appropriate form where the reference is to two or more antecedents representing both persons and things: 'The cabmen and cabs *that* are found in London.' However, we use also *which* here and this form must be used where a preposition stands before the relative: 'The Company had indeed to procure in the main for themselves the money and the men by *which* India was conquered.'

As relative pronouns have the same form for both numbers and all three persons, their number and person can be gathered only from the number and the person of the antecedent. This becomes important wherever the relative is the subject of its clause, for it then controls the number and person of the verb: '*I, who am* your friend, tell you so,' where *am* is in the first person singular agreeing with its subject *who*, which agrees with its antecedent *I*. 'For help I look up to *thee who art* all-powerful and able to help.' 'The *road that leads* to the shore is sandy.' 'The *roads that lead* to the shore are sandy.' An antecedent which is in the vocative, i.e., in the case of direct address, is felt as being in the second person: 'Dark *anthracite, that reddenest* on my hearth!'

The relative often in loose colloquial speech, sometimes even in the literary language, agrees incorrectly with some word closely connected with the antecedent instead of agreeing with the antecedent itself, since this word lies nearer the thought of the speaker or writer than the grammatical antecedent, with especial frequency in the case of a plural partitive genitive that is dependent upon the numeral *one*, which is erroneously felt as the antecedent: 'That is *one* of the most valuable books (true antecedent but here not felt as such) that *has* (instead of the correct *have*) appeared in recent years.' 'Tyranny is *one* of those evils which *tends* (instead of *tend*) to perpetuate *itself*' (instead of *themselves*) (Bryce, *American Commonwealth*, Second Edition, II, 344). The singular form of the verb here is quite old: 'Thauriso, þat is a full fair cytee and a gret and on (one) of the beste þat *is* in the world for marchandise' (Mandeville, *Travels*, Ch. XVII, fourteenth century, MS. Cotton, A.D. 1410–1420).

a. ANTECEDENT IMPLIED IN A POSSESSIVE ADJECTIVE. The antecedent of the relative pronoun is usually a noun or a pronoun, but it is sometimes, especially in older English or in poetry, a person implied in a possessive adjective, which is explained by the fact that the possessive adjective was originally a personal pronoun in the genitive and still always represents a definite person: 'Would you have me . . . Put my sick cause into *his hand that* (now usually *into the hand of him who*) hates me?' (Shakespeare, *Henry the Eighth*, III, I, 115).

b. VERB IN AGREEMENT WITH SUBJECT OF PRINCIPAL PROPOSITION. Where the antecedent is a predicate noun in the principal proposition, the verb of the relative clause sometimes, especially in older English, agrees in person and number with the subject of the principal proposition if it be a personal pronoun: 'I am no orator, as Brutus is, But, as you know me all, a plain blunt man, *That love my friend*' (Shakespeare, *Julius Cæsar*, III, II, 221), now usually *that loves his friend*.

c. VERB IN THIRD PERSON WITHOUT REGARD TO ANTECEDENT. In older English, the verb of the relative clause was sometimes in the third person without regard to the antecedent of the relative: 'My Lord of Burgundy, We first address toward you, who with this king *Hath* (now *have*) rival'd for our daughter' (Shakespeare, *King Lear*, I, I, 192). This usage still lingers: 'To me, who *knows* the capacity of human muscle, these men are a miracle' (Norman Douglas, *South Wind*, Ch. X). 'Above all, no compulsion is offered to yourself, dear Elizabeth, who rightly *resents* anything of the sort' (Hugh Walpole, *Wintersmoon*, A.D. 1928).

d. FALSE ATTRACTION. Writers and speakers not infrequently place the relative pronoun in the accusative under the false impression that it is the object of the following verb, while in reality its grammatical function demands the nominative form: 'Instinctively apprehensive of her father, *whom* she supposed it was, she stopped in the dark' (Dickens). Here *whom* is incorrectly used for *who*, the predicate of the relative clause *who it was*, which is the object of the verb *supposed*. This incorrect usage was very common in Shakespeare's time: 'Arthur, *whom* they say is kill'd tonight On your suggestion' (*King John*, IV, II, 165).

9. **Position and Repetition of the Relative.** To avoid ambiguity the relative should be placed as near as possible to the antecedent: 'The *figs which* we ate were in wooden boxes,' not 'The *figs* were in wooden boxes *which* we ate.' If this cannot be done, the sentence must be altered so that the thought becomes clear: not 'Solomon, the son of David, *who* built the temple,' but 'David's son Solomon, *who* built the temple.' In older English, an antecedent in the genitive might precede its governing noun, but today it follows the governing noun and stands immediately before the relative: 'I shall not confine myself to *any man's rules* (now *the rules of any man*) that ever lived' (Sterne, *Tristram Shandy*, I, p. 10).

Though in general the relative pronoun introduces the clause, we sometimes for the sake of emphasis put some other word in the first place: 'So we get this charming little book, the *newest thing about which* is, perhaps, its method' (*London Times, Literary Supplement*, 29/10, 1914). 'It amounts to this that they are ready to undertake work the *results of which* they can visualize' (*ib.*, 19/10, 1916). 'A deeply interesting book is this ancestor of the modern dictionary, to *describe which* adequately would take far more time than the limits of this lecture afford' (Sir J. Murray, *Evolution of English Lexicography*). If the relative is the object of a preposition the latter frequently precedes: 'He is the man *upon whom* I am depending.' The preposition often stands at the end of the clause. See **62** 4.

Where the construction in two or more successive relative clauses is the same, and there is no particular reason to contrast them or emphasize each statement, the relative pronoun need not be repeated: 'John Jones, who was born and buried in London.' In older English, the relative pronoun was often not repeated even where the construction in the different relative clauses was different: ''Tis like a Potion *that* a man should drinke, But turnes his stomacke with the sight of it' (Ben Jonson, *Euery Man out of*

His Humour, I, i, 9, A.D. 1600). The relative is now repeated when the case or government is changed: 'Originality in politics, as in every field of art, consists in the use and application of the ideas *which* we get or *which* are given to us.' 'Nor do I, either in or out of Cambridge, know any one *with whom* I can converse more pleasantly, or *whom* I should prefer as my companion.' As in these examples, we should always use the same relative when we repeat a relative. There is a natural hesitancy, however, to repeat restrictive *that* when widely separated from its antecedent, as it usually follows its antecedent immediately, not even separated by a pause, so that some prefer *which* where the pronoun is widely separated from its antecedent: 'all the toys *that* infatuate men and *which* they play for' (Emerson). We may avoid this difficulty by using *which* in both cases. On the other hand, if there are two relative clauses in the sentence and one of them is subordinate to the other, a change of relative is helpful to keep the grammatical relations clear: 'He enjoyed a lucrative practise, *which* enabled him to educate his family with all the advantages *that* money can give.'

a. PERSONAL PRONOUN INSTEAD OF RELATIVE. Sometimes, especially in older English, where the grammatical conscience was not so sensitive as today, we find in the second of two coördinated relative clauses a personal pronoun instead of a relative, usually, however, only where the construction in the two clauses is different, which clearly indicates that the personal pronoun has been chosen as a convenient means of avoiding the reconstruction of the second clause: 'Fortune shall cull forth out of one side her happy minion, To whom in favour she shall give the day, And *kiss him* (instead of *whom she shall kiss*) with a glorious victory' (Shakespeare, *King John*, II, i, 391).

b. INDEPENDENT PROPOSITION INSTEAD OF RELATIVE CLAUSE. In older English, we often find a relative in one clause, but do not find in the following clause, which in a formal sense is coördinate with it, a relative expressed or understood: 'At last they were forced into a harbor, where (– in which) lay a French man-of-war with his prize, and *had surely made prize of them also*, but that the providence of God,' etc. (Winthrop, *Journal*, June 15, 1637). In such sentences the second subordinate clause has a subject in common with the first subordinate clause, but there is no relative pronoun that links it to the first subordinate clause, so that it appears to be an independent proposition. Instead of the conjunction *and* the relative pronoun *which* should have been used: 'a man-of-war with his prize, *which* had,' etc.

10. **Asyndetic Relative Construction.** There is in English fairly well preserved the most primitive type of relative construction, the asyndetic relative clause, i.e., a clause without a

connective, without a formal link joining the clause to the governing noun. In a strict sense this is not a relative clause since it does not contain a word which *points back* to an antecedent. It simply lies alongside of it as an appositive clause explaining it. The usual custom of saying that the relative is omitted suggests carelessness and has in fact brought the construction into bad repute with many who are wont to attach value to form. A careful study, however, of the true nature of this favorite old construction, as given at the beginning of II, p. 204, and also in **19** 3, will show at once that it is a good natural English expression, not a mutilated grammatical member but perfect and neatly fitted into the structure of the sentence, performing its function tersely, yet clearly and forcefully, often even with elegant simplicity.

There are two groups:

a. HYPOTACTIC ASYNDETIC CLAUSE. In this, the more common of the two types, the clause is always restrictive, closely linked to its antecedent; in fact so closely that it is indispensable to the thought, hence though not connected with the antecedent by a formal link, it is yet bound to it by such a strong logical tie that the dependent relation is distinctly felt. In most cases there is in the governing proposition a formal indication of subordination, a demonstrative or, more accurately, an adjective or pronominal determinative (**56** A), namely, *the* (definite article), *that, the one,* or some other word with determinative force, the indefinites *a, any,* etc., and the qualitative determinatives *a, one, ones, like that,* or in colloquial language simple *like* (**56** A), pointing to the following asyndetic relative clause. The following groups of examples of this common construction are arranged upon the basis of the function that the relative pronoun would perform if it were expressed.

Direct object of the verb: '*the* book *I hold in my hand*'; '*the* books *I am holding* and *those* (or *the ones*) *you gave me*'; '*that* lovely way *Father has, that* even course *he always pursues*'; '*a* man *we met yesterday*'; '*any* course *you may pursue*'; '*the* need of *a* man *we can trust*'; '*not such a man, but one we can trust.*' 'She makes pies *like those Mother used to make,*' or in loose colloquial speech *like Mother used to make.*

Instead of an indefinite determinative we often simply omit the determinative altogether, since the absence of an article or other determinative imparts indefinite force: '*certain books* (or simply *books*) *we should all read.*'

Although the asyndetic relative clause is most common in the relation of direct object, as discussed above, it not infrequently occurs elsewhere: Cognate (**11** 2) accusative: 'He went back *the* way *he had come.*' Accusative of length of time: 'The length of time *Eskimo dogs can go without food* seems beyond belief.' Indirect object: '*the* man *I wrote to,*' '*the* boy *I gave the knife to.*' Object of a preposition (**62** 4): '*the* pen *I write with,*' '*the* car *I rode on,*' '*the* book *I spoke of,*' '*the* table *the ball rolled under,*' '*the* fence *he jumped over*'; '*the* place *I am going to,*' or *to which I am going,* or *whither* (in a choice literary style) *I am going,* colloquially, *where I am going,* usually only in popular speech *where I am going to,* although outside of relative clauses this form is much more widely used; '*the* place *I came from,*' or *from which I came,* or *whence* (in a choice literary style, or sometimes *from whence*) *I came,* usually only in popular speech *where I came from,* although outside of relative clauses this form is much more widely used. *On* (or *in*) *which* in expressions of time: '*the* day *he arrived,*' '*the* year *you came back.*' *Every* (or *each*) *time that:* '*every* (or *each*) *time he came.*' *While:* '*all the* time *I was there.*' *Why:* '*the* reason *I did it.*' *In which* in expressions of manner: '*the* way *he does things.*' Predicate: 'He is not *the* man *he once was.*' 'She is not *the* cheerful woman *she used to be.*'

Earlier in the period, this construction was not infrequent in the subject relation: 'I haue a neece *is a merchants wife*' (Ben Jonson, *Euery Man out of His Humour*, I, II, A.D. 1600). 'Truth is mans proper good and the onely immortal thing *was given to our mortality to use*' (*id., Discoveries*, p. 4, A.D. 1641). 'I bring him news *will raise his drooping spirits*' (Dryden, *All for Love*, I, 113, A.D. 1678). Though this construction is in general not now used so much in the subject relation as formerly, it is still quite common here in a large number of expressions: 'My children have had every complaint *there is to be had.*' 'There's nothing *makes me so wild* as that continual bawling.' 'Mrs. Jones came to borrow some butter and I gave her all *there was* (or the little *there was*) in the house.' 'I lent to Mrs. Jones all the butter (or the little butter) *there was* in the house.' 'You may keep the money *there is left* after buying your hat.' 'There isn't one of us *really knows* what she's doing it for' (W. D. Howells, *A Hazard of New Fortunes*, II, Ch. I). 'There's going to be several folks *talk too much,* shortly' (H. W. Morrow, *Forever Free*, Ch. XII). Still widely used in popular Irish English, which here, as often also elsewhere, preserves older English idiom: 'It's the like of that talk you'd hear from a man *would be losing his mind*' (J. M. Synge, *The Well of the Saints*, p. 55). Also still quite common in the language of educated Irishmen: 'There's no investment in the world *would give you a return like that*' (Lennox Robinson, *Harvest*, Act I). Also common in the mountain dialect of Kentucky:

'Any man *can't fight for his friends* [had] better be dead' (Lucy
Furman, *Mothering on Perilous*, Ch. XV).

The old asyndetic clause is still not infrequent in subject
clauses which are now felt and treated as relative clauses: 'Who
was it *told you that?*' Other examples in **21** *c*.

The old asyndetic clause was once common after the determinative *that*, but as the form was early interpreted as a relative
pronoun it was later replaced by *what* and *he who, those who*,
the original construction now only lingering on, seldom recognized, in poetry or poetic prose or old saws: 'We speak *that*
(now *what*) we do know and testify *that* (now *what*) we have seen'
(*John*, III, 11). 'A man passes for *that* (now *what*) he is worth'
(Emerson). 'Handsome is *that* handsome does,' now in plain
modern form 'Handsome is *he who*,' etc. 'Of her ancestors there
have been *that* (now *those who*) have exalted and pulled down
Kings' (Digby, *Private Memoirs*, 272, A.D. 1665).

b. PARATACTIC CLAUSE. Here the clause is descriptive, often
quite loosely linked: 'There is a man at the door [, *he*] *wants*
to see you.' 'Here is a little book [, *it*] *will tell you how to raise
roses*.' 'I knew an Irish lady [, *she*] *was married at fourteen*'
(Meredith, *Ordeal of Richard Feverel*, Ch. XXVIII, 226). 'I have
discovered something [, *it*] *Concerns you nearly*' (Bridges, *Humour
of the Court*, III, 2, 2583). In this old paratactic (**19** 3) type two
sentences lie side by side, each with enough independence that
it might stand alone, and yet the second is connected in thought
with the first. In older English, when two such sentences came
into relations with each other, there was often no personal pronoun
in the second sentence referring to a noun in the first. The
context made the thought clear. The suppression of the pronoun
is a primitive means of suggesting subordination. In our present
hypotactic (**19** 3) stage of development we prefer to indicate this
subordination by a relative pronoun, hence this old type is now
little used.

11. **Abridgment of Relative Clause.** The relative clause can
often be abridged. Its contracted form is frequently that of an
appositive noun, adjective, or participle, which, alone or modified, might theoretically be construed as an elliptical clause, as
indicated by the square brackets, but in reality is an abridged
clause (**20** 3), as often becomes evident in clauses containing a
present participle which, as in the examples from Ben Jonson and
Mark Twain, cannot be construed as standing in an elliptical
clause. The subject of the abridged clause is usually some noun
or pronoun in the principal proposition: 'The English, [*who are*]
a practical and energetic people, have spread beyond their islands

and now hold territory in all parts of the world.' 'His companions led Henry V to do many deeds [*that were*] *quite unworthy of a prince.*' 'Opinion is a light, vaine, crude, and imperfect thing, settled in the imagination, but *never arriving* (= *which never arrives*) *at the understanding*, there to attain the tincture of reason' (Ben Jonson, *Discoveries*, p. 6, A.D. 1641). 'It (i.e., the circus) was all one family — parents and five children — *performing* (= *who performed*) *in the open air*' (Mark Twain, *Letter to His Wife*, Sept. 28, 1891). 'Pride [*which is*] *joined with many virtues* chokes them all.' 'Geoffrey says his speech on the Poor Law was head and shoulders the best [*that was*] *made*' (Galsworthy, *The Patrician*, p. 338). 'Well, Father, there's Rocket (name) [*who has*] *come for you*' (Hugh Walpole, *The Green Mirror*, p. 29). 'First (**58**, 6th par.) [*who has*] *come*, first [*who will be*] *served.*' 'First [*who has*] *come*, first [*who will be let*] *in.*'

There is also another kind of abridged relative clause which has come into wide use. Wherever there is a modal idea involved, a relative clause, in accordance with **7 D 2**, can be abridged to an infinitive clause when the infinitive serves as the predicate and some noun or pronoun in the principal proposition as subject: 'He is not a man *to trifle with*' (= *who is to be trifled with, can be trifled with*). 'That isn't anything *to censure*' (= *that should be censured*). 'The sights *to be seen* (= *which can be seen*) are not impressive.' As explained in **7 D 2**, the infinitive here is often active in form but passive in meaning. In oldest English, active meaning was quite rare in this construction, but it is now quite common: 'John is the boy *to do it*' (= *who should do it*). 'Did you ever see anything *to beat it?*' (= *that could beat it*). 'It is the glory of Trinity that she has an abundance of famous men *from whom to select*' (= *from whom she can select*, or in simpler form *to select from*). 'He is a poor old man *soon to become* (= *who must soon become*) *a burden to his family.*' There is often here a future force in connection with the modal. See **7 D 2** (2nd par.).

When the reference is general or indefinite, the infinitive here has no subject: 'It is not a night *to turn a dog from the door*' (= *in which one should turn a dog from the door*). 'He has no following *to speak of.*' 'What is there *to do?*'

Not infrequently, the subject is indicated by the context: 'Clearly the minute had come *at which to speak plainly*' (Basil King, *The Side of the Angels*, Ch. XIII) (or in simpler form *to speak plainly* = *at which he should speak plainly*).

Where the subject of the infinitive is not general or indefinite, or is not implied in some word in the principal proposition, or is not indicated by the context, the infinitive has a subject of its own introduced by *for*, as explained in **21** *c*: 'She wasn't terrible, she wasn't really anything except a kind of peg *for all sorts of traditions to hang on to'* (Hugh Walpole, *The Duchess of Wrexe*, Ch. XII). 'The thing *for you to do* is to go to bed.' 'What is there *for us to do?'*

OBJECT CLAUSE

24. Object clauses are divided into genitive, dative, accusative, and prepositional clauses. In the prepositional clause the preposition and the following clause form a unit called a prepositional clause, which as a whole serves as the object of some verb or adjective.

GENITIVE CLAUSE

24 I. A genitive clause performs the function of a noun in the genitive, used as the object of a verb or an adjective: 'I reminded him *that he had promised it*' (= *of his promise*). 'I am sure *that he will support me*' (= *of his support*).

The genitive clause is introduced by: *that; but, but that,* or in colloquial speech *but what,* after a negative proposition instead of *that not;* the indefinite relative (**23** II 1, 2, 3) pronouns and adverbs *who, what, whether, how,* etc. The genitive clause does not usually have a distinctive form. We recognize it by the fact that a corresponding noun or pronoun object is in the genitive, as in the two examples given above. If, however, it is introduced by an indefinite relative other than *whether,* it has the genitive sign *of:* 'I reminded him *of what he said.*' 'Are you sure *of what you say?*' 'Are you sure *of who he is?*'

Examples:

I am not sure *that he will come.*

I am not sure *that he may not decline* (or *but that,* or *but what, he may decline*).

I cannot convince myself *that she isn't alive* (or *but that,* or *but what, she is still alive*).

I cannot persuade myself *that she does not still love me* (or *but that,* or *but what, she still loves me*).

They robbed him *of what he had on his person.*

He was not sure *whether he had left his umbrella at school or on the playgrounds.*

He was mindful *of how kindly they had treated him.*

As many people feel the genitive clause now as a prepositional clause, these examples might all be classed under IV, p. 253.

a. ABRIDGMENT OF GENITIVE CLAUSE. A *that-*clause may sometimes be abridged to an infinitive clause, but it is much more freely abridged to a gerundial clause, since the gerund can naturally assume the genitive form: 'He is worthy *to receive such honor'* (or *to be thus honored*). 'I reminded him *of his having promised it.'* 'I convinced him *of his* (or *my*) *being able to do it.'* 'He is not convinced *of being defeated.'* 'I am not quite sure *of his having said it.'*

DATIVE CLAUSE

24 II. The dative clause performs the function of a noun which is in the dative after a verb or an adjective:

He told the story *to whoever would listen.*
He told the story *to whomever he met.*
He was unkind *to whoever opposed him.*
This is like *what we saw yesterday.*
The explosion took place near *where we stood.*

The relative pronoun in the subject relation is sometimes incorrectly put into the dative after the dative sign *to,* the writer or speaker for the moment not noticing that the pronoun is subject of the dative clause: 'The original papers . . . are in my possession and shall be freely exhibited to *whomsoever* (instead of the correct *whosoever*) may desire a sight of them' (Hawthorne, *Scarlet Letter,* The Custom House).

As *like* and *near* may be construed also as prepositions, the clause following them may be construed as the object of a preposition, preposition and clause together forming a prepositional clause: 'This cloth does not wear *like what we bought of him before.'*

'The bridge crosses the river *near where we live.*' Compare **50** 4 *c bb* and **24 IV.**

a. ABRIDGMENT OF DATIVE CLAUSE. This clause is sometimes replaced by a participle: 'He is unkind *to all opposing him,*' instead of *to whoever opposes* (sometimes *oppose*) *him.*

ACCUSATIVE CLAUSE, OBJECT OF A VERB

24 III. Conjunctions. This clause performs the function of a noun in the accusative used as the object of a verb: 'I saw *what he did*' (= *his deed*). There are sometimes two direct objects — one a noun or pronoun, the other a clause: 'I entreated *him that he spare me this humiliation.*' As the double accusative is not now a common construction, we prefer a prepositional object instead of the accusative of the noun or pronoun, wherever this is possible: 'Pas straight desired *all the company* they would beare witnes' (Sir Philip Sidney, *Arcadia*, Book III, p. 65, A.D. 1593), now usually *of all the company.* But the accusative of the noun or pronoun is the more common form when the clause is an infinitive clause: 'I desire *all the company* to bear witness.'

This clause is introduced by: *that,* in popular speech still often replaced by *as* (**27** 2, 2nd par.), as sometimes in older literary English; in older literary English sometimes *as that* instead of the usual *that; lest,* from older *thy* (old instrumental case of *that*) *less the,* literally, *on that account that* with the negative *less* (= *not*) inserted to indicate that the person in question wishes that the action may not take place; sometimes still, as in older English, used after verbs of fearing instead of *that; but, but that,* or in colloquial speech *but what,* often used instead of *that not* after a negative or interrogative proposition containing a verb of knowing, thinking, believing, expecting, fearing, or saying; an illogical *but, but that,* or in colloquial speech *but what,* sometimes used instead of the more common *that* after a negative or interrogative proposition containing a verb of doubting, wondering, earlier in the period also a verb of denying and gainsaying, in all four cases verbs which though positive in form are negative in meaning; an illogical *but* or *but that* instead of *that* after a negative or interrogative proposition containing a verb of hindering or preventing, verbs which though positive in form are negative in meaning, a construction once common but now replaced by a positive gerundial clause after the preposition *from;* in older English, an illogical *that not* instead of *that* after such verbs as *to forbid, hinder,* etc., which though positive in form are negative in meaning; after verbs of remembering, recalling, thinking, knowing, learning, perceiving, hearing, and relating often *how* instead of *that*, or, especially earlier in the period, with double expression, *how that*, in popular speech often replaced by *as how* or *that how;* often introduced by the indefinite relative (**23** II 1, 2, 3) pronouns *who* (in older English also *who that*), *what* (in older English also *what that*), *that* (in older English, now replaced by *what*), *which*, *whichever*, *what(so)ever*, *whatso* (in older English); the indefinite relative adjectives *which*, *whichever*, *what* (more indefinite than *which*), *whatever;* the indefinite relative adverbs *where*, *when*, *whence* (in a choice literary style, usually replaced by *where — from*, *from where*) or sometimes *from whence*, *whither* (in a choice literary style, usually replaced by *where*, or often in colloquial speech by the more accurate *where — to*), *why* (in older English also *why that*), *how* (in older English also *how that*), *whether* (originally a pronoun meaning *which of the two*) or *if*, or in older English sometimes *and* or *an; whether — or whether*, in older English also *if — or*, also *if — or whether*, also *if — or whether that; whether — or*, used when the second member has its subject, or verb, or both suppressed, but in older English we find here also *whether — or whether;* in indirect questions introduced by *whether* or *if*, or in older English sometimes *and* or *an; whether — or whether*, in older English also *if — or whether*, *whether* (or *if*) *— or whether that; whether — or*, in older English also *if — or;* in indirect questions also introduced by the interrogative adverbs *why* (in older English *why that*), *how* (in older English *how that*), *whence*, *where — from*, *whither*, *when*, *where*, etc., or the interrogative pronouns and adjectives, *who*, *what*, *which*, etc.; in indirect exclamations introduced by *what a.* Examples illustrating the use of these conjunctions are given below. One of these conjunctions — *if* — needs a historical explanation. In older English, it was used in both substantive and conditional clauses. Its original meaning of doubt or uncertainty was felt as appropriate for both categories. Today in the literary language we usually distinguish the two categories by a distinctive form, preferring *whether* to *if* in substantive clauses and reserving *if* for use in conditions. The old usage of employing *if* also in substantive clauses is still widespread in colloquial speech. But even here *if* is not used if the substantive clause precedes the principal proposition or if the substantive clause stands in the attributive relation, i.e., is an attributive substantive clause (**23** I): '*Whether* (not *if*) *he comes himself or sends a substitute* is immaterial to me.' 'The question *whether* (not *if*) *he should come himself or send a substitute must be decided soon.*'

An understanding of the nature of a direct and an indirect

question is necessary to appreciate the form and meaning of some of the examples given below. The nature of an indirect question is discussed in **21** and **23** II 1 (last par.). The forms employed to introduce direct and indirect questions are used also to introduce other object clauses where there is not the slightest reference to a question or an answer, as in 'I told him *how* (relative adverb) he should do it.' There is, however, a close relation between these interrogative and indefinite relative forms. Both groups were originally indefinites and still retain their original meaning. An interrogative is an indefinite that assumes the additional function of asking information concerning indefinite relations. The interrogative, however, never ceases to be an indefinite. Compare *c*, p. 247, and **23** I and II 1 (last par.). For the use of the terms *relative* and *interrogative* see **21** (4th par.).

Although the accusative clause usually has declarative form, it sometimes has the form of a direct command or a direct question: 'And I say to mankind, *Be not curious about God!*' (Walt Whitman, *Leaves of Grass*, p. 90). For examples of interrogative form see *c*, p. 247.

Examples of Accusative Clauses after Verbs:

'I know *that he has come*,' originally 'I know *that: he has come*,' where the *that* is a determinative pronoun pointing to the following explanatory appositional sentence.

Is it sufferable that the Fop of whom I complain should say *as* (now *that*) *he would rather have such-a-one without a Groat than me with the Indies?* (Steele, *Spectator*, No. 508, p. 6, A.D. 1712).

MISS OPHELIA. You ought to be ashamed of yourselves. — MR. ST. CLAIRE. I don't know *as* (now *that*) *I am* (Harriet Beecher Stowe, *Uncle Tom's Cabin*, Ch. XVIII).

I don't know *as* (now *that*) *it would be proper for me to mention the grown-up people over the way* (Louisa Alcott, *Aunt Jo's Scrap-Bag*, 197).

I don't know *as* (in popular speech replacing, as here, literary *that*) *I should want you should marry for money* (W. D. Howells, *The Minister's Charge*, Ch. XX).

Pray let her know *as that* (instead of the usual simple *that*) *I will present her . . . my Lancashire Seat* (Richardson, *Clarissa*, IV, 259, A.D. 1748).

I feared *that it might anger him* (or *lest it should*, or *might, anger him*).

I don't know *but* (or *but that*, or *but what*) *it is all true* (= *that it isn't all true*).

Who knows *but* (*but that*, or *but what*) *it is all true?* (= *that it isn't all true?*).

I could hardly believe *but* (*but that*, or *but what*) *it was all real* (= *that it wasn't all real*).

Take the money — there is no saying *but* (*but that*, or *but what*) *you will need it*.

That wouldn't say *but what I'd be foolish* (= *that I shouldn't be foolish*) to feel that way (Victor Appleton, *Don Sturdy in Lion Land*, Ch. IV).

Thus we lived several years in a state of much happiness; [I will] not [say] *but that we sometimes had those little rubs which Providence sends to enhance the value of its favors.*

Also, he did a big piece of work in his clean-up of camps all over California, and in awakening, through countless talks up and down the state, some understanding of the I. W. W. and his problem. (*Not but what it seems now to have been almost forgotten.*) (Cornelia Stratton Parker in *Atlantic Monthly*, April, 1919.)

Who doubts *that* (or now less commonly *but, but that,* or *but what*) he *will win.*

'I do not doubt *that* (or now less commonly *but,* or *but that,* or *but what*) *the catastrophe is over,*' but with the indefinite *whether* to bring out the idea of doubt, uncertainty: 'I doubt *whether* (or *if*) *the catastrophe is over.*'

'What hinders then *but that thou find her out?*' (Addison, *Cato*, III, vii, 18), now, 'What hinders *you then from finding her out?*'

He forbade *that not* (now simple *that* without *not*) *anybody should use a silver drinking cup* (W. Burton, *Comment. Itin. Antonin.*, 121, A.D. 1658).

'I saw *how* (= *that*) *he was gradually falling behind in the race,*' quite different from 'I asked him *how he did it*' (indirect question).

Tell John *what* (relative adjective) things ye have seen and heard; *how that* (= simple *how* or *that*) *the blind see, the lame walk* (*Luke*, VII, 22).

Seeing *as how* (for literary *that*) *the captain had been hauling him over the coals* (Marryat, *Peter Simple*, XIII).

Miss Dorritt came here one afternoon with a bit of writing, telling *that how* (in popular speech for literary *that*) *she wished for needle work* (Dickens, *Little Dorritt*).

I should like to ask *who* (interrogative pronoun) *did it* (indirect question).

I told him *who* (relative pronoun) *did it.*

He told me *whom* (relative) *he blamed for it.*

I asked him *whom* (interrogative) *he blamed for it* (indirect question).

I asked him *who* (interrogative; see **11** 2 *e*; better *whom*) *he plays with* (indirect question).

'I may neither choose *who* (now *one whom*) *I would* nor refuse *who* (now *one whom*) *I dislike*' (Shakespeare, *The Merchant of Venice*, I, ii, 24). Today we avoid simple indefinite *who* where we desire to describe rather than to point out.

Give me *what* (relative) *you have in your hand.*

Tell me *what* (interrogative) *you have in your hand.*

That (relative; now *what*) *thou doest,* do quickly (*John*, XIII, 27).

Whatever he threatens he performs.

'I'll tell you soon *which* (relative) *plan,* or *which* (relative) *of the plans, we finally settle on,*' or where the thought is more indefinite 'I'll report to you later *what* (or *whatever*) *changes we make in our plans,*' or a little more definitely 'We are ready to adopt *whichever of these plans you recommend.*'

I asked him *which* (interrogative) *plan he had settled on,* or *which* (interrogative) *of the plans he had settled on.*

I told him *why* (relative) *I did it.*
I asked him *why* (interrogative) *he did it.*
I wonder *why he doesn't come!* (indirect speculative question; see **21**, 3rd par.).
I wonder *what he is going to do now!* (indirect speculative question).
I told him *when* (relative) *I was going.*
I asked him *when* (interrogative) *he was going.*

I have seen, *When* (now a case, or cases in which), *after execution, judgement hath Repented o'er his doom* (Shakespeare, *Measure for Measure*, II, ii, 10).

I see *whither* (relative; in poetry and choice prose not infrequent) *your question tends* (*Concise Oxford Dictionary*).

I told him *where* (relative; in poetry and choice prose *whither*) *I was going.*

I asked him *where* (interrogative; in poetry and choice prose *whither*) *he was going.*

I told her *where* (relative) *I came from* (or in poetry or choice prose *whence I came*).

'Nobody knew *where* (relative) *he came from,*' or to emphasize *where* by withholding it until the end: 'He came from nobody knew *whére*' (George Eliot, *Silas Marner*, Ch. II).

'I should like to know *where* (interrogative) *she came from*' (or in poetry and choice prose *whence she came*), a polite indirect way of asking a question; but in a direct question we often for emphasis bring the interrogative, *who, what, where, where — from*, etc., forward from the subordinate clause and put it at the beginning of the sentence: '*Who* did she say wrote it?', '*Who* do you think it is?', '*What* do you think has happened?', '*Where* did she say she put it?', '*Where* did she say she came from?'; instead of: 'Did she say who wrote it?', 'Do you think who it is?', 'Do you think what has happened?', 'Did she say where she put it?', 'Did she say where she came from?'

'I have heard, *Where* (now *conversations in which*) *many of the best respect* (rank) *in Rome, Have wish'd that noble Brutus had his eyes*' (Shakespeare, *Julius Cæsar*, I, ii, 59). This old use of *where* with the force of a noun + *in which* is still heard in colloquial speech: 'This morning I read in the Tribune *where* (in the literary language *an account in which*) *a boy killed his father.*'

Of many things that have been taken for granted men are beginning to ask, *Are they true?* (direct question), or *whether they are true* (indirect question).

He decided that he would go and see *whether* (relative) *Rachel were in* (Hugh Walpole, *The Duchess of Wrexe*, p. 261).

I asked him *whether* (or *if;* interrogatives) *he was coming.*

In 'She found herself wondering at the breath she drew, doubting *that* another would follow' (Meredith), the writer employs *that* to indicate that, though there was doubt in the mind of the person described, there is really no doubt about the fact in question; but it is more natural here to use *whether* (or *if*) to portray vividly the doubt in the mind of the person described.

'I doubt *whether* (or colloquially *if*) *he was there,*' but 'I do not doubt *that* (or sometimes *but,* or *but that,* or colloquially *but what*) *he was there*' and '*Do you doubt that* (or *but,* or *but that,* or *but what*) *he was there?*'

Good sirs, looke *and* (now *whether* or *if;* relative) *the coast be cleere,* I'ld faine be going (Ben Jonson, *Euery Man out of His Humour,* V, III, A.D. 1600).

Aske him *an* (now *whether* or *if;* interrogatives) *he will clem* (starve) *me* (Ben Jonson, *Poetaster,* I, II, A.D. 1601).

I do not know *whether* (relative) *he will come himself, or whether he will send a substitute* (or *whether he will come himself or send a substitute*).

Know of the Duke *if* (now usually *whether*) *his last purpose hold, Or whether since he is advis'd by aught To change the course* (Shakespeare, *King Lear,* V, I, 1).

I do not know *whether* (relative) *he is better or worse.*

'We may choose *whether we will take the hint or not*' (or sometimes as in older English also *no*), or 'We may choose *whether or not* (or *no*) *we will take the hint.*'

'Confessing not to know *whether there were gods, or whether not*' (Milton, *Areopagitica,* 7), now simply *or not.*

Then while the king debated with himself *If* (now usually *whether*) *Arthur were the child of shamefulness, Or born the son of Gorlois,* etc. (Tennyson, *Idylls of the King,* 237).

I asked him *whether* (interrogative) *he would come himself, or whether he would send a substitute* (or *whether he would come himself or send a substitute*).

'And hark thee, villain, observe *if his cheek loses color or his eye falters*' (Scott, *Talisman,* Ch. XV). This *if* — *or* is still common in colloquial American English, but in the literary language *whether* — *or* is the usual form.

Then judge, great lords, *if* (now usually *whether*) *I have done amiss, Or whether* (relatives) *that such cowards ought to wear this ornament of knighthood* (Shakespeare, *I Henry VI,* IV, I, 27).

Every one knows *what a scene takes place when a Ministry is defeated in the House of Commons.*

Little did she foresee *what a difference this would make.*

The object clause is often complex, i.e., consists of a principal and a subordinate clause, the one being often embedded in the other: 'Let us now consider *what we said was the supreme characteristic of a highly developed age — the manifestation of a critical spirit, the endeavor after a rational arrangement and appreciation of facts.*' Here the principal proposition of the complex clause, *we said,* is embedded in the subordinate. The clause is often only in a formal sense complex since the principal proposition has the force of a sentence adverb, as described in **16** 2 *a* (p. 132): 'I now desire to discuss what *I feel* is the main issue.'

a. ANTICIPATORY OBJECT OR OBJECT POINTING BACK. There is often an anticipatory word such as *this, it, one thing,* etc., in the principal proposition, pointing to the following object clause: 'I know *this, one thing,* that he will never do that again.'

If the principal proposition is placed at the end for emphasis, it often contains a pronominal object which points back to the object clause, which is the real object: 'Whom I honor, *him* I trust.' 'What the light of your mind pronounces incredible, *that* in God's name leave uncredited' (Carlyle).

b. Omission of 'That.'   As in **21** *a, that* is often omitted: 'He always answers us *he is well.'* This always takes place when the principal proposition is embedded in the accusative clause: 'God himself, they devoutly trusted, would shelter his servants in the day of battle against the impious men who were less their enemies than his' (Gardiner).   Sometimes the principal proposition follows the accusative clause, which has been placed first for emphasis: 'You've an appointment at the tailor's, remember' (Pinero, *The Thunderbolt,* Act I).

It is a characteristic of American popular and dialectic speech to employ a full clause after *want* (= *desire*), usually with suppressed *that,* while in the literary language the abridged form of the clause, according to *d,* p. 249, is always used: 'He wanted *Luke should go with him'* (Amy Lowell, *East Wind,* p. 110), but in the literary language always: 'He wanted Luke *to go with him.'*

c. Accusative Clause in the Form of a Question.   In colloquial and popular speech it is common to employ here a blending of direct and indirect discourse — the form of a direct question instead of the usual literary accusative clause introduced by the interrogatory conjunction *whether* or *if,* with the important modification, however, that a present tense form under the influence of a past tense is changed to a past tense form: 'He spoke of Pen's triumphs as an orator at Oxbridge, and asked *was he coming into Parliament'* (Thackeray, *Pendennis,* p. 286). 'He had asked the boy Micky *had any one gone to see them'* (De Morgan, *When Ghost Meets Ghost,* Ch. XXIX). 'He wants to know *is the newspaper man here'* (George Bernard Shaw, *The Doctor's Dilemma,* Act IV). 'Mr. Man up'n ax' 'im *is* (= *has*) *he got a bad cole'* (Joel Chandler Harris, *Nights with Uncle Remus,* p. 125).   This construction is spreading from popular speech.   It is especially common in popular Irish English.   It is used there even when the principal proposition is a question, so that both propositions have question form: 'Would you say *would that lad grow too high in himself to go into the kitchen to oblige me?'* (Lady Gregory, *The Dragon,* p. 91).

As explained in **21** (3rd par.), question form here sometimes denotes not a formal question but mere doubt, uncertainty: 'She cast about among her little ornaments to see *could she sell any to procure the desired novelties,'* instead of the usual *if* (or *whether*) *she could sell any,* etc. Very often in popular Irish English: 'Mad, am I? Bit by a dog, am I? You'll see *am I mad!'* (Lady Gregory, *The Full Moon*), instead of the usual *if* (or *whether*) *I am mad.* In the literary language we often find here a question followed by the formal principal proposition *I wonder,* which in reality, however, is not the governing proposition but a sentence adverb (**16 2 a,** p. 132) which gives the sentence the coloring of uncertainty: 'Am I getting deaf, *I wonder?'* (Edith Wharton, *The Glimpses of the Moon,* Ch. XXI).

In all these cases there is sometimes not only a change of tense but also a change of person: (direct) 'Will you call again?' (indirect) 'Would I call again? she asked.' 'Ned put his flat and final question, would she marry him, then and there' (Hardy, *Life's Little Ironies*).

Similarly, after the interrogatives *when, where, what, why,* etc., we sometimes find here question form instead of the usual word-order of the accusative clause: 'Then he asked *where was King Phillip'* (M. H. Hewlett, *Richard Yea-and-Nay,* 228), instead of *where King Phillip was.* 'Dey ax' 'im, dey did, *wharbouts wuz Brer Fox'* (Harris, *Nights with Uncle Remus*). 'My sister asked me *what was the matter'* (Doyle, *Sherlock Holmes*). As above, question form here sometimes denotes not a formal question but mere doubt, uncertainty: 'I wonder *what way did that lad make his way into this place'* (Lady Gregory). 'He realized that it would be best to see *what was the matter'* (Robert Herrick, *The Common Lot,* Ch. XXVI) (or more commonly *what the matter was*). As above, we often find here in the literary language a question followed by the formal principal proposition *I wonder,* which in reality is not the governing proposition but a sentence adverb which gives the sentence the coloring of uncertainty: 'Why do you dislike having servants and being waited upon so much, *I wonder'* (Mrs. H. Ward, *Lady Rose's Daughter,* Ch. XII).

Furthermore, question form is often employed where there is no desire either to report indirectly actual questions or to express doubt, uncertainty. When a speaker or writer presents a topic for consideration, he frequently first puts it in the form of a question and then proceeds to discuss it: 'To come to closer quarters we may ask, What are the chief general characteristics of sixteenth-century English?' (H. C. Wyld, *History of Modern Colloquial English,* p. 100).

Of course, question form is used when a direct question is quoted: '"Where are you going?" she asked.'

d. ABRIDGMENT OF ACCUSATIVE CLAUSE. This accusative clause can be abridged to an infinitive clause when its subject is identical with the subject or an accusative, prepositional, or dative object in the principal proposition: 'I hope *to see him today.*' 'I don't know *how to do it'*; but in older English sometimes without *how:* 'since I knew *to love'* (Thomas Godfrey, *The Prince of Parthia,* I, III, A.D. 1765). 'I didn't know *whether to laugh or cry.*' 'I beg you (acc.) *to go.*' 'I beg of you (prepositional object) *to go at once.*' 'I showed him (dat.) *how to do it.*' 'Tell him (dat.) *to come at once.*' 'I told him (dat.) *where to find it.*' 'I taught him (dat.) *to swim'* (or *swimming,* or *how to swim*). 'I have taught *how to swim* to many boys' (dat.). 'I·taught him (dat.) *what to say'* (or *what he should say*). 'He allows (or permits) me (dat.) *to do it.*' 'That makes it hard for me (dat. of reference; see **12** 1 B *a*) *to do it.*' As explained in **7** D 2 (3rd par.), the *to*-infinitive here often has modal force: 'I do not know what *to do'* (= *I am to do,* or *I should do*). 'I should be happy if I knew how *to accomplish* (= *I might accomplish*) this.'

Originally, the infinitive was only a modifier of the verb, but in course of time a close relation developed between it and the subject or the object of the principal verb, so that the infinitive and the subject or object of the principal proposition came to be felt as an abridged clause, in which the subject or object of the principal proposition was the logical subject and the infinitive the logical predicate. This construction has become thoroughly established where the subject of the infinitive is the subject of the principal proposition or the accusative, dative, or prepositional object of the principal verb; indeed in many cases it has spread beyond these early limits of the construction, for the infinitive is often used with an accusative subject after the verbs *want, wish, desire, like, order, request, know, think, believe, suppose, take* (= *suppose*), *image, expect, report, represent, reveal, cause, enable, permit, grant,* etc., where the accusative is felt as the subject of the infinitive rather than as the object of the principal verb: 'I want *you to go away and stay away.*' 'I want *you to wait for me until six o'clock,*' but with descriptive force, 'I want you *to be waiting for me with the car when my train arrives.*' 'I expect, desire *him to go.*' 'I desire *the rubbish to be removed.*' 'He ordered *the house to be pulled down.*' 'I know him *to be an honest man.*' 'I know *it all to be true.*' 'I thought, supposed *him to be the owner* of the house.' 'I thought, supposed *it to be him'* (**7** A *a* (1)), or more commonly with a clause with a finite verb, 'I thought, supposed *it was he,*' or in loose colloquial speech *him,* as explained in **7** C *a.* 'He thought, supposed *Richard to be me'* (or *that Richard*

was I, or in loose colloquial speech *me*). 'I took him *to be nearer
sixty than fifty.*' 'The big table enables *maps and documents to
be laid out* with ease' (*Strand Magazine*, No. 325, 16*a*). 'He
doesn't allow (or permit) *the books to be taken out of the library.*'
In Middle English and early Modern English, the list of these
verbs was longer, including *to say, tell, allege, fear, promise, do*,
etc. This usage with the last of these verbs survives in archaic
'We do you *to wit*' (= *know*); i.e., 'We give you to understand,
inform you.' In the passive form of statement, however, the old
construction is generally preserved: 'Nobody could be said *to
understand* the heath who had not been there at such a time'
(Hardy, *The Return of the Native*, I, Ch. I). Though the old
active form with *say* has gone out of use, the old passive form of
the same construction survives. Compare **7 D 1 *b.***

Except with the list of verbs given above we now follow the
simple rule that the *to*-form of the infinitive is used when its subject is the subject or object of the principal verb, and that elsewhere, according to **21 *e***, the infinitive has a subject of its own
introduced by *for;* sometimes also in the case of some of the verbs
in the above list, as the simplicity and clearness of this newer
usage has a strong appeal and is gaining favor: 'I planned *to go
myself*,' but 'I planned *for him to go.*' 'I hope *for the book to make
its mark*' (Meredith, *Letters*, 550). 'I beg *for dear little Molly to
stay on here*' (Mrs. Gaskell, *Wives and Daughters*, I, Ch. VII).
'Harry, Mrs. Roosevelt would like *for you to lunch at the White
House* today' (Archie Butt, *Letter*, Dec. 7, 1908), or also as in
older English with the simple accusative as subject of the infinitive: 'You mean you would like *Captain Lay to lunch at the White
House today*' (*ib.*). 'I hate *for them to whine* like that,' or sometimes still as in older English with a simple accusative as subject
of the infinitive: 'I had rather they would whine — though I
hate *them to whine*, too' (Mary Johnston, *Hagar*, Ch. II); but we
usually prefer to construct the clause so that the subject of the
infinitive is the subject of the principal proposition: 'I hate *to
hear* them whine like that.' In older English, there was another
kind of *for to* used, as explained in **21 *e***, a mere substitute for simple
to: 'The markis (marquis) cam (came) and gan (began) hir *for to*
(now in the literary language simple *to*) calle' (Chaucer, *The
Clerkes Tale*, 233). This old usage lives on in popular speech.

Just as in principal propositions an emphatic subject follows
there is, as in 'There is here some mistáke,' so in abridged clauses
the emphatic subject follows *there to be:* 'I don't want *there to be
any mistáke*' (Stanley Houghton, *Hindle Wakes*, Act III). Similarly, an emphatic subject — especially when modified by a phrase

or clause — follows a passive infinitive: 'Little did the fathers of the town anticipate this brilliant success when they caused to be imported from further in the country *some straight poles with the tops cut off, which they called sugar maple trees*' (Thoreau, *Journal*, XI, p. 218).

The *to be* of the passive infinitive is often omitted, especially in American English: 'I want these letters [*to be*] *stamped and mailed* at once.' 'He ordered a family in Shanty Town [*to be*] *quarantined*' (Sinclair Lewis, *Arrowsmith*). The fact that *to be* is often omitted here indicates that this construction is influenced by the objective predicate construction in **15 III 2**.

In older English, an infinitive with modal force could stand after *doubt not but:* 'He doubted not but *to subvert* any villainous design' (Fielding), now 'He didn't doubt *that he could subvert*,' etc.

With the group of verbs in **15 III 2 B** the simple infinitive without *to* is the usual form, now as well as in older English, although there is a tendency to use here the form with *to*, or in older English also *for to*.

In early Modern English, the old simple infinitive is occasionally still used here as in the case of the verbs in **15 III 2 B**. This old usage lingered longest where there was present in the mind some analogy of meaning with the verbs in **15 III 2 B**: 'But first I *forc'd* him *lay* his weapons downe' (Kyd, *The Spanish Tragedy*, I, II, 158, A.D. 1585), after the analogy of 'I *made* him *lay* his weapons down.' Sometimes where there is at present no verb in the list to serve as an analogy, for in older English this list was larger and the feeling for the old simple infinitive was livelier than today: 'And yesternight [she] sent her Coach twise to my lodging to entreat me *accompanie* her' (Ben Jonson, *Euery Man out of His Humour*, II, III, A.D. 1600). This old usage still lingers where there is some analogy in mind: 'Elementary humanity *forbade* him *leave* (after the analogy of the simple infinitive after *bade*, which is here associated with *forbade*) his lame old godmother one moment unattended' (Agnes and Egerton Castle, *The Lost Iphigenia*, Ch. I). The simple infinitive is now most common here where it is felt as an imperative: 'And you, Quentin, I command you *be silent*' (Scott, *Quentin Durward*, II, 193) (or more commonly *to be silent*). 'I was going to say *wait for us*, and then we could all have been married together' (De Morgan, *When Ghost Meets Ghost*, Ch. XI).

The gerund clause is often used here instead of the infinitive, almost regularly so when the verbal idea is felt as the direct object of the verb, while the infinitive is more common when its expressed subject is felt as having relations with the principal proposition: 'I don't remember *ever being scolded by her*' (or *ever having been scolded by her*). 'I shall not tolerate *your talking so to Mother*,' but 'I shall not allow *you to talk so to Mother*.' The verb *to tolerate* in this meaning usually takes a single object of the thing, while *to allow* usually takes an indirect object of the person and a direct object of the thing, and hence may take an infinitive, since its indirect object can serve also as the subject of the infinitive. We can either say, 'My convictions do not permit *my taking part in this*' or 'My convictions do not permit *me to take part in this*,' for *to permit* admits of either a single object of the thing or an indirect object of the person and a direct object of the thing. We can say, 'I planned *going myself*' or 'I planned *to go myself*,' since we feel that the subject of the infinitive, though unexpressed, has close relations with the principal proposition, for it is the subject of the principal proposition. We can either say 'I don't like *the boy to come here so often*,' or better with the newer form of the infinitive construction, *for the boy to come here so often*, or with the gerundial construction, *the boy's* (or often, *the boy; see* **50** 3) *coming here so often*. 'I aim *to be* (American), or *at being* (British), brief.'

After *help* in its negative meaning *avoid, prevent*, we employ either the infinitive or more commonly the gerund: 'He could not help *to weep and sigh*' (Kingsley, *Hereward the Wake*, II, XVI) (or more commonly *weeping and sighing*). Much more common than the *to*-infinitive is *but* + the simple infinitive: 'He could not help *but laugh*' (S. Weir Mitchell, *Hugh Wynne*, Ch. III). 'He could not help *but see them*' (Hugh Walpole, *Jeremy*, Ch. XI, 2). 'He could not help *but believe me*' (Lord Alfred Douglas, *Oscar Wilde and Myself*, Ch. XXIV, 290). 'I could not help *but feel that*,' etc. (Theodore Dreiser, *The Bookman*, Sept., 1927, p. 8). This construction is an abridged form of the full clause introduced by *but that* following a verb of preventing. Examples of the full clause are given in **24** III, p. 244. The use of *but* + the simple infinitive has been criticized by American grammarians, but it is constructed after an old pattern once widely used. Moreover, it is still employed by good British and American authors. It is common in American colloquial speech. *Choose* has the same meaning and construction, but is not so common: 'He could not choose *but love* her' (Meredith, *Ordeal of Richard Feverel*, Ch. XXV). In older English *to* was sometimes used before the infinitive: 'I could not chuse *but to forgive her*' (Richardson, *Pamela*, III, 70). The *to* should always stand before the infinitive, but the construction has been influenced by the elliptical con-

struction with *but* described in **49** 4 E (4th par.). In older English
this construction was used after other verbs of preventing: 'You
shal not faile *but find* them' (T. Wilson, *Rhetoric*, 81, A.D. 1553).
'She can not miss *but see* us' (Paget, *Tales of Village Children*,
II, 96, A.D. 1844). These examples have been taken from the
Oxford Dictionary under *But* 22, where there is a fuller list. Where
the *but* is not employed in the abridged clause, the *to* before the
infinitive is better preserved. *Fail* usually takes a *to*-infinitive,
but sometimes also a gerund, either in the accusative or the
prepositional genitive, the old genitive of goal (**13** 3): 'Don't
fail *to come.*' 'He never failed *coming* to inform them of this'
(Jane Austen, *Pride and Prejudice*, Ch. XXX). 'My proposals
will not fail *of being* acceptable' (*ib.*, Ch. XIX). *Miss* now usually
takes a gerund, but a little earlier in the period also a *to*-infinitive:
'I would not miss *seeing* it.' 'I was in pain Lest I should miss *to
bid* (now *bidding*) thee a good morrow' (Keats, *Isabella*, XXVI).
Prevent takes either a gerund after the preposition *from* or an
accusative participial or gerundial clause with an accusative or a
genitive subject: 'The troops tried *to prevent the enemy from
crossing the river*' (or *to prevent the enemy,* or *enemy's, crossing
the river*). *Hinder* takes either a gerund after the preposition
from or less commonly a *to*-infinitive: 'The noise hindered her
from going to sleep again.' 'He don't hinder you *to tell*' (Charles
Reade), now more commonly *from telling.* *Avoid* now usually
takes a gerund, though in older English it often has a *to*-infinitive:
'I avoided *discussing* (in older English also *to discuss*) the matter
with him.' 'I cannot forbear *expressing* (or *from expressing,* or
to express) my surprise.'

After verbs and the adjective *worth* (**11** 2 *g*) the gerund sometimes, in accordance with older usage, has active form though the
meaning is passive: 'It won't bear *thinking about*' (Conan Doyle,
Tragedy of the Korosko, Ch. II) (or *being thought about*). 'He
deserves *hanging* for that.' 'He preferred *burning* to recantation.'
'These acts are worth *recording.*' The gerunds in these cases are
felt as nouns, rather than as verbal forms. Compare **50** 1, 2.

PREPOSITIONAL CLAUSE, OBJECT OF VERB
OR ADJECTIVE

24 IV. If we resolve the prepositional clause into its constitu-
ent elements, we find a preposition and a group of words forming
a unit, a clause with the force of a substantive (noun) — a substantive (noun) clause. This clause has the peculiar form of a
substantive clause, i.e., it is introduced by the usual conjunctions

and conjunctive pronouns, adjectives, and adverbs found in substantive clauses. These connectives are given below. This substantive clause is the object of the preposition, hence is an object clause. But we do not feel it as a direct object. Preposition and substantive clause together form a unit, a prepositional clause. This prepositional clause modifies a verb, verbal phrase, participle, or adjective. Sometimes this clause is felt as the prepositional object, i.e., the necessary complement, of the verb, verbal phrase, participle, or adjective which it modifies: 'Your success will largely depend *upon what you do* and *how you do it.*' 'He had wisely made up his mind *as to what could no longer be avoided.*' 'He is conscious *of what a fine opportunity he has.*' 'He gets furious *against whoever opposes him.*' 'I am curious *as to what he will say.*' Sometimes the prepositional clause is much less closely related in thought to the modified word, so that it is felt as an adverbial element rather than as an object or indispensable complement: 'I walked over *to where she sat*' (adverbial prepositional clause of place). 'But you do as you like with me — you always did, *from when first you begun to walk*' (George Eliot, *Silas Marner,* Ch. XI) (adverbial prepositional clause of time). '*From what I know of him* (adverbial prepositional clause of condition = *If I may judge by what I know of him*) I should say that he is unreliable.'

An anticipatory object, *it* or *this,* often precedes the clause, the real object: 'I took his word *for it that he would make an effort.*' 'I am counting *on it that you will come.*' 'You may rely *on it that I shall help you.*' 'It has come *to this, that he can't support his family.*' The conjunction *that* may be suppressed here, as in **21** *a*: 'Molly's punishment had got *as far as this: she longed for her mother at this time*' (Owen Wister, *The Virginian,* Ch. XXXIV).

In older English, in clauses with adverbial force, the anticipatory, or determinative (**56 A,** 3rd par.), object was often *that,* which soon formed with the preceding preposition a compound, the two words developing into an adverbial conjunction. This old type is preserved in a number of adverbial conjunctions: 'He did not really know what he was going to say, *beyond that* (**31**) the situation demanded something romantic.' Likewise in the case of *in that* (**28 1**), *instead of that* (**28 3**), *besides that* (**28 3**), and sometimes *for that* (**30**). In older English, there were many such conjunctions. Compare **27** 3 (7th par.).

The preposition is often suppressed: 'He boasted [*of it*] *that he did it.*' 'I give you my word [*for it*] *that I wasn't there.*' 'I believe he made up his mind [*to it*] *that I was heartless and selfish*'

(Ruskin, *Praeterita*, II, 189). 'She hesitated [*as to*] *whether she should break in on his affliction*.' 'I don't care [*for*, always omitted] *who marries him*.' 'I wonder [*at it*] *that* (often omitted) *he didn't kill you*.' 'She was not aware [*of*] *how wide a place she filled in his thoughts*.' 'Be careful [*as to*] *how* (= *in what manner*) *you do that*.' 'The hawkers are wary [*of it*] *how* (= *that*) *they buy an animal suspected to be stolen*' (Mayhew, *London Labour*, II, 62, A.D. 1865). 'I shall write you as soon as I have made up my mind [*to*] *what I should do*.'

The substantive clause contained in the prepositional clause is introduced by: *that, what a*, and the indefinite relative pronouns, adjectives, and adverbs *what, whatever, who, whoever, which, whichever, where, when, how, why, whether*, etc. The forms with *–ever* have more indefinite force: 'I am pleased *with what he has done*, and I know I shall be pleased *with whatever he undertakes in the future*.' 'A gentleman has informed me *of who were engaged in the affair*, and he will inform me *of whoever in the future will engage in anything similar*.' 'I have made up my mind *as to which plan I prefer*, but I shall probably be contented *with whichever plan Father will adopt*.' Interrogatives are not used in this clause. Even in such sentences as 'I inquired about *what* he was doing and *how* his experiments were turning out' *what* and *how* are relatives, not interrogatives; for the statement here is not an indirect report of a direct question, but a declaration that information was sought with regard to certain matters.

In parallel clauses introduced by *what* the *what* needs to be repeated only when the construction is different in the two clauses: 'His name is associated with *what* is probably the best, and [*what*] has certainly proved to be the most popular, of English anthologies,' but 'He is entirely ignorant of *what* the house is and *what* its work consists of.'

In colloquial and popular speech the preposition often stands before a clause not formally introduced by a conjunction or an indefinite relative pronoun, adjective, or adverb: 'My head has been people-tired, I think, but my heart is just satisfied with being full of "I'm so glad you're better"' (Clyde Fitch, *Letter*, 1904). Usually, however, there is in such sentences a subordinating conjunction present. The preposition itself serves as a conjunction. The subordinate clause is of the old type described in the third paragraph, only that *that*, the anticipatory or determinative (**56 A**, 3rd par.) object of the preposition, has been suppressed, as in **27 3** (7th par.), so that the preposition itself serves as the conjunction, an adverbial conjunction: 'Q. You don't know Mr. Scope? A. [I] Do not, *outside of* [*that*] *I have*

seen him here about town' (*Tennessee Evolution Trial*, p. 12, July 10,
1925). 'I'm just fat *by* [*that*] *I eat so much victuals lately*' (Julia
Peterkin, *Scarlet Sister Mary*, Ch. III). 'They'd figgered on
making him their victim *on account* [*of that*] *he was the handiest*'
(Will James, *Smoky*, Ch. IV). The *that* is sometimes expressed:
'But, then, credit had to be handed to the little horse *on account
that*, even though he still had a powerful lot to learn, *he sure was
all for learning*' (*ib.*, Ch. VIII). Compare **27** 3 (7th par.).

Examples:

I insist *upon it that he go, should go, must go, shall go.*
He is worrying *about what we shall do next.*
Jones and I had a bet [*as to*] *who would stick out the longer.*
The crowd was elated or dejected *according to which of the two antag-
onists got the upper hand.*
They were praised or scolded *according to how they had done their work.*
I am not informed [*as to*] *whether he went, why he went, when he went,
where he came from.*
Instead of the clumsy correct 'I am curious as to *with whom* she is going
tonight,' many who try to talk correctly say *whom she is going with tonight*, but in loose colloquial speech we usually hear *who* (see **11** 2 *e*) *she
is going with tonight.*
He looked from one to the other of us, as if uncertain [*as to*] *which he
was to address* (or simply *which to address*).
Let them take care [*as to*] *what they say.*
'She is worrying *about it*,' or 'She is worrying *that he doesn't come*'
(or *because he doesn't come*). There is often in the *that*-clause, as in this
example, the idea of cause, which leads to the use of *because* instead of
that. Compare **30** *a.*

a. ABRIDGMENT OF PREPOSITIONAL CLAUSE. The original
concrete meaning of movement toward a person or thing found in
the preposition *to* is still discernible in the *to* of the infinitive in
infinitive clauses which form an indispensable complement to a
verb, adjective, or participle: 'His father forced him *to make his
own living.*' 'I persuaded, induced, got him *to do it.*' 'He is
eager *to go.*' 'He is inclined *to take offense easily.*' Often also
where the relation to the verb is not so close: 'He prevailed
upon his wife *to join in the deceit.*' 'I am counting upon John
to do it.' As in these examples, the subject of the infinitive is
often the subject of the verb of the principal proposition, or it
is the object of the verb or the preposition following the verb.
The subject of the infinitive is not expressed if it is general or
indefinite: 'The work is hard *to translate.*' If the infinitive has
a subject of its own *for* is placed before it: 'I am anxious *for you
to succeed.*' In all these cases the infinitive has more or less the

force of a prepositional object. It is interesting to observe that
the gerund after *to* often replaces the infinitive after *to* here,
while it cannot be used after *to* at all in the adverbial constructions
described below: 'Hunger forced him *to steal*' (or *to stealing*).
'I am accustomed *to do it this way*' (or *to doing it this way*). In
many adverbial clauses the *to* of the infinitive is still a preposition,
but its original force has faded away to different shades of abstract meaning. Purpose: 'He worked hard *to get through early.*'
The idea of purpose sometimes becomes quite dim: 'Look out!
I am going *to shoot.*' Adverbial infinitive clauses of purpose are
treated more fully in **33** 2. Result: 'He has come *to see the error
of his ways.*' 'He (i.e., the little son) is exactly like Hugh (i.e.,
the father, a general in the army) — he only wants a uniform *to
be put on the Staff at once*' (De Morgan, *Joseph Vance*, Ch. XXX).
After *to be born* the infinitive often has active form where the force
is passive: 'You was born *to hang*' (Jack London, *The Call of the
Wild*, Ch. I). Compare **28** 5 *d* (4th par.). The infinitive after
to expresses also other adverbial relations: 'I was pleased *to see
him*' (cause). 'I should be glad *to go*' (condition). 'You couldn't
do that *to save your life*' (concession). This infinitive is a terse
convenient means of expression, but, as it hasn't a distinctive
form in all the categories, it can be used only where the context
makes the thought clear. In the categories, however, where
there is a distinctive conjunction the expression is not only terse
but also clear, as in clauses of purpose (**33** 2), modal result (**28** 5 *d*,
29 2 *a*), and exception (**31** 2, 5th par.).

The infinitive clause is often used after other prepositions than
to if it is introduced by an indefinite relative pronoun, adjective,
or adverb: 'I am thinking *of what to do next* (= *of what I should
do next*), *of what course to pursue* (= *of what course I should pursue*), *of how to do it*' (= *of how I should do it*). 'They could not
agree *as to whom to select*' (= *as to whom they should select*). 'She
hesitated [*as to*] *what to reply*' (= [*as to*] *what she should reply*).
The infinitive in such clauses is, of course, not a simple infinitive,
object of the preposition *to*, but a modern formation, a *to*-infinitive
in an abridged prepositional clause. As can be seen by the forms
in parentheses, the infinitive here, as in **24** III *d*, often has modal
force.

After other prepositions than *to*, in clauses not introduced by
a relative, the gerund is used exclusively or alongside of the
prepositional infinitive: 'I am afraid of *doing him an injustice.*'
'He is dead set against *doing anything for me.*' 'They have often
talked about *going to America.*' 'The prisoner rescued himself
by *making a rope out of his coat and letting himself down on it from*

the window.' 'He was dismissed from school on account of *setting the boys up to so much mischief.'* 'She blamed herself for *having been such a dull companion.'* 'She was worried over *her little boy's* (or, according to **50** 3, *boy*) *having to cross the railroad on the way to school.'* 'His present poverty comes from *neglecting his earlier opportunities.'* In all these cases a thing is the object of the preposition, namely, the gerund. A gerund is usually employed here where the sense requires a thing as object, but the prepositional infinitive is here preferred, as in **24** III *d*, when the sense requires as object a person who is at the same time felt as the subject of the infinitive: 'He insisted upon *his wife's joining in the deceit,'* but 'He prevailed upon his wife *to join in the deceit,'* since we insist upon a thing but prevail upon a person. 'I am counting on *John's doing it'* or 'I am counting on *John to do it,'* as *to count on* takes an object of either the thing or the person. The infinitive here is the object of the preposition *to* that stands before it, as in the first paragraph, not the object of the preposition that stands before the subject of the infinitive.

There is sometimes a difference of meaning between gerund and infinitive: 'He is afraid *of dying'* (= *that he shall die*). 'He is afraid *to die,'* literally, in the direction of dying. The real difference here lies in the use of different prepositions rather than in the verbal forms themselves.

After certain prepositions the gerund sometimes, in accordance with older usage, has active form though the meaning is passive: 'I tried vainly to soothe her and reason with her; she was past *soothing* or *being soothed.'* 'He was past *saving.'* 'He tried her patience beyond *bearing.'* 'He got much sympathy in the constituency for his rough *handling* by a band of hooligans' (*Manchester Guardian*, IV, No. 10, 185, quoted by Poutsma in his *Grammar*, IV, p. 481). In such cases the gerund is felt as a noun rather than as a verbal form. Compare **50** 1, 2.

As in older English, a participle employed as a predicate appositive can still often be used instead of a gerund after a preposition: '*Holding* on to the rope firmly, I came safe to land' (= *By holding* on to the rope firmly, etc.). The gerund is more accurate, but the participle is more graphic. In lively style we still use our simpler older forms of expression, since they are usually more concrete and impressive.

CHAPTER XVI

ADVERBIAL CLAUSE

25 1. Different Types of the Adverbial Clause. There are two different types, one introduced by a conjunction, the other dependent upon a preposition. Conjunctional clause: 'I met him *as I was coming home.*' Prepositional clause: 'The light came straight *towards where I was standing.*' The conjunctional type is by far the more common type, so that for many centuries the prepositions in the prepositional clauses have been developing into conjunctions. Compare **24 IV** (3rd and 7th parr.) and **27 3** (7th par.). The prepositional clause is discussed in **24 IV**. The conjunctional clause is treated in detail in the following articles.

2. Origin and Development of the Conjunctional Clause. An adverbial clause performs the function of an adverbial element: 'He went to bed *as soon as he came home*' (= *upon his return home*). We now feel the group of words *as soon as* as a unit, as a subordinating conjunction introducing the subordinate clause of time. Originally, however, here as elsewhere in adverbial clauses, the expression was much more concrete. In the first stages of its development the clause under consideration was of the old determinative (**56 A,** 3rd par.) type. There were two forms.

In the older form the determinative adverb *so* stood after the adverb *soon,* pointing as with an index finger to the following explanatory remark: 'He went to bed *soon, so: he came home.*' The determinative *so* stood in such close relations to the adverb *soon* that the two words early fused into a compound. As this compound stood immediately before the explanatory remark of time, in close relations with it, it was often early felt as a part of it, serving as its connective, binding it to the principal proposition and thus developing into a subordinating conjunction; *so* now, however, in most categories appearing with its later, strengthened form *as* (from *all so,* i.e., *quite so*): 'He went to bed *soon as he came home.*' '*Soon as the evening shades prevail,* The moon takes up the wondrous tale' (Addison, *Hymn on Creation*). In many sentences the adverb or adjective does not fuse with *as* into a compound conjunction that introduces the subordinate clause, as in these examples, but the adverb or adjective remains in the principal proposition, while *as* has been drawn into the subordinate clause as the introductory conjunction: 'Thoughts . . . Glance quick *as lightning* through the heart' (Scott, *Rokeby,* I,

XIX). 'My good lady made me proud *as proud can be*' (Richardson, *Pamela*, III, 241). 'The desert was still *as the sky*' (Wallace, *Ben Hur*, I, Ch. V). This old type of expression with a single *as* was once common here, but is now largely replaced by the type with *as — as*.

Alongside of the old simple determinative *so* was a double determinative *so — so*, pointing as with two index fingers to the following explanatory remark: 'He went to bed *so soon, so:* he came home,' now *as soon as he came home*. The group of words *so soon so* early fused into a unit and became a part of the subordinate clause, serving like *soon so* as its introductory conjunction. This type of expression with double *as*, as in *as long as, as soon as, as early as*, has long been the usual form in this group: 'I stayed *as long as I could*.' 'I come home *as early as I can*.' In many sentences, however, the adverb or adjective does not fuse with *as — as* into a compound conjunction that introduces the subordinate clause, as in these examples, but the first *as* + adverb or adjective remains in the principal proposition, while the second *as* has been drawn into the subordinate clause as introductory conjunction: 'I threw it *as far* from me *as I could*.' 'He is *as strong* now *as he has ever been*.'

The introductory subordinate conjunction — both the simple and the double type, from the old single determinative *so* or the double determinative *so as* or *so that* — not only stands in close association with an adverb or adjective in the principal proposition, as in all the preceding examples, but it may be associated also with the verb of the principal proposition: 'I am going to bed, *as I'm very tired*,' originally 'I am going to bed, *so* (= *it is thus*): I'm very tired.' In some categories the old determinative form *so* is preserved: 'You may go where you like *so* (or with double determinative form *so that*) *you are back by dinner time*.' 'I went early *so* (or with double determinative form *so that*) *I got a good seat*.' 'Many came unto them from diverse parts of England, *so as* (now *so that*) *they grew a great congregation*' (Bradford, *History of Plymouth Plantation*, p. 40, A.D. 1630–1648).

The double determinative is characteristic of primitive expression, a double sign for the same thing, as the double negative still heard in popular speech, or the older double determinative forms *who that, which that* (**23** II), where we now use simple relatives, *who* and *which*. We still, even in the literary language, often prefer the double determinative forms to the simple ones: '*the* book *that* I hold in my hand,' often used rather than '*the* book I hold in my hand'; '*as soon as* I came home,' much more common than '*soon as* I came home.' Double expression arose in the desire to make thought and feeling clearer. Oldest English is characterized by the liberal use of determinatives, spoken gestures freely used, like gestures in general, to explain the intended meaning, so that the expression was markedly concrete. Later, expression lost much of its concreteness and became more abstract, so that words that once had concrete force and were useful lost their meaning, and later as useless words without a function disappeared. In other cases, words that had lost their concrete meaning were nevertheless retained since they had acquired a new abstract force and hence were useful. In the development from the concrete to the abstract, expression became less exuberant and picturesque, more simple and exact. The double forms were often replaced by simple ones; on the other hand, the simple forms were often replaced by double ones, for a combination of words contained greater possibilities of shading the thought than a single form. Modern expression is averse to excess of expression, but it is fond of accuracy and hence does not avoid a combination of words merely because it is long. These general principles will in the following articles be illustrated by many concrete examples.

3. **Classification.** Conjunctional adverbial clauses are subdivided into classes corresponding to those of adverbial elements — clauses of place, time, manner, degree, cause, condition and exception, concession, purpose or end, and means.

CLAUSE OF PLACE

26. Conjunctions. A clause of place indicates the place where the action of the principal verb occurs: 'Corn flourishes best *where the ground is rich.*' This clause is now introduced by: *where; nowhere (that),* see **27** 3 (5th par.); *whereas* (see page 265 and **27** 4); *as,* in older English = *where,* now only used in a few expressions; *whence* or *from whence* in poetry and choice prose, or more commonly *where — from, from where, from what place* or *source; whither* in poetry and choice prose, or more commonly *where; whereso,* now archaic, now usually *wherever, everywhere, everywhere that* (**27** 3, 5th par.), or the less common but more emphatic *wheresoever; whencesoever* in poetry and choice prose, more commonly *wherever — from, from whatever place* or *source; whithersoever* in poetry and choice prose, more commonly *wherever, everywhere, everywhere (that)* (**27** 3, 5th par.), archaically also *whereso.* The parentheses around *that* in these conjunctions indicate that *that* may be used or suppressed.

Examples:

We live *where the road crosses the river.*
I will go *nowhere that* (**27** 3, 5th par.) *she cannot go.*
It is right in front of you *as* (= *where*) *you cross the bridge.*
Here, *as* (now *where*) *I point my sword,* the sun arises (*Julius Cæsar,*
II, I, 106).
'Go *whence* (or *from whence*) *you came,*' now usually *where you came from.*
For *whither* (now *where*) *thou goest* I will go (*Ruth,* I, 16).
She is the belle and the spirit of the company *wherever she goes.*

Clauses of place with general or indefinite meaning often have concessive force and might be classed as well as concessive clauses: 'It would have cost my poor uncle no pang to accept Blanche's fortune, *whencesoever it came'* (Thackeray, *Pendennis,* II, Ch. XXVI). '*Wherever* he went, he was kindly received.' Compare **32.**

In clauses of place, as in **22** (1st par. under Examples), there is sometimes, especially in older English, a demonstrative in the principal proposition, pointing back to some word in the preceding subordinate clause: '*Where* your treasure is, *there* will your heart be also' (*Luke,* XII, 34). 'Then *whither* he goes, *thither* let me go' (Shakespeare, *Richard the Second,* V, I, 85).

In Old English, we often find in the subordinate clause instead of *where* the form *there:* 'Wuna þær þe leofost ys' (*Genesis,* XX, 15) = 'Dwell where it is most pleasant to thee,' literally, 'Dwell *there:* it is most pleasant to thee.' The *there* was originally a determinative (**56 A**), pointing to the following explanatory remark, later gradually becoming closely associated with it, forming with it a subordinate clause of place and serving as its connective, binding it to the principal proposition and thus becoming a relative conjunction. Although the old determinative had become a real relative, standing in the subordinate clause and often pointing backward to the principal proposition, it kept its old determinative form until the sixteenth century: 'It had been better for hym to have taryed *there* (now *where*) he was' (Lord Berners, *Huon,* LXIV, 221, A.D. 1534).

As can be seen by the form in parentheses *there* has been supplanted by *where.* Indefinite *where,* which here replaces older definite *there,* suggests in a general indefinite way the idea of place, but at the same time points to the following explanatory clause, so that in fact the reference becomes definite. This passing from the unknown to the known was a new means of expression that soon found favor here as well as in **23** II 1 and **27** 1. The new form began to appear in Old English: '*Hwer* am ic þer þegn min biþ' (*John,* XII, 26, Rushworth MS.), i.e., 'where I am, there will also my servant be.' In accordance with older English fondness for double or triple expression this indefinite determinative *where* was often accompanied by the double determinative *swa — swa* (later *so — so*), often simplified to a single *swa: 'Sua huer* ic am þer þegn min biþ' (*ib.*, Lindisfarne MS.). In this example the single *swa* precedes *where*, but it often followed, and this form survives in our emphatic indefinite *wheresoever*. The old determinative *so* has survived here because it has a function, namely, the expression of indefiniteness, and hence is useful, but where the reference is more definite it has disappeared, as explained below.

Similar to the use of *swa* in connection with *hwer* for the sake of double expression, is the doubling of the determinative *there* in the subordinate clause, so that instead of *sua huer* in the last example in the preceding paragraph we find a double *there* in the same passage in the Corpus MS.: 'Min þen biþ þær þær ic eom.'

In Middle English, both the single and the double determinative type survive: 'Hir eyen (eyes) caste she ful lowe adoun *Ther* (now *where*) Pluto hath his derke regioun' (Chaucer, *The Knightes Tale*, 1223). In the double determinative type Old English *swa* appears in Middle English as *so* or *as* (contracted from *all so*, i.e., *quite so*), the former with its old indefinite force, the latter with more or less definite force: 'And red *wherso* thou be, or elles songe, That thou be understonde I god beseche!' (Chaucer, *Troilus and Criseyde*, V, 1797) = 'I beseech God that thou ("Troilus and Criseyde") mayst be understood *wheresoever* thou mayst be read or sung.' 'He came alone a-night *ther as* (now simple *where*) she lay' (*id.*, *The Clerkes Tale*, 408). *There* and *there as* were at this time often replaced by *wher* and *wher as:* 'Let see *wher* the cut wol falle' (*id.*, *The Pardoners Tale*, 466) = 'Let us see where the lot will fall.' 'This frere cam, as he were in a rage, *wher as* (now simple *where*) this Lord sat eting at his bord' (*id.*, *The Somnours Tale*, 458). In the principal proposition there is often a *ther* pointing back to the *ther as* or *wher as* in the subordinate clause: '*Ther as* (now simple *where*) myn herte (heart) is set, *ther* wol (will) I wyve' (marry) (Chaucer, *The Clerkes Tale*, 117).

With verbs of motion the double determinative forms *thider as, thider that, whider as, wider that* were sometimes used in Middle English: 'I moot (must) go *thider as* (now in choice English *whither* or in plain prose *where*) I have to go' (Chaucer, *The Pardoners Tale*, 421). Instead of *thider as* here *thider that, whider as*, or *wider that* might have been used.

In Old English, the usual relative adverb of place with definite reference is *þær*. The usual Old English form for indefinite or general reference is *hwær* or *so hwær so*. In Chaucer's language *ther* is still employed for definite reference, but also *wher* is used, or *ther* or *wher* accompanied by one or two determinatives — *ther as, ther that, ther as that, wher as, wher that*. Indefinite or general force is expressed by adding *so* or *so ever* to *wher: wherso, wherso ever*. Thus at this time determinative forms are used for definite or indefinite reference, but the forms are differentiated in meaning — *as* and *that* with more or less definite force, *so* or *so ever* with indefinite or general force.

After the different determinative constructions with definite *there* and *where* had developed into a relative construction, the *there* and *where* becoming relative conjunctions, pointing backward or forward to the principal proposition and linking the clause of place to it, the demonstrative *there* in the principal proposition, pointing back to the clause of place, lost its function and hence its usefulness and gradually disappeared, likewise the determinative adverbs *as* and *that* in the clause of place. This development became more marked after *where* had supplanted *there* as relative conjunction. The dropping of the formal particles *there* in the principal, and *as* and *that* in the subordinate, proposition made the sentence as a whole much more compact. The old type of expression is parataxis, the new type hypotaxis, as explained in **19 3**. The old double determinative construction, however, lingered on for a long time, so that we find traces of it in the present period after both *there* and *where*, i.e., we find the relatives *there* and *where* occasionally followed by *as:* 'He came *there as* (now simple *where*) she was' (Lord Berners, *Huon*, I, p. 100, A.D. 1534). '*Whereas* (now simple *where*) the Ebrewe speache seemed hardly to agree with ours, we haue noted it in the margent' (*Geneva Bible*, A.D. 1578). This older use of *whereas* survives in two derived meanings, namely, *while* (*on the other hand*) and *as* (with causal force): 'Those who are well assured of their own standing are less apt to trespass on that of others, *whereas* nothing is so offensive as the aspirings of vulgarity' (Washington Irving). '*Whereas* Mr. James Smith has been employed in my service from . . . to . . . I hereby testify,' etc. On the other hand, the indefinite determinative *so*, described in the preceding paragraph, did not disappear as did the definite determinative *as*. It has survived not as a determinative but as an indefinite particle felt as useful to stress the idea of indefiniteness: *wheresoever*, more emphatic than *wherever*.

a. ABRIDGMENT OF CLAUSE OF PLACE. The full clause of place is sometimes abridged to a predicate appositive clause, in which the subject of the principal proposition is the subject and a participle is predicate: '*Where having nothing*, nothing can he lose' (Shakespeare, *III Henry VI*, III, III, 152). But in '*Wherever* [*it has been*] *feasible*, the illustrations have been taken from standard literature' we have to do with an ellipsis. Compare **20** 3 (5th par.) and **27** 5 (2nd par.).

The old verbless appositional type of sentence described in **6** B *a* is sometimes found here: 'Least said, soonest mended' = 'Where there is least said, there things are soonest mended.'

CLAUSE OF TIME

27. Conjunctions. A temporal clause limits the time of the action of the principal verb, which is thus represented as taking place simultaneously with, or before, or after that of the temporal clause. The following conjunctions introduce the temporal clause: *soon as* (**25** 1), now more commonly *as* (or *so*) *soon as*, in older English also *anon as* with the same meaning; *as soon as ever*, an emphatic *as soon as; as* (or *so*) *long as; as* (or also *so* in older English) *often as; whenso*, archaic, now usually *whenever*, or the less common but more emphatic *whensoever; so surely as; if* (= *whenever*); *as; when*, or, in older English, *when as*, or *when that; the time* (*that*); *by the time* (*that*) or in older English *by that, by then* (*that*), or *by*, the last form surviving in Scotch dialect; *until*, in dialect often used with the force of *by the time that; the year* (*that*), *the month* (*that*), *the week* (*that*), etc.; *every time* (*that*), *the next time* (*that*), *at the same time* (*that*), *what time; while* or, in older English, *whiles*, an old adverbial genitive from which has come a form with an excrescent *t*, *whilst*, still in use; in older English *during* (*that*), now replaced by *while; now* (*that*), *once, directly, immediately, instantly; since; after, again* (in older English) or *against* (now usually replaced by *by the time* or *before*), *ere* (archaic, poetic, or choice prose), *before, till, until*, all earlier in the period followed by *that;* in older English *fore* (*that*), *afore* (*that*), now replaced by *before; no sooner — than, scarcely — but* (see page 274). The parentheses around *that* in these conjunctions indicate that *that* may be used or suppressed.

In older English, *that*, like French *que*, was used as a substitute instead of repeating a conjunction that had already been used, a *that* thus repeating a preceding *when, since, because, if*, etc.: 'When one of the parties to a treaty intrenches himself in ceremonies and *that* (used to avoid the repetition of *when*, which has already been used) all the concessions are on one side' (Burke, *Letters on a Regicide Peace*, III, Works, VIII, 330). In older

English *that* is used also as a regular conjunction with the force of *when* after *hardly, scarcely, not yet fully, not so soon:* 'The kyng had not yet fullych eten *that* (now *when*) ther come in to the halle another messagyer' (Caxton, *Chronicle English*, CCVII, 189, A.D. 1480). *But* (*that*), however, was more common here: 'So she was not so soone there *but* there came a Knyghte of Arthurs courte' (Malory, *Le Morte d'Arthur*, Book X, Ch. XXXVIII, A.D. 1485). Compare **27** 3 (last par.).

Examples:

I came *as soon as I heard of it.*

Anone as (now *as soon as*) *the kyng wyst that*, he took the quene in his hand and yode (went) unto syr launcelot (Malory, *Le Morte d'Arthur*, Book XVIII, Ch. VII, A.D. 1485).

'*As soon as I saw his face*, all my fears vanished.' Here a causal idea blends with the temporal.

I shall come *as soon as ever I can.*

'*As long as the general spirit of the administration was mild and popular*, they were willing to allow some latitude to their sovereign' (Macaulay, *History*, I, Ch. I). Here a strong causal idea blends with the temporal. Sometimes the causal idea overshadows the temporal. Compare **30.** Sometimes the idea of extent overshadows that of time: 'I have stood it *as long as I can.*' Compare **29** I A *d.*

'*So long as men believe that women will forgive anything*, they will do anything' (Sarah Grand, *Heavenly Twins*, I, 120). Here a strong restrictive idea blends with the temporal. Compare **29** 1 A *c.* There is often in *so long as* also a strong conditional idea: 'I do not care *so long as* (= *provided*) *you are happy.*' Compare **31.**

I visit him *as often as I can.*

Whenever (or *if*) I feel any doubt, I inquire.

So surely as she came into the room, however, Martin feigned to fall asleep (Dickens, *Martin Chuzzlewit*, Ch. IV).

When you are done, let me know.

I shall be ready *by the time* (*that*) *you get back.*

After this course settled and *by that* (now *by the time that*) their corne was planted, all their victails were spente (Bradford, *History of Plymouth Plantation*, p. 147, A.D. 1630–1648).

Now was it eve *by then that* (now *by the time that*) Orpheus came Into the hall (Morris, *Jason*, III, 503, A.D. 1868).

It was done *by* (for literary *by the time that*) we came home (modern Scotch).

He will be ready *till* (= *by the time that*) you are (dialect).

Other examples are given in the following pages in connection with the further treatment of these conjunctions.

Clauses of time with general or indefinite meaning often have concessive force and might be classed as well as concessive clauses: '*Whenever they attack*, they shall find us ready.' Compare **32.**

1. *History of 'When'.* When has become established after a long
competition with other forms. In Old English, the most common
temporal conjunctions were *þonne* and *þā*, both originally determinative adverbs with the force of *then*, pointing to the following
explanatory clause, later gradually becoming closely associated
with it, forming with it a subordinate clause of time and serving
as its connective, binding it to the principal proposition: 'Ic
næbbe nanne man þæt me do on þone mere *þonne* wæter astyred
biþ' (*John*, V, 7, A.D. 1000), literally, 'I have no one to put me into
the pool *then: the water is troubled,*' now *when the water is troubled.*
'Þā se hælend geseah þæt heo weop he geomrode on hys gaste'
(*John*, XI, 33, A.D. 1000), literally, 'Then: the Saviour saw that
she was weeping, he groaned in his spirit,' now '*When he saw her
weeping,* he groaned in his spirit.' In Middle English, *þonne*
appears as *than* or *then* and *þā* appears as *thō:* '*Then* (now *when*)
hys howndys began to baye, That harde (= heard) the jeant
there (now *where*) he lay' (*Sir Eglamour*, 286, A.D. 1440). 'Þis was
þō (now *when*) in Engoland Britones were' (Robert of Gloucester,
Chronicle, I, 2, A.D. 1300). Even in Middle English, *then* and
thō were little used, although the corresponding older forms *þonne*
and *þā* were the most common conjunctions of time in the Old
English period. Early in Middle English, *when* began to supplant
than, *then*, and *thō*, all three of which have entirely disappeared
as subordinating conjunctions of time.

This new relative conjunction of time, now so common, was
little used in Old English, but even in this early period it had
begun to develop out of the old indefinite determinative adverb
when: '*Hwænne* ic bræc fif hlifas . . . hu fela wylegena ge namon
fulle?' (*Mark*, VIII, 19, A.D. 1000) = 'When I broke the five
loaves how many basketfuls took ye up?' Indefinite *when*, which
here replaces older definite *þā*, suggests in a general indefinite way
the idea of time, but at the same time points to the following
explanatory clause, so that in fact the reference becomes definite.
This passing from the unknown to the known was a new means
of expression which soon found favor here as well as in **23** II 1
and **26** (6th par.). In older English, in accordance with older
fondness for double expression, *when* was sometimes accompanied
by two determinatives, *so — so*, later often simplified to a single
so: '*Weonne so* ich beo uorþ faren, Hengest eow wul makien
kare' (Layamon, *Brut*, 2, 206, A.D. 1205) = '*When* I am gone,
Hengest will cause you trouble.' The old determinative *so* appears here later in the form of *as*. Also *that* was used as a
determinative, so that the new definite temporal conjunction *when*
accompanied by its determinatives appeared as *when as* and *when*

that. Later, after definite *when* became a relative conjunction, pointing often backward to the principal proposition, linking the temporal clause with it, the determinative lost its function and hence its usefulness and finally disappeared. Instead of *when*, however, we still find a little earlier in the present period *when as* and *when that*, i.e., *when* in connection with a determinative, which indicates that the old determinative construction was at this time in part still preserved: '*When as* (now simple *when*) the Palmer came in hall Nor lord nor knight was there more tall' (Scott, *Marmion*, I, XXVIII). 'My gracious liege, *when that* (now simple *when*) my father liv'd, Your brother did employ my father much' (Shakespeare, *King John*, I, I, 95). In Middle English and early Modern English, the determinatives were for the most part differentiated. The form *so* had general or indefinite force, while *as* or *that* had more or less definite meaning. Today we still use *so* for indefinite reference, as in *whensoever*, or more commonly *ever*, as in *whenever*. For definite reference we now employ simple *when*, dropping the old determinative *as* or *that*.

2. *Original Meaning of 'As' and Its Present Uses*. *As* is one of the commonest conjunctions in our language. It is not at all confined to clauses of time, but is found in a number of different kinds of clauses. In its oldest form *so* it was a determinative adverb pointing to a following explanatory statement. In this explanatory statement lay the idea of time, manner, result, cause, etc. These ideas did not lie in *as*. The *as* originally simply indicated that a following statement would explain the meaning that was to be conveyed. In the following paragraphs the use of *as* in clauses of time is illustrated, also its employment in several other kinds of clauses to give a general idea of the meaning of this favorite word and the simple concrete conception that lies at the base of all its meanings.

In oldest English, the determinative adverb *so*, or in strengthened form *all so* (i.e., *quite so*), later contracted to *as*, could stand after a verb pointing to a following explanatory clause. This clause did not have a distinctive meaning and still in our own day varies in force according to the context. The *so* standing immediately before the explanatory remark became gradually very closely associated with it, forming with it a subordinate clause and serving as its connective, binding it to the principal proposition and thus becoming a relative conjunction, now with its old form *so* only in the categories of condition, purpose, and pure result, elsewhere with its modern form *as*. Condition: 'You may go where you please *so you are back by dinner time*.'

Purpose: 'They hurried *so they wouldn't miss the train.*' Pure result: 'He went early *so he got a good seat.*' Manner clause of modal result, in older English with *as*, which still survives in popular speech but in the literary language is replaced by *that:* 'I gained a son, And such a son *as* (now *that*) *all men hailed me happy*' (Milton, *Samson*, 358). Degree clause of modal result, in older English with *as*, which survives in popular speech but in the literary language is replaced by *that:* 'I feel such a sharp dissension in my breast *as* (now *that*) *I am sick*' (Shakespeare, *I Henry VI*, V, v, 84). Manner: 'He does *as I tell him.*' Accompanying circumstance: 'The enemy devastated the fields *as he retreated.*' Contemporaneous event: 'He returned home *as I was leaving.*' Cause: 'He stayed at home *as he was ill.*' Proportionate agreement: 'One advances in modesty *as one advances in knowledge.*' Alternative agreement: 'stones whose rates are either rich or poor *As fancy values them*' (Shakespeare, *Measure for Measure*, II, II, 150). Place: 'It is right in front of you *as* (= *where*) *you cross the bridge.*' In older English, *as* was used in purpose clauses. See **33**. *As* was also once common in substantive clauses instead of *that*, now surviving only in popular speech: 'I don't know *as* (for literary *that*) *I should want you should marry for money*' (W. D. Howells, *The Minister's Charge*, Ch. XX).

In oldest English, simple *so* could stand after a noun or pronoun, pointing to a following explanatory remark, so that it gradually became very closely associated with this remark, forming with it a relative clause and serving as its introductory relative pronoun, now always with its modern form *as*. In the literary language relative *as* has never been widely used, but is well established in certain categories, especially after *the same* (pp. 219, 222) and *such* (pp. 219, 222), also in descriptive clauses where the reference is to a preceding or following statement as a whole, or to the idea contained in a preceding word, as illustrated in **23** II 6 (next to last par.). In popular speech *as* is widely used as a relative where the literary language has *who, that,* or *which*, as illustrated in **23** II 5 (toward end of 1st par.).

In the concrete expression of oldest English there are often two determinatives, pointing, as it were, with two index fingers to the following appositional clause which explains their meaning. Since the two determinatives stood immediately before the explanatory remark, they gradually became very closely associated with it, forming with it a subordinate clause and serving, both forms merged into a unit, as its connective, binding it to the principal proposition and thus becoming a relative conjunction.

This development took place: (1) in manner clauses of modal result introduced by *as that*, described in **28** 5 (8th par.); in degree clauses of modal result introduced by *as that* and *so as*, described in **29** 2; (2) in clauses of pure result introduced by *so that* and *so as*, described in **28** 5 (6th and 9th parr.) and **28** 5 *d*; in clauses of comparison introduced by *so as*, described in **28** 2; in clauses of extent introduced by *so as*, described in **29** 1 A *d*; in purpose clauses introduced by *so that* and *so as*, described in **33** and **33** 2; (3) in clauses of place introduced by *there as* and *where as*, described in **26** (last par.); (4) in clauses of time introduced by *when as*, described in 1, p. 269. In the natural development toward greater simplicity the old double determinative has in several cases here as elsewhere been replaced by a simple form, as in the case of *there as* and *where as* replaced by simple *where*, as described in **26** (last par.), or *when as* replaced by simple *when*, as described in 1, p. 269, but in most of the cases already described and in others described in the following pages double or triple form has been retained as useful in differentiating the thought.

The two determinatives often modified an adverb and in course of time became so intimately associated with it that the three words have formed a unit, as: (1) in clauses of time: 'I visited him *as often as* I could'; (2) in clauses of extent: 'He held on *as tight as* he could'; (3) in clauses of restriction: 'They were all pleased *so far as* I know.'

In many other cases the two determinatives have entered into close relations with an adjective or adverb, but the first determinative and the adjective or adverb still belong to the principal proposition, while the second determinative is now a subordinating conjunction of degree: 'He is *as* tall *as* I am.' 'I threw it *as* far from me *as* I could.'

Determinative *as* points as with an index finger not only to a following clause but often also to a following noun which expresses the idea in mind, thus always indicating *oneness with*, *identity*, as in 'I regard him *as* a true friend.' In older English, either single or double *so* is used here. Compare **15** III 2 A.

a. ACCUSATIVE INSTEAD OF NOMINATIVE. In elliptical adverbial clauses introduced by *as — as*, where the finite verb is not expressed, the nominative of personal pronouns is often replaced by an accusative, as so often elsewhere in elliptical expressions, as described in **7** C *a*: 'The post would have been *as soon as me*' (De Morgan, *The Old Madhouse*, Ch. XXVII), instead of *as soon as I*.

3. *Temporal Phrases and Adverbs Used as Conjunctions*. In 1, p. 268, we have seen how determinative *then* developed relative

force and was later replaced by the indefinite relative *when*. The old determinative construction, however, is still common in a number of words. Thus a bit of the older life of our language is not only preserved but is still seemingly thriving amid the changed conditions of another age. The old determinative *that*, of the same stem as *then*, still follows a noun, as in oldest English, pointing to a following explanatory clause: 'I bought my coat *the year that I was in Europe.*' 'I met him *the week* (or *the day*) *that I was in Chicago.*' *The hour that our committee met; the moment that I reached the platform of the car; the minute that I set eyes on him; the instant that he arrived; from the time that I first met him,* etc.

In popular speech we often hear the determinative *as* here instead of *that: the moment as I set eyes upon him.*

In all the cases described above the definite article before the noun has so much determinative power that the *that* or the *as* following the noun may be omitted: '*the year* I was in Europe,' '*the minute* I set eyes upon him,' etc. Instead of the definite article before the noun we often find *next* and *every* and sometimes *what* as determinative: '*next time, every time* I see him.' 'It would be eminently reasonable to refreshen our memories of Dr. Kane's plucky endeavors in northern icepacks *what time* the sun is doing his best to remind us of Central Africa' (periodical in the hot summer of 1911). *What time* was once more common.

There is one case where both the *the* before the noun and the *that* after the noun have disappeared: 'John worked *while Henry played*'; a little earlier in the period *the while* (still lingering in poetry and choice prose), *the while that*, or *while that*, or *while as* (the determinative *as* taking the place of the determinative *that*) *Henry played*. Thus *while* has developed out of the determinative construction into a relative conjunction of time. Also the other expressions, *the day* (*that*), *the week* (*that*), *the moment* (*that*), etc., are now, like *while*, in fact relative conjunctions of time, but the old determinative form *that* is still often used after *day, week, moment*, etc., and the definite article before the noun is still always retained, so that in a formal sense the development hasn't gone as far as in the case of *while*. In early Modern English, *while* not only indicated duration, as in current speech, but also pointed to the point of time at the close of the waiting, i.e., it could have the force of *until*, now in this meaning always replaced by *until*: 'Nothing is more short-liv'd then (now *than*) pride: It is but *while* (expressing duration) their clothes last; stay but *while* (= *until* and now replaced by it) these are worne out, you cannot wish the thing more wretched or dejected' (Ben Jonson, *Discoveries*

p. 59, A.D. 1641). Adiel Sherwood in his *Gazetteer of the State of Georgia* (A.D. 1837) lists this usage as a provincialism, and gives an example: 'Stay *while* I come.'

After the analogy of using all these expressions of time as relative conjunctions of time we often employ certain adverbs of time and place as relative conjunctions of time and place, some with or without *that*, as in the case of *now (that)*, *anywhere (that)*, *nowhere (that)*, *everywhere (that)*; some without *that*, as in the case of *once, directly, immediately, instantly*: '*Now* (or *now that*) we are at last gathered together, I desire to lay before you for your consideration an important family matter.' 'And *everywhere That* (or simply *everywhere*) a thought may dare To gallop, mine has trod' (Cale Young Rice, *Far Quests, The Mystic*). '*Once* that Manchurian Campaign was over (*after* that Manchurian Campaign was *once* over), I never put pen to paper — in the diary sense — until I was under orders for Constantinople' (Sir Ian Hamilton, *Gallipoli Diary*, Preface). '*Once* (= *after once*) a beast of prey has licked blood, it longs for it forever.' '*Directly* I uttered these words there was a dead silence.' '*Immediately* (or *instantly*) the button is pressed the mine explodes.' *Directly, immediately, instantly* are largely confined to British usage. In *now* and *now that* the idea of cause mingles with that of time, often overshadowing it. Compare **30**.

In a number of cases the determinative following a preposition has almost or entirely disappeared. In *since* — the reduced form of *sithen* (Old English *siþþan* = *siþ* 'after' + *þan* 'that') + *s* (gen. ending) — the determinative element is now so fused with the preposition that we do not feel its presence: 'I haven't seen him *since we were boys together*,' originally *since that: we were boys together*. In older English, also the longer form *sithens* was used. Also forms without *s*, *sithen* and the shortened forms *sith* (or *syth*) and *sin* (or *syn*), were once widely employed.

After a number of prepositions the determinative *that* was used in older English, but has since disappeared: '*After that* (now simple *after*) things are set in order here, we'll follow them' (Shakespeare, *I Henry VI*, II, II, 32). 'From Oxford haue I posted since I dinde (dined), To quite (punish) a traitor *fore that* (now *before*) Edward sleepe' (Robert Greene, *Frier Bacon*, III, I, 957, A.D. 1594). After the preposition — *after, against* (or in older English also *again*), *before, ere, till* or *until*, and in older English *fore, afore* (= *before*) — had developed into a relative conjunction, often pointing backward to the principal proposition, the determinative no longer having a function to perform naturally dropped out as a useless form. This development began in Middle English and was still going on in early Modern English, the new form without *that* being used alongside of the old form with *that* and gradually supplanting it: 'And rightful folk shal go, *after* they dye, To heven' (Chaucer, *The Parlement of Foules*, 55). 'Bid your fellowes get their flailes readie *againe* (now *by the time*) I come' (Ben Jonson, *Euery Man out of His Humour*, I, III, A.D. 1600). 'No, stab the earle, and *fore* (now *before*) the morning sun Shall vaunt him thrice ouer the loftie east, Margaret will meet her Lacie in the heuens' (Robert Greene, *Frier Bacon*, III, I, 1019, A.D. 1594). 'They will be here *afore* (now *before*) you can find a cover' (J. F. Cooper, *The Prairie*, I, III, A.D. 1827). 'She gathered fresh flowers to deck the drawing room *against* (now more commonly *before* or *by the time*) Mrs. Hamley should come home' (Mrs. Gaskell, *Wives and Daughters*, Ch. VII). Compare **24 IV** (3rd par.).

In the case of *than* the old demonstrative form has been retained, but every vestige of feeling for it has disappeared: 'He is taller *than* I,' literally, 'He is taller, *then* I come.' *Than* is the old form of the adverb *then*. In older English, before a fixed differentiation had taken place between temporal *then* and comparative *than*, *then* was often used in comparative clauses: 'That is more *then* (now *than*) is in our commission' (Marlowe, *The Jew of Malta*, l. 251, about A.D. 1590). In this older English, the common use of the comma before *then* often makes the original temporal nature of the clause clearer: 'Yet of the two, the Pen is more noble, then [comes] the Pencill' (Ben Jonson, *Discoveries*, p. 59, A.D. 1641). As *than* now differs in meaning from *then* we no longer feel *than* (**29 1 B**) as temporal, but construe it as a comparative conjunction. *Than* is now used with temporal force only after *no sooner;* where, however, it is quite natural since it follows a comparative: 'I had no sooner done it *than* I regretted it.' As, however, the temporal force here is sometimes felt, the temporal conjunction *when* is sometimes improperly used instead of *than*. After other words of similar meaning but without comparative form, as *scarcely*, *hardly* (both = *no sooner*), *not long*, *not far*, *not half* (an hour, etc.), *not* + verb + object or adverbial phrase, we regularly employ *when* or *before:* 'I had scarcely done it *when* (**20 1**, 3rd par.) I regretted it.' 'Randal had scarcely left the house *before* Mrs. Riccabocca rejoined her husband' (Lytton, *My Novel*, II, IX, Ch. XII). Sometimes *than* is improperly used here instead of *when:* 'The crocuses had hardly come into bloom in the London Parks *than* (instead of *when*) they were swooped upon by London children.' In older English, *till* was sometimes used instead of *when* or *before:* 'I had not been many hours on board *till* (in England now usually *when* or *before*) I was surprised with the firing of muskets' (Defoe, *Voyage round World*). In the *Oxford Dictionary* this usage is represented as now confined, in England, to dialect, but in America *till* is sometimes still used here alongside of *before* and *when*. Earlier in the period the negative form of the principal proposition often suggested the use of *but* here instead of *before, when,* or *than:* 'Aurora shall not peepe out of the doores, *But* (now *before*) I will haue Cosroe by the head' (Marlowe, *Tamburlaine,* II, ii, A.D. 1590). 'Scarce have I arrived *But* (now *when*) there is brought to me from your equerry a splendid richly plated hunting dress' (Coleridge, *Piccolomini,* I, 9). 'I no sooner saw this venerable man in the pulpit, *but* (now *than*) I very much approved of my friend's insisting upon the qualifications of a good aspect and a clear voice' (*Spectator,* CVI). Compare **29 1 B** (last par.). *When,* so often used after negative expressions, is sometimes employed with similar force after positive statements, where, however, it has the function of a relative pronoun (**23 II 6,** next to last par.): 'There they repose, . . . *When* from the slope side of a suburb hill . . . came a thrill of trumpets' (Keats, *Lamia*).

4. *Adversative Conjunctions.* In *while, whilst, when, at the same time that,* and in older English *while as* (*II Henry VI,* I, i, 225), *while that* (*Henry the Fifth,* I, ii, 178), *when as* (*III Henry VI,* V, vii, 34), the original temporal meaning is often overshadowed by the derived adversative force, just as in *whereas* and in older English, as in Shakespeare's *Coriolanus,* I, i, 104, also simple *where* the original local meaning is often overshadowed by the derived adversative force: '*Whereas* (or *while,* or *at the same time that*) in applied physics we hold our own, in applied chemistry we have lost much ground' (*British Review*). 'I am really very cross with you for sticking to your work, *when* you ought to be away having a change and a good rest.' Simple *where* sometimes still has adversative force: 'Twenty years ago I used to see a dozen or more (bald eagles) along the river in the spring when the ice was breaking up, *where* I now see only one or two, or none at all' (John Burroughs, *Far and Near,* p. 155). Compare **20 1** (3rd par.).

5. *Abridgment of Clause of Time.* The full clause of time is often abridged to a predicate appositive clause, in which the subject of the principal proposition is subject and an adjective, noun, or participle is predicate: '*When young* (or *when a boy*) I looked at such things quite differently.' 'She always sings *when doing her work.*' 'In those days, *when not knowing how to proceed in an emergency,* he would consult his father.' 'Experience,

when dearly bought, is seldom thrown away.' 'John, don't speak *until spoken to.*' 'Do not read *while eating.*' '*While regretting the sorrow which had fallen upon him,* Miss Cuthbert was nevertheless glad that her brother was free' (R. Bagot, *Anthony Cuthbert,* VI, 51). 'But there was no spite in her quizzes, and Esther felt that *while seeming to make a mock of her,* she was defending her' (George Moore, *Esther Waters,* Ch. III). '*While resembling in some general traits the Yorkshire countryman,* he (the Yankee) has developed in dress, mannerisms, and speech into a figure quite independent of foreign influence' (Marie Killheffer in *American Speech,* Feb., 1928, p. 222). 'The consciousness of his descent from good American stock that had somehow been deprived of its heritage, *while a grievance to him,* was also a comfort' (Winston Churchill, *The Dwelling-Place of Light,* Ch. I, 1). '*Going down town* I met an old friend.' '*Having once acquired* (= *after one has once acquired*) a taste for good things' one doesn't give them up readily.' '*Having finished* (= *after I had finished*) my task' I went to bed.'

In oldest English, the predicate was always a noun or an adjective. If a participle was used, it was an adjective in force. Today the participle has tense like a finite verb, as in the last two examples, where it is in the perfect tense. This development began with the present participle which had both adjective and verbal force. The strong verbal force in the present participle led later to the use of the perfect participle with the full force of a verb in the present perfect or the past perfect tense. The conjunctions *when, until, while, before,* as found in the first eight examples, are modern introductions, not appearing until the sixteenth century. In contrast to older English, the abridged clause here has the features of tense and conjunction which characterize the full clause. In English, the evident tendency has been not to discard the old primitive predicate appositive type of clause but on account of its terseness to retain it, adapting it to the modern need of accuracy of expression by giving the participle an appropriate tense form and conjunction in order to indicate precisely the time relations. Compare **20** 3 (5th par.) and **30** *b.*

Instead of the participial construction we may often use the gerund, which vies with it in terseness. The gerund cannot be used with *when* and *while,* which are pure conjunctions, but on the other hand is freely employed after conjunctions which are also prepositions, for here as elsewhere the gerund is a natural form after prepositions: 'I must write my exercise *before going to school.*' '*Since* finishing these studies he has not taken up a new line of work.' The gerund competes with the simple appositive participle after the prepositions *in* and *after:* '*In going down town* (or *Going down town*) I met an old friend.' '*After having finished my work* (or *Having finished my work*) I went to bed.'

The participle is a favorite in lively language since it is more concrete and impressive, especially the present participle with its descriptive force, even though it cannot mark the time relations accurately: '*Passing* (= *having passed,* but with more descriptive force) through the wall of mud and stone they found a cheerful company assembled' (Dickens, *A Christmas Carol*, II, 65). In both the participial and the gerundial constructions the subject of the principal proposition is also the subject of the abridged clause. The gerund with *after* or *before*, however, may take another subject: 'After *his* (or *John's*, or *my neighbor's*, or *my neighbor*) (**50** 3) acting in that way I can believe almost anything of him,' where the idea of time mingles with that of cause. Also after *on:* 'On *someone's asking* him derisively if he were a partner of mine, he replied,' etc. (Thomas Nelson Page, *John Marvel, Assistant*, Ch. VII).

Also the absolute nominative construction may be employed in abridged clauses of time: '*This disposed of*, I turned at once to something else.' Compare **17** 3 A *a*.

Sometimes the temporal clause can be abridged to an infinitive clause with *to* when the subject of the principal proposition can serve as the subject of the infinitive: 'Imagine how I felt *to find* (= *when I found*) *that you had actually gone off without filling my traveling inkstand*' (Mark Twain, *Letter to Mrs. Crane*, Sept. 18, 1892). 'He was surprised *to see this*' (= *when he saw this*). The idea of time here often mingles with that of cause, as in the second example.

The temporal clause is often abridged to a prepositional phrase: 'She died almost immediately *upon her arrival*' (= *after she arrived*).

CLAUSE OF MANNER

28. A clause of manner describes the manner of the action of the principal verb. This clause may define the action in each of the five following ways:

1. **Manner Proper.** An adverb or adverbial phrase of manner stands in the principal proposition, the adverb or some word in the adverbial phrase pointing forward as a determinative to the following appositional statement, which explains it: 'I interpret the telegram *so* (or *thus*, or *in this way*): *he is coming tomorrow, not today*.' In oldest English, there was often here a double *so*

(Old English *swa swa*), the old double determinative construction found so often elsewhere. The second determinative in this construction is now always *that*, which, however, is now felt as a conjunction introducing the subordinate clause: 'I interpret the telegram *so* (or *in this way*), *that he is coming tomorrow, not today.*' Instead of *so* or *in this way* we often use *in this*: 'This form of speech differs from the various regional dialects in many ways, but most remarkably *in this*, that it is not confined to any locality.'

The determinatives *in what manner, in whatever manner, how, in that* (in older English also simple *that*), and *as*, standing as they do immediately before the explanatory remark, have become closely associated with it, forming with it a subordinate clause and serving as its connective, linking it to the principal proposition and thus developing into relative conjunctions: 'They strove to escape *in what manner they might*,' originally *in what* (a determinative like *that*, but with indefinite force) *manner: they might*, the determinative *what* pointing to the following explanatory clause. We employ the same construction after *how*, which is an old contracted form from the same root as *what* and hence has the same indefinite meaning: 'Do it *how* (or *in what manner*, or *in whatever manner*) *you can.*' 'We must get on *how we can.*' 'A man has a right to spend his money *how he pleases.*' The determinatives *that* and *as* have more definite meaning, but they have the same construction: 'He differed from his colleagues *in that he devoted his spare time to reading*,' originally 'He differed *in that: he devoted his spare time to reading.*' 'Thou hast well done *that thou art come*' (*Acts*, X, 33), now *in that you have come* or more simply *in coming*. 'Do *as* (from older *all so*, i.e., *quite so*) *you think best*,' originally 'Do *all so: you think best*,' i.e., 'Act after the manner that your best thought will suggest to you.' 'Do *as you please.*' 'He described the scene to me *as* [*it*, i.e., the description] *follows.*' For the omission of the pronoun *it*, see **5** *d*. Since *as* has so many meanings, one often shading off into another, it is not always possible to distinguish this *as* from the one in 2, p. 280. This *as* expresses manner pure and simple without a thought of a comparison of one act with another, as in 2. The *as*-clause denotes manner pure and simple when it can be replaced by a participle in the predicate appositive or objective predicate relation: 'I must go *just as I am*' (or *dressed in these clothes*). 'I bought the house *just as it stood*' (or *unrepaired and unpainted*). The commonest use of this *as* is to indicate the manner in which a statement is made, so that the *as*-clause, like a sentence adverb (**16** 2*a*, p. 132), modifies the governing proposition as a whole rather than the verb and, like a sentence adverb, usually stands between subject and verb, or at the beginning or the end of the sentence or proposition: 'Mr. Barkis's wooing, *as I remember it*, was altogether of a peculiar kind' (Dickens, *David Copperfield*, Ch. X). '*As I view them now*, I can call them no less than coward's errands' (Thackeray, *Henry Esmond*, II, Ch. IV). 'If he comes tonight, *as we all expect he will*, it will be a happy household.' 'It is ten miles from here, *as the crow flies*.' 'I protest (declare) to you, *as I am a gentleman and a souldier*, I ne're chang'd wordes with his like' (Ben Jonson, *Euery Man in His Humour*, I, v, 86, A.D. 1601, ed. 1616).

    a. ABRIDGMENT OF CLAUSE OF MANNER PROPER. This clause is quite commonly abridged to the predicate appositive or objective predicate construction with a present or perfect participle as predicate appositive or objective predicate whenever the subject of the participle is the subject or the object of the principal verb: 'She came into the house *singing, crying, carrying an armful of clothes*,' etc. 'He stood *leaning against a tree*.' 'We sat *vacantly looking at each other*.' 'Well, that is just our way, exactly — one half of the administration busy *getting the family into trouble*, the other half busy *getting it out again*' (Mark Twain, *Letter to Mrs. Grover Cleveland*, Nov. 6, 1887). 'He was (= was busy) two years *writing this book*' (Galsworthy, *Caravan*, 421). 'Five languages in use in the house (including the sign language, the hardest-worked of them all), and yet with all this opulence of resource we do seem to have an uncommonly tough time *making ourselves understood*' (Mark Twain, *Letter to Mrs. Crane*, Sept. 30, 1892). 'Don't bother *answering this*' (James Gibbons Huneker, *Letter*, Aug. 11, 1918). 'It was kind of you to bother yourself *asking her*' (*id.*, *Letter*, July 15, 1919). 'Will you never be done *getting me into trouble?*' (L. M. Montgomery, *Anne of Avonlea*, Ch. III). 'Are you through *asking questions?*' 'I beat him *jumping*.' 'I must go *dressed in these clothes*.' 'I bought the house *unrepaired* and *unpainted*.' While a full clause can often be abridged to the participial construction, the latter is often older and hence independent of it, and often still much more common. The present participle is exceedingly frequent. It is here one of the tersest and most convenient constructions in our language. It specifies some activity that characterizes or specializes the act or state.

    The participle is often introduced by *as*: 'I rejoice that I am on record *as having repudiated the financial part of it*' (i.e., the political platform) (James A. Garfield, *Letter to J. H. Rhodes*, May 15, 1868). 'Pray do not understand me *as having lost hope*' (Woodrow Wilson, *Letter to Thomas D. Jones*, 1910).

In older English, the simple infinitive was the common form after *come*, where we now use the present participle: 'Thenne he looked by hym and was ware of a damoysel that came *ryde* (now *riding*) ful fast as the hors mighte ryde' (Malory, *Le Morte d'Arthur*, Book II, Ch. VI, fifteenth century).

The gerundial construction after a preposition is much used: 'He differed from his colleagues *in spending his spare time in reading.*' 'The fight began *by John's calling William names.*' 'He spends his spare time *in reading*' (or with the participle, *reading*).

The prepositional phrase is often simple — with an ordinary noun after the preposition instead of a gerund: 'The assembly was opened *with prayer.*' The phrase often specifies a detail or details in the statement — a phrase of specification: 'The brothers differ *in disposition.*' The phrase often serves as a sentence adverb (**16 2 a**): 'The statement is *without doubt* exaggerated.'

2. Comparison. The action of the principal verb is compared with that in the subordinate clause: 'Do at Rome *as the Romans do,*' originally 'Do at Rome *all so* (older form of *as*): *the Romans do,*' where the determinative *so*, like an index finger, points to the following explanatory clause. 'He treated me *as a father would have done.*' 'You do not act *as you speak.*' 'Let us do our duty *as our predecessors did theirs.*'

In older English, there was often a double determinative here: 'Euen *so* betide my soul *as I vse* him' (Marlowe, *Edward II*, l. 2135, A.D. 1590, ed. 1594). In accordance with this older usage we still sometimes find a *so* in the principal proposition pointing to the *as* in the subordinate clause: 'The committee was not *so* constituted *as* he had expected.' In older English, the *so* was sometimes brought over from the principal proposition and placed before *as* in the subordinate clause: 'to see thy power and thy glory, *so as* (now simple *as*) I have seen thee in the sanctuary' (*Psalms*, LXIII, 2).

In another case the double demonstrative is quite common. The *as*-clause often precedes when it is desired to hold the principal proposition a while in suspense for emphasis, in which case the latter is introduced by *so*, pointing back to the subordinate clause: '*As* it is the nature of the kite to devour little birds, *so* it is the nature of such persons as Mrs. Wilkins to insult and tyrannize over little people' (Fielding, *Tom Jones*). In this form of the clause the idea of cause sometimes mingles with that of comparison: '*As* a madman's epistles are no gospels, *so* it skills (matters) not much when they are deliver'd' (Shakespeare, *Twelfth Night*, V, 294). As in this example, the clause of comparison was much used in older English to convey the idea of cause. Compare **30 a.**

The clause of comparison is often elliptical: 'She plays with him *as a cat [plays] with a mouse.*' 'Of course, our winters here in Chicago are not mild *as [they are] in your native California.*' 'Everything had happened exactly *as [had been] expected.*'

Instead of *as* we often find *like as* in older English: '*Like as* a father pitieth his children, so the Lord pitieth them that fear him' (*Psalms*, CIII, 13). Here *like* is an adverb with the meaning *in the same manner*. *As* performs the function of conjunction. But early *like as* became felt as a unit, and later *as* began to disappear since *like* was felt as expressing clearly alone both the meaning and the function. The *like-as* clause has the great advantage over the *as*-clause that *like* has a clear, distinctive meaning, while *as* has so many meanings that it is often difficult to discover what it means in the case in hand. Shakespeare, among other earlier writers, used *like* here as a short form for *like as*, just as *after, while*, etc., were used for older *after that, the while that*, etc., so that, just as the preposition *after* and the noun *while* have become subordinating conjunctions of time, the adverb *like* has become a subordinating conjunction of comparison, in accordance with sound grammatical analogies which have long been at work in English: '*Like* an arrow shot From a wel-experienc'd archer hits the mark' (*Pericles*, I, i, 163). Our grammarians have recognized *after, while*, etc., but still combat *like*. They demand the use of *as* here. *Like*, however, is widely used in colloquial and popular speech, since its vivid concrete force appeals to the feelings more than the colorless *as*. It is, of course, very common also in literature which reflects colloquial usage: 'They don't marry *like we do*' (A. Marshall, *Abington Abbey*, Ch. XIII). 'Suppose we do knock militarism out of Germany, *like we did* out of France' (Jerome K. Jerome, *All Roads Lead to Calvary*, Ch. XVI). In ordinary use the simple form *like* has entirely supplanted older *like as*, the older form now appearing only in archaic or poetic language, or in dialect.

On the other hand, where there is no finite verb expressed or understood, and there is present a noun or pronoun, *like* is not opposed by grammarians; it is indeed the usual form even in the best literary style, here felt as a preposition, forming with its object a prepositional phrase: 'He treats his wife *like a child.*' 'His coat fits him *like a glove.*' 'He laughs *like her.*' In elliptical clauses *as* was once used before a noun with the same force as *like*, only differing in grammatical structure, the preposition *like* taking an object, the conjunction *as* standing before a nominative which is the subject of a suppressed verb: 'And the desert shall rejoice and blossom *as the rose* [*rejoices and blossoms*]' (*Isaiah*, XXXV, 1). Today we employ *like* here. We avoid the use of *as* in such elliptical clauses, since *as* is so often used in sentences of this form to introduce a predicate appositive (**7 A** *b* (3)), where it has quite a different meaning, indicating not mere *similarity* but *complete identity, oneness with*. If, however, a word or words follow this nominative which show that the nominative is not a predicate appositive but the subject of a suppressed verb, *as* is the usual literary form, not *like:* 'She took to the multiplication-table *as a duck* [*takes*] *to water*,' or in colloquial speech '*like* a duck [takes] to water.' In poetical style *like as* is still used here instead of *as:* 'My spirit rises before it *like as the lark awakened by the dawn*' (Hall Caine, *The Deemster*, Ch. XLII). *Like as* survives here also in popular speech.

    a. 'AS IF' AND 'AS THOUGH.' Before *if* and *though* all of the clause of comparison is usually suppressed except the conjunction *as*, since the thought is always suggested by the context: 'He acts *as* [*he would act*] *if* (or *though* = *if*, as in older English) he were in love with her.' The verbs *look, seem*, and *be* are much used in this category. They are not copulas here but full verbs: 'He looks (= has an appearance, acts) *as if* he were going through a great crisis.' 'They seemed (= seemed to act) *as if* they had never missed Sylvia' (Mrs. Gaskell, *Sylvia's Lovers*, Ch. VI). 'It seemed to me (= impressed me) *as if* they had never missed Sylvia.' 'It was (= seemed) almost *as if* people had sensed at once that she could never be held accountable for what she said and did' (Eleanor Carroll Chilton, *Shadows Waiting*, p. 28). The present indicative is used here to indicate greater confidence: 'He acts as if he *is* [in love with her]' (Tarkington, 'Juliette,' *Ladies' Home Journal*, Aug., 1925). 'It does look as if the very crisis *is* here' (Walter H. Page, *Letter to Arthur W. Page*, April 28, 1917).

    Originally, *if* was not used here. In older English, the form of clause without *if* is common: 'He laye there nighe half an houre *as* [*if*] he had ben dede' (Malory, *Le Morte d'Arthur*, Book XVIII, Ch. XII, A.D. 1485). 'He looks *as* [*if*] he had seen a ghost' (Coleridge, *Wallenstein*, I, V, A.D. 1800). This older usage survives in the set expression *as it were:* 'She took him over *as it were* into her confidence.'

    In popular speech *like as if* is much used instead of *as if:* 'She holds him round the neck, *like as if* she was protecting him' (Dickens, *Our Mutual Friend*).

    In older English, *like as* is sometimes used instead of *as if:* 'Yet once methought It lifted up its head and did address Itself to motion, *like as* it would speak' (Shakespeare, *Hamlet*, I, II, 217). The present tendency in colloquial and popular speech is to simplify these forms to *like:* 'It looks *like he was afraid*' (or to express greater confidence *like he's afraid*).

b. ABRIDGMENT OF CLAUSE OF COMPARISON. This clause is often abridged to the predicate appositive construction, in which the subject is the subject of the principal proposition and the predicate is an adjective, participle, or prepositional phrase: 'She hurriedly left the room *as though angry.*' 'He lay for several hours *as though stunned.*' 'She looked pleadingly at her parents *as though entreating forgiveness.*' 'She looked about *as if in search of something.*' 'The clouds had disappeared *as if by magic.*' The *if* or *though* is sometimes lacking, as originally: 'Then the herald raised his eyes *as seeking approval of someone far off*' (Wallace, *Ben Hur*, Ch. XI). 'Some birds, such as the true thrushes, impress one *as being of a serene, contemplative disposition*' (John Burroughs, *Far and Near*, p. 192). 'Walter S. Smith, not having completed his work, did not graduate with his class in 1924; but in the following year, finishing his work, was at his request graduated *as of the class of 1924.*'

If the predicate is a verb, the clause is often abridged to an infinitive clause: 'He raised his head *as if* (or *as though*) *to command silence.*' 'When I appear upon the scene, the female (sapsucker) scurries away in alarm, calling as she retreats, *as if for the male to follow*' (John Burroughs, *Under the Apple-Trees*, Ch. I). In older English, *if* is often lacking here, as originally: 'Mr. Peters and Mr. Williams are to be here, *as [if] to breakfast with me*' (Richardson, *Pamela*, I, p. 385). Older usage lingers on: 'She paused a moment *as [if] to collect herself for an effort*' (De Morgan, *The Old Madhouse*, Ch. XIII).

We sometimes find here the primitive verbless type of sentence described in **20** 3: 'Lightly won, lightly lost' = 'Just as something is lightly won, it is lightly lost.'

3. **Attendant Circumstance.** The action of the principal verb is accompanied by some attendant circumstance which is contained in the subordinate clause. The conjunctions here used are: *as; without that* (only in older English); *that — not, but, but that,* and colloquially *but what* and *without* (in older English a literary form); *moreover that* (especially in older English, as in Shakespeare's *Hamlet*, II, II, 2); *besides that, in addition to the fact that; apart from the fact that, independently of the fact that, instead of that;* sometimes *instead of* in contrasting two verbs and in elliptical clauses with verb understood; often also the temporal conjunctions *while* or *whilst, at the same time that.*

Examples:

The enemy devastated the country *as he retreated.*

'This seemed to be done *without that the King was fully informed thereof'* (Lord Herbert, *Henry VIII*, 162, A.D. 1648), now replaced by the gerundial construction described in *a* below.

'The artist, of whatever kind, cannot produce a truthful work *without he understands the laws of the phenomena he represents'* (Spencer, *Education*, Ch. I), still heard in colloquial and popular speech, but in the literary language now replaced by the gerundial construction described in *a* below.

He never passed anybody on the street *that he didn't greet him* (or *but, but that, but what,* or *without, he greeted him*).

It never rains *but it pours.*

I can't think housekeeping will be any great addition to your expenses, and I am sure it will give some respectability to your house, *besides that it will be much more agreeable than living in a boardinghouse* (George Mason, *Letter to His Son John*, May 14, 1789).

Still we were grateful to him, for, *besides that he showed an example of contentment to us slaves of unnecessary appetite,* he sold vegetables (T. E. Lawrence, *Revolt in the Desert*, p. 70, A.D. 1927).

If Carlyle had written, *instead of that he wanted Emerson to think of him in America,* that he wanted his father and mother to be thinking of him at Ecclefechan, that would have been well (Ruskin, *Praeterita*, 1, 252).

I saw that you were the real person; someone I admired as well as loved, and *respected instead of — well, patronized* (Eleanor Carroll Chilton, *Shadows Waiting*, p. 286).

When I paint a picture, you think the net result is I and the picture, *instead of [it is] I alone* (Edward F. Benson, *The Judgment Books*, 162).

You ought to have told me this *instead of I [told] you* (Reade, *Cloister and the Hearth*, Ch. IX) (or *instead of my having told you*).

Now they rule him *instead of him* (incorrectly used for *he*) *them* (Sarah Grand, *Heavenly Twins*, 42) (or *instead of his ruling them*).

'I should be his prisoner *instead of he being mine'* (Doyle, *Strand Magazine*, Dec., 1894, 571), incorrectly used for *instead of he mine* or *instead of his being mine.* Mr. Doyle's clause is a blending of the elliptical and the gerundial clause.

He was drowned *while he was bathing in the river.*

At the same time that our trials strengthen us, they make us more tender and sensitive to the sufferings of others.

The idea of attendant circumstance and that of result are often so closely associated that it is difficult to distinguish them. Hence we often find the same conjunctions for both, so that some of these conjunctions will also occur in 5, p. 289.

a. ABRIDGMENT OF CLAUSE OF ATTENDANT CIRCUMSTANCE. An *as*-clause and a *while*-clause can be abridged to the predicate appositive construction with the present participle as predicate appositive whenever its subject is identical with that of the prin-

cipal proposition, or the participle may be replaced by *in* with
the gerund: '*Retreating* (or *in retreating*) the enemy devastated
the country.' 'He was drowned *bathing in the river*' or *while*
(**20** 3, 5th par.) *bathing in the river.*

Also elsewhere a predicate appositive has the force of a clause
of attendant circumstance: '*Far from receiving help*, he gave it.'
'*So far from doing any good*, the rain did a good deal of harm,'
a blending of '*Far from doing any good*, the rain did a good deal
of harm' and '*The rain was so far from doing any good* that it did
a good deal of harm.' '*So far from intending you any wrong*, I
have always loved you as well as if you had been my own mother.'
'The certainty as to the amount of mineral wealth, *so far from
having improved the situation*, made it distinctly worse.'

A clause that in older English was introduced by *without that*
has been replaced by the gerundial construction: 'This seemed
to be done *without the King's having been fully informed of it.*'
A clause introduced by *that* — *not, but, but that*, or *without* is
quite freely abridged to the gerundial construction with *without*,
whether its subject is identical with that of the principal proposition or not: 'He never passed people *without greeting them*' and
'He never passed people *without their greeting him.*' Though
without is now avoided in the literary language in the full clause,
it is common in the gerundial clause. The conjunctions *besides
that, apart from the fact that, independently of the fact that, in addition to the fact that* can be freely replaced by prepositions or prepositional phrases with the gerundial construction: '*Besides being
rich*, she is very pretty.' '*Besides John's* (or *my son's*, or *son;*
see **50** 3) *helping me with the heavy work*, several of the neighbors
lent a helping hand.' '*Quite apart from* (or *quite independently of*)
saving a good deal of money in drawing the illustrations myself, I
derived much pleasure from it.' '*In addition to being charged
with high treason*, he was charged with fraud.' '*In addition to
John's being blamed for this*, he was blamed also for breaking the
window.' After *instead of* we usually employ the abridged form
of statement, rarely the full clause: '*Instead of doing it himself*,
he got a man to do it.'

The gerundial construction is also common after the preposition
so far from, which is thus used not only as a predicate appositive
adjective, as illustrated above, but also as a preposition: '*So far
from the rain doing any good*, it did a good deal of harm.' '*So
far from there being any danger or need of accentuated foreign
competition*, it is likely that the conditions of the next few years
will greatly facilitate the marketing of American manufactures'
(Woodrow Wilson, May 20, 1919).

When two clauses have a gerund in common, the expression is sometimes elliptical where the thought would not be endangered. The gerund may be expressed in the first clause and understood in the second: 'Of course, boys cannot work together in a common cause *without some doing too much and others [doing] too little.*' The subject of the gerund here is always the accusative, never the genitive. We employ the elliptical construction when we desire to contrast the two subjects. Compare **50** 3 (6th par.). In colloquial speech we often find in the second clause a nominative used as subject: 'The sleeping inmates of the room accompanied my recital with a snoring duet or tercet without my interfering with their sleep or *they* with my reading' (Vambéry, *My Struggles*, 93). The nominative here indicates the influence of the full clause with a finite verb. The correct elliptical structure here requires *two* accusative subjects: 'without *me* interfering with their sleep or *them* with my reading.'

A prepositional phrase may often take the place of the full clause: 'We went out *without permission.*' 'I shall act *without regard to* (or *regardless of*) *consequences.*' 'He sang *with the window open,*' not *by the open window,* which indicates a place, not attendant circumstance. Compare **17** 3 A *d.*

Instead of a full clause we often find here the absolute nominative construction described in **17** 3 A *d.*

4. Clause of Alternative Agreement. The action of the principal proposition is in alternative agreement with that of the subordinate clause. The conjunctions here used are *as* (in older English and sometimes still) and the more common *according as:* 'stones whose rates are either rich or poor *As fancy values them*' (Shakespeare, *Measure for Measure*, II, II, 150). 'The shadow cast by an object is long or short *according as the sun is high up in the heavens or near the horizon.*' 'Things are often good or bad for us *according as we look at them.*' This idea can also often be expressed by a prepositional clause: 'They were praised or scolded *according to how they had done their work.*'

5. Manner Clause of Modal Result and Clause of Pure Result. In manner clauses of modal result the subordinate clause is represented as something which has resulted from the manner of the activity expressed in the principal proposition. There are two forms of the clause. In one form there is in the principal proposition a determinative — *súch* or *só* — pointing to a following explanatory clause, originally an independent proposition, hence without an introductory subordinating conjunction: 'He has always lived *súch a life: he cannot expect sympathy now,*' or 'He has always lived *só: he cannot expect sympathy now,*' where the determinative *súch* or *só* points as with an index finger to the following explanatory clause. This old type of clause without an introductory conjunction is still in use; in colloquial speech is even common: 'Here lies our good Edmund, whose genius was súch, *We can scarcely praise it or blame it too much*' (Goldsmith, *Retaliation*). 'His manner was súch *I could not help thinking he was unfriendly to Sherman*' (J. B. Foraker, *Notes of a Busy Life*, Ch. VI). 'I tried to arrange só *the sections would be far enough apart to allow each ample time to unload, feed, water, and load the horses at any stopping place before the next section could arrive*' (Theodore Roosevelt, *The Rough Riders*, Ch. II).

Alongside of this type of sentence there is another with a double determinative, in accordance with older English fondness for double expression, a *súch* or *só* in the principal proposition and *that* in the clause of result: 'He has always lived *súch* a life *that he cannot expect sympathy now*,' originally 'He always lived *súch* a life, *thát: he cannot expect sympathy now*,' the two determinatives *such* and *that* pointing as with two index fingers to the following explanatory clause. The second determinative *that*, standing immediately as it does before the explanatory remark, became early closely associated with it, forming with it a subordinate clause of result and serving as its connective, binding it to the principal proposition, and thus developed into a subordinating conjunction. Modern English has often rejected parts of older double determinative constructions as excessive expression, but the second determinative *that* has been retained here since it has developed into a conjunction and thus performs a useful function, marking the unity of the words in the clause, so that this form is now more common in the literary language than the simpler form of the clause without a conjunction. The old determinative *that* was originally an adjective element and could only be used when it could refer to a preceding noun as in this example referring to 'such a *life*'; but its function as determinative or conjunction was early felt more vividly than its function as adjective, so that since the earliest historical records it has been used as determinative or conjunction even when the preceding word is an adverb: 'He has always lived *só that he cannot expect sympathy now*.' This explains the extensive use of the conjunction *that* in adverbial clauses of modal result whether of manner or degree. It is used also in clauses of pure result, as described below.

In oldest English, the determinative *so* was often used in the clause of result instead of *that*. These old determinatives — *so* and *that* — have throughout the history of our language been competitors in a number of different kinds of subordinate clauses. *That* is now the literary form in the clause of result, but *as* (from *all so*, i.e., *quite so*), the modern representative of older *so*, was common earlier in the period: 'A man should study other things to make his base such *as* (now *that*) no tempest shall shake him' (Ben Jonson, *Discoveries*, p. 57, A.D. 1641). This old usage survives in popular speech, as illustrated on page 290. Of course, we today feel *that* and *as* merely as conjunctions and have so little feeling for their older concrete force that we do not feel *as* as containing the old determinative *so*.

In older English, the *such* of the principal proposition was often replaced by the determinative adjective *that:* 'From me, whose love was of *that* dignity That it went hand in hand even with the vow I made to her in marriage' (Shakespeare, *Hamlet*, I, v, 48). 'She sat and looked on, keeping out of the way of her bustling aunt as far as possible; but Miss Fortune's gyrations were of *that* character that no one could tell five minutes beforehand what she might consider "in the way"' (Susan Warner, *The Wide, Wide World*, Ch. XXII, A.D. 1851).

In all its modal meanings the *so* of the principal proposition is heavily stressed and usually follows the verb, but not infrequently the verbal idea becomes prominent and is heavily stressed, so that *so* has a little less stress than the verb and, like a sentence adverb (**16 2 a**), stands immediately before the verb or in a compound tense or modal form before the part of the verb containing the verbal meaning, thus indicating that the verbal idea is more important than the idea of manner: 'It *só háppened* that I was present.' 'We should *só áct* in this matter that we shall have nothing to regret.'

The *so* of the principal proposition often loses its stress and is brought over to the subordinate clause, so that the modal idea of manner disappears entirely and the subordinate clause becomes a clause of pure result; in the literary language usually introduced by *so that*, in colloquial speech often still by simple *so*, as in older English: 'He went early *so that* (or simple *so*) he got a good seat.' 'She sat directly before me, *so that* (or simple *so*) I could not see the expression on her face.' 'He didn't go early, as he ought to have done, *so that* (or simple *so*) he didn't get a good seat.' 'I would to heaven I were your son, *so* you would love me, Hubert' (Shakespeare, *King John*, IV, I, 23). 'With those (generals) present were their respective staffs, *so* (now more commonly *so that* in literary language) there were enough of them, all told, to make up a pretty large company' (J. B. Foraker, *Notes of a Busy Life*, Ch. VII). 'A man ought to have a settled job, with an office in some fixed place, *so* (for literary *so that*) you always know where he is' (Christopher Morley, 'Thunder on the Left,' in *Harper's Magazine* for Sept., 1925, p. 397). 'You write that letter to Ninian, and you make him tell you *so* (colloquial for *so that*) *you'll understand*' (Zona Gale, *Miss Lulu Bett*, Ch. V). The subordinate clause introduced here by simple *so* is differentiated from the coördinate clause introduced by simple *so*, described in *c*, p. 291, by less stress and a slighter pause before it. We often use here a question instead of a negative *so-that* clause: 'He no longer has any backing, *why should you fear him?*' (or *so that there is no need of your fearing him*).

On account of its lack of distinctive form simple *that*, one of the oldest conjunctions used in clauses of pure result, has become rather rare and choice, although earlier in the period more common: 'Pray let your youth make hast; for I should haue done a business an hower since, *that* (now usually *so that*) I doubt (fear) I shall come too late' (Ben Jonson, *Euery Man out of His Humour*, IV, IV, A.D. 1600). 'The image of a bear stood out upon a Sign-Post, perk'd up on his Arse with a great Faggot-bat in his Claws, *that* (now usually *so that*) he look'd like one of the City Waits playing upon the Double Curtel*' (Ned Ward, *The London Spy*, p. 120, A.D. 1700, ed. 1924). 'A fire scorch'd me *that* (now usually *so that*) I woke*' (Tennyson, *Lucretius*, 66). Simple *that*, however, is quite freely used when the clause of result follows a statement of the cause or the assumed cause couched in the form of a declarative sentence or very commonly a question: 'Something is wrong *that he hasn't come before this*,' or 'What is the matter *that he hasn't come before this?*' 'I must have been blind *that I didn't see that post*,' or 'Where were my eyes *that I didn't see that post?*' Often after an indirect question: 'I should like to know what the matter was *that he didn't come*.' In negative clauses after a question, a negative, or a word with negative force, as *scarcely*, we may still use *that not*, or *but*, or *but that*, or in colloquial and popular speech *but what* or *without*, or instead of a subordinate clause often, even in the literary language, a principal proposition after *and*: 'Can you touch pitch that *you do not defile yourself?*' (or *but*, or *but that*, or *but what*, or *without*, *you defile yourself?* or *and not defile yourself?*). 'He scarcely ever played with the children *that a quarrel didn't follow*' (or *but*, or *but that*, or *but what*, *a quarrel followed*). *Without that* was once employed here, but it is now little used: 'It was next to impossible that a casket could be thrown . . . *without that she should have caught intimation of things extraordinary*' (Brontë, *Villette*, 107), now in colloquial speech sometimes *without she should catch intimation*, etc., but usually in colloquial and literary language *without her catching intimation*, etc.

As described on page 288, *as* was once common instead of *that* in clauses of result. Modal result: 'I gained a son, And súch a son *as* (now *that*) all men hailed me happy' (Milton, *Samson*, 358). 'At last they were forced into a harbor, where lay a French man-of-war with his prize, and (**23** II 9 *b*) had surely made prize of them also, but that the providence of God so disposed *as* (now *that*) the captain knew the merchant of our bark' (Winthrop, *Journal*, June 15, 1637). Still in popular speech: 'But you said they depended on you, papa!' — 'So they do, but of course not *so's* (i.e., *só as*, current popular form for *só that*) they couldn't get along without me' (Tarkington, *Alice Adams*, Ch. IV). 'They planted th' tree *so's* (i.e., *só as*) no one wouldn't ever be buried in that spot agin' (Amy Lowell, *East Wind*, p. 89). In older English, there was a double determinative here, *as that* instead of *as*, in accord with the old fondness for double expression: 'The difficulty certainly is, how to give this power in súch manner *as that* (now simple *that*) it may only be used to good, and not abused to bad, purposes' (Richard Henry Lee, *Letter to George Mason*, May 15, 1787). This usage survives in popular speech: 'There is boarders who is always laying in wait for the days when the meals is not so good as they commonly be, to pick a quarrel with the one that is trying to serve them só *as that* (for literary *that*) they shall be satisfied' (Oliver W. Holmes, *The Poet at the Breakfast Table*, XII).

Similarly, *as* or *so as* was once common in the literary language in clauses of pure result instead of *that* or *so that*: 'And matchlesse beautiful, *as* (instead of *that*, now more commonly *so that*), had you seene her, 'twould haue mou'd your heart' (Marlowe, *The Jew of Malta*, 629, A.D. 1590, ed. 1633). 'He miscarried by un-skilfulness, *so as* (now *so that*) the loss can no way be ascribed to cowardice' (Hobbes, *Thucydides*, 120, A.D. 1628). 'Many came unto them from diverse parts of England, *so as* (now *so that*) they grew a great congregation' (Bradford, *History of Plymouth Plantation*, p. 40, A.D. 1630–1648). This usage survives in popular speech: 'P-pay anything *so's* (for literary *so that*) you get it' (Winston Churchill, *Coniston*, Ch. VII). In older English, we sometimes find three determinatives in clauses of pure result: 'On that night ashes were thrown into the porridge, *so as that* (now *so that*) they could not eat it' (Increase Mather, *Remarkable Providences*, Ch. V, Jan., 1684).

The determinative *so* in the principal clause has not a clearly defined meaning, denoting often manner or degree. Hence the *so* in the example from Tarkington on page 290 may mean degree instead of manner and then would belong to **29** 2.

a. 'TILL' INSTEAD OF 'SO THAT.' *So that* is often replaced by *till* where the idea of time seems more important to our feeling than that of result: 'The dogs fought *till* the hair flew.'

b. RELATIVE CLAUSE INSTEAD OF ADVERBIAL. An adverbial clause of pure result is often replaced by a descriptive relative clause introduced by *whence, wherefore, why,* or more commonly *on account of which:* 'This bird (shrike) has a strong bill toothed at the end, and feeds on small birds and insects, *whence* or *on account of which* (= *so that*) it is known as the butcher-bird.' 'I demand . . . What rub or what impediment there is, *Why that* (old form = *why* = *on account of which*, or more commonly *that*) the naked, poor and mangled Peace . . . Should not . . . put up her lovely visage' (*Henry the Fifth*, V, II, 32).

A relative clause is often used with the force of a clause of pure result when the reference is to a negative: 'Nobody knew him *who didn't love him,*' or in adverbial form, *that he didn't love him,* or *but* (or *but that*) *he loved him.* Compare **23** II 5 (2nd par.).

A restrictive relative clause often has the force of a clause of modal result when it is introduced by the relative pronoun *as* or *that* (expressed or understood) and there is in the principal proposition the determinative *such* or *a* expressing a kind or degree: 'He lent his antagonist *such a box on the ear as made him stagger to the other side of the room*' (or *a box on the ear that made him stagger to the other side of the room,* or in adverbial form, *such a box on the ear that it made him stagger to the other side of the room*). 'We'll each of us give you *such a thrashing as you'll remember*' (or *a thrashing that you'll remember,* or *a thrashing you'll remember,* or in adverbial form, *such a thrashing that you'll remember it*).

c. COÖRDINATION INSTEAD OF SUBORDINATION. Instead of a principal proposition and a subordinate clause of pure result introduced by *so that* we often find two principal propositions connected by *and:* 'My health is excellent, and I could settle down to a stiff task with ease.' Instead of coördination with *and* we may coördinate with *so* (coördinating conjunction; see **19** 1 *e*): 'My health is good, *so* I could settle down,' etc. *And* and *so* may be combined: 'My health is good, *and so I* could settle down,' etc. Compare **19** 3.

d. ABRIDGMENT OF MANNER CLAUSES OF MODAL RESULT AND CLAUSES OF PURE RESULT. After *such* and *so* a *that*-clause of modal result can usually be abridged to an infinitive clause with *as to* when the subject of the principal proposition can serve as the subject of the infinitive: 'This is not *súch* weather *as to encourage out-door sports.'* 'He lays out his work each day *só as to be able to finish it by six o'clock.'* The *as* is not found here in oldest English, which clearly shows that it later entered the abridged clause under the influence of the *as* which introduced the full clause. In the literary language the *as* has been replaced by *that* in the full clause, but it survives in the abridged clause.

In older English, a *so-that* clause of pure result could be abridged to an infinitive clause with *so to* when the subject of the principal proposition could serve as the subject of the infinitive: 'Here it (giddiness of head) increased upon me to an alarming degree, *so to render me incapable of moving from my seat'* (Joseph Farington, *Diary*, Nov. 29, 1810).

A *so-that* clause of pure result is now usually contracted to an infinitive clause with *so as to* when the subject of the principal proposition can serve as the subject of the infinitive: 'Put on your gloves *so as to be ready!'* The *so as* is not found here in oldest English, which clearly shows that it later entered the abridged clause under the influence of the *so as* which introduced the full clause. In the literary language the *so as* has been replaced in the full clause by *so that*, but it survives in the abridged clause.

A simple *that* clause of pure result can be abridged to a *to*-infinitive clause, and is often even more common than the full clause by reason of the concrete force of *to*, which here has one of its common derived meanings, end, result: 'He did not see Stenning again *to speak to'* (A. Marshall, *Anthony Dare*, Ch. III) (or more commonly *to speak to him*). 'A catbird sang *to split its throat'* (Mary Johnston, *Hagar*, Ch. V). 'Five of their six sons lived *to grow up.'* 'How old do you have to be *to be grown up?'* (Christopher Morley, *Thunder on the Left*). 'You have only to ask *to get it.'* 'Whole tracts of the Excursion (poem by Wordsworth) require considerable patience on the part of the reader *to appreciate.'* 'Poetry should not require considerable patience *to be appreciated.'* The infinitive here may now have a subject of its own introduced by *for:* 'In Ireland just now one has only to discover an idea that seems of service to the country *for friends and helpers to spring up on every hand'* (Yeats, *Plays and Controversies*, p. 3). In this very common infinitive clause the form with *to* or *for to* is now the common one, but the old simple infinitive still lingers: 'How came you *take* (now usually *to take*) up such an absurd habit?' (Susan Warner, *The Wide, Wide World*, Ch. XLIX).

In older English, a simple *as*-clause of pure result could be abridged to a *to*-infinitive clause introduced by *as:* 'Where is now the soul of god-like Cato? ne that durst be good when Caesar durst be evill; and had power *As not to live his slave*, to dye his master' (Ben Jonson, *Sejanus*, I, I, 89, A.D. 1616). We now suppress the *as* here.

The simple *that*-clause that follows a statement of the cause of the result, couched in the form of a declarative sentence or very commonly in the form of a direct or an indirect question, can often be abridged to a *to*-infinitive clause: 'I suppose you think I am a very bad mother *to be amusing myself* while Joy is suffering' (Galsworthy, *Joy*). '*Who was I to go tearing through peaceful towns with my execrated locomotive and massacring innocent people?*' (W. J. Locke, *The Joyous Adventures of Aristide Pujol*, Ch. I). 'When his old friend John Street's son volunteered for special service he shook his head querulously and wondered what John Street was about *to allow it*' (Galsworthy, *The Man of Property*, 86). Also the present participle is used here: 'What's got into you *wanting* all of a sudden to get married?' (Mary Heaton Vorse, *Woman's Home Companion*, Aug., 1927, p. 18).

A clause of pure result introduced by *that— not, but,* or *but that* can be abridged to a *to*-infinitive clause: 'None knew him *but to love him.*' After most verbs the negative clause is more commonly abridged to a gerundial clause with *without:* 'The children never played together *without getting into a fight.*' Though *without* is now avoided in the literary language in the full clause, it is common in the gerundial clause.

A full *so-that* clause of pure result that has considerable independence of thought can often be abridged to a participial clause, 'He mistook me for a friend, *so that he caused me some embarrassment*' (or *causing me some embarrassment,* or with a formal expression of the idea of result: *thus causing me some embarrassment*). The use of *thus* here has been unjustly criticized on the ground that a coördinating conjunction should not link a subordinate clause to the principal proposition. But such a clause of pure result is logically a principal proposition, for it does not in any way modify the meaning of the principal proposition, and can be replaced by a principal proposition.

The idea of result is often expressed by an objective predicate (**15** III 2, **15** III 2 A): 'She boiled the egg *hard.*' 'The President made him *a general.*' 'He got the machine *running*' (or *to running*). 'The garrison was starved *into surrender.*' 'He worked himself *into a frenzy.*' 'He smoked himself *into calmness.*' Compare **20** 3 (last par.).

The result in all the above cases is represented as the effect of the activity or state indicated in the principal proposition. The *to*-infinitive is often employed to express an entirely different kind of result, namely, a result which is the natural outcome of events or plans which are independent of the action described in the principal proposition: 'They parted never *to see each other again.*' 'He waked *to find all this a dream.*'

CLAUSE OF DEGREE

29. Clauses of degree define the degree or intensity of that which is predicated in the principal proposition. The degree can be expressed in the following ways:

1. **Comparison.** It is expressed in the form of a comparison:

A. **Positive Clause,** signifying a degree equal to that of the principal proposition:

a. A Simple Comparison. We sometimes employ *as* here: 'She is true *as* gold.' This corresponds closely to Old English usage, where we find *swa*, i.e., *so*, in the place of our *as*, which is a contraction of *all so*, i.e., *quite so*. Thus originally this was a determinative construction, the *so* pointing forward to the following explanatory word or remark: 'She was true, *so:* gold [is].' As the *so*, now *as*, stood immediately before the explanatory remark it early became closely associated with it and was felt as a conjunction introducing the subordinate clause. This simple type is not so common now as in older English, but it still lingers on: 'There's the boy with the basket, punctual *as clockwork*' (Dickens, *Pickwick*, Ch. IX). 'Quick *as thought* he seized the oars.' Compare **25** 1.

Alongside of the old simple determinative construction with *so* was a double determinative construction with *so — so*, as described in **25** 1. In oldest English, this double type was not common in the category of comparison, but it has gradually become the common form of expression here. In its present form it has the following two sets of correlatives, where the first correlative of each set belongs to the principal proposition and the second correlative of each set is now felt as a subordinating conjunction introducing the subordinate clause: *as — as* in positive sentences to express complete equality and *so — as* in negative statements and questions with negative force to indicate inequality: 'I am *as* tall *as* she [is]' (equality). 'Is she *as* tall *as* I [am]?' (question simply inquiring whether there is an equality). 'She is not *so* tall *as* I' (inequality). 'But are you *so* tall *as* she?' (question with negative force). 'I am always *as* busy *as* I am now,' but 'I am not always *so* busy *as* I am now.' 'She wears her clothes *as* gracefully *as* a coat-rack wears the coats hung on it.'

This differentiation between *as — as* and *so — as*, though recommended by grammarians, has not become established in the language. In fact there has long been a fluctuation of usage here, since the two forms *so* and *as* have the same origin and meaning and hence are naturally used interchangeably. In the colloquial speech of our time there is a strong drift in the direction of greater simplicity and uniformity, a trend to employ *as — as* in both positive and negative statements, following the simple principle that *as — as* expresses equality and *not . . . as — as* denies the existence of an equality: 'I am *as* tall *as* she' and 'I am *not as* tall *as* she.' We often, however, employ *so* as the first correlative instead of *as* when we desire to stress not equality or inequality but the unusually high degree: 'You can't get one *só góod* as this.' 'In a country *só lárge* as the United States there must be a great variety of climate.'

Where the things compared are not concrete but mere conceptions, the clause of comparison may be introduced by *as that:* 'Trying hard and failing is not *so* bad *as* [*is*] *that one should not try at all.*' 'Nothing vexes me *so* much *as* [*does*] *that I cannot see in what I can be serviceable to you.*' In older English, the form with simple *as* could be used: 'Nothing vexeth me *as* (now *so much as*) that I cannot see wherein I can be servisable unto you' (Sir Philip Sidney, *Arcadia*, Book I, Ch. XIV, A.D. 1590). The subject of the clause of comparison here is itself a clause — a subject clause. The abridged form of the subject clause is more common here than the full clause. See *bb* below.

aa. ACCUSATIVE INSTEAD OF NOMINATIVE. In elliptical clauses where the finite verb is not expressed, the nominative of personal pronouns is often in loose colloquial language replaced by the accusative, as so often elsewhere in elliptical expressions, as described in 7 C *a:* 'What, the one as big *as me?*' (Dickens, *A Christmas Carol*, Stave V), instead of *as I.*

bb. ABRIDGMENT OF CLAUSE OF SIMPLE COMPARISON. The full subject clause introduced by *that* is little used. It is largely replaced by the infinitival or the gerundial construction. When the subject is indefinite, the subject of the infinitive and the gerund is always understood: 'To go ahead resolutely and fail (or Going ahead resolutely and failing) is not *so* bad *as not to try at all* [*is*],' or *as not trying at all* [*is*], or less commonly *as* [*is*] *that one should not try at all.*

If the subject of the subject clause is definite, there is often some noun or pronoun in the principal proposition which serves as the subject of the infinitive or the gerund: 'There is nothing *so* natural to him *as to crave recognition* [*is*],' or *as craving recognition* [*is*]. If there is no word in the principal proposition that can serve as the subject of the infinitive or the gerund, they have a subject of their own. The subject of the infinitive is an accusative after the preposition *for*, as explained in **21** *e*; the subject of the gerund is a possessive adjective or a noun in the genitive: 'Nothing could be *so* unwise *as for him to attempt it* [*would be*],' or *as his attempting it* [*would be*], or *as John's attempting it* [*would be*]. The gerund is sometimes replaced by the absolute nominative construction described in **17** 3 B with the absolute nominative as subject and a present participle as predicate: 'Nothing alters the case *so* much as [*does*] *your saying* (gerund; or sometimes *as* [*does*] *you saying;* present participle) you are sorry.' 'Nothing cheers us *so* much *as* [*does*] *things going* (present participle) *right.*' 'Nothing reduces men's political power *so* much *as* [*does*] *women having* (present participle) *the vote.*' In older English, the subject of the infinitive here was often the absolute nominative instead of the accusative after *for:* 'That it (i.e., the child) shall [be found], Is all *as* monstrous to our human reason *As my Antigonus to break his grave*' (Shakespeare, *The Winter's Tale,* V, I, 40), now *as for my Antigonus to break his grave.* Compare **17** 3 B (2nd par.).

b. Proportionate Agreement. This clause is introduced by the following conjunctions: *as, according as, in degree as, in the same degree as, in proportion as, but as, except as,* the instrumental correlatives *the — the* (**16** 4 *c*), and the following more formal and stately correlative forms with the same meaning, which were much more used earlier in the period than now: *in what degree — in that degree, by how much — by so much, so much the* + comparative — *by how much the* + comparative, *the* + comparative — *by how much* + comparative, in older English also *as — so,* later entirely replaced by *as, according as, in proportion as.*

The old instrumental correlatives *the — the,* though now void of distinctive form, are still by reason of their terse and telling parallelism much used. They still, as in Old English, have two forms: 'This stone gets the harder *the longer it is exposed to the weather,*' originally 'This stone gets in that [degree] harder, in that [degree]: *it is longer exposed to the weather.*' Here we have the old double determinative described in **27** 2 for the similar use of *as.* Here the two *the*'s point as with two index fingers to the following explanatory subordinate clause. Here as so often elsewhere, the second determinative was early felt as belonging to the subordinate clause and became its introductory conjunction.

In the other form of this construction the subordinate clause precedes to make way for the emphatic principal proposition: '*The more money he makes* the more he wants.' originally '*In that*

[*degree*]: *he makes more money*, in that [degree] he wants more.'
The first *the* is a determinative, pointing to the following subordinate clause. The second *the*, like the *that* in **24** III *a* (2nd par.), is a demonstrative, pointing back to the preceding subordinate clause. In Old English, there was here in this form of the construction a complete parallelism between the two propositions, so that the subordinate clause had no clear formal sign of dependence. At the close of the Old English period a *that* was inserted to indicate subordination: '*The* more money *that* he makes the more he wants.' The double determinative, as here *the* — *that*, is characteristic of older English. In many cases it has disappeared, but it still survives here, since it clearly marks the clause as dependent and hence performs a useful function: '*The* more shy *that* Michael became, the more earnestly did this young man press him with intimate questions' (Compton Mackenzie, *Youth's Encounter*, Ch. VIII). But the old form that expresses complete parallelism is still, as in older English, the favorite. The form with inserted *that* in the subordinate clause is found also in the first form of this construction: 'This stone gets the harder the longer *that* it is exposed to the weather.'

The *the* — *the* of the second form may often in choice prose and poetry be replaced by the longer form *in what degree* — *in that degree*, since it distinguishes by its form the subordinate clause from the principal proposition and hence is often more suitable for accurate expression. For most purposes, however, even in poetry, *the* — *the* by reason of its terse forcefulness, dramatic parallelism, and elegant simplicity is still the favorite.

Examples:

'One advances in modesty *as one advances in knowledge*,' with the emphasis upon the subordinate clause, but the principal proposition stands last when emphatic or important: '*As I grew richer* I grew more ambitious.'

'We can earn more or less *according as we work*,' or in the form of a prepositional clause *according to how we work*.

'His humid eyes seemed to look within *in degree as* (or *in the same degree as*, or *in proportion as*) *they grew dim to things without*,' with the emphasis upon the subordinate clause, but the principal proposition stands last when emphatic or important: '*For just in proportion as the writer's aim, consciously or unconsciously, comes to be the transcribing, not of the world, not of mere fact, but of his sense of it*, he becomes an artist, his work fine art' (Walter Pater, *Style*).

I desire no titles *but as I shall deserve 'em* (Fletcher, *Prophetess*, II, III, A.D. 1622).

When we come to the improvement of the teacher in service, can that be done right *except as the teacher is a participant in the effort for improvement?* (Mary McSkimmon in *National Educational Association*, 1925, p. 104).

The more money he makes the more he wants.

'*In what degree we get self under foot*, in that degree we get a larger view of life'; or much more simply '*The more we get self under foot*, the larger view of life we get.'

Being thought so much the more assured to their Master, *by how much the more he sees them grow hateful to all men else* (Sir Walter Raleigh, *Historie of the World*).

Which deserveth the more accurate handling, *by how much it touches us more nearly* (Bacon, *Advancement of Learning*).

As they excelled in abhominacion, so preferred he theim (Elyot, *Image of Governance*, 8, A.D. 1541).

The full clause is often abridged to a prepositional phrase: 'The price of manufactured articles must rise *in proportion to the cost of labor*.'

A primitive form of this clause is preserved in old saws, as in '*The more*, the merrier,' where we still find the old verbless type of sentence described in **6** B *a* and **20** 3.

c. Restriction. The following conjunctions are used to indicate a restriction of the action or the state of the principal proposition: *so* (or sometimes *as*) *long as; so* (or sometimes *as*) *far as; in so far as;* or sometimes simple *as*.

Examples:

He answered quietly that if I gave the order he would take possession of the mines and would guarantee to open them and to run them, *so long as I told him to stay* (Theodore Roosevelt, *An Autobiography*, Ch. XIII).

So long as a people retains its vigor and its vital energy, its language never grows old (Brander Matthews, *Essays on English*, p. 5).

So far as (or *as far as*) *I could see or judge*, they were all satisfied with the arrangement.

'His efforts were *so far* successful *as they reduced the percentage of deaths*' (H. W. Fowler, *Modern English Usage*, p. 170), or more commonly 'His efforts were successful *so far as they reduced the percentage of deaths*.'

The outlines of the proposal, *in so far as* (or *so far as*) *they interest the general public*, are well known.

'Mr. Carlton is not a prudent man *as* (**5** *d*, p. 18) *regards money matters*' (or *with regard to money matters*, or *so far as money matters go*).

He recognized it for a fact, *as* (**5** *d*, p. 18) *regarded the past*, no more was to be said.

Why, Hal, thou know'st, *as* (= *so far as*) *thou art but man*, I dare; but *as* (= *so far as*) *thou are Prince*, I fear thee *as* (= *as much as*) I fear the roaring of the lion's whelp (*I Henry IV*, III, III, 165).

She's not a bad servant, *as servants go* (Mrs. Wood, *East Lynne*, I, 281).

In poetical language, there is sometimes a *so* in the principal
proposition where the subordinate clause is introduced by an *as*
that has the force of *so far as:* 'But if I live, So aid me heaven,
when at mine uttermost, *As* I will make her truly my true
wife!' (Tennyson, *The Marriage of Geraint*, 501). There is a
more common form of this old adjuration, which is also old:
'So (= to this extent) help me God, I will make her my wife!'
'[*I*] Wouldn't take a sou less, so help me' (Jack London, *The
Call of the Wild*, Ch. I).

aa. CLAUSE OF RESTRICTION REPLACED BY OTHER CONSTRUC-
TIONS. A restriction is often contained in a substantive relative clause introduced by the relative pronoun *that* (or in popular
speech *as*), which is used either as an adverbial accusative or as an
object, object of a preposition that stands at the end of the clause:
'He had never seen Hall *that he knew* before that day' (Dasent,
Jest and Earnest, II, 343), literally, *as to what* (= *so far as*) *he
knew*. 'An injunction to restrain such proceeding has never *that
I know of* been granted since 1851' (Sir N. Lindley in *Law Report*,
31 Chanc. Div. 367). 'It has never been done before *that* (or in
popular speech *as*) *I ever heard of*.'

A restriction is often expressed also by a prepositional phrase
consisting of *for* and a pronoun (*aught, anything*, or now more
commonly *all* or *what*) or noun modified by a relative clause, or
instead of this construction we may employ a subordinate clause
introduced by *so far as*, especially after a negative proposition:
'He may be dead *for aught (that)* — or *for anything (that)*, or more
commonly *for all (that)*, or *for what* — *I know*,' but 'He isn't dead *so
far as I know*' rather than 'He isn't dead *for aught (that)* — or *for
anything (that)*, or *for all (that)*, or *for what* — *I know*,' although the
prepositional construction sometimes occurs, as seen in the next
two examples. '*For aught that I could ever read, Could ever hear by
tale or history*, The course of true love never did run smooth'
(Shakespeare, *A Midsummer-Night's Dream*, I, i, 132). '*And for
all we know*, Xantippe had no mother to whom she could go and
abuse Socrates' (J. K. Jerome, *Idle Thoughts*, 155). 'She seldom
quitted her cabin; a pair of shoes may have lasted her five years
for the wear and tear she took out of them' (Frederick Marryat, *Jacob
Faithful*, I) = *so far as the wear and tear she took out of them was
concerned*. 'But his ship might have sunk with all on board *for any
sign he gave*' (G. Atherton, *Sleeping Fires*, Ch. XXVI). The relative
may be omitted after the governing pronoun or noun, and is always
omitted after *what*. After a personal pronoun the relative clause
is omitted as unnecessary: ' "She's got a pretty waist and a brown
eye, Davy, and she's seventeen." ' — ' "She may *for me*" (= *for all*

I care), said Davy' (Mrs. H. Ward, *David Grieve*, II, II). Similarly, after a possessive adjective, since the possessive adjectives have developed out of personal pronouns: 'The boy is clever *for his age.*' 'I *for my part* agree.'

Restrictions are often expressed by a phrase introduced by such prepositions as *with* (or *in*) *regard to*, *with reference* (or *respect*) *to*, *as to*, *as for*, *touching*, *in the case of*, *of*, *as compared with*, etc.: 'It is true, at least, *with regard to* (*in the case of*, or *of*) *John.*' '*As compared with the last season*, there is an improvement in the catch of whales.' *As for* and *as to* are differentiated in meaning: When we desire to call attention to some particular person or thing in order to say something of that person or thing, we employ *as for* or *as to;* but when we desire to restrict the statement in some particular, we employ *as to* (not *as for*): '*As for* (or *as to*) myself, my adversity was a blessing in disguise.' '*As for* (or *as to*) *cleverness*, there isn't her like in all the county.' But 'He was invariably reserved *as to* (not *as for*) *his private affairs.*'

bb. ABRIDGMENT OF CLAUSE OF RESTRICTION. The full clause of restriction is often abridged to a participial clause introduced by a conjunction, usually *so far as*, or sometimes simple *as:* 'The inquiry, *so far as showing that I have favored my own interests*, has failed.' 'The facts *as* (= *so far as*) *affecting the army* are: The regular army at its present strength,' etc. (Editorial in *Chicago Tribune*, Feb. 19, 1925). But the construction after *so far as* may be construed as gerundial, for *so far as* is now sometimes used as a preposition. See next paragraph.

The full clause of restriction may be abridged to a gerundial clause after the preposition *so far as:* '*So far as its having been premeditated or made for the purpose of insult to the court* I had not the slightest thought of that' (Clarence Darrow in *Tennessee Evolution Trial*, July 20, 1925).

We still sometimes find here the old verbless type of sentence described in **20** 3: 'So far, so good.'

d. Extent, Degree, Amount, Number. Conjunctions: *as long as; as* (or *so*) *far as; as* (or *so*) *far as that; to such an extent as, to the degree that, so as*, or quite commonly simple *as; as fast as, not so* (or *as*) *fast as; as proud as, not so* (or *as*) *proud as*, etc., now only rarely *proud as* (with a single *as*), etc., as in older English; *as much as*, sometimes *so much as; inasmuch as* in older English, now usually with causal force; *as many as*. Here as in *a*, p. 294, we employ the old determinative construction in both of its forms, either with a single or a double determinative. The single determinative *as*, as in the eleventh and twelfth examples (p. 301), is now in the subordinate clause, serving as its introductory conjunction.   In the double determinative construction — now the common form — the two determinatives, as in the first two examples below, have often formed a compound and have often further entered into close relations with the accompanying adverb, forming with it a compound, as described in **25**.   This compound now usually stands in the subordinate clause, serving as its introductory conjunction.   Where, however, the word standing between the two determinatives is not an adverb, but an adjective, as in the ninth and tenth examples below, the development has not gone so far.   The first determinative and the accompanying adjective are still in the principal proposition, while the second determinative is in the subordinate clause, serving as its introductory conjunction.

Examples:

I have stood it *as long as I can.*

I followed him with my eyes *as* (sometimes *so*) *far as I could.*

I have gone *as* (or *so*) *far as that I am collecting statistics for my investigation.*

I know these people about here, fathers and mothers, and children and grandchildren, *so as* (or *to such an extent as*, or simple *as*) *all the science in the world can't know them* (Oliver W. Holmes, *Elsie Venner*, Ch. XV).

To the degree that the reader recognizes the force of these observations, he will feel impelled to discount the author's condemnation of the course pursued by the Mexican authorities (Milo Milton Quaife in 'Historical Introduction' to Kendall's *Narrative of the Texan Santa Fé Expedition*).

He ran *as fast as he could.*

He spends his money *as fast as he gets it.*

He will stand at the end of the class *as sure as* (or *as surely as*) *the end of the month comes around.*

This morning my leg is as stiff *as* [*it*] *ever* [*was*].

He was not so (or 'as') patient *as he might have been.*

My good lady made me proud (now usually 'as proud') *as proud can be* (Richardson, *Pamela*, III, 241).

His method of taking in Blackstone seemed absorbing (now usually 'as absorbing') *as it was novel* (Meredith, *The Ordeal of Richard Feverel*, Ch. XVI).

I had as much *as I could bear.*

The poorest memory will retain so (more commonly 'as') much *as that* (C. E. Pascoe, *London of Today*, 241).

Let them blaspheme in private *as* (= *as much as*) *they please*, it hurts nobody but themselves (Mrs. H. Ward, *Richard Meynell*, Ch. V).

Inasmuch as ye have done it unto one of the least of these my brethren, ye have done it unto me (*Matthew*, XXV, 40).

Bring me as many flowers *as* (**5** *d*, p. 18) *you can find.*

aa. ABRIDGMENT OF CLAUSE OF EXTENT. A clause of extent introduced by *as* (or *so*) *far as that* is often abridged to an infinitive clause: 'I have gone *as* (or *so*) *far as to collect statistics for my investigation.*' Here *as far as* is a conjunction, but, as explained in **29** 1 B *b* (2nd par.), it is now used also as a preposition. As the gerund can stand after a preposition, the infinitive after the conjunction *as far as* can be replaced by the gerund after the preposition *as far as:* 'I have gone *as far as collecting statistics for my investigation.*'

Extent is often expressed by the adverbial accusative of a substantive form of a superlative with its modifying relative clause: 'She sang *the best (that) she could.*'

We still sometimes find here the primitive verbless type of sentence described in **20** 3: 'so many men, so many minds.'

B. **Comparative Clause.** Following a comparative, introduced by the conjunction *than* (in older English also with the form *then*, see **27** 3, last par.), in older English also by *as*, which survives in popular speech. In older English, in Scotch, and elsewhere in dialect, also *nor* was used, which survives in popular speech. The northern dialectic form *an* — an apocopate Danish form of the same word as English *than* — sometimes appears in older literary English in the erroneously expanded form *and*, having been confounded with conditional *an* or *and* (**31**).

Examples:

'Nothing could be more disagreeable to me *than that I should have to do that [would be]*,' or *than to have to do that [would be]*. The subject of the comparative clause here is itself a clause — a subject clause. Compare **29** 1 A *a* (last par.).

'A heavier task could not have been imposed *than I* (**17** 3 B, 2nd par.) *to speak my griefs unspeakable [would be]*' (Shakespeare, *Comedy of Errors*, I, i, 32), now *than for me to speak my griefs unspeakable [would be]*.

It is better that ten criminals should escape *than that one innocent man should be hanged.*

I'd have done anything rather *than [that] you should know* (Sheila Kaye-Smith, *Johanna Godden Married*, II, Ch. XXIV).

He was more shy *than [he was] unsocial.*

She is better *than [she was] when I wrote you last.*

'He more frequently ran *than [he] walked* to his work,' where we speak of different acts, but in 'He ran rather *than [he] walked to the house*' we speak of two descriptions of one act, one of which is represented as more appropriate.

The English love their liberties even more *than [they do] their kings.*

She eats less *than a bird [does].*

His tolerance for people younger, or less instructed, or both, *than [he] himself [was]* was as unfailing as his courtesy to great and small.

No leader of a party in recent modern days has kept himself in greater detachment from the thought and the sentiment of his party *than has the late Prime Minister* (subject at the end for emphasis).

'He was more beloved than Cinthio, but not so much admired,' not 'He was more beloved, but not so much admired, as Cinthio.'

He will never be other *than he is now.*

We are other *than we should be.*

Nought is more high, Daring, or desperate *then* (now *than;* see **27 3**, last par.) *offenders found;* Where guilt is, rage and courage doth abound (Ben Jonson, *Sejanus,* II, ii, 119, A.D. 1616).

No thynge may sooner moue a man to be meke and shewe mercy *as* (now *than*) *whan the persone whiche hath trespassed ayenst hym, lowly will submytte hymself, fall downe at his fete and mekely aske of him forgyuenes* (John Fisher, *E.E.T.S.,* Ex. Ser., XXVII, p. 161, early sixteenth century).

'A (he) made a finer end . . . *and* (now *than*) *it had been any Christom* (Chrisom) *child* (Shakespeare, *Henry the Fifth,* II, iii, 11).

When the verb in the subordinate clause is suppressed, the construction is often the same as in the principal proposition: 'We are moved by other *than* [*by*] *pure motives.*' 'Give it to someone else *than* [*to*] *me.*' 'I love him more *than* [*I love*] *her.*' 'She is regarded more highly *than he* [*is regarded*],' or *he is* [*regarded*]. Often, however, the person of the verb in the subordinate clause is different and has a different subject, thus requiring a different construction: 'I regard her more highly than *he* [does],' but 'I regard her more highly than [I do] *him.*' The person is sometimes incorrectly changed where there is no need of it: 'I have left Jack to tell a part of my life which I am glad to leave to another *than I* [am]' (S. W. Mitchell, *Hugh Wynne,* Ch. XXVIII, p. 531), instead of *than me.* The personal part of the verb is often necessary to make the thought clear: 'Tom likes me better than he *does* Harry,' but 'Tom likes me better than Harry *does.*' A preposition is often necessary to make the thought clear: 'Evanston is nearer to Chicago than *to* Fort Sheridan.' If the *to* after *than* were omitted, the sentence might be felt as meaning, 'Evanston is nearer to Chicago than Fort Sheridan is,' which of course is false.

Other as a comparative formation takes *than* after it, as illustrated in the examples given above. Since *different* has the same meaning as *other*, many improperly employ *than* after it instead of the preposition *from:* 'Your idea is different *than* (instead of the correct *from*) mine.' On the other hand, *different* often improperly influences *other*, so that many use *from* after *other:* 'Yet dress, habits, politics, other things, were still, as it were,

of another world *from ours'* (Saintsbury, 'Introduction' to Thackeray's *Virginians*), instead of the correct *than ours.*

Examples of dialect and popular speech: 'I like play better
nor work' (George Eliot, *Adam Bede*, Ch. I), literally, 'Of the two
I like play better, not work.' '[the baby] Ain't bigger *nor* a
derringer' (Bret Harte, *The Luck of Roaring Camp*, p. 4). 'I
would rather see him *as* you' (U. S. A., *Dialect Notes*, 1895, 376).
'I'd ruther see a railroad train *as to eat*' (Lucy Furman, *Mothering
on Perilous*, Ch. III), for literary *than eat.*

After a negative or a question *but* is sometimes employed in
older English after a comparative instead of *than:* 'If Mohamet
should come from heauen and sweare My royall Lord is slaine
or conquered, Yet shoulde he not perswade me otherwise *But*
that he liues and will be Conquerour' (Marlowe, *Tamburlaine*,
III, III, A.D. 1590). Sometimes still: 'What more natural *but*
(now usually *than that*) there's something for yourself?' (Hall
Caine, *The Manxman*, 138). After *sooner* this usage was once
common: 'He was no sooner landed, *but* (now *than*) he moved
forward towards me' (Defoe, *Robinson Crusoe*, 102). 'And it
(i.e., the spindle) was no sooner got into her hand, *but* (now *than*)
the other people then present beheld that it was indeed a Real,
Proper, Iron Spindle' (Cotton Mather, *Wonders of the Invisible
World*, A.D. 1693). The preceding negative or question here
suggested the use of *but*, which usually stands after a negative
or a question, but its negative force here in an affirmative proposition was later felt as inappropriate. Compare **27** 3 (last par.).

a. ACCUSATIVE INSTEAD OF NOMINATIVE. In elliptical clauses,
where the finite verb is not expressed, the nominative of personal
pronouns is often replaced by an accusative, as so often elsewhere
in elliptical expressions, as described in **7** C *a:* 'They're more
serious *than us*' (A. Marshall, *The Old Order Changeth*, Ch. XXXI),
instead of *than we* [*are*]. 'It is sometimes greater *than me*'
(George Bernard Shaw, *Back to Methuselah*, p. 16), instead of *than
I* [*am*]. The use of the accusative here should be avoided, for it
is often ambiguous. In such examples as 'I regard her more highly
than *he* [*does*]' and 'I regard her more highly than [I do] *him*'
only the correct use of the nominative and accusative forms can
make the thought clear. Compare **31.**

b. ABRIDGMENT OF COMPARATIVE CLAUSE. This clause is often
abridged to an infinitive clause with *to* when the subject of the
principal proposition can serve also as the subject of the infinitive:
'I knew better *than to mention it.*' 'I didn't dare go farther *than
merely to suggest it*' (or *to merely suggest it*). The infinitive is much
used also when the reference is general: 'Nothing pays better

than to be (or *being*) *kind* [*does*].' 'To trust in Christ is no more *but* (now *than*) *to acknowledge him for God*' (Thomas Hobbes, *Human Nature*, Ch. XI, A.D. 1650).

Sometimes the gerund seems to stand in a comparative clause, while in reality the construction is a prepositional clause: 'I didn't dare go *farther than merely suggesting it.*' 'It hasn't gone *any farther at present than me* (or *my;* see **50** 3) *promising not to marry anyone else*' (De Morgan, *Somehow Good*, Ch. XLVII). The use of the gerund here after *farther than* and *any farther than* indicates that these combinations of words are felt as compound prepositions, for the gerund can stand here only after a preposition. After the analogy of 'He has never gone *to,* or *beyond,* Chicago' we say, 'He has never gone *as far as* (*farther than, any farther than*) Chicago,' treating *as far as, farther than, any farther than* as prepositions. Compare **29** 1 A *d aa.*

We often find in the subordinate clause a simple infinitive instead of the form with *to:* 'Age and good living had disabled him from doing more than [that he did] *ride* to see the hounds thrown off and *make* one at the hunting dinner' (Washington Irving, *Sketch-Book*, X). 'I had (or better *would;* see **43** I B) rather go than [I had or would] *stay.*' As can be seen by these examples, such clauses are elliptical, not abridged. For fuller information see **49** 4 E. After *rather than* we sometimes find the simple infinitive even though no word can be supplied in thought which would require the simple infinitive, since the simple infinitive is so often properly used after *rather than,* as in the preceding example, that it sometimes becomes associated with it: 'He ought to have come by steerage *rather than not* [*to*] *have started* the same day' (Theodore Roosevelt as quoted by Archie Butt, *Letter,* Oct. 20, 1908). Compare **49** 4 E (5th par.).

2. **Degree Clause of Modal Result.** This clause never indicates pure result as in **28** 5, but always a result in association with the modal idea of degree.

The conjunctions are: *that* (**28** 5, 2nd par.) preceded by the determinative *so* or *such* or an adverb of degree; a little earlier in the period and in still older English *as, as that,* or *so as,* instead of *that,* as in **28** 5, a usage still surviving in popular speech; after a negative the forms *but that, but what,* or *that — not* preceded by a determinative in the principal proposition; in descriptive clauses *insomuch that* (or, earlier in the period, *insomuch as*), *to such a degree that, to such an extent that, so much so that,* which differ from the preceding conjunctions in that the determinative has been brought over to the subordinate clause from the principal proposition. Earlier in the period and sometimes still *than that* is used after a comparative to indicate result: 'For the bed is shorter *than that a man can stretch himself on it'* (*Isaiah*, XXVIII, 20). The abridged infinitive clause is a little more common than the full clause form of this construction: 'I think more highly of him *than to suppose he would do that.*' 'He knows better than *to do that.*' In a formal sense such clauses are clauses of degree after a comparative, but the idea of result is present and this has led to the replacing of the comparative by *too* + the positive of the adjective or adverb and the blending of the old comparative construction with the clause of result: 'The inquiry is too momentous *than that it should be abandoned.*' This blended and the old comparative construction are now for the most part replaced by an abridged infinitive clause after *too* + the positive of the adjective or adverb: 'The inquiry is *too momentous to be abandoned.*' 'I think *too highly* of him *to suppose that he would do that.*'

Earlier in the period, the determinative adjective *that* or *those* was often used in the principal proposition instead of *so great* or *such:* 'This enlivened us to *that* degree that we were mighty good company' (Duchess of Queensberry, *Letter to Countess of Suffolk,* A.D. 1734). 'The town was reduced to *those* straights that, if not relieved, it must have surrendred in two daies time' (Luttrell, *Brief Relation,* I, 567, A.D. 1689).

Examples:

He is speaking *so* loud *that I hear him even from here* (actual result).
He is *so* badly injured *that he must die* (inevitable result).
He is *so* badly injured *that he will probably die* (probable result).
He is *so* badly injured *that he may die* (possible result).
He is *so* badly injured *that he might die* (a result faintly possible).
He is *so* badly injured *that he shall be taken to the hospital at once* (a result determined upon by the speaker).
He is *so* badly injured *that he should be taken to the hospital at once* (a desired result expressed modestly).
He was *so* excited *that he couldn't sleep.*
He spoke *so* loud *that I could hear him upstairs.*
He spoke in *such* a loud tone *that I could hear him upstairs.*
His efforts were *so far* successful *that they reduced the percentage of deaths.*
Steerforth laughed to *that* degree *that it was impossible for me to help laughing too* (Dickens, *David Copperfield,* Ch. XXII).
John is not old *enough* (or *sufficiently* old) *that we can send him with this message.*
She worried *so that she couldn't go to sleep.*
I feel *such* a sharp dissension in my breast, *As* (now *that*) *I am sick* (Shakespeare, *I Henry VI,* V, v, 84).
He was *so* bad a scribe *as* (now *that*) *his hand was scarce legible* (Bradford, *History of Plymouth Plantation,* p. 181, A.D. 1630–1648).

We should have so much faith in authority *as* (**5** *d*, p. 18; now *that it*) *shall make us repeatedly observe and attend to that which is said to be right* (Ruskin, *Modern Painters*, Part III, Sec. I, Ch. III).

It is still in our power to direct the process of emancipation and deportation (of our slaves) peaceably, and in *such* slow degree *as that* (now simple *that*) *the evil* (of slavery) *will wear off insensibly* (Thomas Jefferson, *Autobiography*, p. 73).

Your informant seems to have given you no very clear idea of what you wish to hear, if he thinks that these discussions took place *so* lately *as that* (now simple *that*) *I could have been of the party* (Shelley, *Banquet*).

But they made *so* pore a bussines of their fishing *so as* (now simple *that*), *after this year, they never more looked after them* (Bradford, *History of Plymouth Plantation*, p. 201, A.D. 1630–1648).

It's far *enough* from the Union Station *so's* (i.e., *so as*, popular form for literary *that*) *they haven't got any warehouses* (Sinclair Lewis, *Elmer Gantry*, Ch. XXII, IV).

I shall never be *so* busy *but that* (or *but what*) *I shall find time to answer your letters* (or *that I shall not find time to answer your letters*).

Between spelling and pronunciation there is a mutual attraction, *insomuch that* (or *to such an extent that*) when spelling no longer follows pronunciation but is hardened into orthography, *the pronunciation begins to move toward spelling* (Earle).

Now this did more increase the people's good opinion of his sufficiency and wise conduction of an army, *insomuch as* (now *insomuch that*) *they thought him invincible* (North, *Plutarch*, 181, A.D. 1579).

Aldous silently assented, *so much so that Hallin repented* (Mrs. H. Ward, *Marcella*, III, 227).

The examples given above with a determinative in the principal proposition and *that* in the clause of result are the double determinative type described in **28 5**. The single determinative type without an introductory conjunction, described in **28 5**, is also used here, especially in colloquial speech: 'I was *so much* upset *I couldn't fix my mind on it*' (Henry Arthur Jones, *Mary Goes First*, Act II). 'She was *so* tired *she could not go another step*' (Mary Heaton Vorse in *Good Housekeeping*, Sept., 1929, p. 42).

a. ABRIDGMENT OF DEGREE CLAUSES OF MODAL RESULT. Clauses of degree to express a simple result can be abridged to an infinitive clause with *as to* when the subject of the principal proposition can serve as the subject of the infinitive and there is a determinative in the principal proposition: 'He was *so* kind *as to help me.*' 'You can't be *such* a fool *as to be jealous of her!*' The origin and meaning of *as* here is the same as in **28 5** *d*. In older English, the *as* is lacking here: 'there is No woman's heart so big, *to hold so much*' (Shakespeare, *Twelfth Night*, II, IV, 98). 'I wish you'd be so kind *to fetch me a rod and baits*' (Richardson, *Pamela*, Letter XXXII). The present use of *as* here shows that it has entered the abridged clause under the influence of the *as* which once introduced the full clause, as described on page 305.

We sometimes find the simple infinitive here instead of the form with *to:* 'I wouldn't have made so free as *drop* (more commonly *to drop*) a hint of,' etc. (Dickens, *Dombey and Son*, Ch. XXII). In the majority of such examples the simple infinitive is employed since it is felt as an imperative: 'If you'll only be so good as *try* (more commonly *to try*) me, sir!' (*ib.*, Ch. XLII).

A clause introduced by *so much so that* can be abridged to an infinitive clause introduced by *so much so as to* when the subject of the principal proposition can serve as the subject of the infinitive: 'Her attendant kept herself modestly in the background, *so much so as hardly to be distinguished*' (Scott, *Count Robert*, XVIII).   Similarly, clauses introduced by *so much — that* are abridged to an infinitive clause with *as to:* 'Take *so much* leisure *as to* peruse this letter' (Scott, *Kenilworth*, Ch. XXXIX), or more commonly 'Take enough time *to read this letter.*' In older English, the *as* is lacking here, which clearly shows that it later entered the abridged clause under the influence of the *as* which once introduced the full clause.   The older form of the abridged clause without *as* survives in poetry: 'Though I have not so much grace *To bind* again this people fast to God' (Swinburne, *Bothwell*, II, IX).

After *enough* and *too* the clause can be abridged to an infinitive clause with *to* when the subject of the principal proposition can serve as the subject of the infinitive and to an infinitive clause with *for . . . to*, when the infinitive has a subject of its own: 'I was not *near enough to distinguish his features.*' 'I was *too near to avoid him.*' 'He was *too tactful to mention it.*' 'I knew *too well to disturb him in these silent moods.*' But: 'He was not *near enough for me to distinguish his features.*' 'He was *too near for me to avoid him.*' Similarly, after other words indicating a degree: 'He came *in time* (= *early enough*) *to help me*,' but 'He came *in time for me to help him.*' 'The walls were *high enough to keep out a foe*,' but 'The walls must have been very high *for the foe to have been kept out.*' Compare **21** *e*. In older English, there is sometimes a superfluous *than* before the infinitive after *too:* 'You that are a step higher than a philosopher, a Devine, yet have *too* much grace and wit *than* to be a bishop' (Pope in a letter to Swift). For an explanation see 2, p. 306.

The idea of modal result is often expressed by a prepositional phrase: 'My emotion is too great *for words*' (= *to be expressed by words*).

CLAUSE OF CAUSE

30. Conjunctions. The subordinate clause contains the cause or reason, the principal proposition, the result or conclusion. This clause is usually introduced by the conjunctions: *that*, in popular speech often replaced by *as; as*, in older English sometimes *as that; because* (from *by the cause that* and in older English still often found with *that*, as in *because that* — Shakespeare, *Comedy of Errors*, II, ii, 26), now in popular speech often reduced to *acause* and *cos; not that — but because* (or simple *but*); *not that not — but because* (or simple *but*); *not that not* (or *not but that*, or *not but what*) — *but because; since* (compare **27** 3, 6th par.), in older English also in the form of *sithen, sithen that, sith, syth, sith that, sin, syn, sin that, syn that, sithens, sithens that, since that; now* or *now that; for the reason that*, or *by reason that; on the ground that; when*, in older English also *when as; after; once; as long as; whereas* (**26**, last par.), in older English also simple *where; inasmuch as*, in older English sometimes also *insomuch as; for fear, for fear that*, or *lest* (the reduced form of the old double determinative construction *thy* [old instrumental case of *that*] *less the*, literally, *on that account, that*, the two determinatives *thy* and *the* pointing as with two index fingers to the following explanatory statement describing a threatening occurrence, with the negative *less* [= *not*] inserted between the two determinatives to express the wish that the threatening occurrence may not take place); *in that;* in older English or still lingering on in poetic or archaic style: *for* or *for that*, reduced forms of Old English *for þæm* (dative of *that*) *þe*, an old double determinative construction, literally, *on account of that, that*, the double determinative pointing to the following explanatory statement, in older English introducing either a subordinate causal clause with the meaning *because*, or, on the other hand, an independent explanatory remark, in the former function now surviving only in poetic or archaic style, while in the latter function simple *for* is still widely used, as described in **19** I *d; for why* or *for why that* (= *because*), originally *for why?* (i.e., literally, *for what?*), a question in two words followed by a clause which was the answer to *for why?; for because* (Shakespeare, *Richard the Second*, V, v, 3); *for cause* or *for cause that; forasmuch as*, in older English also with the form *forsomuch as*, as in *St. Luke*, XIX, 9; *by that*, now obsolete; *in regard* (*that*), now replaced by *because*. Chaucer's *cause why* (*The Reues Tale*, 224) survives in Irish English and in a limited way also in British dialect: 'I didn't go to the fair *cause why* the day was too wet' (Joyce, *English as We Speak It in Ireland*, 81).

Examples:

'I am sorry *that he is going*,' but in popular speech *that* is often replaced by *as:* 'I'm sorry *as he dudn't tell you*' (Sheila Kaye-Smith, *Green Apple Harvest*, p. 35).

I rejoice *that he is prospering.*

The securing of the walrus had indeed been a Godsend, *as it relieved their most pressing needs* (Victor Appleton, *Don Sturdy across the North Pole,* Ch. XVIII).

All this was gall and wormwood to Jake, the more so *as the disparaging sneers that he had ventured to offer on the subject had been resented with hot indignation or cold contempt (ib.,* Ch. XIV).

Greatly pitying her misfortune, so much the more *as that* (now simple *as*) *all men had told me of the great likeness between us,* I took the best care I could of her (Sir Philip Sidney, *Arcadia,* Book I, Ch. VII, A.D. 1590).

The crops failed *because the season was dry.*

She was suspected partly *because that* (now simple *because*), *after some angry words passing between her and her neighbours, some mischief befel such neighbours in their Creatures* (John Hale, *A Modest Inquiry,* A.D. 1697).

The Englishman is peculiarly proud of his country's naval achievements, *not that he undervalues* its military exploits, *but simply because England* is essentially maritime.

'He rarely ever saw the squire and then only on business. *Not that* the squire had purposely quarreled with him, *but* (or *but because*) Dr. Thorne himself had chosen that it should be so' (Trollope, *Dr. Thorne,* I, Ch. VIII). 'Not a word had been said between them about Mary beyond what the merest courtesy had required. *Not that* each did *not* love the other sufficiently to make a full confidence between them desirable to both, *but* (or *but because*) neither had the courage to speak out' (*ib.,* II, Ch. VI).

I am provoked at your children, *not that they didn't behave well* (or *not but that,* or *not but what they behaved well*), *but because they left us too early.*

He cannot be tired *since he has walked only half a mile.*

And *sith* (now *since*) *in cases desperat there must be vsed medicines that are extreme,* I will hazard that little life that is left to restore the greater part that is lost (John Lyly, *Campaspe,* III, v, 54, A.D. 1584).

And *syn that* (now simple *since*) *the cryminell Geant Corfus is dede,* All the Remenaunt is as good as vaynquisshid (Caxton, *History of Jason,* p. 34, about A.D. 1477).

The idea of Marner's money kept growing in vividness, *now the want of it became immediate* (George Eliot, *Silas Marner,* Ch. IV, 30).

Now that he is sick, we shall have to do the work.

The blame cannot be put upon me, *for the simple reason that I was not present and had nothing to do with the affair.*

He refused to participate, *on the ground that he was not in sympathy with the cause.*

How convince him *when he will not listen?*

How can he be expected to be a scholar, *when he has spent his whole life in a dancing-school?*

For were a lady blinde, in what can she be beautiful? if dumbe, in what manifest her witte? *when as* (now simple *when*) the eye hath euer bene thought the Pearle of the face, and the tongue the embassadour of the heart (John Lyly, *Euphues and His England*, Works, II, p. 167, A.D. 1580). I don't think much of John *after he has treated me (in) that way*. *Once* (or *after*) *you have made a promise*, you should keep it. *As long as you act so mean*, you can't expect anybody to do anything for you. *And where* (= *whereas*) *heretofore there hath been great diuersitie . . . within this realme:* Now from henceforth, etc. (*Book of Common Prayer*, Preface, A.D. 1548). *Whereas the Royal Kennel Club of Great Britain has stopped the exhibiting of dogs with cut ears*, be it resolved that the American Humane Association ask the American Kennel Club to take like action. He cannot be expected to know much Latin, *inasmuch as he has been educated at a village school*. To be sure, the present law is inoperative, *insomuch* (now *inasmuch*) *as the universities contain teachers who have never subscribed this famous confession* (*Westminster Review*, XXIV, 105, A.D. 1836). Flashman released his prey, who rushed headlong under his bed again, *for fear they should change their minds* (Hughes, *Tom Brown*, I, Ch. VI, 125). But he did not want to ask any questions now *for fear that Jake would think he was taking advantage of the debt he owed him* (Victor Appleton, *Don Sturdy across the North Pole*, Ch. XXV). Tom dared not stir *lest he should be seen*. I was fearful *lest my hostess should suggest the medieval church as a topic* (Meredith Nicholson, *The Siege of the Seven Suitors*, Ch. IV). Middle English spelling . . . is to a certain extent phonetic, *in that there is often a genuine attempt to express the sound as accurately as possible* (H. C. Wyld, *History of Modern Colloquial English*, p. 28). And *for that wine is dear* We will be furnished with our own (Cowper, *John Gilpin*). And, *for* (= *because*) *himself was of the greater state*, Being a king, he trusted his liege-lord Would yield him this large honor all the more (Tennyson, *Gareth and Lynette*, l. 387). But for a time there was no need of additional territory *for that already hers stretched from the Atlantic to the Rocky Mountains* (Ephraim Douglass Adams, *Great Britain and the American Civil War*, p. 12, A.D. 1925). This death's livery (soldier's uniform), which walled its bearers from ordinary life, was sign that they had sold their wills and bodies to the State and contracted themselves into a service not the less abject *for that its beginning was voluntary* (T. E. Lawrence, *Revolt in the Desert*, p. 317, A.D. 1927). I weep for thee, and yet no cause I have, *For why thou left'st me nothing in thy will* (Shakespeare, *The Passionate Pilgrim*, l. 137). *For cause* (now *because*) *also the paynes of purgatory be moche more than the paynes of this worlde*, who may remembre god as he ought to do beyng in that paynfull place? (John Fisher, *E.E.T.S.*, Ex. Ser., XXVII, p. 15, early sixteenth century).

Forasmuch then as we are the offspring of God, we ought not to think that the Godhead is like unto gold, etc. (*Acts*, XVII, 28).

By that hee cals him virum mortis, I may conclude, etc. (Earl Northampton in *True and Perfect Relation*, Rr 4*b*, A.D. 1606).

He keeps himself a bachelor *by reason he was crossed in Love* (Steele, *Spectator*, No. 2, A.D. 1711).

There was a motion to put up a trading house there; but *in regard the place was not fit for plantation*, we thought not fit to meddle with it (Winthrop, *Journal*, July 12, 1633).

The idea of cause sometimes finds expression in an attributive element, either in the form of an attributive adjective or an attributive relative clause: 'The *crúel mán* didn't pay any attention to their pleadings' = 'The man didn't pay any attention to their pleadings *since he was cruel.*' 'John didn't mind the sharp words, but Mary, *who was of a very sensitive nature*, burst out into tears' = but 'Mary burst out into tears *since she was of a very sensitive nature.*'

A principal proposition is often used instead of a subordinate: 'I'm not going tonight. *I'm very tired.*' 'Round Audrey Noel's cottage they (the owls) were as thick as thieves and almost seemed to be guarding the mistress of that thatched dwelling — *so numerous were their fluttering rushes, so tenderly prolonged their soft sentinel callings*' (Galsworthy, *The Patrician*, Ch. XIII). 'Even now many teachers do not realize, *so great is the hold of tradition*, that English nouns rarely have gender.' '*These wares come from Russia.* That is why they cost so much' = 'These wares cost so much *because they come from Russia.*' Compare **19** 3.

a. ORIGIN OF THE CONJUNCTIONS OF CAUSE. The *that*-clause here performs the function of an old instrumental, genitive, or prepositional phrase of cause. The clause is the old double determinative type found so often elsewhere in English: 'These indications of inward disturbance moved Archer *the* (instrumental case of *that*) more *that* he felt that the Mingotts (name) had gone a little too far' (Edith Wharton, *The Age of Innocence*, Ch. V), literally, *moved Archer more on that account, that: he too felt that the Mingotts had gone a little too far*, the two *that's* pointing as with two index fingers to the following explanatory clause. After the second determinative *that* had developed into a conjunction of cause, the first determinative was felt as excessive expression and was dropped except before a comparative, as *more* in the example just given: 'I rejoiced *that he came.*' 'I am glad *that I went.*' The *that*-clause in all these cases always denotes pure cause;

but, as its form is not distinctive, it is not now in wide use where accuracy of expression is required. The *that* in colloquial and lively literary language is often suppressed: 'Winston was disappointed *we didn't dash away yesterday*, but we have not really let much grass grow under our feet' (Sir Ian Hamilton, *Gallipoli Diary*, I, 16). Except in such sentences as the preceding where the clause with or without *that* gives the cause of some feeling or emotion we now more commonly employ *because:* 'I am urging his name *because* I believe in him.'

It has always been common in English to indicate the reason *for* an act by simply placing after a statement an explanatory sentence: 'You had better be thankful *your life is spared*, young man' (Oemler, *Slippy McGee*, Ch. II). Although such sentences are in a formal sense independent there is a logical tie that binds them together. In an early stage of our language development this was sometimes indicated by placing the determinative adverb *so* at the end of the principal proposition, which after the manner of concrete primitive speech pointed as with an index finger to the following explanatory remark: 'I am going to bed, *so* (= *it is thus*): *I am very tired*.' The *so* standing immediately before the explanatory remark early became closely associated with it, forming with it a subordinate causal clause and serving as its connective, linking it to the principal proposition and thus developing into a causal conjunction, now always in the form of *as* (from older *all so*, i.e., *quite so*): 'I am going to bed, *as I'm very tired*.' 'I saw I had said something wrong, *as they all laughed*' (De Morgan, *Joseph Vance*, Ch. XI). '*As he refuses*, we can do nothing' (*Pocket Oxford Dictionary*).

Causal *as* (in Old English usually in the old simple form *swa*, i.e., *so*), although identical in form with the *as* introducing clauses of time and manner, maintained itself in Old English, Middle English, and early Modern English as an occasional form, and later gradually became common in colloquial speech and not infrequent in the literary language: 'We þe lofiaþ, *swa þu hœlend eart*' (Grein, *Hymnen und Gebete*, 7, 116) = 'We love thee, *as thou art our Savior*.' 'Lete me fro this deth fle, *As* I dede nevyr no trespace' (*Cov. Myst.*, 181, A.D. 1400). 'But att the laste, *as a man may not euer endure*, Syre Launcelot waxed so faynt of fiȝting but (= absolutely) he mighte not lyfte vp his armes for to gyve one stroke' (Malory, *Le Morte d'Arthur*, Book XV, Ch. V, A.D. 1485). 'And at our highest neuer joy we so, *as we both doubt and dread our ouerthrow*' (Kyd, *Spanish Tragedy*, III, I, 6, A.D. 1585) = 'And even when we kings are at the height of our power, we never joy in having it so, *as we fear and dread our overthrow.*' 'If earthlie Kings reuenge any little wrong done to theyr Embassadours, now how much more shall the King of Kings reuenge the death and slaughterdom of his Embassadours? The Angels in heauen, *as they are the Lordes Embassadours,* would prosecute (revenge) it though he should ouerslip it' (Thomas Nashe, *Christs Teares ouer Iervsalem,* Works, II, p. 24, A.D. 1593).

As can be seen by the preceding examples, *as* is now as in older English peculiarly appropriate where it is desired to give an easy, natural, almost self-evident explanation of the statement in the principal proposition.

In early Modern English, a favorite way of expressing cause was to employ an *as*-clause of comparison that always preceded the principal proposition, which itself was always introduced by a *so* pointing back to the *as*-clause: '*As a madman's epistles are no gospels,* so it skills (matters) not much when they are deliver'd' (Shakespeare, *Twelfth Night,* V, 294). Compare **28** 2 (3rd par.). Today we avoid this once common causal construction, as we feel that its peculiar form, so closely associated with the idea of comparison, doesn't give clear expression to the idea of cause.

The very common *as*-clause of manner, which is much used as a sentence adverb (**28** 1), often contains causal force, so that the idea of manner mingles with that of cause: 'He has made me some offers, but, *as I am circumstanced,* [I] cannot accept them' (Nicholas Cresswell, *Journal,* June 15, 1777), or more clearly according to *b,* p. 315: '*circumstanced* (or more commonly *situated*) *as I am,* I cannot accept them.'

Where there is a clear desire to emphasize cause, *because* is the common form: 'He will succeed *because* he is in earnest.' We always employ *because* after the emphatic *it is* described in **22** *a:* 'It is only *because* I regard it as absolutely necessary that I take such harsh measures.' Usually also when the clause is in the form of a question: 'It would have been very unreasonable in the girl to say anything, *because why on earth shouldn't Robert fasten up Vicey's glove if it got unbuttoned?'* (De Morgan, *Joseph Vance,* Ch. X).

Temporal *since* often assumes causal force since what precedes an act is naturally construed as its cause: '*Since* John has lied to us several times, we cannot believe him any more.' The causal force in *since* is stronger than that in *as,* but not as strong as that in *because:* 'You shall have them cheap *since* there is little demand for them.' '*Since* these men could not be convinced, it was determined that they should be persecuted.'

The coördinating conjunction *for* has causal force approaching that of subordinating *as* and *since:* 'He could not have seen me, *for* I was not there.' The proposition introduced by coördinating *for* is in current English always a remark loosely added to a preceding proposition to explain it. Hence it can never precede the main proposition as an *as*-clause or a *since*-clause. For also differs from *as* and *since* in that it can introduce an explanation that does not contain the idea of cause: 'It is morning, *for* (not *as* or *since*) the birds are singing.' Compare **19** 1 *d*.

Inasmuch as is more formal than *since*, also more guarded, qualified: '*Inasmuch as* the debtor has no property I abandon my claim.' *Whereas*, as a pure causal conjunction, is largely confined to legal or official style. An example is given on page 311.

b. ABRIDGMENT OF CLAUSE OF CAUSE. A causal clause introduced by *since, because, as,* and *in that* can sometimes be abridged to a participle, adjective, noun, or prepositional phrase when the subject, predicate, or object in the principal proposition is the subject of the subordinate clause: '*Being poor*, he could not afford to buy books.' '*Knowing him so well from childhood*, I feel that I can recommend him strongly.' '*Feeling that he disliked me*, I avoided him.' '*Seeing that he was in trouble*, I went to his aid.' '*Discovering that the next train didn't leave till late*, I decided to stay and take a morning train.' '*Having passed through severe trials myself*, I have at last learned to sympathize with others in their struggles.' 'In time these voluptuous experiences had their effect, *calling up a hitherto undeveloped sensuousness*' (Sheila Kaye-Smith, *The Challenge to Sirius*, p. 84) = *in that they called up a hitherto undeveloped sensuousness.* '*Conceding this point* (or employing a gerundial construction, *in*, or *by, conceding this point*, or a full clause, *in that you concede this point*) you destroy your entire argument.' 'The enemy, *now in possession of all the bridgeheads*, can be expected to advance soon.' 'She is quite a different woman now, *deprived of her wealth and her beauty*.' 'Dora did not reply, *gentle creature that* (relative pronoun) *she was*.' 'She makes the first advances, *dear kind soul as* (relative pronoun) *she is*' (Pinero, *Mid-Channel*, Act III). 'This is a very rare event, *occurring as* (relative pronoun) *it does only once in many years*.' 'He has made me some good offers, but, *situated as* (adverbial conjunction of manner) *I am*, I cannot accept them.' 'A suppressed excitement in his manner convinced me, *used as* (adverbial conjunction of degree) *I was to his ways*, that his hand was upon a clue.' '*As* (**7** A *b* (3)) *possessors of the bridgehead*, they now had a decided advantage.' 'He was shunned *as* (introducing the predicate appositive, as in the preceding example, but here, perhaps, felt as a causal conjunction) *a man of doubtful character*.' 'Our remaining horse was utterly useless *as* (used as in the preceding example) *wanting an eye.* 'They criticized the boy *as* (used as in the two preceding examples) *having no interest in his work.* 'I mightily approve Lady Craven's blending the dairy with the library *as* (used as in the preceding sentence) *an example to her sex*, who at present are furiously apt to abandon the churn totally' (Horace Walpole, *Letter to Thomas Walpole*, July 21, 1788). 'But if you shall once more make me a tender Of that love which at your Castle I refus'd, *As* (causal conjunction) *being then a prisoner to anothers beauty*, Assure your selfe I shall redeem that errour' (Ludowick Carlell, *The Fool Would Be a Favourit*, Act IV, A.D. 1657). 'It is an unpardonable slight *since* (causal conjunction) *intentional.*' 'The Sophists were hated by some *because* (causal conjunction) *powerful*, by others *because* (causal conjunction) *shallow.*'

The adjective, participle, noun, or prepositional phrase is the predicate of the abridged causal clause. This is the old verbless type of clause described in **6** B *a* and **20** 3, but now after the analogy of usage elsewhere a copula is often inserted: '*Sick and tired*, I went to bed,' now often '*Being sick and tired*, I went to bed.' The copula, however, conforms to the old type in that it takes participial form as a predicate appositive to the subject of the principal proposition. The insertion of conjunctions, *as*, *since*, and *because*, in many of these abridged clauses indicates the influence of the full clause upon this old type. Compare **27** 5 and **20** 3 (5th par.).

Where the reference is indefinite, we often employ the present participle absolutely, i.e., without a subject, as explained in **17** 4, **31** 2, and **32** 2: 'Which isn't to be wondered at, *seeing* (= *as one can see*) *that he has just finished six weeks of examination work*' (Hughes, *Tom Brown*, II, VIII). 'And it would be rather hard for him to overcome this handicap, *seeing* (= *as one could see*) *that other boys with better homes were being trained for special kinds of work*' (T. Dreiser, *An American Tragedy*, I, 14). 'It is no wonder that he learns so little at school, *seeing that he doesn't work*' (= *as one sees that he doesn't work*).

Another kind of participial clause is very common here, a clause with an absolute nominative (**17** 3 A *b*) as subject and a participle as predicate: '*The rain having ruined my hat*, I had to buy a new one.' 'She was named for my father, *there being no son in the family*' (Meredith Nicholson, *The Siege of the Seven Suitors*, Ch. IV). '*It being very stormy*, she stayed at home.' The absolute nominative construction is often replaced here by a prepositional phrase: 'She is lonely, poor thing, *with her husband so much away.*'

Instead of a full causal clause we can often after a preposition employ a gerundial clause: 'The Gunnings are not only resettled in St. James's Street as boldly as ever, but constantly with old Bedford, who exults *in having regained them*' (Horace Walpole, *Letter to Miss Mary Berry*, July 7, 1791). 'I can't do anything *for thinking of her.*' 'He quarreled with her *for saying it.*' 'You will be scolded *for having torn your clothes.*' 'We feel kindly toward him *for* (or *because of*) *his waiting so patiently under such trying circumstances.*' 'I haven't been invited *in consequence of my being a profligate sinner.*' 'I can't leave home *on account of having a visitor.*' 'He dared not fire *for fear of hitting someone.*' 'I don't think much of John *after his treating me (in) that way.*' 'Some of your suggestions could not be followed out *from their not fitting into the plan I have adopted.*' '*Owing to his* (or *John's,* or *the lad's,* or *the lad;* see **50** 3) *bringing me word so late* I couldn't go.' 'Hayward was lionized in London society *on the strength of having written a prose version of about one-half of Goethe's masterpiece.*' At this point the full clause is often avoided since it is often far inferior by reason of its clumsy form: 'Owing to John's bringing me word so late I couldn't go' rather than 'Owing to the fact that John brought me word so late, I couldn't go.'

The abridged clause often has the form of an infinitive clause with *to* if there is some word in the principal proposition that can serve as the subject of the infinitive: 'I was pained *to hear it.*' 'I was glad *to see him.*' 'Mary, hang the idiot *to bring me such stuff!*' The present participle is often used alongside of the present infinitive: 'You ought to be ashamed *stealing from a little widow*' (Joseph Hergesheimer, 'Collector's Blues,' in *Saturday Evening Post,* Oct. 2, 1926) (or *to steal from a little widow*). The subject of the infinitive is sometimes not expressed but merely suggested by the context, as in exclamations where the inference is that the speaker is the subject: '[I'm a] Fool! *to have looked for common sense on such an earth as this!*' The subject is understood if it is general or indefinite: 'To looke backe at Ills begets a Thankefulnesse *to have escap'd them*' (Thomas Dekker, *London, Looke Backe!* p. 1, A.D. 1630). Where the infinitive has a subject of its own, it is introduced by *for . . . to:* 'I know how deeply she must have offended you *for you to speak like that.*'

CLAUSE OF CONDITION OR EXCEPTION

31. Conjunctions. This clause states the condition upon which the action of the principal clause hinges, or adds an exception, i.e., a fact or proviso that qualifies in some particular respect the preceding statement. It is introduced by the following conjunctions:

CONJUNCTIONS OF CONDITION: *if, on condition (that); if not, were it not that, if it were not that; except that = were it not that; only that = if not, were it not that,* in this meaning often replaced by adversative *only* (see 1 *e*, p. 328), in older English also with the meaning *unless; unless,* in older English *on lesse* (or *lasse*) *than* (or *then*), *on lesse that,* i.e., *on less interference than, on a less favorable condition than, short of;* in popular speech *less'n,* representing older *on lesse than; without,* in older English and still in colloquial speech = *unless; save* or *saving,* in higher literary style = *if not, unless; except* and *excepting,* in older English and sometimes still in archaic language = *if not, unless; but, but what* (colloquially and popularly), sometimes still as in older English = *if not, unless; but that* (in older English sometimes simple *but*) = *if not, were it not that,* often replaced by adversative *but* (see 1 *e*, p. 328); *provided* or *provided that, provided only, providing* or *providing that* (both forms now less common than *provided* or *provided that*); *so that,* or in older English and still in popular speech *so as,* or in older English and still often in colloquial speech simple *so,* now also *so only* — all these forms now usually with the meaning *provided (that), on condition (that),* but the *so*-forms in older English could also mean *if, in case; so be it = provided; so long as* or sometimes *while; in case* or *in the event that; when* = *in case; granted that; given that; once = if once.* In older English: *and* or *an = if,* still in certain dialects; *if that, if so (that), if so be (that); if so be as; so be (that); so be as; if case be (that), if case that; conditionally (that); but if (that) = unless; but that (= if not),* after *it is* (or *were*) *pity; foreseen that = provided;* in dialect *gin* and *gif = if.* The parentheses around *that* in these conjunctions indicate that *that* may be used or suppressed.

In older English, after *no wonder, no marvel,* or the negative or interrogative form of the verbs *wonder, marvel, be sorry, care,* a concessive clause introduced by *though* often lost its concessive force and developed into a conditional clause, so that *though* is now replaced by *if:* 'Oh, how can love's eye be true, That is so vex'd with watching and with tears? No marvel then, *though* (now *if*) I mistake my view' (Shakespeare, *Sonnets,* CXLVIII). 'What [do I care] *though* (now *if*) She strive to try her strength, Her feeble force will yield at length' (*id., The Passionate Pilgrim,* 317). 'He cares not *though* the Church sinke' (Gillespie, *English Popish Ceremonies,* Ep. A. II. *b,* A.D. 1637), now 'He doesn't care *if* the Church goes down.' This old *though,* however, is preserved in the elliptical construction with *as:* 'He looks *as* [he would look] *though* (or *if*) he were sick.'

CONJUNCTIONS OF EXCEPTION: *but that* or less commonly simple *but; except that, except* (or *but*) *for the fact that; beyond that* (with the force of *except that*), after a negative proposition or a question; *save that, saving that; only that,* in colloquial speech also simple *only;* in elliptical clauses the simple forms *but, except, save, saving, than,* and sometimes *unless* (next par.).

In elliptical clauses of exception where there is no finite verb, we often find an accusative form employed in the subject relation: 'Nobody was there but *me*' = *but* [*that*] *I* [*was there*]. Many grammarians explain the accusative here by construing the *but, except* (**17** 3 A *c*), or *save* before it as a preposition. Since, however, in choice language it has long been customary to employ in the subject relation the nominative of a personal pronoun after all these words but *except*, it is evident that in our collected moments we feel them as conjunctions. *Except* has not been long felt as a conjunction here, but it is now being drawn into this group by the force of its meaning, which is the same as that of *but*. The common construction of these words as prepositions when an accusative follows is an inadequate explanation, for we find the accusative in many elliptical expressions where the word before it cannot possibly be construed as a preposition: 'They're more serious *than us*' (A. Marshall, *The Old Order Changeth*, Ch. XXXI) = *than we are*. The use of the accusative instead of a nominative in elliptical clauses of exception after *but, except, save,* is simply an illustration of the widespread employment of the accusative of personal pronouns instead of the nominative found everywhere in elliptical expressions not containing a finite verb, as described more at length in **7** C *a*. The frequent accusative after *except* is explained in part also by the fact that many feel *except* as the imperative of the transitive verb *except*. Compare 1 *d aa*, p. 328. The tendency toward the accusative is very strong in elliptical clauses of exception, especially after *except*, but many careful authors resist this drift and employ in choice language the nominative where the pronoun is used as subject, especially after *but*. The case is quite different with simple *excepting*, which is still, as it has always been, a present participle taking an accusative object or a clause. Alongside of it is the transitive verb *except*, which takes an accusative object. The present participle *excepting*, with the full force of the transitive verb *except*, is often used absolutely, as illustrated in 2 (4th par.), p. 330. This absolute participle has been often mistaken for a preposition. Also *saving* is a present participle, but no longer a live one. There is alongside of it no transitive verb *save* with the meaning *except*. Even in early Modern English *saving* was construed as a conjunction, as illustrated on page 325 by the examples from Harvey and Spenser. As it is now little used, we have no live feeling as to how it should be treated, whether as a conjunction or as a preposition. Of all these forms *except* is the favorite before a prepositional phrase or an adverbial clause: 'I take no orders *except from the King.*' 'He is never to be found *except in the wrong place.*' 'I never do such things *except when I have plenty of time.*' 'He is everywhere *except where he ought to be.*' Sometimes, now rather infrequently, *unless* is used in both of these categories instead of *except*. Here we may construe *except* and *unless* as conjunctions standing in an elliptical clause or we may regard them as prepositions governing the following phrase or clause. *Unless,* unaccompanied by *when,* is often used in clauses with the force of *except when:* 'I take a walk every day *unless it rains.*'

Examples of Conditional Clauses:

They'll not go tomorrow *if it rains.*

If the person who wrote the book is not wiser than you, you need not read it; *if he be,* he will think differently from you in many respects (Ruskin).

In literature, in art, in politics a man is exceptionally fortunate *if he 'arrive'* (or more commonly *should arrive*) *by the time he is forty (British Review).*

If ever anyone on this earth was simple and unaffected, Moltke was (Sidney Whitman).

Of course *if the king was in the right,* Fox was in the wrong.

If I were rich, I would travel.

I should have done it before *if I had had time.*

Lord, *if thou hadst been here,* my brother had not died (*John,* XI, 21).

You can have it for a few days *on condition (that) you return it next week some time.*

John is very much disheartened, and *if I did not encourage him* (or *were it not that I encourage him*) he would give up entirely.

'It might have passed unnoticed, *except that he had made enemies by his readiness to saber foes with his speech*' (Will Durant, *The Story of Philosophy,* p. 158), or *had it not been that,* or *had it not been for the fact that,* he had made enemies, etc.

I would come *only that I am engaged.*

She (i.e., the black heifer) let a drive with her horns, and *only that I gave her a belt with the stick I had in my hand,* she'd have her (i.e., the white cow) pinned against the wall (Lennox Robinson, *Harvest,* Act I).

I wille not graunte the thy lyf, said that knyghte, *only that* (now *unless*) *thou frely relece the quene* (Malory, *Le Morte d'Arthur,* Book XVIII, Ch. VII).

I shall go *unless* (in older English *onless*) *it rains* (literally, *on less interference than rain*, i.e., *short of rain*).

Robert will not suffre hym to be laten (let) to baile *on lasse than* (now *unless*) *he will make a generall acquytaunce* (A.D. 1500, quoted from *Oxford Dictionary*).

Ne would I gladly combate with mine host . . . *Vnlesse that* (now without *that*) *I were thereunto enforst* (Spenser, *Faerie Queene*, VI, III, XXXIX, A.D. 1596).

Haue a man neuer (now *ever*) so moche lyght of faythe *onlesse* (now *unless*) *he haue also this hete of charyte sterynge his soule and bryngyng forthe lyfely workes*, he is but a dead stock and as a tree withouten lyfe (John Fisher, *E.E.T.S.*, Ex. Ser., XXVII, p. 326, early sixteenth century).

Don't you ever let on I told you, *less'n* (current popular form representing older *on lesse than*, now replaced by *unless* in the literary language) *you want to see me kilt* (Lucy Furman, *Mothering on Perilous*, Ch. XXIII).

Mrs. Taylor told him last Sunday that, *without* (now usually *unless*) *he understands Latin*, he will never be able to win a young lady of family and fashion (Philip Vickers Fithian, *Journal*, March 15, 1774).

You will not have better health *without* (better *unless*) *you take better care of yourself*.

Who wept and said, That *save they could be pluck'd asunder*, all My quest were but in vain (Tennyson, *Holy Grail*).

For *saving I be join'd To her that is the fairest under heaven* I seem as nothing in this mighty world (*Coming of Arthur*, l. 85).

Thou couldest have no power at all against me *except* (now in plain prose *unless*) *it were given thee from above* (*John*, XIX, 11).

Scindiah certainly could have done nothing *excepting* (now *unless*) *he could bring his brigades to Poonah* (Wellington, A.D. 1804, quoted from *Oxford Dictionary*).

The whiteness of this shadow was not like any other whiteness that we know of, *except* (archaic for *unless*) *it be the whiteness of the lightnings* (Mark Twain, *Joan of Arc*, I, Ch. VI).

'May I die,' cried Montague, *'but I am shocked'* (Dickens, *Martin Chuzzlewit*, Ch. XL) = *if I'm not shocked*.

It shall go hard *but I will get there* = I am willing that it shall go hard with me *if I can't get there otherwise*.

We will drain our dearest veins *But they shall be free!* (Burns, *Scots, wha hae*, V).

I'd burn the house *but* (or *but what*) *I'd find it* = I would burn the house *if I couldn't find it otherwise*.

We'll des nat'ally pull de groun' out *but w'at we'll get deze creeturs out* (Joel Chandler Harris, *Nights with Uncle Remus*, p. 235).

'Ten to one but he comes' (= 'I bet ten to one *if it doesn't turn out that he comes*'), now usually replaced by 'Ten to one he comes,' since we now feel the clause as positive.

But (= *unless*) *I be deceiv'd*, our fine musician groweth amorous (Shakespeare, *Taming of the Shrew*, III, I, 62).

Virtue is the very heart and lungs of vice; it cannot stand up *but* (= *unless*) *it lean on virtue* (Thoreau, *Journal*, I, p. 78).

No man ever did or ever will work, *but* (= *unless*) [*he worked*] *either from actual sight or sight of faith* (Ruskin, *Modern Painters*, IV, Ch. VII, 5).

We should have arrived sooner *but that we met with an accident.*

But that I saw it, I could not have believed it.

I would have told you the story, *but that it is a sad one and contains another's secret* (Thackeray, *Pendennis*, II, Ch. XX).

I should never have repeated these remarks, *but that they are in truth complimentary to the young lady whom they concern* (*id.*, *Vanity Fair*, I, Ch. XII).

And, *but* (now *but that*) *she spoke it dying,* I would not believe her lips (Shakespeare, *Cymbeline*, V, v, 41).

I will come *provided* (or now less commonly *providing*) *that I have time* (or *provided* or *providing I have time*).

Once the travelers were shut up in the *Advance* (submarine), they could exist for a month below the surface, *providing no accident occurred* (Victor Appleton, *Tom Swift and His Submarine Boat*, Ch. IV).

The Romans were well enough satisfied with this, *provided only they might remain inactive* (Hale and Buck, *Latin Grammar*, p. 283).

You may go where you like *so that you are back by dinner time.*

I accept thy submission and sacrifice *so as* (now *so that* = *provided that*) *yerelie at this temple thou offer Sacrifice* (John Lyly, *Midas*, V, iii, 75, A.D. 1592).

PUFF. It would have a good effect efaith! if you could exeunt praying! SNEER. Oh, never mind — *so as* (now *so that*) *you get them off!* I'll answer for't the Audience won't care how (Sheridan, *The Critic*, II, ii, 186, A.D. 1781).

He could play 'em a tune on any sort of pot you please *so as* (in popular speech instead of *so that*) it was iron (Dickens, *Bleak House*, Ch. XXVI).

Schiller seized the opportunity of retiring from the city, careless whither he went, *so he got beyond the reach of turnkeys* (Carlyle, *Life of Schiller*, I, 44).

Let them hate, *so they fear* (G. M. Lane, *A Latin Grammar*, p. 338).

Let him go *so only he come home with glory won* (*ib.*).

So (now *if* or *in case*) *thou hadst been still with me,* I could have taught my love to take thy father for mine (Shakespeare, *As You Like It*, I, ii, 11).

So that (now *if* or *in case*) *you had her wrinkles and I her money,* I would she did as you say (*id.*, *All's Well That Ends Well*, II, iv, 20).

So as (now *in case*) *thou liv'st in peace,* die free from strife (*id.*, *Richard the Second*, V, vi, 27).

I also pray that that fine elevation and expansion of nature which ventures everything may go with us to the ends of the earth, *so be it we go to the ends of the earth carrying conscience and the principles that make for good conduct* (Woodrow Wilson, Dec. 2, 1900).

I do not care *so long as you are happy.*

Nothing matters *so long as we are not found out.*

The brothers, and other relatives, might do as they would, *while they did not disgrace the name* (Meredith, *The Ordeal of Richard Feverel*, Ch. I).

In case it rains (or *in the event that it rains*) we can't go.

When (= *in case*) *great national interests are at stake,* the party system breaks down.

Granted that he actually did it, we may now seek to explain his conduct.

Given that he and they have a common object, the one test that he must apply to them is as to their ability to help in achieving that object (Theodore Roosevelt, *The Strenuous Life*, p. 74).

But there's no dealing with him, *once he's got a notion in his head* (Brand Whitlock, *J. Hardin & Son*, Book III, Ch. VII, 2).

They will set an House on Fire, *and* (now *if*) *it were but to roast their Egges* (Bacon, *Essays*, 97, A.D. 1625).

An (= *if*) *I could climb and lay my hand upon it,* Then were I wealthier than a leash of kings (Tennyson, *Gareth and Lynette*, l. 50).

'*An* (= *if*) *you do that,* we're lost.' *An* is still to be heard in our southern mountains and here and there in New England.

If that (now simple *if*) *you conquer,* I live to joy in your great triumph (Byron, *Sardanapalus*, IV, I, 482, A.D. 1822).

I told them that to come to a publike schoole . . . it was opposite to my humour, but *if so they would giue their attendance at my lodging,* I protested (declared) to doe them what right or favour I could (Ben Jonson, *Euery Man in His Humour*, III, VIII, 26, A.D. 1601, ed. 1616).

If so be the Lord will be with me, then I shall be able to drive them out (*Joshua*, XIV, 12).

If so be that I can get that affaire done by the next post, I will not fail for to give your Lordship an account of it (Chesterfield, *Letters*, II, CCIII, 269, A.D. 1749).

If so be as (older English preserved in dialect) *he's dead,* my opinion is he won't come back no more (Dickens, *Dombey and Son*, Ch. XXXIX).

I care not what I meet with in the way, *so be I can also meet with deliverance from my burden* (Bunyan, *Pilgrim's Progress*, 20).

It ought nat to be applyed, *but yf case be that the pacyente were faynte herted* (R. Copland, *Gydon's Quest. Chirurg.*, A.D. 1541).

If case some one of you would fly from us, etc. (Shakespeare, *III Henry VI*, V, IV, 34).

I here entail The crown to thee *Conditionally that here thou take an oath To cease this civil war* (Shakespeare, *III Henry VI*, I, I, 196).

But if remedee Thou her afford, full shortly I her dead shall see (Spenser, *Faerie Queene*, III, III, XVI).

Inasmuch as things which are præternatural do more rarely happen, it is pity *but that they should* (now *if they should not*) *be observed* (Increase Mather, *Remarkable Providences*, Ch. V).

I shal bere it as patiently as to me is possible *foreseen* (now *provided*) *that ye shall promyse me,* etc. (Caxton, *History of Jason*, p. 88, A.D. 1477).

Gin ye promulgate sic doctrines, it's my belief you will bring somebody to the gallows (Scott, *St. Ronan's Well*, XXXIV).

Dash me *gif I can tell ye wha* (= *who*) *he is* (Gorden, *Carglen*, 33).

Examples of Clauses of Exception:

I don't believe that God wants anything *but that we should be happy.*

What can I say *but that I hope you may be contented.*

Here we live in an old rambling mansion for all the world like an inn, *but that we never see company.*

Nothing would content him *but I must come.*

My boy is quite as naughty as yours, *except that he always begs my pardon when he has done wrong.*

The copy was perfect *except that* (or *except*, or *but*) *for the fact that*, the accents were omitted.

He did not really know what he was going to say, *beyond that the situation demanded something romantic* (Francis R. Bellamy, *The Balance*, Ch. I).

He could not distinguish its meaning (the meaning of the cry), *save that it seemed to convey an urgent appeal for help* (Victor Appleton, *Don Sturdy on the Desert of Mystery*, Ch. I).

I've nothing against the man, *only that I hate him* (Marion Crawford, *Katharine Lauderdale*, II, Ch. VIII).

'Is anything the matter with my Madeline?' — 'No, papa, *only I have got a headache*' (Trollope, *Orley Farm*, II, Ch. III).

I don't know anything, *only he hasn't any folks and he's poor* (Louisa Alcott, *Little Men*, Ch. VI).

Only (now usually *only that*, or more commonly *except that* when the subordinate clause precedes) *he is very melancholy*, he would be agreeable (H. Martin, *Helen of Glenross*, II, 226, A.D. 1802).

Who is glad *but he?* (Chaucer, *The Marchantes Tale*, 1168).

Apone this yt chaunced that vppon a day ther was no persone att dynner with vs *but we* three and Masone (Sir Thomas Wyatt, *Declaration to the Councell*, A.D. 1541).

Damon is the man, none other *but he*, to Dionysius his blood to pay (Richard Edwards, *Damon and Pithias*, l. 1590, A.D. 1571).

Who *but thou* alone can tell? (Spenser, *Faerie Queene*, Book VII, Canto VII, II).

It was I and none *but I* (Sir Philip Sidney, *Arcadia*, Book V, p. 174, A.D. 1593).

Methinks nobody should be sad *but I* (Shakespeare, *King John*, IV, i, 13).

Who hath hindered him from cutting it downe *but I?* (Thomas Nashe, *Christs Teares ouer Iervsalem*, Works, II, p. 19, A.D. 1593).

Who knows *but He* whose hand the lightning forms (Pope, *Essay on Man*, Epistle I, 157).

There's nobody home *but I* (or in colloquial speech more commonly *me*).

The boy stood on the burning deck whence all *but he* had fled (Mrs. Hemans, *Casabianca*).

No one ever knew *but I* (Dickens, *David Copperfield*, Ch. XI).

Who *but he* had betrayed me? (F. B. Aldrich, *The Story of a Bad Boy*, Ch. XX).

No one knows it *but you and I* (W. D. Howells, *A Modern Instance*, Ch. XXXVII).

Nobody knew her *but I* (Pinero, *His House in Order*, Act IV).

Who can have done it *but I?* (Hardy, *The Return of the Native*, V, Ch. I).

There's not a soul in my house *but me* tonight (*id.*, *Far from the Madding Crowd*, Ch. XXXIV).

There is none to claim me *but he* (Meredith, *Rhoda Fleming*, Ch. XLI).

None in the world shall ever know *But I* who am his wife (Cale Young Rice, *Far Quests, The Wife of Judas Iscariot*).

There is none evil *but I* (Alfred Noyes, *The Paradox*, II).

Everybody is to know him *except I* (Meredith, *Tragic Comedians*, 28).

Every one, *except me*, seemed to dislike him (Beatrice Harraden, *The Fowler*, II, Ch. IV, 111).

Now he had lost her, he wanted her back, and perhaps everyone present, *except he*, guessed why (Kingsley, *Westward Ho!* Ch. XXV).

'*Saue I* and a frere, In Engeland ther can no man it make' (Chaucer, *The Chanouns Yemannes Tale*, Ellesmere MS., 802), but in the accusative relation 'Ne I ne desire no thyng for to haue, Ne drede (nor dread I) for to leese (lose) *saue oonly thee*' (*id.*, *The Clerkes Tale*, Ellesmere MS., 451).

None can helpe *saue we* (John Heywood, *The Play of the Weather*, l. 1136, A.D. 1533).

None heard *save I* (Bridges, *Demeter*, Act II).

All *save he and Murray* have pleaded guilty (*Chicago Tribune*, Nov. 12, 1924).

All were reddi *saving I and Sir Flower* (Gabriel Harvey, *Letter to Dr. Young*, Nov. 1, 1573).

All this worlds glory seemeth vayne to me, and all their showes but shadowes, *saving she* (Spenser, *Amoretti*, XXXV, 14, A.D. 1594).

Anybody *but a fool* (may be construed as nominative or accusative since the form is not distinctive) would understand.

She loved no one *but* (or *except*, or much less commonly *unless*) *him* (in the accusative relation, as here, always accusative, usage never varying).

He did not believe that he would ever obtain anything *unless* (now usually *but* or *except*) *a species of elevated poor-law system of government* (*Pall Mall Gazette*, Aug. 4, 1886).

Society can have no hold on any class *except through the medium of their interests* (Buckle, *Civilization*, I, XI, 632).

He is everywhere *except in the right place.*

There were two ponies in the stables of the Great House which they were allowed to ride and which, *unless* (now usually *except*) *on occasions*, nobody else did ride (Trollope, *Small House*, I, Ch. II).

'I take a walk every day *except when it rains.*' Sometimes, now rather infrequently, *unless when* is used here. On the other hand, *unless* unaccompanied by *when* is often used here instead of *except when:* 'I take a walk every day, *unless it rains.*'

He is to be found everywhere *except where he is needed.*

A beautiful horse, jet black, *unless* (now usually *except*) *where he was flecked by spots of foam* (Scott, *Rob Roy,* Ch. V).

A prophet is not without honor, *save* (more commonly *except*) *in his own country.*

He does nothing *but* [*that he does*] *laugh.*

He couldn't do anything *but* [*that he did*] *mournfully acquiesce.*

What could she do *but* [*that she did*] *love him?*

Such procedure cannot [*do anything*] *but hurt his cause.*

No one *other than an Englishman* dare do that.

He could not do otherwise *than* [*that he did*] *assent.*

Nor could his private friends do other *than* [*that they did*] *mournfully acquiesce.*

He will do anything *except* [*that he should do*] *work hard.*

For the explanation of these elliptical forms see **49** 4 E. Note also the following: 'Who *but* (conjunction) *he* (or *besides* — preposition — *him,* or *else than he,* or *other than he*) could have done it?' 'No one *but* (conjunction) *he* (or *besides* — preposition — *him,* or *else than he,* or *other than he*) could have done it,' or sometimes a blending of two constructions: 'Who *else but he* (or *else besides him*) could have done it?' 'No one *else but he* (or *else besides him*) could have done it.'

The use of *than* in a number of the examples given above indicates that the subordinate clause has developed out of a comparative clause (**29** 1 B) and in a formal sense is still a comparative clause.

In older English, the negative *ne* (**16** 2 *d*) often stood before the principal verb: 'He *nis* (= *ne is*) but a child.' By the later omission of *ne,* as in 'He is *but* a child,' the old conjunction *but* has acquired the meaning of *nothing but,* and is now often felt as an adverb with the force of *only* and thus can now as an adverb be employed where it was not used in older English: 'We pass through life *but* (or *only*) once.' In older English, this *but* could be strengthened by *only:* 'I find *but only* (now simple *but* or *only*) two sorts of writings' (Milton, *Areopagitica,* 36).

1. **Clauses of Condition and Exception Replaced by Other Constructions.** These clauses may be replaced by the following constructions:

a. We often employ a relative clause instead of a conditional clause introduced by *if:* 'Any boy *who should do that* would be laughed at' = 'Any boy would be laughed at *if he should do that.*'

b. Instead of a conditional clause introduced by *if* we sometimes use a clause with question word-order, originally an independent question and in rhetorical style still occasionally appearing as such: '*Is any among you afflicted?* let him pray' (*James*, V, 13). '*Don't you love Nature because she is beautiful?* He (i.e., Thoreau) will find a better argument in her ugliness' (James R. Lowell, *Literary Essays*, I, p. 372). 'You would see for yourself, *were you here.*' '*Had I the time,* I would go.' 'There are other articles, to which, *did time permit,* we might draw attention.' 'People will gather by hundreds outside a police court on the chance of catching a glimpse of a criminal; *do they see but a corner of his hat,* they go away happy.' '*Were I to be late,* would you wait for me?' '*Should you find them,* kindly let me know.' '*Would space allow,* I should like to quote the notice in full.' This construction is now for the most part employed only where the verbal predicate is compound, made up of an infinitive or a participle and an auxiliary. Only in the case of *be* and *have* is it used with a simple verb. In older English, this construction was much more common than today. It could be used also with any simple verb of complete predication, where today, if the question form is used at all, an auxiliary verb must be used in connection with an infinitive: 'Call me their traitor! Thou injurious tribune! Within thine eyes *sat* twenty thousand deaths, . . . I would say "Thou liest"' (Shakespeare, *Coriolanus*, III, III, 69), now, if used at all, 'Did twenty thousand deaths *sit* within thy eyes,' etc.

c. A conditional clause may be replaced by a wish impossible of fulfilment, with question word-order: '*Could I see her once more,* all my desires would be fulfilled.' '*O had he only come,* how different would tnings now be!'

In older English, the conditional clause in *b* and *c* was sometimes confounded with the *that*-clause, so that instead of the question word-order the normal order was employed and *that* suppressed, as so often in *that*-clauses: 'I should be glad *this compromise were made*' (Southey in *Life*, III, 26). 'What would I give *I could avoid it* when people speak of you?' (Dorothy Osborne, *Letters*, 279, A.D. 1654).

d. One of two independent sentences linked by conjunctions or unlinked is often equivalent to a conditional clause or a clause of exception.

aa. Where there are two sentences linked by *and* or unlinked, one of which is an expression of will containing an imperative or a volitive (**43** I A) subjunctive, the sentence containing an expression of will has the force of a conditional clause and may be replaced by such: '*Give him an inch* and he'll take a mile.' '*Stir and you are a dead man.*' '*One step further* (= *take one step* *further*) and you are lost.' 'But *enter a Frenchman or two* and a transformation effected itself immediately' (Du Maurier, *Trilby*). 'She had no room for anything but pity; but *let Alessandro come on the stage again*, and all would be changed' (Helen Hunt Jackson, *Ramona*, Ch. XIV). '*Do it at once*, you will never regret it.' '*Suppose* (or *say* = *suppose*, or *assume*) *that he took a real fancy to you*, would you accept him?' In accordance with older literary usage the volitive subjunctive is still often employed in quaint dialect where it is not now used in the literary language: '*Come* (= *if it comes, happens*) [that] we can't get the big things (i.e., trees) and their shade, we're proud to take the little flower-things and their sweetness' (Maristan Chapman, *The Happy Mountain*, Ch. XVI). 'Old maids (a kind of flower) they's going to be — *happen* [that] they get their mind set to blooming ere frost' (*ib.*).

Sometimes there is no expression of will at all in a sentence, and yet it has the force of a conditional clause: 'You don't have to be tender of my feelings. You can't *and be honest*' (= *if you are honest*) (Eleanor Carroll Chilton, *Shadows Waiting*, p. 273).

A sentence containing an imperative is often used instead of a clause of exception: '*Bar Milner's speech* there has scarcely been a word about our policy in the whole of the debate.' 'She is the best housekeeper in town *bar no one*.' *Except* (**17** 3 A *c*) is often felt as an imperative: 'All men are fallible *except the Pope*.'

bb. Where there are two sentences linked by *or, otherwise, else*, or *or else*, the first of which is an expression of will, the sentence containing the expression of will is often equivalent to a conditional clause: '*Do that at once, or* (or *otherwise, else*, or *or else*) you will be punished' = '*If you do not do that at once* you will be punished.'

cc. Where there are two unlinked expressions of will, the first often has the force of a conditional clause: '*Love me*, love my dog' = '*If you love me*, love my dog.' '*Bestow nothing*, receive nothing. *Sow nothing*, reap nothing. *Bear no burdens*, be crushed under your own.' '*Waste not*, want not.'

dd. Where there are two independent declarative sentences linked by a disjunctive (*or, else*, or *otherwise*; see **19** 1 *b*), the first sentence is often equivalent to a conditional clause: '*He cannot be in his right mind, or* (or *else*, or *otherwise*) he would not make such wild statements' = '*If he were in his right mind*, he would not,' etc.

e. After the conclusion of an unreal condition (**44** II 5 C) we often employ an independent sentence instead of a conditional clause. This independent sentence is coördinated with the preceding conclusion by means of adversative *but* or *only* (**19** 1 *c*): 'The one (airship) that fell in Virginia would have made a safe landing all right, *but the metal nose came up against an electric light wire and set fire to the gas*' (Victor Appleton, *Don Sturdy across the North Pole*, Ch. IV) = *if the metal nose had not come up against*, etc. 'And we'd have done better, *only we struck a hard wind against us about two miles up in the air*' (*id.*, *Tom Swift and His Submarine Boat*, Ch. I) = *if we had not struck*, etc.

2. Abridgment of the Clause of Condition or Exception. When the subject of the principal proposition and that of the subordinate clause are identical, the subordinate clause introduced by *if*, *provided*, or *unless* can be abridged to a participle or an adjective, which is a predicate appositive to the subject of the principal proposition: '*Born in better times*, he would have done credit to the profession of letters.' 'Such things are better *left unsaid*.' 'It is best *forgotten*.' '*Left to herself*, she would have been drawn into an answer.' 'This same thing, *happening* (= *if it should happen*) *in wartime*, would amount to disaster.' 'I have an income large enough to take care of me, *living* (= *provided I live*) as I live' (Carrie Jacobs-Bond, *Ladies' Home Journal*, Sept., 1927, p. 141). The participle *failing* belongs here in a formal sense, but it is now really a preposition, for it is no longer in this construction vividly felt as the present participle of *fail*. 'They would prefer to come to us; *failing* that, they would have us visit them.'

The frequent insertion of *if*, *unless*, and *except* in these abridged clauses indicates the influence of the full clause upon this old type of expression: 'Thus will I save my credit in the shoot: Not wounding, pity would not let me do 't; *If wounding*, then it was to show my skill' (Shakespeare, *Love's Labor's Lost*, IV, I, 26). '*Unless meeting with unexpected difficulties at the office today*, I shall be home early tonight.' 'He will do it *if properly approached*.' 'The child is never peevish *unless sick*.' 'The whole Road from Hartford to Springfield is level and good, *except being* too sandy in places' (George Washington, *Diary*, Oct. 21, 1789). Compare **20** 3 (5th par.). It is possible to construe the third and fourth examples as elliptical: 'He will do it *if* [*he is*] *properly approached*.' 'The child is never peevish *unless* [*it is*] *sick*.' In the second and last examples *unless* and *except* may be construed as prepositions governing the following gerund. But *unless* is now little used as a preposition. Compare **31** (5th par.).

An elliptical clause is often used if its subject is situation *it* (**4** A): 'Come tomorrow *if* [*it is*] *possible*.'

Where the reference is general or indefinite, the present participle is often used absolutely, i.e., without an expressed subject, in accordance with the general principle observed with participle, infinitive, and gerund that there is no need of a subject if the reference is indefinite: '*Strictly speaking* (= *if one must speak in a strict sense*), that is not true.' '*Mildly speaking*, that is an exaggeration.' '*Setting aside the £10,000* (= *if one set aside the 10,000 pounds sterling*), it did not appear that she was at all Harriet's superior' (Jane Austen, *Emma*, Ch. XXII). '*Judging* (= *if one judged*) *from the traces of their* (i.e., the beavers') *work*, it (the beaver dam) had once held a large colony of beavers' (Theodore Roosevelt, *Hunting Trips of a Ranchman*, Ch. II). '*Excepting a few of Jonson's earlier creations*, I cannot see but that these (the characters in *Magnetic Lady*) are about as successful as the majority of the personages of his earlier plays' (H. W. Peck, Introduction to Jonson's *Magnetic Lady*, p. xxxiv). '*Looking at his life from another point of view*, his actions become intelligible.' 'It cannot be denied that, *granting the difficulty of the undertaking*, Mrs. Davis has done her work with great skill' (Gamaliel Bradford in *Harper's Monthly*, Aug., 1925). '*Considering the circumstances*, he is doing well.' '*Assuming the hearty coöperation of all the members* (or *that all the members will heartily coöperate*), it is reasonable to expect that the celebration will be successful.' 'Objections to this plan, *supposing there should be any*, should be reported to the committee at once.' '*Barring accidents*, he will arrive tomorrow.' Some call the participle here a preposition or a conjunction, but it has in these and many other examples too much live verbal force to be regarded as crystallized into the rigid state of a preposition or a conjunction, as in the case of *bating*, which, no longer felt as a participle since the verb *bate* has become obsolete, has become a preposition. Similarly, *providing* is now felt as a conjunction, since the verb is not now commonly used in the special meaning contained in the participle: 'I shall go *providing* (not now *if you provide*) it doesn't rain.' In clauses of exception the preposition *except*, the subordinating conjunction *except*, and the second person imperative *except* (1 *d aa*, p. 328) cannot be used at all if the clause is negative. Here *except* must be replaced by the absolute present participle *excepting*: 'All men are fallible, not *excepting the Pope*' or *the Pope not excepted* (**17** 3 A c). The present participle can be freely used here, as the reference is general or indefinite.

The full clause is often abridged to an infinitive clause with *to* in clauses of condition and *but to* or *except to* in clauses of exception, provided there is some word in the principal proposition which can serve as the subject of the infinitive: 'It would hurt us *to act hastily.*' 'I should be glad *to go.*' 'There is nothing left to us *but* (or *except*) *to go.*' 'What am I here for *but to talk*' (Henry Watterson, *Editorial*, Feb. 19, 1908). The full clause can also often be abridged to a *to*-infinitive clause when the subject of the infinitive is general or indefinite, in which case the subject is usually understood: '*To judge by his outward circumstances* he must be very rich' = *if one may judge*, etc. '"I was thinking of asking £30 for the month" (for the use of the boat). — "The boat is not worth it *to buy*"' (G. A. Birmingham, *Spanish Gold*, Ch. II) = *if one should buy it for that price.* 'The reason of man differs from the instinct of animals in that it can form abstract conceptions — conceptions that float free, *so to speak* (= *if one may use such an expression*), dissociated from particular concrete objects.' 'His language is irreverent, *not to say* (= *if one may not say*) blasphemous.' Often an indefinite pronoun in the principal proposition serves as the subject of the infinitive: 'I'm sure, nobody *to read this* would ever imagine I was an almost grown-up girl' (De Morgan, *Joseph Vance*, Ch. X). If the infinitive has a subject of its own, the subject is introduced by *for:* 'It would be delightful to me *for us to work together.*' 'I should be glad *for Mary to go.*' 'There was nothing now *but for him and the footman to get into the carriage.*'

The *to*-infinitive is much used in exclamatory conditional sentences with the principal proposition suppressed. The conditional clause has the form of an abridged *to*-infinitive clause with the subject unexpressed, as the natural inference is that the speaker is the subject: '*Oh, to be in England* now that April's there!' (Browning, *Home-thoughts from Abroad*, I) = 'Oh, how happy I should be *if I were in England*,' etc. We often employ here a prepositional phrase introduced by *for:* '*Oh, for a friend to help us and advise us!*' (Wilkie Collins, *The Woman in White*, p. 222) = 'Oh, how happy I should be *if we only had a friend to help and advise us!*'

The absolute nominative construction described in **17 3 A c** often takes the place of a conditional clause.

Sometimes the conditional clause has the form of an attributive adjective: 'A *true* friend would have acted differently' = 'A friend would have acted differently *if he had been true.*' 'There is little, *if any*, difference between them.' The adjective sometimes follows the noun as an appositive: 'With what species (of birds), *if any*, the marriage unions last during life, I do not know' (John Burroughs, *Leaf and Tendril*, VII).

Sometimes we find a prepositional phrase instead of a clause of condition or exception: *'Without him* I should be helpless.' *'Bating a little wilfulness* I don't know a more honest or loyal or gentle creature.' *'In a thorough analysis* we shall find that there is some good in every man.'

Instead of *were it not for, had it not been for* it is common to employ *but for, except for, save for,* or, in older English and still in colloquial speech, *only for,* which are now felt by many as compound prepositions but which historically are elliptical expressions introduced by the conjunctions *but, except, save,* or *only:* *'But [it were] for the thick trees* the bitter wind would blow the house to pieces.' 'We should have died *but* (or *except,* or *save*) *for him.'* *'Only for my tea,* I should have had the headache' (*Ora and Juliet,* I, 30, A.D. 1811). 'We should have died *only for him'* (in colloquial speech for *but for him*).

After the preposition *without* the *to*-infinitive may be used provided the preposition has an object which can serve as the subject of the infinitive: 'But he couldn't [have sat up], *without me to raise him'* (De Morgan, *Joseph Vance,* Ch. XXXVI) = *if I hadn't raised him,* or we can also use the gerund here: *without my raising him,* or *without my having raised him.* The gerund is, in general, common after prepositions: *'In case of John's* (or *the boy's,* or *the boy;* see **50** 3) *finishing the work tonight,* let me know.' 'How many critics would be able, *on being shown this drawing,* to say from whose pencil it had emanated.' *'Short of committing suicide,* he does his best to keep out of the way.'

A verbless conditional clause is sometimes contained in the old verbless appositional type of sentence described in **20 3**: *'Forewarned, forearmed!'* *'Small pains,* small gains!' *'Once a gambler,* always a gambler!' *'Better dead!'* (Galsworthy, *The First and the Last,* Scene III) = 'It would be better *if we were dead!'* *'No song,* no supper.'

CLAUSE OF CONCESSION

32. Conjunctions. The concessive clause contains a conceded statement, which, though it is naturally in contrast or opposition to that of the principal proposition, is nevertheless unable to destroy the validity of the latter: *' Though he is poor,* he is happy.'

The concessive clause is introduced by the following conjunctions: *if, even if; though, tho, even though, even tho, although, altho;* in older English, *thof* (a variant of *though*), surviving in dialect; the adversatives (**27** 4) *while, when, whereas,* in older English also *where; as* (as in *bad as he is,* in older English *so — as,* or *as — as,* as in *so bad as he is,* or *as bad as he is*); *in spite of the* *fact that, despite that, notwithstanding (that)*; relative pronoun or adverb + *ever* or *soever; for all* or *for all that; for as little as; granted that* (**17** 3 A *c*). In older or archaic English: *albeit* (i.e., *all be it = be it entirely) that* or simple *albeit, albe; al,* with inverted word-order; *howbeit (that)*; *and* or *an* (= *if*); *so* (= *even if*).

A pair of concessive clauses is usually connected by *whether* (in older English a pronoun = *which one of the two,* as in *Matthew,* IX, 5) — *or, whether — or whether, if* (more commonly *whether*) — *or,* simple *or,* in older English *or whether — or.*

As can be seen by the use of *if,* the concessive clause has in part developed out of the conditional clause with which it is often closely related.   On the other hand, the concessive clause has affected the conditional clause, as can be seen in *as though,* which is often used with the force of *as if:* 'He looks *as* [he would look] *though* (= *if*) he were sick.'

The use of *though* in concessive clauses indicates a relation with the older adversative coördinating conjunction *though,* which still as in oldest English stands in an independent proposition that expresses a contrast to the preceding statement: 'This medicine is good for you; it is a little bitter *though.*' 'I have no doubt he will understand — *though* you never know.' 'He is an ingenious lad, *though his brother is more ingenious*' (or *his brother though is more ingenious*).   When such an adversative statement loses somewhat of its independence and becomes logically subordinate to the other proposition, it becomes a concessive clause: '*Though this medicine is a little bitter,* it is good for you,' or 'This medicine is good for you *though it is a little bitter.*'   '*Big though he was,* he was not ashamed to learn,' or 'He was not ashamed to learn, *big though he was.*'   '*Coward though he is,* do not bully him,' or 'Do not bully him, *coward though he is.*'   Where the *though* clause precedes, as in the first alternate form of each of these examples, the subordination is evident, but where it follows, as in the second, the subordination can often be indicated only by a rapid enunciation.   Coördination can often be marked by putting *though* within the proposition or at the end, as illustrated in the examples given above.   In Old English, the subordinate clause was usually distinguished by the volitive (**43** I A) subjunctive: 'He bið þonne undeaþlic, þeah he ær deaþlic *wære*' (*Blickling Homilies,* 21, A.D. 888) = 'It (the body) will then be immortal, though it *was* mortal before.'   In older English, subordinating *though* was often indicated by putting a determinative, in Old English *the,* later *that,* after *though,* pointing forward to the following explanatory group of words, marking it thus as a subordinate clause: '*Though that the queen on special cause is here,* Her army is mov'd on' (Shakespeare,

King Lear, IV, vi, 219). The form *although* is always a subordinating concessive conjunction.

A common form of the concessive clause originated in the clause of degree: '*Bad as he is*, he has some good points,' in older English '*As* (or *so*) *bad as he is*, he has his good points,' where *as — as* (= Old English *swa — swa*, i.e., *so — so*) contains an indefinite idea of degree, so that the clause has the force of *however bad he is*. '*Rashly* (in older English *as* or *so rashly*) *as he acted*, he had some excuse.' In these clauses of degree we now often use the volitive (**43** II A) subjunctive, once much less common: '*Bad as he may be*, he has some good points,' literally, '*Let him be ever so bad*, he has some good points.' In all these examples the *as* or *so* that once stood before the strongly accented word which introduced this clause has disappeared. After the old double determinative construction with *as* (or *so*) — *as* had developed concessive force and the original function of the double forms had become obscured, the first determinative *as* or *so* was dropped as a useless form, so that the heavily stressed word after it might stand in the important first place. The *as* after the heavily stressed word is now felt as a concessive conjunction.

In 'Boy *as* he was, he was chosen king' *as* is a relative pronoun with the force of *that*, but since *boy* is a predicate appositive with concessive force, as explained in 2, p. 339, this group of words is felt as a concessive clause, and *as* is construed as a concessive conjunction. Similarly, relative *that*, which is often used here instead of relative *as*, is often construed as a concessive conjunction: '*Apt scholar that he was*, they were equally apt teachers, never allowing him to linger long in error' (Jack London, *The Call of the Wild*, Ch. II).

Another common form of the concessive clause makes use of an indefinite relative pronoun, adjective, or adverb + *ever* or *soever:* 'He was resolved to defend himself, *whoever should assail him.*' '*Whose-ever* it is, I mean to have it.' 'His love will not fail, *whoever else's may.*' 'We will go on with the war, *whatever it costs*' (*cost*, or *may cost*). '*Whatever may be his weaknesses*, he is generally liked.' 'I am going to pursue this course, *whatever sacrifice it may demand.*' 'He will find difficulties, *whichever way* (or *whichever of these ways*) he may take.' 'Human beings, *of whichever sex they may be*, will do amazing things.' '*However sick he is* (or *may be*), he always goes to his work.'

Examples:

'I don't care *if I do lose*,' or in rather choice English 'I don't care *though I lose*.'

I couldn't be angry with him *if* (or *though*, or stronger *even if*, or *even though*) *I tried*.

He is very kind-hearted, *even if* (or *even though*) *he is outwardly a little gruff*.

He will start tomorrow, *though it rain cats and dogs*.

Foolish though she may be, she is kind of heart.

A gentle hand . . . *róugh-grained and hárd though it was* (Dickens, *Old Curiosity Shop*, Ch. XV).

Strangely enough, *stáunch Róyalist though he was*, Thomas Chicherley must in early life have been brought into contact with Oliver Cromwell (Lady Newton, *Lyme Letters*, Ch. I, A.D. 1925).

A sailor will be honest, *thof* (now *though*) *mayhap he has never a penny of money in his pocket* (Congreve, *Love for Love*, III, IV, 288, A.D. 1695).

Though (or *although*) *he promised not to do so*, he did it.

Though they worked never (once common in concessive clause, but since the later seventeenth century gradually replaced by *ever*) *so hard*, it was all in vain (Dickens, *Martin Chuzzlewit*, Ch. XLII).

Her mother, *while she laughed*, was not sure that it was good to encourage the pert little one.

We sometimes expect gratitude *when we are not entitled to it*.

Whereas I was black and swart before, With those clear rays which she infus'd on me That beauty am I bless'd with which you see (Shakespeare, *I Henry VI*, I, II, 84).

And where thou now exact'st the penalty, Thou wilt . . . Forgive a moiety of the principal (*id.*, *Merchant of Venice*, IV, I, 22).

Stupid as he is, he never loses his profit out of sight.

The world, *as censorious as it is*, hath been so kind (Swift).

Dr. Johnson admitted Boswell into his intimacy *in spite of the fact that the latter was a Scotchman*.

The amount of money in the family threatened to increase from year to year, *despite that* (or *despite the fact that*) *Mr. Middleton's good works were continued* (L. Zangwill, *Beautiful Miss Brooke*, 33).

Notwithstanding that he is being lionized, he still keeps a level head.

He's a scoundrel, *whoever he may be*.

She is always cheerful *in whatever condition her health is*.

Whichever you do here, *whether you go or stay*, you will have reasons to regret it.

Whatever (more indefinite than *whichever*) *you finally decide to do*, tell your father about it before you act.

I shall be quite content *however and whenever you do it*.

However lightly he treated the approaching trial (or *Lightly as he treated the approaching trial*), he became a different man afterwards.

However bad the weather may be (or *Bad as the weather may be*), we shall have to confront it.

However we may assess the merits or defects of the Confucian philosophy (or *Assess the merits or defects of the Confucian philosophy as we may*), the subject of China's religion must always form a subject of the widest interest.

For all that (or simply *for all*) *he seems to dislike me*, I still like him.

They spoke in tones so low that Francis could catch no more than a word or two on an occasion. *For as little as he heard* (or *Although he heard little*) he was convinced that the conversation turned upon himself and his own career (R. L. Stevenson).

Granted that he had the very best intentions, his conduct was productive of great mischief.

Albeit she was angry with Pen, against his mother she had no such feeling (Thackeray, *Pendennis*, Ch. XXI, 275).

. . . of hem alle was ther noon y-slayn, *Al were they sore y-hurt* (Chaucer, *The Knightes Tale*, 1850).

The Moor, *howbeit that I endure him not*, Is of a constant, loving, noble nature (Shakespeare, *Othello*, II, i, 297).

If I have broke anything, I'll pay for 't, *an it cost a pound* (Congreve, *Way of the World*, V, 8).

'Should I lie, madam?' — 'O, I would thou didst, *So* (= *even if*) *half my Egypt were submerged*' (Shakespeare, *Antony and Cleopatra*, II, v, 94).

Whether he succeed(*s*) *or fail*(*s*), we shall have to do our part.

Whether he comes or not, I am not going to worry.

He promised him that, *if* (now usually *whether*) *he fell on the field or survived it*, he would act in a manner worthy of the name of George Osborne (Thackeray, *Vanity Fair*, I, Ch. XXXV).

Stewart was perhaps the most beloved member of Trinity, *whether he were* (**43** II A, last par.) *feeding Rugger blues on plovers' eggs or keeping an early chapel with the expression of an earthbound seraph* (Compton Mackenzie, *Sinister Street*, Ch. V).

Whether I go alone, or whether he go (or *goes*) *with me*, the result will be the same.

Or whether his fall enrag'd him, or how 't was, he did so set his teeth and tear it (Shakespeare, *Coriolanus*, I, iii, 68).

In older English, there was a marked tendency to employ correlatives in concessive sentences, an adversative, *yet*, *still*, *nevertheless*, etc., in the principal proposition corresponding to the concessive conjunction in the subordinate clause: '*Although* all shall be offended, *yet* will not I' (*Mark*, XIV, 29). This adversative often seems superfluous to us today, since this idea is suggested by the context, hence we usually suppress it, following the modern drift toward terse, compact expression; but under the stress of strong feeling we still often employ it: '*Although* it may seem incredible, it is *nevertheless* true.'

1. **Concessive Clause Replaced by Other Constructions.** This clause is often replaced by the following constructions:

a. The concessive adverbial clause is often replaced by a principal proposition, which may be:

aa. An expression of will in the form of an imperative sentence, which, though independent in form, is logically dependent:

'*Laugh as much as you like*, I shall stick to my plan to the bitter end.' 'The massive person of Mr. Bradlaugh is entirely excluded from sight, *crane your neck as you may*.' 'Marietta's the best fore-and-aft, up-and-down little housekeeper on the island, *bar none* and *challenge all comers*' (Wallace Irwin, *Seed of the Sun*, Ch. XII). This is parataxis (**19** 3). We often employ coördination here with two sentences linked by *and*, the first of which is a command: 'Take any form but that *and* my firm nerves shall never tremble.'

The different personal forms of the imperative are quite common here: Third person singular: '*Let him be* the greatest villain in the world, I would not keep from wishing to do some little thing to benefit him.' The old simple subjunctive, a mild volitive subjunctive (**43** II A), frequently serves here as a mild imperative, often with suppressed subject. First person: 'There is no task to bring me; no one will be vexed or uneasy, *linger I ever so late*' (Gissing, *Henry Ryecroft*, II, p. 10). *Willy-nilly*, i.e., *will he, nil* (= *ne will*, the *ne* being an old negative) *he* (= *whether he will or not*), now, however, used as a mere adverb with reference to all persons and numbers, as in '*I, you, he, we*, must go, *willy-nilly*,' but in Shakespeare's time still with the proper person: '*And, will you, nill you*, I will marry you' (*Taming of the Shrew*, II, 273). '*Sink [I] or swim [I]*, I shall undertake it.' '*Say [I]* what I will to the contrary, he tells the story everywhere.' Plural: '*Detest [we]* him as we may, we must acknowledge his greatness.' '*Argue [we]* as we like, *dogmatize [we]* as we please, *experiment [we]* up to the extinction of the canine race, no fellow can ever understand the mysteries and the vagaries of idiosyncrasy.' Third person: 'We cannot receive him, *be he* who he may.' 'Home is home *be it* ever so homely.' 'The business of each day, *be it* selling goods or shipping them, is going on pleasantly.' 'My mental vision is limited as is every man's to a greater or less degree, therefore there are certain great books that have for me no charm, *charm they* ever so many others whose opinions I respect and accept.' 'I shall have to buy the coat, *cost [it]* what it may.' 'I shall go *rain [it]* or *shine [it]*.' 'But *hate [he]* Walpole as he might, the king was absolutely guided by the adroitness of his wife, Caroline of Anspach' (Green). '*Comfort [he]* himself as he would, however, *dream [he]* as he would, Meynell's conscience was always sore for Hester' (Mrs. H. Ward, *Richard Meynell*, Ch. XIV). The suppression of the subject of the volitive forms here is modern. It has resulted from the analogy of the genuine imperative, where the omission of the subject has always been the rule.

bb. As in primitive speech, the concessive idea is still often in colloquial language expressed by simple declarative parataxis (**19** 3): 'The meat is good; *it is a little tough, though* (= *although it is a little tough*). 'I cannot keep these plants alive; *I have watered them well, too*' (= *although I have watered them well*). '*No matter* (= *it is of no importance*) *what he says* (or *it doesn't matter what he says*), I am going' = '*Whatever he may say* (concessive clause), I am going.'

Coördination is also employed here: 'Being the larger, she (the female squirrel) could have whipped him *and not half tried*' (= *even though she hadn't half tried*). 'I cannot keep these plants alive, *and I have watered them well, too.*' We often find here the old appositional type of sentence after *and*, i.e., subject and predicate adjective, participle, or noun lying side by side without being connected by a copula: 'They ne'er car'd for us yet: suffer us to famish, *and their store-houses cramm'd with grain*' (Shakespeare, *Coriolanus*, I, ɪ, 81). This construction is especially common in popular speech. See **19** 3.

cc. Instead of a concessive clause we sometimes find a clause in question word-order, which was originally an unreal wish. This construction was first used in unreal conditional sentences, as described in **31** 1 *c*, and was later transferred to the concessive clause, as in the case of other features of the conditional clause which were employed also in the closely related concessive clause: '*Were the danger even greater*, I should feel compelled to go.' Some adverb, as *even* in this example, now differentiates the concessive from the conditional clause. This form of the concessive clause is unknown in Old English.

As described in **31** 1 *b*, a clause with question word-order, originally an independent question, is used as a conditional clause. This construction is sometimes employed in the closely related concessive clause: 'I, marrie, here comes majestie in pompe, Resplendent Sol, chief planet of the heauens: He is our Seruent, *lookes he ne're* (now *ever*) *so big*' (Thomas Nashe, *Svmmers Last Will and Testament*, l. 443, A.D. 1600). 'Mr. Gibson bowed, much pleased at such a compliment from such a man, *was he lord or not*' (Mrs. Gaskell, *Wives and Daughters*, II, p. 114, A.D. 1865).

b. The concessive idea sometimes finds expression in a relative clause: 'Many American boys *who* (= *although they*) *have had few advantages in their youth* have worked their way into prominence.'

2. Abridgment of Concessive Clause. The abridgment of the concessive clause is very common. Often in the form of a predicate appositive participle, adjective, or noun, sometimes as in primitive speech without a subordinating conjunction, sometimes under the influence of the full clause with a subordinating conjunction, as explained in **27** 5 and **20** 3: 'From dawn till dark in this car, *driving* or *riding*, you'll never feel that you have put a whole day's miles behind you' (Advertisement). '*Well or sick, calm or worried* (or *whether well or sick, calm or worried*), she is always restrained in her expression.' '*Though sick,* she went to school.' 'For lovers' hours are long, *though seeming short*' (Shakespeare, *Venus and Adonis,* 842). 'His critics, *though outvoted,* have not been silenced.' 'The statutes, *if not good,* are tolerable.' 'The rumor, *however incredible,* was believed by the natives.' '*Vagabond or no vagabond,* he is a human being and deserves pity.' '*While admitting that he had no sympathy with private capitalists,* M. Dzerjinski said Soviet Russia could not exist without the participation of private traders in the general trade of the country' (*Chicago Tribune,* April 4, 1925).

As explained in **32** (7th par.), a predicate appositive noun in connection with a following relative clause often forms a concessive clause: '*Whig as* (relative pronoun = *that*) *he was and rather a rancorous one at that,* Creevey was a welcome person even to the Duke of Wellington.' '*Strong man that he is,* General Botha has been severely put to the test during the past few weeks.'

The participle is sometimes in apposition with a pronoun contained in a possessive adjective: '*Waking or sleeping,* this subject is always in *my* mind.'

Where the reference is general or indefinite, the present participle is here, as in the closely related conditional clause in **31** 2, often used absolutely, i.e., without an expressed subject, sometimes accompanied by *even,* which clearly differentiates the concessive from the conditional clause: '*Granting that this is true,* the difficulty is not removed.' '*Even assuming a great willingness on the part of the members to work,* few are properly prepared for the task.' '*Admitting* (or *even admitting*) *that the Governor was provoked,* his procedure is censurable.' '*Conceding his superiority as a scholar,* it is evident that he is inferior as a man.' Compare **17** 4.

The appositional construction is sometimes still verbless as in primitive speech: 'Right or wrong — my country.'

The adjective here sometimes appears as an adherent (**10** I) adjective instead of a predicate appositive: 'With a dogged perseverance and a keen, *if narrow,* insight into affairs President Kruger has worked with a single object.' 'This *óld wóman* dolls herself up like a young lady' = 'This woman dolls herself up like a young lady, *although* she is old.' The adjective is often in the substantive relation (**57** 1), i.e., stands alone, like a substantive, pointing to a following or preceding noun with which it is associated in thought: 'It is one of the most spacious, *if not the most spacious*, of salons.' 'It is one of the finest poems produced in recent years, *if not the finest.*'

The abridged statement is sometimes an elliptical form of the full clause: '[*whether he*] *Drink or* [*do*] *not drink* he must pay.' 'The navy exists for the sole purpose of ensuring, [*whether there be*] *war or no war*, that the British people shall be properly fed.' 'Mr. Cecil Chesterton's article, "Israel a Nation," resolved itself into an attack on the political status of the Jews in the British commonwealth, while my reply to some of his statements must, *albeit* [*it is done*] *unwillingly*, assume a more or less defensive attitude' (*British Review*). '*Whatever the immediate result* [*may be*], there can be no doubt that the dispute has raised issues which can no longer be ignored.' In the last example, however, the subordinate clause may be the absolute nominative construction described in **17** 3 A *f*.

The abridged form is often that of a prepositional phrase, especially one containing the word *all:* 'His wife clung to him *with all his faults.*' '*With all I've done, and all I've spent on my garden*, it's fussy compared to this.' '*For all his learning* he is a mean man.' 'Well, if I did, I shall do as I like *for all him*' (Thomas Hardy, *Jude the Obscure*). 'It's clearing up *after all.*' 'The rain spoiled a part of our fun, but we had, *after all*, a fine time.' 'He is a blunt man, but he is kind of heart *after all.*' Often in connection with a gerund: 'But we haven't got any wind, *for all the barometer falling*' (Joseph Conrad, *Typhoon*, Ch. VII). Often after *in spite of, despite,* or *notwithstanding,* even where there is no *all* present: '*In spite of* (or *despite*, or *notwithstanding*) *his untiring devotion to the community*, he has not received the recognition he deserves.' Instead of *in spite of that* we sometimes use *at that:* '*At that* (i.e., in spite of the very heavy duties of her social position) Mrs. Coolidge gets a good deal of fun out of her life in the White House' (Winifred Mallon in *Liberty*, Feb. 28, 1925).

The concessive clause can sometimes be abridged to an infinitive clause when the subject of the infinitive is the same as that of the main proposition: 'You couldn't do that *to save your life.*'

CLAUSE OF PURPOSE

33. Conjunctions. *The clause of purpose* or *final clause*, as it is often called, states the purpose or direct end of the action of the principal proposition. It is introduced by the conjunctions: *that*, old but still often used, more commonly now, however, replaced by the more expressive forms *in order that* (i.e., *with the purpose that*), quite modern but by reason of its distinctive form in wide use in choice language, and the old but still very common *so that* or in colloquial speech simple *so; as*, much used in older English, but now replaced by *that; for the purpose that, to the end that; till = in order that* in Irish English, which preserves here an older literary meaning; *in the hope that;* after a negative or a question *but that* or more commonly *unless that;* three forms to express apprehension, *that — not, for fear, for fear that,* and sometimes *lest*, which is from older *thy* (old instrumental case form of *that*) *less the*, literally, *on that account that — less* (with negative force = *not*); in older English with the force of *that, so that, in order that,* also the following conjunctions: *because, for, for that, for because, to the intent that.* Also another conjunction, *so as,* was once widely employed and to a limited extent is still a living form. It corresponds to Old English *swa swa* (i.e., *so so*), and thus has been in use from the oldest period to our day. At present it is for the most part confined to popular speech in the full clause, while in the abridged clause it is widely used also in the literary language. In Old English, it was not used at all in the abridged clause, which shows that it entered the abridged clause later under the influence of the full clause at a time when it was in use in the full clause.

The conjunctions *that, so that, so as,* and simple *so* are also used in the closely related clause of result. In both clauses they perform the same function and have the same origin, as described in **28 5**. The two clauses are, in the literary language, often differentiated not by their conjunctions but by the use of different moods. The indicative in the clause of result often represents the statement as an actual result, while in the clause of purpose *may, might, shall, should,* or sometimes the simple subjunctive form of the verb, represents the result as only planned or desired: 'Turn the lantern só *that we may see what it is*' (clause of purpose), but 'He turned the lantern só *that I saw what it was*' (clause of result). 'I am going to the lecture early *so that I may get a good seat*' (clause of purpose), but 'I went to the lecture early *so that I got a good seat*' (clause of result). There is often, however, no formal difference between the two clauses, the meaning alone distinguishing them. The subjunctive is frequently used in clauses of result to represent the result as possible or as desired or demanded: 'It has cleared up beautifully, so that he *may* (or *might*) come after all.' 'You must proceed in such a manner that it *shall* not offend the public.' On the other hand, the indicative is often used in clauses of purpose to indicate confidence of realization, especially in colloquial language: 'He is going to the lecture early so that he'*ll get* a good seat.' A pause here before the conjunction *so that* converts the clause of purpose into a clause of pure result: 'He is going to the lecture early, so that he'*ll get* a good seat.' A clause of pure result is logically an independent proposition and requires a slight pause to indicate its independence.

The clause introduced by *for fear* was originally a causal clause, but the idea of cause here is often overshadowed by that of purpose: 'She walked softly *for fear she should wake the baby.*'

Examples:

He told it só *that it might not hurt our feelings.*

I wish to haue them speake só *as* (now *that*) *it may well appeare that the braine doth gouerne the tonge* (Roger Ascham, *The Scholemaster*, p. 4, A.D. 1570).

They are climbing higher *that* (or *so that*, or *in order that*) *they may get a better view.*

They climbed higher *that* (*so that*, or *in order that*) *they might get a better view.*

'They are hurrying *that* (*so that*, or *in order that*) *they may not miss the train*,' or in colloquial speech *so that* (or simple *so*) *they won't miss the train.*

'They hurried *that* (*so that*, or *in order that*) *they might not miss the train*,' or in colloquial speech *so that* (or simple *so*) *they wouldn't miss the train.*

If a man be asked a question to answer, but to repeat the Question before hee answer is well, *that hee be* (now more commonly *may be*) *sure to understand it, to avoid absurdity* (Ben Jonson, *Discoveries*, p. 6, A.D. 1641).

Come here now *till* (= *in order that*) *I beat you* (an Irish mother to her child, quoted from Hayden and Hartog's *The Irish Dialect of English*).

He never comes *but that* (or *unless that*) *he may scold us.*

'He is keeping quiet *that he may not disturb his father*' (or *lest*, or *for fear*, or *for fear that, he disturb*, or *shall disturb*, or much more commonly *may*, *should*, or *might*, *disturb his father*, but *for fear he will disturb his father*, when the desire is to indicate that this result will surely follow if great care is not taken to prevent it).

He jotted the name down *for fear* (or *lest*) *he should* (or *might*) *forget it.*

Say as little as possible about it to Sybel *lest she repeated* (or more commonly *should* or *might repeat*) *my account of the Happy Valley to that scoundrel Patterne* (Sir Harry Johnston, *The Man Who Did the Right Thing*, Ch. XVII, p. 308).

They axed him . . . *because* (= *that*) *they might acuse hym* (Tyndale, *Matthew*, XII, 10).

And *for* (= *that*) *the time shall not seem tedious*, I'll tell thee what befell me (Shakespeare, *III Henry VI*, III, i, 9).

For that our kingdom's earth should not be soil'd With that dear blood which it hath fostered . . . Therefore, we banish you our territories (Shakespeare, *Richard the Second*, I, iii, 125).

Also he weped not onely, but also very sore and pytefully *for bycause he might wasshe euery synne in hym with his bytter teres* (John Fisher, E.E.T.S., Ex. Ser., XXVII, p. 17, early sixteenth century).

Syth so good and so holy a man desyred of god to be sharpely punysshed in this lyfe rather than after this lyfe, *to thentent* (= *the intent*) *he myght be able* to haue the everlastynge kyngdome of heauen (*ib.*, p. 41).

'What have you done to your neck?' — 'Oh, my wife put that in it *so's* (= *so as* = literary *so that*) *I'd remember to get some things from town*' (Punch).

Father has the first one (i.e., first whistle) blown at half-past six, *so's* (= literary *so that*) *the men can have time to get their things ready* (Dorothy Canfield, *The Brimming Cup*, Ch. VI).

With words nearer admiration then (now *than*) liking she would extoll his excellencies, the good lines of his shape, the power of his witte, the valiantnes of his courage, the fortunatenes of his successes, *so as* (now *so that*) *the father might finde in her a singular love towardes him* (Sir Philip Sidney, *Arcadia*, Book II, Ch. XV, A.D. 1590).

1. Adverbial Clause of Purpose Replaced by Other Constructions. We often prefer to express the idea of purpose by a grammatical form other than an adverbial clause of purpose, namely, by:

a. A relative clause: 'Envoys were sent *who should sue for peace.*' Compare **43** II B *e.*

b. Instead of a subordinate clause of purpose we often employ an independent coördinate proposition connected with the preceding proposition by *and:* 'Won't you come *and see us?*' Compare **19** 3.

2. Abridgment of Clause of Purpose. In this category abridgment often takes place, usually in the form of an infinitive clause with *to* when the subject of the principal proposition or some other word in it can serve as the subject of the infinitive, and in the form of an infinitive clause with *for . . . to* when the clause has a subject of its own: '*I* am waiting *to go with John when he comes,*' but '*I* am waiting *for them to go* before I speak of the matter.' 'I rang *to them to come up,*' but 'I rang *for breakfast to be brought up.*' Even where there is some word in the principal proposition that might serve as the subject of the infinitive, the infinitive often has a subject of its own to remove all ambiguity and make the thought perfectly clear: 'The lad had pulled at his mother *for her to take notice of him.*'

Instead of the infinitive with *for . . . to* here we often find in older English a *to*-infinitive with a nominative as subject: 'Pray to thy Son aboue the sterris clere, *He* (now *for him*) *to vouchasef* by thy mediacion, To pardon thy seruaunt' (John Skelton, ed. by Dyce, I, 14).

Instead of the infinitive with *to* it is now also quite common to place *so as*, *in order*, or *on purpose* before the old *to*-form to bring out more clearly the idea of purpose: 'I am going early *so as to* (or *in order to*) *get a good seat.*' 'I went to Germany *on purpose to study this question.*'

In older English, a *so-that*-clause of purpose could be abridged to an infinitive clause with *so to* when the subject of the principal proposition could serve as the subject of the infinitive: 'Finding by his wisdome that she was not altogether faultlesse, he pronounced she should all her life be kept prisoner among certaine women of religion like vestall nonnes *so to* (now *so as to*) *repaye their touched honour of her house with well observing a stryctt profession of chastitie*' (Sir Philip Sidney, *Arcadia*, Book V, p. 173, A.D. 1593).

In older English, an *as*-clause of purpose could be abridged to an infinitive clause with *as to:* 'The messinger found Argalus at a castle of his owne sitting in a parler with the faire Parthenia, he reading in a booke, she bye him *as to heare him reade*' (Sir Philip Sidney, *Arcadia*, Book III, Ch. VII, A.D. 1590), now *to hear him read.*

Before the *to* of the infinitive, which has for its subject some word in the principal proposition, we find occasionally in Old English and frequently in Middle English and early Modern English a *for* of different origin from the *for* described on page 343 and more in detail in **21** *e*. This *for*, like *to*, meant purpose and was placed before *to* merely to bring out this idea more concretely; but, as its force was not vividly felt, it was gradually replaced by the more expressive forms *so as*, *in order*, *on purpose:* 'Are ye come out as against a thief with swords and staves *for to* (now simple *to*, or *in order to*) take me?' (*Matthew*, XXVI, 55). This old literary usage is well preserved in popular Irish English: 'There will a car be sent and two boys from the Union *for to* bear her out from the house' (Lady Gregory, *McDonough's Wife*). Also in English popular speech: 'She's an orphan, studying *for to* be a governess' (Pinero, *The Schoolmistress*, Act I). For a description of the historical development here and its reason see **21** *e*.

In oldest English, we often find the simple infinitive here, a usage which even in present-day speech in certain set expressions still lingers on quite generally in all parts of the territory: 'I'll go *see*' (Tarkington, *Alice Adams*, Ch. IV). For the original meaning of this form see **11** 2.

The principal proposition upon which an infinitive clause with *to* depends is often suppressed: '*To be sincere,* [I must tell you] you have not done your best.' *'To tell the truth,* [I have to say] the lecture was a great disappointment to me.'

The full clause is often replaced by the gerundial construction after the preposition *for* and the prepositional phrases *for the purpose of, with the object of, with the intention of:* 'We planted a hedge *for preventing the cattle from straying.*' 'I am not here to-night *for the purpose of making a speech.*' 'I didn't come *with the object* (or *intention*) *of destroying the good feeling prevailing among you.*' Instead of the gerund we often use the prepositional phrase *in support of* (= *to the end that he, they, may, might support*): 'Several representative citizens volunteered their services yesterday *in support of the traction ordinance.*'

To indicate continued activity we employ the present participle: 'He went *hunting, fishing, swimming.*' 'He took me out *riding.*' 'Axemen were put to work *getting out timber for bridges*' (U. S. Grant, *Personal Memoirs,* II, 47). 'Joe had been sitting up nights *building facts and arguments together into a mighty unassailable array*' (Mark Twain, *Letter to W. D. Howells,* Christmas Eve, 1880). 'The populace were up there *observing her fortunate performance and rejoicing over it*' (*id., Joan of Arc,* II, Ch. XVIII).

In the early history of our country a gerundial construction was often employed where we now use a present participle — a gerund after *on* or *to:* 'In the beginning of March they sent her (i.e., the pinnace) well vitaled to the eastward *on fishing*' (Bradford, *History of Plymouth Plantation,* p. 165, A.D. 1630–1648). 'Then all went *to seeking of shelfish,* which at low water they digged out of the sands' (*ib.,* p. 149). At this early time the present participle was used here alongside of the gerund, later for the most part replacing it.

CLAUSE OF MEANS

34. The clause of means indicates the means by which the effect mentioned in the principal proposition is produced: 'I recognized him *by the fact* (a formal introduction to the following clause) *that he limped,*' or in abridged form, *by his limping.* 'All strove to escape *by what means they might.*' 'I have been guided more *by what I myself know of the situation* than *by what he said.*' In such constructions there is always a preposition, so that the clause in fact is a prepositional clause and is identical in form with the prepositional clause in **24** IV. Hence it is not further discussed here.

Abridgment to a gerundial or participial clause is very common here: '*By holding* (gerund) *on to the rope firmly,* or *holding* (present participle) *on to the rope firmly,* I came safe to shore.' '*By John's holding the ladder firmly,* I succeeded in climbing onto the roof.' 'He left a considerable fortune — made it *selling* (present participle) *pictures.*'

WORD-ORDER

35. The word-order has been a matter of constant attention throughout the syntax, so that the details have already been presented under the different grammatical categories. Attention is here directed to only the general larger outlines.

In English there are three word-orders: the verb in the second, the third, or the first place.

1. Verb in the Second or Third Place. In older English, the verb in a normal declarative sentence was usually in the second place; but now under certain conditions, described on page 349, it is usually in the third place.

The most common order is: subject in the first place, verb in the second: '*The boy loves* his dog.' This is called *normal order*.

If any other word for emphasis, or to establish a nearer relation with what goes on before, or because it lies nearer in thought, stands in the first place, the verb often still maintains the second place, followed by the subject in the third place. This is called *inverted order*. This order, once common in English, is now as a living force pretty well shattered. It is now most common in the case of emphatic adverbs and other emphatic modifiers of the verb which are made prominent by being put into the first place in the sentence. We cannot, however, freely place emphatic adverbs and objects into the first place immediately before the verb. We usually do this when not only the adverb or object is emphatic but also the verb. In such cases we usually employ auxiliaries, so that the real verb appears in the form of an infinitive or participle which contains only the verbal meaning and hence when stressed calls especial attention to the activity in question: '*Séven times* did this intrepid general *repéat* his attack.' '*Bítterly* did we *repént* our decision.' '*Gládly* would he now have *consénted* to the terms which he had once rejected.' '*Particularly* did Florian *rejóice* in the tale of the saint's birth' (Cabell, *The High Place*, Ch. II). '*Néver* had I even *dréamed* of such a thing.' 'Bitter as

347

the pill was, *rárely* did he *fáil* to force it down.' 'Only *ónce* before have I *séen* such a sight.' 'Only *twó* had merciful death *reléased* from their sufferings.' '*Whóm* did you *méet?*' '*Whén* did you *méet* him?' '*Whére* did you say she *pút* it?' where the interrogative adverb *where* is even brought forward from the subordinate clause to introduce the sentence. The light auxiliary in all such cases has become attached to the strongly stressed adverb or object, so that the inverted order has become fixed here.

By glancing at the examples it will be noticed that the most common forms causing inversion are negatives, interrogatives, and adverbs expressing restriction. We today feel these three elements as the cause of inversion — not the accent, for we invert in questions when neither the interrogative nor the verb is stressed: 'When will you go *néxt?*' We invert in all questions introduced by an interrogative object or adverb simply because inversion has become fixed here. Similarly, we invert after a restriction of any kind, even after a clause, so that it cannot be a strongly stressed *word* that causes the inversion: 'Only when the artist understands these psychological principles *can he* work in harmony with them' (Spencer). Originally, the accent was the controlling force and still is felt here, but the controlling force now is the association of inversion with negatives, interrogatives, and restrictions.

When the principal proposition is inserted in a direct quotation or follows it, the principal verb may sometimes still, in accordance with the old inverted order, uniformly stand before the subject, but it is now more common here to regulate the word-order by the modern group stress, so that the heavier word, be it subject or verb, stands last in the group, just as elsewhere the heaviest word stands last: '"Harry," *contìnued the old mán*, "before you choose a wife, you must know my position,"' but '"George," *shè excláimed*, "this is the happiest moment of my life."' '"You have acted selfishly," *wàs her cóld retórt*,' but '"You have acted selfishly," *shè replíed*.' In accordance with this principle the subject here almost always stands before a compound tense form or a combination of verbal forms: '"You must think that over again," our dear *mòther would sáy*.' The word-order is similarly regulated by the modern group-stress in the case of a sentence which is inserted with the force of a sentence adverb (p. 132) within a sentence or a subordinate clause: 'The wind whistled and moaned as if, *thòught Míchael*, all the devils in hell were trying to break into the holy building' (Compton Mackenzie, *Youth's Encounter*, Ch. V), but 'The wind whistled and moaned as if, *it séemed to him*, all the devils in hell were trying to break into

the holy building.' As the word-order verb before the subject
is so often found with quotations, as just described, it has become
associated with quotations, so that it is sometimes employed at
the beginning of a sentence to introduce a quotation: 'In Phila-
delphia I met the black author, publisher, and sidewalk retailer
of a work entitled "The Ethiopian-American of Ancient and
Modern Education." *Writes he*, "The name Ethiopian-American
was founded and edited in order that we might discontinue the
nickname Negro"' (Rollin Lynde Hartt in *World's Work* for
July, 1924, p. 321).

Where the old inverted word-order is seemingly preserved, it
is usually, except in the cases described in the three preceding
paragraphs, not in a strict sense inversion. The subject instead
of standing before the verb has been put at the end of the sentence for emphasis, as explained in **3** *a*, p. 4: 'Now comes *my bést
tríck.*' 'To the list may be added *the fóllowing námes.*' 'Down
the street came *a gírl and a dóg, rather a small girl and quite a
behemothian dog*' (H. Sydnor Harrison, *Queed*, Ch. I). In this
still very common construction, the introductory words are not
usually emphatic. Sometimes, however, they are stressed, but
usually less strongly than the following stressed subject: '*Thén
came the dréaded énd!* And *fást* into this perilous gulf of night
walked *Bosínney* (name) and *fást* after him walked *Géorge*' (Galsworthy, *The Man of Property*, p. 321). '*Súch* are *the life and
cháracter of this man!*' Though this construction is in general
quite common, it has its limitations, as described in **3** *a*, p. 4.

One feature of the old inverted order is still well preserved
in declarative sentences. We still quite commonly put into the
first place a heavily stressed word in the predicate other than
a finite form of a verb; but now, except after a negative or a
restriction, or where there is a heavy subject, as described above,
the subject usually follows the introductory word or phrase, and
is itself followed immediately by the verb: 'The gallant fellow
fought for appearances and *dówn* he went' (Meredith, *The Ordeal
of Richard Feverel*, Ch. II). '*Cantánkerous cháp* Roger always
was!' (Galsworthy, *The Man of Property*, p. 24). '*Very gráteful*
they were for my offer.' '*Lúcky it is* that we know her name.'
'*This thréat* he was quite unable to carry out.' We sometimes find
the infinitive or participle of a compound verbal predicate in the
first place followed immediately by the subject: '*Grówl you* will,
but *gó* you must.' '"If you telegraph at once, he can be stopped,"
said the Inspector. And *stópped* he was.' It should be noted,
however, that where the subject is quite heavy it *must* stand
after the verb at or near the end, even though the sentence is

introduced by an emphatic element: 'Úp went *this róaring drágonfly in which Peter was sitting* . . . Úp they went and úp, until the world seemed nearly all sea, and the coast was far away' (H. G. Wells, *Joan and Peter*, Ch. XIII), where in the first proposition the subject stands after the verb on account of its length and heaviness, but in the second proposition stands before the verb in accordance with the general rule. In all these sentences the verb stands in the *third place*, which, except after an interrogative, or negative, or where there is a heavy subject, is the usual position for the verb in a sentence introduced by an emphatic modifier of the verb or a predicate noun or adjective.

There is another common word-order here where we desire to put some important word (subject, object, adverb, adverbial phrase, predicate noun, or adjective) in the important initial position. We construe the emphatic word or phrase as a predicate whether it is actually a predicate or not and place it after *it is*, so that, though in a formal sense the predicate stands in the third place, the verb in the second place, the subject in the first place, the emphatic word in reality stands in the first place, for it is preceded only by *it is*, a mere formal introduction: 'It is *Jóhn* that is guilty.' 'It was *on Sáturday* that I saw him.' For fuller description of this construction see **4** C II (p. 12) and **21** *c*.

The word-order with the verb in the third place has not only in large measure destroyed the inverted order in declarative sentences, as described on page 349, but it has also for the same reason displaced it for the most part in exclamations, where inversion is very old but now little used: 'What good friends *horses have been* to us for thousands of years!' 'What cheek *he has!*' 'How diligent *you are!*' We sometimes, however, still find the old inverted order here, especially in choice prose and poetry: 'How pleasant *is this híll* where the road widens! And how beautiful, again, *is this pátch of cómmon* at the hilltop with the clear pool!' Here again, as illustrated for the declarative sentence, the old inverted order is only seemingly preserved. In most cases the subject instead of standing before the verb in its usual position has been put at the end for emphasis. Occasionally, however, the old inverted word-order is still employed: 'Judith, Judith, how lovely *are you!*' (Mary Johnston, *The Long Roll*, Ch. XVII). The old inverted word-order, of course, is used regularly where the expression approaches the nature of a question, especially where the answer is self-evident and no answer is expected: '*Won't she* live to know what she has done! I can tell her of one that won't pity her' (Trollope, *Prime Minister*, Ch. XVI). Exclamations containing a negative usually have inverted order, as they contain a question: 'How many times *had she* not sat there, in white frocks, her hair hanging down as now!' (Galsworthy, *Free-lands*, Ch. XV), a blending of 'How many times *she had* sat there!' and '*Had she not* sat there many times?'

Originally, the normal word-order, i.e., the subject in the first place, was identical with the inverted order, that is, the subject stood in the first place for emphasis, or to establish a relation with what preceded it. This is not now its usual force. The normal word-order has become the form of expression suited to the mind in its normal condition of steady activity and easy movement, from which it only departs under the stress of emotion, or for logical reasons, or in conformity to fixed rules.

a. ORIGIN OF THE WORD-ORDER WITH THE VERB IN THE SECOND PLACE. In oldest English, the verb didn't stand in the second or third place so regularly as today. We often find it at or near the end of the sentence. This oldest word-order, as illustrated also in 6 A, is still possible: 'This under such circumstances I often *do*.' The verb is here at the end preceded by its modifiers. This principle of placing the modifiers of a word before it is still very common in old compounds or group-words, which represent the oldest type of expression in the language: hóme-màde = made at home, táble-lèg = leg of the table, éar-rìng = ring for the ear, éyelàshes = lashes of the eye, etc. Such words arose at a time when there was no inflection, so that the fixed word-order alone indicated the grammatical relations. In oldest English, this old word-order was still in use, although the rich inflection at this time now made it possible to deviate from the old word-order. The stress on the first element of old compounds indicates clearly that the modifier was more strongly stressed than the governing word. This explains the frequent changes in the word-order of the sentence, which ever became more common from the oldest historic times on. The emphatic modifiers of the verb were often put at the end of the sentence after the verb in order to create the feeling of suspense and thus increase the emphasis. As the verb was thus not the center of attention and was often weakly stressed, it gradually settled into the weakly stressed position after the subject or the strongly accented object or adverb which often introduced the sentence.

Besides this rhythmical principle, there was also a psychological force active in establishing the verb in this position. The verb contains the basic idea of the predication, so that there was often, especially in long sentences, a tendency to bring it near the subject in order that the subject and predicate together might at the outset make clear the general line of thought and thus relieve the tension somewhat and make it possible to concentrate the attention upon the important details which were to be presented later. This new word-order with the verb following the subject must not, however, be thought of as something English. It took place long before the historic period, and is indeed very old. In our oldest literature both word-orders — the verb following the subject and the verb at or near the end — were in use, but gradually the newer word-order with the verb after the subject supplanted the older. Thus it gradually became usual to place the subject first, the verb next, and then after them arrange the modifiers of the verb in positions in accordance with their importance and the grammatical relations, so that the word-order gradually assumed the functions of the old case endings, which now for the most part as useless forms little by little disappeared. The originally emphatic order with the modifiers of the verb after the verb became the new normal or inverted order as they exist today, the latter of which has in large measure been replaced by the word-order verb in the third place. These new types, however, are not entirely rigid since we often put an adverb between subject and verb, as in 'I *often do* that' and sometimes even put the verb in the last place, as illustrated on page 351.

The present word-order became established in the principal proposition first. The old word-order with the verb at the end lingered on in the subordinate clause for centuries. The evident reason is that the subordinate clause is felt as a grammatical unit, a subject, object, or adverbial element. The attention is directed not so much to important details as to the thought as a whole. In the old word-order with the verb at the end, the verb contained the basic thought and, standing as it did in the important position at the end, had a distinct stress, though often not so much as its important modifiers. Though this old word-order was at last given up also in the subordinate clause and the word-order in general conformed to that employed in the principal proposition for the sake of the advantages of that word-order in making the grammatical relations clear, the strong stress of the verb still often distinguishes the subordinate clause: '*As soon as I éntered the* room, I nòticed the disórder.' Where as here the subordinate clause is clearly felt as a unit with a definite function in the sentence, the verb receives a little stronger stress than its modifiers, while in the principal proposition the modifiers are usually stressed more strongly than the verb. Of course, however, the more independent a clause becomes the more the attention is usually directed towards the important details. On the other hand, if the attention in the principal proposition is directed to the thought as a whole the verb or verbal phrase of the predicate receives the stress: 'A brave man never *forsákes his post.*'

2. **Verb in the First Place.** As seen on page 347, the first place in the sentence is emphatic. In oldest English, however, this emphatic position was not only reserved for the subject and important objects and adverbs, as in the examples given in 1, but also an emphatic verb could stand in the first place. This older order of things survives in wishes, in expressions of will containing an imperative and often in those containing a volitive subjunctive, also in questions that require *yes* or *no* for an answer: '*Wére* he only here!' '*Hánd* me that book!' '*Cóme* what will.' '*Cóst* what it may.' 'Did he *gó?*' in older English '*Wént* he?'

In questions requiring *yes* or *no* for an answer only the outward

form of the older usage is preserved; the spirit is lost. In these
questions, the personal part of the verb now stands in the first
place, as in older English the simple verb. As a mere auxiliary
it hasn't strong stress. But notice that in both the older and the
newer usage the real verb is stressed. Today we prefer to secure
emphasis in questions by the employment of another old Germanic
principle. We introduce the sentence by an unimportant word,
in this case an unstressed auxiliary, and withhold for a time the
real predicate, the infinitive, thus creating the feeling of suspense,
which imparts emphasis.

If in questions requiring *yes* or *no* for an answer the question
is asked in a tone of surprise, the form is that of a declarative
sentence; but it is spoken with rising inflection: 'You *are going?*'
We may employ the declarative form also when we do not understand a statement and ask for the repetition of it: 'He *went*
whére?' = 'Whére did you say he *went?*'

In oldest English, the verb could stand in the first place also
in lively narrative, since action is here the conspicuous feature.
As illustrated in **4** II C, p. 13, the spirit of this old principle is still
preserved, since we now in lively narrative place the verb as near
the beginning of the sentence as possible, sometimes even put it
in the first place, as in oldest English.

CHAPTER XVIII

TENSES

36. Tenses and Their Sequence. There are four absolute tenses (present, past, present perfect, and future), which express time from the standpoint of the moment in which the speaker is speaking without reference to some other act; and two relative tenses (past perfect and future perfect), which express time relatively to the preceding absolute tenses.

Originally, there were only two tenses in English — the present and the past. The six tenses now in use are made up of a combination of verbal forms, but in each tense there is always a present or a past tense. A tense containing a present tense is called a present tense form: he *writes*, he *is* writing, he *has* written, he *will* write, etc. A tense containing a past tense is called a past tense form: he *wrote*, he *was* writing, he *had* written, etc.

In English, there is a general rule of sequence when a past tense form precedes. When the governing proposition has a past tense form, a past tense form usually follows whether it is suitable to the occasion or not: 'He *says* he *is* going tomorrow,' but 'He *said* he *was* going tomorrow.' 'He *says* he *will* go tomorrow,' but 'He *said* he *would* go tomorrow.' 'He *says* he *has* often done it,' but 'He *said* he *had* often done it.' 'He *will* surely *decide* to do it before his father *comes*,' but 'He *decided* to do it before his father *came*.'

This fixed sequence, however, is often not observed if it is

354

desired to represent something as customary, habitual, characteristic, or as universally true: 'He *asked* the guard what time the train usually *starts*.' 'He *told* me that Mary *is* quite diligent, *works* hard, *sings* beautifully.' 'I *remembered* that boys *will be* boys, and that you *cannot* put old heads on young shoulders.' 'He *didn't* seem to know that nettles *sting*.' 'Columbus *proved* that the world *is* round.' It is also not observed after a past subjunctive, as this form indicates present time: 'I *should say* that this book *meets* your requirements.'

There is a modern tendency to disregard the old sequence in certain subjunctive categories, as described in **43 II B** *a*, *b*, **44 II 3**, **44 II 5 A** *a* (2nd par.), **44 II 10**.

There is also a tendency in indirect discourse to break through the old sequence when a more accurate expression suggests itself. Thus instead of the first example in the third paragraph we may with greater accuracy say: 'He *said* he *is* going tomorrow.' Other examples are given in **44 II 3** *a*.

37. Uses of the Tenses. The following articles apply principally to the tenses of the indicative. The tenses of the subjunctive are treated under the head of the subjunctive mood, **41–44.**

1. Present Tense.

a. It represents an action as now going on, or a state as now existing: 'He *is* writing.' 'There he *comes*.' 'He *is* quite sick.'

b. It represents an act as habitual, customary, repeated, characteristic: 'He *lives* in town in winter, in the country in summer.' 'I *call* on him whenever I *go* to town.' 'He *writes* beautifully.' 'He *loves* his mother tenderly.'

c. It expresses a general truth: 'Twice two *is* four.'

d. HISTORICAL PRESENT. In narrative, especially in a lively style, the historical present is much used to make more vivid past events and bring them nearer the hearer: 'Soon there *is* a crowd around the little prostrate form, the latest victim of reckless speeding. A strong man *holds* the little fellow in his arms. The crowd *makes* room for a little woman who *cries* out, "Give me my boy!"'

The historical present, though now a favorite in a lively literary style, was almost unknown in the literature of the Old English period. It did not become common in the literary language until about 1300. From then on its frequent use indicates that its evident advantages in lively description had at last become appreciated in the higher forms of literature.

Somewhat similar to the historical present is the *annalistic present*, which registers historical facts as matters of present interest: 'It *is* not till the close of the Old English period that Scandinavian words *appear*. Even Late Northumbrian (of about 970) *is* entirely free from Scandinavian influence . . . With the accession of Edward the Confessor in 1042 Norman influence *begins*' (Sweet, *New English Grammar*, I, p. 216).

e. USE OF THE PRESENT TENSE FOR THE FUTURE. As in oldest English, when there was no distinct form for a future tense, the present is still often used for the future, especially when some adverb of time, or conjunction of time or condition, or the situation makes clear the thought: 'I *am going*.' 'He *is coming* (compare **38** 1, 9th par.) soon.' 'I want to see you and talk something over, so I *am running* (compare **38** 1, 9th par.) down on Sunday afternoon' (Galsworthy, *The Country House*, I, Ch. VII). 'I *am leaving* (compare **38** 1, 9th par.) Rose Cottage today' (Mrs. Craik, *John Halifax, Gentleman*, Ch. XV). 'When *does* the ship sail?' 'It *sails* tonight.' 'When *does* the train start?' 'When *does* the lease run out?' 'When *can* you start?' 'When *must* you be back?' 'The sooner you *come* back, the better it will be.' 'When you *try* it a second time, you'll succeed better.' 'We are waiting until he *comes*.' 'If you *move*, I shoot.' This old use of the present tense for future time is best preserved in abridged infinitival and gerundial clauses, where it is the regular future: 'He is planning *to go*.' 'He promises *to do* it.' 'I am counting on his *doing* it.'

The idea of futurity often lies in the present tense form *am* (*is*, etc.) *going* in connection with a *to*-infinitive, originally a clause of purpose or result, so that the conception of intention or result is often still felt alongside of the idea of futurity: 'I *am going to walk* to Geisingen; from there I shall go by train to Engen.' 'What *are you going to be* when you are grown up?' Often to express an earnest purpose: 'I *am going to put* my foot down on that!' The idea of futurity is often associated with that of immediateness: 'Look out! I *am going to shoot*.' 'I *am going to call* on him soon.' 'I am afraid *it is going to rain*.' This future form often points to a result either near at hand or farther off with the implication of the certainty of fulfilment: 'This show *is going to attract* a good deal of attention.' 'He is an unusually bright boy, and is moreover very energetic and diligent. He *is going to be* an important man sometime.' Compare **38** 2 *b ee* (4th par.).

The idea of futurity and immediateness lies in the present tense of *to be on the point* (or *verge*) *of* in connection with the gerund: 'She is *on the point of crying*.' 'He is *on the verge of breaking down*.'

The present is often employed in the subordinate clause with the force of the future to indicate that something as yet merely desired or planned for the future is confidently expected to be realized, the present indicative here representing an older present subjunctive: 'I'll see you *get* there' (Edith Wharton, *Ethan Frome*). Compare **43** 2 B *a* (1st par.).

The idea of futurity often lies in *am* (*is*, etc.) in connection with a predicate *to*-infinitive, usually, however, mingled with the modal force described in **7** D 2: 'He *is to be* there.' 'He *is to be hanged.*' 'There *is to be* a dance after the program.' 'The children *are to have* a holiday tomorrow.' Compare **38** 2 *b ee* (4th par.).

f. The present is often used where the reference is to a past act and the present perfect might be used. The speaker uses the present tense as though the words had just been spoken, since he feels the matter as one of present interest: 'We *read* in the paper that you are going to Europe soon.' 'We *hear* that you have had some good luck.' 'I *learn* that you are going to sell your house.' Similarly, we quote an old author when we feel that his words have weight in questions of the hour: 'Homer *says* that,' etc.

g. The present is sometimes used instead of the present perfect to express that an action or state that was begun in the past is still continuing at the present time, usually accompanied by some adverbial element, such as *these many years, these forty years, long since, long ago:* 'Lo, these many years *do* I serve thee,' etc. (*Luke*, XV, 29). 'Nicholas Vedder! Why he *is* dead and gone these eighteen years' (Washington Irving, *Sketch-Book*, V). 'Did you ever see any scalping, or anything horrible yourself, my dear?' — 'Oh no, Miss Tarlton, all that *is* over long ago. The Indians are in the reservations now' (Mrs. Humphry Ward, *Daphne*). 'When was that, Joan?' — 'It *is* nearly three years ago now' (Mark Twain, *Joan of Arc*, I, Ch. VII) = 'It *has been* nearly three years.'

In Irish English, the present progressive form accompanied by a temporal adverbial expression is much used, corresponding to the literary present perfect: 'I *am sitting* here waiting for you *for the last hour*' (Joyce, *English as We Speak It in Ireland*, 85).

h. In adverbial clauses the present tense is often used instead of the future perfect: 'Telegraph me as soon as he *arrives.*'

2. **Past.** It is used to represent an act as done, or as regularly or habitually done, or as going on in time wholly past at the present moment, although it may have been performed only a few seconds before; but, if this tense is employed, the time of the act must be stated accurately or indicated clearly by the context, so that the idea of indefiniteness or generality is entirely excluded: 'I *bought* this bronze when I was in Naples.' 'I *misplaced* my

pencil a moment ago and can't find it.' 'This man *was* rich in days past.' 'The lightning *struck* a house yesterday.' 'Last week I *went* to town every day.' 'I *was working* in the garden when he *came*.' This is the common tense of narrative, where one event is represented as going on in connection with another.

3. **Present Perfect.** The present perfect tense represents an act as completed at the present moment: 'I *have* júst *fínished* my work.' 'I *have written* a lóng létter to Fáther.' Stress upon the tense auxiliary emphasizes the idea of the reality of the attainment: 'Why don't you fínish your work?' — 'I *háve* finished it.' We belittle or ridicule the attainment by stressing the auxiliary and speaking in a sarcastic tone: 'Well, you *háve* made a figure of yourself' (Susan Warner, *The Wide, Wide World*, Ch. X). Compare **6** A *d* (1).

The present perfect has developed out of the present tense of transitive verbs: 'I *have written* the letter,' originally 'I *have* the letter *written*,' i.e., in a written state. As having the letter in a written state implies previous action, *have written* gradually acquired verbal force, serving as a verbal form, pointing to the past and bringing it into relations with the present. Originally the Germanic past tense had a similar force, but gradually the idea of the past so overshadowed that of the present that a desire arose for a new form that would express a close relation between past and present. In early Old English this desire found an expression in the formation of the new present perfect tense. Similarly, in Latin and Greek the idea of the past so overshadowed that of the present in the perfect tense that it led in popular speech to the creation of a new perfect, a present perfect formed with the auxiliary *have*, which survives in the Romance languages and Modern Greek. In the original form of the English construction the past participle, as *written* in the sentence given above, was an objective predicate participial adjective and as a predicate had a strong stress. Even in oldest English the participle sometimes assumed strong verbal force, transferring to the preceding noun its strong stress, since the object is usually more forcibly accented than the verb. Later, the strongly accented object was placed after the participle, in accordance with the general tendency to place strongly accented words after words with weaker stress. Thus arose a clear formal differentiation between 'I *have* the letter *wrítten*,' the old present tense, and 'I *have written* the létter,' the new perfect tense. The development of the perfect tense suggested the formation of the new past perfect: 'I *had written* the letter.' Thus English was enriched by the creation of two new tenses, the present perfect and past perfect, which were added to the two original English tenses, the present and the past. Durative (**38** 1) intransitives followed the analogy of transitives: '*I have* worked' and '*I had* worked.'

Point-action (**38** 2) intransitives, however, did not at once participate in this development. The present perfect remained in reality a present tense, the perfect participle serving as a predicate adjective indicating a state, the present tense of the copula performing the function of predication: 'The tree *is fallen*' = 'The tree *is in a fallen state*' and 'The tree *has fallen*.' Similarly, 'The tree *was fallen*' had the meaning 'The tree *was in a fallen state*' or 'The tree *had fallen*.' This old order of things continued throughout the Old English period and into the Middle English period, but in Middle English there began to appear alongside of the forms with *is* and *was* forms with *has* and *had* wherever the perfect participle had clear verbal force. The forms with *is* and *was* slowly disappeared, but a few survivals are still to be found, especially in poetic language and in a few set expressions: 'The melancholy days *are* come.' 'We *are* (or *have*) assembled here to discuss a difficult question.' 'Our friend *is* (or *has*) departed' (i.e., is dead). 'The messenger *is* (or *has*) gone.' 'This morning the police found the nest of the thieves, but the birds *were* (or *had*) flown.' Today we only, as in these examples, use *is* and *was* when we feel the perfect participle as expressing more or less clearly the idea of a state and hence as having the force of an adjective. Earlier in the period, however, *is* and *was* could still be used where the perfect participle had clear verbal force: 'The King himself *is rode* to view their battle' (Shakespeare, *Henry the Fifth*, IV, III, 2). 'I *am* this instant *arrived* here' (Witham Marsh, *Letter*, written at Albany, N. Y., April 18, 1763, to Sir William Johnson). We must now in plain prose say here *has ridden*, *have arrived*. The older usage of employing a present tense form for the present perfect lingered also in the passive: 'Besides I met Lord Bigot and Lord Salisbury, With eyes as red as new-enkindled fire, And others more, going to seek the grave Of Arthur, whom (**23** II 8 *d*) they say *is* (now *has been*) *kill'd* to-night On your suggestion' (Shakespeare, *King John*, IV, II, 162). 'Since writing I *am* (now *have been*) credibly *informed* that,' etc. (Sir William Johnson, *Letter*, written at Johnstown, N. Y., Feb. 9, 1764, to John Penn).

Although the present perfect is no longer a present tense, it still preserves much of its original meaning in that it is usually employed when the time is felt as not wholly past but still at least in close relations with the present: 'My brother *bought* two hats this morning,' but 'My brother *has bought* two hats this week,' since the speaker feels that the period in question is not yet closed. 'I *went* to the theater last night,' but 'I *have been* ill all night and do not feel like going to work this morning,' since the speaker still feels the effects of the night's illness. The present perfect can be used of time past only where the person or the thing in question still exists and the idea of past time is not prominent, i.e., where the reference is general or indefinite: 'John *has been punished* many times' (general statement), but 'John *was punished* many times last year' (definite). 'I *have been* in England twice' (indefinite time), but 'I *was* in England twice last year.' 'England *has had* many able rulers,' but 'Assyria *had* many able rulers,' since Assyria no longer exists as an independent country. 'It was one of those epidemic frenzies which *have fallen* upon great cities in former ages of the world' (Hall Caine, *The Christian*) (general and indefinite). 'I *have* in times past more than once *taken* my political life in my hands' (*Daily Telegram*, Sept. 8, 1903) (general and indefinite). There is often a marked difference of tone between the past and the present perfect tense. In referring to something that has taken place, the speaker uses the past when he speaks in a lively tone with a vivid impression upon his mind of what has occurred, while he employs the present perfect when he speaks in a calmer, more detached tone: '*Did you* ever *see* anything to beat it?' (Tarkington, *Napoleon Was a Little Man*), but in a calmer, more detached tone: '*Have you* ever *seen* anything to beat it?'

a. Present Perfect to Represent an Act as Still Continuing. On account of the firm relation of the present perfect tense to present time it is much used to indicate that an act begun in the past is still continuing: 'He *has been working* hard all day,' but when the time is wholly past 'He *worked* hard all day yesterday.' 'How long *have you been studying* German?' 'She *hasn't left* her bed for a week.' 'I *have known* him for years.'

b. Present Perfect with Force of Present. With one verb, namely, *get*, the idea of present time in the present perfect tense often overshadows that of past time, so that the form has the force of a present tense: 'I *have got* (= *have*) a cold, a new car,' etc. 'I *have got* (= *have*) to do it.' *Have got*, however, is not an exact equivalent of *have;* it has more grip in it, emphasizing the idea of the possession or the necessity as the result of some recent occurrence: 'He *has* a blind eye,' but 'Look at John; he *has got* a black eye.' But in colloquial and popular speech the development has gone farther: *has got* often has the meaning of simple *have:* 'What *have you got* (= *have you*) in your hand?'

In Negro dialect *got* (elliptical for *have got*) sometimes has the *s*-ending of the present tense, *gots* serving for all persons and numbers, as described in **8** I 1 *h:* 'I *gots* good news' (Du Bose Heyward, *Porgy*, p. 54). The negative form is *ain't gots:* 'Such as yuh *ain't gots* no use fuh he' (*ib.*, p. 53).

Similarly, the past-present verbs (Accidence, **57** 4), *can, may,* etc., are now felt as present tense forms, although in fact they are old past tense forms. The Germanic past tense once had the force of our present perfect. In the past tense of most verbs the idea of past time finally overshadowed that of present time, but in these few past tense forms the idea of present time overshadows that of past time.

c. PRESENT PERFECT IN POPULAR IRISH. This tense is here often formed by placing the present of the verb *be* before the preposition *after* + a gerund, if one desires to indicate that something has taken place only a short while or immediately before the time one is speaking: '*I'm after walking* up in great haste from hearing wonders at the fair' (J. M. Synge, *The Well of the Saints,* p. 8). Elsewhere the regular present perfect form is used. Occasionally, however, in the case of transitive verbs, Irishmen place the object before the perfect participle instead of after it, which gives a peculiar flavor to their language: 'Have you your tea taken?' (Lennox Robinson, *The Whiteheaded Boy,* Act I, p. 11).

To express that an action that was begun in the past is still continuing, the present progressive is often used in popular Irish instead of the literary present perfect progressive. For an example see 1 *g,* p. 357.

d. 'BE' FOR 'HAVE' IN DIALECT. In certain British dialects *be* is used as tense auxiliary instead of *have.* Also in certain American dialects: '*Is* you seed any sign er (of) my gran'son dis mawnin?' (Joel Chandler Harris, *Nights with Uncle Remus,* p. 55).

4. **Past Perfect Tense.** This form represents a past action or state as completed at or before a certain past time: 'After he *had* finished the book, he returned it.' For the origin and the earlier form of the past perfect tense see 3, p. 358.

In colloquial speech, the past tense is still often used for the past perfect, as in the early period before the creation of a past perfect: 'After he *finished* the book, he returned it.' This usually occurs, as in this example, where the verb has point-action (**38** 2) force. Even in the literary language the past is used instead of the past perfect where some other idea overshadows that of the exact time relations: 'John was punished because he *broke* a window.' Of course, John broke the window before he was punished for it, but the fact of the breaking, in and of itself, is what is uppermost in the mind, not the exact time relations. In 'As soon as he *heard* that, he turned pale' *heard* cannot be replaced by *had heard,* although in fact the person in question heard the bad news before he turned pale. The use of the past perfect here would stress the time relation too much and call the attention away from the close relation of the two acts, the one following the other immediately.

In popular Irish English, the past perfect idea is expressed by the past of *be* + *after* + gerund: 'To hear the talk of you, you'd think I *was after beating* you' (Synge, *The Well of the Saints*, Act II).

5. **Future Tense.** This form represents an action or state as yet to take place or to come into being: 'I *shall be* sorry if you do not come.' 'You *will be* sorry if you do not come along.' 'He *will do* it tomorrow.' This is the pure future.

The future is often used in commands. See **45** 4 *c.*

The future often, most commonly, however, in the English of England, indicates a present probability, the future form implying that upon investigation the truth of the statement will become apparent: '"This *will be* your luggage, I suppose," said the man rather abruptly when he saw me, pointing to my trunk in the passage' (Charlotte Brontë, *Jane Eyre*, Ch. XI). 'At Okehampton a brisk young-looking man with a clean-shaved face appeared before Elizabeth. "You*'ll be* Miss Densham, I reckon," he said slowly' (Phillpotts, *The Beacon*, I, Ch. II, p. 13). 'It's not like Jolyon to be late! I suppose it*'ll be* June (name) keeping him' (Galsworthy, *The Man of Property*, p. 48). 'Mother *will be expecting* me.' The future perfect in such expressions, of course, points to the past: 'You *will have seen* from my postcard that we were at Ostend.'

a. FORM OF THE FUTURE TENSE. The contracted forms *'ll, 'd* represent usually reductions of *will, would,* never contractions of *shall, should:* 'I*'ll* go, we*'ll* go, I*'d* go.' In 'I*'d* better go' I*'d* stands for *I had.* The negative form *will not* appears often as *won't,* representing an older variant form of *will,* namely *woll, woll not* becoming *won't.* The contracted form of *shall not* is *shan't.* The written forms *I shall, we shall* are often in rapid speech pronounced *Ishl, weeshl.* In dialect *I shall* is often reduced to *I'se:* '*I'se* lay a wager he was christened John Trotter' (Smollett, *Roderick Random*, Ch. XII).

In spite of the great importance of a pure future, English has not yet developed such a form. Our future tense is made up of modal auxiliaries which are not only used as future forms but are sometimes employed elsewhere with their old modal meanings, so that they sometimes do not convey the pure idea of tense but are associated also with modal conceptions. The following forms have grown up and are now recognized as a literary standard, but they are far from representing the usage of educated people in all parts of the English-speaking territory. They are followed in England proper better than anywhere else, but not uniformly even there.

In the declarative form, *shall* is used in the first person and *will* in the second and third persons: 'I *shall* die, we *shall* die, you *will* die, he *will* die, they *will* die.'

The use of *shall* in the first person as a pure future has developed out of one of its modal meanings, *am to*, indicating a constraint of circumstances, duty, or the will of another, a meaning still common: 'I'm bad enough, God knows, and I'm afraid, I *shall* (= *am to, must*) find my way to hell some day' (Eggleston, *Circuit Rider*, p. 323). The idea of constraint in the first person is often overshadowed by the conception of future occurrence, which is often implied in the idea of constraint: 'I *shall* return tomorrow.' Thus the modal force often yields in the first person to the conception of pure futurity. *Shall* in the first person, singular and plural, is the standard usage in England, though not uniformly observed, and is still the preferred form in the higher grades of the literary language in America, though now not so uniformly used as it once was. In American colloquial speech *will* is now the more common form in the first person as well as in the second and the third: 'We *will* be terribly poor, I know' (Floyd Dell, *This Mad Ideal*, IV, Ch. VI). In the English of England *will* is used in the first person as a pure future only when in a compound subject *I* or *we* is preceded by a pronoun in the second person, or by a noun or pronoun in the third person: 'You and I *will* get on excellently well' (Dickens, *Martin Chuzzlewit*, Ch. V). 'Eddie and I *will* be delighted to come on Monday' (A. Marshall, *The Greatest of These*, Ch. X). The preceding pronoun or noun in the second or third person here influences the selection of the auxiliary. But we employ *will* here also to express willingness, intention, so that the tone of the voice or the situation must decide the meaning: 'John and I *will* assist you.'

The use of *will* in the second and third persons as a pure future developed out of its modal meaning of *wish, desire*. The idea of desire was overshadowed in the second and third persons by the conception of future occurrence, pure futurity, which is often implied in the idea of *desire*. If a person desires to do something, we may often infer that he will do it: 'He *will* go to town tomorrow.' The use of *will* in the second and third persons in the last centuries to express pure futurity in contrast to the older use of *shall* here has resulted from a feeling of politeness, a desire to represent the act, not as a command of the speaker, but as springing from the will of the person addressed or the person spoken of. Though we now usually employ *will* in the second and third persons as an auxiliary to indicate pure futurity, it is still sometimes used with its older modal force expressing desire, willingness, determination: 'You *will* help me, I am sure.' 'They *will* not look the question in the face.' 'The Court cánnot and *will* not stand journalistic personalities about its members' (*Nineteenth Century*, Dec., 1891, p. 859).

If we use *will* in the first person, it is not a future tense auxiliary, but a modal auxiliary indicating a desire, intention, willingness, inclination, determination: 'I'*ll* send it to you next week' (promise). 'I *will* do it for you,' but 'I *shall* be glad to do it for you,' for we do not desire to say that we *are willing* to be glad but that we *shall* be glad, employing a pure future to express confidently a future result. 'I *will* subscribe to your fund.' 'I'*ll* never give my consent to that' (resolution).

In the first person alongside of modal *will*, which represents a resolution as sprung from the feeling of the moment, is modal *shall*, which represents the resolution as the result of previous deliberation, or deep conviction, or deeply rooted feeling, and represents the execution as assured — not future *shall* as claimed by some English grammarians, but a genuine modal *shall*, for it is used by Americans who use *will* for the pure future: 'Then, Patty, since you make me choose, I *shall* not give up the Lord even for you' (Eggleston, *Circuit Rider*, Ch. XIX). 'I *shall* (= *have decided to*) send my two boys to Harvard.' 'I *shall* stand my ground as firmly as I can.' 'I *shall* do nothing of the kind' (peremptory refusal). In questions *shall* in the first person often inquires after the will of the person addressed: 'What *shall* I do next?' But stressed *shall* often has quite a different meaning here: 'What *shåll* I (= *am I to*) do?' Stressed *will* expresses determination in all three persons: 'I *will* go, no matter what you say.' 'You *will* (he *will*) act foolishly, in spite of my advice.' Unstressed *will* is often used in one of its old meanings *inclined to* when we desire to indicate an action as customary: 'John *will* often sit for hours alone on the porch.' 'Courage *will* come and go.' 'Whenever I asked Edward about his adventures he *would* begin to talk about something else.' A strong stress here indicates a strong inclination, tendency: 'Children *will* be noisy.' 'Accidents *will* happen.'

Just as *will* is a future tense auxiliary only in the second and third persons, *shall* is a future tense auxiliary only in the first person. Hence, when *shall* is employed in the second and third persons, it must be a modal auxiliary. As a modal auxiliary it indicates the will of someone other than its subject, representing its subject as standing under the will of another who commands him, promises or assures him something, wishes something to be arranged to suit him, threatens him, resolves to do something for

his benefit or injury, or it represents the speaker as determined to
bring something about or prevent it: 'Thou *shalt* not kíll' (com-
mandment). 'I won't do it.' — 'You *sháll* [do it]!' (a strong expression of will, of a command). 'You *shall* páy me at your
convenience,' i.e., 'you *are to* pay me, it is my desire that you pay
me at your convenience.' 'You *shall* háve some cake' (promise).
'If you trust him you *shall* not mispláce your confidence' (a personal assurance, a usage once common but now usually replaced
by the future, *you will not misplace*). 'You *shall* not cátch me
again!' 'You *shall* páy for that!' (threat). 'She *shall* not regrét
her kindness to me' (resolution). 'He *shall* páy for that!' (resolution). 'I mean it; nothing *shall* stóp me!' 'You (or he) *shall* not
háve any' (refusal). The constraint is often that of authority,
convention, good usage, etc.: 'Immigrants *shall* be tréated with
kindness and civility by every one' (notice posted at different
points on Ellis Island). 'Why *shall* he (the pupil) not sáy, "He
or I are going"?' (P. Chubb, *The Teaching of English*, p. 214).
(Because it is illogical and is forbidden by good usage.) The
constraint is often that of circumstances: 'I'll sell my new
red cloak sooner than yo' (=you) *shall* (=*must*) gó unpaid'
(Mrs. Gaskell, *Sylvia's Lovers*, Ch. V). It represents the speaker
as proclaiming the will of God or destiny in a prophetic or oracular
announcement of something that shall take place: 'Heaven and
earth *shall* pass away, but my word *shall* not pass away' (*Matthew*,
XXIV, 35). 'The time shall come when Egypt *shall* be avenged!'
(Lytton, *Pompeii*, II, Ch. VIII). Often in rhetorical and deliberative questions (p. 212): 'When doctors disagree, who *shall* (= *is
to, can*) decide?' 'Who *shall* (= *is to, can*) tell of what he was
thinking?' (Galsworthy, *The Man of Property*, p. 367). 'Which
of these views *shall the student of English* (= *is the student of
English to*, or *ought the student of English to*) accept?'
  In independent questions, *shall* and *will* are used as pure futures
in the first and third persons, as in the declarative form, but in
the second person that auxiliary is used which is expected in the
answer, so that also in questions we must carefully distinguish
between *tense* and *modal* auxiliaries: '*Shall* (tense auxiliary) we
have the pleasure of seeing you tomorrow?' '*Will* (tense auxiliary) he come tomorrow?' '*Shall* (tense auxiliary) you have
time enough tomorrow to do this for me?' corresponding to the
expected answer, 'I *shall* have time enough'; but '*Will* (modal
auxiliary) you do this for me?' i.e., 'are you willing to do this
for me?' corresponding to the expected answer, 'I *will* do it for
you.' Instead of the present tense *will* here we often use the past
subjunctive *would*, the polite volitive (**43** 1 A), in order to put the

question more modestly or politely: '*Would* you tell me the time, please?' If, however, the question is not a real one expecting an answer, but a so-called rhetorical question, we do not use *shall* anticipating a *shall* in the answer, but we employ *will*, the usual second person form: '*Will* you ever live to realize all these dreams?'

Shall is much used in questions in the first and third persons as a modal auxiliary to ascertain the will, idea, or thought of the person addressed: 'What *shall* he do next?' 'What *shall* I help you to?' (at the table). '*Shall* we go?' but 'We *won't* pay till the end of the week — *will we?*' since *won't* has preceded, expressing the will of the speaker, and *will* is added to invite, as it were, the concurrence of the person addressed. Similarly: 'We *would* do it for you, *wouldn't* we, Graham?' But 'We *will* do it for you, *shall* we?' since the speaker leaves the decision entirely with the person addressed.

In dependent statements and questions containing a pure future the auxiliaries are used in accordance with the general rule, *shall* in the first person and *will* in the second and third, usually entirely without regard to the auxiliary used in the direct form of statement: 'He says that I *shall* (in American colloquial speech *will*) surely fail,' direct 'You *will* surely fail.' 'He fears he *will* not arrive in time,' direct 'I *shall* not arrive in time,' or sometimes here in the third person with the auxiliary used in the direct statement, as explained more fully in **44 II 3 *a***: 'He fears that he *shall* not arrive in time.' On the other hand, in the case of modal auxiliaries we always use the auxiliary employed in the direct form, without regard to the person: 'He says he *will* do it,' direct 'I *will* do it.' 'He often asks me whether I *will* do it for him,' direct '*Will* you do it for me?' Of course, in all these cases after a past tense *shall* becomes *should* and *will* becomes *would:* 'He said that I *should* (in American colloquial speech *would*) surely fail,' direct 'You *will* surely fail.' 'He feared he *would* not arrive in time,' direct 'I *shall* not arrive in time,' or sometimes here in the third person with the auxiliary used in the direct statement: 'He feared he *should* not arrive in time.' On the other hand, in the case of modal auxiliaries we always use the auxiliary employed in the direct statement: 'He said he *would* do it,' direct 'I *will* do it.' 'He often asked me whether I *would* do it,' direct '*Will* you do it?' Compare **44 II 3 *a***.

Wherever the idea of uncertainty enters into our conceptions of the future, as in the principal proposition of a theoretical conditional sentence (**44 II 5 B**), we employ as future subjunctive forms to indicate a future result the past potential (**41**, 2nd par.) *should*

in the first person and the past potential *would* in the second and
third. 'If he should go away without speaking to me, I *should* be
grieved.' 'If I should go away without speaking to him, he *would*
be grieved.' This use of *should* and *would* as potential subjunctive
futures is modern. In older English, *would* in all three persons
was often used in the principal proposition of a theoretical conditional sentence with its old volitive (**43** I A, 7th par.) force, expressing desire, willingness, intention, and this old usage still
not infrequently occurs: 'If he should treat me in that way, I
just *wóuldn't* stand it.' 'If we should treat you in that way,
you just *wóuldn't* stand it.' 'If we should treat him in that
way, he just *wóuldn't* stand it.' Compare **44** II 5 B.

Instead of the first person form *should* in the principal proposition of these theoretical conditional sentences we sometimes use
would, provided it has just been used by someone in speaking
to us, since we feel a desire to reply to him in his own terms,
catching up the very word he used: 'You *would* think so yourself
if you were in my position.' — 'No, I *wouldn't*,' or '*Would* I
though?' or with the regular form 'I *should* not.'

We often use the regular form of the principal proposition of
a theoretical conditional sentence as a form to express an opinion
modestly, employing *should* in the first person and *would* in the
second and third: 'I *should* regard this course as unwise.' 'I
should think so.' 'It *would* (sometimes, in accordance with older
usage, *should*) seem so.' Compare **44** I and II 5 D. Such modest
expressions containing the future subjunctive of result should
not be confounded with modest expressions containing the modal
should, which indicates that the subject is under some kind of
constraint, the constraint of duty, circumstances, or the will of
another: 'I *should* (ought to) help him.' 'I *should* (under the
circumstances) go.' 'You *should* (ought to) go.' 'We *should*
hurry' (admonition). *Should*, however, often becomes quite emphatic: 'You *should* go if I had my way.' 'You *should* mind your
own business.' This modal *should* is used in all three persons.

In all expressions of desire with reference to the immediate
future, the past subjunctive *would*, a modest optative (**43** I B),
is milder in force than *will:* 'I *would* not have you think unkindly
of me.' 'Your present plan may have its advantages, but I
would suggest quite a different course.' '*Would* you pass the salt?'
'I think he *would* do it for you.' 'I am sure your father *would*
not have you neglect this opportunity.' But in the first person
we usually employ *should* in 'I *should* like to go' and 'I *should*
prefer to stay at home,' for the idea of desire is expressed in *like*
and *prefer* and to use *would* here would be expressing this idea

twice. We usually employ the pure future form *should* here, as we desire something for the immediate future and wish to express this desire modestly. Similarly, we employ *should* in questions where we expect *should* in the answer: 'How *should* you like to go to New York?' corresponding to the expected answer 'I *should* like to go to New York.' '*Should* you prefer to stay at home?' corresponding to the expected answer 'I *should* prefer to stay at home.' Even good authors, however, often use *would* improperly in the first person in declarative statements and in the second person in questions, not feeling the tautology: 'I *would* like to show you my den' (Mrs. H. Ward, *Richard Meynell*, II, Ch. X). In questions this tendency to use *would* instead of *should* is especially strong: '*Would* you like to go to New York?' Some employ in the first person *should* instead of *would* when the auxiliary is associated with *rather*, feeling that the adverb contains the idea of desire: 'They bury men with their faces to the East. I *should rather* have mine turned to the West' (Kingsley, *Westward Ho!* Ch. XVI). But *would* is the proper form here, for *rather* has other common meanings and hence does not of itself express desire or preference: 'I *would rather* stay at home.' In all declarative statements we, of course, always use *would* with *like, prefer, rather*, etc., in the second and third persons, for *would* is here a pure future: 'I know *you would like* to go.' 'He *would prefer* to stay at home.' 'He *would rather* stay at home.'

The usage described above began to take definite shape in the southeast of England in the second half of the sixteenth century, and became fairly well fixed there in the course of the seventeenth. Although at this time *will* had become the usual pure future form in the second and third persons, older *shall* still continued to be used alongside of it, usually with a slight modal tinge: 'What will you say if I make it so perspicuously appeare now that yourself *shall* (now in plain prose *will*) confesse nothing more possible' (Ben Jonson, *Euery Man out of His Humour*, IV, v, A.D. 1600). Similarly, in theoretical conditions *should* was still often used at this time in the second and third persons: '[if we should act so] This *should* (now *would*) be treacherie' (Marlowe, *Tamburlaine*, Second Part, II, I, A.D. 1590). The pure future form *shall* was at this time fairly well fixed here in the first person: 'Gentlemen, you three take one Boat, and Sogliardo and I *will* (modal) take another: we *shall* (pure future) be there immediately' (Ben Jonson, *Euery Man out of His Humour*, IV, v). 'But I *will* (modal) say that unless you take some speedy and effectual resolution in this particular, I *shall* (pure future) look like the veriest rogue' (Sir William Temple, *Letter*, Oct. 13, 1665).

As there was a strong immigration into our country from the southeast of England at this time, *shall* was often used as a pure future sign in the first person, so that at the very beginning of our literary language it became more or less firmly established as the literary form, although *will* was sometimes used here, and later became the common form in colloquial and popular speech: 'I *shall* not need to name perticulers, they are too well known to all' (Bradford, *History of Plymouth Plantation*, p. 299, A.D. 1630–1648). The Englishman, Sir William Temple, quoted on page 368, employs *shall* in the third person of indirect discourse, corresponding to a *shall* in the first person of direct discourse, as described on page 366: 'He says, if he failes in his enterprise, he *shall* esteem his condition not at all the worse' (*Letter*, Sept. 6, 1665). This use of *shall* (or, after a past indicative, *should*) in indirect discourse is in British English still not infrequent, but is not so common as *will* (or *would*). In American literary English, this use of *shall* or *should* is still less common. In our older American literature, however, it often occurs: 'Their answer was, as before, that it was a false calumniation, for they had many amongst them that they liked well of, and were glad of their company; and *should* (now usually *would*) be of any such like that should come amongst them' (Bradford, *History of Plymouth Plantation*, p. 184, A.D. 1630–1648). 'He used to tell his friends after his release that he verily believed, if he had not taken this method, he *should* (now usually *would*) have lost his senses' (Benjamin Franklin, *Writings*, II, p. 70). The use of *shall* or *should* in the first and third person, as illustrated above, is preserved in part in the native popular and colloquial speech of New England: 'Give wut they need, an' we *shell* git 'fore long A nation all one piece, rich, peacefle, strong' (J. R. Lowell, *The Biglow Papers*, No. XI). 'He sez he *shall* vote for Gineral C.' (*ib.*, No. III). 'Charley Marden remarked that he *shouldn't* be surprised if,' etc. (Thomas Bailey Aldrich, *The Story of a Bad Boy*, Ch. VIII). 'I *shall* go mad 'fore long if somethin' don't happen' (Amy Lowell, *Selected Poems*, p. 179).

Our present literary usage is characterized by a much less frequent employment of *shall* in the second and third persons than found in early Modern English, since *shall* in these persons is so intimately associated with the idea of the constraint of circumstances or the will of another than the subject that it is now avoided here as an unclear form in favor of *will*, which in these persons is not so charged with modal force.

The expression of future time in our common colloquial English follows, in general, the usage of England, as described above, but differs from it in one important point, namely, *will* and *would*

are used as the signs of the pure future, not only in the second and
third persons, but also in the first person: 'Patty, I tell you I'm
wretched and *will* be till I die' (Eggleston, *Circuit Rider*, p. 290).
'Do you really think we *would* (for literary *should*) be happy [if
we should marry]?' (Floyd Dell, *This Mad Ideal*, IV, Ch. VIII).

Under the influence of the strong national drift, *will* and *would*
often occur here also in the literary language of prominent Americans: 'I have come to believe that should I violate this law (i.e.,
the law he had made for himself never to ask for an office) I *would*
fail' (James A. Garfield, *Journal* for December, 1880). 'If men
cannot now, after this agony of bloody sweat, come to their self-
possession and see how to regulate the affairs of the world, we *will*
sink back into a period of struggle in which there will be no hope,
therefore no mercy' (Woodrow Wilson, March 5, 1919). 'If I
could feel that our laws and the administration of our laws were
in the future to be such as would be conducive to the health and
morals, the prosperity and happiness, of the average citizen of
our country, I *would* feel confident, wholly confident of the future'
(William E. Borah in the U. S. Senate, 1916).

The use of *will* as a sign of the pure future in all three persons
is also a marked characteristic of popular Scotch, Welsh, and
Irish English. This usage was already in early Modern English
fairly well established in the popular English of Scotland and
Wales and in general also of the intervening western shore country.
After the invasion of Ireland in the twelfth century English colonies
were established in the southeast. English spread in the thirteenth century, but in the next centuries declined. Still later,
in the seventeenth century, new life came into the colonization of
Ireland. The Irish English of our time rests for the most part
upon this later stream of immigration. As these colonists were
largely from the western part of Great Britain, the *will*-future
became established in these colonies. In the seventeenth century
under James I a large part of Ulster in North Ireland was given
over to Scotch settlers, who, of course, brought their *will*-future
along with them. Settlers from southwestern Lancashire carried
it to the Isle of Man. Scotch, Irish, and Welsh immigrants have
furthered this usage in American colloquial speech.

The use of *will* as a pure future sign in the first person as well
as in the second and third is, however, not unknown in the English
of England proper: 'An (= if) bad thinking do not wrest true
speaking, *I'll* offend nobody' (Shakespeare, *Much Ado about
Nothing*, III, IV, 33). 'Very well; then I *will* be the miserablest
woman in the world' (Hardy, *Return of the Native*, I, Ch. V).
Thus the forces that have been operating in the English-speaking

territories outside of England have long been felt also in England itself. *Will,* now everywhere used in the second and third persons, is being carried by the force of leveling into the first person.

If the present widespread use of *will* in all three persons as a sign of the pure future should become finally established in the literary language, it would be a distinct gain to English expression in the direction of greater simplicity. We should, however, in this event lose some useful distinctions in the first person. These distinctions are not so intricate that they could not be grasped by most people, for in England the uneducated, in general, observe them. But the great mass of English-speaking people are today at this point borne along unconsciously by the strong drift toward a greater simplicity of expression. Grammarians, in general, and many educated people in the English-speaking territories outside of England proper still follow the usage of England, feeling that it is superior. Which force shall ultimately prevail?

Though the English-speaking territories outside of England proper, in general, go together in the colloquial use of *will* as the sign of the pure future, they differ somewhat in the use of *will* and *shall* as modal forms, so that peculiar uses here characterize different sections. Thus, Irishmen often attract our attention by their use of *will* instead of *shall* in inquiring after someone's will or desire: '*Will* I cut another piece for you?' (St. John Ervine, *John Ferguson,* Act II). This same usage is common also in Scotland: 'Will you tell her, man, or *will* (instead of *shall*) I?' (J. M. Barrie, *Tommy and Grizel,* Ch. XII). Also in the Isle of Man: '*Will* (instead of *shall*) I go home with ye?' (Moore, *Anglo-Manx Dialect,* p. 202). This is a modern development. In America older *shall* is here as well preserved as in England proper. On the other hand, the Irish cling conservatively to older usage in expressing dutiful assent by *shall:* 'Please have breakfast for me at 8 o'clock.' — 'I *shall,* sir,' where we today in literary speech usually employ *will* since there now prevails here the desire to express the idea of willingness to comply with the request.

b. OTHER MEANS OF EXPRESSING THE IDEA OF FUTURITY. The idea of futurity is still, as in older English, often expressed by the present tense, as described in 1 *e,* p. 356.

6. **Future Perfect Tense.** This form represents that an action or state will be completed at or before a certain time yet future: 'I *shall have completed* the task by evening.' 'He *will have completed* the task by evening.' The same use of *will* and *shall* is observed here as described for the future tense in 5 *a,* p. 362. Of course, *shall* and *will* here become *should* and *would* after a past

tense form: 'I said I *should have reached* home before Easter.' 'I was sure they *would have finished* my house by then.'

Will and *would* are often replaced in temporal clauses by *shall* and *should* to give the statement modal force, the idea that the future act is the result of a natural development, or is arranged, planned, desired: 'Our salvation will come when the search for friendship *shall take* (or *shall have taken*) the place of the search for wealth.' 'I shall pay him as soon as he *shall finish* (or *shall have finished*) the work.' 'I was to pay him as soon as he *should finish* (or *should have finished*) the work.' Compare **43** II B *c*.

In principal propositions the future perfect is used in choice, accurate language, but in colloquial speech it is avoided as too formal. This form is a late and learned development which has not yet become established in simple expression. It is not found in the language of Shakespeare. In informal speech we employ here the future in connection with a perfective adverb or a perfect participle to indicate completion: 'I *shall have finished* the work before you return,' or in colloquial speech 'I *shall* (or in America *will*) *be through* with the work (or I *shall*, or in America *will*, *have* the work *finished*) before you return.'

The future perfect is avoided still more in the subordinate clause. Here it is usually replaced by the present or future, the present perfect, the past or past perfect: 'He is standing there reasoning out the steps to be taken when the fog *lifts*' (or *shall lift* = *shall have lifted*). 'I shall pay him as soon as he *has finished* (= *shall have finished*) the work.' 'I was to pay him as soon as he *finished* (or *had finished* = *should have finished*) the work.'

ASPECT

38. Aspect indicates the aspect, the type, the character of the action. The following classes occur:

1. Durative Aspect. This type represents the action as continuing. We usually employ here the progressive form: 'He *is eating.*' To express different shades of the idea of continuance also other forms are often used, especially *remain, keep, keep on, go on, continue* with a present participle as predicate after an intransitive, and an infinitive or gerund as object after a transitive: 'Don't you see, you foolish girl, that he'll *remain hanging* (participle) about?' 'He *kept working* (participle) until he was tired out,' or 'He *continued to work* (object of transitive *continued*), or *working* (predicate participle or gerund object according as *continued* is felt as intransitive or transitive), until he was tired out.' 'He was tired, but he *kept on working*' (participle). 'I could *go on writing* (participle) about it forever if I only had time.' Other forms of expression are given in *a*, p. 377. In older English, the present active participle was used also with passive force: 'The books continue *selling*' (Priestley, *Rudiments of English with Notes and Observations*, p. 111, A.D. 1769), now *being sold* or *to be sold.*

In older English, the simple form of the verb often had durative force, but it now usually represents an action as a whole, i.e., is terminate (3, p. 385). It still often implies the idea of duration, but this conception is now never the leading one here. It expresses the idea of a general truth, an act as a fact or as a whole, or an act as habitual, customary, characteristic, while the progressive form stresses the conception of continuation, repetition, the frequent exercise of a habit at the present moment or at a definite past time: 'Dogs bark' (a characteristic act), but 'Dogs are barking' (act now going on). The copula is expressed in the progressive form when the subject is a nominative, as in the last example.

But it is regularly lacking when the present participle is predicated of an accusative object: 'I saw *him working* in the garden.' 'I kept *him waiting.*' Compare 15 III 2 (2nd par.), 15 III 2 A, and 48 2 (3rd and 4th parr.).

As the present participle in the progressive form has not only verbal force, but is also a predicate adjective, it frequently, like an adjective, has descriptive force and by reason of its concrete meaning and the emphasis or peculiar tone often associated with it is charged with feeling, indicating that the speaker is affected by something, often expressing joy, sorrow, pleasure, displeasure, praise, censure, also emphasis, implying that the person in question is convinced of the truth or importance of the statement, i.e., the progressive form often differs from the simpler form in that it has modal force: 'John *bothers* me a good deal' (fact). 'John *is bothering* me a good deal of late and *keeping* me from work' (spoken in a complaining tone). 'John *does* fine work at school' (fact). 'John *is doing* fine work at school' (spoken in a tone of praise). 'When Elizabeth put Ballard and Babington to death, she *was* not *persecuting*' (Macaulay, *Essays*) (important statement spoken in tone of conviction).

Stress upon the copula often emphasizes the idea of actuality, usually with feeling: 'Why aren't you studying?' — 'I *ám* studying.' Compare 6 A *d* (1).

In questions with the stress upon the present participle or some more important part of the predicate, the progressive form often indicates curiosity: 'What are you *dóing*, children?' Feeling of different kinds: 'Why aren't you *stúdying?*' (censure). 'How are you *féeling* this morning?' or 'Are you feeling *bétter* this morning?' (sympathy, concern). Stress upon the copula here often indicates a marked displeasure with the condition of things: 'Children, what *áre*.you doing?' Compare 6 A *d* (1).

It is very common to use the simple form to express a general truth, as in 'Twice two *is* four,' but it is also common to employ the progressive form here in lively style when we feel the truths as living forces, always at work, usually accompanied by some adverbial expression, as *always, forever*, to indicate their incessant action: 'True taste *is for ever growing, learning, reading, worshiping, laying* its hand upon its mouth because it is astonished' (Ruskin, *Modern Painters*, Part III, Sec. I, Ch. III). 'You are not surprised to see his (i.e., the chipmunk's) face so clean, because he *is washing* it on all occasions' (John Burroughs, *Field and Study*, Ch. IX).

It is very common to employ the simple form to express a fact or an act as a whole, either in present or past time: 'The town *lies* on a river' (a fact, a permanent situation), but 'The wounded man *is* still *lying* on the ground' (continuation). 'He made a home of our house, while he *stayed* in our town' (act as a whole), but 'While my father *was trying* to make me a good merchant, my good mother *was seeking* all the while to make a musician out of me' (emphasizing the unceasing efforts upon both sides). 'There he *comes*' (a fact), but 'He *is coming* down the road' (descriptive). We should, however, not be misled by the word 'descriptive.' The simple past and present tenses are the usual tenses of narrative and description; they relate and describe, but they represent events only as facts in a development and describe persons and things only as details in a picture, so that they are immediately replaced by progressive forms when the narrative becomes a description of unfolding events or unfolding details in a picture: 'We reached (fact in a description) the lake just as the sun *was rising* (unfolding event) above it.' 'A blow well given now would not only disperse the mob and set the Nazarene free; it would be a trumpet-call to Israel, and precipitate the long-dreamt-of war for freedom. The opportunity *was going* (unfolding event); the minutes *were bearing* (unfolding event) it away; and if lost! God of Abraham! Was there nothing to be done — nothing?' (Wallace, *Ben Hur*, VlII, Ch. IX). As can be seen by the last example, it is absolutely necessary in narrative to employ the past progressive when it is desired to represent a past act as unfolding at a definite point of time, for the simple past tense here would represent the act as completed. In general, however, in description the simple tenses are the rule in narrative, as the described persons and things are felt as details of a picture: 'She *seemed* about fifteen, and *had* her apron full of pears.' 'Beside her on the table *lay* a large pan.' This is normal narrative or description, but in lively style we often employ here the progressive forms since we feel the phenomena, not as actual events and persons and things known to us but as unfolding before us, in the vivid play of the imagination arising and taking form: 'I *coughed* all night' (objective statement), but 'I *was coughing* all night' (vivid style). 'It is the representation of a lady. She *lies* on a couch. At her side *sits* a woman in grief' (objective statement), but 'It is the representation of a lady. She *is lying* on a couch. At her side *is sitting* a woman in grief' (vivid style).

'I *live* (or *am living*) in Chicago,' a habitual, customary act at the present time, often as here without an essential difference of meaning between the two forms, but the progressive form becomes more natural when feeling of any kind enters into the statement: 'I am now living in a very pleasant flat' (feeling of satisfaction, arising perhaps from a change of residence for the better). The progressive form is a favorite in the lively description of things going on at the present time: 'We are tramping over the hills and reading and writing and having a restful time' (Jean Webster, *Daddy-Long-Legs*, 225). The simple present tense here would be only an objective statement of fact.

The present tense of the progressive form often represents, not an act as actually taking place, but a person as looking forward to it with a lively feeling of expectancy: 'Aunt *is coming* soon.' 'We *are having* a few guests tonight.'

Instead of the simple present we often use the present of *will* (= *apt to, inclined to*) in connection with a dependent infinitive: 'John *will* often *sit* on the veranda alone for hours, or *will go* off alone into the woods.' We stress *will* here to indicate a strong tendency to do certain things: 'Children *will* be noisy.' 'Accidents *will* happen.'

With the aid of appropriate adverbs both forms of the present perfect, the usual tense form and the progressive, may express a habitual act in a time past but connected with the present: 'Recently John has done his work regularly' (fact), but in a tone of praise or censure we say: 'Recently John *has been doing* his work quite regularly, or very slovenly.' The usual present perfect tense form expresses a habitual act after the subordinating conjunction *after:* 'After I *have seen* her, I feel encouraged' (Mildred E. Lambert in *American Speech*, Oct., 1928). Similarly, after the subordinating conjunction *until:* 'I don't go to bed *until* I *have finished* my work.'

Past habit: 'Even when a little girl she *ran* (*used* — now in contrast to older English only used in the past tense — *to run*, or *would run*) after the boys' (fact), but in a tone of censure: 'Even when a little girl she *was always running* after the boys,' where we usually have to employ an adverb, as *always, all the time, forever*, to make the situation clear. 'I knew John smoked (a fixed habit, well known and characteristic of John, but here merely stated as a fact without reference to its exercise at any particular time), but he emphatically declined to do so in my presence'; but to emphasize the frequent exercise of the characteristic habit at some particular period of time we say: 'In those days John *was always smoking.*'

Both forms are used with reference to the future: 'We shall soon have plenty of rain' (something so confidently expected that it is here stated as a fact), but to express the displeasure that the thought arouses in us we say: 'We shall soon be having rain, rain, and nothing but rain.'

a. Often to emphasize the idea of duration we add *on*, or *on and on*, to the simple verb, or we add *and* and repeat the verb: 'When the Elsmeres were gone, Hester *sat on* alone in the drawing-room' (Mrs. H. Ward, *The Case of Richard Meynell*, III, Ch. XVII, 359). 'The prayers and talks (in the prayer-meeting) *went on and on*' (W. S. Cather, *The Song of the Lark*, Ch. XVII). 'When they (i.e., Mexican women) are in trouble, in love, under stress of any kind, they *comb and comb* their hair' (*ib.*, Ch. VI).

Intermittent action is expressed by *off and on:* 'I slept *off and on* all the way to Chicago.'

b. In older English, after *be* the progressive idea was sometimes expressed by the prepositional infinitive, which originally was an infinitive of purpose but finally often became a mere parallel of the progressive form: 'AMIENS. He hath been all this day *to look you* (= *to look for you*). — JAQUES. And I have been all this day *to avoid him*' (*As You Like It*, II, v, 34–35). Compare **7 D 3**.

c. The progressive form has been steadily spreading at the expense of the simple form. Earlier in the present period we often find the simple form where we now use the progressive: 'The whole fleet that went from hence *rides* (now *is riding*) now before the enemies' harbours' (Earl of Clarendon, *Letter*, Aug. 2, 1666).

2. Point-action Aspects. The point-action aspects call attention, not to an act as a whole, but to only one point, either the beginning or the final point. There are thus two classes:

a. INGRESSIVE ASPECT. This point-action type directs the attention especially to the initial stage of the action or state: 'He *awoke* early,' i.e., came into a waking state early. 'The boat *slowed up* as it came in.' 'They went the moment *it cleared.*' This idea is expressed in various ways:

aa. The ingressive aspect is often expressed by *begin, commence,* or *start* in connection with an infinitive or gerund as object. The simple present tense form of *begin, commence, start* (in colloquial American also *start in*), *start out* indicates that the beginning is habitual: 'When we scold her, she *begins to cry*' (or *begins crying*). The progressive form of *begin, commence, start, start out, start in* (in America used of a prolonged activity) denotes the beginning of an activity in present time: 'It *is beginning (starting) to rain.*' 'The baby is *beginning (starting) to cry.*' 'He *is starting out to write* his report without knowing all the facts.' The simple past tense represents the beginning of an act in past time as a fact; the progressive past represents it as an unfolding event: 'When I said that, she *began to cry.*' 'When the horses got stuck with the load, the driver *started to abuse* (or *abusing*) them.' 'It *was just beginning to rain* as I awoke.' 'The United States commis-

sioner for Dakota *started in to give* the world a comprehensive idea
of the resources of the territory' (*Lisbon Star*, Jan. 2, 1885). The
infinitive after *start in* and *start out* has adverbial force expressing
purpose. To express the idea of beginning work on something we
employ here *set about:* 'As soon as the flood was over, they *set about*
(preposition) *repairing* (gerund) the damage' or 'they *set about*
(adverb) *to repair* the damage.' Compare **50** 4 *c dd*. Of things
we use here *set in* to express steady, continued action, development: 'It *set in to rain*.' 'It had *set in snowing* (predicate
appositive participle) at breakfast.' 'A reaction *set in*.' *Start*
is often used in connection with a direct object and an objective predicate participle: 'It *started him coughing*.' Compare
15 III 2 A. See also *hh*, p. 380.

The ingressive aspect is often expressed by *to break out, burst out*
in connection with a present participle: 'He *broke out laughing*.'
'She *burst out crying*.'

The present tense of *be about* (**7** F) in connection with a *to*-
infinitive and the present tense of *be on the point* (or *verge*) *of* in
connection with a gerund indicate an action that will take place
in the immediate future in accordance with some plan, or as the
result of circumstances, or a natural development: 'I *am about
to leave* for Europe.' 'He *is about to break down*.' 'It *is about
to rain*.' 'She *is on the point of crying*.' 'She *is on the verge of
breaking down*.' The gerund is sometimes used after *is about*.
See **50** 4 *c dd*.

bb. The ingressive idea is often expressed by the ingressives
get, grow, fall, turn, wax, become, run, go, come, set, start, take
(take up as a habit) in connection with a predicate adjective,
participle, noun, or a prepositional phrase: 'He often *gets* sick.'
'Things often assume distorted forms when we *get* to worrying
about them.' 'It *is growing* dark.' 'She *turned* (*became, got,
grew*) pale.' 'Our funds *are falling* short.' 'He *waxed* hotter.'
'The captain's voice *came* (*got*) thick.' 'He *fell* asleep' (from
older *on sleep*). 'He *fell* again *to speculating* (less commonly *fell
speculating;* in older English also *fell on speculating, fell a-specu-
lating,* or *fell to speculate*) on the probable romance that lay behind
that loneliness and look of desolation.' 'The cow *ran* (or *went*)
dry.' 'The engine *went* dead.' 'He *went* to sleep.' '*Go* to work.'
'They *went* to housekeeping.' 'He *started* the ball rolling.' 'That
set me thinking' (or *to thinking*). 'He *took* to drinking.' 'He
took to going out nights and coming home at late hours.' Often
after *am* (*was*) *going to:* 'Look out! I *am going to shoot*.' In
older English, *going to* could follow the present participle *being*,
while today we suppress *being:* 'I do assure you that nothing

would surprise me more than to hear of their *being going to be married'* (Jane Austen, *Sense and Sensibility*, II, Ch. VII). Compare *b ee*, p. 383, and **37** 1 *e.*

In the preceding paragraph the gerund is used after *take*, but the infinitive is sometimes employed here: 'She *has taken to like him'* (Meredith, *One of Our Conquerors*, III, XI, 233). In older English, instead of the meaning *take up as a habit* the ingressive *take* had the general force of *start, proceed*, employed usually of vigorous action with the implication that the action would be carried through successfully. In the thirteenth century co-ordination (**19** 3, 4th par.) was employed here instead of the infinitive: 'He *tok* (took) *and wente'* (*Genesis and Exodus*, 1751). This usage is still common in popular speech: 'Ever since Mallie *tuck'n* (took and) *died* in Aprile, hit's been the same old story' (Lucy Furman, *The Quare Women*, Ch. V). 'He *tuck'n sot* a trap for Brer Rabbit' (Joel Chandler Harris, *Uncle Remus*, p. 142).

Verbs made from adjectives have ingressive force: 'They went out the moment it *cleared.*' 'The milk *soured.*'

cc. We often use *catch* and *take* here in connection with an object: 'I *caught sight* of him.' 'I *caught a cold.*' 'The plant *took root.*' 'He *took heart.*'

dd. Ingressive force often lies in the adverbs *up, down, out, off, in, away*, in the prefix *a–* and the suffix *–en:* 'He stood *up.*' 'He hurried *up.*' 'He didn't *show up'* (colloquial = *appear*). 'He sat *down.*' 'Children, quiet *down!'* 'The lilacs have come *out.*' 'He dozed *off.*' 'His regular breathing told that he had gone *off'* (= *fallen asleep*). 'He jumped onto his horse and rode *away.*' 'Then a heated discussion *arose.*' 'Her face *reddened* with anger.' 'He *quickened* his pace.' Borrowed verbs often have ingressive force by virtue of their prefixes: *appear, introduce*, etc. *In* is much used in American colloquial speech to indicate the beginning of a prolonged activity: 'When are you going to begin your new work?' — 'I start *in* tomorrow.' Compare *aa*, p. 377. *Pitch in, sail in, light in* have the additional idea of energetic action: 'When he has a job to do he *pitches* (or *sails*, or *lights*) *in* at once' (*Crowell's Dictionary of English Grammar*).

ee. The imperative of all verbs, durative as well as point-action verbs, usually has ingressive force, since the expectation is that the action will be begun or performed at once: '*Run!*' '*Come in!*' '*Hand* me that book!' The progressive form is much used in lively style, where feeling of different kinds enters into the expression: '*Let euery man* take his wife and his children and *be goying'* (Coverdale, *I Samuel*, XXX, 22, A.D. 1535). '*Be tredging* (trudging) or in faith you bere me a souse' (*Jack Juggler*,

50, A.D. 1562). *Leat vs be trudging!* (John Heywood, *Proverbs and Epigrams*, 37, A.D. 1562). 'Up, *be doing* everywhere, the hour of crisis has verily come!' (Carlyle, *Latter-Day Pamphlets*, 28). *Let's be going! We must be going!*

On the other hand, the negative form of the progressive imperative usually has durative force: '*Don't be trying* to make me a participator in your wickedness!' (Meredith, *Sandra Belloni*, 297). '*Don't be talking!* Let me just suck this in as we go along!' (Phillpotts, *Beacon*, I, Ch. V).

The progressive imperative is a conspicuous feature of popular Irish English: '*Be taking* your rest!' (Synge, *In the Shadow of the Glen*, 11). '*Let you not be telling* lies to the Almighty God!' (*id.*, *The Well of the Saints*, Act III).

The *be* of the progressive form has ingressive force in the imperative as often elsewhere, as described in *ff* below. In the imperative it is often rather literary, replaced in colloquial speech by *get:* '*Get* goin', Bozo!' (*Chicago Tribune*, Harold Teen Cartoon, Jan. 20, 1929). An ingressive particle is often used instead of an ingressive copula: 'Hurry *up!*' 'Brace *up!*'

ff. The verb *be* has had for many centuries both durative and ingressive force, but the former has so overshadowed the latter that we do not now have a vivid feeling for the latter. For the most part *be* as an ingressive copula or auxiliary is now replaced by other ingressive forms, such as *become, get*, etc., but its old ingressive force still lingers: 'He *was* (= *became*) both out of pocket and out of spirits by that catastrophe' (Thackeray, *Vanity Fair*, Ch. XXXVII). 'I must *be* going' (Kingsley, *Hypatia*, I, 246). In the actional passive, *be* still regularly has ingressive force. Compare **47** *b*. It often has the same force in the progressive form. See *ee*, p. 379, and *hh* below. It is often a full verb with ingressive force = *come into being, take place:* 'It *was* not until they had turned aside that she asked him why he was so quiet' (Tarkington, *The Plutocrat*, p. 292).

gg. The ingressive idea sometimes lies in the meaning of the verb: 'The buds will soon *show*' (make their appearance). 'The real test *begins* tomorrow.' 'We *start* tomorrow at six.'

hh. The progressive form, though usually durative in force, often with ingressives indicates the beginning of an activity: 'It *is clearing*.' 'The lilacs *are* just *coming out*.' 'I *am getting* tired of it.' 'I *was getting* tired of it.' 'The children *are quieting down*.' 'He *is quickening* his pace.' 'It *is starting* to rain.' In English, it has become necessary to employ the progressive form to express the beginning of an activity at the present moment or to represent the activity as unfolding at some moment in the past.

With ingressives we employ the progressive form of the ingressives themselves. With duratives we employ the progressive form of *start, begin,* etc., as in the last example. Compare *aa,* p. 377. For the use of *be* here in the progressive form with ingressive force see *ff,* p. 380. Compare *b hh,* p. 385.

b. EFFECTIVE ASPECT. This point-action aspect directs the attention to the final point of the activity or state, to a result that has been reached, hence it often indicates attainment or failure: 'The two friends *fell out.*' 'He *knocked* him *out* in the fourth round.' 'I at last, becoming discouraged, *gave up* hope.' 'The plan *fell through.*' In these examples the verbs have point-action force. They are pure effectives. A durative in connection with an effective particle has durative-effective force, indicating that the action continues to the end and often implying attainment, thoroughness: 'I *hunted* him *up.*' 'We must *clean up* here.' The effective idea is usually expressed by:

aa. Adverbs and prefixes. Pure effectives: 'He set *up* in the school a new standard of attainment.' 'He put the rebellion *down.*' 'He passed *away* quietly in the night.' 'The rumor turned *out* false.' 'It will turn *out* all right.' 'Our finances gave *out.*' 'His right leg gave *out.*' 'I at last found *out* what the matter was.' 'They were paid *off* and discharged.' 'I'll lay *off* (colloquial = *cease work*) for a month' (James Gibbons Huneker, *Letter,* Oct. 11, 1918). 'The company laid *off* ten men today' (*Crowell's Dictionary of English Grammar*). 'Several banks have gone *under* this year.' 'We hope to bring it *about* soon.' 'He got *by* with it' (American slang = *succeeded*). 'He got *there*' (American slang = *succeeded*). 'He put the nefarious design *through.*' 'They put it *across*' (colloquial American). 'They put it *over* on him' (colloquial American). Durative effectives: 'He not for his own self caring but her, Her and her children, let her plead in vain, So grieving held his will, and bore it *through*' (Tennyson, *Enoch Arden,* 167). 'I'll fight it *out* on this line if it takes all summer.' 'It requires exceptional courage to stand *out* against a popular cry.' 'He held *out* although it was a severe test.' 'They sat *out* the next dance.' 'The result of the sad experiences was that he pined *away.*' 'He kept his courage *up.*'

The English adverbs here have in general strong concrete force, but they are acquiring abstract ingressive or effective force, as can be clearly seen in *up.* We say 'I ate the apple *up,*' although we know very well that the apple went *down* and not *up.* This shows that *up* has lost its old concrete force and has become a point-action particle. Similarly, *a* in *arise* (see *a dd*) once meant *out,* but we now have no feeling for its old concrete meaning.

Some point-action verbs take no effective particle since the simple form has effective force, as in the case of *die*, *win*, *stop*, etc.: 'He *died* this morning.' 'He *won* by a head.' 'He *stopped* in the middle of the sentence.' 'My watch *has stopped*.' *Die out* and *win out* are durative-effectives: 'My interest in the subject *died out*.' 'A good cause often makes little headway at first, but in time it *wins out*.' *Stop* in connection with a prepositional phrase is much used in colloquial speech as an effective-durative: 'We *stopped at the Pennsylvania Hotel*.' 'I *have been stopping in Cornwall with friends*' (*Concise Oxford Dictionary*). The prepositional phrase indicates that a sojourning takes place after the journeying ceases. Some criticize the use of *stop* here and suggest that it be replaced by *stay*, but *stay* does not say so much as *stop* does.

bb. The effective idea is often expressed by a prepositional phrase instead of an adverb: 'He shot the hat *to pieces*.' 'He developed *into a strong man*.' 'He worked himself *into a frenzy*.'

cc. The final point in an activity is also indicated by *cease*, *stop*, *leave off* (or in older English also simple *leave*), *finish*, *quit* (American), or *do*, with an infinitive or gerund as object: 'She *ceased to cry*' (or *ceased*, or *stopped*, *crying*). 'I *have left off* (or in older English also simple *left*) *sleeping* (in older English sometimes *to sleep*) with the windows shut.' 'I *have just finished reading* the book.' 'I *have quit smoking*.' '*Quit teasing her*.' 'I *have* (in America, Scotland, Ireland often *am*) *done packing*.' In the American construction, *done* is a predicate adjective, and *packing* is a present participle employed as a predicate appositive expressing manner or specification — a very common construction, which is illustrated in **28** 1 *a* by a number of examples. In this construction the adverb *through* is often used as predicate instead of *done:* 'I am *through trying* to please her' (Mildred E. Lambert in *American Speech*, Oct., 1928).

In the passive form of statement the present participle usually has passive form: 'I finished *sowing* my clover field yesterday' (active form). 'My clover field was finished *being sown* yesterday' (passive form). In older English, the participle often had active form: 'Upon inquiring [I] found that my Clover Field was finish'd *sowing* and *rolling*' (George Washington, *Diary*, May 1, 1760).

dd. With transitive point-action verbs the final result is often indicated by an object or an object in connection with an objective predicate: 'He has *won great fame*.' 'We shall *reach the city* within an hour.' 'They *got the thief*.' 'I remember them, but I

forget their names,' literally, 'I fail to get hold of their names.'
'He has *made himself skilful* in this kind of work.'

In colloquial speech, to express the cessation of an activity, *it*
is often used as object, referring to something being done by
another or others, usually in a tone of disapproval: 'Cut *it* out!'
'Quit *it!'* 'Drop *it!'* (principally British).

ee. After point-action copulas, like *become, catch* (**6 B, 7 F**),
come, get, turn, etc., we use a predicate noun, adjective, or prepositional phrase to indicate the final goal or state: 'He *became a
lawyer.'* 'I was behind him for a while, but I *have caught up*
(adverb used as predicate adjective; see **7 F**) with him.' 'His
prediction *came true.'* 'They at last *came to terms.'* 'He *got to
be rich, my best friend, a great lawyer.'* 'He *turned out to be a rascal.'*
'He *turned traitor.'* As we have seen in *a ff,* p. 380, *be* is sometimes
used as a point-action copula with ingressive force. Like a number
of other ingressive forms, it points also to the final point in the
development: 'He wants to *be* (= *become*) a lawyer.' The extensive use of ingressive and effective copulas is a marked feature of
modern English. They are often used where in other languages a
prefix is employed in connection with the verb. For a full list of
these copulas see **6 B.**

In colloquial speech, we are very fond of speaking of an attained
state, employing a predicative perfect participle after *get,* where
in more formal language we speak of an act, employing a simple
finite verb of complete predication: 'It will be ten o'clock before
we *get started'* (or in more formal language *start*). 'We all lost
our patience before we *got started'* (or simply *started*). 'I was tired
long before I *got done* (colloquial American) with my work' (or
more formally '*finished* my work').

It is usually necessary to employ here a copula and an adjective
to predicate a quality of a person or thing, but in verbs made
from adjectives the verb performs the functions of copula and
adjective: 'Her hair *grayed* and *whitened.'*

The infinitive is much used after *be, stand, get, be growing, be
coming,* and *be going* (**37 1 e**), or simple *grow, come, go,* to indicate
the actual or forthcoming result, outcome of some action, influence,
development, or state of things: 'Better things *are to follow.'*
'You must get down to work if you *are* ever *to accomplish* anything.'
'The situation is such that we *stand* (indicating imminence) *to
lose* a large sum of money.' 'We gazed in despair, for we were
only three hundred yards from the railway, and *stood to lose* the
car when the enemy came along in ten minutes' (T. E. Lawrence,
Revolt in the Desert, p. 272). 'I *got* him *to do it.'* 'I *got to talk*
with him.' 'I *got* the machine *to run.'* 'I *am growing to believe*

(or I *am coming to believe*) that my sacrifice has been in vain.'
'He *is going to be* rich.' 'I *am going to injure him* (purpose) all
I can,' but 'Don't you see that you *are going to injure him* (result)
by this course?' 'Naturally, being fond of boxing, I *grew to
know* a good many prize-fighters' (Theodore Roosevelt, *An Autobiography*, Ch. II). 'Sooner or later the world *comes round to see
the truth and do the right.*' 'I went *to help him* (purpose), but now
it is quite evident that I actually *went to disturb his peace of mind*'
(result). After *got* the infinitive here is regularly replaced by a
gerund or a predicative present participle when the force becomes
descriptive, i.e., when it is desired to represent the resultant
activity as proceeding steadily rather than merely to state a bare
result as a fact: 'I got the machine *to running* (or simply *running*)
smoothly.' 'The machine got *to running* (or *running*) smoothly'
in contrast to 'The machine *was running* smoothly.' 'Uncle
Gus's got *going*' (Harriet Connor Brown, *Grandmother Brown's
Hundred Years*, 359), i.e., he got to singing the favorite songs of
his earlier years and overpowered by memory couldn't stop. The
substitution of the infinitive *to go* here for the participle *going*
would change the meaning entirely: 'Uncle Gus *has got to go*,'
i.e., *must go*. 'The machine *has got to go*,' i.e., 'I am determined
that the machine *shall go*.' The infinitive expresses result after
all these verbs except the present perfect tense of *get*, which has
the force of *must*. The verbs *stand, be growing, be coming, be
going, grow, come, go* are usually found with the infinitive, as in the
above examples, since the idea of an actual result is prominent.
There is here often a modal force associated with the effective
force. Compare **43** I A (6th par.), **43** II B *c*.

ff. The same form is often used for both point-action aspects.
The context alone can then indicate whether the expression is
ingressive or effective: 'The children *quieted down*' (ingressive),
i.e., came into a quiet state, but 'He put the rebellion down'
(effective), the final result of the action. 'He became sick' (ingressive), entrance into a new temporary state, but 'He became
rich,' final state, final result of a development.

gg. In all point-action verbs, ingressive as well as effective, the
perfect participle of intransitives was in compound tenses originally
felt as a predicate adjective expressing a condition, either a resultant state or a new state just entered upon, hence it was linked to
the subject by the copula *be*. Compare **37** 3. This older usage
still occasionally occurs since the original construction is still
dimly felt: 'The melancholy days *are come*' (Bryant). 'You
knew I *was returned* to London, Major Winter?' (Galsworthy,
Beyond, I, Ch. VI, 57). 'Many of our apples *are fallen*,' i.e., are

lying on the ground in a fallen state. 'He *is gone*,' always so in 'My money *is gone*.' This older usage also survives in the present perfect imperative 'Be gone!' See also **45** 6. Point-action intransitives are now usually conjugated with *have* since verbal activity and tense are now more prominent here than state and aspect. We now use *be* only when we feel the idea of state strongly.

hh. To indicate that the final point of the activity, or that attainment, is approaching at the present moment or was approaching at some moment in the past, we employ the progressive form of a pure effective in the case of pure effectives and the progressive form of *cease, stop*, etc., in the case of duratives: 'He *is dying*.' 'I *am catching up* with him.' 'My strength *is giving out*.' 'They *are putting* it *across*' (colloquial American). 'I *was winning* him to all that was good when I fell sick.' 'It *is ceasing to rain*.' Compare *a hh*, p. 380.

3. **Terminate Aspect.** A large number of simple and compound verbs indicate an action *as a whole*. Such verbs are called terminates. This aspect is especially associated with the simple form of the verb just as the durative aspect is associated with the progressive form. In 1, p. 373, examples have been given illustrating the difference of meaning between the simple form of the verb with terminate force and the progressive form with durative force. In terminates the action often begins and terminates within a limited period: 'He *motioned* to me.' 'He didn't even *wince*.' 'He *hit* the mark.' 'He *handed* me a book.' 'He *shot* a duck.' 'The bullet *pierced* his heart.' 'She *sighed*.' 'A snowflake *lit* upon his nose.' 'He *stumbled* and *fell*.' 'The thugs *killed* him, *took* his money, and *threw* him into the river.' 'An idea *flashed* on me.' 'This news *dashed, shattered*, our hopes.' 'She *misunderstood* me.' 'I *overlooked* this item in my calculation.' The terminate aspect is the largest category, and hence is associated with many verbs of quite a different meaning from those just mentioned. Any verbal form that represents the act as a finished whole is a terminate whether the duration of the act be long or short: 'He *went* (here thought of as a finished whole, not as continuing) to church this morning.' 'Last summer I *built* a fine new house.' 'Next summer I expect to *build* a fine new house.'

A terminate indicates an action as a whole, while a point-action verb indicates only a point in the activity. In 'As soon as I shot, I saw the bird *drop*' *drop* is a terminate, for the action is considered as a whole. But in 'She *dropped* asleep' *dropped* is an ingressive, for it indicates the point of entrance into a new state. In 'She *dropped* dead' *dropped* is an effective, for it indicates the point of entrance into a final state. In 'He *put* the book upon the table' *put* is a terminate, for the action is considered as a whole; but in 'He *put* the nefarious design *through*' *put through* is an effective, for it calls attention to the final point in the activity. A terminate expressing momentary action often becomes a point-action verb when it stands in progressive form. In 'I couldn't see where I *stepped*' *stepped* is a terminate, but it is an ingressive in 'He *is* just *stepping* into his car,' for it indicates the beginning of the action. The point-action aspect is closely related to the terminate aspect. The point-action idea is present when the conception of a point becomes more prominent than that of the action as a whole. On the other hand, in a point-action verb we often lose sight of the point and feel the action as a whole, shifting the stress from the particle to the verb: 'He is just *getting úp*' (ingressive), but 'This morning I *gót up* (terminate) early.' 'I bought his shoes only a few weeks ago, but he's about *worn* them *óut*' (effective), but 'He *wéars out* (terminate) shoes faster than any boy I know.' 'It is just *setting ín* (ingressive) to rain,' but 'It *séts in* (terminate) to rain here in April.' 'They have just *paid óff* (effective) the debt on their house,' but 'Honest people *páy off* (terminate) their debts as fast as they can.' 'He has *fooled awáy* (effective) all his money,' but 'Shiftless people *fóol away* (terminate) their money.'

The terminate aspect has relations also to the durative aspect. A terminate often becomes a durative when it stands in the progressive form: 'The mercury *is* slowly *falling*.'

4. **Iterative Aspect.** This type indicates an indefinitely prolonged succession of like acts: 'He *pooh-poohs* at everything.' 'He threw his head back and *haw-hawed*.' 'Outside the wind blew gustily and set a loquacious tassel *tap-tapping* against a pane' (Maud Diver, *Desmond's Daughter*, I, Ch. V, 36).

The suffixes *–le*, *–er* are often used to suggest repetition, but we have no strong feeling for their meaning and cannot use them freely with any verb, employing them only in certain words where they have become fixed: 'The fire *crackles*.' 'Geese *gabble*.' 'Hens *cackle*.' 'Girls *giggle*.' 'The flame *flickers*.' 'He went off *muttering* something to himself.'

We often use the auxiliary *keep* along with a present participle: 'He *kept looking back* as he ran,' but the idea of repetition here is only inferred from the meaning of the verbal stem of the participle, for with many verbs this same form indicates duration: 'He *kept working* until it became dark.'

Repetition is also expressed in other ways: 'She sang it *over* and *over again*' (or *again* and *again*). 'He is (or was) *accustomed* (or in choice language *wont*) to think before he speaks' (or spoke):

or we can employ *be used* here, sometimes with the infinitive or more commonly with the gerund: 'He *is* (or *was*) *used to think* (or more commonly *to thinking*) before he speaks' (or spoke). 'What things *have* they *been used* (or *accustomed*) to tell you?' (Mark Twain, *Joan of Arc*, I, Ch. VII). 'She looked at him pretty much as Mrs. Pipchin *had been used* (or *accustomed*) to do' (Dickens, *Dombey and Son*, Ch. XII). 'And you are to know that in Hampshire they *use* (now only used in the past tense) *to catch* Trouts in the night by the light of a Torch or Straw' (Izaak Walton, *Compleat Angler*, p. 128, A.D. 1653), now '*are accustomed to catch* trout in the night,' or '*are used to catching* them in the night.' 'You *don't use* (now *are not accustomed*) to be so shy to speak your mind' (Richardson, *Clarissa*, IV, 164, A.D. 1768). 'She *used* (still common in the past tense) to sing it,' now usually, however, with the implication that the habit has ceased. 'She was *in the habit of* singing it.' 'Courage *will* come and go.' 'She *would* sing it upon every occasion.' 'I've *tried and tried*, but I've not succeeded.' 'We *insisted* and *insisted* and *insisted*, not once but half a dozen times, at the very beginning of the war, on England's adoption of the Declaration of London' (W. H. Page, *Letter to Edward M. House*, Aug. 4, 1915). 'He *is always getting* angry.' 'I *have often got* the machine *to running* smoothly.' 'He *is perpetually complaining.*' In the second from the last example repetition is associated with the ingressive aspect, in the next to the last example with the effective aspect, in the last example with the durative aspect. Thus the iterative aspect is often associated with other aspects.

The past tense and past participle *used*, employed in the preceding paragraph in illustrative examples, is pronounced *ūst* as a result of assimilation with the unstressed *to* of the infinitive that always follows it. As it is thus pronounced *ūst* to indicate repetition, while it is pronounced *ūzd* in its more general meanings, it is evident that *ūst* is now felt as having a special function, namely, that of an iterative aspect auxiliary: 'He *used* (*ūst*, iterative auxiliary) to visit us frequently,' but 'The whistle was *used* (*ūzd*, full verb) to call the dog.'

5. **Aspect in Popular Scotch and Irish English.** The progressive form in Scotch and Irish English is used to express any kind of action, hence it is here often used where the literary language requires the simple verb: 'I *was* never *knowing* such a girl, so honest and beautiful' (R. L. Stevenson, *David Balfour*, Ch. XXI). 'Try again, Martin, try again, and you'*ll be finding* her yet' (J. M. Synge, *The Well of the Saints*, p. 31). In Irish English the idea of duration or habit is expressed by using *do* in connection

with the progressive form. 'It's small joy we'd have hearing the lies they *do be telling* from the gray of dawn till the night' (J. M. Synge, *The Well of the Saints*, p. 91). 'The young and silly *do be* always *making* game of them that's dark' (blind) (*ib.*, p. 4). In the case of the copula *be* the idea of habit is expressed by *do* and the infinitive *be:* 'I *do be* at my lessons every evening from 8 to 9 o'clock' (Joyce, *English as We Speak It in Ireland*, p. 86).

CHAPTER XX

MOOD

39. Mood is a grammatical form denoting the style or manner of predication. There are three moods, the *indicative, subjunctive,* and *imperative.*

INDICATIVE

40. The indicative, the mood of simple assertion or interrogation, represents something as a fact, or as in close relations to reality, or in interrogative form inquires after a fact. A fact: '*The sun rises* every morning.' In close relation to reality: 'I shall not go, if it *rains.*' The indicative *rains* here does not state that it *is* raining, but indicates that the idea of rain is something close to a reality, for the speaker feels it is an actual problem in the near future with which he has to reckon and is reckoning. We sometimes still, as very commonly in older English, use the present subjunctive here, 'if it *rain,*' which has about the same meaning as the indicative *rains,* only representing a little different point of view. The subjunctive indicates that the idea of rain is merely a conception, but at the same time represents the act in question as something with which we may have to deal. There is at present also a stylistic difference between the two forms. The present indicative is everyday expression; the present subjunctive, like old forms in general, belongs to a choice literary style. The common preference for the indicative in this category and a few others has led some grammarians to talk about the slovenly use of the indicative and the slighting of the subjunctive in present-day English, while in fact the increasing use of the indicative in these categories doesn't indicate carelessness, but rather a change in our way of thinking. Today we decidedly prefer to look at many things, not as mere conceptions, but as things near to us, as actual problems with which we must deal. The indicative is never a substitute for the subjunctive, but is always felt as an indicative. Even when used as an imperative (**45** 4 *c*) it does not lose its old indicative character, for it represents the command as executed, the desired act as an actuality. Though the indicative, in common expression, is supplanting the subjunctive in certain categories, the subjunctive in general is not on the decline. Indeed, we are coining new subjunctive forms to express ourselves more clearly and more accurately. In life we have to deal not only with facts but with conceptions of many kinds.

SUBJUNCTIVE

41. Classification of the Meanings and the Use of the Tenses. The function of the English subjunctive is to represent something, not as an actual reality, but only as a desire, plan, demand, requirement, eventuality, conception, thought; sometimes with more or less hope of realization, or, in the case of a statement, with more or less belief; sometimes with little or no hope or faith. The subjunctive is also often used of actual facts, but it represents them as conceptions of the mind, general principles rather than as facts. See **44** II 1 (2nd par.), 3 (last par.), 10. Thus, though the subjunctive has a number of distinct functions, they are all united in a higher unity — they all represent the action or state as a conception of the mind rather than as a reality.

The different uses of the subjunctive may be classified under two general heads, which are hereby only briefly outlined, but are treated more fully in the following articles: (1) The *optative* subjunctive, which represents the utterance as something which is desired or planned, a *present tense form* (**36**) indicating hope of fulfilment; a *past tense form* (**36**) indicating little or no hope of fulfilment. We frequently avoid a blunt expression of will by using a past tense form of the subjunctive, thus indicating that we do not count upon the fulfilment of our wish. Here the past tense forms lose in large measure the element of unreality and are called *the subjunctive of modest wish*. (2) The *potential* subjunctive, which represents the statement, not as an actual fact, but only as a conception of the mind, a *present tense form* indicating that the speaker or writer feels the conception as probably conforming to fact or reality, or regards the occurrence of the act in question as likely, probable, sometimes, however, indicating doubt as to the matter of fact or the occurrence of the act; a *past tense form* indicating decided doubt as to the matter of fact and pronounced improbability as to the occurrence of the act. We frequently avoid a blunt expression of our opinion by using a past tense form of the subjunctive, thus expressing hesitation. Here the past tense forms of the potential subjunctive lose in large measure the element of doubt and uncertainty and are used to state an opinion modestly, politely, or cautiously in a less positive and abrupt way than in the indicative. This is the polite subjunctive, or the subjunctive of modest or cautious statement.

The two groups of tenses employed in the subjunctive — the present tense forms (present, present perfect, or *will, may,* or *shall* with a dependent infinitive) and the past tense forms (past, past perfect, or *would, might,* or *should* with a dependent infinitive) — stand out in general quite distinctly from each other. The different tenses within each group mark different distinctions of time, while the tenses of one group as compared with those of the other group do not mark different distinctions of *time*, but differ only in the *manner* in which they represent the statement. Thus the present and the past subjunctive both denote present or future time, but they usually differ in the manner of the statement, the past tense indicating a greater improbability, or even unreality: 'If there *be* a misunderstanding between them, I don't know of it,' but 'If there *were* a misunderstanding between them, I should know of it.' 'If it *rain*, I'll not go,' but 'If it *were to rain*, I wouldn't go.' Likewise the present perfect and the past perfect subjunctive both denote past time, but differ in the manner of the statement: 'I ask that every man of any standing in Rome be brought to trial even if he *have remained* (a quite probable case) neutral' (Masefield, *Pompey the Great*, Act II). 'Even if he *had been* (contrary to fact) here, I should have said the same thing.' We feel the distinctions of manner today most vividly in the auxiliaries. *Will, may, shall*, on the one hand, and *would, might, should*, on the other hand, all represent present or future time, but the two groups differ markedly in the manner in which they represent the thought: 'I am hoping that he *may* come this evening,' but 'I think he *might* come this evening but I am not expecting him.'

In oldest English, when there were only two tenses, the present and the past, the past subjunctive, like the past indicative, pointed to the past, differing from it only in that it represented the act as a mere conception or as contrary to reality. It is sometimes still employed for reference to the past where it is desired to represent something not as a concrete reality but as conceivable, probable, as occurring. Interesting examples are given in **44** II 5 A *b* (last par.). It is no longer employed for reference to the past when it is desired to express unreality, for we now have much better means of expression here and moreover have found a better use for this old form. In Old English, it was still used for reference to the past to express unreality: 'Gif þu *wære* her *nære* min broðer dead' (*John*, XI, 21, A.D. 1000) = 'If thou *hadst been* here, my brother would not have died.' The past subjunctive form with the peculiar idea of unreality that had become associated with it was sometimes used also for reference to the future, as the present subjunctive forms could not express this idea. Later when the past perfect indicative came into use, its subjunctive gradually assumed the functions of the old past subjunctive where the reference was to the past, and the past subjunctive was reserved for reference to the future. As the modal auxiliaries, however, are defective verbs that have never had a past perfect subjunctive, we have to employ here another means to express unreality when the reference is to the past, namely, the past subjunctive of the auxiliary in connection with a dependent perfect infinitive: 'He *might have succeeded* if he had tried' (past perfect subjunctive). Similarly, the present tense subjunctive forms of these auxiliaries with their implication of greater probability may be used for reference to the past if they are associated with a perfect infinitive: 'The train *may have arrived* by this time.'

As indicated on page 391, the tense of the subjunctive employed is a point of vital importance. Unfortunately, however, this feeling for the meaning of the subjunctive tenses is only active after a *present tense form* (**36**). After a *past tense form* (**36**) it is entirely destroyed by the law of the sequence of tenses described in **36**: 'I *am* hoping that he *may* come this evening,' but 'I *was* hoping that he *might* come that evening.' Here *might* does not have the usual force of a past subjunctive, for it is a present subjunctive that has been attracted into the form of a past tense after a past tense.

42. Subjunctive Form. Since the time of the earliest records the simple subjunctive forms have lost much of their original distinctiveness, so that they now cannot always be distinguished from indicative forms. The forces that called the original forms into being, however, did not cease their activity. As described on page 390, the subjunctive is an important means of expression, vital to an accurate expression of thought and feeling. As the simple subjunctive forms in the course of a long phonetic development lost their distinctive endings, modal auxiliaries were pressed into service to express the same ideas. In large measure they are subjunctive forms, although not recognizable by a distinctive ending. In fact, however, whether indicative or subjunctive in form, they perform the function of the older simple subjunctive and are here treated as our modern subjunctive forms. For clear formal proof that a number of these so-called modal auxiliaries have entirely ceased to be verbs and are now in reality mere grammatical forms to color the statement, see **44** I. In the same way the original endings of the simple subjunctive forms had been pressed into service to color the statement. The mind seeks until it finds a means to express its thought and feeling. The first means which the mind employs to express itself are usually concrete in meaning. The endings of the old simple subjunctive were doubtless originally more concrete than they were even in oldest English. They had become mere abstract symbols, so that even in the Old English period the English mind was already seeking a more concrete and a more accurate expression for its subjunctive ideas, and began to employ the auxiliaries which are now so much used. The fact that some of these auxiliaries were employed at a time when the subjunctive had distinctive endings shows clearly that they did not come into use on account of the lack of distinctive subjunctive forms. The use of the auxiliaries evidently indicates a desire for a more concrete and a more accurate expression of thought and feeling. The auxiliaries have more and brighter shades of meaning than the old simple subjunctive forms.

OPTATIVE SUBJUNCTIVE

43. This subjunctive is used in the following expressions of will:

I. In Principal Propositions:

A. VOLITIVE SUBJUNCTIVE. The old simple subjunctive is, in general, now little used in decided expressions of will — the volitive subjunctive. Third person: '*Suffice* it to say that,' etc. '*Perish* the colonies rather than a principle!' '*Be* this purse an earnest of my thanks!' (Lytton, *Rienzi*, I, Ch. III). '*Laugh* those that can, *weep* those that may!' (Scott, *Marmion*, 5, 17, l. 3). It is most common with a subject of general or indefinite meaning: 'Everybody *stand* up!' 'Please *forgive* me everybody!' (Pinero, *His House in Order*, Act II). It is also still quite common where the subject is a substantive limiting adjective modified by a partitive genitive of a personal pronoun: 'One of you *go* and *hasten* it!' (Alfred Noyes, *The Torch-Bearers*, p. 24). It is also frequently used with *witness* in the sense *serve as proof, be the proof:* 'The literary works that have fascinated mankind abound in strokes of invention: *witness* Homer, Shakespeare,' etc. (Bain, *Rhetoric*). 'The drama of literary moralizing is growing increasingly, as *witness* the plays by Mr. Shaw, Mr. Barker, Mr. Galsworthy' (*Bookman*). We now usually employ here *let* (imperative) with a dependent infinitive clause: 'Someone is inquiring for you.' — '*Let* him *come* in!' '*Let* them *take* care what they say!' The form with *let* here is the modern subjunctive form corresponding to the old simple subjunctive. In popular speech, *leave* is often used here instead of *let;* always without *to* after the analogy of *let:* '*Leave* him *come* in.' In the negative form of statement, we use here the present subjunctive of *do* with a dependent infinitive: '*Don't* everybody *talk* at once!' '*Don't* anybody *tell* me that!' '*Don't talk* to me anybody!' (Pinero, *Sweet Lavender*, Act III). The first person plural of the old simple subjunctive is now possible only in poetry: '*Part we* in friendship from your land' (Scott, *Marmion*, 6, 13), now expressed by the new *let*-form: '*Let us* part!' Compare **45** 3.

To convey stronger force we employ *must:* 'You *múst* go!' '*He múst* go!' 'We *múst* go!' 'The world *múst* be made safe for democracy' (Woodrow Wilson, April 2, 1917). 'It *múst* succeed!' Often, however, with the stress upon the form that has the verbal meaning where the verbal meaning seems important to the mind: 'We must *gó!*' Also *have to* and *have got to* are used here. The latter is the more emphatic of the two, but is for the most part confined to the present tense and to colloquial language. Although *have to* and *have got to* usually denote an objective necessity that lies in circumstances, they are also not infrequently used to indicate that the objective necessity lies in the will of another, hence the speaker often employs them instead of *must* when he desires to represent his will or, in the language of kindness and politeness, his wish as an objective necessity that constrains another or brings about some result: 'I order it and you *have to* do it; this is my last word.' 'You *have to* (or *have got to*) come to our cottage over Whitsuntide.' 'It *hás to* succeed.' They often denote the constraint of another than the speaker: 'I don't want to do it, but I *have to*' (or *have got to*). We often have to use *had to* and *have had to* as *must* has no clear forms for reference to the past: 'I *had to* do it.' 'I *have* often *had to* do it.' Compare **45** 4 *e*. Alongside of this common use of *have to*, *have got to*, and *must* is their common use to indicate the constraint of circumstances: 'We *have to* (or *must*) sell our house.' 'In life we *have to* (or *must*) do many things we do not desire to do.' Perverse constraint: 'Just when I was dropping off, a door *had to* (or *must*) bang.' *Must* was originally a past subjunctive. We now feel it as a present tense. Where the reference is to the will of a person the force is that of a volitive subjunctive. Where the reference is to the constraint of circumstance the force is thought by some to be that of the indicative, though the form was originally a subjunctive. On the other hand, *have to* was originally an indicative indicating the constraint of circumstances, but it is now used also with subjunctive force indicating the will of a person. In both forms, however, there is always present the idea of a constraint of some kind, so that there is a unity of meaning in all the examples. There is a certain volitive force here, for the aim is not to express the act of a free subject, but to represent the act as determined by another, or by circumstances, or by natural law. Sometimes other forms of expression, *need*, *want* (popular), *am obliged*, *am compelled*, etc., are employed to express this modal idea: 'He *need* not wait.' 'You *want* (= *need*) to keep your eyes open in the city or you will be taken in' (Krapp, *Comprehensive Guide to Good English*). 'I *am obliged* to be away tomorrow.' Also sentence adverbs (**16** 2 *a*) have this modal force: 'He will *necessarily* (or *of necessity*) arrive late.'

Am (or *is, are*) *to* is often used instead of *must* or *have to,* usually with a little milder force: 'You *are to* stay here until I come back.' Sometimes in sharper tone: 'You *are* always *to* shut the door when you enter this room!' For a fuller description of this modal force see **7** D 2. Compare **45** 4 *f. Going to* has the same general meaning, but is more forcible: 'All policemen *are going to* go to work or get off the force' (words of the Chief of Police in Chicago, July 16, 1930).

To indicate the will of the speaker with reference to the future we use *will* in the first person and in questions also in the second person, but in declarative statements employ *shall* in the second and third persons: 'I *will* do all I can' (promise). 'I *won't* have you children playing in my study!' In '*Will* you sit down?' and in still more friendly tone '*Won't* you sit down?' the force is kind, but in '*Will* you children be quiet!' the words and tone have the force of a command. 'You *shall* have some cake' (promise). 'You *shall* smart for it' (threat). 'You *shall* do as I say!' (command). A mild form of expression of will is found in permissions: 'You *may* go.' The *Concise Oxford Dictionary* gives *must not, cannot* as the usual negative forms of *may:* 'You *must not* (or *cannot*) *go.*' This corresponds closely to our colloquial American usage: '*May* I (or *mayn't* I) play ball this morning?' — 'No, you *cannot;* but you *may* play this afternoon' (Kittredge and Farley, *Advanced English Grammar,* p. 126). But *may not* is sometimes used here, especially in the literary language: 'Why *mayn't* I say to Sam that I'll marry him? Why *mayn't* I?' (Hardy, *Life's Little Ironies,* I, II, 29). 'Would he break faith with one I *may not* name?' (Tennyson, *Lancelot and Elaine,* 681). 'Now the dilemma is acute, and settlement *may not* be deferred' (editorial in *Chicago Tribune,* Dec. 9, 1929). 'Rooms *may not* be sub-rented' (*The University of Chicago Announcements,* Jan. 15, 1930, p. 18). *May not* is most common here when the word *may* immediately precedes: 'It is not always easy to know what we *may* do and what we *may not* do.' '*May* I go now?' — 'No, you *may not!*' *Can* is not infrequently employed also in positive permissions: 'You *can* go' (*Concise Oxford Dictionary*). Of course, also in the subordinate clause: 'Why won't you say when I *can* see you again?' (Tarkington, *Mirthful Haven,* Ch. XIV). In questions *may* and *can* here have the force of a request: '*May* I come in?' 'I may come and see you, *mayn't* I?' (Susan Warner, *The Wide, Wide World,* Ch. XIII). '*Can* I come in?' (Rider Haggard, *Mr. Meeson's Will,* Ch. VIII). The positive form of statement with *may* or *can* often has the force of a mild command: 'PRETTY COUSIN. — "Bobby, how dare you give me a kiss?"' BOBBY (unabashed).

— "Well, if you don't like it, you *can* (or *may*) give it me back again"' (*Punch*). Compare **45** 4.

To ascertain the will of a person to whom we are speaking, we employ *shall* or *am* (or *is*, *are*) *to*: '*Shall I* (or *he*) come again tomorrow?' '*Am I* (or *is he*) to come again tomorrow?' Compare **37** 5 *a* (pp. 366, 371).

Shall or *am* (or *is*, *are*) *to* is employed to predict that some-thing will come about in accordance with the will of God or des-tiny: 'Heaven and earth *shall* pass away, but my word *shall* not pass away' (*Matthew*, XXIV, 35). 'The time *shall* (or *is to*) come when Egypt *shall* be avenged' (Lytton, *Pompeii*, II, Ch. VII). Similarly, *shall*, *am* (*is*, *are*, *was*, *were*) *to*, *going to*, and *come to* are used to represent an act or state as the inevitable outcome of events or as the natural result of a development: 'We *shall* then (or *are* then *to*) be partners with all the business men of the country, and a day of freer, more stable property *shall* have come' (Woodrow Wilson, Aug. 7, 1912). *Is to* cannot replace *shall* in the future perfect relation, as in the case of the second *shall* here, but elsewhere it is the common form in everyday language, while *shall* is the favorite in higher diction: 'Better days *are* soon *to* (or *shall* soon) follow.' 'The worst was over. Better days *were* soon *to* (or *should* soon) follow.' These forms point to the future — from the present or from a point of time in the past. *Going to* points to the future from the present: 'We *are going to* lose all that we have earned in a lifetime.' In the case of *come to* all the different time relations can be expressed, as *come* has retained enough of its original concrete meaning to point, like any verb, to the present, past, or future: 'He *is coming* (*came*, *has come*, *will come*) *to* see the error of his ways.' In the case of *is coming*, *came*, *has come* the reference is to actual events, but these forms express something more than actual events. They contain a modal idea. They represent the events as the result of the con-straint of educating personal experiences. This modal idea is often expressed by a sentence adverb (**16** 2 *a*): 'Our cause will *ultimately* (or *eventually*) prevail.'

The past subjunctive *should* is much used as a modest or polite volitive: 'You *should* go at once,' much milder than '*Go* at once!' or 'You *shall* go at once!' 'He *should* go at once.' 'We *should* go at once.' This form, however, sometimes becomes quite em-phatic: 'You *should* go if I had my way!' 'You *should* mind your own business!' The past subjunctive *would* is here usually associated with the idea of politeness, modesty: 'I *would* speak a few words to you, sir.' '*Would* you tell me the time, please?' 'Mrs. Ralston, also Mr. Brown *would* like a cup of tea' (indirect polite request), but, according to **37** 5 *a* (p. 367), we say 'I *should* like a cup of tea' (direct polite request) to avoid expressing the idea of desire twice. The past subjunctive *would* is sometimes quite sharp and emphatic: 'If he should treat me in that way, I just *wóuldn't* stand it.' The past subjunctive *might* is much used in polite and modest requests: 'You *might* call at the baker's and get some bread.' 'Aunty, *might* (or *could*) I bother you again with a few questions?' *Might* sometimes becomes sharp and emphatic: 'You *might* offer to help me!' Compare **45** 4. For reference to the past we employ the perfect infinitive: 'You should *have gone* at once.'

The past subjunctives *ought* (past subjunctive of *owe*), *must*, and *should* are often used to express modestly and politely the idea of constraint of duty, i.e., moral necessity or obligation: 'We *ought* (literally, *should owe*) *to* (or *must*, or *should*) do something to help him.' Ideal constraint, i.e., fitness and expediency: 'She *ought to* (or *should*) be praised for that.' 'A liar *ought to* (or *should*) have a good memory.' *Should* is often used ironically: 'He — as he put it colloquially to himself — *should* worry!' (Lawrence Perry, *Collier's*, Sept. 3, 1927, p. 32) = 'It wasn't anything he should worry about.' 'You'll get a good thrashing for that.' — 'I *should* worry' = 'I'm not worrying about that.' Compare **44** I *a*. For reference to the past we employ the perfect infinitive: 'We ought *to have done* something to help him.'

A polite expression of will often takes the form of a simple question calling for a statement of fact: 'Who lives here?' See **2** (3rd par.), p. 1.

B. SUBJUNCTIVE OF WISH. The present subjunctive is often used to express a wish which in all probability may be realized, the sanguine subjunctive of wish: 'God *bless* you!' 'The Lord *have* mercy upon us!' 'The Lord *save* us!' 'Thy kingdom *come!*' 'Heaven *forbid!*' Often in oaths as an expression of irritation: 'God *damn* you!' (or it). '*Be damned* to you!' a blending of '*Be* [*you*] *damned!*' and '*Woe* [*be*] to you!' Often with milder words: '[God] *Confound* you!' (or it). 'The devil *take* him!' 'Plague *take* them!' 'Grammar *be hanged!*'

In general, the new subjunctive form with *may* and a dependent infinitive clause is more common: '*May* you see many happy returns of this occasion!' '*May* he return soon!' '*May* I never see such a sight again!' 'So *mote* (archaic present subjunctive of *must*, once used here with the force of *may*) it be!' In oaths and mild imprecations *will* with a dependent infinitive clause is often used in the first person: 'I'*ll be damned* (*hanged*, or *dashed*) if I do it!' '[I'*ll be*] *Dashed* if I like it.'

A past tense form, the unreal subjunctive of wish, conveys the idea of unreality, indicating that fulfilment is not expected: 'O *were* he only here!' 'O *had* I wings!' '*Would* God that thou couldst hide me from myself!' (Tennyson, *Guinevere*, 117), now usually 'I *would* to God that,' etc., after the analogy of 'I *wish* to God.' Modal auxiliaries are now more common here, serving as the modern subjunctive forms: 'Too late! O *might* I see her just once more!' '*Could* we only look forward in life and see as clearly as we do looking backward in memory!'

The past tense often expresses a modest wish (**41**): '*Might* this little book contribute something toward arousing interest in this important question.' 'I *would* not have the affair known for all the world.' 'I *would* rather stay than go.' Instead of *would rather* we often employ the past subjunctive *had* with *rather:* 'I *had rather* err with Plato than be right with Horace' (Shelley, *Essays*, II, 155). The adverb *rather* has displaced here older *liefer*. The newer form began to appear here in the fifteenth century, but the older lingered on for a long while: 'Far *liever* would I face about, and step back to my Emperor' (Coleridge, *Piccolomini*, IV, V, A.D. 1800). It survives in dialect. Earlier in the present period the positive of this old form was still in use: 'I *would as lief* go there as anywhere' (Thackeray, *Henry Esmond*, I, VI). It survives in colloquial speech. In more formal language we use *as readily* here. In less formal language older *liefer, as lief* are now represented by *sooner, as soon:* 'I *would* (or *had*) *sooner* die than let him find it out.' 'I *would* (or *had*) just *as soon* stay at home as go.' In all these cases *had* is now less common than *would*. The past optative *had* with an adverb should be distinguished from the past potential described in **44 I** (10th par.). The past potential is associated with an adjective, not with an adverb: 'I *had better* (objective predicate adjective) go,' literally, 'I *should* regard going as better.' 'I *had best* go.' In the potential category *had* is much more common than *would*. The latter, however, is sometimes used. Examples are given in **44 I** (10th par.).

In all these examples the past subjunctive expresses a desire of the speaker, but it is often employed to report the desire of another: 'He *would* gladly do it.' 'He *would* rather stay at home.'

For reference to past time we employ the past perfect subjunctive, or in the case of auxiliaries use the perfect infinitive instead of the present: 'O *had* he only *been* here!' 'O *might* I *have known* it in time!' 'O *could* I *have understood* him better!' 'I *would* gladly *have done* it.' 'I *should have liked* a glass of water.' 'He *would* gladly *have done* it.'

C. SUBJUNCTIVE OF LOGICAL REASONING. In logical reasoning in laying down one or more desired propositions from which conclusions are to be drawn, the present tense of the simple subjunctive is now entirely replaced by *let* with the infinitive: '*Let* the figure abc *be* an isosceles triangle and bd a perpendicular line on the base,' etc.

D. SUBJUNCTIVE OF PLAN. *Am* (or *is, are*) *to* and *shall* are much used to represent the act as merely planned, but usually with the implication that the plan will be carried out: 'I *am to go* by train to Jerusalem tonight. There I *am to meet* Ellington' (Sir Walter Raleigh, *Letter to H. A. Jones*, March 22, 1922). 'There *shall* (or more commonly *is to*) *be* a girth of buildings down the avenue that leads to the woods below, and there *shall* (or more commonly *is to*) *run* by those buildings a path which leads to the open quadrangles of the professional schools' (Woodrow Wilson, Dec. 9, 1902).

To express an unrealized past plan we employ *was to* followed by a perfect infinitive: 'He *was to have dined* with us today.'

The finite verb in the case of *am* (or *is, are, was*) *to* is always in the indicative. It indicates the time of the action — future or past. The subjunctive or modal idea lies in the *to*-infinitive in connection with the verb *be* (*am, is, are, was*). Compare **7** D 2.

II. **In Subordinate Clauses.** Here the optative subjunctive represents the action as conceded or desired.

A. ACTION CONCEDED. The present subjunctive is often used as a weak imperative, a mild volitive. Originally, these propositions were independent sentences and may still be regarded as such, but as their logical dependence is evident they may be regarded as subordinate clauses: '*Say* [he] what he will, he cannot make matters worse,' or '*Let him say* what he will,' etc. Other examples in **32** 1 *a aa*.

Also in really subordinate concessive clauses: 'Though he *make* (*shall make*, or more commonly *may make*) every effort, he cannot succeed.' 'But whether the extensive changes which I have recommended *shall be thought* desirable or not, I trust that we shall reject the Bill of the noble Lord' (Macaulay). 'However hard it *rain* (*shall rain*, or more commonly *may rain*, or *rains*, if we desire to indicate that we are reckoning with this factor), we shall have to go.' 'Whosoever he *be* (now more commonly *may be*) that doth rebel, he shall be put to death' (*Joshua*, I, 18). 'I ask that every man of any standing in Rome be brought to trial even if he *have remained* neutral' (Masefield, *Pompey the Great*, Act II). The past tense forms convey the idea of unreality: 'Even if (or though) it *were* more dangerous, I should feel com-

pelled to go.' 'Even though (or if) he *were* here, I should say the
same thing.' Improbability: 'Though he *might* (or *should*) make
every effort, he could not succeed.' The past subjunctive of the
simple verb or the past subjunctive *might* or *should* in connection
with a present infinitive points to the present or the future. If
the reference is to the past, we must use the past perfect subjunctive or the past subjunctive *might* or *should* in connection
with a perfect infinitive: 'Even if (or though) it *had been* more
dangerous, I should have felt compelled to go.' 'Even if he *should
have made* every effort, he could not have succeeded.'

The past subjunctive sometimes, as in **44** II 5 A *b* (last par.),
has the modal force of the present subjunctive, indicating that the
statement is probably true, but it differs from it in that it refers
to the past: 'Stewart was, perhaps, the most beloved member of
Trinity, whether he *were* feeding rugger blues on plovers' eggs or
keeping an early chapel with the expression of an earth-born
seraph' (Compton Mackenzie, *Sinister Street*, Ch. V). In older
English, the past subjunctive often pointed to the past. See **44**
II 5 A *b* (last par.). Now we more commonly employ the past
indicative here, since we feel that we have to do with actual facts.

B. ACTION DESIRED. A present tense form represents the
statement only as desired or planned, but implies the expectation
that the desire or plan will be realized. It expresses various shades
of the volitive and the sanguine subjunctive of wish described in
I A and B. A past tense form represents the thing desired or
planned as a mere conception of the mind, not resting upon any
expectation of realization, or, on the other hand, by thus using
here a past tense form and thus indicating that we are not counting
upon a realization of our expectations we can often modestly
express earnest wishes and plans which we inwardly hope to see
realized.

The subjunctive of action desired occurs in the following categories:

a. In substantive clauses:

In object clauses after verbs of advising, beseeching, warning,
praying, wishing, willing, demanding, deciding, providing, seeing
to, taking care, etc., also after adjectives of similar meaning:
'Pray God it *last* not long!' (S. Weir Mitchell, *Roland Blake*,
Ch. II, p. 15). 'She desires that he *do* (or *may do*) it,' or with
milder force, 'She begs that he *will* (consent to) do it,' 'that I
will do it.' 'I hope (= desire and expect) that he *may recover*.'
'I tell you what *let's do*: let's all run away' (Margaret Deland,
The Iron Woman, Ch. II). 'I insist that he *be* allowed his freedom.' 'I require that you *be* here by eight.' 'We demand that

this burden *must* (or *shall* — a modern subjunctive, originally the
present indicative of the modal auxiliary *shall,* hence stronger
than *may*) *be removed.*' 'I will arrange that another consultation
shall be held.' 'The doctor insists that I *shall give up* smoking.'
'The will provides that the estate *be* (or *shall be*) *divided* among
his children.' 'Let him that hath ears and understanding see
that he *hear* (now more commonly *hears*) God's word regard-
fully' (Baxter, *Paraphrase on the New Testament, Mark,* IV, 23,
A.D. 1685). 'See to it that my boots *be* (or *shall be*) *blacked,*' but
more commonly *are blacked,* to indicate that we are counting on it.
'Take care that she *may* not *jilt* you,' or more commonly *doesn't
jilt you,* since we are reckoning with this factor. 'But mind your
human debts *are paid*' (Edwin A. Robinson, *Collected Poems,*
'Ballad by the Fire'), the indicative emphasizing the absolute
necessity of complying with this injunction.

As described in **7** D 2, there is a peculiar modal force in the
indicative forms *am to, is to, are to;* also *shall* often has this same
force: 'Father has finally decided that Fred *is to go,* that we *are
to go.*' 'I stipulate that I *shall,* you *shall,* he *shall* do it.' 'I beg
that I *shall* not suffer from it.' *Shall* is especially common here
to represent an act or state as the inevitable outcome of events
or as the natural result of a development: 'I trust that you *shall*
have no cause to regret making this appointment' (Charles P.
Taft, *Letter,* Jan. 29, 1887). *Am to, is to, are to* often have about
the same meaning here and elsewhere, but there is a little difference in the style. *Is to, are to* are more common in everyday
language.

The future indicative, so often used in direct commands, as
described in **45** 4 *c,* is often used also in indirect form here in
object clauses: 'I desire you *will do* no such thing' (Jane Austen,
Pride and Prejudice, Ch. I). The form *will* is often found here
with milder meaning, but it is, of course, modal *will,* not the
future tense auxiliary: 'I beg that you *will* draw your chair up
to the fire' (Conan Doyle, *Sherlock Holmes,* I). 'He begs that I
will do it.'

A past tense form in this category often conveys the idea of
unreality: 'I wish I *were* dead!' or here often in colloquial speech
with the past subjunctive form *was,* after the analogy of other
past subjunctives which all have the same form as the past indicative, the reference to the present or the future alone distinguishing the subjunctive here from the indicative: 'I wish it
was to-morrow!' (Farjeon, *London's Heart,* I, 188). 'I wish I *had*
wings!' 'They afterwards wished they *had* arrested him,' where,
however, in popular speech a *have* (frequently in the contracted

form of *a* or *of*) is often inserted after the *had* of the past perfect subjunctive to distinguish here the subjunctive from the indicative and thus impart the clear modal idea of unreality, as explained in **49** 3 *b* (3rd par.) and **44** II 5 C (last par.): 'They did most earnestly wish they *had of* arrested him' (A. S. M. Hutchinson, *This Freedom*, p. 370). The past subjunctive *might* is much used here: 'I too wish our efforts *might* be successful, but I scarcely expect it.' A past tense subjunctive form is often a modest expression of desire: 'I wish I *might* not have my labor in vain!' 'I wish you *would* stay a little longer!' 'He wishes I *would* go and visit him.' 'I wish that success *might* come to you speedily!' 'I would rather he *took* (or *should take*) me over the crossing.' 'Which would you rather *took* you over the crossing? Me or Papa?' (May Sinclair, *Mary Olivier*, p. 88). 'Would you rather I *went* on to the house?' (Mary Johnston, *The Long Roll*, Ch. XVII). Polite command: 'I (a physician) desire the patient *should* have a bath every day.'

After a past indicative tense form the distinction of meaning between present and past tense forms usually disappears entirely: 'She desired that he *might* come at once.' 'We demanded that the burden *should* be removed.' In recent literature and present colloquial usage, however, the tendency occasionally found in early Modern English to break through our rigid sequence and employ the simple present subjunctive even after a past tense has grown stronger, since the simple present subjunctive with its implication of early and immediate execution has become associated with the expression of will in general without reference to the tense of the principal verb: 'I *desire, demand,* or *suggest,* or I *desired, demanded,* or *suggested,* that action *be postponed.*' 'She insisted that he *accept,* and, indeed, *take* her with him' (Edgar Rice Burroughs, *Tarzan of the Apes*, Ch. I, 3). 'He was glad his sisters had suggested that the Holtons *be invited*' (Meredith Nicholson, *Otherwise Phyllis*, Ch. X).

The subjunctive is found with verbs with these meanings not only in object clauses, but also often in subject clauses: 'It has long been desired by us all that this privilege *be extended* to others.' ''Twere to be wish'd not one of them *survived*' (Robert Rogers, *Ponteach*, I, II, A.D. 1776), or *should survive.* 'It seems to be fixed that Fred *is to go* to college' (George Eliot).

This subjunctive is much used in subject clauses also after nouns and adjectives with these meanings: 'It is my ardent wish, or very desirable, that he *come* (or *may come,* or *shall come*) at once.' 'The essence (= thing required) of originality is not that it *be* new' (Carlyle). There is a tendency here to disregard the old sequence and employ a present subjunctive after a past tense in the principal proposition, especially when immediate action seems desirable: 'It was more than ever imperative now that he *forestall* that desperate action' (Brand Whitlock, *J. Hardin & Son*, III, Ch. X, 4). 'For our good name it was essential that they (the notes) *be* early *redeemed*' (T. E. Lawrence, *Revolt in the Desert*, p. 121).

This subjunctive is much used also in attributive substantive clauses after nouns with these meanings: 'Father's advice that Mary *wait* until next week is quite reasonable.' 'The Committee on Curriculum presents the recommendation that the cases of all students who do not fully meet the requirements for a degree *shall be considered* by a committee consisting of the Dean, the Registrar, and the Committee on Registration.' 'When one runs against a post like that, one can't help expressing the wish that the post *were* in the infernal regions.' 'She has left the written request that you *would* (or stronger *should*) *come* soon.' 'He has given the order that the patient *should have* a bath every day.' Of course, with a past indicative the present subjunctive is attracted into the form of the past: 'I promise secrecy on the understanding that the thing *end*' (or *shall end*), but 'On the understanding that the thing *ended*, secrecy was promised' (Jerome K. Jerome, *Harper's Monthly*, July, 1925), or 'on the understanding that the thing *should end*.' Often, however, here, as above, a present subjunctive after a past tense: 'He issued the order that the work *be done* at once.'

The past tense subjunctive forms are often used in the subordinate clause where the principal proposition is suppressed: 'Oh! that I *were* young again!' 'Ah! that your excellency but *saw* the great duel which depends on you alone!' (Kingsley, *Hypatia*, Ch. II). 'Oh! that I *had* but known!' (Hall Caine, *The Deemster*, Ch. XVIII).

In the preceding examples the idea of wish, desire, demand is expressed by the meaning of the verb or some noun or adjective in the principal proposition as well as by the subjunctive form of the verb in the subordinate clause. Often, however, the idea of wish, desire, demand is expressed only by the subjunctive form of the verb in the subordinate clause.

In object clauses: 'Therefore they thought it good you *hear* a play' (Shakespeare, *The Taming of the Shrew*, Induction, II, 136), or more modestly '*should hear* a play.' 'He thought it good that a young man now and then *hear* (or *should hear*) a play.' 'We regard it of the highest importance that Kinney *be nominated*' (*Chicago Tribune*, April 12, 1926). 'Mary will telegraph him that he *is to* (*shall*, or more modestly *should*) come at once.' It can be seen by the first examples that the old sequence is not always observed here.

In subject clauses: 'It is a matter of the highest importance to the whole world that there *shall be* a free ballot and a fair count' (J. B. Foraker, *Notes of a Busy Life*, Ch. XVI). 'It is biologically important that the sex-complex *leave* nothing to chance' (George A. Dorsey, *Why We Behave as Human Beings*, p. 438). 'It is best that he *go* at once.' 'It is sufficient, not sufficient, that he *read* his lesson over only once.' 'The only form of independence that is possible or desirable for a woman is that she *shall be* (or simple *be*) dependent upon her husband, or if she is unmarried, on her nearest male relative' (St. John Hankin, *The Last of the DeMullins*, Act III), or more modestly '*should be dependent* upon,' etc.

In predicate clauses: 'What this country needs now more than it ever did before, what it *shall* (or *is to*) *need* in the years following is knowledge and enlightenment' (Woodrow Wilson, Dec. 9, 1902). The force of *shall* and *is to* in this example is the same as in the example from Charles P. Taft on page 402.

In attributive substantive clauses: 'It is high time that he *go*' (or more modestly *went*, or *were going*, or *should go*). 'It is time that you either *showed* your authority or openly *confessed* you had none.' As *were* is the only distinctive past subjunctive in the language, in all other verbs the past subjunctive having the same form as the past indicative, we sometimes even in the literary language and frequently in colloquial speech find the past indicative used as a past subjunctive: 'It's really time something *was* done' (Marion Crawford, *The Undesirable Governess*, Ch. I).

b. In adverbial clauses of purpose introduced by *that, so that, in order that, for fear that, lest*, with the same use of forms and tenses as in *a*: 'In order that this measure *be* useful, it must be put into force at once.' 'I move that the case be adjourned until tomorrow in order that further inquiries *may be made*.' 'I locked myself into my study that I *might* not *be disturbed*.' 'I would give all my goods that it *had* never *happened*' (Dasent, *Burnt Njal*, II, 118), or more commonly '*might* never *have happened*.' For other examples see **33**.

As in object clauses, as described in *a* (5th par.), there is also here in adverbial clauses of purpose, especially those introduced by *lest*, a tendency after a past tense to break through our rigid sequence and employ the simple present subjunctive to indicate more vividly that the thing feared is felt as imminent: 'We helped down the Indians from their burdened camels that no sound *betray* (instead of *might betray*) us to listening ears' (T. E. Lawrence, *Revolt in the Desert*, p. 177). 'And lest she *disobey* (instead of *disobeyed*, or more commonly *should disobey*), he left her' (Amy Lowell, *Men, Women, and Ghosts*, p. 111). 'He desired rather to keep free of these follies lest they *confuse* him and *make* him soft' (Sinclair Lewis, *Arrowsmith*). The use of *may* instead of *might* after a past tense is a prominent feature of colloquial Irish English: 'Last week when I set out on my long train journey I brought a book that I *may* read as I traveled along' (Joyce, *English as We Speak It in Ireland*, 84).

Shall, here as elsewhere in purpose clauses, has a strong force. It represents something as yet only conceived, but at the same time as something that *must* be attained: 'They (i.e., the trappers) go about their business in a stealthy manner for fear that any *shall* see where they set their traps' (Thoreau, *Journal*, XI, p. 456). 'The one command laid upon him (i.e., the real playwright) is to see things nobly — that his deeper vision *shall* help the crowd' (L. Merrick, *The Actor-Manager*, Ch. I, p. 13). 'He brushes his hair up over his head from behind, so that it *shall* not be seen how bald he is' (Anne Douglas Sedgwick, *The Little French Girl*, Part III, Ch. IV).

c. In temporal clauses after *until, till, when, whenever, as soon as, before, against* (= *before*), *ere* the subjunctive *shall* is sometimes employed to represent a future act, not as a fact, but only as the result of a development, the outcome of circumstances, or as planned, desired: 'Is she going to keep a lonely vigil till that time *shall* come?' (Florence Montgomery, *Thrown Together*, I). 'Do my errand when it *shall* be most convenient for you in the course of the day' (Stevenson, *Dr. Jekyll*, Ch. IX). 'There is much to be done before every child in the country *shall* speak English as could be wished' (H. C. Wyld). 'There is a month yet, and I promise you to be back ere it *shall* have elapsed.' *Come to* is often used here instead of *shall:* 'It will be a better and a happier world when greater numbers of men *come to* (or *shall*) see the need of serving others.' Of course, *shall* and *come to* become *should* and *came to* after a past indicative: 'Many years passed by before he *should* (or *came to*) realize his error.'

In older English, the simple subjunctive was used here: 'The tree will wither long before it *fall*' (Byron, *Childe Harold*, III, XXXII). 'The most forward bud Is eaten by the canker ere it *blow*' (Shakespeare, *The Two Gentlemen of Verona*, I, I, 45). This usage lingers on in poetry and choice prose: 'Not though all men call, Kneeling with void hands, Shall they see light fall Till it *come* for all Tribes of men and lands' (Swinburne, *Songs before*

Sunrise, 'Christmas Antiphones,' III). 'I am now going down to Garden City and New York till the President *send* for me; or, if he do not send for me, I'm going to his house and sit on his front steps till he *come* out!' (Walter H. Page, *Letter to Irwin Laughlin,* August, 1916). 'It follows that all gods must pass until — perhaps — a god *be* found who satisfies the requirements of this disastrously exigent human dreaming' (Cabell, *The High Place,* XXIX).

After the past subjunctive forms *ought, might, should,* etc., the present subjunctive is usually attracted into the form of the past: 'You ought not to decide this matter until you *were* (or *should be*) calmer.' 'You ought to be beaten until you *fell* down' (Hergesheimer, *Cytherea,* p. 288) (or *should fall down*). 'She might say it until she *dropped* dead before me, and I should know it wasn't true' (Alice Brown, *The Winds between the Worlds,* Ch. XXIII). 'You should be kept at this work until you *finished* it.'

The present indicative is now more common here than the form with *shall* or the simple present subjunctive, since we desire to represent the thought, not merely as something planned or desired, but as an actual factor with which we are reckoning: 'When he *comes,* bring him into the room.'

d. The old simple volitive subjunctive (I A) is still sometimes used in a proposition which, though formally independent, has the logical force of a temporal *when*-clause: 'She will be eighteen years old *come Easter'* (= when Easter shall come), literally, *Let Easter come.* 'I almost think if I could do like you, Drop everything and live out on the ground — But it might be, *come night* (= when night should come) I shouldn't like it' (Robert Frost, *North of Boston,* p. 71).

e. In relative clauses expressing shades of the volitive subjunctive and the subjunctive of wish:

Often to express purpose: 'Envoys were sent who *should sue* for peace.' 'The system of Divine Providence leaves it open to us, by humble and loving ways, to make ourselves susceptible of deep delight from the meanest objects of creation — a delight which *shall not* (= *is not intended to*) separate us from our fellows, nor require the sacrifice of any duty or occupation, but which *shall* bind us closer to men and to God' (Ruskin, *Modern Painters,* Part III, Sec. I, Ch. III).

Often in choice language to represent a future act or state as the inevitable outcome of events or as the natural result of a development: 'May my beloved old college have the unspeakable privilege of helping on my country towards the days when its people *shall* respond to the world that invests it, by learning its laws and obeying them, by loving its beauty,' etc. (Sir Henry Jones, *Letter*, May 7, 1920). 'It is hard to construct an argument here which *shall* not be heated' (Woodrow Wilson, Jan., 1901). *Am* (or *is, are*) *to* often has the same force. Of course, the past subjunctive form must be used after a past indicative: 'The year was now at hand in which he *should* draw the proconsulate of Africa as his lot' (Hale and Buck, *Latin Grammar*, p. 268).

Often as a strong volitive: 'I am engaged in an enterprise that *must* and *shall* succeed.' 'But even more do we need criticism which *shall* be truthful both in what it says and in what it leaves unsaid' (Theodore Roosevelt, *The Strenuous Life*, p. 74). Also with milder force: 'After a time she was telling herself that she did love the Butler (name) of that remote past, but that, as (see **23** II 6, next to last par.) *witness* what had just occurred, she did not love the Butler of the present' (Cameron Mackenzie, *Mr. and Mrs. Pierce*, Ch. XIX).

Also the subjunctive of wish is common: 'Moreover, the work in which this appears is not intended for the enjoyment of erudite scholars, whom God *preserve*, but for the enlightenment of the ordinary innocent weakling who is only too easily led away from the faith.' Also when the antecedent is a previous clause or statement: 'its interest to be paid to her if she's a spinster at thirty . . . which Heaven *forbid*' (Granville Barker, *The Madras House*, Act IV).

The past tense forms are used here to express a modest wish: 'I hear a voice I *would* not hear, a voice that now *might* well be still' (Byron, *Away, Away, Ye Notes of Woe!*).

f. Optative Subjunctive in Adverbial Clauses of Modal and Pure Result. May indicates a desired result: 'We should proceed in such a manner that the public *may* indorse our cause.' Here *shall* is employed to indicate a result determined upon or demanded by the speaker: 'He is so badly injured that he *shall* be taken to the hospital at once.' 'A hundred and twenty little incidents must be dribbled into the reader's intelligence in such a manner that he *shall* himself be insensible to the process' (Trollope, *Is He Popenjoy?* Introductory). 'We should have so much faith in authority as (**5** *d*) *shall* make us repeatedly observe and attend to that which is said to be right' (Ruskin, *Modern Painters*, Part III, Sec. I, Ch. III). We employ *should* here to state the desired result modestly: 'He is so badly injured that he *should* be taken to the hospital at once.' Compare **29** 2 (Examples).

We express the constraint of circumstances or natural forces by *have to, must*, or *come to;* the outcome of events and natural developments by *shall, come to,* or *is to:* 'The seed corn has come up so poorly that (or very poorly so that) the farmers *have to* (or *must*) plant over again.' 'The world sometimes treats us so roughly that we *come to* be contented with things that once made us miserable.' 'Can human progress ever advance so far that justice *shall* (or *is to*) come to all men?' 'I believe that the mind can be profaned by the habit of attending to trivial things, so that all our thoughts *shall* (or *come to*) be tinged by triviality' (Thoreau, *Journal*, II, p. 290). In older English, the simple subjunctive of result was in use here: 'He that smiteth a man so that he *die* shall be surely put to death' (*Exodus*, XXI, 12). Where it is desired to represent the result not as the constraint of circumstances but as a simple fact, we still, as in older English, employ the indicative: 'The seed corn has come up so poorly that the farmers *are planting* over again.'

g. *Optative Subjunctive in Adverbial Clauses of Condition.* We often employ the unreal subjunctive of wish (I B, p. 398) in the condition of conditional sentences. Examples are given in **44 II 5 C** *a*. Also the volitive subjunctive is used in conditions. See **44 II 5, 44 II 5 A** *a, b*.

POTENTIAL SUBJUNCTIVE

44. The potential subjunctive (**41**) shows the same use of the tense forms which have been described in **41** and illustrated in the different articles of **43**. Here as elsewhere the old sequence (**36**) usually destroys after a past tense form all the fine distinctions observed after a present tense form. The following categories occur:

I. **Potential Subjunctive in Principal Propositions.** *Can,* though an indicative form, has potential force. It is much used to express ability to perform an act: 'Mary *can* walk, *can* write.' *Will* is sometimes used in the same meaning: '[His] words, though they *will* bear, yet do not warrant, such a translation' (R. Simpson, *Life of Campion*, IX, 279, A.D. 1866). *Can* and *will,* though indicatives, do not express action here. They express only the possibility of an action. They have in a certain sense the force of the potential subjunctive, but they have retained a good deal of their original concrete meaning. Also their past tense forms *could* and *would*, like past indicatives, can point to the past.

The present indicative *may* is now very commonly used as a present potential subjunctive to mark the thoughts which are busying the mind at the present moment as mere conceptions: 'It *may* rain today.' 'He *may* come today.' 'You *may* be right.' This old indicative is now rarely used as an indicative with its original meaning *to have power, to be able:* 'Try as he *may* he never succeeds.' 'Try as he *might* he never succeeded.' Here *might* refers to the past.

The fact that *might* now usually refers to the present or future indicates clearly that it is prevailingly employed as a subjunctive. The past tense form was employed as an indicative and as a subjunctive in oldest English, a slight difference of form distinguishing the two functions, but only the subjunctive survives in wide use, so that *might*, now with the same form for indicative and subjunctive, is felt as a subjunctive referring to present or future time, which thus prevents its use as an indicative referring to the past. The present tense *may*, though originally an indicative and still possessing somewhat of its older concrete force, has developed into a present subjunctive, widely used in principal propositions and subordinate clauses to correspond to the past subjunctive *might* in the same positions, the former in accordance with the nature of the present subjunctive expressing a greater degree of probability: 'It *may* rain today,' where *may* expresses more probability than *might* in 'It *might* rain today.'

Grammarians usually consider *may* a present indicative when it stands in a principal proposition, but the fact that we do not use it in the past indicative except in a few rather rare expressions shows clearly that we do not feel it as an indicative. We do not have the least inclination to use it with reference to the past, as in the case of *would* and *could*, which, though their indicative and subjunctive are alike in the past tense, are much used as indicatives and subjunctives, referring to either the past or the present. *Might*, like *should*, has lost its indicative function. *May* and *might*, like *shall* and *should*, are both felt as subjunctives, both referring to the present or future, differing from each other only in the degree of probability which they express.

Must and *ought* are old past subjunctives which are not felt as related to other forms from the same stem. They differ from the other modal auxiliaries in that they do not have alongside of them a present tense form with a different shade of meaning. The one form must perform both functions.

May, might, shall, should, must, and *ought* are not now felt as belonging to a conjugational system like other verbs. They indicate present or future time when associated with a present infinitive, but point to the past when associated with a perfect infinitive, so that it is not they but the infinitive that indicates the time. All these forms are usually called modal auxiliaries, but they differ markedly from the modal auxiliaries *will* and *can*, and from all the modal auxiliaries in the closely related German in that they rarely have an indicative form and cannot show time relations. They are used with an infinitive, which indicates the verbal meaning and the time relations, while they themselves only give a touch of color to the statement, each having a distinct shade, which is again in the case of *may, might, shall, should* differently shaded according as the form is in the present or the past tense: 'He *may* miss the train' (future possibility). 'He *might* miss the train' (faint future possibility). 'He *may* have missed the train' (past possibility). 'He *might* have missed the train' (faint past possibility). *Shall* and *should* are differentiated in the same way and have the same use of the dependent infinitive forms. *Shall* is little used in the potential category, but is very common in the optative category (**43**). *Should* is common in both categories, also *may* and *might*. The only function of *may, might, shall, should, must*, and *ought* is to color the statement. They perform the same functions as the subjunctive endings in Latin, but as there are a number of different auxiliary verbs in English and each verb retains a little of its original concrete meaning and the present and the past tense forms *may, shall, might, should* have a different shade of meaning, the English coloring is more varied and considerably richer. Compare Accidence, **57** 4 A *h.*

The auxiliary *can* is developing in the direction of *may.* It has become a subjunctive form when it expresses a possibility due to circumstances, having here the same force as *may*, only stronger, and, like *may*, not capable of indicating past time when used in the past tense: 'We *can* (stronger than *may*) expect opposition from vested interests' (*London Times*). 'It *cannot* (or with much weaker force *may not*) be true.' '*Can* it be true?' In '*Could* this be true?' *could*, though a past tense, refers to the present.

Can is often also a subjunctive when used of the possibility that lies in the ability of a person. 'I *am* at last *able* to do it' is an objective statement of fact, but in 'I *can* do it!' *can* is a subjunctive when spoken by someone who is confident of his ability to do something that he has never as yet done. It expresses here the abstract subjunctive idea of possibility.

While *would* and *could*, like past indicatives, often point to the past, they can do this only when the context clearly indicates that the reference is to the past: 'I tried to get it into my suitcase, but it *wouldn't* (= *couldn't*) go in.' 'He tried to get it into his suitcase but *couldn't.*' Where the context does not clearly indicate that the reference is to the past, *would* and *could* point to the present or the future, like other modal auxiliaries, and, like them, are now usually felt as subjunctive forms: 'We *could* never get that into the suitcase! It *wouldn't* (= *couldn't*) go in.' Thus *would* and *could* are developing in the direction of the other modal auxiliaries, i.e., they cannot now of themselves indicate time relations and are becoming mere coloring forms. *Can, could, will, would* are used in both the optative and the potential category and with the same differentiation of the tenses as found in the other modal auxiliaries.

The past subjunctive forms are widely used in principal propositions in the potential category. Possibility that lies in the ability of a person or in circumstances: 'He *could* easily do it.' 'It *couldn't* possibly be done.' 'It *might* possibly be true.' 'He *might* come today.' Doubt or uncertainty: '*Could* he mean it?' The polite subjunctive of modest or cautious statement: 'It *were* wise to be silent.' 'I *had* better (objective predicate adjective) go,' literally, 'I should hold or regard going as better.' 'I *had* best (adjective) do it now.' 'I *had* as good (adjective) do it now,' or sometimes 'I *had* as well (adverb) do it now' after the analogy of 'I *might* as well (adverb) do it now.' 'All's over for us both; 'Tis vain contending; I *would* (not so widely used here as *had*) better go' (Browning, *A Soul's Tragedy*, I). 'We *would* (not so widely used here as *had*) better wait and see if they wish to come' (Mary Roberts Rinehart, *The Circular Staircase*, Ch. VI). 'I think you *would* (not so widely used here as *had*) better read it aloud' (Willa Cather, *Death in the Desert*, p. 293). 'I *should* (**37** 5 *a*, p. 367) think so.' 'I *should* hope so.' 'It *would* (**37** 5 *a*, p. 367) seem that the War Office is not as it ought to be.' 'This *would* seem to confirm his statement.' 'The royal power, it *should* (now more commonly *would*) seem, might be intrusted in their hands' (Hume, *History of England*). 'That *would* be rather difficult.' 'Your refusal to come *might* give offense.' *Should* is often used in all three persons to express modestly a strong probability: 'We *should* be there within an hour.' 'He *should* (or *ought to*) succeed this time.' In *should* the tone of modest assurance is often intensified to that of positive affirmation: 'Is anybody deceived by such words?' — 'I *should* say not.' In rhetorical questions (p. 212) *should* is often used after *how* to express impossibility: 'How *should* I know that?' (Tarkington, *The Magnificent Ambersons*, Ch. XXII) = 'I couldn't possibly know that.' Compare II 5 D, p. 428.

The form *should* is sometimes not a direct past subjunctive but the indirect form, corresponding to a first person present subjunctive of the direct, as described in 3 *b*, p. 419: 'He sat brooding. What *should he* (in the direct *shall I*) say when Father came (in the direct *comes*) home?'

With reference to the past, the perfect infinitive is used instead of the present. Possibility: 'He *could* easily *have done* it.' 'He *might have missed* the train.' Doubt or uncertainty: '*Could* he *have meant* it?' '*Might* he *have missed* the train?' Subjunctive of modest or cautious statement: 'I *should have thought* it rather unfair.' 'He *would have thought* it rather unfair.' 'That *would have been* rather difficult.' 'He *should have succeeded*.'

In the potential category there are other quite different means of expression. The copulas *seem, appear,* and often *look* represent the statement as uncertain: 'He *seems* (or *appears*) friendly.' 'He *looks* perplexed.' Also sentence adverbs (**16** 2 *a*) are employed to express this idea: 'He is *apparently* friendly.' Since there are a large number of such adverbs or adverbial phrases, as *seemingly, to judge by appearances, as far as we can see,* etc., with different shades of meaning, the adverb is a highly prized means of expression.

a. 'OUGHT' AND 'MUST.' These past tense subjunctive forms are usually optatives with volitive force, as described in **43** I A (2nd and next to last parr.). Not infrequently, however, they have potential force. Strong probability: 'You have no occasion whatever to worry. He is an old experienced man and *ought to* (or *must,* or *should*) know what he is about.' 'Eclipse (horse) *ought to* (or *should*) win.' Inferred or presumed certainty: 'You *must* (or *should*) be aware of this.' 'You *must* (or *should*) have been aware of this.' With a tinge of doubt: 'He *must* come soon.' 'He *must* have missed his train.'

In neither potential nor volitive (**43** I A) meaning do *ought* and *must* now have alongside of them a past indicative or a present indicative or subjunctive to make us feel that they are past subjunctives. As they usually point to the present, they have gradually come to be felt as present subjunctives; but we still have enough feeling for their old meaning to use them in dependent sentences as past subjunctives, as in older English; i.e., like every other past subjunctive they can be freely used in indirect discourse after a past tense, thus here pointing to a past duty or a past necessity: 'I thought he *ought* to do it and told him so.' 'I thought it *must* kill him' (Meredith, *The Ordeal of Richard Feverel,* Ch. XLV).

Sometimes under the influence of this common construction *must* is used elsewhere with reference to the past, in independent sentences as well as subordinate clauses, in some cases seemingly as a past indicative; but in fact in such instances it always stands in the neighborhood of some other verbal form which clearly points to the past and is thus in reality the means of conveying the idea of past time: 'A commander like Mansfield, who could not pay his soldiers, *must,* of necessity, plunder wherever he was. As soon as his men had eaten up one part of the country, they *must* go to another, if they were not to die of starvation' (Gardiner, *Thirty Years' War,* 47). '[In reading the fine books in the British Museum] My hunger was forgotten, the garret to which I *must* return to pass the night never perturbed my thought' (Gissing, *Henry Ryecroft*, Ch. XVII). Compare II 3 *a*, p. 418.

The common people often replace the unclear old past subjunctive *ought* by a clear modern past subjunctive, employing the past subjunctive auxiliaries *should, had*, or *did:* 'A woman *should ought* to be modest' (Sheila Kaye-Smith, *Joanna Godden*, p. 31). 'You *should ought* to have seen them' (*ib.*, p. 29). 'He'*d oughter* (i.e., *had ought to*) know better.' 'He'*d oughter*'ve known better.' 'And now the old lady downstairs is turning down the gas; she always does at half past ten. She *didn't ought*' (H. G. Wells, *Mr. Britling Sees It Through*, II, Ch. IV). 'There *didn't ought* to be such things.' 'He *didn't ought* to have done it.' Instead of adding the negative to the auxiliary, as in the last examples, it is sometimes added to *ought*, as the auxiliary and *ought* are together felt as a unit, a new clear past subjunctive form: 'D'you claim he'*d* (= *he had*) *oughtn't?*' (Owen Wister, *Extra Dry*, last page). To convey greater assurance the common people place the present tense *do* before the old past subjunctive *ought*, and have thus created a new present subjunctive form: 'He *don't ought* to go.' Alongside of the past subjunctives *might, should, would* are the present subjunctives *may, shall, will* for more positive assertion. There is in the literary language no present subjunctive corresponding to the old past subjunctive *ought*. The common people feeling the deficiency of form here have created two clear subjunctive forms, a present and a past, with the usual differentiation of subjunctive meaning. They have thus given clarity to English expression at a point where the literary language is regularly unclear. The common people instead of neglecting the subjunctive, as is so often claimed, are creating new and clearer subjunctive forms in accordance with their natural tendency toward concrete expression. Compare **49** 3 *b* (3rd par.).

II. Potential Subjunctive in Subordinate Clauses.

1. POTENTIAL SUBJUNCTIVE IN SUBJECT CLAUSES. It represents the thought which is busying the mind as a mere conception; but the indicative is used to indicate that the thought appears almost as a reality, as a practical problem with which we must deal: 'It is not impossible that he *may* change his plans.' 'It seems quite probable that it *may* (or with different force the indicative *will*) rain today.' 'What he *may* do next is now the absorbing theme.' *Shall* is employed to indicate a future contingency: 'Whoever *shall* violate the law shall pay the penalty.' 'My one great fear is that he *shall* some day return.' The past tense *might* indicates uncertainty: 'It is possible that it *might* rain.' Modest statement: 'It is easily conceivable that he *might* outstrip them all.'

We often use *should* even of facts, as the abstract conception, the principle involved, is more prominent in the mind than the concrete fact: 'That many men *should enjoy* (or of course also *enjoy*) it does not make it better' (Matthew Arnold, *Essay on*

Keats). 'It is extraordinary, Dorian, that you *should have seen* (or, of course, also *saw*) this in the portrait' (Wilde, *Dorian Gray*, 190). 'It is surprising that *I, you, he should be* (or *should have been*) so foolish.'

After a past indicative, of course, in accordance with the law of sequence (36), we employ a past tense of the subjunctive instead of the present: 'At that moment it seemed quite probable that it *might* rain.' 'My one great fear was that he *should* some day return.'

2. POTENTIAL SUBJUNCTIVE IN PREDICATE CLAUSES: 'My health is not what, under favorable circumstances, it *may* (probability) or *might* (possibility) be.'

3. POTENTIAL SUBJUNCTIVE IN OBJECT CLAUSES. In object clauses introduced by the interrogative or indefinite *whether* or *if*, we sometimes still in choice prose and poetry employ the simple subjunctive, as in older English, to express the doubt in our mind, but in plain prose we now use the indicative, since we feel the reality, the actuality, of the problem stronger than the idea of doubt as to the proper solution: 'We doubt whether it *be* (in plain prose *is*) possible to mention a state which on the whole has been a gainer by a breach of faith' (Macaulay). 'She'll not tell me if she *love* (in plain prose *loves*) me' (Tennyson). 'I some-times wonder if it *be* (in plain prose *is*) understood in the United States' (Walter H. Page, *Letter to Woodrow Wilson*, Jan. 12, 1915).

After a past tense we, of course, employ a past tense form of the subjunctive. This past subjunctive which results from attraction seems a little more common than the present subjunctive after a present indicative: 'That's just the answer Tertius gave me when I first asked if she *were* (in plain prose *was*) handsome' (George Eliot). 'He decided that he would go and see whether Rachel *were* (in plain prose *was*) in' (Hugh Walpole, *The Duchess of Wrexe*, p. 261). 'Esther trembled like one grown suddenly old. She did not know whether it *were* (in plain prose *was*) with pleasure or fear' (Max Pemberton, *Doctor Xavier*, Ch. IX). There is a modern tendency after *lest* to disregard the old sequence where the thing feared is felt as imminent: 'Each was playing a part and dreading lest the other *suspect it*' (G. Atherton, *Sleeping Fires*, Ch. XX) (or *should suspect it*).

We sometimes in choice prose and poetry use the simple subjunctive after other interrogatives and indefinites, *what, how, where, why*, etc., but we now usually employ the indicative, as in the second paragraph: 'A wise horseman should, in such a case, take care how he *pull* (in plain prose *pulls*) the rein' (Lytton,

Rienzi, II, Ch. III). After a past indicative the simple subjunctive — of course here the past subjunctive — seems a little more natural: 'I could not, when the scheme was first mentioned the other day, understand why a visit from the family *were* (in plain prose *was*) not to be made in the carriage of the family' (Jane Austen, *Mansfield Park*, I, Ch. VIII).

In older English, the simple subjunctive could be used not only after interrogatives and indefinites, but also in indirect statements: 'I think the King *be* (now *is*) stirring, it is now bright day' (Richard Edwards, *Damon and Pithias*, l. 132, A.D. 1571). 'I think it *be* (now *is*) not so' (Chapman, *All Fooles*, IV, I, 223, A.D. 1605). 'I fear me "faire" *be* (now *is*) a word too foule for a face so passing fair' (John Lyly, *Sappho and Phao*, I, IV, 6, A.D. 1584). 'I think my daughter *be* (now *is*) an exception' (Scott, *Fair Maid of Perth*, Ch. XXIX). The past subjunctive of modest statement is better preserved and can still be used in choice language: 'But I should say that men generally *were* (in plainer style usually *are*) not enough interested in the first-mentioned sciences (i.e., botany, anatomy, mathematics, chemistry) to meddle with and degrade them' (Thoreau, *Journal*, III, p. 326).

On the other hand, when the idea of doubt or uncertainty is strong we still quite commonly employ the subjunctive in all kinds of object clauses, even in the categories discussed above; now, however, in its modern form with an auxiliary: 'The doctors do not yet know whether there *may be* any change in his condition during the night.' 'I am going to ask him whether there *may be* any chance of an opening in his business for me.' 'I fear that he *may* not *recover.*' 'I now believe it possible that he *may recover.*' 'He now feels (or thinks) that he *may be* mistaken about it.' 'I have heard that he *may return* soon.' However, we use the indicative wherever we desire to indicate that the statement is felt not as a mere conception but rather as a reality, truth, sure result: 'He now feels that he *is* mistaken about it.' 'I fear that he *will* not *recover.*' 'I think this *will meet* with your approval.' In all these cases a past tense form is, of course, employed after a past tense: 'I *feared* he *might* not *recover.*' 'I *had heard* that he *might return* soon.' 'I *feared* that he *would* not *recover.*' 'He *felt* that he *was* mistaken about it.'

The past tense forms of the simple subjunctive and the modal auxiliaries are much used after a present tense with different shades of meaning. Possibility: 'Whether such a development *were* possible or not is not for me now to discuss.' 'I see that that *might* have proved disastrous.' Often to put the thought upon a basis of pure imagination: 'Suppose he *were* here?' 'Suppose that I *were* to tell you that you had no need to be alarmed' (Black, *Daughter of Heth*, I, 270). Modest statement: 'I think that *might* (or *should*) please anybody.' 'I think you *would* be better pleased with this book.' The past subjunctive is often used instead of the present indicative since the abstract principle is felt as more important than the concrete fact: 'I regard it as the saddest of things that a man *should be allowed* to bring up his son in that way.'

a. *Indirect Discourse after Verbs of Saying, Reporting, Remarking*, etc. After these verbs we now employ the subjunctive in indirect discourse only where it is used in the direct form. Direct: '*I may* finish the work tomorrow.' Indirect: 'He says he *may* finish the work tomorrow,' or 'He said he *might* finish the work tomorrow.' We employ the indicative uniformly in all indirect statements where the indicative is used in the direct form. Direct: '*I am* sick.' Indirect: 'John says he *is* sick' or 'John said he *was* sick.' There is often here an element of uncertainty or unreality. Today we feel this as amply expressed by the meaning of the verb in the principal proposition and the change of person and tense in the subordinate clause. These characteristic features of indirect discourse show us that we have to do with an indirect, hence not necessarily reliable, statement. In Old English, as still in modern German, the subjunctive was used here to indicate uncertainty or unreality: 'Oft us men secgaþ þæt hi unsynnige *beon*' (Ælfric, *Homilies*, II, 330) = 'Often men tell us that they are without sin.' 'Nu cwædon gedwolmen þæt deofol *gesceope* sume gesceafta' (*ib.*, I, 16) = 'Now heretics said that the devil created some creatures.' But in this oldest period the subjunctive was often used also of actual facts: 'Ic gehyrde secgan þæt hwæte *wære* on Egypta lande' (*The Heptateuch, Genesis*, XL11, 2) = '1 have heard that there *is* corn in Egypt' (King James Version). The potential idea has here entirely disappeared, the subjunctive expressing merely indirectness of statement. This subjunctive survives in German, but has been discarded in English as superfluous expression. At least one of the characteristic features of indirect discourse described above is always present and indicates indirectness of statement.

The following additional examples are given to illustrate present usages more fully:

Direct	Indirect
I come as often as I *can*.	He says he comes as often as he *can*.
I *will* do it for you.	He says he *will* do it for me.
I would come if you *should* ask me.	He says he *would* come if I *should* ask him.
It *may* rain.	He thinks it *may* rain.
Am I making progress?	He often asks me whether he *is* making progress.

There is no difficulty here except in the case of the pure future, which has different forms for the different persons. In the indirect statement we here usually, without regard to the auxiliary used in the direct statement, employ *shall* in the first person and *will* in the second and the third, in accordance with the usual way of using these forms in the future tense:

Direct	Indirect
You *will* surely fail.	He says I *shall* (or in American colloquial speech *will;* see p. 369) surely fail.
I *shall* return tomorrow.	He says he *will* return tomorrow.

There is, however, a tendency here, especially in the third person of the indirect statement, to retain the auxiliary used in the direct, just as we do everywhere else:

Direct	Indirect
I *shall* come to stay at Diplow.	Sir Hugo says he *shall* (usually *will;* see pp. 366, 369) come to stay at Diplow (George Eliot).

Of course, after a past tense, in accordance with our law of sequence (**36**), a present tense form becomes past. The only difficulty here is the proper treatment of the pure future forms. The rules given in the preceding paragraph apply here, except that every present form becomes past: 'He said I *should* (in American colloquial speech *would;* see p. 369) surely fail'; direct: 'You *will* surely fail.' 'He said he *would* return tomorrow'; direct: 'I *shall* return tomorrow,' or sometimes with the auxiliary used in the direct: 'He told her plainly he *should* be a prince before he died' (Kingsley, *Westward Ho!* Ch. I); direct: 'I *shall* be a prince before I die.'

In the case of modal auxiliaries the auxiliary used in the direct is always retained in the indirect statement, the present, however, becoming past: 'I told him I *would* help him if he needed it.' Direct: 'I *will* help you if you need it.' *Must* and *ought* do not change their form after a past tense since, according to I *a*, p. 413, they are past subjunctive forms: 'I thought it *must* kill him' (Meredith, *The Ordeal of Richard Feverel*, Ch. XLV). 'I thought he *ought* to do it and told him so.'

A past tense subjunctive of the direct is, of course, not affected by a preceding past tense when the statement becomes indirect: 'My reason often asked harshly why I *should* be so desolate.' Direct: 'Why *should* I be so desolate?'

The present perfect of the direct statement usually becomes past perfect in the indirect, but the present perfect may be retained to emphasize the close relations of the act to the present: (direct) 'I *have been* sick,' but in the indirect form: 'I met John on the street this morning and he told me that he *had been* sick,' or in the form of a subject clause: 'His first remark was that he *had been* sick.' Direct: 'The painters *haven't finished* work on the house yet,' but in indirect form: 'John told me this morning that the painters *hadn't* (or often *haven't*) finished work on his house yet,' or in the form of a subject clause: 'His greatest worry this morning was that the painters *hadn't* (or often *haven't*) finished the work on his house yet.'

Similarly, the present and the future of the direct discourse may be retained in the indirect to indicate that the act is still continuing and will go on for some time: (direct) 'The painters *are* still at work on the house and *will be* for some time,' and in indirect form: 'He told me this morning that the painters *are* still at work on his house and *will be* for some time,' or in the form of a subject clause: 'His first remark this morning was that the painters *are* still at work on his house and *will be* for some time.' Often also where the reference is to a point of time still vividly felt as future at the time of speaking: 'He told me this morning that he *is going* (or *will go*) with us tomorrow.'

Moreover, the present must be used to represent something as habitual, customary, characteristic, or as universally or locally true: 'I told him that the morning train *leaves* at nine, that John *is* diligent and energetic.' 'I told him where the post office *is*.' 'He asked me what the properties of acetylene *are*.'

There is one point in indirect discourse not covered by the above description. In reporting indirectly a command we never employ the imperative, but an optative — the volitive — subjunctive or an infinitive with the force of a volitive subjunctive: (direct) '*Come* at once.' (indirect) 'He said *I should come* at once' (or *I was to come* at once), or 'He told me *to come* at once.' We say also: 'He wrote, telegraphed, to me *to come* at once' (or *that I should come* at once). In American English it is common to say also: 'The teacher *says* (= *tells us*) *to come* early' (or *that we must come* early). 'When the Federal Board says *for it* (the stabilization corporation) *to do so* (or *that it must do so*), it borrows money from the Government and casts it into the wheat pit' (Garet Garrett in *The Saturday Evening Post*, June 21, 1930, p. 6). In the *Oxford Dictionary* this use of *say* for *tell* is marked obsolete. It was once literary usage in England.

Of course, a direct quotation is given exactly as it is spoken and is distinguished by quotation-marks: 'He extended his hand to me and said, "I am grateful to you for all that you have done for me,"' but in indirect form: 'He extended his hand to me and said that he *was* grateful to me for all that I *had done* for him.'

b. Independent Form of Indirect Discourse. In a lively style, the author often strips off all formal signs of subordination and reproduces the thoughts, feelings, dreams, impressions, fears, etc., of another in grammatically independent form. The words are not represented as a free report of the author or speaker, but as a close, though indirect, reproduction of the thoughts, musings, reveries, etc., of another. The tenses are the past tense forms usually employed in narrative: the past tense to correspond to the present indicative or subjunctive of the direct discourse, whether used as a present or a future, or with reference to the future we may use *would* + infinitive without regard to the auxiliary employed in the direct statement, or sometimes *should* instead of *would* where *shall* is used in the direct; the past perfect indicative to correspond to the past or the present perfect of the direct; the past subjunctive of simple verb or modal auxiliary to correspond to a past subjunctive of the direct where the reference is to the moment at hand, i.e., the moment the writer is describing, but the past perfect subjunctive or the past subjunctive of a modal auxiliary (*could, should,* etc.) in connection with a dependent infinitive in the perfect tense may also be used here if the feeling prevails that the words are a narration of a past musing: 'James looked at his daughter-in-law. That unseen glance of his was cold and dubious. Appeal and fear were in it. Why *should he* (direct *should I,* with reference to the moment described by the writer) be worried like this? It *was* (direct *is*) very likely all nonsense; women *were* (direct *are*) funny things! They *exaggerated* (direct *exaggerate*) so, you *didn't* (direct *don't*) know what to believe; and then nobody *told* (direct *tells*) him (direct *me*) anything, he *had* (direct *I have*) to find out everything for *himself* ' (direct *myself*) (Galsworthy, *The Man of Property,* Ch. III). 'When he came out of Timothy's his intentions were no longer so simple. *He would* (direct *I will*) put an end to that sort of thing once for all . . . A divorce! The word was paralyzing. She *would* (direct *will*) pass out of *his* (direct *my*) life, and he — he *should* (direct *I shall*) never see her again!' (*ib.,* Ch. VI), or instead of *should* in the third person more commonly *would* corresponding to *shall* in the first person in the direct form: 'He considered whether it wouldn't be wiser to go to his room and lock himself in. But then he *would* (direct *I shall*) miss Miss Corner' (H. G. Wells, *Mr. Britling Sees It Through,* I, Ch. III). 'He ordered himself, too, the very dinner the boy had always chosen — soup, whitebait, cutlets, and a tart. Ah! *if he were* (direct *if he were*) only opposite now!' (Galsworthy, *The Man of Property,* Ch. II), where the use of *were* indicates that the writer is referring to the moment that he is describing, but under the influence of narrative, as often elsewhere in this book, he might have said: 'Ah! if he *had* only *been* opposite!' 'In a few kindly words the Field-Marshal (Moltke) told me he *was* (direct *I am*) unable to fathom the source of my apparent intimate knowledge of the Prussian army. How *could a stranger have grasped* (direct *could a stranger grasp*) the spirit which *pervaded* (direct *pervades*) it?' (Sidney Whitman, *German Memories,* Tauchnitz Collection 4393, p. 127). The first sentence of the last quotation is the usual form of indirect discourse. In the second sentence the writer passes over into the independent form, representing the words as a report of the musing of Moltke.

This form of indirect discourse is widely used also by newspaper men, who in this manner report indirectly the things that have been told them: 'Bishop Charles P. Anderson, primate of the Episcopal Church of America, critically ill with heart trouble, *was beginning* to show signs of exhaustion this afternoon, though otherwise his condition *was* unchanged. This was stated in a bulletin issued by Dr. James B. Herrick' (*The Chicago Daily News,* Jan. 25, 1930). It is used also in novels instead of ordinary indirect discourse: '"What can I do for you?" Swithin asked ironically. The Hungarian seemed suffering from excitement. Why *had Swithin left* his charges the night before? What excuse *had he* to make? What sort of conduct *did he call* this? Swithin, very like a bulldog, at that moment, answered: "What business *was* it of *his?*'" (Galsworthy, *Salvation of a Forsyte*, p. 218). In the last sentence the proposition in which this construction stands is not independent as usual but dependent, object of a verb, as in the case of ordinary indirect discourse.

4. POTENTIAL SUBJUNCTIVE IN ADJECTIVE CLAUSES:

a. Attributive Relative Clause: 'It is a book that *may* (or the indicative *will* to indicate that the speaker is counting on a positive favorable result) help many a poor struggling fellow.' 'Here is a book that *may* (or more modestly *might*) interest you.' In Masefield's *The Everlasting Mercy*, p. 65, there is an example of the older simple subjunctive here, but it may have been chosen for the sake of the rime: '[he] Has got his dirty whores to speak to, His dirty mates with whom he *drink* (for *may drink*), Not little children, one would think.'

Shall is used to express a future contingency: 'I offer a reward to anyone who *shall* give me the desired information.'

Should is often employed to express a strong probability: 'He is a bright young man who *should* succeed.' *Would* and *should* are used to represent something as merely conceived: 'I should like to see the man who *would* dare to insult me in Illfracombe's presence' (Florence Marryatt, *A Bankrupt Heart*, II, 62). 'He was not the kind of a man whom a servant *would* ever *have dared* to express any sympathy with' (Sarah Grand, *The Heavenly Twins*, I, 85). In the preceding examples the relative clause has the force of a conclusion to a condition. It may have the force also of a condition: 'A man might pass for insane *who* (= *if he*) *should* see things as they are' (Channing). 'Two months ago I should have scouted as mad or drunk the man *who* (*if he*) *had dared* tell me the like' (Kipling, *The Phantom Rickshaw*, 9).

Unreality: 'Here is a man that *might* have become a power in the land.'

b. Attributive Substantive Clause: 'The thought that he *may miss* his train is worrying her.' 'He dismissed the suspicion that she *might be deceiving* him.'

5. SUBJUNCTIVE AND INDICATIVE IN CONDITIONAL SENTENCES. For practical considerations conditional sentences of all kinds are here treated together. In some of the categories the indicative and the subjunctive are employed side by side, while in others the subjunctive alone is used. The potential subjunctive is the more common subjunctive use, especially after *if, unless, in case.* Examples are given in A, B, C, D. But also the volitive subjunc-

tive (**43** I A) occurs, especially after *provided, on condition that, so, so only, so that,* often after *unless:* 'I will help him *provided* (or *on condition that*) he *do* (*shall do,* or more commonly *does;* indicative) what I say.' 'I will not help him *unless* he *do* (*shall do,* or more commonly *does;* indicative) what I say.' Besides the examples given below there are others in **31**.

A. *Practical Condition.* This category has to do with the things of practical everyday life — things with which in our world of action and thought we may have to do in the immediate future or with which we may have to do in the present moment. This category has to do also with the things of the past, for the things of the past often affect us in one way or another. When the things with which we are dealing or shall soon deal present themselves to the mind under the aspect of facts, we employ the indicative. Many of the mere conceptions that are passing through the mind are felt by us at the time as realities even though they have not as yet become facts. They are so near to us that they appear to us under the aspect of facts; so near often that we base conclusions on them. Often, however, in our more composed moods we feel these things as conceptions, as things near to us but yet as mere conceptions, and when we speak of them we use the subjunctive. This attitude of mind was more common in older English, so that the subjunctive here was more common then.

a. *Future Time.* When the action or state expressed in the condition seems of practical importance to us, something which in the near or more remote future will concern us, hence something well within the realm of reality, we usually employ in the condition the present indicative, which here as so often elsewhere has future force; in the conclusion we use *will* in the first person to express intention and in all three persons employ the future indicative to indicate a future result: 'If it *rains* (or *is stormy*) I'*ll* not go.' 'If it *rains* (or *is stormy*) we *shall* (in American colloquial speech *will*) all *be* very much discouraged' (or 'they *will* all *be* very much discouraged'). 'They *will* go unless it *rains.*'

In the condition alongside of the present indicative with future force there has always been employed here a present subjunctive with future force, with the same meaning as the indicative, only representing a little different point of view. The present indicative represents the assumed act or state as so near to us that we regard it as a future actuality or at least as something with which we may have to deal: 'If it *rains,* I'*ll* not go.' The present subjunctive represents the act or state as a mere conception but at the same time marks it as something with which we

may have to deal — the potential subjunctive — or after *provided,
so, so that, so only, on condition* (*that*) as something desired or required — the volitive (**43** I A) subjunctive: 'The gathering will
be large if (or in case) the weather *be* (or *is*) good' (or 'unless the
weather *be*, or *is*, bad'). 'Let him go, so only (= provided)
he *come* (or *comes*) home with glory' (G. M. Lane, *A Latin Grammar*, p. 338). 'I'll lend it to him on condition he *return* (or *returns*)
it tomorrow.' Sometimes after a past indicative there is a tendency to disregard the old sequence (**36**): 'She was granted a
year's probation on condition she *send* (instead of *should send*,
or *sent*) her son to school' (*New York Evening Post*, July 12, 1929).
In everyday life the indicative is the common form in all these
cases, but the subjunctive is still in use in choice language.

Alongside of the simple present subjunctive we often find in
older English the newer form with *shall*, and in those palmy days
of the simple subjunctive it was much needed, for the simple
subjunctive can frequently not be distinguished from the indicative: 'If ye *shall* ask anything in my name, I will do it' (*John*,
XIV, 14). *Shall* is still often used here in one special case, namely,
to represent the act as the assumed final outcome of events, or the
assumed result of a development, where in choice language it is
not infrequently preferred to either the present indicative or the
present subjunctive: 'If annihilation *shall end* (or *ends*, or *end*)
our joys, we shall never regret the loss of them.' 'If you *shall fail*
to understand What England is . . . On you will come the curse
of all the land' (Tennyson). In everyday language *is to* (**43** I A,
6th par.) is common here: 'It (the government) will have to
maneuver skilfully if it *is to* avoid being caught in a snap vote'
(*The New York Times*, July 7, 1929).

b. Present and Past Time. Often in our daily life we are forced
to draw conclusions from what seem to us, so far as our practical
experience goes, to be facts of the present and the past. Here
we often employ in both condition and conclusion a present,
past, or present perfect indicative, thus for the time being in the
absence of fuller evidence recognizing the reality of the assumed
act or state, but not committing ourselves to this view: 'If he
is doing this, he *is doing* wrong.' 'If this *is* true, that *is* false.'
'If he *lies*, he probably *cheats* also.' 'If he *did* this, he *did* wrong.'
'If the weather *was* pleasant (and you admitted it was) why
*did*n't you go to school every day?' 'If it *has thundered*, it has
also *lightened*.' Condition and conclusion are often in different
times: 'If he *did* this, he *is* in the wrong.' 'If he *had* fair warning,
he *has* nothing to complain of.' 'If he *has found* it, he *will send* it.'

In older English, we often find here instead of a present, past, or present perfect indicative the corresponding tense of the subjunctive with about the same meaning, only from a little different point of view.   The subjunctive represents the statement as a mere conception but at the same time marks it as probably or presumably true.   The present subjunctive after *provided, so long as, so that,* and often *unless, but* (= *unless*) represents the action as desired or required, as illustrated in the next paragraph, hence has volitive (**43** I A) force.   The indicative recognizes the act or state as a reality.

To express present time or a general truth the present subjunctive is still common in choice language: 'But the slight, if there *be* one, was unintentional' (Stevenson, *Treasure Island*). 'But I confess, so long as (= provided) a volume *hold* together, I am not troubled as to its outer appearance' (Gissing, *Henry Ryecroft*, Ch. XII).   'We care little what he (i.e., man) believes or disbelieves, so that he *believe* in sobriety, justice, charity, and the imperativeness of duty' (John Burroughs, *The Light of Day*, Ch. XIV, VI).   'Virtue is the very heart and lungs of vice: it cannot stand up but (= unless) it *lean* on virtue' (Thoreau, *Journal*, I, p. 78).   The present subjunctive as well as the present indicative can be used of actual facts, the subjunctive form representing the assumed act or state as a general conception, i.e., as a general principle rather than as a particular concrete act or state: 'If God so *clothe* the grass . . . how much more will he clothe you?' (*Luke*, XII, 28).   'If a straight line *be* bisected,' etc. (Mansford, *School Euclid*, 95).   'If the planet *be* close to the sun, its speed increases.'   In all these examples we may use the indicative instead of the subjunctive.   The difference is one of style rather than of meaning.   The subjunctive is characteristic of choice language and elevated discourse.

The present perfect subjunctive was much used in older English to represent a past act or state as only conceived but at the same time to mark it as probably a fact: 'If experience *haue* not taught you this, you haue lyued long and learned lyttle' (John Lyly, *Euphues*, Works, I, p. 193, A.D. 1578).   This older usage is still occasionally found in choice language: 'It ought to weigh heavily on a man's conscience, if he *have* (in plain prose *has*) *been* the cause of another's deviating from sincerity' (W. J. Fox, *Works*, III, 283).

If the reference is to time wholly past, the past indicative is the usual form for the condition.   But the past subjunctive is sometimes employed in choice language.   It has the same modal force as the present and the present perfect subjunctive.   It represents the statement as a mere conception but at the same time marks it as probably true: 'If it *were* so, it was a grievous fault' (Shakespeare, *Julius Cæsar*, III, ii, 84). 'If ever poet *were* a master of phrasing, he (Tennyson) was so' (A. C. Bradley, *Commentary on Tennyson's 'In Memoriam,'* Ch. VI). 'No Thanksgiving dinner was quite complete unless there *were* a baby on hand belonging to some branch of the family' (George F. Hoar, *Autobiography*, I, 57). Similarly, in the closely related concessive clause: 'If the cavern into which they entered *were* artificial construction, considerable pains had been taken to make it look natural' (W. Black, *Daughter of Heth*, II, Ch. XVI). The past subjunctive here for reference to the past is much less common than the present subjunctive for reference to the present and future, for it is contrary to the now almost universally recognized principle that the past subjunctive refers to the present or the future. In older usage the past subjunctive was often used here for reference to the past: 'She wolde wepe, if that she *sawe* a mous Caught in a trappe, if it *were* deed or *bledde*' (Chaucer, *Prologue*, 144). The past perfect subjunctive is impossible here since it represents the statement as contrary to fact, so we now usually employ the past indicative. Compare **41** (4th par.).

B. *Theoretical Condition.* In the theoretical condition, or less vivid condition, as it is often called, the action or state seems less near to us, seems to us of only theoretical nature with no prospect of our having to deal with it practically, hence we employ here a past tense form of the subjunctive, namely, *should*, to indicate that the situation is only conceived, and in the conclusion we use the past volitive (**43** I A, 7th par.) subjunctive *would* in all three persons to express intention or willingness, and employ the past potential *should* in the first person and the past potential *would* in the second and third persons as future subjunctive forms to indicate a future result: 'If it *should* rain tomorrow, I *wouldn't* go.' 'If he *should* treat me in that way, I just *wóuldn't* stand it.' 'If he *should* treat you in that way, you just *wóuldn't* (volitive) stand it.' 'If we *should* treat him in that way he just *wóuldn't* (volitive) stand it.' 'If he *should* go away without speaking to me, I *should* be grieved,' but 'If I *should* go away without speaking to him, he *would* (potential) be grieved.' It should be noticed that in the second and third persons there are in the conclusion a volitive and a potential *would* with quite different meanings. Compare p. 367. Instead of the first person form *should* we sometimes use *would*, provided it has just been used by someone in speaking to us, since we feel a desire to reply to him in his own terms, catching up the very word he uses: 'You *would* think so yourself if you were in my position.' — 'No, I *wouldn't*,' or '*Would*

I though?' or with the regular form 'I *should* nót.' In the subordinate clause of all these conditional sentences, we normally employ potential *should*, but instead of the *should* we may use the simple past subjunctive, or *were to*, usually, however, with the differentiation that simple past subjunctive, *should*, and *were to* indicate decreasing grades of probability: 'If we *missed* (or *should miss*, or *were to miss*) the train, we should have to wait an hour at the station.' We sometimes find in the condition a *would* instead of a *should*, since the clause in which it stands is a conclusion to a suppressed condition: 'If you *would* be patient for yourself [if occasion should arise], you should (= *ought to;* see next par.) be patient for me.'

A *should* in the condition always indicates that the subject acts, not of his own free will, but under the constraint of circumstances, business, etc., as in 'If he *should* fail, I would help him,' but if he acts of his own free will, we must use *will* here: 'I should be (or he would be) glad if she *would* (expressing desire) only come.' If the subject in the conclusion acts under the constraint of duty *should*, not *would*, must be used: 'He *should* (constraint of duty) go, if his father *should* (constraint of circumstances) call him.' *Should* in the conclusion often indicates the desire of the speaker: '*You* (or *he*) *should* go, if it were left to me.' '*You* (or *he*) *should not* go, if it were left to me.' The condition may be according to A and the conclusion here according to B: 'If he *lies*, he *should* be punished.'

The past subjunctive *could* and *might* are often used in the conclusion to express the idea of possibility, the former the possibility that lies in the ability of a person, the latter the possibility that lies in circumstances: 'He *could* do it if he tried.' 'We *might* miss the train if we walked slower.' 'If he could hold out a little longer, he *might* succeed.' *Might* also has optative force indicating the possibility of a permission: 'You *might* go if you would only behave a little better.' *Could* is used also in the condition, as in the third example. To express the idea of constraint we now employ *should* (or *would*) *have to*, not *must*, as we no longer vividly feel the latter as a past subjunctive: 'If he should not come, I *should have to* do the work.' 'If I should not be able to come back in time, he *would have to* do the work.'

C. *Condition Contrary to Fact.* In conditions contrary to fact, or unreal conditions, as they are often called, we employ the simple past subjunctive in the condition, and in the conclusion use *would* or *should*, as described in B: 'If he *were* here, I *would* speak to him.' 'If father *were* here and *saw* this, we *should* have to suffer for it.' 'If father *were* here and *saw* this, he *would* punish

us.' 'He looks as [he *would* look] if he *were* sick.' In poetry and
rather choice prose, we sometimes still use the old simple past
subjunctive *were* in the conclusion instead of the newer, now more
common, form *should be, would be:* 'It *were* (= *would be*) different
if I had some independence, however small, to count on' (Lytton,
My Novel, I, III, Ch. XIX).

As the past subjunctive has through phonetical change become
identical in form with the past indicative in all verbs except *be*,
we often in loose colloquial speech find the past indicative singular
was used as a past subjunctive singular instead of the regular
were, after the analogy of other verbs in which the past subjunctive
is identical in form with the indicative: 'If it *was* (instead of
were) not so cold, he would be allowed to go out.' Sometimes
even in choice language: 'What appears more real than the
sky? We think of it and speak of it as if it *was* as positive
and tangible a fact as the earth' (Burroughs, *The Light of Day*,
Ch. XIV, VIII). In older English, this usage was much more common than now: 'I shall act by her as tenderly as if I *was* her
own mother' (Richardson, *Pamela*, Vol. II, p. 216, and often elsewhere in this work). '*Was* I in a desert, I would find out wherewith in it to call forth my affections' (Sterne, *A Sentimental
Journey*, 'Calais'). This use of *was* as a past subjunctive arose
in the seventeenth century: 'She told him if he *was* not a
fool he would not suffer his business to be carried on by fools'
(Pepys, *Diary*, July 12, 1667). In spite of the long use of *was* in
the literary language as a subjunctive form it has not become
established there with this meaning. *Were* is still the usual
form.

When the reference is to past time, we usually employ in the
condition the past perfect subjunctive and in the conclusion the
same auxiliary used for present time, *should, would, could, might*,
but put the dependent infinitive in the perfect tense instead of
the present: 'If it *had rained*, I *would* not *have gone*.' 'If he *had
gone* away without speaking to me, I *should have been grieved*.'
'If I *had gone* away without speaking to him, he *would have been
grieved*.' 'He *should have gone*, if it *had been* left to me.' 'If he
had been present, I *would have spoken* to him.' 'He *could have
done* it if he *had tried*.' '*We might have missed* the train if we *had
walked* slower.' In older English, the past perfect subjunctive
was used in both propositions: 'If thou *hadst been* here, my
brother *had* not *died*' (*John*, XI, 21). This older usage lingers on
in poetry and choice prose: 'Her anger frightened him. It *had
been* no surprise to him if she *had fallen* dead at his feet' (Max
Pemberton, *Doctor Xavier*, Ch. XX). The condition is sometimes

abridged to a prepositional phrase: 'Mrs. Doria, an amiable widow, *had* surely *married* but for her daughter Clare' (Meredith, *Richard Feverel*, Ch. XIII) = 'if it had not been for her daughter Clare.' The condition is sometimes implied in the context: ''Tis mercy that stays her hand, Else she *had cut* the thread' (Thomas B. Aldrich, *The Bells at Midnight*). In lively style, the past indicative sometimes takes the place of the regular subjunctive form in the conclusion, since the past act does not seem to us a mere conception, but something so close to us that we feel it as a reality which we relate: 'Surely if they had been zealous to pluck a brand from the burning, here *was* a noble opportunity' (W. Gunnyon, *Biographical Sketch of Burns*, 41).

In strong contrast to the tendency in colloquial and popular speech to neglect an opportunity to distinguish between indicative and subjunctive by the use of distinctive forms in the case of *was* and *were* is the decided tendency to distinguish in the past perfect tense the subjunctive from the indicative by the insertion of *have* after *had*, as explained in **49** 3 *b*: 'If they had '*a*' said so, you'd '*a*' sat and listened to 'em' (De Morgan, *Alice-for-Short*, Ch. II). The reason that the tendency to distinguish between *was* and *were* here is so weak is that all the analogies in the language are against a distinction, the past tense indicative and subjunctive always being alike except in the case of *was* and *were*, while after *had*, as described in **49** 3 *b*, there are analogies favoring a distinction between indicative and subjunctive. Compare **43** 2 B *a* (4th par.) and **44** I *a* (last par.).

a. Optative in Conditions. It should be noted that in unreal conditions the past tense forms are often optative, not potential: '*Were* he only here, I would give all that I have!' '*Had* he only *been* here, I would have given all that I had!' This is the unreal subjunctive of wish (**43** I B).

D. *Subjunctive in Elliptical Conditional Sentences.* A sentence that is seemingly independent is often in fact the conclusion of a conditional sentence with the condition suppressed: '*I should say* [if I were asked] that it were better to say nothing about it.' In this sentence *that it were better* serves as an object clause, the object of the verb *say*, but *it were better* is also the conclusion to the condition *to say nothing about it* = *if one said nothing about it.* The apparently independent sentences in I, p. 409, are in fact largely conclusions with the conditions suppressed. The condition in most cases can easily be supplied. Sometimes a blending has taken place: 'The face is a curious mixture: the soft dreamy eyes contrast so sharply with the firm, *I had almost said*, hard little mouth' (Florence Montgomery, *Thrown Together*, I, 72), where *I had almost said* is a blending of *I almost said* and *I had said if I hadn't checked myself.*

6. POTENTIAL SUBJUNCTIVE IN CLAUSES OF MANNER. *May* is much used here to mark the thoughts which are busying the mind at the present moment as mere conceptions: 'It looks *as if* (or *as though*) it *may* rain,' or indicating more doubt and uncertainty: '*as if* it *might* rain.' Modest statement: 'It seems to me as though he *might* (or a little more positively *should*) outstrip all the others.' '"The world is not your nursery, Angel!" Agatha closed her lips very tightly, as who (= one who) *should* imply: "Then it ought to be!"' (Galsworthy, *The Patrician*, p. 298). Often with more positive force: 'I feel as if (or though) I *were going* to fall.'

7. POTENTIAL SUBJUNCTIVE IN ADVERBIAL CLAUSES OF MODAL AND PURE RESULT. In clauses of modal result *may* is used to express a possible result and *might* a result only faintly possible: 'He is so badly injured that he *may* (or *might*) die.' Compare **29 2**.

In clauses of pure result *may* or *might* indicates a possible result: 'It has cleared up beautifully, so that he *may* (or *might;* faint possibility) come after all.'

8. POTENTIAL SUBJUNCTIVE IN COMPARATIVE CLAUSES. The simple subjunctive is often used here in choice language to represent something as a mere conception: 'Nor is there fairer work for beauty found Than that she *win* in nature her release From all the woes that in the world abound' (Bridges, *The Growth of Love*, 8), or now more commonly the modern form with the past tense of a modal auxiliary, *should win.*

9. POTENTIAL SUBJUNCTIVE IN CLAUSES OF EXTENT. The simple subjunctive is much used here in older English to represent the act as a mere conception, while today we usually employ the indicative, as we feel the act as a fact: 'The onely triall that a ladie requireth of her louer is this, that he performe as much as he *sware*' (John Lyly, *Euphues and His England*, Works, II, p. 168, A.D. 1580), now *promises.*

10. POTENTIAL SUBJUNCTIVE IN CAUSAL CLAUSES. We often use *should* here to express an abstract conception, an abstract principle. We use it even of facts, since the abstract conception, the principle involved, is more prominent in the mind than the concrete fact: 'Yes, [I am] ashamed that I *should have* (or, of course, also the simple present indicative *have*) a mother who could show so little thought for another's feelings' (J. Hartley Manners, *The Harp of Life*, Act II).

After *for fear (that)* and in choice language *lest* we sometimes find the simple subjunctive here, now more commonly the modern

form with the past tense of a modal auxiliary, to represent something as a mere conception: 'Let us act and not shrink *for fear*
(*that,* or *lest*) our motives *be* (or *should be*) misunderstood.' 'I
tremble *for fear that* (or *lest*) you *should* be seen.' 'In England
many legislators are uneasy *for fear that* (or *lest*) they *should* not
get away to the country for the grouse shooting.'

Sometimes after a past indicative there is a modern tendency
to disregard the old sequence (**36**) in clauses introduced by *lest*
where the thing feared seems imminent: 'People dared not venture into the street lest they *be shot*' (G. Atherton, *Sleeping Fires,*
Ch. III), or *should be shot.*

IMPERATIVE

45. The imperative is the mood of command, request, admonition, supplication, entreaty, warning, prohibition. This is one
of the oldest grammatical categories. Forms for the expression
of will are older than those for the expression of actual fact. The
simple imperative, as in *eat, sit,* etc., antedates inflection. It is
an old uninflected form, which along with interjections, like *O!
ouch!* belongs to the oldest forms of spoken speech. Though the
oldest imperative form, it is still widely used, but now it is only
one of many forms, for today the expression of one's will is no
longer a simple matter as in the earliest period when men were
less differentiated and less sensitive.

The following categories indicate the means we now employ to
express our will:

1. **Old Simple Imperative Form.** In direct address we usually
employ in commands, admonitions, requests, supplications, wishes
the simple stem of the verb without a subject, as the direct address
of itself suggests the subject: '*Hurry!*' '*Shut* the door!' '*Keep*
quiet!' '*Come* in!' '*Mind* your own business!' '*Shut* up!' '*Be*
here at noon!' '*Study* your failures and *be* instructed by them.'
'*Pass* me the bread, please.' '*Give* us this day our daily bread.'
The one form here with its many meanings represents the simplicity of primitive speech. The meaning here is not conveyed by
the form alone, but also, as in primitive speech in general, by the
situation, the accent, and the tone of voice. Often to suggest a
course of action politely we make the real command an object
clause after the imperative *suppose,* thus presenting the command
merely as a case for discussion: 'Gerry found a friend there last
night. Very likely he's walked up to say goodbye to him. *Suppose you go to meet them!*' (De Morgan, *Somehow Good,* Ch. XLVI).

The simple imperative is often used to express a wish: 'Good night. *Sleep* well!' (Galsworthy, *Indian Summer of a Forsyte*, Ch. V). Such a permutation —'here clothing a wish in the language of a command — imparts a sprightliness and hopefulness of tone not found in the usual forms of wishing.

The subject is often expressed:

a. In older English, where we now and in oldest English find the simple imperative: '*Enter ye* in at the strait gate . . ., because strait is the gate and narrow is the way' (*Matthew*, VII, 13). There are survivals of this older usage: '*Mind you*, he hasn't paid the money as yet.' Especially common in the colloquial expression 'Look-a-here!' for 'Look you here!' The subject here follows the imperative. In certain dialects, as in Scotch English, this older usage is still quite common: 'Sit ye doon' (George Macdonald, *Robert Falconer*, Ch. XLII).

b. In present English, in order to indicate a contrast, usually with the subject before the imperative: 'I don't know what to say. Norah, *yóu go.*' '"*Yóu watch* her," the doctor said to his assistant, "I shan't be back before eight."' 'I must go about my work. *Yóu amuse* yourself in any way you like.'

c. In lively language, to indicate that the person addressed should take an interest in something, or that it is intended especially for his good or for his discomfiture, or that it should concern or not concern him especially: 'Yóu márk my words. It's a certainty.' 'Yóu bét,' in slang = 'You may risk a bet on that.' 'He's not an unpleasant fellow at all.' — 'Just yóu get better acquáinted with him and sée!' 'Yóu fóllow my advice and don't you go!' 'It'll never work!' — 'Just yóu wáit and sée!' 'Yóu léave that alone!' 'Never yóu mínd, Master Impertinent!' Similarly, in negative *do*-form: 'Dón't yóu be cocksure!' 'Dón't yóu dare to touch a single thing!' 'Dón't yóu say that again!' Compare 2 *b*, p. 432.

2. Modern *Do*-Form:

a. Negative commands are expressed by the rorm with unstressed *do:* 'Don't tálk so lóud!' In popular Irish English *let* is often the auxiliary here: '*Let* you not be a raving fool, Mary Doul!' (Synge, *The Well of the Saints*, Act III). Compare 3, p. 432.

In older English, the simple imperative is employed here. This older usage survives in connection with the adverb *never* and sometimes elsewhere in solemn language and in poetry: 'Never méntion it again.' 'Téll me not in mournful numbers . . .' This older construction is in harmony with the old Germanic principle of putting emphatic words at or near the beginning. The modern use of *do* with dependent infinitive, which contains the

verbal meaning, has in part resulted from the desire to suspend
the real verb for a time in order to create the feeling of suspense
and thus increase the emphasis: 'Don't you ever téll!' See also
6 A *d* (2), (3).

b. The form with *do* is often employed in entreaties and as
an emphatic prohibition or a negative entreaty, here usually with
stressed *do:* 'Dó go, please!' 'Dón't go!' 'Give me a penny,
Papa!' — 'I have nothing for you.' — 'Dó give me just one penny!'
'Dó get up, it's very late.' 'Sit down for a moment, pray, dó!'
When the tone becomes that of an emphatic prohibition or a
negative entreaty, the subject, according to 1 *c* is often expressed:
'Dón't yóu do that!' 'Dón't yóu forget!' or to call attention to
the verbal activity: 'Don't forgét.' But 'Don't thínk it for a
minute!' (Mildred E. Lambert in *American Speech*, April, 1928,
p. 332) is not a prohibition at all but an emphatic denial. Also
in positive entreaties we stress the infinitive to emphasize the
activity: 'Do fínish your work!' 'Do húrry!' In popular Irish
English *let* is often the auxiliary here: '*Let* you make haste; I
hear them trampling in the wood' (Synge, *The Well of the Saints*,
Act III). 'Oh, *let* you not endanger yourself!' (Lady Gregory,
The Full Moon). 'O Hilaria, you who are blind, *let* you open your
eyes!' (Donn Byrne, *Blind Raftery*, p. 145).

Also the progressive form is used here. See **38** 2 *a ee.*

3. **Subjunctive Forms in Commands.** In older English, the
volitive (**43** I A) subjunctive forms were used instead of the imperative when the subject was in the first or the third person.
'*Climb we* not too high, Lest we should fall too low' (Coleridge).
These subjunctive forms survive only in set expressions, now in
contrast to older English usually with suppressed subject after
the analogy of the old imperative: '*Say* [*I*] what I will, he doesn't
mind me.' '*Say* [*we*] what we will, he doesn't mind us.' '*Say*
[*he*] what he will, no one believes him.' '*Cost* [*it*] what it may, I
shall buy it.' '*Try* [*they*] as they may, they never succeed.' In
a few expressions with the subject expressed: 'She *be hanged!*'
(De Morgan, *The Old Madhouse*, Ch. XXVII). The subject is
most commonly expressed when it is a general or indefinite pronoun. For examples see **43** I A.

Instead of the simple form of the subjunctive we now usually
employ here the modern form with the unstressed modal auxiliary
let (originally the stressed imperative of the verb *let* = *allow,
permit*) and a dependent infinitive: 'There is a man at the door
wants to see you.' — '*Let* him cóme ín!' quite different in meaning
from '*Lét* (= *allów, permit*) him come in!' '*Let* me sáy what I
will, he doesn't mind me.' '*Let* us gó!' '*Let* them gó!' *Let* can

be used with all persons but the second. It can, however, be used with the second if combined with another person: '*Let* you and me *go* by ourselves!' In popular Irish English, *let*, after the analogy of the first and third persons, can be used also with the second person, where the literary language requires the simple imperative of the second person: '*Let* you *quit* mocking and making a sport of me!' (Lady Gregory, *The Bogie Man*, p. 18). '*Let* you *get* up out of that!' (Synge, *The Well of the Saints*, Act III).

The *let*-form often occurs in a substantive relative clause: 'Ah'll (I'll) tell you *what let's do*, Miss Leighton!' (W. D. Howells, *A Hazard of New Fortunes*, II, Ch. II). 'I tell you *what let's do:* let's all run away!' (Margaret Deland, *The Iron Woman*, Ch. II). Compare **43** II B *a* (1st par.).

When we speak in a pleading tone, we place the imperative *do* before the *let*-form: '"I say, Ellen! Suppos'n we follow the brook instead of climbing up yonder again!" — "Oh, *do let's,*" said Ellen' (Susan Warner, *The Wide, Wide World*, Ch. XII).

Negative form: '*Let's* not *dó* that!' When we speak in a pleading tone, we employ the *do*-form, or often also the regular negative form with a *don't* as negative instead of *not:* '*Dón't* let us *do* that!' '"*Let's dón't* (prolonged, i.e., drawled out) *be* serious, George," she begged him hopefully. "Let's *tálk* of something pleasant!"' (Tarkington, *The Magnificent Ambersons*, Ch. XVII).

Instead of a *let*-form we often, to suggest a course of action politely, make the real command an object clause after the imperative *suppose*, or sometimes the present participle *supposing* (**31** 2), originally an elliptical condition with the conclusion suppressed: '*Suppose* (or sometimes *supposing*) we all go together and ask him about it! [would it be agreeable to you?]'

Past subjunctive forms are used in polite admonitions: 'We *should* do it' or 'We *ought* (old past subjunctive) to do it.' 'You *should* do it,' 'You *ought* to do it,' or 'You *had* better do it.' 'I thought to myself: "Old chap, you *had* better look into this matter."' For another form of admonishing one's self see 4 *b*, p. 434. To convey mild force we often use *might:* 'Perhaps you and I *might* run round to Sir Thomas' (Henry Arthur Jones, *Mary Goes First*, Act II).

4. Auxiliary Verbs in Expressions of Will. The use of auxiliary verbs here has been touched upon above. A number of other auxiliaries, such as *will*, *shall*, *must*, etc., have clear modal force, likewise certain verbal formations containing auxiliaries, such as the future tense and the progressive form:

a. A present tense of a modal form is used in connection with the old imperative, especially common in requests: 'Just hold the light for me a moment, *will* you?' *Can* is used when the request is spoken in impatient tone: 'Come down quietly, *can't* you?' But *will you?* is often used when the utterance is more an exclamation than a request: 'Look at that, *will you?*' (Mildred E. Lambert in *American Speech*, April, 1928, p. 332).

b. USE OF MODAL 'WILL' AND 'SHALL' INSTEAD OF 'LET.' Instead of *let* (see 3, p. 432) we often use modal *will*: 'Everybody *get* (subjunctive imperative) ready, we'*ll* try again!' = 'let us try it again!' '"Granny," said Barbara, "you must go quietly on to the stile. When you're over I'll come too." — "Certainly not," said Lady Casterley, "we *will* go together"' (Galsworthy, *The Patrician*, p. 86). '"We'*ll* carry these (i.e., the bookshelves) longways," Sabre (name) directed, when the first one was tackled' (Hutchinson, *If Winter Comes*, p. 25). When we are not so sure of assent and desire to defer to the wishes of others, we use modal *shall* here and employ the question form: '*Shall* we try it again?' In an admonition to one's self, where there is, of course, no fear of opposition, we employ *will* and declarative form, as in the first example: 'I said to myself: "I'*ll* go and see."'

c. USE OF THE FUTURE AND THE PROGRESSIVE. We employ the future indicative when we desire to speak courteously and at the same time indicate that we are confidently expecting that our wish will be fulfilled: 'Heads of departments *will submit* their estimates before January first.' When spoken in earnest tone the future becomes almost a command: '"You *will do* nothing of the sort!" she (grandmother to grandchild) said' (Galsworthy, *The Patrician*, p. 87). On the other hand, since we feel a certain bluntness in the future we often soften the force of the expression here by the use of *please, kindly, perhaps, I know*, etc.: 'Intending subscribers *will please* to note the following terms on which the Graphic will be posted to any part of the world' (*Graphic*). 'You *will kindly excuse* me as I must go back to my work.' 'As you are going to the post office, you *will, I know* (or *perhaps*), mail these letters for me.' We often soften the expression by employing modal *will* and question form in connection with a negative: 'Mrs. Jones, *won't* you sit down?' 'You'll stay to tea, *won't* you?' The use of the past subjunctive *would* in a dependent clause is a still more modest form of expression: 'I wish you *would* come over soon to see me.'

As described in **38 1**, the progressive form often has modal force. Hence its imperative is often charged with feeling: 'Up, *be doing* everywhere, the hour of crisis has verily come!' (Carlyle, *Latter-Day Pamphlets*). Compare **38 2 a ee.** As the present indicative of the progressive form of *go* often indicates a prospective action which is to take place in the immediate or near future, it is often used in expressions of will to indicate that the command is to be carried out at once or soon and is usually charged with feeling: 'John, you*'re going* to bed early tonight!' 'You sit down! You*'re* not *going* yet!' (George Bernard Shaw, *Candida*, Act III).

d. Shall is used in commands issued in a tone of authority: 'Thou *shalt* not steal!' '"No, my dear, you had better stay in." — "But I should like to go." — "Well, you *shall* not go!"' 'Positively, you *shall* not do that again!' 'We *shall* have courteous language or none at all.' The past subjunctive *should* has very much milder force, representing the words as friendly advice kindly given: 'You *should* go at once!' 'We *should* go at once!' 'He *should* go at once!' Negative question form has still milder force: '*Should* you *not* go over all the factors in the case once more very carefully before you make a final decision?'

e. Must is much used in commands or prohibitions to indicate that something should be done or not done since it is proper or improper: 'John, we have company today. You *must* behave!' 'You *must*n't knock against the table in that way when I'm trying to write!' 'You *must* not talk so loud!' As explained in **43 I A** we may use also *have to* here in positive commands. *Must* often denotes a strong determination. See **43 I A**.

f. Are to. This form is much used to convey the will of someone other than the subject, representing the order as something that has already been determined upon and here is simply transmitted: 'You *are to be* up at six!' 'You *are* always *to shut* the door when you enter this room!' 'You *are to come* down! Mamma wants you.' Compare **43 I A**.

5. In lively language, expression is often terse, since the situation makes the thought clear, so that nouns, adverbs, prepositional phrases, etc., serve as imperatives: 'The *salt*, please!' 'All *aboard!*' '*Down* in front!' 'Hats *off!*' '*Forward*, brave companions!' A noun or a noun and an adjective often serve as a warning: 'Danger!' 'Fresh paint!' Compare **2 *a***, p. 1.

The gerund preceded by *no* has the force of a negative command: '*No parking* here' = 'Do not park here.'

6. **Tenses of the Imperative.** Commands, such as have been treated in the foregoing articles, usually have reference to the present moment or the future. We sometimes use also the present perfect tense of the imperative to represent the action as already performed: *Have done!* or in popular speech '*a*' *done!* '*Have done* with such nonsense!' In the tone of entreaty the imperative of *do* is used here in connection with the perfect infinitive: '*Do*

have done with this nonsense!' Found also in popular speech: 'Now, Mother, *'a'* done do wud such silly talk!' (Sheila Kaye-Smith, *Green Apple Harvest*, p. 117). As described in **38** 2 *b gg*, the tense auxiliary *be* is still sometimes used, with point-action (**38** 2) intransitives in the present perfect and past perfect tenses of the indicative and subjunctive. This older usage survives here intact in the present perfect imperative *Be gone!*

7. **Passive Imperative.** The positive passive is, in general, avoided: 'We *welcome* you,' not '*Be welcomed* by us!' '*Listen to* your higher nature!' or also '*Be guided* by your higher nature!' '*Heed* my warning!' rather than *Be warned!* (Phillpotts, *Eudocia*, I, II). Of course, in some cases the passive is common, especially the colloquial form with *get:* '*Get shaved* before you come home!' Also the negative imperative with *do* is common: '*Don't be swayed* by such considerations!' or perhaps more commonly '*Don't allow yourself to be swayed* by such considerations!' A present perfect passive is sometimes used: '*Don't have been told* anything about it!' (De Morgan, *The Old Madhouse*, Ch. XVI), i.e., 'Arrange it so that you have not been told anything about it.'

VOICE

46. Active Voice. A marked peculiarity of present-day English is the freedom with which a transitive verb is used without an object — either absolutely or with reflexive, intransitive, or passive force.

We often use a transitive verb absolutely, without an object, because we are not thinking of a particular person or thing as receiving the action, but have in mind only the action itself, pure and simple: 'He likes *to give*.' 'As a teacher, he not only *interests* and *inspires*, but also *stimulates* and *incites* to further investigation.' 'No doubt extraordinary men are in a measure the result of happy accident. There are *determining* or *favoring* factors — race, climate, family inheritance, and so on' (John Burroughs, *Under the Apple-Tree*, XIII, IV). 'It is my turn *to milk* [the cow].' 'I'm *laying* [an ambush] for that Encyclopedical Scotchman' (Mark Twain, *Letter to W. D. Howells*, Oct. 24, 1880). 'He never *laid* [his sword] about him in his imaginary battles in a more tremendous way than he did in this real one' (*id.*, *Joan of Arc*, II, Ch. XVIII). 'The hens *are laying* [eggs] again.'

English shares this feature with a number of tongues, but the wide use of this principle in English has led to distinctive features. For many centuries there has been a growing tendency to employ transitive verbs intransitively without an object for the purpose of predicating an act pure and simple of some particular person or thing: 'He is very weak this morning, *is breaking* fast.' 'The bread *baked* too long.' 'The turkey *is roasting* nicely.' 'Stir till the pulp *cooks* to a marmalade.' 'The cloth *tears* at a touch.' At this point has arisen a long list of new intransitives, which in many cases have developed a peculiar meaning, as described on page 440.

In English, there has arisen another peculiar group of intransitives made from transitives. We say, 'Mary *is dressing*,' or 'Mary *dresses* plainly,' although it is quite evident that Mary acts upon herself. Modern German and other languages use in these cases a reflexive pronoun as object: 'Mary *dresses herself*.' We say, 'Her eyes *filled* with tears,' 'The thick fog *lifted*,' while in German in many such cases where the subject seems to act of itself the subject is personified, i.e., a reflexive pronoun is used as object, as if the subject were a person acting upon himself: 'Her eyes *filled themselves* with tears.' We sometimes find the reflexive form in English: 'round which the heart's best affections *have twined themselves*' (Robertson, *Sermons*, III, XVII, 216). 'Some such impression *conveyed itself* to the two men who were walking with Mrs. Reffold' (Beatrice Harraden, *Ships That Pass in the Night*, I, Ch. III). 'In a few years the population of the town *doubled*' (or *doubled itself*). 'The convulsion soon *exhausted itself*.' With reference to persons the reflexive pronoun in its older, shorter form was once very common where there is now no reflexive object at all: 'Which way will I *turne me?*' (Lyly, *Euphues and His England*, Works, II, p. 142, A.D. 1580), now simple *turn*. 'I met a fool; who laid him down and *bask'd him* (now simple *basked*) in the sun' (Shakespeare, *As You Like It*, II, vii, 15). 'At the breach of day we sixe *made vs* [go] for the mountaine' (Lithgow, *Travels*, VI, 261, A.D. 1632), now 'We six *made* for the mountain.' 'We *put* (for older *put us*) up at the hotel.' In older English, *set* was used reflexively or intransitively in the sense of *seat one's self, sit down:* 'My doughter, *sette you* here by me' (*Mélusine*, 154, A.D. 1500). 'He made them *set* vpon a benche' (Caxton, *Sonnes of Aymon*, XVI, 377, A.D. 1489). The intransitive form is still common in popular speech: '*Set* by me.' '*Set* down.' 'Our hen *is setting*.' Intransitive *set*, developed out of reflexive *set*, occurs also in the literary language in many set expressions, for the most part figurative or abstract: 'Plaster of Paris *sets* quickly.' 'His character has not yet *set*.' 'About a dozen fruit *set*, of which six ripened.' 'The sun *is setting*.' 'The tide *sets* in' (out). 'They *set* about repairing the bridge.' 'We *set* off (or out) together for the base of the mountain.' After a number of verbs, *absent, bear, bestir, betake, bethink, busy, comport, compose, conduct, demean, deport, intoxicate, perjure, pique, plume, pride*, etc., the reflexive pronoun is still the rule, of course, now in its modern compound form: 'She *prides herself* on her cooking.' With a number of verbs the reflexive pronoun can be used or omitted: *Behave*, or *behave yourself*. 'I *dressed*' (or *dressed myself*). 'I *hid*' (or *hid myself*). 'I *overslept*' (or now rarely *overslept myself*). 'I *overate*' (or now rarely *overate myself*). 'The horse *reared*' (or less commonly *reared himself*). 'She likes *to show* off,' or 'She likes *to show herself* off.' 'A sweet smile *spread* (or *spread itself*) gently over his face.' 'I *rested* (or *rested myself*) an hour or two.' 'I *washed, bathed*' (or *washed myself, bathed myself*). 'A new sense of duty *is developing* (or *is developing itself*) in him.' In America we say, 'He *hired out* to a farmer,' while in England it is still, as in older English, usual to say, 'He *hired himself*.' In the case of the one verb *rest* the intransitive is the older form.

In general, we use the reflexive or the reciprocal pronoun when we think of a person or thing as acting on himself or itself, or as having mutual relations with another, while we employ intransitive form when the idea of an action pure and simple, or a development or result presents itself to our mind: 'I *applied myself* to my difficult task,' but 'I *applied* to my friend for advice.' 'I *qualified myself* (= *made myself fit*) for the position,' but 'I *qualified* (= *passed the examination*, or *gave a bond*) for the office.' 'A door can't *open itself*,' but 'The door suddenly *opened*.' 'He *proved himself* to be worthy of the place,' but 'He *proved* intractable' and 'He made acquaintance with a lady who *proved* to be the Countess of Drogheda' (Macaulay). 'He *felt himself* degraded,' where we feel the thought of the subject as turned in on himself; but we say 'He *felt* disgusted,' as we feel *felt* as a mere copula. There is the same fluctuation in the use of the reciprocal pronoun: 'They *kissed each other* tenderly,' but without the pronoun to express action pure and simple: '*Kiss* and be friends.' 'Our letters *crossed*' (or *crossed each other*). 'They *met* (or sometimes *met each other*) at the gate,' but 'They *separated* at the gate.' This fluctuation between reflexive or reciprocal and intransitive with a general drift in the direction of the intransitive is old, for it is not only going on now, but it was going on also in Old English: 'Hie *gedældon hie*' (or simply *gedældon*, i.e., *they parted*). 'Hie oft *gemetton hie*' (or simply *gemetton*, i.e., *they often met*).

There has been here a steady development away from reflexive form toward intransitive wherever there has been a development of reflexive meaning into intransitive. As, however, the old transitive meaning of such verbs often maintained itself alongside of the new intransitive, the same verb often had either transitive or intransitive force according to the connection. Thus early in the history of our language there began to be felt the principle, now widely observed, that the same verb may be used both transitively and intransitively. Even in Old English, there were a number of such verbs. In many other cases transitive and intransitive verbs had in this early period the same stem but were slightly differentiated in form. Later, through natural phonetic development and under the influence of the growing feeling that a difference of form was not necessary here, both transitive and intransitive form became in many words identical.

There is often a further development here. Since many of the new intransitives from the two groups described in the third and fourth paragraphs, as well as many old intransitives, represent something as naturally developing or accidentally entering into a new state, or as having the power or fitness to enter it, consequently as affected or capable of being affected, they acquire passive force, so that now passive force is often associated with intransitive form: 'Muscles, nerves, mind, reason, all *develop* (or *are developed*) under play.' 'This cloth *has worn* (or *has been worn*) thin.' 'This cloth *feels* (i.e., is felt as being) soft.' 'The first consignment *sold out* (or *was sold out*) in a week.' 'He *graduated* (or *was graduated*) last year.' 'The wheat in our northern states often *winterkills*.' 'The boat *upset*' (= *was upset*). 'The right to rule *derives* (= *is derived*) from those who gave it.' 'The two of them *traced* (= *were traced*) back to a Samuel Lincoln who had come two hundred years before to Hingham' (Carl Sandburg, *Abraham Lincoln*, I, p. 82). 'Women could go *hang* (i.e., *to be hanged*), because she did not want them' (W. J. Locke, *The Glory of Clementina*, Ch. II). 'My hat *blew* (or *was blown*) into the river.' 'These plans *are working out* (or *are being worked out*) successfully.' 'The plans *worked out* (or *were worked out*) successfully.' 'The eggs *hatched out* easily.' 'My coat *caught* (or *got caught*) on a nail.' 'The door *doesn't lock*' (or *can't be locked*). 'Such houses *rent, sell* (or *can be rented, sold*) easily.' 'Ripe oranges *peel* (or *can be peeled*) easily.' 'Sugar *dissolves* (or *can be dissolved*) in water.' 'The vessel *steers* (or *can be steered*) with ease.' 'These colors *do not wash* (or *cannot be washed*) well.' 'This cloth *doesn't cut* (or *cannot be cut*) to advantage.' 'This cake *doesn't break* (or *cannot be broken*) evenly.' 'This paper *doesn't tear* (or *cannot be torn*) straight.' 'This wood *doesn't split* (or *cannot be split*) straight.' 'The bread *doesn't bake* (or *cannot be baked*) well in this oven.' 'The travel-book *did not finish* (or *could not be finished*) easily, and more than once when he (Mark Twain) thought it completed, he found it necessary to cut and change' (Albert B. Paine, *Mark Twain's Letters*, II, p. 644). 'I don't know that I can write a play that *will play*' (or *can be played*) (Mark Twain, *Letter to W. D. Howells*, Jan. 22, 1898). 'This play *reads better than it acts*' (or *should be read rather than acted*).

The boundary line between the new passive and the older intransitive force is often quite dim and cannot be accurately determined by a distinctive formal mark of any kind nor by any inner shade of meaning, for intransitive and passive force are so closely related that the one shades imperceptibly into the other. Thus the examples from Robertson and Beatrice Harraden given in the fourth paragraph may be construed not only as intransitive but also as passive. Similarly, when the reflexive has been dropped and the form becomes outwardly intransitive the inner meaning often hovers between intransitive and passive. In many cases, however, the passive idea here is so strong that intransitive can be replaced by passive form as indicated on page 440 in parentheses. But these two passive forms are often not identical in force. The passive with passive form represents a person or thing as being affected by an agent working under resistance vigorously and consciously to a definite end, while the passive with intransitive form represents an activity as proceeding easily, naturally, often almost spontaneously. Compare 47 a.

The development of form and meaning here is often uneven. The original reflexive form here is often retained although the meaning after having become intransitive has finally become passive: 'No progress can *establish itself* (i.e., *be established*) without a partial retrogression.' 'The fire *communicated itself* to the next house.' 'He fell down and *hurt himself*' (i.e., *was hurt*).

As can be seen from the above account, a large number of intransitives or passives with intransitive or reflexive form have developed out of transitives, so that the same verb can be used actively, intransitively, or passively without a change of form. In contrast to this group there is another in which transitive verbs have developed out of intransitives. There was in Old English, in a number of cases, a difference of form between a transitive causative and the intransitive from which it was derived: 'bærnan' (trans.), *to make something burn, to burn up*, but 'beornan' (intrans.) *to burn;* 'sencan' (trans.), *to make something sink*, but 'sincan' (intrans.), *to sink*, etc. There are still a few cases where there is here a difference of form between the transitive causative and the intransitive from which it is derived: 'He *fells* (literally, *makes fall*) the tree' and 'The tree *falls*' (intrans.). In other cases where the two forms are preserved we do not now feel their original force: 'The storm *drenched* our clothes' (literally, *made our clothes drink*) and 'He *drank* (intrans.) deeply.' 'He *sets* (literally, *makes sit*) the pot on the stove' and 'He *sits* (intrans.) by the window.' 'He *lays* (literally, *makes lie*) his book on the table' and 'The book *lies* (intrans.) on the table.' 'Her family *reared* (or in Danish form *raised;* literally, *made rise*) a sumptuous mausoleum over her remains' and 'He *rose* to the occasion.' In a special sense also *rise* is used as a causative: 'We *rose* many birds in the course of the day's hunt.'

In this category we now employ usually in most cases, in accordance with the usage so common elsewhere, only one form for both transitive and intransitive function: I *burned* up the rubbish' and 'The rubbish *burned* up.' 'He *sinks* the boat' and 'The boat *sinks*.' In all these cases the verb was originally intransitive, but the corresponding transitive causative was already in oldest English in common use, at first with a somewhat different form, later usually with the same form.   Of course, when causatives were later formed from originally intransitive verbs they assumed the form of the intransitive, as in the case of *fall* (in older English), *swim, starve, stand, fly, gallop, leap, run, drop, march, flash, jingle, grow, stay, walk, sit, rise*, etc.: 'A little child learning to walk often *falls*' (intrans.). 'The common executioner, Whose heart the accustom'd sight of death makes hard, *Falls* (trans. caus.) not the axe upon the humbled neck But first begs pardon' (Shakespeare, *As You Like It*, III, v, 5). 'The horses plunged into the river and *swam* (intrans.) over.' 'We in the Evening *Swam* (trans. caus.) our horses over' (George Washington, *Diary*, March 20, 1748). 'They had so little to eat that they almost *starved*' (intrans.). 'He *starved* (trans. caus.) his old father to death.' 'They *starved themselves* (reflex.) to buy books.' 'Here once *stood* (intrans.) a huge oak.' 'I *stood* (trans. caus.) my rifle against the oak.' 'The kite *is flying* (intrans.) high.' 'The boy *is flying* (trans. caus.) his kite.' 'She (airship) *flew* (intrans.) to Spitzbergen, where she replenished her supplies' (Victor Appleton, *Don Sturdy across the North Pole*, Ch. XXV). 'Croil (name) *flew* (trans. caus.) me to Suez' (T. E. Lawrence, *Revolt in the Desert*, p. 192). 'He *flies* (trans. caus.) his own plane.' 'He *sprang* (intrans.) up from his seat.' 'He loves to *spring* (trans. caus.) surprises on us.' 'The horse *galloped* (intrans.) away and *leaped* (intrans.) over the fence.' '. . . the horsemanship of the cavalry, who *galloped* (trans. caus.) their horses at full speed over the ground and *leaped* (trans. caus.) them over formidable obstacles' (Theodore Roosevelt, *The Winning of the West*, Vol. IV, Ch. V). 'The water *ran* (intrans.) off.' 'He *ran* (trans. caus.) the water off.' 'He *ran* his canoe ashore.' 'He *dropped* the letter into the box.' 'The guard *marched* the prisoner off.' 'From a little handmirror he *flashed* sun into their eyes.' 'He *jingled* the loose coins in his pockets.' 'He *grows* vegetables for the market.' 'Who can *stay* the hand of death?' 'He drew me out of my study and *walked* me off to the woods.' 'He (Voltaire) was refused Christian burial in Paris; but his friends *sat* him up grimly in a carriage, and got him out of the city by pretending that he was alive' (Will Durant, *The Story of Philosophy*, p. 275). 'We *rose* many birds in the course of the day's hunt.'

In most cases, however, the causative idea is now expressed by placing the auxiliary *make* or *have*, or in a number of expressions, as in older English, the auxiliary *let*, before the infinitive of the verb in question: 'Money *makes* the mare *go*.' 'That *makes* you *look* miserable.' 'I'll *make* him *take* it back.' 'I'll *have* him *do* it.' 'I'll *let* you *know* tomorrow.' '*Let* him *see* that you are dissatisfied.' '*Let* him *feel* it.' When the infinitive is to have passive force, the usual causative auxiliary is *have* in connection with the past participle of the verb, which contains the passive force: 'I *had* a new suit *made*.' Compare **15** III 2 B (4th and 5th parr.). In accordance with older usage *let* is sometimes still employed as auxiliary here, in connection, however, with the passive infinitive: 'He *let* it *be known* to only a few friends.' 'He soon *let* his power *be felt*.' In older English, the active infinitive was used here with passive force: 'Hę *lete make* a proclamacion þorʒ (through) all his Empire' (*Gesta Romanorum*, I, VI, 15, A.D. 1440). Compare **15** III 2 B (4th and 6th parr.). In older English, the causative idea could be expressed by *do* with an infinitive: 'Sometimes to *do* him *laugh* she would essay To laugh' (Spenser, *The Faerie Queene*, II, VI, VII).

There is another group of transitives that have developed out of intransitives — intransitives that take an accusative object to complete their meaning. This group of verbs is treated in **11** 2 (4th par.).

47. Passive Voice. The passive forms in English are used to express two quite different things, *action* and *state*.

a. ACTIONAL PASSIVE. The simpler passive form with *be* and the perfect participle is used to denote an act as a whole: 'The house *is painted* every year.' 'The house *was painted* last year.' 'Since we have lived here, the house *has been painted* every year.' 'For as the sun is daily new and old, So is my love still telling what *is* (now *has been;* see **37** 3, 3rd par.) *told*' (Shakespeare, *Sonnet* LXXVI).

The progressive form is employed to represent an act as going on. In the literary language, it is made up of the progressive form of the verb *be* and the perfect participle of the verb to be conjugated: 'The house *is being painted*.' This progressive form arose in the fifteenth century: 'Wyne (wine) is being *y-put* (old perfect participle for *put*) to sale' (in a letter of John Shillingford, about 1447). It spread at first very slowly and did not really become established in the literary language until about

1825. During this period (1447–1825) there were two other competing progressive forms, a gerundial and a participial: (gerundial) 'The house is *in building*,' or in contracted form *a-building;* (participial) 'The house *is building*' (the present participle with passive force). The gerundial construction in its contracted form, 'The house is *a-building*,' survives only in popular speech; in the literary language it was earlier in the period gradually supplanted by the participial construction.

Between 1700 and 1825 the participial construction (*is building*) gained temporarily the ascendency in the literary language and was widely used also in colloquial speech. Thus in colonial times and the early days of the Republic this passive form was the common one: 'Some of the Peas are up and some *are* now *sowing*' (Richard Smith, *A Tour of Four Great Rivers*, II, 19, A.D. 1769), now *being sown.* 'This being the Anniversary of American Independence and being kindly requested to do it, I agreed to halt here this day and partake of the entertainment which *was preparing* (now *was being prepared*) for the celebration of it' (George Washington, *Diary*, July 4, 1791). From 1825 on, however, the form with *being* + perfect participle began to lead all others in this competition, so that in spite of considerable opposition the clumsy *is being built* became more common than *is building* in the usual passive meaning, i.e., where it was desired to represent a person or thing as affected by an agent working under resistance vigorously and consciously to a definite end: 'The house *is being built.*' 'My auto *is being repaired.*'

On the other hand, the form with the present participle did not now disappear, but continued to be widely used. This was because the present participle had been gradually developing a peculiar passive meaning, which was felt as distinctive and useful. While this peculiar force of the present participle rendered it unfit to express the usual passive meaning, it came into wide use in its own distinctive field, namely, to represent an activity as proceeding easily, naturally, often almost spontaneously: 'These books *are selling out* fast.' 'Our plans *are working out* successfully.' 'Dust *is blowing in* at the open door.' The development of passive force here out of active form is explained in **46** (7th and 8th parr.)

Thus the form with *being* and the form with the present participle were at first competing constructions without a difference of meaning, but later became differentiated, enriching the language. This differentiation, however, is incomplete, for the form with *being* is used only in the present and the past tense: 'The house *is being built, was being built.*' In the compound tenses the construction with the present participle is still, as in older English, employed in the usual passive meaning: 'The house *has been building, had been building, will be building.*' The form with *being* is employed in the present and the past tense for the sake of its accuracy, but we hesitate to extend this principle of accuracy to the compound tenses, where the accumulation of auxiliary forms would be intolerable. For a similar reason we avoid the form with *being* in the imperative, infinitive, participle, and gerund, since the use of *being* after the form *be* or *being* would sound too harsh. In older English, the form with the present participle could be used in the infinitive: 'After passing Beverly we come to the Cotton Manufactory, which seems *to be carrying* (now *carried*) on with spirit by the Mr. Cabbots' (George Washington, *Diary*, Oct. 30, 1789). In the dialect of the southern counties of Scotland, the form with the present participle is still, as in older literary English, employed also in the present and the past tense in the usual passive meaning: 'The hoose *is buildan.*' This older usage still occasionally occurs also in the literary language: 'My horse!' — 'My Lord, he's *shoeing*' (George H. Boker, *Francesca da Rimini*, V, ii, A.D. 1856). Most commonly, however, where the idea of conscious agent is little felt, overshadowed by that of natural development or process: 'Tea *was preparing* in the kitchen' (A. Marshall, *Anthony Dare*, Ch. X).

The gerundial construction survives only in popular speech, now only in contracted form: 'The house *is a-building.*' This contracted form was once in use in the literary language: 'Now we have shown our power, Let us seem humbler after it is done Than when it *was a-doing*' (Shakespeare, *Coriolanus*, IV, ii, 3). Likewise the full form was once common in the literary language: 'Forty and six years *was* this temple *in building*' (*John*, II, 20).

Alongside of the literary passive with *be* and the past participle is a common, more expressive, colloquial form conjugated with *get* instead of *be:* 'Our house *gets painted* every year.' 'Our house *is getting painted.*' Compare *b* below.

Besides the various means of expressing the passive idea described above, there are still others, described elsewhere. See **15** I 2 *a* (last par.), **15** III 2 B (4th, 5th, 6th parr.), **46** (next to last par.), **7** D 2.

b. STATAL PASSIVE. The simpler passive form is also used to denote a state: 'The house *is painted.*' Past state: 'The house *has been painted*, although no trace of paint can now be detected upon it.' 'The door *was shut* at six when I went by, but I don't know when it *was shut.*' The first *was shut* in the last sentence is used to denote a state, the second *was shut* to denote an act.

Thus the one form is employed to denote two quite different things. For many centuries the verb *be*, whether used as copula or passive auxiliary, has had a twofold meaning, expressing on the one hand the idea of state, on the other hand the idea of ingression (**38** 2 *a ff*) with the meaning of *become*, hence used in the passive to express action: 'Our house *is* (expressing state) painted.' 'Our house *is* (= *becomes*, hence expressing action) painted every year.' In *be* the idea of state so overshadows that of ingression or action that its establishment as an auxiliary in the actional passive is a great misfortune for our language. This lack of an adequate form in the literary language to express action has led in colloquial speech to the use of a more expressive actional form, namely, *get* with ingressive force, like *become*, hence fitted for the expression of action: 'I fear that all books that really do their work *get used* up' (Sir Walter Raleigh, *Letter to Evan Charteris*, May 9, 1917), i.e., 'a good book *gets read* so much that it *gets used* up.' 'A man *gets driven* into work' (H. G. Wells, *The New Machiavelli*, p. 207). 'Your nature is an overbearing one, Sophia, and for once you *got punished* for it' (A. Marshall, *Many Junes*, Ch. I, p. 2). 'The poor little fellow *gets punished* almost every day.' — 'He's never yet *got punished* enough. Some day he'*ll get punished* the way he deserves.' 'I suppose it *will get whispered* about and they'll hear it' (Tarkington, *Gentle Julia*, Ch. XVIII). 'And now what was this wonderful game where so many people *got killed?*' (Rupert Hughes, *Clipped Wings*, Ch. I). If this expressive, actional, passive form with the auxiliary *get*, already quite common colloquially, ever becomes established in literary English, it will be a decided gain to the language. Our present use of *get* as the auxiliary of the actional passive alongside of *be* corresponds closely to the Old English use of *weorþan* as the auxiliary of the actional passive alongside of the *be* forms. *Weorþan* was an ingressive with the force of our modern auxiliary *get*, which at that time had, of course, not yet come into existence, hence was not available. *Weorþan* was superior to *be* in expressive power, but its form was so heavy that even in the Old English period it began to be replaced by its lighter competitor. Our present wide use of *get* here shows plainly that we feel the inability of *be* to express our thought clearly. *Get*, unlike Old English *weorþan*, is a light, handy word that gives promise of a long period of usefulness.

The past participle of certain verbs have almost pure adjective force. The use of *get* or *become* with such past participles does not indicate action at all, but merely the beginning of a temporary or a final state: 'I *am getting* (or *becoming*) tired.' 'Dialectic

expressions sometimes *become* established in the literary language.'
Compare **38** 2 *a bb* and **38** 2 *b ee*. The use of the auxiliary *be*
with such participles indicates an actual state: 'I *am* tired.'
'The expression *is* established in the literary language.' The auxiliary *stand* here has the force of *be* with the implication that the
state is the result of a decision or act that has just preceded:
'The meeting *stands* adjourned to five o'clock.' 'I *stand* corrected.'
'We *stand* committed to this action.' 'The delegates *stand*
pledged to this course.' 'He took the key and opened the lid,
when the cakes and wine *stood* revealed in all their damning pro-
fusion' (Anstey, *Vice Versa*, Ch. V). Sometimes *stand* indicates
readiness: 'I *stand* prepared to dispute it.'

CHAPTER XXII

THE INFINITE FORMS OF THE VERB

In contrast, in a formal sense, to the finite forms of the verb, i.e., those limited by person, number, and mood, are the infinite forms, i.e., those not thus limited, verbal forms without person, number, and mood. There are three such forms — participle, infinitive, and gerund. The extensive use of these forms is an outstanding feature of English. No other part of our grammar is at the present time developing so vigorously. Compare **20 3**.

PARTICIPLE

48. The participle, true to its name, participates in the nature of an adjective and a verb.

1. Functions Other than Those with the Force of a Finite Verb. There are five categories:

a. Participle Used as an Adjective with More or Less Verbal Force. Attributively with active meaning and descriptive stress (**10 I 1**): a *gràsping* náture; a *càptivating* mánner; the *rìsen* sún; often in connection with a modifier (adverb, object, etc.) or a predicate adjective: a wèll-*meaning* bóy; a wèll-*behaved* bóy; a wèll-*read* mán; a wèll-*dressed* wóman; an ùn*relenting* wóman; a fùll-*blown* róse; a bèautifully *dressed* wóman; a hèart-*breaking* scéne; a hèalthy-*looking* bóy; but in the predicate relation the adverb is usually stressed less than the participle; of course, also in the attributive relation if the adverb is unstressed

in the compound verb: 'The boy is well-*méaning*, well-*beháved*.'
'The woman is well-*dréssed*, un*relénting*.' 'The rose is full-*blówn*.'
'The woman is beautifully *dréssed*.' 'An over*drèssed* wóman'
and 'The woman is over*dréssed*,' since in the compound verb
overdréss the verbal form is stressed. Attributively with passive
meaning: a *bròken* cháir; a wèll-*known* mán; a fùlly *equipped*
ármy; an ùn*opened* létter; a wèll-*dressed* little gírl (i.e., 'a little
girl who *has been* well *dressed*,' while in 'a wèll-*dressed* wóman' the
participle has active meaning); an ìvy-*clad* cástle; a stòrm-
tossed shíp; a lòng-*looked*-for occásion; ùn*heard*-of wónders;
carved-in-wòod ídols; but in the predicate relation: 'The man
is well-*knówn*.' 'The army is fully *equípped*.' 'The letter is un-
ópened.' 'The little girl is well-*dréssed*.' Attributively with
classifying or distinguishing stress (**10** I 1): the first of *living*
àrtists; the *fóllowing* dày; (with passive meaning): *wáshing* tìes
(i.e., ties that wash, are washed); *cóoking* àpples (i.e., apples that
cook well, can be cooked). Appositively after the noun: 'the
little boy *sitting* on the last chair,' 'a new sect lately *risen* in India.'
Predicatively: 'He is always *reserved*.' 'The book is *interesting*.'
As objective predicate (**15** III 2, **15** III 2 A): 'I find the book
interesting.' As predicate appositive (**6** C): 'He awoke the next
morning *rested* and *refreshed*.'

b. Participle Used as a Noun. As an adjective the participle
can be used as a noun: the *wounded* and *dying;* the *deceased;*
my *intended*, etc. Compare **58**.

c. Participle Used as an Adverb. The participle is used also
as an adverb: *boiling* hot; *piercing* cold.

d. Participle Used as a Pure Adjective. In a number of cases
the adjective nature of the participle has entirely overshadowed
the verbal nature, so that the words are now felt as adjectives
pure and simple and have, in the case of perfect participles, become
differentiated in form from the participle by the retention of the
older participial form in *–en*, while the participle with verbal force
has developed a new form, if it is preserved: one's *bounden* duty;
a *cloven* hoof; *sunken* eyes; a *graven* image; a *drunken* man;
a clean-*shaven* or clean-*shaved* face, etc.

e. Participle Used with More Verbal than Adjective Force. The
participle now for the most part has more verbal force than
formerly. The present participle in connection with an auxiliary
is much used in the progressive form of verbs, where, though still
a predicate adjective, it has the full force of a verb: 'He *is writing*
a letter.' 'He *was, has been, will be, writing* a letter.' This form
often has passive meaning: 'There *is* a new house *building* on the
corner.' 'These books *are selling* out fast.' For a fuller treatment

of this passive construction see **47** *a*. The progressive form has become a powerful construction by the fusion of the gerundial construction with it: 'as she *was writing* (older form *in writing*) *of it*' (Shakespeare, *As You Like It*, IV, III, 10), now 'as she *was writing* it,' the dropping of *in* and *of* indicating that the gerundial construction has merged into the participial. This fusion of the two constructions was made possible by the earlier fusion of their endings and the general similarity of their meaning. In the fourteenth century, the participial ending *–inde* became confused with the gerundial ending *–inge*, so that *–ing* became the common ending for both forms. In the dialect of Northumberland and the southern counties of Scotland the two forms still have different endings, *–an* (pronounced ǝn) for the participle, *–in* for the gerund. The fusion of the two forms in the literary language often makes it difficult to distinguish them: the form in *–ing* a gerund in *dining*-car (i.e., a car for dining), *ironing*-board (i.e., a board for ironing), but a present participle with passive (**47** *a*, **46**) force in *cooking*-apple (i.e., an apple that cooks well, can be cooked), breech-*loading* gun (i.e., a gun that loads, is loaded at the breech).

The present participle is much used as predicate also after the copula *seem:* 'Instead of offering any explanation he seemed *waiting* for her to say something.' The predicative infinitive of the progressive form competes with the predicative participle: 'He seemed *to be waiting* for her to say something.'

Also the past participle is much used in verbal forms as a predicate adjective, namely, in the passive: 'The house is *painted*.' Here the participle has almost pure adjective force expressing a state. But it often has strong verbal force: 'The house is (or gets) *painted* every year.' There is here also a progressive form: 'The house is being (or getting) *painted*.' Compare **47** *b*. In older English, also the past participle of point-action (**38** 2 *b gg*) intransitives was used as a predicate and occasionally is still so used: 'My money is all *gone*.' 'The leaves are all *fallen*.' 'The melancholy days are *come*.' After the verbal force here had overshadowed the adjective force, *is, are, was*, etc., were gradually replaced by *has, have, had*, so that we today usually employ a present perfect or a past perfect tense where our ancestors used an adjective construction: 'Much snow *has* (once *is*) *fallen*.' 'Much snow *had* (once *was*) *fallen*.' Compare **37** 3 (3rd par.).

2. Functions with the Force of a Finite Verb. Our English ancestors made a liberal use of the two participles when they fashioned our conjugational systems, and the following generations continued this work by employing both participles in abridged clauses (**20** 3), which they began to develop more carefully to replace, for practical purposes, the more formal subordinate clause with a nominative subject and a finite verb as predicate, so that participles were used to *build up* the verbal systems and later *to replace* these same systems.

After a noun a participle often forms with the words near it an attributive clause, in which the preceding noun serves as subject and the participle as predicate. Here the participle is not in a formal sense a predicate adjective after a finite copula or auxiliary, as in 1 *e*, p. 449, but predicates of itself, just like a finite verb: 'It (the circus) was all one family — parents and five children — *performing* (= *who performed*) *in the open air.*' 'Good things *long enjoyed* (= *which have long been enjoyed*) are not easily given up.' 'The large building *being constructed* (= *which is being constructed*) *in the field yonder* is the new schoolhouse.' 'The bridge *seized* (= *which had been seized*) *two hours before by the enemy* was now retaken.' 'We shall arrive too late to catch the train *leaving* (= *which will leave*) *at eight.*' The participle, though it has fewer forms than the finite verb, expresses the time relations quite accurately.

The participle is often employed to predicate something of the object of the principal verb, i.e., it serves as an objective predicate (**15** III 2, **15** III 2 A). In this construction the object of the principal verb and the participle together form a kind of subordinate clause, in which the object serves as the subject and participle as the predicate. The participle performs the function of predicate just as in the progressive form and in the passive of finite verbs, but there is present in this construction no finite auxiliary verb to serve as a formal sign of predication. The participle predicates of itself: 'I saw him *lying* under a tree.' 'I have my work *done.*' 'I had my work *done.*' This use of the past participle as objective predicate has led to one of the most important developments in the history of our language. By simply changing the word-order in such sentences as the last two we have developed the present perfect and the past perfect tense of transitive verbs: 'I *have done* my work.' 'I *had done* my work.' Compare **37** 3 (2nd par.). The use of *have* and *had* here in the new present perfect and past perfect tenses proved so useful that they were similarly employed with intransitives, so that *has, have, had* are now used uniformly with all verbs. Compare **37** 3.

The predicative past participle out of which the present perfect and past perfect tenses developed had a good deal of adjective force, expressing a condition or state. This old participle is still widely used with the same force: 'I had the letter *written* before he came.' 'I got my work *done* before twelve o'clock.' Both the present and the past participle, however, often have here almost pure verbal force: 'I watched the net *being hauled* in.' 'I saw the thing *shaping*' (active form with passive force; see **15** III 2 B, 6th par.). 'He felt himself *seized* by a strong arm from behind.' 'She represents him as *having* ever *struggled* for the best things.' The form *shaping* represents the original condition of things as far as the form is concerned. It was originally an adjective and has still its old adjective form, but it has acquired a good deal of verbal force. *Being hauled* has the force of a passive verb and has been given passive form to express it. *Having struggled* has the force and the form of the present perfect active. We often employ the present infinitive instead of the present participle, but each form has a little different shade of meaning. The participle has descriptive force, expressing duration or repetition, while the infinitive represents the action as a finished whole, a fact: 'I heard him *coming* slowly up the steps as if under a heavy load' (duration), but 'I heard him *come* up the stairs a few minutes ago' (a fact). 'We should be sorry to see English critics *suggesting* (repetition, one critic suggesting in one periodical, another in another periodical) that they ought to or could have acted otherwise.' Compare **50** 3 (3rd par. from end). The present participle has this force also when it is used to predicate something of the object of a preposition: 'Do not send any more of my books home. I have a good deal of pleasure in the thought of *you looking* on them' (Keats). Compare **50** 3 (4th and 5th parr. from end).

The most common use of the participle is to employ it as a predicate appositive (**6** C). We bring it into relation to the subject or the object of the principal verb that it may predicate something of it and at the same time, as a predicate appositive, serve as an adverbial element indicating some adverbial relation, such as time, cause, manner, condition, purpose, means, etc. The participle has the force of a finite verb. Its subject is not expressed but implied in the subject or the object of the principal verb: '*Going* (= *while I was going*) *down town* I met a friend.' '*Having finished* (= *after I had finished*) *my work* I went to bed.' '*Being* (= *as I was*) *sick* I stayed at home.' 'I feel it as a rare occasion, *occurring as it does only once in many years*' (= *since it occurs only once in many years*). 'I beat him *jumping*' (clause of manner, indicating manner, respect in which he excelled). 'He went *hunting*' (clause of purpose). In older English, instead of 'He went *hunting*' it was common to say, 'He went *on hunting*.' Compare **33** 2 (last par.). Thus the more accurate gerundial construction has been replaced by the simpler participial form. Simplicity is a marked characteristic of English. Compare **20** 3 (3rd par.).

Hampered by their original adjective nature and form, these participles have not yet developed forms for mood and have not as many tenses as verbs have. Thus, the same participle must often serve as an indicative and a subjunctive: 'This thing, *happening* (= *since it happened;* past indicative) at the right time, has helped our cause' and 'This same thing, *happening* (= *if it should happen;* past subjunctive) in wartime, would amount to disaster.' Again, the present participle must serve, not only as a present tense, but also as a future: 'My train starts at six, *arriving* (future time) in Chicago at ten.' Similarly, the perfect participle must serve as a present perfect and as a past perfect: '*Having been* (= *as I have been*) sick so much, I have learned to take good care of my health.' '*Having finished* (= *after I had finished*) my work, I went to bed.' Compare **27** 5.

As the participle never assumes a form to indicate person, number, and mood, and in these categories never has a subject of its own expressed, the construction is an exceedingly simple one. The great ease of movement associated with it explains its wide use. While it is terse and convenient, there is often in it no clear expression of the adverbial relations. Instead of rejecting it as inadequate for accurate purposes we have for a long time been trying to improve it by introducing into it features, i.e., the conjunctions, of the full clause: '*While* going down town I met an old friend.' Compare **20** 3 (5th par.). On the other hand, in lively style, as illustrated in **24** IV *a* (last par.) and **27** 5 (4th par.), the simpler older form is still often preferred, since it is more concrete and impressive.

a. Voices of the Participle. There are active and passive forms. Examples are given in 2, p. 450.

b. Tenses of the Participle. Though the participle has fewer tenses than the finite verb, it can express the time relations quite accurately. Examples are given in 2, p. 450.

c. Subject of the Participle. In all the categories described in the preceding pages the subject of the participle is always understood, never expressed. It is usually implied in some noun or pronoun that stands near it, which at the same time performs some function in the principal proposition, usually that of the subject or the object of the principal verb. Examples are given in 2, p. 450.

Sometimes the subject of the participle is not implied in any word in the sentence, as the reference is general and indefinite. Such a participle is called an absolute participle. This construction is described in **17** 4.

Sometimes the participle has a subject of its own, which is usually in the nominative. This is the so-called absolute nominative construction. It is described in detail in **17** 3 A, B, C.

3. **Complete Outline of Functions.** In accordance with its importance, the participle has been carefully discussed under the different grammatical categories treated throughout the syntax. The following references are given in order that the student may get a clear view of the entire field of its present usefulness in the language: **4** I *c*; **6** C; **7** B *a, b, c*; **10** I 1; **15** III 2 A, B; **17** 3 A *a, b, c, d*, B, C, 4; **20** 3; **21** *e*; **23** II 11; **24** IV *a* (last par.); **27** 5; **28** 1 *a*; **28** 2 *b*; **28** 3 *a*; **28** 5 *d*; **29** 1 A *c bb*; **29** 1 A *d aa*; **30** *b*; **31** 2; **32** 2; **33** 2; **34**; **47** *a, b*; **58**.

THE INFINITIVE

49 1. **Origin.** The infinitive is a verbal noun which for many centuries has been gradually acquiring more and more verbal force. In Old English, the infinitive was still inflected as a noun except in the genitive, which was lost in the prehistoric period: Nominative and accusative *writan* (*to write*), dative *to writenne* or *writanne*. The dative consisted of a distinctive dative form, *writenne*, etc., and the governing preposition *to*, which in Old English usually took a dative object, not an accusative object as today. The remnant of this older inflection is the so-called infinitive with *to*, which retains the *to* of the old dative form but has lost the infinitive suffix *–en* and the dative sign *–e*, so that the dative now, aside from its distinctive *to*, is identical in form with the nominative and accusative. The old dative *–e* was dropped in the twelfth century. After the dative sign *–e* disappeared, there still survived the infinitive suffix *–en*, which now served as the infinitive ending not only when the infinitive was used as the subject or the object of a verb but also when it was the object of the preposition *to*. In all these grammatical relations it was becoming ever more common to place *to* before the infinitive, as *to* had come to be felt as the sign of the infinitive. The suffix *–en* was often reduced to *–e*, as in *to aske*, and in this form remained in use in the South and the Midland until the sixteenth century, when it disappeared, *to aske* becoming *to ask*, since the *to* before the infinitive was felt as sufficiently distinctive. After auxiliaries, as in 'It may *rain*,' 'I shall *go*,' 'He will *go*,' the simple infinitive, as in these examples *rain* and *go*, is no longer felt as an infinitive, but as a component element of a subjunct've form or the future tense form.

The infinitive with *to* was originally a noun in the dative governed by the preposition *to*, hence was in the first stages of its development a prepositional object modifying the verb. This *to*, as can still be seen in many sentences, originally meant *toward* and pointed to *that* toward which the activity of the principal verb was directed: 'Jealousy drove him *to do it*,' i.e., *drove him toward the doing of it*. Similarly, after adjectives: 'I am ready *to do it*,' i.e., *ready in the direction of doing it*. As described in **24** IV *a*, the *to* of the prepositional infinitive is still in a number of grammatical categories more or less vividly felt as the preposition *to* or upon reflection can be recognized as such. This *to*, however, is now often not felt as a preposition but rather as a part of the infinitive itself, and hence the prepositional infinitive is now no longer confined to a prepositional relation, but may be used also as the subject or the object of a verb, where *to* cannot be construed as a preposition governing the infinitive: '*To err* is human.' '*Learn to labor* and *to wait*.'

As the prepositional infinitive originally stood in a close relation to the verb or adjective, it gradually came to be felt as the proper form to use with a verb or adjective to complete its meaning. In oldest English, the prepositional infinitive was still in large part a prepositional phrase in which the preposition *to* still had its original meaning. Preposition and infinitive together formed a unit, a prepositional object, which completed the meaning of the verb. The simple infinitive was often employed to complete the meaning of a transitive verb, performing the grammatical function of a direct object: 'Þa ongan he *wepan*' (object), now 'Then he began *to weep*.' As can be seen by the translation of this example, the Old English simple infinitive in the object relation is now replaced by the prepositional infinitive. The development had already begun in the Old English period. Gradually the prepositional infinitive came to be felt as the proper form to complete the meaning of the verb in all categories. As the prepositional infinitive had come to be felt as a unit, a verbal noun, it became natural to employ it not only as the object of the verb but also as the subject, for a noun may be used as either the subject or the object of the verb. This development was greatly favored by the distinctive form of the prepositional infinitive. The simple form would not be equal to the difficult task ot performing all the delicate work now done so well by the prepositional form. The simple infinitive survives as a fossil in various categories described in the following pages.

2. Form of the Infinitive Clause.

a. Subject of the Infinitive. For centuries the *to*-infinitive and
its modifiers have been developing into a distinct subordinate
clause of a new type, which has been crowding more and more
out of common use the older *that*-clause with a finite verb, so
that the *to*-infinitive has acquired functions unknown to the simple
infinitive. Today the infinitive clause introduced by *to* is a form
of expression which is felt and used as a more convenient subordinate clause than the more formal clause introduced by *that*,
followed by a nominative subject and a finite verb. In a grammatical sense they are two expressions for the same thing. The
to of the infinitive has become in all such abridged clauses a conjunction, so that we speak of a *to*-clause just as we speak of a
that-clause: 'I am not eager *to go*' (or *that I should go*). Originally,
the subject of the infinitive was not expressed but was contained
in some noun or pronoun of the principal proposition, as in this
example in *I*, the subject of the sentence. As described in detail
in **24** III *d* and **24** IV *a*, the subject of the infinitive may be the
subject of the principal verb or an accusative, dative, or prepositional object of the verb. In the earliest stages of development
the subject of the infinitive always performed thus some function
in the principal proposition and was only by implication also
subject of the infinitive. This terse older form of the clause is
still very common. The simple compact form of this construction
brought it from the start into ever greater favor.

In the fourteenth century, as described in **21** *e*, there arose a
desire to extend the use of the convenient infinitive construction,
and people began to give the infinitive a subject of its own when
there was no noun or pronoun in the principal proposition which
could serve as a subject. The subject was put before the old *to*-
form of the clause and *for* was used as a formal sign of the introduction of this new element: 'I am not eager *for him to return*.'
This is only a slight variation of the old *to*-form. In the original
infinitive construction, as explained above, the subject was not
expressed but was contained in some noun or pronoun in the
principal proposition. Thus from the very start the subject was
not a part of the infinitive construction; and later when the
infinitive could have a subject of its own, it was placed before
the clause outside of its construction, just as it had always stood
outside of it. The *for*, whose origin is explained in **21** *e*, here
merely indicates that in the case in hand the infinitive has a subject of its own. In older English, there was before the infinitive a
for . . . to of a different origin. This older *for . . . to* hadn't
the functions of the later *for . . . to* but was used interchangeably

with simple *to*. This older *for . . . to* has disappeared from the
literary language but is still widely used in dialect. Examples
are given in **21** *e* (8th par.), **24** III *d* (3rd par.), **33** 2 (6th par.).

When the subject of the infinitive is general or indefinite, it is
often not expressed: 'It is wise *to be* cautious.'

b. Elliptical Form of the Infinitive Clause. In oldest English,
to was still largely felt as a preposition governing the infinitive,
its object, but it gradually became the distinctive feature of the
clause, marking the following group of words as a grammatical
unit, often even representing it alone, the other words dropping
out where the reference is to a thought previously expressed
which is to be briefly repeated in substance in the form of an
abridged infinitive clause: 'I shall go to the celebration tomorrow,
or at least I am planning *to* [*go to it*].' This construction arose in
the fourteenth century, but did not become common until the
second half of the nineteenth century. It gradually developed
power along with the infinitive clause, which it now often represents. In older English, it was more common here to place the
preposition *to* before the neuter pronoun *it*, which pointed back
to the thought previously expressed: 'But shall we dance, if they
desire us *to* '*t?*' (Shakespeare, *Love's Labor's Lost*, V, II, 145). This
old form of expression lives on in popular speech: 'I can't read,
nor I don't want *to it*' (Dickens, *Our Mutual Friend*, I, 31). Besides the common *to*-form described above there is now another
less common elliptical construction, which has no distinctive mark
and consists simply in suppressing the infinitive clause entirely
and leaving us to gather the thought from the context: 'Do you
write to him!' — 'I will since you wish me [*to* do so]' (Marryat,
The Settlers in Canada, 11). 'Meanwhile she opened the little
door of Ellen's study closet and went in there, though Ellen
begged her not' (Susan Warner, *The Wide, Wide World*, Ch. XX,
A.D. 1851), now usually 'begged her not *to*.' On account of the lack
of distinctive form to make the thought clear this construction can
often not be used at all.

c. Split Infinitive, Origin and Development. As explained in
16 2 *a*, the sentence adverb stands before the stressed simple verb
or the stressed verbal phrase and is itself usually unstressed, but
under the influence of strong emotion or on account of its logical
force is often heavily stressed. This peculiar word-order with its
peculiar stress is absolutely rigid for the *that*-clause. Since the
to-clause has the same force as the *that*-clause, there is a widespread
feeling that this peculiar word-order with its peculiar stress should
obtain also in the *to*-clause. The *to* is thus separated from the
infinitive by the adverb, which has led to the expression 'split

infinitive': '*To álmost succéed* (or *That I should álmost succéed*) is not enough.' 'I don't expect *to ever sée him again*' (or *that I shall ever sée him again*). 'I wish *to útterly forgét my past*' (or *that I may útterly forgét my past*). 'It's a sad experience *to always live from hánd to moúth*' (or *when one must always live from hánd to móuth*). The insertion of the adverb here between *to* and the infinitive cannot even in the strictest scientific sense be considered ungrammatical. As explained on page 456, *to*, in certain common categories, has long since ceased to be a preposition, just as *that* in the corresponding *that*-clause has long since ceased to be a determinative pronoun pointing to the following clause. Both *to* and *that* have in the course of the development here lost their old force and have assumed a new function. Both words introduce a clause and naturally all words that belong to the clause should follow. In the newer *for-to*-infinitive construction all words belonging to the predicate similarly follow *to*: 'I am not eager *for him to ever retúrn.*'

In the older form of the infinitive construction the sentence adverb preceded the *to* and this is still the more common form of expression; but, as the feeling grows that *to* should introduce the clause, it becomes more common to place the adverb after the *to*. In the older form with the adverb before the *to* there is no clearly marked beginning to the infinitive clause, which sometimes leads to ambiguity: 'He failed *entirely to comprehend* it.' It is not clear here whether *entirely* modifies *failed* or *comprehend*. We can construe the sentence either way with a difference of meaning. If *entirely* modifies *comprehend* it would be better to place it before *comprehend*: 'He failed *to entirely comprehénd* it.' Thus the split infinitive is an improvement of English expression.

The old position of the adverb before *to* is most common in the case of such distinguishing (**16 2 b**) adverbs as are distinctly felt as belonging to the infinitive clause as a whole rather than to the infinitive itself: 'I've dropped in *just* (or *merely*, or *only*) *to inquire how your father is doing.*' Especially *not* clings to the old position before *to*: 'I desire, *not to discourage*, but to encourage.' But even these adverbs are sometimes placed after *to* when they are distinctly felt as belonging to the infinitive itself. Examples are given on page 460.

The adverb sometimes stands after the infinitive instead of before it, but this change of word-order is always associated with a different shade of meaning, indicating emphasis upon the adverb, as described in **16 2 a**, while in the split-infinitive construction the infinitive itself is the important word and has a strong stress: 'He understood a good deal of it, but he failed to comprehend it *entirely.*' The adverb is sometimes stressed in the split-infinitive construction. There are then two strong accents, both adverb and infinitive receiving a strong stress: 'She wishes to *útterly forgét* her past.' Compare **16 2** *a* (2nd and 3rd parr.).

The split infinitive began to appear in the fourteenth century. The oldest examples do not have the characteristics which mark the construction as we use it today: 'He louied þe lasse auþer *to lenge lye* or *to longe sitte*' (*Sir Gawayne and the Grene Knight*, ll. 87–88) = 'He (Arthur) did not like *to either lie or sit long.*' 'Bot to take þe toruayle to my-self *to trwluf expoun*' (*ib.*, l. 1540) = 'but to undertake the task *to expound true love.*' Today, we put the adverbial modifier and the object here after the infinitive. These interesting old examples show one thing very plainly. The *to* is no longer felt as a preposition, so that adverbs and objects can stand between *to* and the infinitive. The idea of a *to*-clause, which had long lain in English feeling, received here for the first time a formal expression in the language. The future development of the new clause was now possible. Changes soon took place in the word-order which affected also the *to*-clause, so that these early examples now look strange to us, but the important point here is that an interesting development had begun which was to go on for many centuries and is still going on. Late in the fourteenth century two scholars — Wyclif and John Purvey — employed the split infinitive as it is used today, even in the case of *not*, which is still in our day not so thoroughly established here as other sentence adverbs: 'It is good *to not ete* fleisch and *to not drynke* wyn' (*Romans*, XIV, 21, Purvey's ed., A.D. 1388).

In the fifteenth century this construction was used by Pecock and Sir John Fortescue. Pecock employed it in his philosophical writings with as great frequency as it is found in authors of the present time, and with the same force: *for to so leie a side*, etc. (*The Folewer to the Donet*, E.E.T.S., No. 164, p. 97, about A.D. 1454) = *to thus lay aside*, etc. Even in the case of *not*, which is still in our day not so thoroughly established here as other sentence adverbs: 'Y schall . . . swere *to not discouere hem*' (*ib.*, p. 138) = 'I shall pledge myself *to not inform on them.*'

In the next three centuries the split infinitive was used freely by only a few authors, but the construction was spreading. It was employed occasionally by a large number of writers: Thomas Cromwell, Lord Berners, Tyndale, Sir Philip Sidney, Donne, Sir Thomas Browne, Pepys, Bentley, Defoe, Thomas Godfrey, Jr., Robert Rogers, Benjamin Franklin, Dr. Johnson, Burke, Coleridge, Southey, Lamb, De Quincey, and others.

The split infinitive has been censured by grammarians to whom grammar is not an objective study of the living language but a fixed body of rules that has come down to us from the past. Also a number of good writers avoid the split infinitive. Since the fourteenth century, however, the split infinitive, by virtue of its decided advantages, which are unconsciously widely felt, has been gradually gaining ground, in recent times even making headway against deeply rooted prejudices, so that it frequently appears in good authors, among them many of our best, sometimes only occasionally, sometimes more freely. But it is never used with such consistency that it is uniformly employed where it should be. In the feeling of speaker or writer there is a struggle here between older and newer usage. He now follows the one, now the other, but yielding ever more and more to the powerful new drift in the direction of greater precision of expression.

Although this new drift has long been regarded by many who do not understand it as plebeian or vulgar, there have never been any real grounds for such an attitude, for it has never been characteristic of popular speech. Although it is now rapidly spreading in the language of the common people, it was not prominent there in older English, so far as we can judge from the evidence at our disposal. On the other hand, it has long been used in literary and colloquial language. In general, it is more characteristic of our most prominent authors than of the minor writers, who avoid it as they fear criticism. In the last fifty years, however, its use in literature has spread more rapidly than in any previous period of its development. It has become such a necessary form of English expression that we often cannot avoid it if we would employ the infinitive at all: 'This earl would have deemed it a condescension *to so much as invite* me to his house' (Marie Corelli). 'He stood high in the colony, was extravagant and fond of display, and, his fortune being jeopardized, he hoped *to more than retrieve it* by going into speculations in Western lands' (Theodore Roosevelt, *The Winning of the West*, Vol. I, Ch. VI). 'Her husband was sure to enable her *to more than better her old position*' (Edwin Balmer, *The Breath of Scandal*, Ch. II). 'I've heard enough *to about do* for me' (Willa Cather, *The Professor's House*, p. 241).

The split infinitive has become so common that an adequate idea of its extensive employment cannot be conveyed by illustrations, but a large number of characteristic examples, taken from the author's much larger collection, are given here in order that the student may get a general idea of the wide use of the construction by good authors: 'to nobly stém tyrannic pride' (Burns), 'to still further límit the hours' (William Wordsworth), 'without permitting himself to actually méntion the name' (Matthew Arnold), 'of a kind to directly stímulate curiosity' (Walter Pater, *Appreciations*, Sir Thomas Brown, p. 132). 'New emissaries are trained with new tactics, to, if possible, entráp him and hóodwink and hándcuff him' (Carlyle). 'To slowly tráce the forest's shady scene, Where things that own not man's dominion dwéll' (Byron, *Childe Harold*, II, 25). 'In order to fully appréciate Lord Holland' (Macaulay, *Critical and Historical Essays*), 'to still líve ón' (Whittier, Cambridge ed., p. 401), 'being told to just stép ón seven miles farther' (Mrs. Gaskell, *Wives and Daughters*, Ch. VII), 'to half surmíse the truth' (Robert Browning, *The Ring and the Book*, Cambridge ed., p. 513), 'to straightway múrder' (*ib.*, p. 561), 'to longer béar' (*ib.*, p. 563), 'to worthily defénd' (*ib.*, p. 563), 'to bravely disbeliéve' (*ib.*, p. 570), 'to quietly next day at crow of cock Cút my throat' (*ib.*, p. 588). 'Escape? To even wísh that would spoil all' (*id.*, *Pippa Passes;* and many other examples in this and others of his works). 'How much better to thus sáve the money which else we sink for ever in the war' (Abraham Lincoln, July 12, 1862). 'The fury of the Confederate assault soon halted this advance force and ultimately inflicted upon it such loss of men and guns as to seriously crípple McCook's corps' (P. S. Sheridan, *Personal Memoirs*, I, Ch. XI). 'Things which few except parents can be expected to really understánd' (Oliver W. Holmes, *Elsie Venner*, Ch. XIX). 'I wish the reader to clearly understánd' (Ruskin). 'I undertook to partially fíll úp the office of parish clerk' (George Eliot, *Silas Marner*, p. 56). 'To an active mind it may be easier to bear along all the qualifications of an idea than to first imperfectly concéive such idea' (Herbert Spencer, *Philosophy of Style*). 'To further confírm this, Sherman's advance division will march direct from Whiteside to Trenton' (U. S. Grant, *Personal Memoirs*, II, p. 51). 'The commission's scheme to arbitrarily and permanently confíne the channel' (Mark Twain, *Life on the Mississippi*, p. 224). 'I don't ask you to vote at all — I only urge you to nót (not as often found here after the *to* as other sentence adverbs, but with an evident drift in this direction) sóil yourself by voting for Blaine' (*id.*, *Letter to W. D. Howells*, Sept. 17, 1884). 'The cost *has to all cóme* (after the analogy of *must all come*) out of a year's instalments of Autobiography in the N. A. Review' (*id.*, *Letter to H. H. Rogers*, May 29, 1907). 'Enough to thoroughly appréciate' (Ellis, *Early English Pronunciation*, 1875, p. 1087). 'Which women do not like in a woman and men prefer to distantly admíre' (Meredith, *Diana of the Crossways*, London, 1914, p. 103). 'But the tendency of the study of science is to útterly upróot such notions' (John Burroughs, *The Light of Day*, Ch. XIV, I). 'The great point of honor on these occasions

was for each man to strictly límit himself to half a pint of liquor'
(Hardy, *The Mayor of Casterbridge*, Ch. XXXIII); frequently in
this author in the descriptive portions of his works, occasionally
also in the portions reproducing popular speech, for this construction is now affecting the language of the common people:
'Don't let my sins, when you know them all, cause 'ee to quite
forgét that though I loved 'ee late I loved 'ee well' (*ib.*, Ch. XLIII).
'To útterly forgét her past' (Henry James, *Adina*). 'To só ar-
ránge it' (Helen Hunt Jackson, *Ramona*, Ch. I). 'The old man
only similated deafness all these years to one day cátch your
father óut' (De Morgan, *Joseph Vance*, Ch. I, p. 2); here in popular speech, but more commonly in literary language: 'to merely
fíll úp to the brim' (*ib.*, p. 5). 'There can be nothing to — to nót
(not as often found here after the *to* as other sentence adverbs,
but with an evident drift in this direction) tálk about, between
you and me, dear mother' (*id.*, *Alice-for-Short*, Ch. XXXV).
'Which prompts a man to savagely stámp on the spider he has but
half killed' (Kipling, *The Phantom. Rickshaw*). 'I was able once
more to calmly revíew my chances of escape' (*id.*, *The Strange
Ride*). 'The Cavalry were to gently stímulate the break-up which
would follow' (*id.*, *The Drums of the Fore and Aft*). 'To basely
desért his friend' (Du Maurier, *Trilby*, p. 185), 'to honestly féel'
(*id.*, *Peter Ibbetson*, p. 155), 'to selfishly overráte' (*id.*, *The Martian*,
p. 215), 'to thoroughly understánd life' (*ib.*, p. 352), 'to basely
lóng for these' (*ib.*, p. 371). 'I am asking myself how difficult it
will be to quite understánd these people' (Frances Hodgson Bur-
nett, *The Shuttle*, Ch. XXVIII). 'The idlers of the town might
not have been able to accurately defíne the moment when the
drama of defeat lost its interest' (Charles Egbert Craddock, *The
Prophet of the Great Smoky Mountains*, Ch. XII). 'Ask cook to
kindly máke me a sandwich' (C. Haddon Chambers, *The Tyranny
of Tears*, Act IV; also often elsewhere in this drama). 'Unable to
squarely fáce Aurelia's ardent assumption' (Henry Blake Fuller,
The Chatelaine), 'to further cómplicate our problem' (Hamlin
Garland, *A Daughter of the Middle Border*, p. 328), 'to quite fíll
the measure' (John Fox, Jr., *The Kentuckians*, Ch. I), 'to firmly
cárry óut one's ideas' (Margaret Deland, *The Apotheosis of the
Reverend Mr. Spangler*, Ch. I). 'Just sensible enough of his own
callousness to intensely enjóy the humor and adroitness of it'
(George Bernard Shaw, *You Never Can Tell*, Act II). 'The observer who had thoroughly understood one link in a series of incidents should be able to accurately státe all the other ones'
(A. Conan Doyle, *Sherlock Holmes*, I, 211). 'You are to please
cóme óver here' (Mrs. H. Ward. *Marcella*, IV, Ch. VI). 'I've

presumed to call on you in the hope that I may be permitted to modestly réason with you' (Pinero, *The Amazons*, Act I). 'I'm old-fashioned enough to really beliéve there is that difference' (Stanley Houghton, *Hindle Wakes*, Act II). 'And after that he had made up his mind to always stárt on a Friday' (Jerome K. Jerome, *Diary Pilgrim*, 13). 'It really almost frightened the poor girl to suddenly fínd herself in this strange position' (Rider Haggard, *Mr. Meeson's Will*, p. 55). 'She proceeded to securely cóver óver the sunshade' (W. Black, *Highland Cousins*, II, 28). 'She had cause to bitterly repént it' (F. C. Philips, *One Never Knows*, II, 125). 'You appear to me not to quite knów what you are about' (B. L. Farjeon, *London's Heart*, II, 32). 'Why you should have been made to half kíll yourself over the matter is more than I can understand' (W. J. Locke, *The Red Planet*, Ch. XVIII). 'It would have overburdened the text to thére incórporate many details' (G. Hempl, *Modern Language Notes*, XIII, 456). 'To só júdge literature would be tantamount to,' etc. (Edward Sapir, *Language*, p. 24). 'It is doubtful if he had quite listened — he having so much to nót lísten to at the Home Office that the practice was growing on him' (Galsworthy, *Freelands*, Ch. XVI); in general, often found in the works of this author, sometimes even in the case of *not*, as in this example. 'Well, Dad oughtn't to ever lét you háve it' (Sinclair Lewis, *Babbitt*, Ch. II); frequently elsewhere in this book, occurring even in the case of *not:* '[I] Always figured somebody'd come along with the brains to nót léave education to a lot of bookworms' (*ib.*, Ch. VI, III). 'I'll have time to really fínish my research' (*id.*, *Arrowsmith*, Ch. XXIX). 'The truth is I have come to rather dislíke him' (Tarkington, *The Magnificent Ambersons*, Ch. XVIII); in colloquial language found frequently throughout the many books of this writer. 'He decided to again attáck Rivas' (Richard Harding Davis, *Real Soldiers of Fortune*, p. 160). 'But it is hard to álways háve to brace yourself to be a prop to the weak' (Hubert Henry Davies, *Mrs. Gorringe's Necklace*, Act I). 'Nobody dared to even quéstion the truth of that report' (Oemler, *Slippy McGee*, Ch. IX). 'He used to keenly quéstion' (J. R. Green, *A Short History of the English People*, 1911, p. 50). 'Mr. Man, that ought to pretty nearly fíx it' (William Allen White, *A Certain Rich Man*, Ch. XIII). 'I thought I was pretty good to even trý it' (F. Scott Fitzgerald, *This Side of Paradise*, p. 203). 'When I hear gentlemen say that politics ought to let business alone, I feel like inviting them to first consíder whether business is letting politics alone' (Woodrow Wilson, Feb. 24, 1912). 'How satisfactory it must be to really knów,' etc. (W. S. Cather, *The Song of the Lark*, p. 421). 'I do not know that she ever hoped to really sólve it' (Francis R. Bellamy, *The Balance*, Ch. XX). 'Why, it would be such fun to just forgét all about the hours when the sun didn't shine, and remember only the nice, pleasant ones' (Eleanor A. Porter, *Just David*, Ch. X). 'To só áct that,' etc. (*Webster's International Dictionary*, 1921, p. 1301, 13), 'designed to further céntralize government in Washington' (editorial in *Chicago Tribune*, Feb. 28, 1924), 'something that would command me to útterly submít' (De Voto, *The Crooked Mile*, p. 342), 'to publicly baptíze Psalmanazar' (Sir Sidney Lee, *Dict. Nat. Biography, Psalmanazar*, p. 440). 'This knowledge has been so applied as to well-nigh revolútionize human affairs' (Harvey Robinson, *The Mind in the Making*, p. 7). 'I don't want you to even spéak to her' (Floyd Dell, *This Mad Ideal*, II, Ch. VII). 'To devise measures to vigorously restóre and expánd our foreign trade' (Herbert Hoover, Oct. 15, 1928).

If the *to* before the second of two infinitives is suppressed, the sentence adverb invariably stands immediately before the infinitive: 'We pray you to proceed And *jústly* and *religiously unfóld*' (Shakespeare, *Henry the Fifth*, I, ii, 9). This construction, which has been in universal use for many centuries, has facilitated the spread of the split infinitive.

Similar to the prepositional infinitive is the prepositional gerund. The preposition here serves as a conjunction introducing the gerundial clause. Here, as in the case of the infinitive clause or the full clause with a finite verb, sentence adverbs stand before the verbal element, i.e., before the gerund: 'When he looked at her he usually ended by smiling and sometimes by *suddenly láughing*' (A. Marshall, *The Old Order Changeth*, Ch. XIII). When the subject of the gerund is expressed, the sentence adverb, as in a full clause, stands between subject and gerund: 'It (i.e., your case) will rest upon *my áctually háving* no complaint against you' (*ib.*, Ch. XXII). These examples clearly show how closely related a full clause with finite verb, an infinitive clause, and a gerundial clause are. Curiously enough it has never occurred to a grammarian to censure the placing of a sentence adverb before a gerund, while the grammarians who have written our schoolbooks quite generally censure this word-order in the infinitive clause. In full clause, infinitive clause, gerundial clause the same forces are at work; in all three cases the development is natural and in accord with the development in an independent sentence, and should be furthered rather than censured, for it makes for clearer expression.

In all the cases just discussed, the split infinitive is the simple form without an auxiliary. In a compound form containing an auxiliary the sentence adverb usually stands before the stressed form of the verb, which in most cases is the part having the verbal meaning: 'Life's aim is simply to be *always lóoking* for temptations' (Oscar Wilde, *A Woman of No Importance*, Act III). In the passive, the form is slightly different wherever there are two participles, one the passive auxiliary, the other the form containing the verbal meaning. These two participles usually form a unit, so that the sentence adverb cannot stand between them before the stressed verbal form, but for the most part stands before the participial unit: 'She seems to have always *been admíred.*' But even in the case of these participial units we must put the adverb between the participles before the stressed verbal form wherever the adverb indicates the manner or degree of the verbal activity: 'She seems to have always *been* kíndly *recéived.*' 'She seems to have always *been* gréatly *admíred.*' As in these examples, there are often two adverbs, one in the usual position before the passive auxiliary, the other, an adverb of manner or degree, before the stressed verbal form. This form with the sentence adverb before the stressed part of the verb is widely used, even by many who do not split a simple infinitive. It does not seem to be generally felt as a split infinitive, though the adverb plainly stands between the auxiliary and the form of the verb containing the verbal meaning. The word-order, here as elsewhere, corresponds closely to that found in an independent sentence and in the *that*-clause: 'She has always *been* kíndly *recéived.*' 'It seems that she has always *been* kíndly *recéived.*' In the infinitive construction the unsplit infinitive, i.e., the form with the adverb before the *to,* is also used here: 'The former I do not remember *ever to have seen*' (Thomas B. Aldrich, *My Cousin the Colonel*, Ch. I). 'She seems *always to have been* happy.' This construction, however, is often ambiguous: 'I remember plainly to have refúsed his offer.' Here *plainly* may modify either *remember* or *refused.* If we mean the latter, the split infinitive conveys this meaning clearly: 'I remember *to have plainly refúsed* his offer.'

Also when the infinitive is the copula *be* and the real predicate in the infinitive clause is an adjective, noun, or prepositional phrase, we usually place the sentence adverb before the stressed predicate: 'I intend to be *always wátchful*' (a *wátchful obsérver,* or *on the wátch*). Sometimes, however, the sentence adverb stands before the *to,* as in the unsplit infinitive construction: 'The girl seemed *always to be* in half-mourning' (Thomas B. Aldrich, *The Stillwater Tragedy*, Ch. IX).

There is one case where the sentence adverb always precedes the *to,* namely, when the infinitive clause follows the copula **with** the force of a predicate adjective or noun: 'It was *hardly to be expected.*' 'Life's aim is *simply to be* always *looking* for temptations.' As the infinitive clause in each of these sentences has the function of a predicate and thus is felt as a unit, the sentence adverb, which belongs to the sentence as a whole, cannot enter it. Of course, where the sentence adverb belongs only to the infinitive clause, as *always* in the second example, it rightfully stands within the clause.

3. **Tenses and Voices of the Infinitive.** Although the infinitive was originally a noun, it has in the course of time acquired the properties of tense and voice, thus approaching the nature of a verb. Like a finite verb, the infinitive has two voices — active and passive. There are no peculiar difficulties here except in the case of the passive form. The infinitive in passive function gradually developed passive form, but in a few categories retained its original active form in passive function. For fuller information see **7 D 2, 15** III 2 B, **46** (next to last par.).

Unlike the finite verb, the infinitive has only two tenses — present and perfect. As the use of these two tenses presents peculiar difficulties, they are treated in detail in *a* and *b* below.

Although the infinitive has no special forms to indicate mood, it can render fairly accurately some of the relations expressed by the subjunctive forms of the finite verb: 'I wrote him *to come at once*' (= 'that he *should come* at once'). 'I do not know *what to do*' (= 'what I *should do*'). 'I should be happy if I knew how *to accomplish* (= I *might accomplish*) this.'

a. Use of the Tenses of the Infinitive after a Full Verb. The tenses of the infinitive here express time relatively to that of the principal verb. The present tense indicates time contemporaneous or future with reference to that of the principal verb: 'I wish *to do* it.' 'He was very foolish *to do* it,' not usually now as in older English 'He was very foolish *to have done* it.' 'The Indian must have possessed no small share of vital energy *to have rubbed* (incorrectly instead of *to rub*) industriously stone on stone for long months till at length he had rubbed an ax' (Thoreau, *Journal,* I, p. 40). 'I intend *to write* a line or two to her soon.' 'I yesterday intended *to write* a line or two to her, but forgot *to do* so.' 'I managed *to do* it without his help' (i.e., 'I *did* it without his help'). 'It was the fourth case of lockjaw *to occur* (i.e., that *occurred*) within a week.' Of course, the present infinitive refers to the past after the annalistic present (**37** 1 *d*), for the annalistic present itself points to the past: 'This is the fourth case of lockjaw *to occur* (i.e., that *has occurred*) within a week.' The perfect tense of the infinitive indicates time prior to that of the principal verb: '**I am** proud *to have been* able to help.   It gives recreation a better relish *to have* first *accomplished* something' (Harriet Connor Brown, *Grandmother Brown's Hundred Years*, 279).   'He found about a half dozen Seniors whom he did not remember *to have noticed* before.'   'I consider myself lucky *to of* (reduced colloquial form of *have*) *found* out about it before it was too late' (Ring Lardner, *Saturday Evening Post*, July 11, 1914).   Looking backward from the present to a past situation, having in mind one's present state of feeling: 'I should like *to have given* him something' (Dickens, *A Christmas Carol*, II, 41), but (with reference to a past situation, but looking forward) 'I should have liked *to make* her a little present' (Thackeray, *Vanity Fair*, I, Ch. XII).   The principle that the perfect tense of the infinitive should indicate time prior to that of the main verb is not always observed, as will be seen in the following paragraphs, but it is now much better observed than earlier in the present period.   The steadily increasing observance of this principle shows clearly that its importance for English expression is gradually becoming more widely felt.   In our language the infinitive has only two tenses, and unless their use be regulated by some such fixed principle our expression will become unclear.

In unreal conditions, the infinitive is often used as an abridged clause to form the condition or the conclusion, with the same use of the tenses described in the preceding paragraph: 'I should be glad *to go*' (= *if I could go*).   'I should have been glad *to go*' (= *if I could have gone*).   'He would have been foolish *to do* it' (= *if he had done* it).   'What would I give *not to have heard* the calamities fallen on the heads of the King and Queen of France' (Horace Walpole, *Letter to Miss Mary Berry*, June 28, 1791) (= *if I had not heard*, etc.).   'Here was enough *to haue infected* (now usually *to infect* = *that it could have infected*) the whole city, if it had not been taken in time' (Ben Jonson, *Euery Man in His Humour*, V, v, 28, A.D. 1616).   '[it was] A glorious vision to the youth, who embraced it as a flower of beauty, and read not a feature.   There were curious features of color in her face *for him to have read*' (Meredith, *The Ordeal of Richard Feverel*, Ch. XV), instead of the better *for him to read* = *which he could have read if he had observed*.   As can be seen by the examples, there has long been a tendency here after a past tense to employ a perfect infinitive instead of a present infinitive.   This usage seems at present to be less common in good literature than formerly, and it is to be hoped that it will disappear altogether, for it violates the widely observed principle that the perfect infinitive indicates time prior to that of the main verb.

Where, however, the situation clearly shows that the reference is to the future, the perfect infinitive represents the action as completed at a point of time in the future: 'He expects *to have written* the last chapter by tomorrow evening.'

Where it is desired to indicate that a past intention, hope, expectation has not been realized, we often instead of the regular past perfect subjunctives *I had meant, thought, intended*, etc., in connection with a present infinitive, as in 'I *had meant, thought, intended* to write a line to you,' employ, as in older English, the past subjunctives *meant, thought, intended* with a dependent perfect infinitive after the analogy of the past subjunctive *would*, which in older English was used in the sense of intention in connection with a dependent perfect infinitive to indicate that a past intention was not realized: 'I *meant, thought, intended to have written* a line to you' = older 'I *would have written* a line to you,' i.e., 'I *had intended to write* a line to you.' Such a sentence with *would* has developed out of a full unreal conditional sentence, as 'I *would have written* a line to you if I had been able to find the time.' We still use *would* in a full conditional clause, or where we feel the statement as containing an unreal condition, as in 'In your place I *would* have acted otherwise.' We do not now use *would* in an independent sentence where the idea of unreal condition has disappeared and there remains only the idea of unreality, as in 'I *would have written* a line to you.' But in older English, beginning in Middle English, this use of *would* is common: 'For summe of hem *wolden haue take* hym, but no man sette hondis on hym' (*John*, VII, 44, John Purvey's ed., A.D. 1388). 'He, following that faire advantage fast, His stroke redoubled with such might and maine, That him upon the ground he groveling cast; and leaping to him light *would have unlast* (unlaced) His helme to make unto his vengeance way' (Spenser, *The Faerie Queene*, VI, I, XXXIX). The context in both examples clearly shows that *would* with its dependent perfect infinitive expresses an unrealized past intention.

Even as early as the thirteenth century *would* began to be replaced here by *thought, meant*, or *weened* as clearer expressions for this idea. These past tense forms had become very common by the fourteenth century. That these verbal forms were felt as past tense subjunctives with the force of *would* can be seen by the frequent use of the perfect infinitive after them without *to* as after *would:* 'He *thought* (= *would*) *have slaine* her in his fierce despight (anger); But hastie heat tempring with suffrance wise, He stayde his hand' (Spenser, *The Faerie Queene*, I, I, LI). This old use of *meant, thought, intended*, etc., long remained quite common, except that the dependent perfect infinitive later always took *to:* 'Long as this letter is, I *intended to have written* a fuller and more digested one upon this important subject' (George Washington, *Letter to Benjamin Harrison*, Oct. 10, 1784). 'I *intended to have written* a line to you' (Mrs. Gaskell, *Life of Charlotte Brontë*, 299). The old list of past tense forms has been increased by a few others of related meaning: 'I *hoped to have left* them in perfect safety' (Dickens, *A Tale of Two Cities*, III, Ch. IX). 'I *wanted to have seen* you ever so much, but I did not like to trouble you' (F. C. Philips, *Mrs. Bouverie*, 89).

The use of the perfect infinitive to express an unrealized purpose or plan is found not only in object clauses, as in the preceding examples, but also in adverbial clauses, especially in older English: 'Sir Beaumayns felle vpon hym and vnlaced his helme *to have slayne* hym, and thenne he yelded hym and asked mercy' (Malory, *Le Morte d'Arthur*, Book VII, Ch. XVII, A.D. 1485). 'This traine he laid *to have intrap'd* thy life' (Marlowe, *The Jew of Malta*, 2375, A.D. 1590). It is sometimes still found after *am* (*is, are*) *going*, where it was originally an adverbial clause of purpose: 'Were you going *to have walked?*' (Temple Thurston, *The City of Beautiful Nonsense*, Ch. XV).

As the idea of result is closely related to that of purpose, the perfect infinitive is employed to express an unrealized result, especially in older English: 'He was readie *to have striken* his tapster for interrupting him, but for feare of displeasing mee hee moderated his furie' (Thomas Nashe, *Works*, II, p. 212, A.D. 1594). 'I was ready *to have gone* with her, but this will do just as well' (Jane Austen, *Emma*, Ch. XLIII). 'Several times we were like *to have been staved* against Rocks' (George Washington, *Diary*, Dec. 16, 1753), or, in older English, often the incorrect *had* instead of *was* or *were:* 'One thing more remains, which I had like *to have forgotten*' (*id., Letter to Benjamin Harrison*, Oct. 10, 1784). 'The evening liked *to have been* a tedious evening' (J. A. Benton, *California Pilgrimage*, 127, A.D. 1853). The perfect infinitive after *liked*, as in the last example, is still common in popular speech. In the literary language we say, 'The evening *came near to being* tedious.'

In spite of the long and wide use of most of these forms the construction is bad and useless. *Meant, thought, intended, hoped,* etc., are not modal auxiliaries and should indicate past time, not by a dependent perfect infinitive, but by the regular past perfect subjunctive with a present infinitive, also an old construction hallowed by long and good usage: 'I *had* not *thought to see* thy face*, and, lo, God hath shewed me also your seed' (*Genesis*,

XLVIII, 11). 'I *had meant, thought, intended, hoped, wanted, wished to write* a line to you.' With the verbs *intend, mean, hope, think* the past perfect subjunctive is quite common, but with the other verbs we may use also the longer subjunctive form with *should* in the first person and *would* in the second and third in connection with the perfect infinitive: 'I *should have wished* to go to France, but I must take what I can get' (Galsworthy, *Saint's Progress*, IV, I, 354). 'He *would have longed* to give his arm to the fair Blanche' (Thackeray, *Pendennis*, II, Ch. I).

On the other hand, as explained in *b*, p. 472, *would* and the other modal auxiliaries can only indicate past time by means of a dependent perfect infinitive, so that this construction is proper for them. In older English, this usage was improperly extended to *meant, thought, intended,* etc. Alongside of this incorrect usage is the correct one with a past perfect subjunctive and a dependent present infinitive, and this correct usage is widely followed by careful speakers and writers and should finally supplant the incorrect usage: 'I *had meant to go to* China, but,' etc. (Edith Wharton, *The Glimpses of the Moon*, Ch. XIII). Likewise in the case of *like* (= *come near to*), once widely used in the literary language, but now avoided: 'Ellen's tears *had been like to burst forth* again at his words; with great effort she controlled herself and obeyed him' (Susan Warner, *The Wide, Wide World*, Ch. XLVII).

The past subjunctives *meant, thought,* etc., described above, have long been erroneously felt as past indicatives, so that when this construction spread to the verb *be* when used in the sense of an unrealized intention, the form *was to* was employed: 'She *was to have dined* with us here the day after her father's death' (Gissing, *A Life's Morning*, Ch. XIV). The past indicative has become established here and will have to remain as it is, for we cannot here use the past perfect subjunctive *had been*, since it would mean something quite different.

In another respect the infinitive construction after full verbs is often influenced by that found after modal auxiliaries. After modal auxiliaries the perfect infinitive is necessary to convey the idea of time past. After the past perfect subjunctive of *intend, mean, think, hope, want, desire, wish, like, long,* or after their longer subjunctive form with *should* or *would* with the perfect infinitive, we sometimes, after the analogy of usage with modal auxiliaries, find the perfect infinitive instead of the present, which here is sufficient, as the preceding subjunctive clearly indicates time past: 'I had thought, sir, *to have held* (instead of the correct *to hold*) my peace until You had drawn oaths from him not to stay' (Shakespeare, *The Winter's Tale*, I, II, 28). 'The rabble had lik'd *to have pulled* him to pieces' (Mrs. Behn, *Novels*, I, 282, A.D. 1689), now *came very near to pulling him to pieces.* 'I had hoped *to have procured* (instead of the correct *to procure*) you some oysters from Britain' (Lytton, *Pompeii*, I, Ch. III). 'He would have liked *to have hugged* (instead of the correct *to hug*) his father' (Hughes, *Tom Brown's School-Days*, I, Ch. IV). In older English, the *have* of the perfect infinitive here was often suppressed to avoid the heaping up of auxiliary forms: 'My men would have had me [*have*] *given* them leave to fall upon them at once' (Defoe, *Robinson Crusoe*, A.D. 1719), now *would have had me give them leave.* Similarly, the perfect infinitive has often been used instead of a present infinitive in a full subordinate clause that depends upon a past perfect subjunctive: 'I am glad to see you so well, Miss Cardinal . . . I had been afraid that it might *have exhausted* (instead of the correct *exhaust*) you' (Hugh Walpole, *The Captives*, I, Ch. III). The incorrect perfect infinitive in all these cases, though still to be found in current English, is not so common as it once was. Of course, the perfect infinitive is in order when it is desired to indicate that the intention at the time was that a contemplated act should take place prior to another act that is mentioned in connection with it: 'I had meant *to have visited* Paris and *to have returned* to London before my father arrived from America.'

b. Use of the Perfect Infinitive with Modal and Tense Auxiliaries. The present and past subjunctive forms of the modal auxiliaries are now so commonly used to give modal force, the present and the past subjunctive each imparting a distinctly different shade of feeling or thought rather than conveying different time relations, that we feel them now only as modal forms without distinction of time. Both the present and the past subjunctive here indicate present or future time when used in connection with a present infinitive. Reference to the past can be secured only by using a perfect infinitive instead of the present: 'He *may have gone.*' 'He *might have gone.*' As these auxiliaries were once concrete verbs and could indicate time relations like other verbs and in part can still do so, we must always note carefully whether we are using a concrete verbal or a mere modal form. As can be seen by the two examples just given and as explained more fully in **44** I, *may* and *might* are now usually felt as subjunctive modal forms and regularly require a perfect infinitive for reference to the past. Likewise the past subjunctives *ought* and *must* (**43** I A, next to last par.; **44** I *a*): 'He *ought to have done it.*' 'He *must have done it.*'

Similarly, the past subjunctive *had* and in negative statements and in questions usually *need* and sometimes *dare,* which are now felt and used as past subjunctives: 'He *had* better *have taken* a return ticket.' 'She *need* not *have done* it,' but sometimes with the incorrect past indicative form described in *a,* p. 467: 'She hardly *needed to have asked* the question' (Mrs. Gaskell, *Life of Charlotte Brontë,* 209), instead of 'She *need* hardly *have asked* the question.' 'Why *need* he *have gone* so soon?' 'You know you *daren't have given* the order to charge the bridge if you hadn't seen us on the other side' (George Bernard Shaw, *The Man of Destiny*), or more commonly 'You *wouldn't have dared to give* the order,' etc. The indicative *could,* as in 'He tried yesterday, but *couldn't* do it' can point to the past, but the subjunctive *could* can only indicate past time when its dependent infinitive is in the perfect tense: 'He *could have done* it yesterday if he had tried.'

After the analogy of examples like the last, where a perfect infinitive follows a past subjunctive, we often hear in popular speech instead of a perfect participle a perfect infinitive after the past subjunctive *had* of the regular past perfect subjunctive, i.e., 'if they *had have said so*' instead of 'if they *had said* so,' or, stated in other words, a *have* (frequently in the contracted form of *'a'* or *of*) is often inserted after the *had* of the regular past perfect subjunctive: 'If they *had 'a' said* (instead of the correct *had said*) so, you'd *'a'* sat and listened to 'em!' (De Morgan, *Alice-for-Short,* Ch. II, p. 16). Here *had* is a past subjunctive and hence has modal force; but, since the form is the same as the indicative, the common people, unworried by historical considerations and actuated by the desire to impart the modal force which is present in their feeling, insert here *have,* which so often follows a past subjunctive, as in 'you'd *'a'* sat' (= 'you would have sat') in this same sentence. The literary language permits this usage only after modal auxiliaries; popular speech extends it also to tense auxiliaries. This incorrect usage makes the thought clear, so that even educated people sometimes use it unconsciously, but there is at present no tendency in the literary language to use it consciously, hence it is never found in careful speech. Compare **44** II 5 C (4th par.), **43** II B *a* (4th par.), and **44** I *a* (last par.). This *a* should not be confounded with the *a* which is the reduced form of the old prefix of the perfect participle corresponding to German *ge–,* once found in literary English, now surviving only in certain South English dialects: 'I've *a zin* (better written *a-zin* = *seen*) a young chap make a vool ov hisself avore' (Maxwell Gray, *Ribstone Pippins,* 8).

In older English, the *have* of the dependent perfect infinitive was sometimes suppressed: 'I would have sworn the puling girl Would willingly [*have*] accepted Hammon's love' (Dekker, *Shoemaker's*

Holiday, III, 2). This suppression of *have* has become a characteristic feature of our popular speech: 'If Smoky could only [*have*] knowed, there'd [*have*] been a lot of suffering which he wouldn't [*have*] had to've went through' (Will James, *Smoky the Cowhorse*, Ch. IV).

With auxiliaries that point to the future the perfect infinitive represents the action as completed at a point of time in the future: 'I *shall have completed* it before you return.' 'He *will have completed* it before you return.' 'If things go right, they *should have completed* the work by tomorrow evening.'

4. **Functions of the Infinitive.** In order that the student may get a clear view of the entire field of the present usefulness of the simple infinitive and the form with *to* or *for . . . to,* an outline of their different functions is given below along with references which refer to sections where these functions are discussed. From a close study of these references it will become evident that the infinitive is an amazing tangle of the old and the new, now with its modern function or form, now with the function or form of an earlier period. As the infinitive often competes with the gerund, it ought to be studied in connection with the gerund, as presented in **50** 4.

The infinitive is now used as:

A. *Subject,* usually with *to* or *for . . . to:* '*To err* is human.' 'It is better *for you to go.*' Sometimes with its simple form: '[it is] Better *bend* than *break.*' See **4** I *d,* **21** *e* (9th par.).

B. *Predicate,* usually with *to:*

(1) Normal Form:

a. After a copula: '*To do good is to be* happy.' See **7** D 1 *a.*

b. After passive verbs: 'He was made *to shut* the door.' See **7** D 1 *b.*

(2) Modal Form:

After the copula with the modal force described in **7** D 2: 'This story is not *to be repeated.*' 'He is soon *to be married.*'

In the abridged attributive relative clause there is of course no copula before the predicate infinitive: 'Here is the man who is *to be sent,*' but 'Here is the man *to be sent.*' 'I have much *to do*' (= *that I am to do*). Compare **23** II 11 and **7** D 2.

(3) After a copula to express purpose. See **7** D 3.

(4) In the nominative absolute construction. See **17** 3 A *d* (3rd par.) and B (2nd par.).

C. *Object:*

(1) With its simple form:

a. After: *do;* the modal auxiliaries *may, can, shall,* etc.; the future tense auxiliaries *will* and *shall;* often also *dare* and *need;* in older English, sometimes *ought* and *note*. Explanations and examples are given below.

Dare is not only treated as a common verb with the *to*-infinitive after it, but often also, when not standing in the form of a present participle or in a compound tense, is used, like a modal auxiliary, with a simple infinitive after it, especially in the negative and interrogative forms of statement and in the now rare old past tense form *durst* and the new past subjunctive form *dare*, which after the analogy of *must* (old past subjunctive) is now often employed where the context makes the thought clear.

Similarly, *need* is frequently still, as in older English, treated as a common verb with a *to*-infinitive after it; indeed regularly so in positive indicative form; usually also in negative statements and questions in its newer periphrastic form with *do;* or, on the other hand, when not standing in the form of the present participle, or in a compound tense, or in the form with *do*, it may be used as a modal auxiliary with the simple infinitive after it when negatived, qualified, used in a question, and when after the analogy of *must* it takes the past subjunctive form *need*, which is now often employed where the context makes the thought clear.

Examples: 'Why *don't* you *work* hard?' — 'I *do work* hard.' 'I *will do* it,' i.e., 'I will the doing of it.' 'I *must do* it.' 'He *shall do* it.' 'I *shall do* it.' 'He *will do* it.' 'He lay flat on his face, not *daring to look* (not simple *look*) up.' 'He has never *dared to say* (not simple *say*) it.' 'Who *dare set* (or *dares to set*) a limit to woman's tenderness?' '*Didn't* he *dare do* it?' or '*Didn't* he *dare to do* it?' 'He *dare not* (or *does not dare to*) *tell* the truth.' 'He felt that he *didn't dare venture* (or *didn't dare to venture*, or *dared not venture*, or *dared not to venture*, or *dare* — past subjunctive — *not venture*) upon the subject.' 'You know you *daren't* (past subjunctive) *have given* (more commonly *would not have dared to give*) the order to charge the bridge if you hadn't seen us on the other side' (George Bernard Shaw, *The Man of Destiny*). 'Her spirit failed her a little. She *daren't* (past subjunctive; or *dared not*, or *didn't dare to*) *climb* after him in the dark.' (Mrs. H. Ward, *David Grieve*). 'He *durst* (usually *dared*) *not deny* it.' 'If I *durst* (usually *dared*, or *dared to*) *speak*, I should have something interesting to say.' 'Not *needing to hurry* (not *hurry*), I walked along leisurely.' 'He has never *needed to hurry* (not *hurry*) more than now.' 'He *needs to hurry*,' but 'He *need not hurry*,' or 'He *doesn't need to hurry*.' 'He *didn't need to hurry*.' '*Need* he *hurry?*' or '*Does* he *need to hurry?*' 'What more *needs to be* (now more commonly *need be*) *said?*' (Draper, *History of the Intellectual Development of Europe*). 'He only *need inquire* (or *needs to inquire*) of the porter.' 'That is all that *need be* (or *needs to be*) *said.*' 'The waiter was told that he *need* (past subjunctive) *not stay*' (or *did not need to stay*). 'He had a good hour on his hands before he *need* (past subjunctive) *go* back' (A. Marshall, *Anthony Dare*, Ch. XI). 'He hesitated for a moment. *Need* (past subjunctive) *he go?*' (or *Did he need to go?*) 'Had he done his duty in that respect, Lydia *need* (past subjunctive) *not have been indebted* to her uncle' (Austen, *Pride and Prejudice*, 274). The formal proof that *dare* and *need* are felt as past subjunctives is that they can stand after a past indicative: 'He felt he *dare* (like the past subjunctive *must*) *not reply.*' 'I told him that he *need* (like *must*) *not wait* longer.' Compare **44** I *a*.

Ought, by reason of the similarity of its meaning to that of *should*, was, in older English, sometimes drawn into this group of verbs which take after them a simple infinitive: 'Y *ouȝte loue* my neiȝbor' (Pecock, *Folewer*, p. 91, about A.D. 1453). *Ought* is the past subjunctive of *owe*, as explained in **43** I A (next to last par.). The original meaning of *owe* is *have*, *possess;* later, the idea of *having* went over into that of *having to do as a duty*, i.e., *ought*. Under the influence of the verb *have*, which is related to it in meaning, there was in the oldest examples of *owe* or *ought* with the infinitive a *to* before the infinitive, and later, after a long competition with the simple infinitive, this usage became established: 'I *ought to love* my neighbor.' *Ought* now usually takes *to* after it even when combined with modal auxiliaries: 'We should be sorry to see English critics suggesting that they *ought to* or could *have acted* otherwise' (Fowler, *Modern English Usage*) or 'could or *ought to have acted* otherwise' (*ib.*).

In early Modern English, *note* (= *ne wot;* see Accidence, **57** 4 A *e*) was often drawn into this group by reason of its meaning. *Wot* meant *know*, but in connection with an infinitive the meaning *know·how to* often went over into *be able to, can*. This development, however, took place only where the form was negative and the context clearly referred to past time. Here *note*, though a present tense form, had the force of *couldn't*, pointing to the past: 'Ere long so weake of limbe and sicke of love He woxe that lenger he *note stand* upright' (Spenser, *The Faerie Queene*, IV, XII, XX, A.D. 1596) = 'Ere long he became so weak of limb and sick of love that he *couldn't stand* upright any longer.' Similarly, in our own time *ought* (**44** I *a*), *must* (**44** I *a*), *dare*, *need*, though elsewhere felt as present tense forms, often point to the past when the context clearly refers to past time. The explanation is, that these verbal forms are felt as past subjunctives. Compare second paragraph above this, also **44** I *a* (2nd par.).

In older English, the dependent infinitive after *do* was sometimes attracted to the form of the past tense after a past tense: 'He *dyd made* to rayne fourty dayes' (Caxton, A.D. 1483, *Oxford Dictionary* under *Do*, 25 d). This is still common in popular Southern American English: 'I *done tole* you 'bout ole Mr. Benjermin Ram' (Joel Chandler Harris, *Nights with Uncle Remus*, p. 297). A similar attraction took place in older English after a past participle. See E (3rd par.). Compare **6** A *d*, p. 23.

b. The simple infinitive is used also after *had as good, had better, had best, had* (or *would*) *rather*, etc.: 'A man *had* as good *go* to court without a cravat as [he *had*] *appear* in print without a preface.' 'I *had* better *go.*' '*Had* we not best *go* and *ask?*' 'I *had* rather *wait* a day.' In older English, the *to*-infinitive was sometimes used here: 'He knew not whether he *had* best *to run* or *to stand* his ground' (Richardson, *Clarissa*, III, 209), now always *run* or *stand his ground*. In older English, an impersonal construction was much used here: '*Me* (dative) *were as lief, liever, better*, etc., *to go*,' now 'It were *as good, better* (etc., but no longer *as lief, liever*) *for me to go.*' The impersonal construction came in contact with the personal construction, 'I had as *lief*,' 'I had *liever*' (no longer in use), 'I had as *good, better*,' etc., and began to blend with it: 'I *were* better to be married' (Shakespeare, *As You Like It*, III, III, 91), now 'I *had* better be married.' 'I *were* (now *had*) as good haue a quartane feauer follow me now, for I shal ne'r bee rid of him' (Ben Jonson, *Euery Man out of His Humour*, II, III, A.D. 1600). Much less frequently did the personal construction blend with the impersonal: 'Nat longe tyme after that this Grisild Was wedded, she a doughter hath ybore, Al *had hir* lever *have born* a knave child' (Chaucer, *The Clerkes Tale*, 386), now 'although she *had* rather *have born* a male child.' The blended constructions have disappeared. Compare **43** I B (4th par.) and **44** I (10th par.).

After *had* the *have* of the perfect infinitive is sometimes suppressed: 'The country finds itself faced with arrears of legislation which for its peace and comfort had far better [*have*] been spread over the previous years.' The *have* should not be dropped here, for it obscures the construction. The *had been* might be taken for a past perfect tense. The suppression of *have* was once more common than now. Compare 3 *b* (next to last par.), p. 473.

c. With its simple form after a few other verbs, but here only as an objective predicate: 'I heard him *say* it.' See **15** III 2 B.

d. After the one preposition *to*, as explained in 1, p. 456: 'Hunger drove him *to steal food*' = *to the stealing of food*. 'She persuaded, induced, got him *to do it*.' 'I hired him *to do it*.' Historically the infinitive here is a verbal noun, object of the preposition *to*. *To* and the infinitive together form a prepositional object, i.e., an indispensable complement of the verb. Although the infinitive here is still a verbal noun, object of the preposition *to*, it has also the force of a verb, for it takes an object in the accusative case. Compare **24** IV *a*.

This prepositional object construction is common also after adjectives and participles: 'He is ready *to go*, eager *to go*, eager *for you to go*.' 'The question is difficult *to answer*.' 'The room is difficult *to heat*.' 'He is hard *to approach, to understand, to cook for, to get along with*.' 'He is easy *to understand, to get along with*.' 'He is sure *to come*.' 'You would be sure *to dislike* him.' 'He is unfit *to work*, slow *to sympathize* with others.' 'It was sad *to listen to*.' 'It is a calamity hard *to bear*' (or *to be borne*). 'I am ready *to be shaved*.' 'He is worthy *to be* thus *honored*.' 'He is inclined *to take offense* easily.'

After verbs and participles the gerund competes here with the infinitive. See **50** 4 *c dd* (2nd par.).

(2) After other verbs usually with *to:* 'I wish *to go*.' Often in connection with an objective predicate: 'I find *it* difficult *to do* that,' i.e., 'I find the doing of that difficult.' 'I felt *it* useless *to say* anything further.' Here anticipatory *it* points to the following infinitive.

The infinitive as object has a wide field of usefulness in abridged clauses: 'He begged *to go*, begged me (accusative) *to go*.' 'I told him (dative) *to do it*.' 'I planned *for him to go*.' For a full description of these objective clauses and their development see **24** III *d*.

The older simple form of the infinitive, still preserved in (1) *a*, *b*, *c*, was also in part still preserved here in early Modern English in archaic, poetic language, where after a few verbs, especially *begin*, older usage lingered on for a while longer: 'Then gan she *wail* and *weepe*' (Spenser, *The Faerie Queene*, Book I, II, VII), now 'Then she began *to wail* and *weep*.' Sometimes still: 'The sunshine went out of his soul with a thrill, The flesh 'neath his armor *'gan shrink* and *crawl*' (J. R. Lowell, *The Vision of Sir Launfal*, I, V). Other survivals of older usage here are given in **24** III *d*.

D. *As an Adjective Element Modifying a Noun.* See **10** I 2 (next to last par.); **10** V 1, 2, 3; **23** I *a*; **23** II 11; **50** 4 *d* (3rd par.). The prepositional form is always used here.

E. *The Infinitive in Elliptical Constructions.* The simple infinitive is much used in elliptical constructions: 'I [should] *ask* his pardon!' 'Why [should we] not *go* at once?' In older English, the infinitive with *to* was much used in such exclamations, and this old usage lingers on: 'I *to marry* before my brother, and *leave* him with none to take care of him!' (Blackmore, *Lorna Doone*, Ch. XXX). This construction, however, is not elliptical, but the old loose infinitive form of expression, once common and often described elsewhere in this book, which could replace almost any finite form of the verb. Compare 6, p. 481.

The infinitive is much used in another elliptical exclamatory construction, an unreal conditional sentence with the principal proposition suppressed. Here the subordinate conditional clause has the form of an abridged *to*-infinitive clause (3 *a*, 2nd par., p. 468) with the subject unexpressed, as the natural inference is that the speaker is subject: '*Oh to be in England* now that April's there!' (Browning, *Home-Thoughts from Abroad*, I) = 'Oh how happy I should be, were I in England now that April's there!'

Especially common are the elliptical constructions after the conjunctions *but* (= *except*), *except, save, than*. If the construction in the subordinate clause follows closely that in the principal proposition, the verbs *do, had* (past subjunctive), *will, would, can, could* in the subordinate clause are suppressed before their dependent simple infinitives if they have already been expressed in the principal proposition: 'She does nothing *but* [*that she does*] *laugh*.' 'I'll do anything to show my gratitude *but* (or *except*) [*that I do*] *marry* the daughter.' 'All day he has done nothing *but work*' (in older English, often *worked*, which was attracted to the form of the participle under the influence of *done*). 'Since her interview with him she has done little else *than* [*that she does*] *think* about him.' 'You can't do better *than* [*that you do*] *go*.' 'I had rather err with Plato *than* [*that I had*] *be* right with Horace.' 'I would rather (or sooner) die *than* [*that I would*] *yield*.' These constructions arose in older English, and for some of them we no longer have a live feeling, so that today we do not use some of the fuller forms given in brackets. The construction with *do* arose at a time when the *do*-form of the verb was not differentiated in meaning or function from the simple form, as described in 6 A *d*.

In *but*-constructions *anything* is sometimes omitted, often also *anything* and *do*: 'It cannot be [*anything*] but a dishonor and derogation to the author' (Milton, *Areopagitica*, 56). 'Under such circumstances he could not [*do anything*] but fail.' 'I cannot [*do anything*] but admire his courage.' 'I cannot [*do anything*] but be gratified by the assurance' (Thomas Jefferson, *Writings*, IV, 180). The infinitive that follows *but* here is always without *to*, for it is dependent upon a *do* understood, as explained in the preceding paragraph. In this construction there is always the idea present that something cannot be prevented. Instead of a suppressed *do* after *cannot* or *could not* we may employ an expressed verb, namely, *choose:* 'I *could not choose but speak* the truth' (Mrs. Gaskell, *A Dark Night's Work*, Ch. VI). There ought to be a *to* here before the infinitive that follows *but*, for the words form an abridged clause, which regularly requires a *to* before the infinitive. In older English, we sometimes find a *to* here, as illustrated in **24** III *d* (next to last par.). But this clause has the same meaning as the elliptical *do*-construction and has been influenced by it, so that *to* has dropped out. The verb *choose* is not now so common here as earlier in the period. It is now usually replaced by *help:* 'We *could not help but love* each other' (Hall Caine, *The Christian*, IV, Ch. XV). 'The cause of peace *could not help but be advanced* today' (*Westminster Gazette*, No. 9370). 'Their one aim is to push the British empire into a corner where it *cannot help but fight* a foredoomed battle' (F. Britten Austin in *The Saturday Evening Post*, June 7, 1930, p. 165). These are British examples. The construction is quite common also in American English, especially in the language of every day: 'You *can't help but notice* the pride that owners everywhere express for Essex' (advertisement of an auto in *Saturday Evening Post*, July 12, 1930). Examples from our literature have already been given in **24** III *d* (next to last par.). Several American grammarians have censured this construction without giving any grounds whatever. It has long been employed by good writers, and is still supported by good usage. There is, however, another construction — the gerund without *but* — which is now competing with it and is gradually becoming the more common form: 'I *cannot help feeling* gratified by the assurance.' 'We *could not help loving* each other.'

Since we do not have a vivid feeling for the constructions containing *rather*, illustrated on page 477, we have come to feel that the simple infinitive is to be used with *rather*, so that we now sometimes find the simple infinitive with *rather* even though no word has been previously used which could be supplied in thought before it: '*Rather* than *disturb* him she went for a light-box and his cigar-case to his bedroom' (Thackeray, *Pendennis*, I, Ch. XVIII). Similarly, after 'there is nothing *to do but*' and 'we have nothing *to do but*' we often employ the simple infinitive, as it so often elsewhere follows *do but:* 'There is nothing *to do* (or we have nothing *to do*) *but enjoy* ourselves.' But we often use also the *to*-infinitive here, as we feel the construction as an abridged infinitive clause, as in the second paragraph on page 481: 'I am sure we in England had nothing *to do* but *to fight* the battle out' (Thackeray, *The Virginians*, Ch. LXXXIV).

We often suppress the governing noun before its dependent *to*-infinitive if the noun has already been used in the principal proposition: 'I have no choice *but* [the choice] *to accept* the fact.' 'He hath never spoken a word *save* [the word] *to ask* for his food' (Scott, *Kenilworth*, Ch. I).

Except in the case just mentioned the *to*-infinitive constructions after these conjunctions, i.e., *but, except, save, than,* are not elliptical but abridged infinitive clauses of condition or exception (**31** 2) or abridged comparative clauses (**29** 1 B *b*), where the subject of the infinitive, as elsewhere, is usually not expressed but implied in some word in the principal proposition: 'What was left to them *but to drink and get merry?*' 'You ought to know better *than to believe* all the gossip you hear.' If the infinitive has a subject of its own the subject is introduced by *for:* 'There was nothing now *but for him* and *the footman to get* into the carriage.'

F. *As an Adverbial Element,* originally modifying the verb, now along with its expressed or unexpressed subject and its expressed modifiers forming an adverbial clause. This important construction is discussed in detail in **24** IV *a;* **27** 5; **28** 2 *b;* **28** 5 *d;* **29** 1 A *a bb;* **29** 1 A *d aa;* **29** 1 B *b;* **29** 2 *a;* **30** *b;* **31** 2; **32** 2; **33** 2. The prepositional form is always used here except in a few set expressions in clauses of purpose and result. See **11** 2; **28** 5 *d* (4th par.); **29** 2 *a* (2nd par.); **33** 2 (7th par.).

5. **Repetition of 'To' with the Infinitive.** When there are several infinitives with the same or similar construction, it is common usage to employ *to* with the first infinitive and understand it with the next one or the following ones: 'I wished *to finish* my business and [*to*] *get* away' (Meredith Nicholson, *The House of a Thousand Candles*, Ch. I). 'I hoped *to draw* him into the open and [*to*] *settle* with him' (*ib.*, Ch. XI). 'I thought it better *to take* the anthem myself than [*to*] *give* it to a junior, who would be sure to make a mull of it' (Mrs. Wood, *The Channings*, Ch. I, 4). However, whenever the second or later infinitive becomes important by reason of a contrast or a wish to emphasize it in any way, it becomes at once more natural to repeat the *to:* 'It was better *to laugh* than *to cry.*' '*To be* or not *to be*, that is the question.' In involved constructions it is always desirable to repeat *to* to make the grammatical relations and the thought clear.

6. **Infinitive Used to Carry On a Construction.** In older English, it was not uncommon to put a *to* before an infinitive although a preceding infinitive having the same construction was without *to:* 'And bids you, in the bowels of the Lord, Deliver up the crown,

and *to take* mercy on the poor souls' (Shakespeare, *Henry the Fifth*, II, IV, 102). 'She tells me here she'll wed the stranger knight, or never more *to view* nor day nor night' (*id.*, *Pericles*, II, v, 17). The *to*-infinitive is much used in older English, as in the last two examples, to carry on a construction once begun and thus avoid the repetition of verbal forms used in the construction. The second and third propositions may even have a different subject, in which case the subject of the infinitives carrying on the construction is in the nominative: 'Heaven would that she these gifts should have, And I *to live* and *die* her slave' (*id.*, *As You Like It*, III, II, 161). In the following example the *to*-infinitive clause with an absolute nominative subject carries on the preceding concessive clause construction introduced by *though:* 'I could then have look'd on him without the help of admiration, though the catalogue of his endowments had been tabled by his side and *I to peruse him by items*' (*id.*, *Cymbeline*, I, v, 4) = *I could study him by items*.

The infinitive construction was sometimes used in the first dependent clause, even after the conjunction *that*, which always calls for a finite verb: 'Iff all my saide children decesse, I will *that* the saide goodes to them bequethed *to be bestowed* in charitable deades' (*Lincoln Diocese Documents*, p. 138, July 22, 1529).

THE GERUND

50 1. Origin and Development. The gerund was originally a verbal noun in *–ing* (until about 1250 also with the form *–ung*). Thus it differed from the present participle in meaning, which was originally an adjective and until about the fourteenth century had a different ending, namely, *ende* (or *inde, ynde, ande*), so that the two suffixes were farther apart in form and meaning than they are today. They have both in course of time acquired more verbal force, but the gerund is still a noun and the present participle is still an adjective. In Old English, the gerund was a feminine noun with the inflection of a strong feminine, as described in Accidence, **56** 3 *c*. The gerund is still often a simple noun without any of the characteristics of a verb except its verbal meaning. The noun gerund always preserves its original transitive form even where it has strong passive force, and is usually formally distinguished by a preceding adjective, descriptive or limiting, and often also by a following *of*-genitive object: 'He has not committed any act worthy of transportation or *hanging*' (active form with passive force). '*Horsewhipping* (passive force) would be too good for such a scoundrel.' 'His forearms and clean-shaven face were brown from *prolonged tanning* (passive force) by the sun.' 'The candle is in need of *snuffing*' (passive force). '*The singing* was good.' '*The shooting of birds* (genitive object) is forbidden.' A verbal gerund now rarely has an adjective before it and takes after it an accusative, dative, or prepositional object and adverbial modifiers of all kinds: '*Shooting birds* (accusative object) is useless.' 'It is fun *shooting at a mark*' (prepositional object). 'It is dangerous *playing recklessly with fire*' (two adverbial modifiers).

As we have seen above, the gerund was once felt only as a noun and, like a verbal noun, took a genitive object, and still takes a genitive object when it is felt only as a noun. Where, however, the verbal force is strong, it now takes regularly an accusative

object, as in the first of the last three examples just given. The
accusative occurred only rarely in Old English, but became more
common in Middle English. This development was facilitated by
the example of the present participle, which had the same form and
took an accusative object. It was facilitated also by the example
of the closely related infinitive, which, though originally a noun, had
acquired so much verbal force that it took an accusative object, like
a verb. The natural influence of the infinitive upon the gerund was
greatly increased in older English by the confounding of their forms.
The older infinitive in *–n* (**49** 1) and the gerund in *–ing* often had
in the spoken language the same form. However, in older English
literature, the original genitive object in its modern form with *of*
lingered long after the gerund, even where the verbal force was
strong, and in popular speech it still lingers: 'imployed onely in
casting up *of earth* and digging *of trenches*' (Thomas Dekker, *The
Wonderfull Yeare*, p. 32, A.D. 1603), now 'employed in casting up
earth and digging *trenches*.' 'Whom I left [in, i.e., engaged in]
cooling *of the air* with sighs' (Shakespeare, *The Tempest*, I, II, 222),
now 'Whom I left cooling *the air* with sighs.' 'He was by nature
unfortunate and was always a-missing (i.e., in missing) *of everything*' (De Morgan, *Joseph Vance*, Ch. I), now in literary English
'was always missing *everything*.' As can be seen by the present
form appended to the last two examples, the gerund has here
often been replaced by the present participle. Compare 4 *c dd*,
p. 494. On the other hand, where the gerund has an article or
other limiting adjective modifier before it and thus has the characteristic mark of a noun, there is today a strong feeling that a
direct object should be in the genitive, just as nouns in general
take only a genitive object: 'the trusting *of a secret* to a woman.'
Earlier English, however, did not differentiate so carefully between
these two classes of gerunds, and this older usage which admitted
of an accusative after a gerund modified by an article or other
limiting adjective still occasionally occurs: 'the trusting *a* secret
to a woman' (Meredith, *Diana of the Crossways*, Ch. XXXV).

2. **Voice and Tense.** As the gerund in the sixteenth century
was felt as having strong verbal force, it began to appear with
forms for voice and tense, which have become established: 'So
my heart, although dented at with the arrowes of thy burning
affections, shall alwayes keepe his (now *its*) hardnesse and be so
farre from *being mollyfied* that thou shalt not perceiue it moued'
(John Lyly, *Euphues and His England*, Works, II, p. 139,
A.D. 1580). 'In *having known* no travel in his youth' (Shakespeare,
The Two Gentlemen of Verona, I, III, 16, A.D. 1591–1595).

Passive force today usually requires passive form and an ap-

propriate tense, although in older English we find here active
form and we may even still use a present tense for past time,
as originally: 'A Shootynge Gloue is chieflye for to saue a mannes
fyngers *from hurtynge*' (Roger Ascham, *Toxophilus*, Book II,
p. 4, A.D. 1545), now *from being hurt.* 'Shall we send that foolish
carrion, Mistress Quickly, to him, and excuse his *throwing* (now
being thrown, or *having been thrown*) into the water?' (Shakespeare,
The Merry Wives of Windsor, III, III, 205).   By comparing these
older gerunds with the accompanying newer ones and the newer
ones in the following sentences we may see how much our language has gained by the introduction of passive form for the expression of passive force: 'The fact of *being backed* by my friends is
a great comfort' = 'The fact that I *am backed* by my friends is a
great comfort.' 'The fact of his *being* (or *having been*) *convicted*
so promptly is gratifying' = 'The fact that he *was convicted* so
promptly is gratifying.' 'I have read of its *being* (or *having been*)
done before' = 'I have read that it *has been done* before.' 'After
having been so thoroughly *punished* he became more tractable'
= 'After he *had been* so thoroughly *punished*, he became more
tractable.' 'There is no hope of his *being convicted*' = 'There is
no hope that he *will* (or *may*) *be convicted.*'
     The active forms now usually indicate tense, although the older
use of the present tense for past time occasionally occurs: 'His
having such poor health is against him' = 'The fact that he *has*
such poor health is against him.' 'There is a possibility of his
having arrived this morning' = 'There is a possibility that he
arrived this morning.' 'I have heard of his *doing* (or *having done*)
it before' = 'I have heard that he *has done* it before.' 'After
having finished my task I went to bed' = 'After I *had finished*
my task, I went to bed.' 'There is no hope of his *coming* soon' =
'There is no hope that he *will* (or *may*) *come* soon.' 'There is
hope of his *finishing* it by evening' – 'There is hope that he *will
have finished* it by evening.'
     Thus the gerund, though having only two tenses, can express all
the time relations expressed by the more complicated finite verb.
Though it has no special forms to indicate mood, it can render
fairly accurately some of the relations expressed by the subjunctive
forms of the finite verb.   Its great simplicity in connection with
a fair degree of accuracy has made it one of the favorite means
of English expression.   It is the very embodiment of English
practicality.
     3. **Subject of the Gerund.** Like a verb, a gerund may have a
subject, but, like other verbal nouns, its subject is in the genitive,
here, however, only the old subjective genitive in *-s*, or instead of

the genitive the person implied in a possessive adjective, *my*, *his*, etc., which were originally genitives of the personal pronouns and are still often used as such, as illustrated in **10** II 2 D (last par.): 'I am provoked at *John's* talking so rudely' (or 'at *his* talking so rudely'). In older English, the *his*-genitive (**10** II 1) was sometimes used instead of the *s*-genitive: 'The governor and assistants met at Boston to consider of *the deputy his* deserting his place' (Winthrop, *Journal*, May 1, 1632). The development of the gerundial construction is hampered at the present time by the lack of *s*-genitive forms in current English and by the lack of a clear form for the possessive referring to a female. *Her* is either a personal pronoun or a possessive adjective. Many common substantive limiting adjectives, as *this*, *these*, *those*, *any*, *several*, *all*, *two*, *three*, etc., have no *s*-genitive. Here, of course, as the genitive is impossible, we have to use the accusative: 'Was it thou who didst tell the boy this foolishness of *these* being our arms?' (S. Weir Mitchell, *Hugh Wynne*, Ch. VII). 'Some families may possibly have moved away on account of the repeated failure of crops, but I do not know of *any* having done so.' There are also nouns that have no genitive form. Here we must have recourse to the accusative: 'I am not surprised at *young* or *old* falling in love with her' (Thackeray, *Pendennis*, I, 151). 'There is no hope of *good* coming from it.' 'There is no expectation of the *French* withdrawing their demands.' A clause used as a subject always has accusative form, for it is not possible for a clause to indicate the genitive relation by taking an *'s:* 'There is, however, a middle class prejudice against the possibility of *what is ornamental* being useful' (*Cornhill Magazine*, Sept., 1912).

Moreover, many avoid, in the case of common nouns, the genitive singular as subject, for in most words the singular and the plural here both end in –*s*, and thus sound alike to the ear, so that, unless the connection makes the thought clear, the singular is not heard as a singular: 'I don't approve of my *son's* (often replaced by the accusative *son* to make it clear that a singular form is intended) doing that.' In the plural, the accusative is usually employed to bring out clearly the plural idea: 'I don't approve of *cousins marrying*' (Sir Harry Johnston, *The Man Who Did the Right Thing*, Ch. III). 'A stout fox had been turned out of Hartover copse within a few minutes of the *hounds* being put in it' (A. Marshall, *The Eldest Son*, Ch. XXVIII). Even where there is a clear plural form we avoid the genitive subject and usually employ the accusative: 'She would have despised the modern idea of *women* being equal to men' (Mrs. Gaskell, *Cranford*, Ch. II, p. 15). The genitive subject here is rather uncommon:

'It does not at first appear easy to prove that men ought to like one thing rather than another, and although this is granted generally by *men's* speaking of "bad" or "good" taste, yet,' etc. (Ruskin, *Modern Painters*, Part III, Sec. I, Ch. III). In the case of nouns denoting lifeless things or abstract ideas, many avoid the genitive as subject also in the singular, even where the connection makes the thought clear, for in general they use the s-genitive very little of lifeless things and abstract ideas. They employ the accusative here as subject: 'When a man goes back to look at the house of his childhood, it has always shrunk: there is no instance of *such a house* being as big as the picture in memory and imagination call for' (Mark Twain, *Letter to W. D. Howells*, Aug. 22, 1887). 'It was a sweet consolation to the short time that I have left to fall into such a society; no wonder then that I am unhappy at *that consolation* being withdrawn' (Horace Walpole, *Letter to Miss Mary Berry*, Oct. 10, 1790). In circles strongly disposed to use the genitive as subject of the gerund, however, we not infrequently find it even in the case of nouns denoting lifeless things — provided, of course, that the connection makes the thought clear, and the genitive is possible: 'On the *permission's* being granted she left the room.'

Even though the connection should make the thought clear and there is a disposition to use the genitive as subject with the names of lifeless things as well as with the names of living beings, the genitive is not a good, ever ready instrument of thought, for it cannot be used at all when it is modified by a noun, phrase, or clause, in which case we must have recourse to the ever ready accusative: 'On the *permission to go* being repeated she left the room' (George Gissing, *The Unclassed*, p. 6). 'There is danger of a *woman's head* being turned' (Meredith, *Diana of the Crossways*, Ch. VI). 'Have you heard of *Smith the carpenter* being injured?' 'Have you heard of *Smith, who used to be pitcher*, being injured?' 'Did you ever hear of a *man of good sense* refusing such an offer?' 'In spite of Clyde Fitch's *play* "Glad of It" having been a failure, Howells had given a fair appreciative criticism of it in *Harper's Weekly*' (Mildred Howells, *William Dean Howells*, p. 182). 'I remember *each one's* (or *each one*) saying it,' but only 'I remember *each one of them* saying it.' 'Harder than to give up was to be given up, or to be the cause of *some one you love* giving up for you' (Galsworthy, *To Let*, Part II, Ch. IX). 'I hate the thought of *any son* of *mine* marrying badly' (Hardy, *The Return of the Native*, p. 251). In this large category the genitive subject has entirely disappeared. Our feeling today is against the employment of a modified genitive as subject of the gerund. There are no exceptions when the modifier is a noun, phrase, or clause. Our present feeling is also against employing the genitive as subject when followed by an adjective. The only exception is the occasional use of the old genitive of personal pronouns followed by *all:* 'Isn't it dreadful to think of *their all* (or *them all*) being wrong!' (Sir Harry Johnston, *The Man Who Did the Right Thing*, Ch. II). 'I suffer at the idea of *its all* (or *it all*) being rendered useless perhaps by one fault' (Clyde Fitch, *Letter*, Sept. 20, 1905).

In a number of cases the subject of the gerund cannot for a double reason be in the genitive — it has no *s*-genitive form and it is modified by a noun or phrase: 'In this morning's letter I have told you that, in the uncertainty of *any* of my letters reaching you, I must, until I know they do, use many repetitions' (Horace Walpole, *Letter to Miss Mary Berry*, Dec. 17, 1790).

Furthermore, we always use the accusative — never a genitive — subject when the subject follows the gerund: 'He would always ignore the fact of there being a *back-door* to any house' (Mrs. Gaskell, *Cranford*, Ch. VIII).

We regularly use the accusative as subject when the subject is emphatic: 'She was proud of *hím doing it.*' The emphasis often comes from contrasting the subjects: 'We seem to think nothing of *a bóy smoking*, but resent *a gírl smoking.*' Contrasting subjects is frequently associated with elliptical form. See next paragraph.

When the gerund is understood in the second of two clauses having a gerund in common, the subject of the gerund is always an accusative, never a genitive: 'I don't like the idea of *méthod being everything* and *individuálity [being] nothing.*' We employ the elliptical construction when we desire to contrast the two subjects. Compare the second paragraph below this, also **28 3** *a* (5th par.).

Some writers often employ the accusative even where it is not absolutely necessary to make the thought clear, as in the case of names and titles where the genitive could not be construed as a plural: 'At *Elizabeth Jane* mentioning how greatly Lucetta had been jeopardized, he exhibited an agitation different in kind no less than in intensity from any she had seen in him before' (Hardy, *The Mayor of Casterbridge*, Ch. XXIX). 'He gives an account of the stormy scenes in the House of Commons, the Parliament insisting upon the *King* withdrawing or altering his Declaration of Indulgence before any money could be voted for carrying on the war' (Lady Newton, *Lyme Letters*, Ch. V, A.D. 1925).

In one category the accusative has not become so well established as in the others, namely, in personal pronouns. As these pronouns all have a genitive and all the genitives except *your* distinguish singular and plural, there has never been a strong need of the accusative in this group. In older English, it occasionally occurs in good authors: 'Take no displaysure at *me* so presuming' (Caxton, fifteenth century). 'I would haue no mans honestye empayred by *me* tellynge' (Latimer, *Seven Sermons*, p. 160, A.D. 1549). We must still use the accusative when we desire to describe rather than merely to state a fact, i.e., when we desire to represent something as proceeding or as being repeated. But then the form in *–ing* is a present participle, not a gerund: 'I caught a glimpse of *you* (never *your*) *looking* on,' and similarly in 'Do not send any more of my books home. I have a good deal of pleasure in the thought of *you looking* on them' (Keats). 'I couldn't think of *him greeting* (expressing repetition) people kindly as he passes them on the street.' In non-descriptive language the accusative is often employed in colloquial speech also as the subject of the gerund: 'We were talking only the other day of *you* going with us' (Victor Appleton, *Tom Swift and His Submarine*, Ch. VII). In choice language we employ here the possessive adjectives *my*, *your*, etc., which are historically genitives of the pronouns. But we must have recourse to the accusative of the pronoun where the expression is elliptical: 'There is danger of *you* being dismissed as well as *me* [being dismissed].' We employ the elliptical construction when we desire to contrast the two subjects. Compare the fourth paragraph, p. 488.

In Old English, the subject of the gerund was always in the genitive: 'He sæt to þam casere and hi swyðe blyðe wæron for *martines* gereordunge' (Ælfric, *Lives of Saints*, II, p. 258, l. 629) = 'He sat by the Emperor, and they were very cheerful on account of *Martin's* feasting with them.' In Middle English, the genitive often lost its distinctive form, so that it could not be distinguished from an accusative: 'For *the quene* comynge he was fol glad' (Robert Brunne, *Chron.*, 682, A.D. 1338). *Quene* seems to be the indistinctive genitive that was in use at this period. The construction resembles that in the sentence from Ælfric. But this is not at all sure, for *comynge* may be a present participle. Just about this time the present participle in *–and* had through phonetical development lost its old ending and had become identical in form with the gerund. If *comynge* is a present participle its subject *quene* is an accusative, object of the preposition *for*. In the literary language of the North the present participle in *–and* was still in use at this time, so that we can find after prepositions clear examples of a present participle with an accusative subject: 'þe stok nest þe root growand es þe heved *with nek followand*' (Rolle, *Pricke of Conscience*, 676) = 'The stock growing

next to the root was the head *with the neck following.*' After the
ending *–ing* became established in the literary language as a
participial form as well as a gerundial, it was difficult to distinguish the two constructions after prepositions. We still, however,
clearly feel the form in *–ing* here as a present participle when it
has descriptive force, representing something as continuing or as
being repeated: 'It is dreadful to think of him *lying* out there in
his cold grave tonight.' 'From our veranda we can enjoy the
beautiful sight of the waves *beating* on the shore.' But the present
participle does not always have descriptive force. It may, like a
gerund, refer to an act as a whole: 'I am proud of *him acting so
unselfishly*' = 'I am proud of him, *as he acted so unselfishly.*'
Thus, after a preposition the form in *–ing* became associated with
an accusative subject as well as with a genitive subject, and
participle and gerund became confounded here. As the gerund
has always been more common after a preposition than the
participle, we usually feel the form in *–ing* here as a gerund, but
we now use either a genitive or an accusative as its subject.

Similarly, in clauses that are the object of a verb, the gerundial
and the participial clause have been confounded. In 'I remember
his mother's saying it' *saying* is a gerund, as we can see by its
genitive subject. In 'I remember *his mother saying* it' *saying*
was originally a present participle. *Mother* was the accusative
object of the verb *remember* and at the same time the subject of
the present participle *saying*. As the gerundial and the participial
clause have been confounded, we now usually feel the form in *–ing*
as a gerund whether its subject is a genitive or an accusative.
However, where it has descriptive force, representing something as
proceeding or as being repeated, we feel it as a present participle:
'I see *him* (not *his*) *coming* up the road.' 'We could see *him* (not
his) *bowing* graciously to the people as he drove along.' The
uniform use of the accusative here shows that the form in *–ing*
is a present participle. The participial construction is described
in **15** III 2 A. Compare **48** 2 (4th par.).

Thus in choice language the accusative is found as subject of
the gerund or participle only in object clauses that are the object
of a preposition or a verb. In subject and predicate clauses the
gerund with a genitive subject is the usual construction in the
literary language, the accusative subject being confined to popular
speech: 'Does *our* (in popular speech *us*) *singing* in the room
above disturb you?' 'It was *our* (in popular speech *us*) *coming*
late that disturbed him.' The participial clause competes here
with the gerundial, but it is largely confined to colloquial speech:
'*He saying* (present participle) *he is sorry* alters the case,' or in

the literary language usually '*His saying* (gerund) *he is sorry*
alters the case.' For a fuller description of the participial clause
see **17** 3 B.

Often, however, the gerund has no subject of its own, as there
is elsewhere in the sentence a noun or pronoun which is felt not
only as performing its own proper function but as serving also
as the subject of the gerund: 'I am going down there this evening;
so you must excuse *me* for *hurrying* away.' '*I* am afraid of *hurting*
his feelings.' In older English, the subject of the gerund was
often expressed even though it was the same as some word in the
principal proposition: 'Since *her* (now suppressed) being at
Lambton *she* had heard that Miss Darcy was exceedingly proud'
(Jane Austen, *Pride and Prejudice*, III, Ch. II). The suppression
of the subject of the gerund is discussed in detail throughout the
Syntax where the different gerundial categories are described.
In such constructions the gerund should be distinguished from
the present participle. The gerund performs the function of a
noun; the present participle performs the function of an adjective:
'That set me *thinking*' (present participle). 'That set me *to
thinking*' (gerund). Compare **15** III 2 A. When the subject of
the gerund is general or indefinite, it is often not expressed: 'It
is dangerous *playing* with explosives.'

4. **Functions of the Gerund.** In spite of the strong verbal
force of the gerund and its assumption of tense and voice forms,
it remains a noun. It can still stand in the sentence only where a
noun can stand, and it still always performs the function of a
noun. But as it now often has strong verbal force, it may have
accusative objects and adverbial modifiers. These modifiers usually follow the gerund, but sentence adverbs precede it: 'When
he looked at her he usually ended by smiling and sometimes by
suddenly láughing.' Compare **49** 2 *c*, p. 465. On account of the
importance of the gerundial construction it has been treated in
detail under the different categories throughout the Syntax. In
order that the student may get a clear view of the entire field of
its present usefulness, an outline of its different functions is given
on page 492, with references to paragraphs where these functions
are discussed. It often competes with the infinitive in certain categories, as described in the articles referred to in the following pages.

Attempts have been made to prove that there is a differentiation
of meaning between gerund and infinitive where the two forms
compete with each other. It has been claimed that the gerund
is preferred in stating a general fact, while the infinitive is used
in referring to special circumstances of a particular individual act:
'Talking (in general) mends no holes,' but 'To delay (in this

special case) is dangerous.' Actual usage knows nothing of this distinction: 'No letter today! It has a bad air *your forgetting me so early*' (Horace Walpole, *Letter to Mary and Agnes Berry*, June 23, 1789). The reference here is not general, but to the special case in hand. The writer might have used the infinitive here: 'It has a bad air *for you to forget me so early*.' The gerund is similarly used in 'It's (i.e., your pushing your scientific studies is) far more important for us than *getting the Vote*' (Sir Harry Johnston, *Mrs. Warren's Daughter*, Ch. XIII, p. 207), where the speaker in referring to the special case in hand says that it is much more important to women that Professor Rossiter, at this time member of the House of Commons, should return to his scientific studies than that he should stay in politics to secure to women the Vote. The speaker here might have said *to get* instead of *getting*. In the first example we might use the infinitive: 'It doesn't mend holes *to talk*.' In the second example we might employ the gerund: 'It is dangerous in this special case, your *delaying*.' Thus we often may use either the gerund or the infinitive. They are usually competing constructions, although in certain categories the one or the other form is preferred. In colloquial use the gerund is more likely to stand in the first position than is the infinitive. Except after *to*, as described in *d*, p. 495, the gerund is alone used after prepositions. It is also often preferred in accusative clauses, as described in **24** III *d*. On the other hand, where modal force is to be conveyed, the infinitive is usually employed, as described in **7** D 2, although this idea is in a restricted sense found in the gerund, as described in **4** II C (3rd par.). For the one point where the gerund and the infinitive are differentiated in meaning, see *c dd* (3rd par.), p. 494.

The gerund is used as:

a. Subject: '*Seeing* is believing.' See **4** I *e, h*; **4** II C; **21** *e*.

b. Predicate: 'Seeing is *believing*.' See **7** E; **22** *c*.

c. Object:

aa. Accusative object, object of a verb: 'I like *getting up* early.' The *to*-infinitive competes here with the gerund. See **24** III *d*. On the other hand, the object of the adjective *worth* is always a gerund: 'A thing worth *doing* at all is worth *doing* well.'

bb. Dative object, object of an adverb or adjective, or indirect object of a verb: 'He came near *being killed*.' 'Next to *being married*, a girl likes to be crossed in love a little now and then' (Jane Austen). 'I don't feel like *laughing* today.' 'He is devoting his time *to improving* (indirect object) his garden.' The Old English forms corresponding to the adverbs *near* and *next to* and the adjective *like* governed the dative, so that we might call the noun or pronoun following these words a dative object. But as we now feel *near, next to, like* for the most part as prepositions, we may consider the object here as the object of a preposition, the preposition and object together forming a prepositional object. The *to* and the indirect object represent an older dative, but we now often feel them as a prepositional object.

cc. Genitive object, object of a verb or an adjective: 'I convinced him *of his being* able to do it.' 'I am not sure *of having seen* him.' This object may be classified also as a prepositional object.

dd. With a preposition the gerund often forms a prepositional clause, which is used as a prepositional object of a verb or adjective or as a prepositional predicate (**7** F) after a copula: 'They set *about repairing the damage.*' 'I am afraid *of their seeing it.*' 'Her son had not written to herself to ask a fond mother's blessing for that step which he was *about taking*' (Thackeray, *Henry Esmond*, III, Ch. II). 'England seems *about deserting him*' (Carlyle, *Frederick the Great*, IX). After *about* the prepositional infinitive may be used instead of the gerund, but the constructions are not the same, *about* before a gerund being a preposition but before the infinitive being an adverb, for a prepositional infinitive cannot now stand after a preposition: 'They set *about* (adverb) *to repair the damage.*' 'He is *about* (adverb; see **7** F) *to take* (more common than *taking*) *the step.*' 'England seems *about* (adverb; see **7** F) *to desert* (more common than *deserting*) *him.*' There is sometimes a difference of meaning between a gerund and an infinitive, but the difference lies in the use of different prepositions rather than in the verbal forms themselves: 'He is afraid *of dying*' = *that he shall die.* 'He is afraid *to die*' = *He fears dying*, literally, *is afraid in the direction of dying.*

The gerund is much used thus in prepositional clauses that complete the meaning of a verb or an adjective. The gerund is employed quite freely after all the prepositions except the one preposition *to*. After *to* we still often use the infinitive where *to* is not a mere sign of the infinitive but a preposition indicating a movement toward a person or thing: 'Hunger drove him *to steal*' (or *to stealing*). 'I am accustomed *to do it this way*' (or *to doing it this way*). The gerund is often used here alongside of the infinitive, as it is in general natural to employ a gerund after a preposition. But often the gerund cannot be used here at all, as the infinitive is still the favorite form after *to*. In adverbial clauses after *to* the gerund is never used: 'He worked hard *to get* (never *to getting*) *through early.*' On the other hand, the gerund is employed to make it clear that the prepositional construction is a prepositional object, not an adverbial element: 'I am looking forward with pleasure *to seeing you soon.*' Compare **24** IV *a.*

The gerund after the preposition *to* or *on,* when used in the sense of entrance into a state of activity, has the same force as the present participle when used as predicate after an ingressive or an effective point-action (**38** 2 *a bb* and **38** 2 *b ee*) verb, such as *get, fall, burst out, set,* which indicate entrance into a state of activity. After ingressives: 'He fell again *speculating*' (pred. part.), or *to speculating* (gerund), or in older English also *to speculate.* 'She burst out *crying*' (pred. part.), or in popular speech *a-crying,* in older English, a literary form contracted from *on crying* (gerund). 'That set me *thinking*' (objective pred. part.), or *to thinking* (gerund), or as in older English: 'It was what put Cit's back up so two years ago that set me *on thinking* (gerund) it' (De Morgan, *The Old Madhouse,* Ch. XXV). After effectives: 'The machine got *running*' (pred. part.), or *to running* (gerund). 'I got the machine *running*' (objective pred. part.), or *to running* (gerund). The infinitive can be used here instead of the gerund, but it is differentiated in meaning from it. The infinitive represents the activity merely as a result pure and simple, while the gerund represents the resultant activity as proceeding steadily: 'I finally got him *to do* it.' 'I soon got the machine *to running.*' Compare **38** 2 *b ee* (last par.).

In the same way we may use either the present participle or the gerund to represent an action as continuing: 'There is a new church *building*' (pred. part.), or in popular speech *a-building,* from older literary English *in* or *on building* (gerund). Through the suppression of the preposition here the old gerundial construction has merged into the participial. That the preposition has been suppressed here can be clearly seen in older literary English, and still in popular speech by the objective genitive following the form in *–ing,* which thus clearly shows that the form in *–ing* is a gerund, not a present participle: 'as she was [in] *writing of it*' (Shakespeare, *As You Like It,* IV, III, 10). 'She fancied the bull was *a-chasing of her*' (Mrs. Alexander, *For His Sake,* I, Ch. III). The history of these two constructions is given in **47** *a* and **48** 1 *e.*

Similarly, the predicate appositive participle competes with the gerund after *in:* 'I wasn't long *getting* (or *in getting*) out of the room.' 'We must not be late *getting* (or *in getting*) home.'

Instead of construing the gerund as a prepositional object we may often regard it as an accusative object, for the preposition is now frequently felt as a part of the verb, verb and preposition forming a compound, as becomes evident in the passive form of

statement, where the object here, just as any accusative object
of the active, may become the subject: (active) 'They often
laugh at my doing it in this way,' but in the passive 'My doing
it in this way has often been *laughed at*, but it has proved best
after all.'

d. *As an Attributive Element.* The gerund is common here in
three grammatical relations, as an attributive genitive, as an
appositive noun, and as an attributive prepositional phrase.

As an attributive genitive: 'the love *of indulging self*,' 'the fear
of losing his friendship,' 'the hope *of John's coming soon*,' 'the fear
of his wife's mother (accusative subject; see 3, p. 487) *coming*.'
The prepositional infinitive competes with the gerund here: 'It
is the best way *to do it*' (or *of doing it*). 'They approach the subject
with the honest desire *of getting* (or *to get*) at the truth.' In the
last example either the infinitive after *to* or the gerund after *of*
can be used after the noun *desire*, but often the infinitive alone
can be employed when the idea of desire, wish, demand, command,
or modality (**23** II 11, 2nd par.) is present: 'There is a strong
public demand *for him to take the place*,' not *of his taking the place*.
'She has a strict charge *to avoid the subject*.' 'He received the order
to retreat.' 'He is the man *to do it*' = *who should do it*. 'That
is not the way *to do it*' = *in which it should be done*. In such
examples the *to* before the infinitive has its original meaning of
towards, in the direction of, as in the second paragraph below.

In the appositive relation we may use the gerund in the appositive genitive or as an appositive agreeing with its governing
noun in case: 'I now have the pleasant work *of preparing boys
for college*,' or 'I now have very pleasant work, *preparing boys for
college*.' The infinitive competes with the gerund here: 'I claim
the right *to do it* (or *doing it*, or *of doing it*) *in my own way*.' 'What
right's he got *telling* (or *to tell*) *me where I head in*' (Sinclair Lewis,
Elmer Gantry, III, III). Compare **23** I *a* (next to last par.).

The gerund is common also in attributive prepositional clauses:
'His joy *on account of my* (or *John's*) *coming*,' 'his sorrow *on account of his wife's mother* (accusative subject; see 3, p. 487) *coming*,'
'his disappointment *over attaining so little*.' After the one preposition *to*, however, we still often prefer the infinitive where the *to*
is not a mere sign of the infinitive but a preposition with the
meaning of *towards, in the direction of:* 'a strong impulse, or
tendency, *to do it*,' 'an incentive *to do it*' (or *to doing it*), 'an additional stimulus *to do it*' (or *to doing it*), 'a natural reluctance *to
do it*' (or *to doing it*), 'a disposition *to exaggerate*,' 'a strong temptation *to do it*.' But when *to* has the clear meaning of *against* the
gerund is more common: 'his opposition *to my going*,' 'many

obstacles, or objections, *to building now,*' 'an aversion *to shedding blood*' (or *to shed blood*). When the infinitive has a subject of its own, *for* must stand before it: 'That will be an additional inducement *for him to do it.*' Compare *c dd* (2nd par.).

   e. In Abridged Adverbial Clauses. This common use is discussed in detail in **27** 5; **28** 1 *a*; **28** 3 *a*; **28** 5 *d* (7th par.); **29** 1 A *a bb*; **29** 1 A *c bb*; **29** 1 A *d aa*; **29** 1 B *b*; **30** *b*; **31** 2; **32**; **33** 2.

ADJECTIVES

51 1. Functions. Adjectives and participles can be used predicatively, attributively, appositively, and substantively. Some adjectives and participles can be used also as nouns. The nominative predicate is discussed in **6** B *a*; **7** B *a, c*; **17** A *a, b, c*, B, C; the objective predicate in **15** III 2 A; the attributive adjective in **10** I 1, 2, 3, 4; the appositive adjective in **10** I 1 and 1 *a*; the predicate appositive adjective in **6** C; **7** B *b*; **20** 3. Further details with regard to attributive, predicate, and appositive adjectives are given in the following pages, where also the substantive (i.e., pronominal) use and the use as nouns are discussed.

2. Classes. There are two classes of adjectives — descriptive and limiting. A descriptive adjective expresses either the *kind* or the *condition* or *state* of the living being or lifeless thing spoken of: a *good* boy; a *bright* dog; a *tall* tree; a *sick* boy; a *lame* dog. The participles of verbs in adjective function are all descriptive adjectives, since they indicate either an active or passive state: *running* water; a *dying* soldier; a *broken* chair.

A limiting adjective, without expressing any idea of kind or condition, limits the application of the idea expressed by the noun to one or more individuals of the class, or to one or more parts of the whole, i.e., it points out individuals or individual parts: *this* boy; *that* tree; *my* hat; *these* books; *this* part of the country; *other* parts of the country. Limiting adjectives are divided into classes. These classes are described in The Parts of Speech, **10.**

INFLECTION OF ADJECTIVES

INFLECTION OF DESCRIPTIVE ADJECTIVES

52. Inflection in the Positive. The entire loss of adjective inflection in the positive degree at the close of the Middle English period gradually brought to the descriptive adjective a great extension of its boundaries. After the loss of adjective inflection it became possible to place a noun, adverb, prepositional phrase, or even a whole sentence before a noun to modify its meaning as a descriptive adjective, for, since there is no longer an adjective ending present, there is nothing here to call attention to a conflict between the former and the present function of the modifying word: the *stone* bridge; the *down* stroke; an *up-to-date* dictionary; a *go-ahead* city. For fuller information see **10 I 2.**

Although the loss of adjective inflection was, in general, an advantage, it was at points a real loss, as can be seen in its use as a noun, described in **58.** We now feel the disadvantage here and are restoring inflection; of course, not by putting into use again the old forms, but by employing modern means which we understand, as described in **58.**

At another point the loss of inflection was felt so keenly that attempts to restore inflection began in the fourteenth century, namely, in substantive function, i.e., when an attributive adjective stands at some distance from its governing noun, apparently alone, like a substantive, but in fact in relation to a noun, as in 'a black sheep and a *white one*.' The object of inflecting the adjective is to bring it into relation to the governing noun. When the adjective stands immediately before the noun we need no ending to indicate its relation to the noun, but when we remove it from the noun, we need a sign to relate it to the noun. In the fourteenth century, *one* was placed after the adjective to perform this function. At first this *one* had its original concrete meaning, *one*, but, as we now can say 'the black sheep and the *white ones*' it is evident that this *one* no longer denotes *one*, but has developed into an adjective suffix with the same force as the Old English adjective inflectional ending, namely, to bring the adjective into relation to the governing noun. Though this *one* is separated from the adjective in writing, it is suffixed immediately in the spoken language and has the weak stress of a suffix. Similarly, other words in the course of their development have assumed new functions. *Has*, a verb originally denoting possession, is often also used as the sign of the present perfect tense, as in 'He *has* gone.' Likewise the preposition *of* often loses its prepositional force entirely and merely serves as the sign of the genitive, as in 'the father *of the boy*.' Grammarians do not usually call the *one* found after an adjective in substantive function an adjective suffix; but they should, for it is a simple fact, though not generally recognized.

Though the descriptive adjective is not so much inflected as formerly, it is still inflected in the comparative and the superlative and often also in the positive in substantive function and when used as a noun. The detailed description of present usage is given below for the means of indicating comparison. The means of indicating the substantive relation are described in **57**. The inflection of adjectives used as nouns is given in **58**.

COMPARISON OF ADJECTIVES

53. Degrees. There are three degrees — the positive, the comparative, the superlative. The positive is the simple form of the adjective: 'a *strong* man.' The comparative indicates that the quality is found in the person or thing described in a higher degree than in some other person or thing: 'the *stronger* of the two men.' 'This tree is *taller* than that.' The superlative is relatively the highest degree and often indicates that the quality is found in the highest degree in the person or thing described: 'Mt. Everest is the *highest* mountain in the world.' Often, however, the superlative is used in a relative sense, indicating that of the persons or things compared a certain person or thing possesses the quality in the highest degree, which need not be a very high or the highest degree in general: 'John is the *strongest* of these boys, but there are others in the school stronger than he.'

In general, comparison is characteristic of descriptive adjectives, the comparative and the superlative indicating different degrees of a quality. But a number of limiting adjectives are compared. Here the comparative and the superlative do not indicate different degrees, but point out different individuals: the *former;* the *latter;* the *first;* the *last;* the *topmost* round; the *southernmost* island of the group. In the following discussion of comparison, descriptive and limiting adjectives are, for convenience, treated together.

54. Comparison to Denote Degrees of Superiority:

1. RELATIVE COMPARISON. In contrast to the older uniform use of endings to construct the comparative and the superlative, we today with some adjectives employ the old terminational, or synthetic, form in *–er* and *–est;* with others, influenced by our fondness for analytic form, as described in *b,* p. 504, we prefer comparison with *more* and *most;* with others we fluctuate between the old terminational, or synthetic, form and the new analytic form. The wide use of the analytic form with *more* and *most* in modern English is explained not only by its expressiveness, as described in *b,* p. 504, but also by its agreeableness of sound and its ease of pronunciation in the case of long adjectives.

Monosyllabics and a large number of dissyllabics are compared by means of the comparative ending *–er* and the superlative ending *–est: quick, quicker, quickest; sturdy, sturdier, sturdiest.*

While we may thus compare with *–er* and *–est* a number of dissyllabics, especially those in *–er, –le, –y, –ly, –ow, –some,* such as *tender, bitter, clever, sober, able, noble, idle, holy, goodly, narrow, handsome, wholesome, winsome,* and some words accented upon the last syllable, such as *profound, remote,* etc., and also others that cannot be easily described, such as *pleasant, cruel, quiet,* etc., or in these same words and many others may use both the old form in *–er* and *–est* and the newer analytic form with *more* and *most,* as in *pleasanter* or *more pleasant, crueler* or *more cruel, serener* or *more serene,* in many others we usually prefer comparison by means of *more* and *most,* as in the case of *earnest, eager, proper, famous, comic, docile, fertile, hostile, certain, active, content, abject, adverse,* and participles in *–ed* and *–ing* and adjectives in *–ful* and *–ish,* as *learned, strained, charming, useful, childish,* etc.

A few monosyllabics, *like, real, right, wrong,* and *wan,* which do not naturally incline to comparison, are usually compared by *more* and *most* when they are compared, although the terminational form occasionally occurs; in the case of *like,* however, only in older English, and sometimes still in poetry and dialect, never in colloquial or literary prose: 'I'm *liker* (now usually *more like*) what I was than you to him' (Dryden, *All for Love,* I, 247, A.D. 1678). 'Father is *more like* himself today.' 'The figures of Spartacus, Montrose, Garibaldi, Hampden, and John Nicholson were *more real* to him than the people among whom he lived' (Galsworthy, *Freelands,* Ch. X). 'It is wrong to even think it; it is *more wrong* to do it.'

Monosyllabic adjectives, however, are often compared by *more* when the adjective is placed after the noun to give it more emphasis and at the same time impart descriptive (**10** I 1) force:

With classifying force 'There never was a *kínder* and *júster* man,' but with descriptive force 'There never was a man *more kind* and *júst*.'

In ordinary literary language, words of more than two syllables are seldom compared otherwise than by *more* and *most: beautiful, more beautiful, most beautiful.*

a. *Irregular Comparison:*

Positive	Comparative	Superlative
bad, ill, evil	worse, badder (in older English)	worst, baddest (in older English)
far	farther, further	farthest, furthest
fore	former	foremost, first
good, well	better	best, bettermost
late	later, latter	latest, last, lattermost
little	less, lesser	least
much, many	more, or in older English, mo or moe	most
nigh	nigher	nighest, next
old	older, elder	oldest, eldest
	after	aftermost
east, eastern	more eastern	easternmost
end		endmost
hind	hinder	hindmost, hindermost
	inner	inmost, innermost
low	lower	lowest, lowermost
north, northern	more northern	northmost, northernmost
	nether	nethermost
	outer, utter	outmost, outermost
		utmost, uttermost
rear		rearmost
south, southern	more southern	southmost, southernmost
top		topmost
under		undermost
up	upper	uppermost, upmost
west, western	more western	westernmost

In older English, *mo* or *moe* (Old English *mā*) was used instead of *more* when the reference was to number: 'Send out *moe* horses' (Shakespeare, *Macbeth*, V, III, 34).

In a few cases the variant forms indicate a differentiation of meaning or function. The usual comparative and superlative of *old* are *older, oldest;* always so in the predicate relation, but we may use *elder, eldest* in the attributive and the substantive (**57 1**) relation and *elder* as a noun, especially of relationship and rank: the *elder* brother; the *elder* Pitt; I am the *elder;* He is my *elder* in service; the *eldest* brother, etc. 'He is an *elder* in the church.'

We use *farther* and *further* with the same local and temporal meaning, but *further* has also the meanings *additional, more extended, more:* 'The cabin stands on the *farther* (or *further*) side of the brook.' 'I shall be back in three days *at the farthest*' (or *at the furthest*). But: *further* details; without *further* delay. 'After a *further* search I found her.' 'Have you anything *further* (= *more*) to say?' In adverbial function *farther* and *further* are used indiscriminately: 'You may go *farther* (or *further*) and fare worse.' There is, however, a decided tendency to employ *further* to express the idea of additional, more extended action: 'I shall be glad to discuss the matter *further* with you.'

Later and *latter* are now clearly differentiated in meaning.

The terminations in some of these forms, as *lesser, innermost,* etc., express the degree two or three times instead of once. Compare *aa* below.

aa. Older Comparison, Pleonasm, Excess of Expression. In older English, *old* was not the only adjective that might have a change of vowel in the comparative and superlative. Once this change, called mutation, was with certain words the rule. Later, the tendency toward uniformity brought the vowel of the positive into the comparative and superlative. In the early part of the sixteenth century there are still two adjectives which have mutation, but alongside of the old mutated form is the new unmutated, both forms with exactly the same meaning: *long, lenger* or *longer, lengest* or *longest; old, elder* or *older, eldest* or *oldest.* Toward the close of the century the old mutated forms of *long* disappeared, while *old* kept both forms but now with differentiated meaning, as described on page 501.

In older English, the comparative and superlative were formed by means of suffixes, not only in the case of monosyllabics but also in the case of longer adjectives, often where it is not now usual: 'Nothing *certainer*' (Shakespeare, *Much Ado About Nothing,* V, IV, 62); 'one of the *beautifullest* men in the world' (Thomas Fuller, *The Holy State and the Profane State,* V, II, 362, A.D. 1642). Long terminational comparatives and superlatives can still be heard in popular speech, which here preserves older usage: *beautifuler, beautifulest,* etc. This older usage still occurs also in emphatic and excited colloquial speech, especially in the attributive relation: 'The machine was perfect as a watch when we took her apart the other day; but when she goes together again the 15th of January, we expect her to be *pérfecter* than a watch' (Mark Twain, *Letter to Joseph T. Goodman,* Nov. 29, 1889). 'There was no *cráftier* or *cróokeder* diréctor in the habitable world' (Sinclair Lewis, *Arrowsmith,* Ch. XXX, IV). 'Joe Twichel was the *delíghtedest* old bóy I ever saw when he read the words you had written in that book'

(Mark Twain, *Letter to W. D. Howells*, Dec. 18, 1874). 'Our baby is the *bléssedest* little bundle of súnshine Heaven ever sent into this world.' 'It is the *stúpidest* nónsense!' The analytic forms with *more* and *most* began to appear in the thirteenth century in connection with participles, where they are still the most thoroughly established. This tendency to place the comparative and superlative of an adverb before a participle had already begun in Old English, where the forms *swiþor* and *swiþost* were used, which were replaced by *more* and *most* in the thirteenth century. The participles as verbal forms could take adverbs before them just as finite verbs do. The adverbs *more* and *most* were often retained when the participles were used as adjectives, since *more* and *most* as common adverbs had more concrete force than the endings *-er* and *-est*. This new usage spread to adjectives. It was and still is absolutely necessary in the case of nouns, adverbs, and prepositional phrases used as adjectives, as in 'He was *more knave* than fool' and 'I was *more in doubt* about it than any of them.' The general development in the direction of *more* and *most* was facilitated by the strong English trend toward analytic forms and was also furthered by French influence.

The new analytic forms at first gained ground only slowly, not becoming common until the sixteenth century, then gradually establishing themselves in the literary language alongside of the terminational forms, as we find them today.

The new analytic forms occur also in popular speech, but for the most part only pleonastically alongside of the usual terminational forms: a *more abler* man; the *most carelessest* man. Such double forms were once in use in the literary language: 'we will grace his heels With the *most boldest* and best hearts of Rome' (Shakespeare, *Julius Cæsar*, III, i, 120). In older literary English, we often find double comparison in *worser*, which still survives in popular speech. Double comparison still survives in the literary language in *lesser*, which replaces *less* in attributive and substantive function in certain expressions, especially with reference to concrete things: in *lesser* things; the *lesser* grammarians; the *lesser* of two evils; but *less* with more abstract reference, as in *less* degree; at a *less* depth; also to express amount, quantity, and in adverbial use, as in 'He has *less* money than I' and 'He works *less* than I.'

We no longer feel the double comparison in *near* (comparative of *nigh*, but now felt as a positive with regular comparison, *near*, *nearer*, *nearest*) and adjectives in *-most* (now confounded with *most*, but in older English with the form *mest*, which consists of the two superlative suffixes, *-m* and *-est*), as in *foremost*, *hindmost*, *inmost, utmost.* From the superlative *foremost* the comparative *former* has been formed. In *aftermost, hindermost, innermost, nethermost, outermost, uppermost, uttermost,* we have a comparative + the two superlative suffixes *–m* and *–est.*

While we today in general avoid pleonastic comparison, we do not feel such forms as *more perfect, most perfect, deader, deadest, more unique,* etc., as pleonastic, since we have in mind degrees of approach to something perfect, dead, or unique.

Somewhat similar to the pleonasm of older English was its excess of expression in using the superlative of *two,* which still survives in popular and colloquial speech, as in 'the *smallest* of the two.' Sometimes in the literary language: 'They (i.e., the two squirrels) seemed to vie with one another who should be *most bold'* (Thoreau, *Journal,* XIII, p. 189).

b. Advantages of the Analytic Forms. It should be noticed that in the old terminational form the sign of the degree is intimately associated with the stem, so that it is a mere suffix and can never be stressed. On the other hand, in the analytic form the sign of degree, *more* or *most,* is still an independent word and is often stressed. There are here two parts, one indicating the degree, the other the meaning. We here, as in **6** A *d* (1), are fond of using the analytic form, since by means of it we can better shade our thought. We stress the adjective when we desire to emphasize the meaning, but stress the *more* or *most* when we desire to emphasize the idea of degree: 'She is more béautiful than her sister,' but 'She is indeed béautiful, but her sister is still móre beautiful.' 'Of the sisters Mary is the most béautiful and Jane the most belóved,' but 'The sisters are all béautiful, but Mary is by far the móst beautiful.'

c. Different Form for Different Function. The different degrees have different forms when used substantively (**57** 1), the form with *one* being required in the positive, but not always necessary in the comparative and superlative, as explained more at length in **57** 1 (next to last par.): 'This cord is *strong'* (predicate adjective) or *a strong one* (used substantively). 'This cord is *stronger'* (predicate adjective), or in substantive use *the stronger* or *the stronger one,* but always *a stronger one.* 'This cord is *strongest* (predicate adjective) at this point,' but in substantive use 'This cord is *the strongest,'* or *the strongest one.* 'The lake is *deepest* (predicate adjective) at this point,' but in substantive use 'Of these lakes this one is *the deepest,'* or 'This lake is *the deepest one,'* or simply *the deepest.*

In the predicate relation, instead of the adjective superlative, the adverbial accusative (**16** 4 *a*) of the noun made from the

adjective superlative preceded by the definite article is sometimes used here: 'I doubt whether the actions of which we are
the very proudest will not surprise us, when we trace them, as we
shall one day, to their source' (Thackeray, *Pendennis*, Ch. XXXI),
instead of *indeed proudest.* 'The rooks settle where the trees are
the finest' (Lytton, *My Novel*, I, Ch. V), instead of *finest.* 'Of
these specimens my friend is naturally *the móst proud*' (J. Conrad,
A Set of Six), instead of *móst proud.* 'It was, perhaps, at this time
that Mrs. Henry and I were *the móst uneasy*' (R. L. Stevenson),
instead of *móst uneasy.* This superlative is always used when
it is modified by a restrictive relative clause: 'On that day she
looked *the happiest* that I had ever seen her,' or often with suppressed relative pronoun: 'Louise was sitting in a deep chair,
looking *the happiest* [that] I had ever seen her' (Mary Roberts
Rinehart, *The Circular Staircase*, Ch. XXXIV). 'On that day
she looked *the most beautiful* that I had ever seen her.' As
described in **16 5 *a bb*,** this adverbial accusative is sometimes
used with verbs as the superlative of the adverb, hence it is
used also here in the predicate, just as adverbs in general are
often used in the predicate (**7 F**).

In the predicate instead of the simple superlative without *the*
or the adverbial accusative of the superlative with *the*, we may
also use an adverbial phrase with *at* and the superlative modified
by a possessive adjective: 'The steps are *at their steepest* (or
steepest, or *the steepest*) just here' (F. M. Peard, *Madame's Grand-
daughter*, p. 74). 'She knew that she looked *at her best* in this
attire' (C. Garvice, *Staunch as a Woman*, p. 83). Similarly, as
objective predicate: 'She first saw the hill *at its gayest* when that
brief, brilliant hour before autumn bedecked Cosdon' (Phillpotts,
The Beacon, I, Ch. VI). 'In "Doctor Dick" we have the author
at his most useful' (*Literary World*, April 19, 1895, p. 362).

d. Two Qualities of One Person or Thing Compared. In comparing two qualities of one person or thing we usually employ
more: 'She is *more proud* than *vain.*' 'He is *more shy* than *unsocial.*' However, in the case of a few monosyllabics, *long, wide,
thick, high*, we still regularly employ the old simple comparative,
usually with full clause form in the subordinate clause: 'The
wall was in some places *thicker than it was high.*'

e. Comparative of Gradation. To indicate that the quality
increases or decreases at a fairly even rate we place *ever* before
the comparative, or we repeat it: 'The road got *ever worse* (or
worse and worse) until there was none at all.'

f. Comparison of Other Parts of Speech Used as Adjectives. Here
we usually employ *more* and *most:* 'John is *more in debt* than I am.'

'She is *more mother* than wife.' 'Though the youngest among them, she was *more woman* than they.' Where we feel a comparative more as a pronoun than as an adjective we say: 'Charles was *more of a gentleman* than a king, and *more of a wit* than a gentleman.' 'Smith is *more of a teacher* than his brother.'

g. Comparative of Limiting Adjectives Not Used in Predicate. The comparative of limiting adjectives, *inner, outer, former, latter,* etc., cannot be used as a predicate followed by *than,* since, according to the second paragraph of **53,** limiting adjectives do not indicate degrees, but merely point out individuals. The comparative *older* can, as a descriptive adjective, be used as a predicate; but *elder* cannot be so used, for it is a limiting adjective: 'He is *older* (not *elder*) than I,' but 'This is the *elder* brother.'

h. Comparison of Compounds. We compare the first element of a compound where this is possible, usually employing the terminational form, but if the first element is a word that does not admit of this form we use *more* or *most:* 'the *biggest-chested* and *longest-armed* man I ever saw,' but 'This is the most *up-to-date* book I know.' Even if the first element admits of the terminational form, we employ *more* or *most* if the first element has fused with the other component so closely that it is not felt as a separate element with a separate function: *well-*known; *better-*known; but the *more well-to-do* tradesmen.

Of course, we compare the last component if it contains the element capable of comparison, usually employing the form we should use if it were an independent word: *bloodthirstier, bloodthirstiest; praiseworthiest,* or *most praiseworthy,* etc.

2. ABSOLUTE COMPARISON:

a. Absolute Superlative. In all the preceding examples the degrees express superiority in a relative sense, some person or thing excelling all the members of a definite group in the possession of a certain quality, while in fact the higher or highest degree here may be a comparatively low degree: 'John is *the taller* of the two, *the tallest* of them all, but he is notwithstanding quite small.' We may in the case of the superlative, quite commonly, express superiority in an absolute sense, indicating a very high degree in and of itself, not necessarily, however, the very highest.

In lively style, we here often place unstressed *most* before the stressed positive of the adjective or participle: (relative superlative) 'It is the *móst lovely* flower in the garden,' but in an absolute sense: 'He has *the most béautiful* of gardens.' 'Everything about the place tells of *the most dáinty* order, *the most éxquisite* cleanliness' (Mrs. Gaskell, *Life of Charlotte Brontë,* Ch. I). 'It was *a most magníficent* exhibition of courage.' 'We shall soon see George

and *his most béautiful* wife.' '*Most lóvely* flowers everywhere greet
the eye and *most frágrant* perfumes fill the air.' We can distinguish
only by the stress '*Most réputable* (absolute superlative) writers
have now abandoned this claim' from '*Móst* (= the great majority
of) *reputable* writers have abandoned this claim.'

Instead of the usual absolute superlative with *most*, we sometimes in the case of adjectives which admit of the terminational
form employ the simple superlative, often drawling it out and
stressing it: 'Oh, he made *the rú–dest* remark!' 'The letter did
not meet with *the wármest* reception.' 'I'm in *the bést* of health.'
'She is in *the bést* of company.' 'At all times her dress was of
the póorest.' 'Humphrey's ideas of time were always of *the váguest*
order' (Florence Montgomery, *Misunderstood*, Ch. III). 'The
letter was written in *the kíndest* terms.'   Besides such expressions
we find this form sometimes, especially in our own time, when the
superlative is modified by a limiting adjective, *my, any, every,
each, no, some, certain*, etc., or, on the other hand, sometimes when
it is entirely unmodified, especially in the case of abstract and
plural nouns: '*my déarest* darling'; '*any pláinest* man who reads
this' (Trollope, *Framley Parsonage*, Ch. XIV); 'so completely
did it fulfil *every fáintest* hope'; 'there is *no smállest* doubt.' 'It
was perhaps on *some dárkest, múddiest* afternoon of a London
February' (*Times Literary Supplement*, June 9, 1918). 'A stronger
lens reveals to you *certain tíniest* hairlets, which make vortices
for these victims' (George Eliot, *Middlemarch*, I, Ch. VI). 'Michael and Guy left Oxford in the mellow time of an afternoon in
éarliest August' (Compton Mackenzie, *Sinister Street*, p. 760).
'I owed her *déepest* gratitude' (Elinor Glyn, *Reflections of Am-
brosine*, III, Ch. V). 'Our friendship ripened into *clósest* intimacy.'
'From *éarliest* times.'

The most common way to express the absolute superlative is to
place before the positive of the adjective a simple adverb, such as
very, exceedingly, highly, absolutely, etc., or in colloquial speech
awfully, dreadfully, terribly, beastly, etc., sometimes without the
suffix *–ly*, as in the case of *awful*, even regularly so in the case of
real (**16** 4; widely used in America), *mighty, jolly* (British colloquial for *very*), *devilish, damned, bloody* (British), *bally* (British),
etc.: *very cold* weather; an *exceedingly intricate* problem; a *highly
polished* society. 'I am *awfully* (sometimes *awful*) glad,' but after
a verb: 'I dread *awfully* (not *awful*) to go.' 'It's *real cold*.' 'I'm
jolly glad anyhow.' 'It's *damned hot*.' Also *only too, simply too,
just too*, and *just* are so used: 'I shall be *ónly tóo glád* if you accept
my invitation.' 'It's *símply tóo bád* of him!' 'It's *júst tóo áwful!*'
'It's *júst spléndid!*' In older English, *pure* was used with the

meaning of *absolutely:* 'It is *pure* easy to follow god and serue hym in tyme of tranquylite' (Caxton, *Chast. Goddes Chyld*, 89, A.D. 1491). This usage is preserved in certain American dialects: 'Dey hides is *pure tough*' (Julia Peterkin, *Scarlet Sister Mary*). Compare **16** 2 *a*.

b. Absolute Comparative. The absolute comparative is not as common as the absolute superlative: the *lower* classes; the *higher* classes; *higher* education; a *better*-class café; the *more complex* problems of life; 'the mist, like a fleecy coverlet, hiding every *harsher* outline' (H. Sutcliffe, *Pam the Fiddler*, Ch. I).

We usually place here before the positive of the adjective a simple adverb, such as *tolerably, fairly, rather,* etc.: a *tolerably* (or *fairly*, or *rather*) long walk; *somewhat* talkative, etc.

55. Comparison to Denote Degrees of Inferiority. Here we uniformly employ *less* and *least: wise, less wise, least wise.*

INFLECTION AND USE OF LIMITING ADJECTIVES

56. Attributive limiting adjectives are inflected in the positive only in the case of: *this, these; that, those.* These forms are also used substantively. In substantive function *that, those* are now often replaced by *the one, the ones,* comparatively recent formations but now widely used. Many limiting adjectives, such as *many, several, two, three,* etc., have no plural form, but contain the plural idea in their meaning.

A number of limiting adjectives have a comparative and a superlative form, as explained in **53** (2nd par.).

A. Use of Demonstrative Adjectives. Demonstrative limiting adjectives point out persons or things either by gesture, or by the situation, or by an accompanying description.

By gesture: '*Thése* flowers bloom longer than *thóse*,' or in popular speech where there is a great fondness for excess of expression: '*These hére* flowers bloom longer'n *those thére*' (or *them thére*). '*Thóse* (in popular speech often *thém*, or *them thére*) flowers are the finest.' In older literary English, there is here the same fondness for excess of expression as found in current colloquial speech, only in different form, usually with a redundant *same* after the demonstrative: 'Call that *same* Isabel here once again' (Shakespeare, *Measure for Measure*, V, I, 270). In Middle English also *here* and *there* were used redundantly after a demonstrative, as described above for popular speech, where older literary usage survives. Where the persons referred to are supposed to be known and there is no need of identification, the demonstratives are often employed unaccompanied by a gesture and marked by a peculiar tone of voice expressing praise or censure, pleasure or displeasure: 'I am coming soon to see *that* dear little grandson.' 'I hate *that* Johnson boy.' '*These* inexperienced maids are always breaking dishes.' 'I was attacked by one of *those* huge police dogs.' These demonstratives that are charged with feeling have become intimately associated with the lively double genitive (**10** II 1 *b*): '*this* broad land *of ours*,' '*that* kind wife *of yours*.' 'I want you to keep *that* old dog *of yours* at home.'

Where the persons and things referred to are not supposed to be known, demonstratives unaccompanied by a gesture point them out in a twofold way. They either have anaphoric force, i.e., point backward to some person or thing that precedes, as in 'In this old castle there lived once a king who had an only child, a daughter. *The* (or *this*) daughter was very beautiful.' Or they have determinative force, i.e., they point forward to a following remark which defines or describes some person or thing. The determinative is often used substantively (**57** 1), i.e., as a pronoun, preceded by an antecedent or followed by a limiting genitive, prepositional phrase, adverb, or relative or participial clause: 'thís hat and thát (not *the one*) of my brother's'; 'thís book and thát one (or now also quite commonly *the óne*) upon the table in the next room'; 'thése books and thóse (or *the ónes*) upon the table in the next room,' 'thís window and thát one (or *the óne*) upstairs'; 'thése windows and thóse (or *the ónes*) upstairs'; 'thése books and thóse (or *the ónes*) lying, or piled up (or which are lying, or which are piled up) upon the table in the next room'; 'thése books and thóse (or *the ónes*) we bought yesterday.' Instead of thát one's Milton in *Paradise Lost*, V, 808, employs whóse, a survival of the older determinative force of *who*: 'Vengeance is his or whóse he sole appoints.'

The determinative is often used substantively (**57** 1), i.e., as a pronoun, followed by a limiting noun or pronoun and also by a relative clause which limits it as restricted by its limiting noun or pronoun: 'I like thóse of your friends whom I have met.' There is here a double restriction. Compare **23** II 6.

Also a number of indefinites are used as determinatives, especially *one, ones, any,* etc.: 'When you buy a new pen, get *one* with a sharper point' (or '*one* that has a sharper point'). 'When you buy new pens, get *ones* with a sharper point' (or '*ones* that have a sharper point'). 'You may have *any* of the books that you may select.' Compare first paragraph, p. 510.

Of these forms *that* and *those* are either demonstratives proper or determinatives; *the one, the ones, one, ones* are only determinatives.

In loose colloquial speech there is a qualitative determinative, *like* = *that kind:* 'pies *like* mother used to make.' 'I was going to bring some port wine *like* we drink at school in our crowd there' (Tarkington, *The Magnificent Ambersons*, Ch. III). 'When a young gentleman marries, he can't expect to live in a house *like* he was brought up in' (A. Marshall, *Anthony Dare*, Ch. II). Though common, this *like* is confined to the one case that a relative clause with suppressed relative pronoun follows. In the literary language we use here *such* followed by a relative clause introduced by the relative pronoun *as*, or we employ *like that* followed by a relative clause, usually with suppressed relative pronoun: 'pies *such as mother used to make*' (or *like those mother used to make*). Elsewhere we can use either *such as that* or *like that* as a qualitative determinative: 'a house *such as that* of my father's' (or '*like that* of my father's'); 'books *such as those* upon the table' (or '*like those* upon the table'). Where the reference is indefinite, *one, ones* are often used as a qualitative determinative instead of *such*. For examples see next to last paragraph, p. 509, and **57** 5 *b* (3rd par.). In older English, *such* often loses the idea of quality entirely and has the force of *this, that, these, those.* This old usage still lingers where there is a somewhat indefinite reference to a group of persons or things: 'It seems to have cooled the ardor of *such of the Bishops as* (or *those of the Bishops who*) at first tended to favor Sinn Fein as a means of smashing the Irish party' (*London Times, Educational Supplement*, Nov. 18, 1918). There is a tendency to differentiate *those* and *such* here by employing *such* where we feel the reference as more indefinite. Compare Parts of Speech **7** 7 *b* (last par.).

The determinative is often used as an adherent (**10** I) adjective: *the* hat of my brother; *the* book upon the table; *the* window upstairs; *the* boys playing in the street; *those* people who never forget an insult; *such* books as I have. In the singular, *a* is often used as a qualitative determinative instead of *such:* 'We need *a* man that we can trust.'

Also the pronouns *he, they*, or now more commonly *those*, are used as determinatives, pointing to a following relative clause introduced by *who* (or in older English also *that*). For further particulars and examples see **23** II 5 (2nd par. of Examples). *He* and *she* also point to a following genitive of characteristic or a prepositional phrase: '*she* of (or with) the auburn hair.'

B. **Use of the Definite Article.** The definite article *the* is the weakened form of an old demonstrative now represented by *that*, and true to its origin points to a definite person or thing. As a demonstrative it has a twofold function: anaphoric *the*, pointing backward to a person or thing already mentioned, as in 'There lived once in this old castle a powerful king. *The* king had a lovely daughter'; determinative *the*, pointing to a definite person or thing, described usually by a following genitive, adverb, prepositional phrase, or relative clause: *the* hat of my brother; *the* tree yonder; *the* hat on the table; *the* hat which I hold in my hand. Of course, a person or thing which is single in kind needs no description: *the* king; *the* queen.

In oldest English, the definite article was little used with nouns, not even with common class nouns. All things living and lifeless were conceived of as individuals, and were used without the article, just as names of persons had no article. In set expressions there are many survivals of this old usage: 'He is going *to bed, to school, to ruin, on foot, by water,*' etc. Very early, however, the old idea of individuality became much restricted. Many lifeless things were divided into classes, as trees, flowers, stones, rivers, etc. There are usually many individuals in a class; hence in order to point to a definite individual within a class, the definite article was placed before the noun, which was followed by a descriptive genitive, etc., as illustrated above: *the* hat of my brother; *the* hat upon the table. Of course, where a person or thing is single in kind within any definite group, circle, commonwealth, etc., it needs no description: *the* king; *the* queen; *the* mayor; *the* captain; *the* president; *the* army; *the* navy; *the* bridge (where there is only one in the neighborhood); *the* school; *the* post office, etc. Outside of such cases of evident uniqueness we now stress the *the* to mark a person or thing as unique: 'He is *thé* pianist of the day.' 'That is *thé* hotel of the city.'

The names of individuals within a family or a class at school have remained without the article. We still say: John, Mary, etc. This is the old style of individualization. The definite article before a noun also individualizes, but it is felt as individualization within a class. It is the new style of individualization. The idea of a personal, inner individuality is what characterizes the old style of individualization: God, man, woman, and persons in general: Gladstone, Lincoln, John, Mary. By vivid personification we also say gold, silver, copper, honesty, chastity, beauty, antiquity, death, spring, winter, diphtheria, rheumatism, consumption, etc., feeling that they are things single in kind: '*Honesty* is the best policy.' But when we think of the concrete manifestation of honesty we feel these acts as members of a class and hence employ the new style of individualization. '*The honesty* of these boys ought to be rewarded.' On the other hand, the new style of individualization often borders closely on that of the old:

the King; *the* Queen; *the* Duke; *the* Savior, etc. Germans employ the new style for the members of the family: *the* John; *the* Mary, etc., i.e., *the* John, *the* Mary of their circle, individualizations within a class, a circle. In recent English, there is a slight tendency in this direction: '*the* old man' or '*the* governor' (= Father); '*the* dad' (Galsworthy, *In Chancery*, p. 57); '*the* poor old dad!' (*id.*, *The Man of Property*, p. 41); '*the* mother' (De Morgan, *The Old Madhouse*, Ch. XXVII); 'the electrical surprise and gratitude and exaltation of *the* wife and the children' (Mark Twain, *Letter to Oliver Wendell Holmes*, Dec., 1885); '*the* wife' (Hutchinson, *If Winter Comes*, p. 321), etc.

In Old English, it was the rule to say '*the* little John,' an individualization within a class, but in colloquial speech we now usually say 'little John' after the analogy of 'John.' This usage is very common where there is the warmth of interest or personal feeling in the tone: '*Poor Tom* is in trouble again.' '*Good Saint Francis* loved every created thing.' In more formal and dignified literary language, however, the definite article is still the more natural expression: '*the* late Mr. Byron Jones'; '*the* elder Pliny.' Similarly, older '*the* king Arthur' has for the most part become 'King Arthur,' but older usage still not infrequently occurs: 'Tell *the Countess Shulski* I wish to speak to her' (Elinor Glyn, *The Reason Why*, Ch. I, 8). Of course, the article is usually employed when the title is followed by a prepositional phrase designating a place, as the title is felt as an individualization within a class: '*the* Earl of Derby,' but 'Lord Derby' as the words are felt as a name. Wherever the idea of individuality or singleness in kind is strong, we today prefer the form without the article: *January, heaven, hell*, etc. But the development here is quite uneven: *God*, but *the Lord, the devil; Parliament, Congress*, but often *the Congress*, especially in the language of congressmen, senators, etc.; *dropsy*, but *the measles* or simple *measles; Mars* (planet), but *the moon, the earth, the Hudson, the Cape of Good Hope; Genesis*, but *the Bible*.

The article is dropped in a numeration of things or particulars, for here the idea of unit, sovereign individuality, separate item, something single in kind, overshadows all other conceptions: 'He studied the history of early dramatic efforts in *church, university, school, court*.' Similarly, where the words come in pairs: 'He is tired *body* and *soul*.' 'He works *day* and *night*.' 'He is happy in *shop* and *home*.'

On the other hand, the absence of the definite article is today often felt as a contrast to its presence and hence indicates an indefinite portion, amount, or extent: '*the* dust on the veranda,' but in an indefinite sense 'In these dry days we see *dust* every-

where.' The absence of the definite article often suggests the
general conception of class or kind with only a general character-
ization, while the definite article points to something definite,
a definite variety or a definite individual: 'I write with *black*
ink,' but '*the* black ink that this firm makes.' 'She suffers much
from *headache*,' but '*The* headache that she had yesterday has
rendered her unfit for her duties.'

A noun is often without an article in the predicate when the
noun does not designate a definite individual but something abstract, such as an estate, rank, relationship, calling, or capacity
of any kind: 'This thesis — for *thesis* and nothing more it at
present is — would no doubt make the basis of a very keen
discussion in any gathering of naval men.' 'He turned *traitor*.'
'He fell *heir* to a large estate.' 'Williams was *son* of an officer
in the service of the East India Company.' 'Of this society Mr.
Smith is now *president*.' 'Mr. Boyd is *Irishman* first, *critic* next.'
'German tribes deposed the last Roman emperor and proclaimed
their leader Odoaker *king* (objective predicate) of Rome.' Similarly, in abridged clauses: '*Child* though he was, consciousness
of self had come to him.' Predicate appositive: 'In this eventful
year Tennyson succeeded Wordsworth as *poet laureate*.'

Of course, a noun is also elsewhere without the article when
the noun does not denote a definite individual but only an abstract
or general idea: 'He is doing all that *mortal man* can do.' 'Fully
a century has passed since *mason's* hand has touched it.' 'If
ever *poet* were a master of phrasing, he (Tennyson) was so.'
This usage is very old and hence still a favorite in poetry and choice
prose, but the indefiniteness usually present here leads to the
use of the indefinite article in plain prose.

a. DEFINITE ARTICLE WITH GENERALIZING FORCE. The definite article usually has individualizing force; but when there is no
reference to a definite individual, it assumes generalizing force,
i.e., the representative idea becomes more prominent than the
conception of a sharp individualization, one individual representing
a whole class: '*The* rat is larger than *the* mouse,' or also '*A* rat
is larger than *a* mouse.' '*The* child is father of *the* man.' 'He is a
lover of *the* beautiful.' The plural is also used where the plural
idea is prominent: '*The* English are a vigorous people.' In a few
common words indicating individuals with highly developed personality the old style of individualization without the article is
used here: '*Man* is mortal.' '*Woman* is frail.' Also the plural
without the article can be used here, as an articleless plural lacks
definiteness and hence can be used with general force: '*Owls*
cannot see well in the daytime.'

b. USE OF THE DEFINITE ARTICLE IN DIRECT ADDRESS. Today, proper names or common class nouns used in direct address are without the article: '*John*, come here.' '*John*, *dear brother*, I want you to help me.' '*Smith*, *old boy*, truest of friends, I come again to you for counsel.' '*Little boy*, what do you want?' In older English, both common and proper nouns were often used with the definite article, since they were felt as individualizations of the new style. This older usage has come down almost to our own day: '*The last* of the Romans, fare thee well!' (Shakespeare, *Julius Cæsar*, V, III, 99). 'What ho! *The Captain* of the Guard! Give the offender fitting ward' (Scott, *Lady of the Lake*, V, 26).

c. The definite article *the* is sometimes still for archaic effect written *ye*, the *y* representing older thorn (þ), hence pronounced *th:* '*ye* old town.'

C. **Form and Use of the Indefinite Article.** The indefinite article *a* or *an*, the reduced form of the numeral *one*, has preserved the *n* of the original word only before a vowel sound: *a* boat; *a* house; *a* union (yūnyən); not *a* one (wun), but *an* apple; *an* heir (with silent *h*).

There is fluctuation of usage before an initial *h* where the syllable is unaccented. In the literary language of England it has long been usual to place *an* here before the *h:* *an* histórical character; *an* hotél, etc. At the present time, however, this usage is not universal in England. The British scholar H. W. Fowler in his *Modern English Usage* even calls it pedantic. In America it is usual to employ *a* here, although some follow the prevailing British usage. The difference of usage here rests upon an older difference of pronunciation. In America, Ireland, Scotland, and the extreme northern part of England initial *h* has been preserved. In the English dialects it has for the most part been lost, but in standard English under the influence of the written language and Scotch and Irish usage it has been restored. For a long time, however, it was pronounced weakly or not at all in unaccented syllables, which gave rise to the spelling *an* in '*an* histórical character,' '*an* hotél,' etc. Older spelling, such as '*an* hundred crowns' (Shakespeare, *Taming of the Shrew*, V, II, 128), '*an* hill' (*Matthew*, V, 14), shows that in early Modern English initial *h* was not always pronounced in England even in accented syllables.

The indefinite article *a*, true to its origin, singles out one object, action, or quality from among a number. It designates an individual in different ways:

a. It points to an individual person or thing without fixing its identity: 'We met *an* old man on our way here.' 'There is *a* book lying on the table.'

b. In its more indefinite sense *a* is equal to *any,* designating no individual in particular: 'There isn't *a* man in our community in whom I have more confidence.'

c. Like *the* it often has generalizing force. See B *a,* p. 513.

d. It is used as a determinative with the force of *such:* 'It was *a* sight that would make angels rejoice.' 'He is *a* man that must be treated kindly.'

e. Often with its original meaning: '*a* foot long.' 'Wait *a* minute.'

f. It sometimes represents older *on,* hence is the reduced form of a preposition. This *a* occurs in adverbial expressions denoting repetition: 'He goes to the city several times *a* year.' Compare **16** 4 *a* (last par.).

g. It can stand before a proper name in only two cases: (1) to designate one member of a family: 'There isn't now *a* single Jones in our village, although it once seemed full of them'; (2) to convert a proper name into a common class noun: 'He is *a* regular Hercules.'

D. Use of Intensifying 'Myself,' 'Himself,' etc. In Old English, the simple limiting adjective *self* was used appositively after nouns or pronouns to make them more emphatic; in older periods with either weak or strong inflection: 'He *selfa* (weak nominative) hit segþ,' '*He himself* says it.' The dative of a personal pronoun was often in Old English placed between the governing noun or pronoun and *self:* 'He *him* (dative) *selfa* (nominative) hit segþ,' '*He himsélf* says it,' literally, 'He says it *himself, on his own account.*' The dative of interest (**12** 1 B *b*) was inserted here to call especial attention to the person involved in the act by personal interests. We now often employ a modern dative with *for* instead of the old simple dative: 'Few among our statesmen have seen anything of colonial life and colonial institutions *for themselves*' (*London Times*), instead of *themselves.* 'She bade him, if he doubted her, go see *for himself*' (Kingsley, *Westward Ho!*).

In older inflected English, in such a sentence as 'He *him* (dative) *selfa* (nominative) hit segþ,' the *self* used in connection with the simple dative long continued to take the case required by the construction, i.e., was nominative, dative, or accusative according to the case of the noun or pronoun with which it stood in apposition, but it was sometimes attracted into the dative, the case of the *him, her,* or *them* that stood before it, both words thus standing in the dative, indicating that they were felt as one, as a compound. We now regularly construe the two forms as a compound, an appositive to the noun or pronoun to which it refers. As, however, the original grammatical relations here are no longer understood there have arisen two groups of compounds; on the one hand, the group just described, the old simple dative group *himself, herself, themselves* (until about A.D. 1550 *them selfe*), and after the analogy of these also *itself;* on the other hand, a group of nine words of quite different formation replacing the older type, *myself, ourself* (after the plural of majesty *we* and editorial *we = myself), ourselves, thyself, yourself, yourselves,* in the seventeenth and eighteenth centuries also *itsself* (now replaced by *itself*), in dialect also *hisself, theirselves,* all nine after the analogy of *herself,* in which *her,* although originally a dative, was in the thirteenth century falsely construed as a possessive adjective and *self* construed as a noun. Although these two groups are of different form, they both perform the same function, serving as intensifying adjectives. All eleven compounds now have the same function as the old simple adjective *self,* serving as appositives to the noun or pronoun to which they refer: 'I *myself* think so,' or 'I think so *myself.*' 'We think we have hinted elsewhere that Mr. Benjamin Allen had a way of becoming sentimental after brandy. The case is not a peculiar one as we *ourself* can testify' (Dickens, *Pickwick,* Ch. XXXVIII). 'We *ourselves* think so,' or 'We think so *ourselves.*' 'I gave it to John *himself.*' 'I saw John *himself* do it.' For sake of emphasis in lively style the intensifying adjective often stands at the beginning of the sentence: '*Himself* an artist in rhetoric, he (Thoreau) confounds thought with style when he attempts to speak of the latter' (James R. Lowell, *Literary Essays,* I, p. 374). It often also stands within the sentence before the word to which it refers where there is a contrast to what precedes: 'He had always taken it for granted, since he was eighteen, that she would marry him and from that age *herself* she had tacitly accepted the position of his fiancée' (Sir Harry Johnston, *The Man Who Did the Right Thing,* Ch. IV, p. 48).

As the intensifying adjective often emphasizes a personal pronoun and is thus closely associated with it, it has gradually acquired the function of the personal pronoun in addition to its own, so that since the eleventh century the personal pronoun often in certain categories drops out as a useless form and the intensifying adjective becomes an emphatic personal pronoun, especially in the subject relation at the end of the sentence introducing an abridged subordinate clause with the finite verb omitted: 'My boy played with several others who were of about the same age as *himself*' (= *he himself was*). 'Did you ever know a woman pardon another for being handsomer than *herself?*' (= *she herself was*). Quite often also at the end of a full independent proposition for especial emphasis: 'The poor boy of whom I have just related

was *myself* ' (= *I myself*). Frequently also at the beginning of a
full independent proposition, provided the logical subject is expressed in a preceding proposition: 'With a sudden rough movement she all but snatched the child out of the other's arms and
herself saw to Sheila's comfort' (W. J. Locke, *The Glory of Clementina*, Ch. XIX). In the nominative absolute construction: 'But
he did want very much to meet Roy Carrington, whose novel
"Gentlemen, The King" everybody had read, *himself* included'
(A. Marshall, *Anthony Dare*, Ch. III). As predicate: 'You are not
yourself today.' After *like* or a preposition: 'I am a stranger
here *like yourself.*' 'It is satisfactory to them, if not *to us*' (or
ourselves). 'You can't do that *by yourself.*' As object of a verb:
'Most people do not realize how closely the mute creatures of
God resemble *ourselves* in their pains and griefs.' In older English,
it was common where it cannot now be used — namely, at the
beginning of a sentence instead of a personal pronoun, pointing
back to some person already mentioned: 'But *him selfe* (now
simple *he*) was not satisfied therwith' (Bradford, *History of
Plymouth Plantation*, p. 363, A.D. 1630–1648). '*Himself* (now
simple *he*) and Montmorin offered their resignation' (Thomas
Jefferson, *Autobiography*, p. 138). This elliptical construction is
now less common than earlier in the period and grammarians often
oppose it, but it is old and still widely used. A feeling of modesty
often suggests its use instead of the pompous *I myself, me myself*:
'General Lee surrendered the Army of Northern Virginia this
afternoon on terms proposed by *myself*' (U. S. Grant, *Telegram
to E. M. Stanton*, April 9, 1865). The censure of the grammarians
seems justified where the intensifying adjective is used instead of
an ordinary personal pronoun which, though stressed, is not important enough to take after it an intensifying adjective: 'There's
only *myself* and Louisa here' (Hugh Walpole, *The Duchess of
Wrexe*, Ch. XIII), instead of 'There are only Louisa and *I* here.'
'A few moments later *Tommy and herself* (instead of *she and
Tommy*) were speeding westward in a taxicab' (W. J. Locke,
The Glory of Clementina, Ch. XXIII). As in older English, the
intensifying adjective is still in popular Irish English used at the
beginning of a sentence instead of a personal pronoun, pointing
backward to some person already mentioned: 'MILDRED. Dear
me, what's the matter with Jack? — BRIDGET. *Himself* (= *he*)
is vexed about something' (Lennox Robinson, *Harvest*, Act II).
In commercial language simple *self* is often used instead of *myself:*
'Pay *self* or order Ten Pounds' (check). Sometimes also in colloquial speech: 'As both *self* and wife were fond of seeing life, we
decided,' etc. (Sir John Astley, *Fifty Years of My Life*, II, 31) .

As described in **11** 2 *c*, we sometimes still use the objective form of the personal pronouns *me*, *him*, etc., as reflexive pronouns. This was normal usage in Old English and long remained so. To distinguish reflexive from personal pronouns and thus emphasize the reflexive idea, intensifying *self* was in Old English often added to the personal pronoun. These old intensive forms have become the modern normal reflexive pronouns *himself*, *herself*, *itself*, *themselves* (until about A.D. 1550 *them selfe*). This usage, once found with all the reflexives, is now confined to these four words. As early as the thirteenth century *herself*, which originally consisted of *her*, the objective form of the personal pronoun *she*, and intensifying *self*, was sometimes construed as being the possessive adjective *her* and the noun *self*. This conception affected other reflexive pronouns, so that we now employ several reflexives of this type: *myself*, *thyself*, *ourself* (after the plural of majesty and editorial *we* = *myself*), *ourselves*, *yourselves*, instead of *meself*, *theeself*, *usself*, *usselves*, *youselves*. In the seventeenth and eighteenth centuries *its self* was in limited use, but is now replaced by *itself*. In popular speech *hisself*, *theirselves* are common forms.

The simple form *self* survives as a noun made from the old adjective *self*: 'a truth which purifies from *self*'; 'love of *self*.' 'The next morning all the guests at the hotel except *us* (or *ourselves*, or *our two selves*) went back.' 'Have you hurt your little *self?*' 'Baby fell and hurt its dear little *self*.' 'I hope you are your old *self* again.' 'You must not blame anybody but your own *self*.' 'A man's better *self* should lead him.' 'Sometimes one must think of one's own *self*.' The compound forms are sometimes needlessly used here instead of the simple form: '*Himself* is the only consideration with himself' (Meredith, *The Egoist*, 231), instead of '*Self* is the only consideration with him.'

THE SUBSTANTIVE FUNCTION OF ADJECTIVES

57 1. **Use of the Suffix 'One.'** The adjective is used substantively when it stands alone like a substantive. The adjective used substantively, however, differs from a real substantive in that it is not used independently, but always refers to a preceding or following noun. The adjective used substantively sometimes has after it the suffix *one* (by some improperly called 'prop-word') to indicate that it refers to a preceding or following noun; sometimes it has no formal sign to indicate such a relation, the context alone suggesting it.

Pointing backward: 'a white sheep and a *black one*'; 'white sheep and *black ones*'; 'this book and *that one* lying upon the table.'

'Here are two fine pencils. You may have *either*' (or *either one*).
'Here are two fine pencils. You may have *both*.' 'Of these apples
you may select any *two*.'

Pointing forward: '*each* (or *each one*) of the books which I hold
in my hand'; 'to *every* (now *each*) of the ministers one (heifer)
and the rest to the poor' (Winthrop, *Journal*, July, 1634); 'prom-
issing to them and *évery* (now *évery óne*) of them rewards' (Slingsby,
Diary, 420, A.D. 1658); '*évery óne* (or in older English, simple
évery) of the books upon the table'; '*either* (or *either one*) of
these two books'; '*neither* (or *neither one*) of these two books';
'*either* (*either one*, or more accurately *any one*) of these three books';
'*either* (*either one*, or much more commonly *any one*) of these twelve
books'; '*none* of the books,' with singular or plural meaning, more
commonly the latter, while with reference to one we usually say
'*not one* of the books'; '*some* of the boys' with plural meaning,
but 'I don't know *whích óne* of them, but *sóme óne* of them did it.'
'I don't know *which* of the hats is mine.'

In American English and also the English of England, it is
common to say: 'All three boys have a good record at school, but
I do not know *which one's* is the best.' 'Here are the books.
Which one is (or *which ones are*) yours?' 'Here are some new
books. You may have *whichever one* (or *whichever ones*) you
select.' '*Which* (or *which one*) of these books is yours?' '*Which*
of these books are yours?' But, especially in American English,
where the reference becomes more general or indefinite, there is a
strong tendency both in colloquial speech and the literary language to employ *what one*(*s*) or *whatever one*(*s*) in referring backward: 'Our teacher is a stickler for dates but in examinations we
never know *what ones* he will spring on us.' 'About the middle
of the eighteenth century it (i.e., the French Academy) altered
the spelling of five thousand words. Perhaps it would be juster
to say that it indicated, in the case of a number of these, *what one*
should be adopted of several forms which were then in use' (Louns-
bury, *English Spelling*, Ch. I, 51). 'I have made some bad blunders in my life, and I may yet make still worse ones; but I have
the consolation that *whatever ones* I shall make I shall have the
sympathy of my wife.'

In general, the substantive relation is usually indicated by
the accompanying *one*, but *all*, *many*, *few*, *enough*, *both*, and the
cardinals *two*, *three*, etc., never take *one*. The use of *one* here is a
modern innovation that has not yet become established with all
adjectives. In older English, the adjective was inflected, so that
the ending of the adjective in the substantive use was sufficient
to indicate that the adjective had a relation to a preceding or

following noun. In Middle English, the inflection of the adjective was so reduced that it frequently had no ending at all. This often left the descriptive adjective in substantive use without any sign indicating its relation to a preceding or following noun: 'a knight *a worthy and an able*,' now *a worthy one and an able one*, or simply *a worthy and able one*. The feeling of the lack of a clear sign for the substantive relation led in the fourteenth century to the use of *one*. In certain British dialects, as in Scotch English, the old substantive form without *one* is still used: 'He is a fine lad and *a clever*' (George Macdonald, *Robert Falconer*, Ch. V). Also in certain American dialects, as in the mountains of Kentucky: 'A rude race they were, but *a strong*' (Lucy Furman, *The Quare Women*, p. 53).

Grammarians call this *one* a prop-word, but this term is a bad one, for *one* is here not a word at all. It is a suffix to indicate the substantive relation. Of course, *one* was originally a limiting adjective meaning *one*, referring backward or forward to a noun indicating some concrete thing, as can still be seen in our hesitation to use it where the noun to which the substantive form of the adjective refers is not a single object but a coherent mass or a group of individuals massed together, or, on the other hand, something abstract: 'I like bathing in salt water better than in *fresh*.' 'Efficiently trained troops should not be filled up with *the partially trained*.' 'He has no books other than *English*.' 'I judge of his public conduct by his *private*.' 'His religion is the *Mohammedan*.' But, in general, we now add *one* to an adjective in order to indicate the substantive relation, so that *one* assumes an abstract meaning and becomes a suffix. As a suffix, *one* is unstressed and should not be confounded with stressed *one*, which is a numeral, although it often has outwardly the form of the suffix when it follows the limiting adjectives *any, some, no, this, that, my,* etc.: 'You can have *any óne* (or *twó, thrée*) of these apples.' 'She might rescue from the mire *some óne* struggling soul.' 'In *no óne* instance was he your partner in any of these transactions.' 'He doesn't get so much pleasure from his many acres as we get from *this óne*' (or *our óne*). However, in 'I want *évery óne* of you to come' *one* in spite of its accent is not numeral *one* but the suffix of *every*. As can be seen in the third paragraph of this article, *évery óne* represents older *évery*. The double stress here is a common feature of emphatic language in English. We find the same double stress in 'I want the candid opinion of *éach óne* of you.' 'I don't know *whích óne* of them, but *sóme óne* of them did it.'

Since any other part of speech or a group of words is in English

often used as an adjective, as described in **10 I 2**, *one* may be
added as a suffix to any other part of speech or to a group of words
that has the force of an adjective used substantively, pointing
back to some preceding noun: 'You can easily get another
secretary. Another time you shall have a *man one*, as you originally
wanted to' (C. Haddon Chambers, *The Tyranny of Tears*, Act II).
'On a side line was a little train that reminded Peter of *the Treliss*
(town) *to Truro* (town) *one*' (Hugh Walpole, *Fortitude*, p. 57).
'This time it (i.e., the new idea) was *an awfully better than usual
one*' (De Morgan, *The Old Madhouse*, Ch. II). The substantive
form of 'as beautiful a *sight* as' is 'as beautiful a *one* as': 'The
sight was *as beautiful a one as* I have ever seen.' But we say,
'The sight was *one* as beautiful as I have ever seen,' corresponding
to 'a sight as beautiful as I have ever seen.' As a genitive is often
felt as an adjective, it often takes *one* in the substantive relation:
'The higher course is *a two years' one*' (*London Times, Educational
Supplement*, Aug. 8, 1918).

One was introduced much later with limiting than with descriptive adjectives, and with the former class it has not yet in
many cases become established, since three of the limiting adjectives, *these, those, others*, have distinct plural form; a number
of others, *two, three, many, all, several, certain*, etc., have distinct
plural meaning, so that the thought thus through form or meaning
becomes clear; others are accompanied by a gesture which indicates the situation; others are limited by a genitive or a relative
clause which shows the thought, for an attributive genitive or
relative clause can modify only a noun or an adjective used substantively: 'these books and *those*,' rarely *those ones*, but in popular
speech often 'these here books and *those ones*' (or *thosen*, or
them there ones); 'those books and *these*,' rarely *these ones*, but in
popular speech often 'them there books and *these ones*' (or *thesen*,
or *these here ones*); 'these books and *others* upon my table'; 'these
books and *two* upon my table'; 'this chair and *that*' (accompanied
by gesture); 'my book and *that* of my brother'; '*each* of the
books'; '*which* (or *which one*) of the books?' *One*, however, is
employed when it is needed to indicate clearly the thought:
'*ány óne* (quite distinct in meaning from *any óne*) of the books,'
to bring out clearly the singular idea in contrast to the plural idea
in '*any* of the books' and the idea of an indefinite amount in
'[I don't want] *any* of your nonsense'; 'thís book and thát *one*
(or *the óne*) upon the table,' to show that *that* indicates an individual, but 'this sugar and *that* upon the table,' to indicate a mass;
'thís pencil and thát *one* (or *the óne*) in my pocket,' to express the
idea of an individual, but 'The pain of her mind had been much

beyond *that* in her head,' to refer to an abstract conception; 'thése books and *thóse* (or *the ónes*) upon the table,' because the plural form *those* brings out clearly the idea of a number of individuals. 'This butter is better than *that* (mass) we got last week, but it will probably not prove as good as *what* (indefinite mass) we shall get next week.' 'My father is a man of few affections, but *what* (indefinite number) he has are very strong' (Mrs. Gaskell, *Wives and Daughters*, Ch. XVIII). '*Which* (indefinite number) of the books are the most interesting?' In connection with *same* and *such* we may use *one* or *ones* to bring out the idea of a concrete thing or distinct concrete things, but avoid these forms when the idea is abstract or indefinite: 'Her dress was the *same* (or the *same one*) she wore last week.' 'His shoes were the *same* (or the *same ones*) he wore last week,' but 'His condition remains *the same*.' 'His objections remain *the same*.' 'His cell was *such* (or *such a one*) as a convict would now disdain to inhabit,' but 'His kindness was *such* that I could not withstand it.'

There are several other categories of limiting adjectives in which *one* is only slowly gaining ground. In the case of the ordinals we often avoid *one*, since ordinals of themselves clearly indicate a relation to a preceding noun or pronoun: 'William is the second scholar of the class and Henry *the third*.' 'He is *the second* on the list.' Similarly, in expressions where the situation suggests that the substantive adjective stands in relation to a noun, especially in the case of two things that are closely associated: 'The right hand is clean and so is *the left*.' 'The southern dialect is more tenacious of these forms than *the northern*.' Sometimes here even in the case of descriptive adjectives: 'Only two balls — *the red* and *the white* — are used.' Similarly, in contrasts where persons and things of two different kinds are brought into close relations by way of contrast we usually avoid *one*: 'He could not bring himself to tackle new books, and *the old* had lost the potency of their appeal' (G. Cannan, *Round the Corner*, Ch. XXII). The use of *one* here would often weaken the expression.

In popular speech the personal pronouns are often used as adjectives, possessive adjectives, as described in 5 *a*, p. 528. Hence it is only natural that as limiting adjectives they are used also substantively with the *one*-forms, the *one*-forms of the first and second persons often serving as personal pronouns: 'Did *you uns* sleep good last night?' (*American Speech*, II, p. 345). *Them +* *ones* becomes a demonstrative pronoun: 'these books and *them there ones*.'

The *one*-form is, in general, quite firmly established in the case of descriptive adjectives, since it is here needed to indicate substantive function. Examples are given on page 518. There are, however, certain limitations to the use of *one* here. It is still not necessary in case of reference to abstract nouns or nouns denoting a mass, as illustrated on page 520.

The comparative and the superlative of descriptive adjectives often do not need *one*, since in connection with the definite article, the degree ending, and the context they become in large measure limiting adjectives; i.e., they do not merely describe persons and things but assign to them a definite place and thus mark them so clearly as individuals that *one* is not necessary to indicate the grammatical relation: 'Which of the two brothers did it?' — 'The younger' (or 'The younger *one*'). But in '*the younger* of the two brothers,' '*the youngest* of the brothers' *one* is not usually felt as necessary. *One*, however, is now, in contrast to older usage, felt by most people as indispensable after the indefinite article, since the reference is not clear and definite: 'This cord will not do; I need *a stronger one*.' 'I am not looking for a room today. I have just found *a most cómfortable one*.'

The suffix *one* has come to stay because it is useful, but no one feels it as elegant. In choice language we try to avoid it. Hence we say 'mingling playful with pathetic thoughts' rather than 'mingling playful thoughts with pathetic ones.' We not infrequently repeat a preceding noun rather than employ *one:* 'An Oxford man will differ all his life from a Cambridge *man*' (*The New Statesman*, No. 152, 512a).

2. **Difference of Nature between a Pure Pronoun and a Substantive Form of an Adjective.** A form that is used only as a pronoun is a mere substitute for the name of a person or thing. In the case of *I* and *you* the pronoun in connection with the situation indicates the person. The pronouns *he, she, it, they* are mere substitutes for nouns that have already been mentioned. The interrogative *who* is used instead of a noun, since the speaker does not know the person and inquires after him. *Nobody, somebody, nothing, something* are mere substitutes for the names of persons and things so vaguely conceived that no names can be given.

Similarly, forms that are still often used as attributive — descriptive or limiting — adjectives become pronouns in the substantive relation, for they are here mere convenient substitutes for nouns or nouns modified by an adjective: 'the black sheep and the *white one*' (= *white sheep*); 'these books and *those* (= *those books*) on the table.' But the substantive forms of descriptive and limiting adjectives differ from pure pronouns such as *you, I, he, she*, etc., in one important point. They not only perform the pronominal function, but they describe or point out, i.e., they have meaning, while the pure pronouns, meaningless and colorless, are mere conventional symbols standing for persons or things. These substantive forms differ from pure pronouns also in that they are freely modified by adherent (**10** I) adjectives, betraying thus their substantive origin, their relation to some noun understood: 'quaint old houses and *beautiful new ones*'; 'these books and *all those*'; 'these books and *many more*' (*a few more*); '*some fifty* of them'; 'John, Fred, and *some others*'; '*some few* of us,' etc.

3. **The Substantive Forms of Limiting Adjectives Used as Pronouns.**   A number of limiting adjectives when used in the substantive relation become pronouns, referring like a pronoun to a preceding noun or to a following modifying *of*-genitive, prepositional phrase, or a relative clause.   The reference is sometimes definite, sometimes more or less indefinite.   When the reference is intentionally entirely general and indefinite, the indefinite pronoun stands alone without referring to anything that precedes or follows, thus indicating a person or thing in only a vague way.

With definite reference, *this, these, that, those, such* and *such a one, the former, the latter, both, either, neither, the first (one), the second (one), each* (now often replacing older *every*) or *each one, every one* (or earlier in the period simple *every*), *two, three, half,* etc.: 'Work and play are both necessary to health; *this* (or *the latter*) gives us rest, and *that* (or *the former*) gives us energy.' 'Dogs are more faithful animals than cats; *these* (or *the latter*) attach themselves to places, and *those* (or *the former*) to persons.' 'Hand me the books on the table and *those* on the window.' 'You may have these books, but give me *those* you hold in your hand.' 'Associate with *such* as will improve your manners.' 'Oh! it was hard that *such a one* should be chosen.' 'John and Henry, you shouldn't quarrel.   It isn't *either's* book.' 'John and Henry are not working hard.   *Neither's* record at school (or the record *of neither* of them at school) is creditable.' 'There are in this Isle two and twentie Bishops, which are as it wer superentendaunts ouer the church, appoynting godlye and learned Ministers in *euery* (now *each*) of their Seas,' etc. (John Lyly, *Euphues' Glasse for Europe*, Works, II, p. 192).   '*Each* (or *each one*) of us has his just claims.' 'I want *évery óne* (in older English, simple *every*) of you to come.' '*Every* (now *évery óne*) of this happy number That have (now *has*) endur'd shrewd days and nights with us shall share the good of our returned fortune' (Shakespeare, *As You Like It*, V, IV, 178).   '*Half* of the cake is gone.' '*Half* of the cakes are gone.' 'The cake was cut in *half*, or in *two* (both forms limiting adjectives used as plural pronouns), or into *halves'* (plural noun). 'He has a whole apple but I haven't even *half a one.'* Compare Parts of Speech, **7** 7 *b*, and Accidence, **42** *b*.

With indefinite reference, *all* (singular and plural), *none, this one and that*, or *this one and that one, any* (plural), *anyone* (or earlier in the period simple *any*), *any* (= *any amount*), *everyone, some* (= *a fair amount*, and *some people*, earlier in the period also with the meaning of *someone*), *someone* (or earlier in the period simple *some*), *many a one, such* (5 *b*, p. 530), *such and such a one, one, no one, another, others, much*, etc. Examples: *'All* is not gold that *glitters.'* 'I haven't *any* of your patience.' 'A woman's injured honor, no more than a man's, can be repaired by *any* (now *anyone*) but him that first wronged it' (Wycherley, *Country Wife*, V, IV, 100). *'Everyone* knows better than that.' 'I should like to have *some* of your patience.' 'When a great aim miscarrieth, the blame must be laid on *some'* (now *someone*) (Thomas Fuller, *Holy War*, II, 45). *'Some* agree with me, *some* do not.' 'There is *much* to learn.' 'If you want to know who *such and such a one is* (or *such and such are*), ask Jones.' 'He is always ordering me about and telling me to do *such and such.'* Two neuter singulars, *none* and *other*, are treated in 5 *b* and *c*, pp. 532–534. Compare Parts of Speech, **7** 7 *c*, and Accidence, **42** *c*.

The accusative singular of neuters, such as *all, some, any, much, none, a little*, is much used adverbially. See **16** 4 *a*.

Four limiting adjectives — *which, what, whichever, whatever* — are used as indefinite relative pronouns (**23** II, 2, 3): 'Here are two hats, but I don't know *which one* is mine.' 'Here are some new books. I don't know *which ones* to select.' 'By quoting (we will not say whence — from *what one* of her poems) a few verses' (Poe, *Works*, 565). 'Here are a number of books on the subject. You may take *whichever one* (or *ones*) you like.' 'My father will approve these plans and *whatever ones* we may make in the future.' *Which* and *whichever* have an *s*-genitive: 'All three boys have a good record. I don't know *which one's* is the best, but *whichever one's* is declared the best, it will not be much better than that of the others.' Compare 5 *a* (close of 2nd par.), p. 527. When the reference is to an indefinite mass or number *what* and *which* do not take the *one*-form. See 1, p. 522. For fuller treatment of these forms see 1 (4th par.), p. 519; **23** II, 2, 3; Accidence, **38** *b*.

The substantive forms of the interrogative adjectives *which* and *what* are used as interrogative pronouns: 'Here are several interesting books. *Which one* (or *which ones*) do you want?' 'The three sisters all have a good record. *Which one's* is the best?'

'The principal has requested us to propose some themes for future discussion. *What ones* are you going to suggest?' For fuller treatment see Parts of Speech, **7** 6, and Accidence, **41**.

4. The Substantive Forms of Limiting Adjectives Used as Nouns. The substantive forms of certain limiting adjectives are also used as nouns: 'I have spent my *all*.' Other examples are given below under 5 and in **58** (last par.).

5. Special Substantive Forms and Their Use as Pronouns and Nouns:

a. SUBSTANTIVE FORMS OF POSSESSIVE ADJECTIVES. The substantive forms of the possessive adjectives *my, thy* (in current American Quaker speech often *thee;* see p. 528), *our, your, her,* and *their* are *mine, thine, ours, yours, hers,* and *theirs:* '*My* fault is serious' but 'The fault is *mine.*' 'This is *our* house' but 'This house is *ours*' and 'His house is larger than *ours* [is].' '*Their* house is large' but 'This house is *theirs.*' *His* is used both as an attributive and a substantive form: 'It is *his* book' and 'The book is *his.*' *His* was also the usual form for things until the close of the sixteenth century, when *its* (in older English, often with the apostrophe, *it's*) began to replace it here: 'Ye are the salt of the earth: but if the salt have lost *his* (now *its*) savor,' etc. (*Matthew,* V, 13). This old usage lingered on until the close of the seventeenth century. The new form *its* developed out of the old possessive *it,* which arose in the fourteenth century in the western Midland dialects and later about 1600 became common elsewhere. About this time its new genitive form *its* came into use, which by reason of its distinctive genitive ending soon gained favor and supplanted older *it* and the still older *his.* The older form *it* occurs in the Bible of 1611, and in the original editions of Shakespeare: 'of *it* own accord' (*Leviticus,* XXV, 5, in the edition of 1611, in the edition of 1660 changed to *its*). *Its* was first used as an adjective, as in 'The salt has lost *its* savor,' and is now also sometimes used substantively: 'The children's health is poor except the baby's and *its* is perfect.' 'Women take to a thing, anything, and go (= let them go) deep enough, and they're *its;* they never, never will get away from it' (A. S. M. Hutchinson, *This Freedom,* p. 253).

We call these forms today adjectives, but they were originally the genitives of the personal pronouns *I, thou, he,* etc., most commonly a possessive genitive, but also often used in other functions of the genitive. We can often still feel the old genitive force: '*his* (subjective genitive) love of *his* (possessive genitive) children'; '*my* (objective genitive) punishment' (punishment *of me*). In the case of the double (**10** II 1 *b*) genitive the form is still always a genitive: 'that patient wife *of yours.*' In the predicate where the subject is not a noun but an indefinite pronoun, the form can be only the genitive of the pronoun: 'I don't want what is *yours* or anybody else's.' Where a noun is subject, the predicate may be regarded either as a substantive adjective form or the genitive of a personal pronoun: 'This hat is *mine.*' But in such a sentence as '*Yours* is the greater treason, for *yours* is the treason of friendship' *yours* cannot possibly be construed as the genitive of the pronoun, for it is the subject of the sentence. It would be impossible to construe the construction as elliptical, as in '*John's* is the greater treason, for *his* is the treason of friendship,' where we might supply the noun *treason* after *John's* and *his*. The fact that we cannot supply a noun after *yours, mine, hers* shows plainly that the old possessive genitive in all these cases has become a substantive adjective form, or we may call it a possessive pronoun, for in fact, according to 2, p. 523, the substantive form of an adjective is a pronoun. But it should be clearly understood that this pronoun is not the genitive of the old personal pronoun, but the nominative of the new pronoun, formed from the substantive form of the possessive adjective. Likewise the possessive genitive of any noun or pronoun which, unaccompanied immediately by a governing noun, points backward or forward to a preceding or following governing noun, becomes a substantive possessive adjective, or, in other words, a possessive pronoun, for we do not now here place a noun immediately after it: 'My hand is larger than *John's.*' '*Mary's* is a sad fate.' Compare **5** *c*, p. 10. Even the genitive of the substantive form of an adjective used as a pronoun can be employed as a possessive pronoun in the nominative or the accusative: 'Both boys have a good record, but the *younger one's* is a little better.' 'All three boys have a good record. I don't know *which one's* is the best, but *whichever one's* is declared the best, it will not be much better than that of the others.' 'Both John and William have a good record. I regard *the latter's* as a little better.' Although possessive pronouns are freely employed in literary English, they are little used in Irish English: 'Who is this book belonging to?' — 'It's belonging to me, Teacher' (Mary Hayden and Marcus Hartog, *The Irish Dialect of English*) = '*Whose* book is this?' — 'It is *mine*, Teacher.' There are no possessive pronouns in Gaelic; hence in the early Modern English period when the Irish people were struggling to acquire English, they naturally avoided this construction, so that it did not become well established in Ireland.

In older English, *mine* and *thine* were used both attributively

and substantively. In the twelfth century, they began in attributive function to lose their −n before consonants: 'min (mine)
arm,' but 'mi (my) fot' (foot). This phonetic distinction disappeared about 1700, so that my, thy were used before vowels as
well as consonants, thus becoming the regular attributive forms:
my arm, my foot. As the old forms mine, thine had remained in
constant use in substantive function, the differentiation just described became established, i.e., my, thy in attributive, mine, thine
in substantive, function. The old attributive use of mine, however,
still lingers in the language of affection: 'sister mine,' etc. The
old forms in −r — her, our, their — were originally felt as the
genitives of the personal pronouns she, we, they, as can still be felt
in 'We mourn their (objective genitive) loss' (= 'the loss of them').
About 1300 an −s was added to these forms to make the genitive
form more distinctive, her, our, their becoming hers, ours, theirs.
As the old forms, however, continued to be used alongside of the
new, they finally about 1550 became differentiated in function,
as described on page 526. His and its, both originally genitives,
are now the only forms which still perform both attributive and
substantive functions. In the dialects in the south of England
and in the Midland, also here and there in America among uneducated people, we find instead of the substantive forms his,
hers, ours, yours, theirs the forms hisn, hern, ourn, yourn, theirn,
where an n characterizes the substantive forms after the analogy
of −n in the substantive forms mine and thine. In these sections
and circles we find also the substantive form whosen instead of
whose: 'If it ain't hisn, then whosen is it?' In America sometimes
also thisn, thatn, thesen, thosen: 'Thisn is better'n thatn.' 'Thesen
are better 'n thosen.' On the other hand, in the attributive relation
certain British and American dialects employ a personal pronoun
instead of a possessive adjective: 'at us (= our) own fireside'
(Lancashire); 'arter we horses' (Gepp, Essex Dialect Dictionary,
p. 131) = after our horses. 'He roll he (= his) eyeballs 'roun'' (Joel
Chandler Harris, Nights with Uncle Remus, p. 69). 'Look, Margaret, thee's (4 II H, last par., and 8 I 1 h) tearing the skirt of thee
dress' (American Speech, Jan., 1926, p. 118). Similarly, who for
whose: 'SCIPIO. "I been to de trial." VOICE. "Who trial?"'
(Edward C. L. Adams, Congaree Sketches, p. 4).

In the seventeenth century arose the usage of suffixing one to
the possessive adjectives to form possessive pronouns. This
development has never been strong, and is for the most part
confined to British English: 'When a woman is old . . . but
my one! She's not old' (Trollope, The Duke's Children, 3, 163).
This form, however, becomes indispensable when the possessive

pronoun is modified by a genitive: 'leaning back in *his one* of the two Chippendale armchairs in which they sat' (Juliana Ewing, *Jackanapes*, 26).

In older English, and sometimes still, when two possessive adjectives or a possessive adjective and a genitive are connected by *and* and together modify a noun, the first possessive adjective has the substantive form: 'I bought them both the same day, *mine* and *your* ticket' (Sydney Smith, *Moral Philosophy*, 209, A.D. 1804–1806), now usually '*your* and *my* ticket' (or sometimes *tickets*) or more commonly and more clearly '*your* ticket and *mine*'; '*mine* and *her* souls' (Browning, *Cristina*, VI), now usually '*my* and *her* soul' (or sometimes *souls*) or more commonly and more clearly '*my* soul and *hers*'; '*mine* and *my* husband's fortunes' (Middleton-Rowley, *The Spanish Gipsie*, III, II, 125, A.D. 1661), now usually '*my* and *my* husband's fortune'(or sometimes *fortunes*), or more commonly and more clearly '*my* husband's fortune and *mine*.' Sometimes the substantive form cannot be used here at all: '*her* and *my* mutual dislike.' Compare 10 I 4.

The substantive forms are also used as nouns, indicating a family, a friend, a circle of friends, property, personal belongings or deserts, a letter, etc: 'Do no harm to *mine*, and *mine* will do no harm to you.' 'He and *his* are all well.' '*Yours* truly' (at the close of a letter). 'He doesn't seem to know the distinction between *mine* and *thine*.' 'Everything of *mine* is at your disposal.' 'Well, little Miss Stuck-up, you got *yours* at last, didn't you?' (Floyd Dell, *The Mad Ideal*, II, Ch. V) = 'got what was coming to you.' 'I have just received *yours* (= *your letter*) of the eighteenth.'

The idea of possession in the possessive adjectives is often emphasized by adding the adjective *own*, both in the attributive and the substantive relation: 'It is *my own* book.' 'The book is *my own*,' where *my* is attributive and *own* the substantive form. 'It had a value all *its own*.'

In connection with a verb, *own* preceded by a possessive adjective often emphasizes the idea of independent action on the part of the subject: 'She makes *her own* dresses' = 'She makes *her* dresses hersélf.' 'He rolls *his own*' (cigarettes). In the predicate after a copula, *own* preceded by a possessive adjective often emphasizes the idea of independence on the part of the subject: 'I am *my own* master.'

Own preceded by a possessive must often be used instead of a simple possessive to make it clear that the reference is to the subject, not to some noun standing near the possessive: 'He seems to love his brother's son more than *his own*.'

Own preceded by a possessive adjective is often used as a noun: 'I have a house of *my own.*' 'May I have it for *my very own?*' 'I can do what I will with *my own.*' 'He is coming into *his own.*' 'He is holding *his own.*' 'In a period of hard struggle it adds to our strength to feel that *our own* believe in us.' 'She has a will of *her own.*' 'He had reasons of *his own* for doing it.'

b. SUBSTANTIVE FORMS OF 'ONE,' 'No.' *One* is used attributively or substantively without change of form; of course, usually only in the singular: 'I have only *óne* apple.' 'How many apples have you?' — 'I have only *óne.*' Often unstressed with indefinite force, referring to a noun preceded by the indefinite article: 'Take an apple.' — 'I already háve *one.*' *One* is used not only with reference to a noun but also often with reference to a noun and its modifying descriptive adjective: 'It's my town. It could be a mighty good town. It's going to become *one*' (Oemler, *Slippy McGee*, Ch. VI). Attributive *one* often has pronounced indefinite force: 'I met him *one* night, on *one* occasion.'

In the substantive relation, indefinite reference is in the singular expressed by *one* when it is desired to refer back to a noun that has just been mentioned, but *such* is sometimes still as in older usage employed here: 'He is a friend, and I tréat him as *one.*' 'Two or three low broad steps led to a platform in front of the altar, or what resémbled *such*' (Scott, *Aunt Margaret's Mirror*, II), or now more commonly *one*. As indefinite *one* cannot refer back to an abstract noun or any other noun that does not denote an individual, person or thing, it is here usually replaced by *it*, *this*, or *such:* 'I offer you my coöperation if *this* will help you.' Similarly, as indefinite *one* usually has no plural, it is replaced here by *they*, *these*, or *such:* 'I should like to find other examples if *they* are to be had.' 'To call for more facts and experiments, if *such* are possible' (Geike in *Nature*, Sept. 19, 1889).

When the reference is not to an individual or individuals indicated by a preceding noun, but to the idea of specific character or capacity, *such* is the usual pronoun: 'It is needless to demonstrate that a poem is *such* only inasmuch as it intensely excites by elevating the soul' (Poe, *Philosophy of Composition*, p. 4). 'A heroic poem, truly *súch*' (Dryden, *Æneid*, Dedication). 'He is a member of this organization, and as *súch* he deserves a hearing.' But *one(s)* may be employed here when the form is used determinatively (**56** A), pointing to a following clause or phrase: 'Why not plain white for the walls and no curtains at all, until you can get *ones* (or *such as*) you really do like?' (Mackenzie, *Guy and Pauline*, p. 57). 'It is a matter of common notoriety that the habitual drinker, even *one who* (= *such a one as*) drinks in moderation, desires to buy his liquor a drink at a time' (*The Christian Science Monitor*, March 29, 1930). Compare **56** A (5th par.) and Parts of Speech, **7** 7 *c* (3rd par.).

Provided the word is unstressed, the indefinite substantive form drops out in the predicate relation after the copula *be*, regularly in the plural, often also in the singular: 'They are members, and we are too.' 'He is a member, and I am too' (or 'I am *one* too'). But 'They have been friends to us, and *súch* we want to be to them.'

Indefinite *one* is also used as an absolute indefinite pronoun, i.e., without reference to a noun that has been previously mentioned, usually with a genitive in –*s:* 'He died in 1859, leaving his property to *one* Ann Duncan' (i.e., to *a certain one*, namely, Ann Duncan, the name standing in apposition with *one*). 'He looked like *one* [who was] dead.' '*One* must do *one's* duty.' The reflexive form is either *one's self* or *oneself*, the former, the older form, after the analogy of *a man's better self, one's own self, myself* (**56** D, last and next to last parr.), the latter, the newer form, after the analogy of *himself* (**56** D, next to last par.), both forms in common use in America, while in England the newer form is probably more common than the older: 'One should not praise *one's self*' (or *oneself*). Both *one's self* and *oneself*, however, are comparatively recent formations, which do not occur in Shakespeare. In older English, *himself* was used here.

The nominative, genitive, dative, accusative corresponding to indefinite *one* in present-day English are *one, one's, one, one*, but the older forms *he, his, him, him* still linger on: '*One* never realizes *one's* blessings while *one* enjoys them.' '*One* hates *one's* enemies and loves *one's* friends.' 'In life *one* only notices what interests *one*' (but in Galsworthy's *Patrician*, p. 48, we find here *him* as in older English). 'Vulgar habit that is people have nowadays of asking *one*, after *one* has given them an idea, whether *one* is serious or not' (Oscar Wilde, *A Woman of No Importance*, Act I). But *he, his, him* correspond to the numeral *one*, to *one . . . another*, and to *no one, someone, everyone, anyone:* '*One* of these men hates *his* enemies.' '*One* hates *his* enemies and another forgives *his*.' 'If *someone* (or *anyone*) should lose *his* purse, *he* should apply to the Lost Property Office.' Similarly, the reflexive object *one's self*, or *oneself*, corresponds to the indefinite subject *one*, while *himself* corresponds to the numeral *one*, to *one . . . another*, and to *no one, someone, everyone, anyone:* 'One cannot interest *one's self* in everything,' but '*One* of the boys fell and hurt *himself*' and '*No one* can interest *himself* in everything.' We often, however, hear *himself* instead of *one's self* or *oneself*, as in older English: 'One might fall and hurt *himself.*' In careless expression we often find here even in good authors a plural form corresponding to *one:* 'As though *one* went to tea with a woman for the sake of talking about the very things *you* (= *one*) have been doing all day' (Mrs. Ward, *Sir George Tressady*, I, Ch. V). 'One must be on *their* (= *one's*) guard against bargains that are worthless' (Rev. E. J. Hardy, *How to Be Happy Though Married*, Ch. XII, 128).

The substantive form of attributive *no* is *none:* 'Lend me your pencil.' — 'I have *none*,' or 'I haven't *any*.' 'Of all the crimes committed by Englishmen *none* is so hideous as this.' '*None* of the books *is* (or *are*) fit to read,' or to convey emphasis we replace *none* in the singular by *nót óne* but retain it in the plural: '*Nót óne* of the books *is* fit to read,' but '*Nóne* of the books *are* fit to read.' 'I have no fear, if you have *none*.' 'Where are the apples?' — 'There are *none*.' 'Give me another pen!' — 'I have *no other*,' where *no* is attributive and *other* the substantive form. In answer to the question 'Have you four-bladed knives?' it was once common to say 'We have *no such*,' where *no* is attributive and *such* the substantive form. Today the answer in rather choice language is 'We have *none such*,' where *none* is the substantive form and *such* a predicate adjective, *none such* thus having the force of *none that are of that kind.* The more common answer is 'We haven't *any of that kind*' (or *sort*).

In older English, emphatic *nót a óne* is often used instead of *nót óne*, and this older usage survives in colloquial speech: 'There's *nót a óne* of them but in his house I keep a servant fee'd' (Shakespeare, *Macbeth*, III, IV, 131). After the analogy of *nót a bóy*, etc., we say *nót a óne:* 'There is*n't a boy* absent, no, *nót a óne*.' Similarly, *néver a óne* is still sometimes used instead of *néver óne:* 'I have sung many songs, But *néver a óne* so gay' (Tennyson, *Poet's Song*, 19). In popular speech, in England and America, the contraction *nary* (i.e., *ne'er a* from *never a*) is common, often with a repetition of *a*, as it is not felt in the contraction: 'Ask others for a loan. You'll get *nary one* (or *nary a one*, or *nary red* [cent], or *nary a red*) from me.'

The two forms *no* and *none* come from the Old English singular form *nān* = *ne* + *ān*, i.e., *not one*, *ne* being the old negative and *ān* the form corresponding to modern *one*. In Old English, the form *nān* was used both attributively and substantively; in attributive function standing either before a noun beginning with a vowel or one beginning with a consonant. Later, as in the case of the possessives in *a*, there arose two attributive forms, *no* before consonants, as in *no good*, and *none* before a vowel, as in *to none effect* (More, *Utopia*, 87).　Later, about 1600, *no* became established as the attributive form in all positions, i.e., before a vowel or a consonant, while *none* remained in the substantive relation, the differentiation described on the preceding page.　Older usage still lingers on before *other:* 'On these terms it shall be, and upon *none others*' (Allen, *The Woman Who Did*, 57), now usually *no others*, as explained on page 532.

The form *none* is used in older English, and sometimes still in choice language, also as an indefinite pronoun referring to one person.　Today it is more common to use *no one* for *one* person and *none* for more than one: '*No one* (or *nobody*) gave him anything.' '*None* are so deaf as those that will not hear.'

None is used also as a neuter pronoun with the force of *not any:* 'It is *none* of my business.'　'*None* of your cheek, please!' '*None* of your tricks!'　Just as the adverbial accusative of the neuter pronoun *nought* has developed into the negative *not*, so has the adverbial accusative of the neuter pronoun *none* developed the force of a negative with much the same meaning as an emphatic *not:* 'I am *none* the less obliged to you.'　'I was *none* too sure of it.'

c.　SUBSTANTIVE FORMS OF 'OTHER.'　The form remains unchanged in the singular and takes *–s* in the plural, or to emphasize the idea of individual units the form with *one* or *ones* may be used: 'this book and *the other, another, one other, no other*'; 'this book and *two others, the others, several others*'; 'these books and *no others.*'　'These apples are larger and more beautiful than the *other ones.*'　In older English, there was in the simple form no plural ending as a result of the disappearance of the ending which originally was found here: 'Some seeds fell by the wayside. . . . But *other* fell into good ground' (*Matthew*, XIII, 4–8).　This old plural without an ending is still often found alongside of the more common new plural *others* when the noun or pronoun to which it refers follows it: 'many *others* (or *other*) of the men and women I met last night,' but always 'this book and *others* of the same kind,' since the noun to which it refers precedes it.　The old endingless form is still, however, the rule before *than* wherever the noun to which it refers follows it, for it is here used not substantively but attributively: 'I have never heard *other* than laudable things said of him.'　The *other* before *than* is also often not a substantive form but an ordinary predicate adjective: 'These precepts lighted her to conclusions [which were] quite *other* than those at which he had arrived himself.'　'I would not have my boys *other* (objective predicate) than they are.'

In appositive function we often use after pronouns the adverb *else* instead of *other:* who *else;* somebody *else;* anybody *else;*

no one *else;* nothing *else,* etc.; genitive: who *else's* (or whose
else); somebody *else's;* anybody *else's;* no one *else's.* Thus *else*
here now usually forms a compound with the preceding pronoun.
Compare Accidence, **40** and **41.**

Other is used also as a pronoun: 'He and *another,* no *other';*
'they and two *others,* no *others.*' 'The thief was no (or in choice
language still sometimes *none*) *other* than his own son.' 'They
rode for miles in silence, each knowing what was passing in the
other's mind.' 'What understanding of *others'* pains she had!'
'Nor could his private friends do *other* (*anything else*) than mournfully acquiesce.' 'He spoke no more and *no other* (once more
common, now usually replaced by *nothing else*) than he felt'
(A. Hope, *Rupert of Hentzau,* 153). The accusative of the pronoun *other* was once used adverbially with the force of *otherwise*
and this older usage still lingers. Compare Accidence, **42** *c* (4th
par. from end).

When *other* refers to a plural subject, it is used in connection
with *each* or *one* to indicate a reciprocal relation, *each other* (with
reference to two, or often two or more), *one another* (sometimes
with reference to two, usually, however, to more than two):
'These two never weary of *each other,*' or in genitive form '*each
other's* company.' 'The three gentlemen looked at *one another*
with blank faces,' or in genitive form 'The three never weary of
one another's company.'

ADJECTIVES AND PARTICIPLES
USED AS NOUNS

58. In English more easily than in most languages a word can
be converted, i.e., made into another part of speech. This usually
takes place without any modification whatever, except, of course,
the necessary change of inflection. Thus the noun *eye* is converted
into a verb by merely giving it verbal inflection: 'They *eyed* the
prisoners with curiosity.' As adjectives are now always uninflected, the conversion of nouns, adverbs, phrases, and sentences
into adjectives is very easy. Compare **10** I 2. On the other hand,
the conversion of adjectives into nouns is more difficult and irregular. In Old English, adjectives, converted into nouns, often
retained their old adjective form. In many cases this old usage
survived even after the adjective endings had disappeared; in
other cases the loss of the adjective endings brought about new
forms of expression. The breakdown of the adjective inflection
at the close of the Middle English period forced the English people,
who are fond of short-cuts in language, to do something contrary

to their nature — to go a roundabout way to express themselves. If we now say *the good* it can only mean *that which is good*, but in older English, according to the form of article, it could mean *the good man, the good woman, the good thing*. We now regularly use *man, woman*, and *thing* here, but there are numerous individual survivals of the older use of the simple adjective where the situation of itself without the help of the form of article or adjective makes the thought clear. Of persons: the *deceased;* the dear *departed;* my *intended;* the *accused;* the *condemned;* a lover clasping his *fairest;* my *dearest* (in direct address), etc. In a few cases a modern genitive form has been created: the *Almighty's* strong arm; her *betrothed's* sudden death, etc. A number have a genitive singular in *-'s* and a plural in *-s*, since they have become established as regular nouns: a *savage*, genitive a *savage's*, plural *savages*. Similarly, *native, equal, superior, private, male, three-year-old, grown-up, Christian, criminal*, etc. 'She is such *a silly!*' 'They are *such sillies!*'

Alongside of modern plurals here in *-s* are a number of older plurals without an ending, which are the reduced forms of still older inflected forms: my *own* (i.e., my kindred); the *rich;* the *poor;* the really (adverb) *poor;* the seriously (adverb) *wounded;* the worst (adverb) *wounded;* the *living* and the *dead;* the *blind;* our *wounded;* 2000 homeless *poor;* a new host of *workless* walking the streets; four other *accused;* 2000 *killed* and *wounded; rich* and *poor; old* and *young; big* and *little*. These nouns usually have no case ending throughout the plural, taking the modern forms of inflection: *the wounded;* gave food and drink *to the wounded;* the friends *of the wounded*. The *s*-genitive is rare: 'Always just the pausing of folks for the bit of offhand chat and then the hurrying away to their own dinner bells and their *own's* voices, calling' (Fannie Hurst, 'White Apes,' in *Forum* for March, 1924, p. 290).

These nouns without an ending in the plural have been preserved because in the competition between the old and the new plural in older English they became differentiated in meaning. They acquired collective force: 'The *poor* of our city,' but 'the two *poor men* entering the gate'; 'the state of *the heathen* and their hope of salvation,' but 'Smith and Jones are regular *heathens*.' On account of the lack of a plural ending the old uninflected plural, however, is usually ambiguous, so that we often cannot use it at all. We may say 'the *poor* of the South,' but we must say 'the *blacks* (or the *black people*) of the South,' for *the black* now suggests a singular idea since it is sometimes used in the singular, thus now being felt as a noun: '"Fetch a light," she said to *the black*

who opened for us' (S. Weir Mitchell, *Hugh Wynne,* Ch. XXVII).
We say also *'the whites* of the South.' The old form is thus in
quite limited use. A pastor might say to his congregation 'I urge
old and young,' but he could not say 'I desire to meet after our
service *the young.'* He would say *the young people.* But we
say 'a picture of a willow-wren feeding its *young'* (or *young ones).*
In a broad sense *the young* is used also of human beings: 'Men
rode up every minute and joined us, while from each village *the
adventurous young* ran afoot to enter our ranks' (T. E. Lawrence,
Revolt in the Desert, p. 303).

Since the names of some peoples have been made from adjectives,
as *the English, the French,* the old uninflected adjective plural has
become productive here, and is now used with many names of
peoples: the *Swiss* (in older English *Swisses*), *Portuguese* (in
older English *Portugueses*), *Japanese, Chinese,* etc. We sometimes
use the same form for the singular just as we use 'the *deceased'*
for the singular, but we avoid these singulars since we feel these
forms as plurals and prefer to say 'a *Portuguese gentleman, lady,'*
etc. In *Chinaman,* plural *Chinamen* or *Chinese,* we have, for
singular and plural, forms which may become established. The
singular *Chinee,* a back-formation from the plural *Chinese,* is
common in a derogatory sense. We usually say 'three, four
Chinamen,' but '10,000 *Chinese, the Chinese'* (not *the Chinamen,*
although in a narrow sense we may say *'the Chinamen* sitting on
the bench yonder'). The uninflected plural is especially common
with the names of uncivilized or less civilized peoples: the *Iro-
quois, Navaho, Hupa, Ojibwa, Omaha, Blackfoot, Duala, Bantu,
Swahili,* etc. Here the same form is freely used also as a singular:
a *Blackfoot,* etc. We say the *English, French* or *Englishmen, French-
men,* but in the singular only *Englishman, Frenchman.* Many
other words, however, may assume the new, more serviceable,
type with the genitive singular and the plural in *–s:* a *German,*
a *German's,* the *Germans;* an *American,* an *American's,* the
Americans; a *Zulu,* a *Zulu's,* the *Zulus;* and even many of those
given above with uninflected plural: an *Omaha,* an *Omaha's,*
the *Omahas.* The plural of *Blackfoot* is often *Blackfeet.*

In some cases we make nouns out of the substantive form (**57** 1),
i.e., the *one*-form: the *Crucified One;* the *Evil One.* 'He is a
queer one.' My *dear ones;* our *little ones;* my *loved ones;* the
great ones of earth, etc.

In a few cases nouns made from adjectives may drop the article
as in older English: 'My good lady made me proud as *proud* can
be' (Richardson, *Pamela,* III, 241). 'Eleven years *old* does this
sort of thing very easily' (De Morgan, *Joseph Vance,* Ch. XV).

'Sweet *Seventeen* is given to day-dreams.' '*Slow* and *steady* wins the race.' 'For 'tis the eternal law That *first* in beauty should be *first* in might' (Keats, *Hyperion*, II, 228). '*First* come, *first* served.' '*First* come, *first* in.' In plain prose an article is usually placed before the noun: 'He is strong for *an eleven-year-old*.' 'I was *the first one* served.' 'We were *the first ones* served.'

Nouns made from adjectives often denote lifeless things, usually with a meaning more or less general or indefinite. They are usually preceded by the definite article or some other limiting adjective: *the present* (= *the present time*); *the beautiful; the sublime.* 'You ask *the impossible*.' 'He did *his best*.' As such forms, though now employed as nouns, were originally adjectives, they still are often, like adjectives, modified by adverbs: the genuinely *lovable;* the relatively *unknown*, etc. There are still many neuter nouns made from adjectives, but in older English, the tendency to use them was stronger than today. A number of these nouns have since been replaced by other words: 'Let me enjoy my *private*' (Shakespeare, *Twelfth Night*, III, ii, 99), now *privacy*. 'Whereat a sudden *pale* (now *paleness*) . . . Usurps her cheeks' (*id., Venus and Adonis*, 589).

While the neuter nouns made from adjectives now usually have the definite article or some other limiting adjective before them, we still not infrequently find the older articleless form, especially in the case of two adjectives connected by *and:* 'I can spy already a strain of *hard* and *headstrong* in him' (Tennyson). 'That is *good*, but there is *better* to follow.' 'There is *worse* ahead.'

The modified or unmodified form has become fixed in many set expressions: in *the dark;* after *dark;* through *thick* and *thin;* from *grave* to *gay;* to keep to *the right;* to go to *the bad;* to go from *bad* to *worse;* to make *short* of *long;* *the long* and *the short* of it; before *long*. 'After frequent interchange of *foul* and *fair*' (Tennyson, *Enoch Arden*, 529). 'The police came up to see *fair* between both sides' (*London Daily News*, March 11, 1891).

A large number of neuters have become concrete nouns: *German;* Luther's *German;* the *German* of the present time; my *German;* a *daily* (paper), plural *dailies;* a *weekly*, plural *weeklies;* the *white* of an egg, the *whites* of eggs. 'What is *the good* of lying?' 'It is no *good* trying to conceal it,' but the plural *goods* has a much more concrete meaning. A large number are employed only in the plural: *greens, woolens, tights, necessaries, movables, valuables, the Rockies*, etc.

Most of the adjectives used as nouns in the examples given above are descriptive adjectives, but also some limiting adjectives are used as nouns: 'He has lost his *all*.' 'He and *his* (**57** 5 *a*) are all well.' 'I wrote you the details in my *last*' (= *last letter*). 'He was successful from *the first*' (= *the beginning*).   Proper adjectives are limiting adjectives.   They can, of course, be used also as nouns: *a German; a German's; the Germans*, etc.   The use of these adjectives as nouns is treated on page 536.

CHAPTER XXVI

NUMBER IN NOUNS

59. There is often a conflict between form and meaning. A singular form is often plural in meaning and a plural often singular. A form that is a plural in one generation may be interpreted as a singular by the next. Thus there arise certain difficulties in the use of the plural. Some of the more common or more peculiar are treated here.

1. **Collective Nouns.** While in general the singular denotes one and the plural more than one, in certain cases the opposite may be true, namely, that one denotes many and many one. A group of persons or things may be felt as a unit, a whole: the *gentry;* the *army;* the *navy;* the *cavalry;* the *infantry;* the *police;* the *public; fruit; poultry;* a *dozen;* a *score;* a *myriad;* the seaworthiness of the English *craft,* etc. '*Poultry* is high here.' For the number of the verb see **8 I 1** *d.* In spite of the singular form here the idea of a plurality, a number of individuals, is so strong that we not infrequently find before these collective nouns a limiting adjective plural in form or meaning: 'the hostile feelings with which the child regarded all these *offspring* of her own heart and mind' (Hawthorne, *The Scarlet Letter,* 104); 'many *gentry*' (Barrie, *The Little Minister,* 268); 'eighty *clergy*' (Caine, *The Christian,* p. 266); '80,000 *cattle.*' 'Some few *infantry were doubling* out into the defence position' (T. E. Lawrence, *Revolt in the Desert,* p. 275). 'About a dozen *fruit are setting,* of which at least half will ripen.' Such nouns when used as subject quite commonly require a plural verb, as in the last two examples. See also **8 I 1** *d.*

With a number of words there are two forms, a singular to express the idea of oneness, a distinct type, and a plural to indicate different individuals or varieties within a group or type: 'an abun-

dance of good *fruit,* of good *grain,'* but *'the fruits* and *grains* of
Europe'; 'peasant *folk,* gentle*folk,'* but more commonly *folks*
where the idea of individuals is prominent: 'young *folks,* old
folks.' 'It is bedtime for *folks* who want to get up early in the
morning.' 'His *folks* are rich.' 'Why should I expose myself to
the *shot* of the enemy?' but 'Two *shots* hit the mast.' 'We have
just enough *shell* for one more attack' (Sir Ian Hamilton, *Gallipoli
Diary,* p. 340), but 'Two more *shells* exploded not far away.'
'The one half of his *brain,'* but 'He blew out his *brains'* and 'Perhaps I haven't *brains* (intellectual powers) enough to understand
metaphysics.' To indicate the idea of separate units we often use
another word in plural form in connection with the collective
noun: 'our *cattle,'* but 'forty *head of cattle';* 'the *furniture* of our
room,' but 'three *pieces of furniture.'* In a few cases the collective
singular is used also as a plural: 'the English *people'* (collective
singular) and 'Many good *people* (plural) believe this.' 'The
cannon (collective singular) were still thundering at intervals'
(J. T. Trowbridge, *The Drummer Boy,* Ch. XXIII) and 'she did
not seem aware of the gallant figure standing between the two
little bright brass *cannon'* (plural) (Tarkington, *Mirthful Haven,*
Ch. I). Sometimes the plural expresses a part of a whole, hence
has less extensive meaning than the singular: 'She has gray *hairs'*
indicating a smaller number than 'She has gray *hair.'*

Of course, a collective noun can always take plural form to indicate different groups of the same kind: 'the *army* of France,'
but 'the *armies* of Europe'; 'the English *people,'* but 'the *peoples*
of Europe.'

2. **Plural Used as Singular.** A number of individual things
expressed by the plural form of the noun may acquire a oneness
of meaning, so that in spite of the plural form we use the noun
as a singular: *pains* (**8** I 2 *f*); *means* (**8** I 2 *f*); *news* (**8** I 2 *f*);
tidings (**8** I 2 *f*); *amends* (a singular or a plural); *barracks* (sometimes a singular, usually a plural); *links* (sometimes a singular,
usually a plural); *stamina* (Latin plural used as a singular); *odds*
(used as a singular in the meaning of difference; elsewhere a plural;
see **8** I 2 *f*); *works* (usually a plural, but often, especially in England, a singular in *a gasworks, an ironworks,* etc., where Americans
often prefer *plant,* as it can form a plural: *a gas plant, gas plants,*
etc.); *smallpox* (for *smallpocks,* the singular still preserved in
pockmarks); *measles; mumps; lazybones; sobersides; gallows;
innings,* the usual British singular and plural, but in America the
singular is *inning* and the plural *innings* except in such figurative
expressions as 'The Democrats now have their *innings'* (singular)
and 'It is your *innings* (singular = *opportunity*) now'; *a bellows*

(or more commonly *a pair of bellows*); *the bellows* (plural, sometimes singular: '*The bellows* need — sometimes needs — mending'); *two bellows* (or more commonly *two pairs of bellows*); *a rather uncomfortable ten minutes; another two weeks; every five minutes; every five miles.* 'Their (i.e., the rivers') confluence was above the town *a good two miles*' (Owen Wister, *The Virginian*, Ch. XXXV). We say '*desirous of seeing another United States* than that of today' and feel the name of our country often as singular in many other expressions, while in others the plural idea is more natural to us, as in *these United States*, etc. The names of sciences in *-ics* (the singular form in *-ic* still found in *arithmetic, magic, music, rhetoric*), as in *mathematics* (comprising the various branches of this subject), *physics*, etc., are, in spite of their plural form, now usually felt as singulars; while the names of practical matters, as *gymnastics, athletics, politics, tactics*, etc., are now usually felt as plurals. See 8 I 2 *f*. In older English, a number of plurals could be treated as singulars preceded by *much* when the idea of quantity or mass was present: '*much* (now *many*) goods' (*Luke*, XII, 19); '*much* (now *many*) people' (*Acts*, XI, 26). Older '*Much* oats is grown here' is now replaced by '*Large quantities of* (or in colloquial speech *lots of*) oats are grown here.' On the other hand, there are a number of old plurals now regarded as singulars. We treat such plurals as *Des Moines, Athens, Brussels*, etc., as singulars, since we do not feel them as plurals; but certain other proper names we treat as plurals, since we still feel the plural form: '*Kew Gardens*, which *have* become famous throughout the world' (Ferrars, *Rambles through London Streets*, p. 83).

3. **Plural Nouns with Form of Singular.** The Old English plural of neuters had a form like the singular, as still preserved in 'one *sheep*, two *sheep*.' Shakespeare still sometimes used the old plural *horse:* 'I did hear The galloping of *horse*' (*Macbeth*, IV, I, 140), now *horses*. The old plural *horse* survives only in the sense of *cavalry:* 'the enemy's *horse*.' When the new plural in *-s* came into use the old plural lingered for a while and finally became in a number of cases differentiated in meaning, so that this type has been preserved and has even become productive, influencing other words. The plural in *-s* is applied to words taken separately; the one that takes no plural ending, in accordance with its apparently singular form, is, in a few expressions, once more numerous, invested with collective force to express weight and measure, especially in British English and in popular American English: 15 *pound;* a few *ton;* a few *hundredweight* (in universal use) of coal; five *brace* of birds; ten *gross* (in universal use) of buttons; a gross = twelve *dozen* (thought of as a mass; in this sense in universal use);

often *forty head of poultry, cattle; ten yoke of oxen; three score and ten;* a couple of *year* (dialect in mountains of Kentucky). We often hear 'He is not more than *five foot ten.*' 'I should say that *three pound ten* were plenty.' In older English, the plural *pair* was used in the literary language, but today the literary plural is *pairs,* the form *pair* surviving as plural only in colloquial and popular speech. In older English, the plural *sail* (= *ship*) was common: 'a fleet of thirty *sail*' (Hume, *History*, III, p. 448).

On the other hand, in the case of gregarious animals, where the idea of separate individuals is not pronounced, the plurals without –*s* are still common, even increasing. We now regularly say 'a herd of *deer*'; 'two *carp*'; 'two *perch*'; 'a string of *fish*'; 'a boatload of *fish*'; 'I caught six *fish.*' *Vermin* is now used so much as a plural that it has become rare as a singular. The singular form is widely employed by hunters of game also as a plural: to hunt *pig* (but to raise *pigs*); kill *duck* (but raise *ducks*); a jungle abandoned to water *fowl* (but *the fowls* have gone to roost). 'I shot two *elk* and some *antelope*' (Theodore Roosevelt, *Letter to Henry Cabot Lodge,* June 19, 1886). 'There was plenty of *lion* about this camp, but few *buffalo*' (Mary Hastings Bradley, *Caravans and Cannibals,* IX, A.D. 1925). 'Very soon the little dog treed a flock of *partridge*' (E. T. Seton, *Rolf in the Woods,* Ch. XXXI). In older English, the idea of separate individuals was still firm in a number of cases: 'five loaves and two *fishes*' (*Matthew,* XIV, 17). 'We ate the *carps*' (Swift). 'A dish of *trouts*' (Macaulay, *History of England,* I, Ch. III). We still say *crabs, lobsters, oysters, eels, sharks, whales,* etc. Usage here is very capricious.

The plural without –*s,* so common in nouns representing animal life, is sometimes found also in nouns representing plant life, as also here the idea of separate individuals is sometimes not pronounced: 'The crowd had destroyed my pleasure in Azrak, and I went off down the valley to our remote Ain el Essad, and lay there all day in my old lair among *the tamarisk*' (T. E. Lawrence, *Revolt in the Desert,* p. 268). 'In spring and early summer, daffodils, primroses, bluebells, *honeysuckle,* cowslips, are seen on every side' (*Calendar of Historic and Important Events,* A.D. 1930, p. 41).

The noun *ski* often has the same form for the plural when the plural idea is not prominent: 'We traveled on *ski,*' but 'Two broken *skis* were lying on the ground.'

4. **Names of Materials.** Names of materials do not from their very nature admit of a plural in the usual sense: *wine, gold, copper, silver,* etc.

a. The plural is often used to indicate different species, varieties, or grades of the same thing: *French wines, Rhine wines,* etc. Another word in plural form is often used in connection with the material to indicate different varieties: different *teas* or *sorts of tea*.

b. The plural often denotes definite portions of the material: 'He washed his *hair*' (mass), but 'The very *hairs* of your head are numbered.' 'My father is sowing turnip-*seed* (in mass) in the garden,' but 'There are 100 *seeds* in this packet.' 'We are carrying a fine line (or stock) of *linens.*' '*Silks* and *satins* put out the kitchen fire' (proverb). A *glass* (drinking utensil), plural *glasses;* a *copper* (coin), plural *coppers; iron* (for ironing), plural *irons*, etc.

5. **Abstract Nouns.** Abstract nouns do not admit of a plural as a rule: *beauty;* the *beautiful; liberty; disease*, etc.

a. They have a plural when they assume concrete force by representing concrete objects, or by indicating a number of kinds or distinct actions or concrete manifestations: *writing* (in the abstract) without a plural; *writing* in the sense of *book, work*, plural *writings;* thus also *beauties* (of nature); *liberties; diseases.* '*Hopes, suspicions* are entertained.' In words like *filings, sweepings*, we have plurals indicating the concrete results of the abstract actions *filing, sweeping.*

b. The plural of abstract nouns sometimes expresses a part of a whole, hence has less extensive meaning than the singular: '*truth* broader than *truths.*' 'There are a number of pronounced *successes* to his credit, but he has not as yet attained to full *success.*' 'She possessed certain perfectly definite *beauties*, like her hair' (Edwin Balmer, *The Breath of Scandal*, Ch. II). 'No, it wasn't their *manners* that bewildered me, but their *manner*' (Lewis Browne, *The American Magazine*, Jan., 1929, p. 7). 'The *facts* in the case are clear,' but 'In our scientific libraries are vast stores of *fact.*'

Sometimes both singular and plural have abstract force but different shades of abstract meaning: 'He had *nerve* but no *nerves*' (Walter Noble Burns, *The Saga of Billy the Kid*, Ch. V) = 'He had *physical courage* but no *nervousness.*'

c. A number of abstract nouns cannot form a plural in the usual way, but with the help of another noun in plural form can convey the idea of a number of concrete manifestations of the abstract idea: *gratitude, expressions of gratitude; fortune, pieces*, or *strokes, of fortune; death, deaths*, or *cases of death.*

6. **Nouns without a Singular.** Some words occur only in the plural since the things represented are never simple in their make-up, so that the plural idea is uppermost in our minds: *the Alps, annals, ashes* (from the furnace, stove), *athletics, bellows, billiards, the Cyclades, the Dardanelles, dregs, eaves* (**8 I 2** *f*), *entrails, goods, lees, the Netherlands, nuptials, oats, obsequies, pincers, proceeds, the*

Pyrenees, riches, scales (for weighing), *scissors, shears, spectacles* (*eyeglasses*), *stocks* (timbers on which a ship rests during construction), *suds, tweezers, tongs, trousers, victuals, vitals,* etc. The plural *contents* is the usual form of the word, as in the *contents* of a purse, a drawer, a barrel, a book. But the singular is sometimes used in abstract meanings, *holding capacity, substance as opposed to form, sum of inner qualities:* 'Gaugers glance at a barrel to tell its *content.*' 'In this course on English literature we shall turn our attention, not only to structure, but also to the *content* of what is read.' 'Many judge a book by its ethical *content.*' Usually we say, 'the *scissors, pincers,* etc., *are* on the table,' but the singular form of the verb is sometimes used where the tool is thought of as a unit: 'There *is a scissors, pincers,* etc., on the table,' or in careful language much more commonly 'There *is a pair of scissors, pincers,* etc., on the table.'

7. **Plural of 'Kind,' 'Sort,' 'Manner.'** When the reference is to more kinds than one, we employ the plural here: 'There are many *kinds* of apples.' In older English, *manner* often seemingly had no distinctively plural form. In certain expressions it seemingly still has a plural like the singular: 'We played all *manner* of games.' The explanation is that *all* here retains the old meaning of *every,* so that this example really means 'We played *every kind* of game.' Thus the form *manner* here is really a singular.

Where the reference is to only one kind, we often hear the singular form *kind* after the plural limiting adjectives *these, those:* '*these kind* of apples' = 'apples *of this kind.*' In all such expressions *kind* has the force of a genitive dependent upon a governing noun. At the close of the Old English period the genitive was still always used here. The genitive form employed was *cynnes,* the Old English equivalent of *of kind,* but as an *s*-genitive it always stood before the governing noun: '*alles cynnes* deor' = 'animals *of every kind.*' Later *cynnes* lost its genitive ending, becoming *kin:* '*al kin* deer' = 'animals *of every kind.*' The loss of the genitive ending obscured the grammatical relations. At this point of the development *kin* was replaced by *kind.* The new form was construed as the governing noun, and there was placed after it a dependent *of*-genitive: '*al kynde* of fisshis' (*Matthew,* XIII, 48, Purvey ed., A.D. 1388) = '*every kind* of fish.' This construction has become established in the language. Today, however, we prefer to place the dependent genitive in the generic singular instead of the plural, as in this example from the fourteenth century: 'this kind *of shoe,*' 'this kind *of boy.*' 'What kind *of cherry tree* flourishes best in this region?' 'What kinds *of cherry* flourish best in this region?' But the old plural is still used where the idea of number is prominent: 'Our hills are covered with this kind *of trees.*' 'What kind *of trees* are those?' 'How do you like this kind *of people?*' Though the new construction became established in the literary language of the Middle English period, the feeling for the older was not lost. Many felt *kind* as an adjective element modifying the following noun. Its predecessor *kin* was such an adjective element. Many felt *kind* as assuming the function of *kin.* They were not disturbed by the *of* that followed *kind* in the new construction. They even accepted the *of* and joined it to *kind,* treating *kind of* as a compound adjective. This is a blending of the old *kin* construction with the new *kind of* construction. When *kind of, sort of,* etc., came to be felt as attributive adjectives standing before a noun, it followed as a matter of course that the inflected demonstrative before them was regulated in number by the governing noun, also the verb if the governing noun was subject: '*This* kind of *man annoys* me,' but '*These* kind of *men annoy* me.' In both examples the reference is to only one *kind:* 'a man of *this kind,*' 'men of *this kind.*' In older English, this construction is used also where the reference is to more kinds than one: 'To some *kind* (now *kinds*) of men Their graces serve them but as enemies' (Shakespeare, *As You Like It,* II, III, 10). Where the reference is to only one kind, the construction of *kind of* as an adjective has always had a wider currency than where the reference is to different kinds. In early Modern English, it was still commonly used by good authors: 'these *kind of* people' (Sir Philip Sidney, *Trewnesse of the Christian Religion,* Ch. I, A.D. 1587) = 'people *of this kind*'; 'these *kind of* knaves' (Shakespeare, *King Lear,* II, II, 107) = 'knaves *of this kind.*' At the present time this construction is still used in England in colloquial speech: 'these ingenious *sort of* men' (H. G. Wells, *Twelve Stories and a Dream,* p. 116). In America it is now largely confined to popular speech.

Preceded by *a* the expression *kind of* expresses a certain approach to something: 'He is a *kind of* stockbroker.' 'I feel a *kind of* sympathy for him.' This *kind of* is often used in colloquial speech as an adverb with the force of 'to a certain extent': 'I *kind of* expect it.' *Sort of* has the same meaning: 'If I were you, I would hunt him up and *sort of* get in touch with him.' The attributive genitive *of a kind* has quite a different meaning. It expresses contempt: 'We had coffee *of a kind.*'

In choice language the original genitive construction discussed on page 544 is still well preserved, now, of course, in its modern form with *of* following its governing noun, since with names of things we no longer freely use an *s*-genitive before the governing noun; 'an apple *of this kind*'; 'apples *of this kind*'; 'people *of this kind.*'

This literary construction, however, still seems a little strange to us, since the word-order is different from the old familiar word-order. This has led to such expressions as '*this kind* of people'; '*this kind* of apples.' This type of expression preserves the old order, but when the noun becomes subject we see by the singular form of the verb that the construction is not the old type, but a curious mixture of the old and the new: 'Apples *of this kind are* highly prized,' or with the old word-order '*This kind* of apples *is* highly prized.' The latter type of expression has been in use for centuries. In the second paragraph (p. 544) the history of the construction is given and an example is cited from the fourteenth century. *Sort* has followed the same pattern: 'I know *that sorte of* men ryght well' (Daus, *Sleidan's Commentarii*, 63, A.D. 1560). As can be seen, however, by the example from Shakespeare's *King Lear*, given on page 545, the use of the plural form *those* or *these* here before *sorte* would not have been contrary to the literary standard of that time. Both forms — *that* and *those* — were in use, with the verb in the singular or plural if the noun was subject. In British speech the three types are still used: 'Men *of that sort are* highly prized.' '*Those sort of* men *are* highly prized.' '*That sort* of men *is* highly prized.' In America the second type is avoided.

Where there is a reference to more than one in the dependent genitive, we now, as mentioned on page 544, prefer the generic singular, with its abstract general force, to the concrete plural, which, however, in older English was the usual form: 'They do not seem to be the kind (sort) *of horse* (or *horses*) to stand much knocking about.' 'An apple-tree on Luther Burbank's Sebastopol Farm, where, when this picture was taken, 526 varieties *of apple* were ripening' (*The Saturday Evening Post*, April 24, 1926, p. 29). Where the abstract idea is prominent, we do not use the plural at all, as an abstract idea demands singular form: 'You are *the kind* (*sort*) *of man* I want.' 'He is *a kind of fool*.' For many centuries there has been a tendency here in the singular to place the indefinite article *a* before the noun following *kind of, sort of,* and in older English also *manner of* to give it abstract general force: 'Cokodrilles (crocodiles), þat is, a manner of *a* long serpent' (Mandeville, *Travels*, fourteenth century, MS. Cotton, A.D. 1410–1420); 'a kind of *a* knave' (Shakespeare, *The Two Gentlemen of Verona*, III, I, 262); 'a very good sort of *a* fellow' (Fielding, *Tom Jones*). This usage is still common in colloquial speech, but it has not become established in the literary language.

In Middle English, *manner*, like *kin*, was employed as an uninflected genitive preceding the governing noun. This usage still lingered in early Modern English: 'to give notice that *no man-*

ner person Have any time recourse unto the princess' (Shakespeare, *Richard the Third*, III, v, 108). Gradually *manner* was replaced by *manner of* and had the meaning and the constructions of *kind of*, which have been described on page 546. In modern usage *manner of* has been largely replaced by *kind of, sort of*. The words *manner, type*, and *class*, similar to *kind* in meaning and hence influenced by it, have in the singular the same construction when the dependent genitive has abstract force: 'It enabled him to show *what manner of* man he was' (Macaulay, *History*, III, Ch. V). Where the reference is to more than one and the plural idea is strong, many still employ plural form here: 'Mary and Ann represent the new type of *girls*' (or *girl*). The abstract singular is very common here in recent literature. 'It would be easy to multiply examples of *this type of town*' (H. W. C. Davis, *Medieval Europe*, p. 220). '*The usual type of successful teacher* is one whose main interest is the children, not the subject' (Sir Walter Raleigh, *Letter to J. C. Dent*, Oct. 29, 1921). 'The real facts are little known to *either type of theorist*' (Arthur Ruhl in *New York Herald Tribune*, July 8, 1928). 'His rebels show hardly a trace of the arrogant self-sufficiency which makes *that class of person* objectionable' (*Athenæum*, 23/12, 1915). 'Selling for the most part standardized goods, both firms appealed to *the same class of customer*' (E. Phillips Oppenheim, *A Minor Hero*, A.D. 1925).

8. **Plural of Titles.** When a proper name with the title is put into the plural the rules are as follows:

a. The plural of Mr. is *Messrs.* (mĕsərz): 'Messrs. Smith and Brown'; 'the two Mr. Smiths,' or still, in accordance with older usage, 'the two Messrs. Smith'; 'Messrs. Smith's works'; 'Mr. Paul [Smith] and Mr. John Smith,' or '*Messrs.* Paul [Smith] and John Smith.' Similarly, 'Master Smith'; 'the two young Master Smiths,' or still, as in older usage, 'the two young Masters Smith.' The title *Mr.* was originally the same word as *Master*, serving at first as one of its abbreviations. By the close of the seventeenth century *master* and *Mr.* had become differentiated in pronunciation, form, and meaning. *Master*, as in 'Master of Arts,' is still used as a title, representing a certain degree of learning. In older English, it had a much wider meaning, being used of a man of high social rank or considerable learning. On the other hand, it is used of young men, who are not old enough to be addressed as *Mr.*

In the case of *brother* and *sister* we may say: 'the Smiths,' or 'the Smith brothers,' or 'the brothers Smith,' but on a sign without the article 'Smith Brothers'; 'the Smith sisters.' Likewise in the case of other titles of males: 'the two Drs. Brown' or 'the two Dr. Browns.' But if there are two or more names, the title is always plural: 'Drs. William Smith and Henry Brown'; 'Professors Smith and Brown'; '[the] Captains Smith and Brown.'

b. In the case of the title *Mrs.* the name assumes the plural: 'the two Mrs. Smiths,' in contrast to 'the two Misses Smith.' But 'Mr. and Mrs. Smith.' In the seventeenth and eighteenth centuries *Mrs.* was used not only with its present force, but also with the force of our present *Miss.* The form *Miss* itself originated in the seventeenth century, and only slowly became differentiated from *Mrs.* Both *Mrs.* and *Miss* are abbreviations of *Mistress.* Before the present differentiation was effected, *Mrs.* was often used to an elderly maiden lady and *Miss* to a young unmarried woman.

c. In the case of the title *Miss* we may still, in accordance with older usage, say 'the Misses Woodhouse'; 'the Misses Woodhouse's little orchard' (Margaret Deland, *John Ward, Preacher*, Ch. I); especially so in the formal language of invitations, also in business language, as in 'The Misses Smith & Company' (on a sign); also when different Christian names or other titles stand before the name, as in 'the Misses Mary and Ann Brown,' or when the name is followed by others, as in 'the Misses Smith, Brown, and Read'; but elsewhere, just as common or perhaps more so, the newer usage 'the Miss Woodhouses'; 'the Miss Woodhouses' little orchard'; 'both the pretty Miss Gibbses' (Ethel Sidgwick, *A Lady of Leisure*, p. 465); 'the two youngest Miss Fawns' (Trollope, *Eustace Diamonds*, I, 24). We should say 'the numerous Mrs. and Miss Grundys' rather than 'the numerous Mrs. and Misses Grundy' to avoid the plural of Mrs., which is not in use. We should also say *Mrs. Smith and the Miss Smiths*, not *Mrs. and the Miss Smiths*, for it is inaccurate.

GENDER

60. The necessities of life require us still in a large number of cases to indicate sex, but in the literary language there is a marked and growing disinclination to do this with reference to man or beast. In loose colloquial speech, on the other hand, there is a strong tendency to throw off this reserve and go to the other extreme, so that even lifeless things are freely but capriciously endowed with sex. This same inclination is seen also in higher diction, but there is more moderation and more consistency in the use of genders.

1. **Natural Gender.** In English, gender is the distinction of words into masculine, feminine, and neuter. Our nouns follow natural gender. Names of male beings are masculine: *man, father, uncle, boy,* etc. The names of female beings are feminine: *woman, mother, aunt, girl,* etc. The names of inanimate things are neuter: *house, tree, street, whiteness,* etc. Thus natural gender is a grammatical classification of words according to the sex or sexlessness of the persons and things referred to. Sex is denoted by nouns, pronouns, and possessive adjectives in the following ways:

a. The male and the female are in many cases denoted by a different word: man, woman; salesman, saleswoman; foreman, forewoman; horseman, horsewoman; laundryman, laundrywoman; gentleman, lady; Sir, Madam; Lord, Lady; father, mother; papa, mama; dad or daddy, mum or mummy; grandfather, grandpa, granddad, grandmother, grandma, granny; brother, sister; bridegroom, bride; husband, hubby, wife, wifie; uncle, aunt; nephew, niece; monk, nun; king, queen; earl, count, countess; bachelor, old maid or spinster (the *–ster* originally a feminine suffix, but now usually masculine: youngster, teamster, etc.), or now often bachelor girl; wizard, witch; boy, girl or maid, maiden; milkboy, milkmaid; cash boy, cash girl; lad, lass; tom, tabby; dog, bitch or slut; cock or rooster, hen; gander, goose; drake, duck; fox, vixen; sire, dam; buck, doe; hart or stag, hind; ram or wether, ewe; bull, cow; bullock or steer, heifer; stallion, mare; colt, filly, etc.

Some feminine nouns, as *duck, goose,* and many masculine, as *dog, horse, teacher, editor,* are often used to denote either sex where there is no desire to be accurate. Such nouns are said to be of common gender.

There are a number of words that apply only to females without a corresponding word for males: frump, dowd, slattern, termagant, virago, minx, hussy, prude, dowager, etc. On the other hand, there are a number of words which apply only to males: dude, fop, masher, bruiser, ruffian, etc.

b. The male and the female are in many cases distinguished by placing before the noun an adjective or more commonly a noun or pronoun used as an adjective — where, however, the two forms are in some cases written together, since they are felt as forming a compound: woman friend, woman friends (in popular speech lady friend, lady friends); man friend, men friends (in popular speech, gentleman friend, gentlemen friends); boy friend, boy friends; girl friend, girl friends; woman servant, women servants; women students; manservant, menservants; woman doctor (or lady doctor), women doctors (or lady doctors); woman clerk (or lady clerk); women voters; woman witness (or lady witness); girl cashier, girl cashiers; stag party, hen party; hen bird (or lady bird); cock pheasant, cock pigeon, cock robin, cock sparrow, but guinea cock, peacock, turkey cock; hen pheasant, hen pigeon; jenny robin, hen sparrow, but guinea hen, peahen, turkey hen (also a hen turkey); buck rabbit, doe rabbit; dog fox; she bear, he bear; tomcat, tom lion, she cat or tabby cat; billy goat, she goat, nanny goat; he ass, jackass, jenny ass; cow rhinoceros; heifer calf or cow calf, bull calf; the fair singer; fair readers; female (or better woman) novelist; female cat, female dog; bulldog, female bulldog.

c. The female is distinguished in a number of cases by adding *–ess* to the masculine form: god, goddess; count, countess; viscount, viscountess; duke, duchess; peer, peeress; emperor, empress; prince, princess; marquis, marchioness; baron, baroness; ambassador, ambassadress; Lord Mayor, Lady Mayoress (in England); abbot, abbess; prior, prioress; actor, actress; adulterer, adulteress; adventurer, adventuress; ancestor, ancestress; benefactor, benefactress; caterer, cateress; enchanter, enchantress; founder, foundress; giant, giantess; governess; heir, heiress; host, hostess; hunter, huntress; inheritor, inheritress or inheritrix; Jew, Jewess; launderer, laundress; leopard, leopardess; lion, lioness; master, mistress; murderer, murderess; Negro, Negress; ogre, ogress; panther, pantheress; patron, patroness; poet, poetess; priest, priestess; procurer, procuress; prophet, prophetess; proprietor, proprietress; protector, protectress;

shepherd, shepherdess; Quaker, Quakeress; songster, songstress; seamstress; sorcerer, sorceress; servitor, servitress; steward, stewardess; tempter, temptress; tiger, tigress; traitor, traitress; votary, votaress; waiter, waitress; warder, wardress. Other suffixes are used in a few words: hero, heroine; administrator, administratrix; aviator or more commonly flyer, aviatrix; executor, executrix or executress; testator, testatrix; sultan, sultana; czar, czarina; Joseph, Josephine; Francis, Frances, etc.

The ending in –*ess* was once more common. There is a derogatory touch in it which makes it unsuitable when we desire to show respect, but on the other hand appropriate when we speak slightingly. Rather than use it we go a roundabout way: 'wife of the ambassador,' 'wife of the pastor,' etc.; 'woman doctor,' 'lady doctor,' 'woman student,' etc. If we stress the idea contained in the stem of the word, we use the masculine form for females: '*Dr.* Louise Jones.' 'George Eliot is a great *author, writer.*' 'She is an able *editor, teacher,*' etc. The forms in –*ess* have become established in certain titles and a few other words given above, but even some of these are avoided.

Widower is formed by adding –*er* to the feminine form.

d. The male and the female are often distinguished only by a possessive adjective or a pronoun that refers back to the noun: 'The speaker, doctor, teacher, etc., shook *her* head as *she* heard these words.' It is now usual to treat animals as neuter, since the idea of personality is not prominent and the idea of sex doesn't seem important to us, but we not infrequently regard them as masculine, employing masculine pronouns and possessives without regard to sex: 'The camel is inestimable for long desert journeys, for *he* has strong powers of endurance.' 'If you want to kill a tortoise, wait until *he* puts out his head.' 'Probably we have no other familiar bird keyed up to the same degree of intensity as the house wren. *He* seems to be the one bird whose cup of life is always overflowing' (John Burroughs, *Field and Study*, Ch. IV). In contradistinction to other animal life there is a tendency to regard birds as feminine, especially in the case of *swallow, dove, sparrow, lark, thrush*, etc.; sometimes also other little animals and insects, as *mole, bee*, etc.: 'How winsome is the swallow! How tender and pleasing all *her* notes! Is it boyhood that *she* brings back to us old men who were farm boys in our youth?' (John Burroughs, *Field and Study*, Ch. XIII, II). 'Like a skilful surgeon, the wasp knows just what to do, knows in what part of the head to insert *her* sting to produce the desired effect' (*ib.*, Ch. XIII, III). But, for the most part, the masculine prevails if we do not choose to employ the neuter. Of course, the feminine pronoun occurs with reference to all kinds of animal life where the idea of a female animal naturally suggests itself: 'The cat looked from one sister to the other, blinking; then with a sudden magnificent spring leaped onto Agnes's lap and coiled *herself* up there' (Mrs. Ward, *Robert Elsmere*, I, 124). It is quite probable that Burroughs' use of the feminine gender in the examples quoted above rests upon the conception of sex, for he is an accurate observer. The wasp is referred to as a female because only the female wasp has a sting. The bee is often referred to as a female because it is the female bee that is so often seen gathering sweets from the flowers. Compare **23 II 7.**

The masculine pronoun and possessive adjective are usually employed for persons without regard to sex wherever the antecedent has a general indefinite meaning and hence doesn't indicate sex and the situation doesn't require an accurate discrimination: 'Everybody is to do just as *he* likes.' Often, however, the natural feeling here that *he* is one-sided prompts us to use both *he* and *she*, *his* and *her*: 'Everybody is to do as *he* or *she* likes.' 'Each of us must lead *his* or *her* own life.' In choice English, however, this accuracy is often quite out of place, since the idea of the oneness of man and woman is present to our feeling: 'Breathes there the *man*, with soul so dead Who never to *himself* hath said, This is my own, my native land!' not 'Breathes there the man or the woman,' etc. 'Who is a neighbor, *he* who shows love, or *he* who shows it not?' (French, *Parables*). In popular speech, as in the older literary language, *they* is much used, as it is inclusive in gender: 'Everybody is to do just as *they* like.'

With reference to a baby or little child we often use the masculine pronoun *he* or the feminine form *she* according to sex when we happen to think of personality or sex, but usually when we speak of a little child or a small insect we do not think of personality or sex, and hence with reference to either child or insect employ the neuter pronoun *it* and the possessive adjective *its:* 'She had to pass our door where stood Mrs. Todd and the baby. *It* stretched out *its* little arms to her.' 'Something flew on to my neck and I soon felt *it* crawling downward.' Similarly, we find *it* with reference to a person that has been presented to us in only shadowy outlines which do not afford a clear idea of the personality: 'The street was empty but for a solitary figure sitting on a post with *its* legs dangling, *its* hands in *its* trousers-pockets' (Du Maurier, *Trilby*, I, 241). This *it*, thus closely associated with the idea of the lack of personality, is often used disparagingly of persons, similarly also *that* and *what*: 'Would you like to marry Malcolm? Fancy being owned by *that!* Fancy seeing *it* every day!' (Elinor Glyn, *Vicissitudes of Evangeline*, p. 127). 'Well — [she is] the sort that takes up with impossible people — you really never know *What* you may meet in Agnes Hyde's rooms' (Mrs. Cecily Sidgwick, *The Severins*, Ch. XVI). It is also used in kindly humor: 'It's a wise nephew that knows *its* own aunt' (W. W. Jacobs, *The Casta-ways*, Ch. V), where the speaker claims superiority of knowledge and humorously looks down on the person addressed for not knowing his own aunt better. This *its* is also in a playful humorous tone used for *your:* 'There, run along and put *its* (= *your*) pretty things on for the theater!' (Pinero, *Sweet Lavender*, Act II).

On the other hand, *it*, like the relative *which* (**23** II 7, 4th par.), is used to indicate estate, rank, dignity: 'She is a queen and looks *it.*' Likewise *itself:* 'The Gaul asserted *itself* in a shrug, a form of expression rare in him' (Meredith Nicholson, *Lady Larkspur*, Ch. I). The author is here speaking of an old French servant in an American home, but the reference is not to the man but to the Gallic trait of his shrug, which hadn't entirely disappeared in spite of his long American experiences.

2. Grammatical Gender and Gender of Animation. In Old English, as in modern German, there are three grammatical genders. Of nouns denoting inanimate objects one large group was masculine, one large group feminine, a third large group neuter, i.e., neither masculine nor feminine. The original idea of this grammatical gender was that of personification. In the earlier stages of language development the imagination played a much bigger rôle than it does today. In the Indo-European period many inanimate things, such as the sun, the moon, the earth, the sky, the sea, the stars, shrubs, plants, flowers, trees, rivers, winds, water, fire, actions, processes, etc., were conceived as animate beings, while other things were conceived as inanimate. The animate was distinguished from the inanimate by the form, but the animate was not distinguished as to sex, i.e., masculine and feminine nouns and pronouns did not have different endings in the names of either living beings or personified things. This older order of things survives in *who* and *what*. Here as in Indo-European the animate stands in contrast to the inanimate, but there is no distinction of sex. Certain pronouns early developed distinctive forms for sex. Although adjectives originally derived their inflection from that of nouns, they gradually in many languages developed distinctive forms for the three genders. Nouns went much slower in developing distinctive forms for the three genders, but distinctive forms appeared in many words. Even in the period of the first records of the older languages the original conception of grammatical gender based upon personification had in large measure faded away. The inherited gender of nouns representing inanimate things had become a matter of form or meaning, i.e., the nouns were masculine, feminine, or neuter according to their form or their meaning.

The use of grammatical gender in Old English was not so foolish as it might at first seem to a modern English or American boy or girl who is beginning to study Old English. After adjective inflection had disappeared in Middle English, it was soon discovered that something valuable had been lost. The inflection of the adjective so that it always agreed with the noun in gender and case kept the adjective in close relations with its governing noun. After the distinctive endings of adjective and noun had disappeared there was nothing to bring the adjective into relation to its governing noun when it stood at some distance from it in substantive function. It became necessary to insert *one* or *ones* here to relate the adjective to its governing noun, as described in **57** 1: 'a black sheep and *a white one*,' 'black sheep and *white ones*.' Here *one*, *ones* took the place of the old endings that indicated gender and case. Thus the employment of different genders here binding adjectives to their governing nouns was useful, only unnecessarily complicated. We all know how colorless our *one, ones* are. They are mere abstract signs to relate adjective to noun and have nothing whatever to do with gender. The gender endings of Old English used here have seemingly more color than our *one, ones*, but in reality they were not much less abstract. They were, like our *one, ones*, mere formal devices to relate adjective to noun, only more complicated.

After the gender endings had been dropped there was nothing that brought lifeless things into relation to sex, nothing in the form of noun or adjective to guide the memory when it became necessary to refer to the noun by means of a personal pronoun, which still retained its distinctive forms. The old usage of associating lifeless things with sex had to be abandoned in the literary language, and it here gradually became established to refer to lifeless things by a neuter pronoun as being the most natural course under the circumstances, thus avoiding inconsistency and caprice. This new development, however, was not entirely new. Even in Old English, there was a strong tendency to use the personal pronouns in accordance with natural sex or sexlessness. The selection of a masculine or feminine personal pronoun in harmony with the sex was quite common when the reference was to a neuter noun denoting a living being. This strong sense of sex in the Old English period helped develop the idea of sexlessness, so that a neuter personal pronoun was sometimes used when the reference was to a masculine or feminine noun denoting a lifeless thing. Later, at the close of the Old

English period in the North, at the beginning of the thirteenth century in the Midland, and the end of the fourteenth in the Southeast, when article and descriptive adjective had lost their distinctive endings for gender and case, grammatical gender could no longer be distinguished and was replaced by natural gender, which even in Old English was in use with personal pronouns, and now after the disappearance of distinctive forms for grammatical gender in article and descriptive adjective came to be the predominating conception of gender in our language.

The new usage did not come in all at once, but appeared at first alongside of the old historic grammatical gender, at last gradually supplanting it in the normal form of expression. But the old habit of giving lifeless things sex, still common in our playful moods, never died out entirely. In moments of vivid feeling the old association of sex with lifeless things reappeared, no longer, however, influenced by the form of noun and adjective, but entirely under the sway of psychological forces, the mind assigning the gender under the influence of the conceptions suggested by the grammatical gender of Latin and French words, as in the case of rivers, lakes, and mountains, which became masculine as in Latin; as in the case of the vices, which became masculine after the analogy of Old French *vice;* and the virtues, feminine after the analogy of Old French *vertu;* and the word *ship,* feminine after the analogy of Old French *nief.* In this new reign of psychological influences, however, the mind is often swayed by mere caprice. Thus, the grammatical gender of older English has become in modern English the gender of our animated moods; hence we call it here the *gender of animation.*

Although the gender of animation now rests upon a psychological basis, while, in Old English, grammatical gender was closely associated with the form and inflection of nouns, the inner nature of Old English and modern usage is exactly the same — both rest upon a mild personification of lifeless things, not a vivid one born of the imagination. Both are a lively form of speech that has resulted from associating things with sex in a mere formal way for thousands of years; a long step removed from concrete expression, which has at last been attained in modern scientific English, where usually natural gender has full sway. If we have banished this mild form of fancy from our scientific language, we still feel its charm in our poetry and colloquial speech. In our ordinary literary language we often use *sun* as a masculine: 'The sun was shining in all *his* splendid beauty,' etc. (Dickens); but, of course, at any time we may lapse into scientific English again and say: 'The sun performs one revolution about *its* own axis in about 25 days,' etc.

We sometimes in choice prose make the *earth*, the *world*, and the *moon* feminine, but may at any moment become scientific again and treat them as neuter nouns.   We are inclined to make *church*, *university*, *state*, and especially *ship* feminine.   With a good deal of persistency we say of a ship: '*She* behaves well, *she* minds her rudder, *she* swims like a duck,' but lapsing into a scientific mood may say: 'The boat was attacked by a constant fire from both banks as *it* drifted along.'   In higher diction, where we employ grammatical gender more freely than in the ordinary literary language, we are often inclined to treat as masculine mountains, rivers, the ocean, time, day, death, love, anger, discord, despair, war, murder, law, etc.; as feminine spring, nature, the soul, night, darkness, cities, countries, arts, sciences, liberty, charity, victory, mercy, religion.   In our playful moods we have a great fondness for the feminine: 'That helps the blood to draw the wart and pretty soon off *she* comes' (Mark Twain, *Tom Sawyer*); but the masculine is not unknown here: '"You are provided with the needful implement — a book, sir?" — "Bought *him* at a sale," said Boffin' (Dickens, *Our Mutual Friend*).   In American English, there has been for a long while a steady trend toward the feminine in colloquial and popular speech, so that here the feminine is now the favorite form.   The masculine is now rather uncommon except in quaint dialect where older usage is still preserved, as in Maristan Chapman's *The Happy Mountain*, where the hero's 'fiddle' is treated as masculine throughout the book.   The feminine is the usual form even where the masculine is employed in higher diction: 'Sun, *she* rise up en shine hot' (Joel Chandler Harris, *Nights with Uncle Remus*, p. 34).   'I've swum the Colorado where *she* runs down clost to Hell' (Mulford, *Bar*, 10, 115).   The feminine here is characteristic also of Irish and northern British dialects, which through Irish and northern British immigrants into our country may have influenced our American development.

CHAPTER XXVIII

PRONOUNS

61. A pronoun, as indicated by its literal meaning *standing for a noun*, is usually a mere substitute for some person or thing suggested by the situation, as in the case of *I, we, you,* or by a gesture, as in the case of *this, that:* '*This* (or *that*) is a photograph of my wife'; or is a substitute for some person or thing already mentioned, as in the case of *he, she, it, they.* As in these cases, the reference is usually definite, but a number of pronouns contain only an indefinite reference, as in the case of *many, some, somebody, none, nobody,* etc. In the case of the interrogatives *who,* etc., a pronoun is used instead of a noun, as the speaker does not know the fact and inquires after the person or thing in question.

In a series *I,* for politeness' sake, is put last: '*John, Fred, and I* arrived at the same time.' '*You and I* had better go.'

a. Agreement. A pronoun as a mere substitute for a noun agrees with its antecedent in gender, number, and person wherever there is a distinctive form to indicate these conceptions, but, of course, it takes a case form in accordance with the grammatical function it performs in the proposition in which it stands: 'Your *sister* borrowed my dictionary yesterday. *I* met *her* this morning and *she* gave it back to *me.*' When the reference is to the indefinite pronoun *one* the proper pronoun is *one,* not *he:* 'It offends *one* to be told *one* (not *he*) is not wanted.' See **57** 5 *b* (6th par.).

When a pronoun refers to two or more antecedents of different persons, the first person has precedence over the second and third, and the second person precedence over the third: 'You and I divided it between *us.*' 'You and he divided it between *you.*'

Where a pronoun or possessive adjective refers to a word plural in meaning, but in form being an indefinite pronoun in the singular or a singular noun modified by an indefinite limiting adjective, it was once common to indicate the plural idea by the form of the following pronoun or possessive adjective, but it is now usual to put the pronoun or possessive adjective into the singular in accordance with the singular form of the antecedent: '*Nobody* knows what it is to lose a friend, till *they have* (now *he has*) lost him' (Fielding). 'If the part deserve any comment, *every* considering *Christian* will make it *themselves* (now *himself*) as *they go*' (now *he goes*) (Defoe). 'I do not mean that I think *anyone* to blame for taking due care of *their* (now *his*) health' (Addison). Older usage, however, still occasionally occurs: '*Everybody* is discontented with *their* (instead of *his*) lot in life' (Beaconsfield). This older literary usage survives in loose colloquial and popular speech: 'Everybody has *their* (instead of *his*) faults.' 'It is the duty of each student to interest *themselves* (instead of *himself*) in athletics.'

If there is a reference to *your Majesty, her Grace*, etc., usage requires the repetition of the full title or the use of *you, your, he, his*, etc., instead of the grammatically correct *it, its:* '*Your Majesty* can do as *your Majesty* will with *your Majesty's* ships,' or '*Your Majesty* can do as *you* will with *your* ships' (Fowler, *Modern English Usage*). 'His (Her) Majesty can do as *he* (*she*) will with *his* (*her*) ships.' 'Her Grace summoned *her* chef.'

The antecedent is sometimes not a noun or pronoun, but the idea contained in a group of words or a single noun or adjective. See **7** C; **23** II 6 (6th par.).

Some pronouns (relatives, interrogatives, etc.) perform not only the function of a pronoun but also that of a conjunction, linking the clause in which they stand to a preceding word or clause. See Conjunctive Pronouns in Index.

For the agreement of the relative pronoun with its antecedent see **23** II 8 *a, b, c, d*; **21** *c*.

b. Case of the Predicate Pronoun. This subject is discussed in **7** C *a*.

PREPOSITIONS

62. Very closely allied in nature to adverbs are prepositions, which, like adverbs, limit the force of the verb as to some circumstance of place, time, manner, degree, cause, condition, exception, concession, purpose, means. But a preposition and an adverb differ in this, that the latter limits the force of the verb in and of itself, while the former requires the assistance of a dependent noun or some other word: 'Mary is *in*' (adverb), but 'Mary is *in* (preposition) *the house.*' A preposition is closely related also to a subordinating conjunction. It often stands before an abridged clause as a sign of its subordination to the principal verb. See **20 3** (next to last par.).

A preposition and its object perform various functions. They modify a verb and thus serve as an adverbial element: 'I wrote the letter *with care.*' Where they stand in a very close relation to the verb, forming its necessary complement, they serve as an object, a prepositional object(**14**): 'He is shooting *at a mark.*' They often serve as the object of an adjective or a participle, forming its necessary complement: 'He is fond *of music.*' 'He is given *to exaggeration.*' After a noun they form an adjective element: 'the book *upon the table.*' After a linking verb they serve as a predicate adjective: 'The country is *at peace.*' For a fuller statement of the functions of the preposition and its object see **7**, p. 570, and the articles there referred to.

The usual object of the preposition is a noun or a pronoun, the noun or pronoun forming with the preposition a prepositional phrase: 'He plays *with my brother* or *with me.*' If the object of the preposition is an adverb or some other part of speech or a clause, it serves here as a noun or a pronoun: 'after *today*' (an adverb serving as a noun). 'I saw him a year ago, but since *then* (an adverb serving as a demonstrative pronoun) we haven't met.' 'I met him a year ago, since *when* (an adverb serving as a relative pronoun; see **23** II 6, next to last par.) I haven't seen anything of him.' When the object of the preposition is a clause, we call preposition and clause a prepositional clause: 'He is thankful *for what I have done for him.*'

In 'A rat ran out from under the stable' *from* was originally a preposition governing the prepositional phrase *under the stable*, but we now feel *from under* as a compound preposition in which *under* indicates a position and *from* a movement from that position. Similarly, in *into* and *onto* the first component indicates a position and the second a motion into that position. Originally, simple *in* and *on* were used with a following dative noun to indicate rest in a position and with a following accusative noun to indicate a motion toward a position. After adjectives and nouns lost their distinctive endings it became necessary to add *to* to *in* and *on* to bring out the idea of motion toward a position, while simple *in* and *on* were retained to indicate rest in a position.

We often bring a predicate adjective or participle and the preposition that usually accompanies it into relation to a verb of complete predication and thus convert adjective and preposition into a compound preposition. We often indicate the prepositional function of the new compound by giving the adjective adverbial form by the addition of the suffix *–ly:* 'The science has a speculative interest which is *irrespective of* all practical considerations' (Buckle, *Civilization*, III, V, 416), but 'He values them *irrespectively of* the practical conveniences which their triumph may obtain for him' (Matthew Arnold, *Essay in Criticism*, V, 192). 'His actions are *inconsistent with* his professions,' but 'He acts *inconsistently with* his professions.' In many of these compounds, however, the adjective form remains unchanged, or the unchanged form is used alongside of the adverbial: 'I shall speak to him *relative to* the matter.' 'This course will be pursued *regardless of* consequences.' 'The company, *previous* (or *previously*) *to* his majesty's arrival, were all assembled.' 'They will be chosen *irrespective of* age.' 'This was *owing* (adjective) *to* bad luck,' but '*Owing to* (preposition) drought the crops are suffering' (or 'the crops are short'). This process is going on all the time. As can be seen in the last example, a participle or an adjective becomes detached from nouns and is often for convenience attached to a verb or a statement as a whole. Grammarians would often arrest this useful development.

The *Concise Oxford Dictionary* recommends, 'The difficulty is *due* (adjective) *to* ignorance,' but condemns as 'incorrect': 'I came late *due to* (preposition) an accident.' The preposition *due to* is not more incorrect than the preposition *owing to*, which is approved by the same dictionary, but it is not as yet so thoroughly established in the language. Compare **17** 4 (4th par.).

As a preposition usually stands *before* the dependent word it is called a preposition (Latin 'prae' *before* and 'positio' *position*). Where several prepositions connect different words with a common dependent word or object, the object need be expressed only once, standing after the last preposition: 'I do not think a man is fit to do good work in our American democracy unless he is able to have a genuine fellow-feeling *for*, understanding *of*, and sympathy *with* his fellow-Americans' (Theodore Roosevelt, *An Autobiography*, Ch. III). In English, however, we often detach the preposition from the noun or pronoun and place it at the end of the proposition or clause, as described in 4, p. 566.

The preposition now brings a noun or some other word into relation with a verb, noun, adjective, etc.: 'Mary works *in* the house.' Here *in* brings *house* into relation with the verb *works*. Originally, however, *in* was an adverb modifying the verb *works*. The idea now conveyed by *in the house* was at this early period expressed by *house* in the old locative case. The adverb *in* with the meaning *inside* expressed the same idea as the old locative case, but expressed it more concretely, hence more forcibly. Gradually *in* came into a closer relation with *house*, so that it became more intimately associated with *house* than with the verb and thus developed into a preposition, and since its force was stronger than the old locative, the latter gradually disappeared as superfluous. Thus we lost an old case form, but the prepositions *in, inside, within, outside, on, at, by, under*, etc., which took its place, more than made up for the loss, because they have more and finer shades of meaning. In the same way the old instrumental case, denoting association, instrument, and cause, has been displaced by the prepositions *with, by, through, by means of, on account of*, etc. Similarly, the old ablative case, denoting separation, has been displaced by the prepositions *from, out of*, etc. The old simple dative, denoting a *direction toward*, has been in large measure replaced by the prepositions *to, toward, at*, etc. Compare **12** 2. After the disappearance of the locative, instrumental, and ablative, the dative and accusative forms for a long while served as the sign of subordination to the new prepositions, as the prepositions had to govern some case to indicate the relation between preposition and dependent noun. The prepositions themselves indicated the relation between the dependent noun or other word and the verb or the governing noun or adjective. As there is now no distinction of form between dative and accusative, we may say that all prepositions govern the accusative.

The loss of the old case forms and the development of prepositions brought us new and considerably improved means of expression. As we feel the possibilities of this construction, we are constantly forming new prepositions for fuller or more convenient expression of our thought. We form them not only from adverbs but also from nouns and present participles: *beside* (i.e., *by the side of*), *alongside of* or *alongside*, *instead* (i.e., *in the place*) *of*, *on account of*, *during*, *pending*, *regarding*, etc. A perfect participle occurs in *past* and *as compared with*. There is a tendency, as in the first two examples, to suppress parts of the prepositional phrase as unnecessary to the thought. For the origin of the use of participles here see **17** 3 A *c*, 4.

1. **List of Prepositions.**

The most common are:

abaft

aboard, on board of, or simply on board

about

above

abreast of, abreast with

according to

across

adown (poetic for *down*)

afore (now replaced by *before*)

after

against (in older English also *again*)

agreeably to

ahead of

along, alongst (once widely used, but now obsolete)

along of (now replaced by *on account of*)

along with

alongside of, or alongside

amid, amidst (in poetry mid, midst)

among, or amongst

anent

antecedent to

anterior to

apart from

apropos of

around

as against (= against)

as between (= between)

as compared with (**29** 1 A *c aa*)

as distinct (or distinguished) from

as far as ('I traveled with him *as far as* Chicago'; see **29** 1 B *b*, 2nd par.)

as far back as

as for (**29** 1 A *c aa*)

as opposed to

as to (**29** 1 A *c aa*)

as touching (now replaced by *touching*)

aside (now replaced by *beside*)

aside from (American)

aslant

astern of

astride of

at

at the cost of
at the hands of
at the instance of
at the peril of
at the point of
at the risk of
athwart
atop

back of (from *at the back of*),
   colloquial for *behind*
bating (**31** 2, 4th par.)
because of
before
behind
below
beneath
beside
besides
between
betwixt
beyond
beyond the reach of
by
by dint of
by (the) help of
by means of
by order of
by reason of
by the aid of
by virtue of
by way of

care of (in addresses; = in care
   of)
concerning (**17** 4)
concurrently with
conditionally on
conformably to
contrary to
counter to

despite
differently from

down
down at
down to
due to (**62,** 5th par.)
during

east of, to the east (or eastward)
   of
ere
exclusive of

face to face with
failing (**31** 2)
farther than (**29** 1 B *b*, 2nd par.)
for
for fear of
for lack of
for the behoof of
for the benefit of
for the ends of
for the purpose of (**33** 2)
for the sake of
for want of
fore (now replaced by *before*)
forth (now replaced by *from
   out of*)
from above
from among
from behind
from below
from beneath
from between
from beyond
from forth (obsolete)
from in front of
from lack of
from off
from out of, from out
from over
from under

hand in hand with

in
in accordance with

in addition to
in advance of
in agreement with
in back of (= back of), popular American, after the analogy of *in front of*
in behalf of (= in the interest of)
in between
in care of (or in addresses *care of*)
in case of (= in the event of)
in common with
in company with
in comparison with (or to)
in compliance with
in conflict with
in conformity with
in consequence of
in consideration of
in contrast with (or to)
in course of
in default of
in defiance of
in disregard of
in (the) face of
in favor of
in front of
in fulfilment of
in lieu of
in obedience to
in opposition to
in place of
in point of
in preference to
in process of
in proportion to
in pursuance of
in quest of
in re or re (legal term; = concerning)
in recognition of
in regard to (or of)
in relation to
in respect to (or of)

in return for
in search of
in spite of
in support of (**33** 2)
in the case of (= as regards; **29** 1 A *c aa*)
in the event of
in the matter of
in the middle of
in the midst of
in the name of
in the presence of
in the room (or place) **of**
in the teeth of
in the way of
in token of
in under, popular for *under* ('The dog ran *in under* the barn.')
in view of (= considering)
including (**17** 4)
inclusive of
inconsistently with
independently of (**28** 3 *a*)
inside of, or inside
instead of
into
irrespective of

less (**8** I 2 *e*)
like (**28** 2, 6th par., **50** 4 *c bb*)
long of (= along of; both now replaced by *on account of*)

mid, midst, *see* amid
midmost of, midmost
minus (**8** I 2 *e*)

near (**40** 4 *c bb*)
next door to
next room to
next to (**40** 4 *c bb*)
north of, to the north (or northward) of
notwithstanding

of (*o'* in *o'clock*, etc.)
off (in popular speech *off of*)
on account of
on behalf of (= in the name of)
on board of, on board
on pain of
on the face of
on the occasion of
on the part of
on the point of
on the pretense of
on the score of
on the side of, (on) both sides
(of); (on) each side (of), (on)
either side (of), (on) the other
side (of), (on) that side (of),
(on) this side (of), always
with *of* before a pronoun;
(on) both sides *of it*, (on) each
side *of her*
on the strength of
on the top of, or on top of
on top of, or on the top of
onto, or on to
opposite to, or opposite
out of, or less commonly out
out of regard for (or to)
outside of, or outside
over
over against
over and above
overthwart
owing to (**17** 4, 4th par.)

past
pending
per
plus
preferably to, **or in preference to**
preliminary to
preparatory to
previous(ly) **to**
prior to
pursuant to

re, *see* in re
regarding (**17** 4, 4th par.)
regardless of (**28** 3 *a*)
relative to
respecting
round
round about

short of
side by side with
since
so far as (**29** 1 A *c bb*)
so far from (**28** 3 *a*)
south of, to the south (**or south-**
ward) of
subject to
subsequent(ly) **to**
suitably to

thanks to
through
through lack of
throughout
till
to
to and fro
to the order of
touching (**17** 4)
toward or towards

under
under cover of
under pain of
underneath
until
unto
up
up against
up and down
up at
up till
up to
upon

via

west of, to the west (or west-ward) of	with the exception of
with, sometimes withal [1]	with the intention (or object) of
with a view to	with the purpose of
with an eye to	with the view (or intention) of
with reference (or respect) to, or sometimes in respect to	within
	within reach of
	without
with regard to (**29** 1 A *c aa*)	without regard to (**28** 3 *a*)

Some of the old forms listed above, as *afore, along of*, survive in popular speech.

a. The preposition *onto*, or less properly *on to*, corresponds closely to *into*. As it indicates motion toward the upper surface of something, it differs distinctly from *on* or *upon:* 'The boys jumped *onto* the ice and played *on* it until sundown.' The use of *onto* or *on to* ought not to be discouraged, as is done by many grammarians, but strongly encouraged, for it enables us to express ourselves more accurately.

Onto should be distinguished from *on to*, where *on* belongs to the verb: 'We must *struggle on* to victory.' Similarly, *in to:* 'We went *in to* dinner.'

2. Contraction of 'On' to 'A.' The preposition *on* is often contracted to *a: athwart, abreast, aslant, asleep, aglow, aflame, on fire* or *afire, on shore* or *ashore, on board* or *aboard, on top of* or *atop*, etc. Except in established set expressions, like these, this usage is characteristic of popular speech. See **50** 4 *c dd* (4th par.).

3. Omission of Prepositions. Prepositions are often omitted in colloquial speech in set expressions since they are lightly stressed and of little importance to the thought: 'He must never treat you [in] *that way* again.' In such expressions the element as a whole is felt as an adverb, or an adverbial accusative, so that the preposition really has no function any more and drops out. Compare **16** 4 *a* (9th par.). In the same way *of* often drops out of many prepositions, as in *inside* instead of *inside of*. The moment that such a group of words as a whole is felt as a preposition, *of* ceases to have a function and naturally drops out as superfluous.

4. Preposition at End of Sentence. The preposition often seems to stand at the end of the sentence or clause: 'I have lost the pen I write *with*.' According to **19** 3 (3rd par.) this is a sentence containing a primitive type of relative clause in which there is no relative pronoun, since in this old type the subordination is indicated

---

[1] Found only at the end of a relative clause: 'Such eyes and ears as Nature had been pleased to endow me *withal*' (Lowell, *Democracy*, 6).

by simply placing the dependent clause alongside the principal proposition and suppressing the personal pronoun, thus indicating that the person or thing in question is to be supplied from the preceding proposition: 'I have lost the pen: *I write with* [*it*].' In this old type of expression *the*, the weakened form of the demonstrative *that*, not only modifies *pen*, but also by virtue of its old demonstrative force serves as a determinative (**56 A**), pointing as with an index finger to the following explanatory clause. In this old type there are often two determinatives, one before the governing noun and another after it, the two determinatives pointing as with two index fingers to the following explanatory clause: 'I have lost *the* pen *that* (= *that one:*) I write with [it].' 'He should read *such* books *as* (= *that kind:*) we all approve of [them].' The suppression of the personal pronoun here causes us to look to what precedes for the connection and thus marks the clause as dependent. In spite of the fact that we now feel *that* and *as*, not as determinatives, but as relative pronouns, we still retain here the old sentence structure. Similarly, in relative clauses with *which, who, what,* which have developed out of determinative constructions, as described in **23** II 1, 2, 3: 'the pen *which* I write *with.*' 'Lord Hubert Dacey *whom* she ran *across* on the Casino steps' (Edith Wharton, *House of Mirth*). 'It all depended on *what* one was accustomed *to.*' Also in relative clauses where there is no relative expressed: 'That is nothing *to joke about*' = *about which one should joke.* Where, however, the relative clause expresses manner, cause, place, or time, so that the relative pronoun is not vividly felt as an object, the relative *which* is expressed, and the preposition stands before it, or the relative *that* is employed, and the preposition is suppressed as unimportant, especially when the same preposition is used in the same construction in the principal proposition; sometimes also the relative pronoun is suppressed: 'By the sharp tones *in which* he spoke of his brig it was plain to both of us that he was in deadly earnest.' 'I wish you would only see things in the light *that we see them*' (or *in which we see them*). 'He took him for his model for the very reason *that* (or *for which*) he ought to have shunned his example.' 'They now find themselves in the same predicament *that* (or *in which*) *we once found ourselves*' (or *that we once found ourselves in*). 'I was getting ready to leave on the very day *he came*' (or *on which he came*).

We also retain the old determinative structure after the subordinating conjunctions *as* and *than:* 'The case is *as sad as I've ever heard of*,' where originally the two *as's* were felt as pointing forward, like two index fingers, to the following explanatory clause. 'He writes with a worse pen *than I write with*,' originally 'He writes with a worse pen, *then* (modern form of *than*) *I write with* [*a bad one*].'

Thus for many centuries the position of a preposition at or near the end of a proposition has been one of the outstanding features of our language. It is so natural to put the preposition at the end that we have extended this usage beyond its original boundaries. The prepositional dative follows the analogy of other prepositional constructions, so that *to* or *for* often stands at the end of the relative clause: 'That is the man (*that*) *I gave it to*' (or *did it for*). In the case of an emphatic prepositional object we often for the sake of greater emphasis put the object — word, phrase, or clause — into the first place and put, as so often elsewhere, the preposition after the verb at the end, for we hesitate to begin the sentence with an unstressed preposition: '*Where* does he come *from?*' 'Well, *where* that rolling-pin's got *to* is a mystery' (Compton Mackenzie, *The Altar Steps*, Ch. III). '*Which pen* did you write *with?*' 'What is he writing *with?*' '*What* is he *up to?*' '*Who* (instead of the correct *whom;* see **11 2 e**) does this dreadful place belong *to?*' (Mrs. H. Ward, *Robert Elsmere*, II, 141), or '*To whom* does this dreadful place belong?' '*How many scrapes* has he gotten *into?*' also in indirect form: 'I asked him *how many scrapes* he had gotten *into*.' '*They* (instead of the correct *them;* we now use *those* here) who have saluted her (i.e., poetry) on the by and now and then tendred their visits she hath done much *for*' (Ben Jonson, *Discoveries*, p. 27, A.D. 1641). '*These reports* Inglesant does not seem to have paid much attention *to*' (J. H. Shorthouse, *John Inglesant*, Ch. I). '*What I have commenced* I am prepared to go on *with*.'

Similar to these prepositions that stand at the end of a proposition are the prepositional adverbs that often stand at the end of a proposition because of the suppression of a governing noun or pronoun, which is omitted since it is suggested by a preceding noun or by the situation: 'I threw the ball at the *wall*, but I threw too high and it went *over*.' 'John drew the heavy sled up the *hill*, then he and Mary rode *down*.' 'We soon reached the *park* and strolled *through*.' Prepositional adverbs now usually have the same form as the prepositions that stand before a noun, but in older English, they often had a different form and, except in relative clauses, are sometimes still distinguished in the case of *out*, *in*, and *on* in connection with verbs denoting motion from or toward: 'He came *out of* (preposition) the house' and 'This is the house (that) he came *out of*' (preposition), but 'He is now in the house but will soon come *out*' (prepositional adverb). 'From my window I saw him come *into* the house' and 'This is the house (that) I saw him go *into*,' but 'Come *in!*' (spoken by someone from the window of a house to someone passing on the street). 'He jumped *onto* the car just as it started' and 'This is the car (that) he jumped *onto*,' but 'Just as the car started he jumped *on*.' In older English, adverbial form could even stand in a relative clause, where we now use the prepositional form: '*wo* that she was *inne*' (Chaucer, *The Man of Lawe*, 420), now 'the distress that she was *in*.' In older English, *in* was the form for preposition, *inne* for adverb. In the earlier periods when the sentence structure was much more loosely fitted together than today, there was a natural tendency to construe the preposition that stood at the end of the proposition without an accompanying governing noun as an adverb and give it adverbial form. In the more compact sentence of our time, especially in relative clauses, we feel the reference to a preceding noun as indicating a prepositional relation and give the word prepositional form. In the relative clause we feel this so distinctly that the word usually loses the strong stress which characterizes adverbs: 'the fence that he júmped *over*.' Compare 5 below.

In contrast to prepositional adverbs and all the prepositions previously discussed — all of which usually follow the verb — are prepositions which always precede the verb, forming with it a compound: 'The river *over*flowed its banks.' 'A great principle *under*lies this plan.' 'Water *per*meates the ground.' As the object of the preposition always follows the verb, it is now felt as the object of the compound verb. Where the preposition is no longer used outside of these compounds, as in the case of *be–* (= *over, upon*), it is called a prefix: '*to bemoan* (= moan over) one's fate,' '*befriend* (= bestow friendly deeds upon) one,' etc., but with privative force in *behead*.

5. **Prepositional Adverbs.** In older English, certain adverbs had also prepositional force, so that they were not only stressed as adverbs but governed a case like a preposition: 'God *him* com *to*,' now 'God came *to him*.' In Old English, as in this example, the prepositional adverb might follow its object. The prepositional force of such forms has so overshadowed the adverbial that they now regularly stand before the noun which they govern. Not infrequently, however, we feel their adverbial force so clearly that we still stress them: 'He stood bravely *bý* my brother.' 'It becomes necessary to look *into* this matter.' 'I looked straight *át* him.' 'The ball went clear *óver* the house without striking it.' 'The child wants *ín*' (adv.; see **6 A** *a*, 3rd par., p. 21), but 'Belgium wants *in* (prepositional adv.) this protective arrangement' (*Chicago Tribune*, Nov. 10, 1919, p. 8). In poetry these prepositional adverbs not only have their distinctive stress but still, as in older English, may stand after their object: 'Soft went the

music the soft air *alóng'* (Keats, *Lamia*, II, 199). Sometimes in plain prose: 'I have read the letter *thróugh.*' 'I want to think the matter *óver.*' 'Let us pass the matter *bý.*' As described in the last paragraph on page 568, stressed prepositional adverbs still often stand at the end of a proposition where the dependent pronoun has been suppressed, as it is suggested by a preceding noun.

6. **Fluctuation.** With certain words usage fluctuates without a difference of meaning: Thus we say *different from* or *to, averse to* or less commonly *from:* 'It is a *different* sort of life *to* (or perhaps more commonly *from*) what she's been accustomed to' (George Eliot, *Silas Marner*, Ch. IX).

In older English, *beside* and *besides* were not differentiated in sense, being two forms with the same meanings — *alongside of, in addition to, other than.* Now, *beside* has the first meaning and *besides* the others.

7. **Functions of the Prepositional Phrase or Clause.** It is used with the force of:

a. A predicate adjective. For examples see **7** F. In the examples referred to, the object of the preposition is a noun, but it can, of course, be also a pronoun. It is sometimes an *it* that is explained only by the situation or context: 'There was nothing *for it* (= *feasible*) but to grin and bear it.' 'I am glad that I am *out of it.*' 'Their team was *not in it*' (colloquial for *outclassed, had no chance to win*).

b. An attributive adherent (**10** I) adjective: 'an *up-to-date* dictionary.' See **10** I 2. An attributive appositive adjective. For examples see **10** IV, **10** IV *a.*

c. An object of a verb or an adjective. For examples see **14, 24** IV. In the examples referred to, the object of the preposition is a noun, but it can be, of course, also a pronoun. It is sometimes an *it* that is explained only by the situation or context: 'He goes *at it* right.' 'I am sick *of it.*'

d. A prepositional phrase is very often used as an adverb: 'He is working *in the garden*' (place). 'He arrived *in the evening*' (time). 'He wrote the letter *with care*' (manner proper). '*In my opinion* (manner, here a sentence adverb; see **16** 2 *a*, 6th par.) they are wise.' 'He is lacking *in initiative*' (manner, specification; see **28** 1 *a*). 'She passed me on the street *without speaking to me*' (attendant circumstance). 'He worked himself *to death*' (result). 'He is taller *by two inches*' (degree). 'He may be dead *for all I know*' (restriction). 'He was beheaded *for treason*' (cause). '*Without him* (condition) I should be helpless.' 'His wife clings to him *with all his faults*' (concession). 'John works *for grades*' (purpose). 'He cut the grass *with a lawn mower*' (means). 'The trees were trimmed *by the gardener*' (agency). Compare Index under Prepositional Phrase. In these examples the object of the preposition is a noun, but it can be, of course, also a pronoun. It is sometimes an *it* that is explained only by the situation or context: 'He is always putting his foot *in it*.' 'He is trying to lie *out of it*.' 'He was hard put *to it* for an answer.' 'He made a clean breast *of it*.' 'We had a bad time *of it*.' 'Step *on it!*' (slang). Instead of a noun or pronoun we sometimes employ a prepositional phrase as object of the preposition: 'Many place-names do not go back *to before the Norman conquest*' (W. J. Sedgefield, *Introduction to the Survey of English Place-Names*). 'I'll flog him *to within an inch of his life*.' In both examples the prepositional phrase is a noun, object of the preposition *to*.

A prepositional clause is sometimes used adverbially: 'Say, can't you get that husband of yours to come right back *from wherever he is?*' (Hichens, *Ambition*, Ch. XXVII). Compare **16 1, 24 IV, 25 1.**

CHAPTER XXX

GROUPS AND GROUP-WORDS

63. Just as a word has syllables, just so has a sentence groups of words, and just as a word has one syllable more strongly stressed than the others, just so has one word in a group a stress stronger than the others. Group stress, usually in normal groups, rests upon the last member of the group. A group of a noun and its modifiers: 'the lìttle bóy'; 'a whìte hórse'; 'a blàck bérry'; 'Jòhn's hát'; 'the bòok upon the táble.' A verb and its modifiers: 'He càme ín'; 'he wènt óut'; 'he stòod úp'; 'he wrìtes beaútifully'; 'he càme with a friénd'; 'he wròte a létter.' A verb and its subject: 'This sòap flóats'; 'the sùn is rísing.' But, of course, the subject is often more important than the verb and receives a stronger stress: 'Look yonder where the dead *léaves lìe.*' In a normal modern group the chief stress rests upon the last word; the secondary stress occurs near the beginning of the group. In such groups the force is usually descriptive.

In Old English, things were quite different. The chief stress was often upon the first word of a group: 'He *ín càme.*' 'He *úp stòod,*' etc. In the course of the Old English period a great change took place. The heavily stressed word that stood at the beginning of a group took a position at the end of the group: 'He *úp stòod* ' became 'He *stòod úp.*' 'He *a létter wròte* ' became 'He *wròte a létter.*' The old stress has been kept though the word-order has changed. The old word-order and stress are still preserved in group-words, described below. The object of the new development is evident. The heavily stressed word was withheld for a moment to create the feeling of suspense and thus render the word more prominent. It is only a matter of course that groups in which the first member was not heavily stressed did not participate in this change of word-order. There are three classes of such groups. The first member is a genitive with secondary stress: *Jòhn's hát.* The first member is an adjective with secondary stress: *the lìttle hát.* The first member is an adverb with secondary stress: *to ùplíft, ùndergó, òvercóme, òutstríp.* Though these classes of groups did not suffer a change of word-order, they are in perfect harmony with the large class of groups that did suffer a change of word-order. In all of them the heavily stressed member stands in the last place. More-

over, they all have a pronounced descriptive character. The
change of word-order in the one group brought it into harmony
with the three others and established the general character for
the normal English group.

In marked contrast to these normal groups are a very large
number of old groups which represent an older type of English
expression. This type originated in the prehistoric period at a
time when inflection was still unknown. As there were no inflectional forms the grammatical relations of the members of the group
could only be conveyed by the establishment of a fixed word-order:
the modifying member always precedes. The first member is an
uninflected subjective genitive: 'éarthquàke = the quaking of
the earth.' The first member is an uninflected possessive genitive:
'wágon-whèel = wheel of a wagon'; 'trée-tòp = top of a tree.'
The first member has the force of a genitive of origin: 'fírelìght =
light from the fireplace.' The first member is an adverb: íncòming;
óutgòing; fórthcòming; dównfàll. The first member has the force
of a prepositional phrase: 'stórm-tòssed = tossed by the storm';
'a stárlìt heaven = heaven lit up by the stars'; 'tóothpìck = a pick
for the teeth'; 'sléeping-càr = a car for sleeping'; 'drínking-wàter
= water for drinking'; 'íroning bòard = a board for ironing,' etc.
'Let your next car be *púrolator equìpped*' (advertisement) =
'equipped *with a purolator*.' The first member is an object: shóe-
màker; hóuse-clèaning; pléasure-lòving; époch-màking. We often
call such groups compounds, but they are not compounds in
the sense in which *goodbye* (a contracted form of *God be with
you*) is a compound. The syntactical relations of the different
members of the group are just as clear as in a modern group,
although there are no inflectional forms to indicate these relations.
The fixed word-order here takes the place of inflection. They
differ from modern groups, however, in that they have a peculiar
oneness of meaning which resembles the oneness of meaning found
in a word. They have the general characteristics of a group of
words but also the oneness of meaning found in a word, hence we
call them group-words. They have two other features that distinguish them from modern groups — they have the chief stress
upon the first member of the group and most of them have a pronounced classifying or distinguishing force: (with classifying
force) wáter-pòwer, stéam-pòwer; héadàche, báckàche; (with
distinguishing force) Jácksonvìlle, Lóuisvìlle. Though the group-
word construction in all its functions is a survival of prehistoric
usage, it is still, as can be seen by the numerous examples given
above, playing an important rôle in the life of our time. It is a
particular favorite in the headlines of our daily newspapers:

IOWA BATTLES WISCONSIN TODAY FOR *BÍG TÉN LÈAD* (*Chicago Tribune*, Nov. 17, 1928).

This old type of expression was so useful that our ancestors retained it and improved it by introducing inflectional features into it: bírd's-nèst; wásp's-nèst; a chíld's vòice; a wóman's hànd; a móther's lòve; chíldren-lòver; chíldren's lànguage; prínters' èrrors; líce-destròyer; sávings bànk; báckwoodsmàn, etc. We may call these formations younger group-words in contrast to the old group-words. They differ only in inflectional form from the older formations; the typical features of stress and meaning are exactly the same in the older and the younger group. The influence of these old types of expression is still very powerful. When we form new group-words we still usually give them the form of one of these two old types: mén's shòes; wómen vòters; wóman's còllege; tíe ùp; lóck òut. The first three of these examples are in harmony with the spirit of the old type of expression. The last two examples have the form of the old type, but they don't have its spirit. They are decidedly descriptive. We often feel this in forming group-words with descriptive force and hence give them modern form in harmony with their meaning: the wày óut; the wày ín; the rìde hóme; yèllow féver; Nèw Yórk; Hàrper's Férry, etc.

On the other hand, old group-words have in very many cases been influenced by modern groups. Old English group-words of the type of *stánbrỳcg* (*stone bridge*) are often as useful in modern life as in early times, as, for instance, when we desire to classify or distinguish, as in *stóne brìdges, íron brìdges*, etc., or *not an íron brìdge but a stóne brìdge;* but they are often in open conflict with our modern feeling when we describe, hence we have to give them modern form: *a brìdge of dréssed stóne, a stòne brídge.* The last example represents one of the most characteristic changes that have taken place in modern English. The expression *a stòne brídge* is formed after the analogy of *a whìte brídge.* The adjective with secondary stress stands before the strongly stressed noun describing it. Similarly, we now construe *stone*, originally a noun, as an adjective and give it the secondary stress of an adjective, although it was once more strongly stressed than the noun that forms the second member of the group. Thus we have used old material for our modern construction, but have given it modern form. On the other hand, we often use an adjective, adverb, or genitive in –*s* with classifying or distinguishing force, but, of course, we place the stress as in an old group, i.e., upon the first member: *a bláckbèrry; the Whíte Hòuse; Néwcàstle; the réd bòok* not *the ᵇrówn one; áll-wòol; néar bèer* (i.e., almost beer); 'Trusts and

Néar-Trùsts' (heading of an editorial in *Saturday Evening Post,* July 21, 1928); *Píttsbùrg; Jóhnstòwn,* etc. Compare **10** I 2, **10** II 1.

In old compounds and group-words the first component is often a modern descriptive group: 'a dìrty clóthes bàsket' = 'dìrty clóthes + básket'; 'a nèw and sècond-hand bóoksèller' = 'nèw and sècond-hand bóok + séller'; 'a pràctical jóker' = 'pràctical jóke + –er.'

INDEXES

WORD INDEX

The references are to sections and subsections.

it, cont.
  as object (sometimes anticipatory),
    11 2 *b*, **15** III 2 A *a*, **23** I (par. 4),
    24 III *a*, **24** IV, **38** 2 *b dd*,
    40 4 C (2)
  referring to person, **21** *c* (par. 4),
    60 1 *d*
  situation *it*
    as object, **62** 7 *c*
    as predicate, **7** C (pars. 4, 9),
      21 *b, e* (par. 10), **62** 7 *a*
    as subject, **4** II A, **8** I 1 *a*, **31** 2
its, **57** 5 *a*
it's, **57** 5 a (par. 2)
itself, **56** D, **60** 1 *d* (last par.)

J

jingle (verb), **46** (par. 3 from end)
jumping geraniums, **17** 1
Joseph, Josephine, **60** 1 *c*
just, **16** 4
  as distinguishing adverb, **16** 2 *b*

K

keep (copula), **6** B (par. 3), **38** 1
  as auxiliary, **38** 4
keep on, **6** B (par. 3), **38** 1
kind (plural of), **59** 7
kindly
  as adverb, **16** 4 (par. 5)
kind of, **59** 7
kiss, **46** (par. 5)
  two objects following, **15** III 1
know
  objective predicate following,
    15 III 2 B
  accusative subject following,
    24 III *d*

L

late, **16** 4
  comparison of, **16** 5 *a aa*, **54** 1 *a*
later
  in comparison, **16** 5 *a aa*, **54** 1 *a*
  as coordinating conjunction, **19** 1 *a*
latest, lattermost, **54** 1 *a*
latter, **54** 1 *a, g*
  as pronoun, **57** 3

last, **16** 5 *a aa*, **54** 1 *a*
lay, **46** (par. 2 and par. 4 from end)
lay off, **38** 2 *b aa*
lazybones, **59** 2
lead (verb)
  double accusative following,
    15 III 1
leap, **46** (par. 3 from end)
learn
  used with force of *teach*, **15** I 1 *a*
least, **16** 4 *a* (par. 6), **16** 5 *a aa, bb*,
    54 1 *a*, **55**
leave
  = *let* (popular speech), **43** 1 A
  objective predicate following,
    15 III 2 B
leave off, **38** 2 *b cc*
less
  as comparative, **16** 4 *a* (par. 6),
    16 5 *a aa, bb*, **54** 1 *a*, **55**
  as coordinating conjunction, **19** 1 *a*
  as preposition, **8** I 2 *e*, **62** 1
lesser
  in double comparison, **54** 1 *a*, 1 *aa*
less than
  as subject, **8** I 5
lest, **21, 23** I (par. 6), **24** III,
    30, 33, 43 II B *b*, **44** II 10
let, **7** A *a* (1)
  = *allow*, imperative of, **43** 1 A, C,
    45 3, 4 *b*, **46** (par. 2 from end)
  as causative auxiliary,
    46 (par. 2 from end)
  objective predicate following,
    15 III 2 B
let alone
  as coordinating conjunction, **19** 1 *a*
let us say
  as explanatory conjunction, **19** 1 *f*
lie (copula), **6** B (par. 3)
  dative following (*lie me down*),
    12 1 B *b*
lief, liefer, **43** I B, **49** 4 C (1) *b*
lift (verb), **46** (par. 4)
like (adjective or adverb)
  as differentiated from, **7** a *b* (3),
    15 III 2 A (last par. before *a*),
    28 2 (par. 5)
  comparison of, **54** 1
  construed as preposition, **24** II,
    28 2 (last par.), **50** 4 *c bb*, **62** 1
  determinative,
    56 A (par. 3 from end)
  explanatory conjunction, **19** 1 *f*

SUBJECT INDEX

The references are to sections and subsections.

H

I

im-, **16** 1 (par. 3)
imperative mood, **31** 1 *d aa*, **32** 1 *a aa*
  auxiliary verbs in expressions of
    will in, **45** 4
  indicative used as, **40**
  ingressive force of, **38** 2 *a ee*
  modern *do*-form in, **45** 2 (SEE ALSO
    do-forms)
  old simple, **45** 1
  passive, **45** 7
  subjunctive forms in commands
    in, **44** II 3 *b* (par. 2 from end),
    45 3, (mild form) **45** 4 *d*
  tenses of, **45** 4 *c*, **45** 6
imperative sentence, **2** (par. 2)
  accusative clause as, **24** III (last
    par. before examples)
  future indicative expressing,
    43 II B *a* (par. 3)
  simple infinitive expressing, **29** 2 *a*
  subject clause as,
    21 (last par. before examples)
  subject omitted in, **5** *a*
  terse expression as, **45** 5
  verb omitted in, **6** A *a*
impersonal *it*, SEE *it* (Word Index)
in-, **16** 1 (par. 3)
incomplete predication, verbs of, SEE
  verb(s)
indefinite
  adverbs, SEE adverb(s)
  article, SEE article, indefinite
  pronouns, SEE pronoun(s)
independent elements
  defined, **17**
indicative mood, **40, 43** I d,
  43 II B *a* (par. 3), *c* (last par.),
  44 II 5
indirect command,
  44 II 3 *b* (par. 2 from end).
  (SEE ALSO imperative mood;
    imperative sentence)
indirect discourse
  direct blended with, **24** III *c*
  independent form of, **44** II 3 *b*
  subjunctive mood in, **44** I *a*,
    44 II 3 *a*, *b*
  tense in, **36**, **44** II 3 *b*
indirect object, **11** 1 (par. 3), **50** 4 *c bb*
  asyndetic relative clause as,
    23 II 10 *a* (par. 4)
indirect question, SEE question(s)
Indo-European, **10** II 1, **14, 19** 3, **60** 2
infinite forms of verb, SEE verb(s)

infinitive(s), **49**
  in abridged appositional type of
    clause, **20** 3 (par. 9)
  active, with passive function,
    7 D 2, **15** III 2 B (par. 6),
    46 (par. 2 from end), **49** 3
  as adverbial element, **49** 4 F
  appositive force of, **10** V 3
  as attributive adjective modifier,
    10 I 2 (par. 2 from end), **10**, V,
    49 4 D
  difference of meaning between
    gerund and, **24** IV *a* (par. 4)
  in elliptical construction,
    24 III *d* (par. 2 from end), **49** 2 *b*,
    49 4 E
  in exclamatory conditional
    sentence, **31** 2 (par. 6)
  expressing purpose or intention,
    7 D 3, **33** 2 (par. 3), **37** 1 *e*
  for... to construction in,
    21 3 (pars. 3-8), **23** I *a*,
    24 III *d*, IV *a*, **29** 2 *a*, **31** 2 (par. 5),
    33 2, **49** 2 *a*, *c*, **49** 4, 4 A
  functions of, **49** 4
  gerund competes with,
    50 4, 4 *c aa*, 4 *d*
  gerund replaces, **21** *e* (par. 11),
    23 I *a*, **24** III *d* (par. 9), **24** IV *a*,
    38 2 *b ee* (last par.)
  idea of necessity in, **7** D 2
  indicating result, **38** 2 *b ee*
  modal, **7** D 2, **24** III *d*
  as object, **38** 1, **49** 4 C
  as objective predicate, **15** III 2 B,
    49 4 C (1) *c*
  omission of, **6** A *a*
  omission of *to* in, **4** *d*, **23** I *a*
  origin of, **49** 1
  passive, *to be* omitted from,
    24 III *d* (par. 5)
  perfect, **43** I B (last par.), **43** I D,
    44 I *a* (par. 2 from end), **45** 6,
    49 3 *a* (pars. 4-8)
    with modal and tense
      auxiliaries, **49** 3 *b*
  as predicate, **7** D, **17** 3 A *d*,
    3 B (par. 2), **23** II 11, **49** 4 B
    after copula, **7** D 1 *a*
    after passive verbs, **7** D 1 *b*
  repetition of *to* with, **49** 5
  simple, **33** 2 (par. 7), **49** 1, **49** 4 C (2)
    felt as imperative, **29** 2 *a*
  split, **16** 2 *a* (par. 8), **49** 2 *c*